Old Mobile

The Library of Alabama Classics,
reprint editions of works important
to the history, literature, and culture of
Alabama, is dedicated to the memory of

Rucker Agee

whose pioneering work in the fields
of Alabama history and historical geography
continues to be the standard of
scholarly achievement.

Old Mobile

Fort Louis de la Louisiane, 1702–1711

Jay Higginbotham

With a New Introduction by the Author

The University of Alabama Press

Tuscaloosa

Manufactured in the United States of America

∞

The paper on which this book is printed meets the minimum requirements of American National Standard for Information Science-Permanence of Paper for Printed Library Materials ANSI Z39.48-1984.

Library of Congress Cataloging-in-Publication Data

Higginbotham, Jay.
Old Mobile : Fort Louis de la Louisiane, 1702–1711 / Jay Higginbotham ; with a new introduction by the author.
p. cm.—(Library of Alabama classics)
Reprint. Originally published: Mobile : Museum of the City of Mobile, 1977.
Includes bibliographical references and index.
ISBN: 0-8173-0528-9
1. Mobile (Ala.)—History. 2. Southwest, Old—History. I. Title. II. Series.
F334.M6H483 1991
976.1'22—dc20 90-22776
CIP

British Library Cataloguing-in-Publication Data available

For My Father and Mother

Contents

Introduction

OLD *Mobile* bears the influence of the French anti-novel that emerged in the 1950s and 1960s. Still under the spell of the *nouveau roman* in the late 1960s, I did not structure this work through the eye of the historian. The book is not fictional (far from it; I went to absurd lengths to ascertain the facts, once attempting to slip into Cuba from Veracruz to scour burial records in Havana), but then-fashionable theorists such as Alain Robbe-Grillet and Nathalie Sarraute played some part in its design, in the stress on incident, the submergence of explanation. This emphasis of presentation over interpretation, I believed, might add some new dimension to the meaning of the material beyond conventional analysis.

There was a difference, however, in the *nouveau roman* and my own vision of early Mobile. Robbe-Grillet's world was neither absurd nor meaningful; yet the trials of the inhabitants at Mobile did provide an intrinsic theme, and one did not have to analyze it to portray it as fundamental. The omnipresence of conflict, of struggle on every level—settlers against the elements (poverty, hunger, disease), militia against their common enemies (the English, the Spanish, the Indians), individuals against themselves—formed a poignant motif, the place of struggle in the lives of men.

Such design as I had for this work apparently failed, and only one or two reviewers picked up on it; but if the book fell short in this respect, there were other more concrete uses that unexpectedly surfaced, though not until years later. When I completed *Old Mobile* in the fall of 1975, there was, to be sure, not a great deal of interest in the subject. Aside from personal friends (Marcel Giraud, Richebourg McWilliams, Charles O'Neill) there were few parties with whom to discuss the subject. My own fascination stemmed from the fact that my ancestors had lived in the town. Apart from that sense of belonging, there was a certain mystique about the place itself (the quiet isolation, the lonely river drifting by, the wind in the trees above the undiscovered graveyard) that was compelling.

My first visit to the site as an adult was in 1963. I was struck by the fact that while plant construction had taken place nearby and heavy industry loomed around, the land where the town once had stood was still relatively undisturbed. There were a few docks near the bluff, an industrial waste pond and several narrow roads dissecting the property, but the site was in a virgin state compared to those of other French capitals, such as New Orleans or Montreal. Along the roads were bits of broken pottery in the sandy loam, and one could not help visualizing the town's layout, especially the fabled graveyard where supposedly Henri de Tonti and his iron hand yet resided. Still, researchers had found few artifacts here, and no one had made archaeological surveys. It was only natural to wonder if this were indeed the site where La Louisiane's first capital had once stood.

In fact, the exact location of the site caused a running controversy. Because few artifacts had been found at Twenty-Seven-Mile Bluff, local history buffs had long argued that the actual site of Old Mobile was at the mouth of Dog River. Had not a French cannon been found there, as well as numerous French artifacts? And had not several historians of the past century (Albert Pickett among them) made this claim outright?

Even a cursory study of the charts and plans at the Bibliothèque Nationale and the Archives Nationales, however, should have been enough to settle the question. The accuracy of these maps (some quite specific) could not be denied. Drawing on two of the maps, the Iberville Historical Society erected a monument in 1902 at the site of Fort Louis at Twenty-Seven-Mile Bluff. But was the location precise?

Mobile author Peter Hamilton had seen at least four of these same maps from the Archives Nationales near the turn of the century. His book *Colonial Mobile* dealt partly with this settlement, and from these maps, as well as from local probate records, Hamilton had concluded, rightly, that Old Mobile had been located at Twenty-Seven-Mile Bluff. In fact, during a brief excursion to the site in 1902, one of his colleagues, Carey Butt, supposed he had discovered the fort's powder magazine. From Butt's claim, a monument marking the site of the fort was erected to coincide with the 200th Anniversary Celebration of Mobile's founding.

The monument still stands today, yet by the 1970s nothing of major importance had been found at the site. Shortly after my first visit to Old Mobile, I began gathering materials for a work on the original settlement. Throughout the time I was engaged in this research, I made regular visits to the site; yet I remained puzzled about the lack of artifacts found. By 1969 I had reached the conclusion that while the town was surely at Twenty-Seven-Mile Bluff, the fort must have been located slightly south of the marker. The following year the first archaeological survey of the site was conducted by The University of Alabama under the direction of Donald Harris. Over a two-week period, Harris excavated what he assumed were Fort Louis's foundations, just north of the monument. This assumption seemed unlikely to me, and I suggested he might want to try farther south a few hundred yards, where logically, according to my sketches, the fort site should be, on the highest part of the bluff, near where the old McGowan home once stood. To shift the focus of excavation at that time was deemed impractical because of the brevity of the survey and because Courtaulds Fibers, Inc. was the only landowner who had given permission to excavate. A week later, Harris wrapped up his survey and concluded his reports. Shortly thereafter he left Mobile and I continued my research. In 1973, I commenced writing *Old Mobile*, which occupied me for two years, during which time I was able to push through an application making Old Mobile a part of the National Historical Register.

By 1974, I had ceased visiting the site, being more concerned with revising and proofreading my manuscript. When *Old Mobile* was published in 1977 (mainly because of Dr. Samuel Eichold), it came at a timely juncture. That same fall, the city sponsored a 275th anniversary celebration at the site. *Old Mobile* appeared a few weeks later in an edition of some 1,200 regular edition copies and 200 deluxe copies. These editions sold fairly quickly, mostly to libraries and book collectors, and the entire matter receded from my memory. By the end of the 1970s, Old Mobile was for me a forgotten subject. I assumed that few had read the book and that it would never be reprinted. In addition, my own interests had shifted to parenting, poetry, and politics (especially the international peace movement). I had also become director of the Mobile Municipal Archives and chairman of the Society Mobile-Rostov-on-Don, a highly controversial sister city organization.

It was, then, with some detachment that in August 1988 I received a visit from James C. "Buddy" Parnell, an engineer from Courtaulds. Parnell, it seemed, had attended the 275th anniversary celebration and wondered what all the excitement was about. During the festivities, he had wandered down to the riverfront and was astounded to learn that such a renowned colonial capital had once stood on the very property where he was employed. Intrigued, he obtained a copy of *Old Mobile* and with its maps and charts began spending his lunch hours at the site. As the years went by, Parnell began finding artifacts, having concluded, as I had, that the town site must have been slightly farther south than was previously thought. His extensive finds suggested that what Harris had taken for the fort was in all probability a house of one of the Canadians on the north and northwest fringes of the town. As Parnell began locating more artifacts, he occasionally brought his findings by the Archives. By August 1988, however, he was becoming increasingly concerned about where his efforts were leading. I suggested that we ought to inform the University of South Alabama, which had on its faculty two respected archaeologists in the field of French colonial archaeology. Parnell agreed and the next day Professors Noel R. Stowe and Gregory A. Waselkov stopped by my office to discuss the matter. The following day, Waselkov returned with Associate Dean Stephen Thomas who was highly enthusiastic about the university's assuming a major role in the project.

My suggestion was that the Old Mobile project be a community effort involving the County and City of Mobile, as well as the University of South Alabama. Thomas and Waselkov agreed and I contacted John H. Friend, founder of the City of Mobile's Archaeological Committee, who set up a meeting with John Bertolotti, then-current president, and Dr. Samuel Eichold. Friend then informed F. Lawerence Oaks, director of the Alabama Historical Commission, who made a visit to the site.

With these groups agreed, Dean Thomas gained enthusiastic support from university officials, notably President Frederick Whiddon and Arts and Sciences Dean Gene Crossley. Following talks with these officials, an organizational meeting was held at the University of South Alabama on May 16, 1989, to organize formally the Old Mobile Project. The officers elected were: Chairman, Jay Higginbotham; Vice-chairmen, John H. Friend and Samuel Eichold; Secretary, John Bertolotti; Treasurer, Stephen Thomas; and Archaeological Project Director, Gregory A. Waselkov.

Following this meeting, the various landowners—Courtaulds, Dupont, Alabama Power—gave permission to excavate. Funds were solicited from the private sector, with the university providing start-up funds, and Waselkov began excavations in June 1989. Support was also obtained from the Alabama Historical Commission, the Bedsole Foundation, and from numerous individuals. Sizable grants were received from the Alabama State Legislature (thanks to Rep. Taylor Harper) and the National Endowment for the Humanities.

Backed by this support, Waselkov's field operations were successful in unearthing several houses constructed by the Canadians, as well as a hitherto unknown blacksmith's shop. With the location of the fort site, which at this point seems imminent, the team will recover the dimensions of the entire settlement, exactly as they were in 1711 when Bienville abandoned the site and moved downriver. Where the project will turn once the archaeological work is completed is not yet clear, but efforts are being made to obtain the various properties for the public and it is possible that a preservation project similar to Moundville, Jamestown, or even Williamsburg will eventually be realized. Such a project is appropriate, for Old Mobile is as important historically to the Deep South as Jamestown or Williamsburg is to the Atlantic Coast.

Once word reached the news media, the Old Mobile project generated a demand for information about the site and for copies of *Old Mobile*. There were no copies available, nor did any prospects for reprinting the book seem likely.

At this point, The University of Alabama Press offered to reprint the book in its Library of Alabama Classics. For benefit of the project, this plan could not have come at a more favorable time. Bernard Diamond, Jr., President of the Mobile Genealogical Society, had just been selected to head the Friends of Old Mobile, a support group growing out of the Old Mobile Project. This group, formed in the spring of 1990, quickly expanded to hundreds of members, few of whom knew much about the settlement's history. The Library of Alabama Classics edition, issued at this timely moment, will serve to acquaint new members with the facts and kindle enthusiasm for the project.

After I completed *Old Mobile* in 1975, I shifted quickly to other fields of interest, so I was unaware until recently of new accomplishments in the field of French Colonial history. Since 1975, a great deal of close scholarship has added to the literature of the French in Louisiana, especially works by Patricia Galloway,[1] Carl Brasseaux, Robert Weddle, and others. Richebourg McWilliams's translations of Iberville's Louisiana journals appeared in 1981. In addition,

1. In addition to other studies, Galloway has revised and edited two new volumes of colonial documents collected, edited, and translated by Dunbar Rowland and A. G. Sanders. Patricia Kay Galloway, ed., *Mississippi Provincial Archives, French Dominion*, Vol. IV, 1729–1748; Vol. V, 1749–1763 (Baton Rouge and London, 1984). Volumes I–III of this series constitute an invaluable resource, used extensively by every writer on French Louisiana since Jean Delanglez. Dunbar Rowland and Albert G. Sanders, ed. and trans., *Mississippi Provincial Archives, French Dominion*, Vols. I–III (Jackson, MS, 1927–1932).

much new material concerning French families in Louisiana is now available in works by Elizabeth Shown Mills, Winston De Ville, Jacqueline Vidrine, Gary B. Mills, Glenn Conrad, and others. These studies and compilations are the results of careful scholarship, and they dramatically reveal the dispersion of genes throughout the United States and Europe from the mere score or so of families at Old Mobile. Baudreau de Graveline, Étienne Burelle, and François Trudeau are the progenitors of descendants in the thousands, but the Chauvin clan, whose issue have doubtless now spread to every state in the union, is surely the largest of the early Mobile families.[2] Thus the inhabitants of Old Mobile, by their genes as much as by their exploits, have left a lasting legacy in North America, and their progeny (one of whom was Edgar Degas) have made their mark in the New World.

It was the travail of these struggling inhabitants that I attempted to recount in *Old Mobile* in the early 1970s. Whether I described their sufferings well or not, it was not the full story. Nor will future writers, though improving on my efforts, be able to recount these experiences wholly. The integral truth is lost forever, and the best the writer or the archaeologist can do is to seek to recapture some of the fleeting images of particular persons and events. The search for these glimpses will reap new meaning from the experience, from rediscovering the ordeals of these individuals, and will reveal perhaps, as Albert Camus once found, that the struggle itself can make the human heart swell.

Mobile, Alabama J.H.
October 19, 1990

2. Elizabeth Shown Mills, *Chauvin* dit *Charleville* (Mississippi State, MS, 1976); Gary B. Mills, "The Chauvin Brothers: Early Colonists of Louisiana," *Louisiana History*, Vol. XV, No. 2 (Spring 1974), pp. 117–31.

Preface

OLD *Mobile* purports to be neither an institutional study of early Louisiana nor an analysis of French colonial strategy; nor does it offer any novel conclusions or broad interpretations concerning the various forces at work in the eighteenth century New World. It is rather, for the most part, a local history: an attempt to describe in as detailed and accurate a fashion as is presently possible the personalities and events surrounding the establishment and life of the now extinct town known to history as Old Mobile.

Although modern scholars seeking more conceptual studies may quarrel with the straightforward narrative and the more or less chronological framework in which the work is set, I do think that the method employed offers some advantage (continuity of insight, perhaps) to the understanding of the period in question, especially since a detailed narrative concerning the beginnings of French colonization on the Gulf Coast has not heretofore been made available. While the specialist will recognize the enormous amount of labor involved in producing this work (by comparing it with what has previously been published), I have no illusions regarding its permanence: the archives are vast and they may yet have abundant treasures to yield. Like previous works on colonial Louisiana, *Old Mobile* will serve principally to open new avenues of inquiry to those who relish re-discovering the shadowy rims of a particular past.

Archival research of Louisiana's pre-Crozat years is actually yet in embryo. Although nearly 275 years have passed since Pontchartrain and Iberville began to colonize the Mobile River basin, only Jean Delanglez in 1935, Marcel Giraud in 1953, and Charles Edwards O'Neill in 1966, have completed major works based solidly on examination of primary sources. And of these, only Giraud in his *Histoire de la Louisiane* (Vol. I) deals extensively with the period (1702–1711) which this book explores.

Until recent years there have been legitimate reasons for this lack of emphasis. The scholar dealing with the early history of Virginia or Massachusetts Bay found his original materials principally in two or three centers, whereas manuscripts pertinent to early Louisiana were housed in such diverse locales as La Rochelle, Quebec, London and Natchitoches, not to mention Paris, Rome, Sevilla, Mexico City, New Orleans and Nantes. The necessity for searching these various archives dissuaded impecunious scholars who otherwise might have concentrated their efforts on Louisiana, and even those of more comfortable means who had the will, such as Charles Gayarré and Peter J. Hamilton, lacked the time and the guidance of archival finding aids.

Technological advances in the last forty years have somewhat altered all this. Rapid postal service, improved reproduction methods and the publication of excellent guides, inventories and calendars now make it possible to adequately investigate a large number of remote archives in a few years' time.

I have been fortunate to have been able to research most of the archival depositories in person; yet I would never have been able to complete this undertaking were it not for the aforementioned conveniences and the kindnesses of innumerable librarians and archivists. For assistance in exploiting the various repositories I am indebted especially to the following: In London, to P. A. Penfold and F. F. Lambert of the Public Record Office; in Quebec, to Honorius Provost of the Archives du Séminaire de Québec and to Roland-J. Auger and Gilles Durand of the Archives Nationales du Québec; in Sevilla, to Rosario Parra Cala of the Archivo General de Indias; in Rome, to Edm. Lamalle of the Archivum Romanum Societatis Iesu and to Simon Lourdusamy of the Archivio della Sacrae Congregazione Gentium Evangelizatione seu de Propaganda Fide; in Paris, to Edmond Pognon of the Bibliothèque Nationale and to Marie-Louise Boulard, Jean Favier and Marie-Antoinette Menier of the Archives Nationales; in La Rochelle, to Françoise Giteau of the Archives de la Charente-Maritime; in Rochefort, to Marc Fardet of the Archives et Bibliothèque du port de Rochefort; in Mexico City, to J. Ignacio Rubio Mañé of the Archivo General de la Nación; in New Orleans, to John Kemp of the Louisiana State Museum and to Alice D. Forsyth of the St. Louis Cathedral Archives.

For various forms of assistance I am indebted also to Ruth Warren, Mary Anderson, Melissa Bowden and E. Herndon Smith of the Mobile Public Library; to the members of the Bienville Historical Society; to Milo Howard of the Alabama State Department of Archives and History; and to Caldwell Delaney, Charles Edwards O'Neill, Roland Latham, Albert Hunter, William R. Armistead, Mildred Mott Wedel, Richebourg McWilliams, Marcel

Giraud, Glenn Conrad, Jack D. L. Holmes, William S. Coker, Winston De Ville, N. Read Stowe, Yvonne Tardif, Dewey C. Freeman, Samuel Wilson, Jr., Sidney Louis Villeré, G. Douglas Inglis, Samuel Eichold, Jean Couture, Oscar H. Lipscomb and Collin B. Hamer for aid and counsel on numerous technical questions.

Above all, I am indebted to Francis Escoffier and my wife, Louisa, both of whom critically reviewed the final manuscript.

Mobile, Alabama
November 21, 1975

Jay Higginbotham

Abbreviations

AAE	Archives du Ministère des Affaires Étrangères
AAQ	Archives de l'Archevêché de Québec
AC	Archives des Colonies
ACM	Archives de la Charente-Maritime
ADM	Archives of the Diocese of Mobile
AGI	Archivo General de Indias
AGN	Archivo General de la Nación
AGPF	Archivio della Sacrae Congregazione . . .
AJM	Archives Judiciaires de Montréal
AJQ	Archives Judiciaires de Québec
AM	Archives de la Marine
AMT	Archives Municipales de Toulon
AN	Archives Nationales
ANDM	Archives Paroissiales de Notre-Dame de Montréal
ANDQ	Archives Paroissiales de Notre-Dame de Québec
APR	Archives de l'arrondissement maritime et du port de Rochefort
AQ	Archives du Québec
ARSI	Archivum Romanum Societatis Iesu
ASH	Archives du Service Historique de L'Armée
ASJ	Archives de la Province (Société de Jesus) de Paris
ASME	Archives du Séminaire des Missions Étrangères
ASQ	Archives du Séminaire de Québec
ASS	Archives du Séminaire de Saint-Sulpice
AVP	Archives de la Ville de Paris
BHVP	Bibliothèque Historique de la Ville de Paris
BMLR	Bibliothèque Municipale de La Rochelle
BN	Bibliothèque Nationale
BRH	*Bulletin des Recherches Historiques*
CO	Colonial Office
DCS	Délibérations du Conseil Supérieur
DFC	Dépôt des Fortifications des Colonies
DGFC	*Dictionnaire généalogique des familles canadiennes*
FF, NA	Fonds Français, Nouvelles Acquisitions
FLC	*Fleur de Lys and Calumet*

IJAL	*International Journal of American Linguistics*
JR	*Jesuit Relations*
LSMA	Louisiana State Museum Archives
MM	Musée de la Marine
PRO	Public Record Office
RB	Registre de baptêmes
RM	Registre de mariages
SLCA	St. Louis Cathedral Archives
SLUA	St. Louis University Archives
SOCG	Scrit. orig. rif. nelle cong. gen. (in AGPF)
SPO	State Papers Office
SQ	Séminaire de Québec
WO	War Office

Prologue

THE flagship *Renommée* reeled and lurched in the raw December gulf, her bedridden captain, Pierre Le Moyne d'Iberville, lying listlessly below deck, his thoughts swirling among recent and ominous events . . .

On the seventh of November, 1701, Iberville had cast anchor at Cap-français on the Île de Saint-Domingue along with the *Palmier* (commanded by his brother Le Moyne de Sérigny), after narrowly escaping a flotilla of corsairs in the seas above Hispaniola. Shortly before being rescued from the corsairs, the *Palmier* had been struck by lightning, which had split her mainmast, causing a delay at the French port of nearly two weeks. Moreover, on arriving at Cap-français it was discovered that most of the meat on board had been spoiled and had to be discarded.[1]

Perceptive to these incidents was Iberville's younger brother, Le Moyne d'Assigny, who with little taste for adventure and still less for danger, quit the expedition forthwith (much to Iberville's chagrin) and remained on the island where he applied for a position on the local council and where he would shortly expire at the age of twenty.[2]

The recent chain of episodes had been preceded by a series of portentous political discussions in the courts of Versailles and Madrid during which Iberville, with his men and his ships, had been forced to cool his heels the entire summer at the ports of La Rochelle and Rochefort, awaiting final instructions from the

1. Iberville to min., Nov. 14, 1701, AM, B4, 21, f. 540. The *Renommée*, a "vasseau de 4ème rang," had been built at Bayonne in 1698 by the *constructeur* Antoine Tassy. Of 560 tons burden, the vessel measured 118 French feet in length by 32½ in width. AM, G, 13.

2. *Édits, ordonnances royaux, déclarations et arrêts du Conseil d'état du roi concernant le Canada, I,* p.57. *DGFC*, I, p. 379.

minister of marine. When eventually the minister's orders arrived, they were as disappointing as they were welcomed: since the Spanish refused to cede Pensacola (which Iberville had long coveted and which he continually described as "the grandest harbor on the Gulf Coast"), the only alternative was that the expedition move on to the bay of Mobile, a nearby harbor of shallow depth but of strategic rivers.[3]

Once arrived at Cap-français Iberville's spirits were temporarily lifted by the presence in port of the fireship *Enflammé*. Dispatched from France ten months before to replenish Fort Maurepas on the bay of Biloxi and Fort La Boulaye on the lower Mississippi, the fireship had been feared lost by the extraordinary delays she had suffered during her voyage on the northern gulf. Yet this splendent surprise was shortly dimmed when the ship's commander, Denis de La Ronde, submitted to Iberville a recent report from the commandant of Fort Maurepas, Ensign Sauvole. In his report (actually a journal directed to the minister), Sauvole had little good news to offer: another of Iberville's younger brothers, Le Moyne de Bienville, then commandant of Fort La Boulaye, was dangerously short of food and supplies, so improvisioned that he had been forced to send hunters to the bay of Saint-Louis to try to supplement the corn that Sauvole was sending from his own meager supply. Moreover, there was an air of rebellion in the fort, stemming not only from the behavior of the Canadians, described by Sauvole as "unstable, unruly and disobedient," but from the Jesuits, Jacques Gravier and Paul Du Ru, who refused to obey orders to ascend the Mississippi to escort Father Gabriel Marest down river—instructions handed down by Iberville himself. The principal cause for alarm, however, was Sauvole's description of the fever that had spread through the fort, leaving half the garrison in a faint and flaccid condition.[4]

3. Min. to Bégon, Aug. 10, 1701, AM, B2, 155, f. 236–42. Iberville to min., July 30, 1701, AM, B4, 21, f. 532–41. Min. to Ducasse, Oct. 5, 1701, AM, B2, 156, f. 48. Mémoire sur la Misissipi . . . par Iberville, AM, B4, 21, f. 526.

4. Iberville to min., Nov. 14, 1701, AM, B4, 21, f. 540–41. Min. to Bégon, Jan. 12, 1701, AM, B2, 153, f. 39–46. Bégon to Villermont, Feb. 8, 1701, BN, FF, 22810, f.39. The *Enflammé* had left the port of Rochefort on Feb. 7, 1701 with orders to return as soon as her supplies had been delivered. Her return was expected by mid-August of 1701. Min. to Bégon, Feb. 9, 1701, AM, B2, 153, f. 333–41; B2, 155, f. 281–83. Min. to Iberville, Aug. 17, 1701, AM, B2, 155, f. 285. Journal de Sauvole, Aug. 4, 1701, AC, C13A, 1, f. 316–21.

On receiving Sauvole's reports, Iberville acted with characteristic dispatch. He quickly ordered the *Enflammé* on her way to France where the vessel was already six months overdue then sent the large smack which had accompanied the *Renommée* on to Fort La Boulaye with three weeks' provisions to relieve his brother Bienville. By the smack (under command of Jousselin de Marigny), which he ordered to continue on to Fort Maurepas, Iberville dispatched a brief but poignant message to Commandant Sauvole:

> [We will] form a settlement at the bay of Mobile. [Use] the smacks to convey everything at the fort to that place and wait for me there where I will go and join you.[5]

With the expedition's official business thus set in motion, Iberville proceeded in a further distinctive manner: he delayed sailing for the Gulf Coast until he could negotiate a private business transaction. Grown wealthy by the booty in furs he had captured at Hudson's Bay in 1697 and by his considerable peltry trade, Iberville now entered into partnership with a merchant of Saint-Domingue, René Cochon de Maurepas, to purchase a sugar mill and cocoa plantation, a venture that would ultimately gain him over 13,000 *livres* in profits.[6]

Toward the middle of November thereupon, Iberville weighed anchor and departed Cap-français, his next port of call the Spanish Santa María de Galve—the port of Pensacola. Though a course of only some twenty-odd days it was to be the Canadian commander's

5. Iberville to min., Nov. 24, 1701, AM, B4, 21, f. 541–44. Fort La Boulaye, though known commonly as "fort du Mississippi," was officially named to honor the Inspector General of the Marine, Louis-Hyacinthe Plomier, Sieur de La Boulaye. Plomier, whom Iberville knew personally, was in the West Indies during the years 1699–1700 inspecting French fortifications in the islands. AM, 2 JJ 56. Of the two early forts or "blockhouses" built on the lower Mississippi, the first (1700–1707) was located on the southwestern bank of the river near the present community of Myrtle Grove, forty miles below the New Orleans Custom House. Point A La Hache, La. Quadrangle, 1948. N2930–W8945/15. Relation ou Journal du voyage du Père Gravier, Feb. 16, 1701, *JR*, *LXV*, pp. 160–61. Rémonville to min., Aug. 6, 1702, BN, FF, 9097, f. 127. ASH, 7 C 213.

6. *BRH*, *XLII*, p. 90. AM, C7, Iberville dossier, *n.p.* The Hudson's Bay campaign against the English had been Iberville's most glorious exploit. Now, at age forty, he had but one minor blemish on his record: conviction by the Conseil souverain de Québec in October 1688 of fathering an illegitimate daughter by Mlle. Jeanne-Geneviève Picoté de Belestre, for which he was condemned to support the child for thirteen years. *Cf. BRH*, *XXI*, p. 224. *Jugements et délibérations du Conseil souverain*, *III*, p. 258.

most grueling voyage; for, rounding the Île de la Tortue and drifting through the Windward Passage between Cuba and Hispaniola, Iberville began to be more and more agonized by a swelling in his side, a mounting pain that had begun in Cap-français and which had now reached almost unbearable intensity. Overwrought and besieged with fever, Iberville called once more for his surgeon, Pierre Clavery. Clavery's diagnosis was no different than it had been in Cap-français: a deep abscess in the abdominal wall (caused no doubt by an abrasion or small laceration which had subsequently become infected). At this advanced stage, there was but one course of action for the surgeon to follow: he was forced to make an immediate incision—a gash over six inches in length—which allowed the wound to begin draining, leaving the commander's body to fight the infection with what resources it could muster.[7]

Rounding now the western tip of Cuba, the Cabo San Antonio, the *Renommée* plunged directly into the cold, choppy Gulf of Mexico, Iberville's fevered brain reeling uncertainly . . . from his recent reverses to his own torturous side . . . to the shadowy, unknown Mobile River basin, where presently must begin the ordered establishment . . .

By the year 1701, the mysteries of the northern shoreline of the Gulf of Mexico had partially been cleared by the persistent if imperfect attempts of Spanish and French cartographers. It had been, in the main, a late seventeenth century achievement, made more difficult over the years by map publishers in Rome, Lisbon and Sevilla whose chief concern seemed to be the marketing of new charts which at best involved merely the copying of older maps embellished by an exotic name or two and at worst the deliberate altering of landscapes to suggest fresh surveys.[1]

From across the same horizons that Iberville was now crossing

7. Martínez a su magesdad, April 14, 1702, AGI, *México*, L. 618. Journal de Le Sueur, 1702, AM, 2 JJ 56,9. Journal d'Iberville, April 27, 1702, AM, B4, 23, f. 315–21; AC, F3, 24, f. 39–43. Depenses de l'Entretien . . . , AC, F1A, 10, f. 282.

1. *Cf.* Delanglez, *El Rio del Espiritu Santo*, pp. *xi–xiii*. Cumming, *The Southeast in Early Maps*, pp. 1–3. This is not to say there were no responsible attempts made by contemporary cartographers during the years 1500–1650, but for the most part the results of those efforts were too inaccessible during the last quarter of the seventeenth century.

had once returned scores of sixteenth and seventeenth century adventurers, seekers of gilded, undiscovered kingdoms. Returning to the old ports of Verapaz, San Cristóbal and Puerto Real, they told of marvelous villages and pearl-laden savages, of scepters of burnished bronze and fountains of everlasting youth. They told too another tale, of another treasure that hard-headed rulers who doubted the existence of more Inca and Aztec gold found much more credulous yet no less worthy of pursuit. They spoke of a fabulous bay of the north, a magnificent harbor capable of sheltering a hundred ships, on which a bustling port could be developed to exploit the riches of an untapped interior.[2] To many of these wandering seamen, the great northern bay lay at the center of the gulf crescent; to others it was much farther west or only slightly east of center. Of those who sailed in search of the fabled harbor were some who perhaps never reached it but found another, who discovering an inlet and certain it was the same, brought back similar tales of grandeur: it was wide and deep, opening from a narrow entrance to a vast expanse of calm; capable of protecting innumerable vessels from the most rigorous storms of the sea; its shorelines crowded with mysterious savages. No more certain than the bay's location was its appellation which varied (from one reporter to another) as "Mar pequeña," "Ochuse" or "Bahía del Espíritu Santo."[3]

Into that veritable unknown (apparently in the year 1520) had by government decree first been sent Álvarez de Pineda whose expedition (complete with map-maker) skirted closely the northern shoreline before returning to Veracruz bringing a somewhat crude drawing which indicated near the north-central-most point of the gulf arc a plainly unfinished outline of a conspicuous inlet.[4]

2. Dawson's arguments to the contrary, the hypothesis of "unknown navigators" seems more an inescapable conclusion than an "easy solution." The early seamen could not possibly have explored the entire gulf. Maps of this period were strewn with non-existent islands not because of false reports but merely to ornament. *Cf.* Dawson, *The Saint Lawrence Basin and its Borderlands*, pp. 54–55.

3. Fernández de Oviedo y Valdés, *Historia General y Naturel de las Indias, Islas y Tierra-firme del Mar Océano, II*, p. 143.

4. The unsigned, undated, untitled original is preserved at the Archivo General de Indias in Sevilla. AGI, *Patronato*, L. 26. Fernández de Navarette, *Colección de los Viajes . . . III*, pp. 148–49. *Colección de documentos inéditos relativos al descubrimiento, conquista y colonizatión de las posesiones españoles en América y occeania . . .* Vol. XXVIII, p. 500. Consejo de Indias, June 4, 1521. *Colección de documentos inéditos . . . Ultramar, XVIII*, p. 28.

At nearly that same time, an expedition sent out by Fernando Cortés returned from the gulf with a more definitive map showing in the same general vicinity a large unnamed bay into which emptied the broad Río del Espíritu Santo.[5]

Following the efforts of Pineda and Cortés came new, more confident expeditioners. Pánfilo de Narváez and Hernando de Soto, additions-to-be to a long necrology of ill-fated *voyageurs*, penetrated the southern interior en route to the renowned bay only to fall victim to the disasters of ambush and disease.[6]

Though Soto's expedition yielded little permanent knowledge, and Narváez's even less, a new legend was born of the *antelantado's* campaign—a newly discovered province 180 leagues upstream from the mysterious bay—a rich and abundant district called Coza.[7] Partly with the desire to rediscover Soto's province (whose reputation had swollen through the years) and partially with the idea of blazing an overland trail to the Atlantic, a new expedition was sent out from Veracruz in the summer of 1559, bound for a harbor which Soto's men had called Ochuse (considered the same which Guido de las Bazares, sent out the previous year to reconnoitre the coast more carefully, had named Bahía Filipina in honor of his sovereign). It was Bazares who had first pinpointed the bay of Mobile, who had described so fully the northcentral gulf that he left little doubt as to where he had been.[8] It is thus on the basis of Bazares' intelligence that the movements of Tristán de Luna can be accurately traced, not the case with any previous Gulf Coast exploration.

Receiving Bazares' reports, Luna had departed the port of Veracruz in 1559 in 13 ships with 500 soldiers, 1,000 colonists and 240 horses—the most ambitious enterprise yet undertaken in the New World.[9] Anchoring at Mobile Bay (Bazares' Bahía Filipina), Luna, however, summarily rejected the recommended site; for among

5. The original of this map is lost; an engraving, presumably after the original sketch, appeared in Peypus, *Praeclara* . . . in 1524. Earlier maps such as those by Waldseemüller, Canerio and Cantino cannot with certainty be accepted as actual representations of the northern gulf shoreline, despite similarities.

6. *Relación que dio Alvar, nuñez cabeça de vaca* . . . , pp. 36–97. *Relaçam verdadeira . . . feida per hũ fidalgo Delvas*, pp. *lxv–lxxv*.

7. Garcilaso de la Vega, *La Florida del Ynca, Historia del Adelantado Hernando de Soto* . . . , pp. 346–91.

8. Relación que hizieron Guido de las Bazares y los pilotos . . . 1559, AGI, *Gobierno*, L. 12.

9. Luna a su Majestad, May 1, 1559, AGI, *México*, L. 97.

his chosen crew were four survivors of Soto's expedition who quickly convinced him to sail farther east, to the bay of Ochuse where the veterans assured him was a finer harbor into which a mighty river flowed.[10]

Disembarking his cavalry near present-day Bon Secour, Luna dispatched the horsemen overland, while he and his ships moved on to a rendezvous at the appointed inlet. No sooner had Luna unloaded his vessels, however, and begun his establishment than he realized the broad river emptying into his harbor was a stream of little source. He may have been questioning whether to return to the larger but shallower Bahía Filipina when an awesome hurricane struck the coast disproving reports of "a bay which could resist all winds," forcing him to move inland in search of food, to a native village called Nanipicana on the river of Piachi (the present day Alabama).[11] After a disastrous year in the interior, during which Luna failed to achieve even the least of his objectives, the beleaguered commander moved his colony down the river of Piachi, back to Mobile Bay to a point on the lower eastern shore where two years earlier he had disembarked his cavalry.[12] Here he made another settlement, more because of the fish and clams that could temporarily support him than because of any strategic advantage. A few months later, failing of food and morale, he moved his distraught colony back to Ochuse from where the expedition disbanded and sailed to Spain by way of Havana.

While the Mobile Bay area was once again devoid of Europeans, contact with the harbor was not entirely broken although it now came to be known as the bay of Mobila[13] in consequence of the

10. At Luna's departure from Veracruz, he was uncertain whether Bazares' "Bahía Filipina" was Soto's "Ochuse." Upon arriving at Bazares' bay, however, he was easily convinced by Soto's veterans that the two were not the same and that Ochuse was superior. Soto himself had no knowledge of Mobile Bay. He believed that the Alabama River which he was following to the gulf would eventually lead him to the bay described by Maldonado as "Ochuse." Maldonado knew that a broad river emptied into Ochuse but he greatly overestimated its length. Velasco a Luna, September 13, 1560, AGI, *Justicia*, L. 1013.

11. Velasco a Luna, May 6, 1560, AGI, *Justicia*, L. 1013.

12. Los Capitanes al campo del Sargento Mayor, 1560, AGI, *Justicia*, L. 1013.

13. The name had been recorded by the chroniclers of Soto's expedition as "Mabila, Mavilla and Mauvila," according to Rangel, Elvas and Garcilaso de la Vega respectively. By 1693 the name had become fairly standardized as "Mobila" or "Movila" in Spanish documents. Diario de Torres y Ayala, Panzacola, Aug. 5, 1693, AGI, *México*, L. 616. Diario de Barreda,

natives (descendants of a village Soto partially destroyed in 1540) that moved into the area in the late sixteenth century. In the years after St. Augustine was founded in 1565, Franciscan missionaries had begun drifting from that port into the province called Apalache and from there occasionally made contact with natives from the bay of Mobile.[14] If, however, the missionaries of Apalache and the participants in Luna's adventure held a rough idea of the terrain so temporarily settled, the years between Luna's abandonment of Mobile Bay in 1561 and the Spanish reconnaissance missions of 1685–1693 saw a hazy obscurity return to Spanish Gulf Coast geography due to lack of official interest in the area and to the activities of unscrupulous cartographers whose altered names and indiscriminate indentations in the coastline were baffling even to the most experienced pilots. New world navigators (without accurate pilot maps), with little chance of reconciling the numerous discrepancies, were still confused when the Spanish began a new reconnaissance effort in 1685 brought on by reports of French intrusion on the gulf.

The search for the great bay (into which emptied a powerful river) was begun anew with numerous expeditions by sea from 1686 to 1693 and by such inland *jornadas* as the missions of Marcos Delgado [15] and Torres y Ayala.[16] On the 22nd of May 1687, Martín de Rivas entered Mobile Bay and came to the reluctant

---

Aug. 3, 1693, AGI, *México*, L. 616. While Tonti in 1686 and Châteaumorand in 1699 followed the Spanish "Mobila," the French, after 1700, began recording "Mobile" or "Mobille," a word which used adjectively meant "capable of moving or of being moved," in French as in English. Iberville to min., Sept. 7, 1700, AM, B4, 20, f. 371–73. Iberville to min., February 15, 1703, AM B4, 25, f. 372–75. "Mobile," however was not a French rendering of the Spanish "Movíle." The Spanish claimed that the natives themselves gave the name "Mobila" to the bay. Carta de Francisco Martínez, April 14, 1702, AGI, *México*, L. 618. Iberville, thanks to Claude Delisle, was familiar with the narratives of Garcilaso de la Vega and the gentleman of Elvas. Notes de Claude Delisle sur la géographie de la Louisiane (Questions sur la Route de Soto), vers 1703, AM, 2 JJ 56, 17.

14. Antonio Matheos al gobernador y capitán-general de la Florida, May 19, 1606. In Serrano y Sanz, *Documentos históricos de la Florida y la Luisiana*, p. 197. Alonso de Benavides, *Memorial Que Fray Juan de Santander de la Orden de San Francisco, Comissario General de Indias, presenta a la Magestad Catolica del Rey don Felipe Quarto Nuestro Señor*, pp. 93–96.

15. Delgado a Cabrera, Sept. 19, 1686, AGI, *México*, L. 616. Matheos a Cabrera, Sept. 29, 1689, AGI, *México*, L. 616.

16. Diario de Torres y Ayala, August 5, 1693, AGI, *México*, L. 616.

conclusion that here must be the mythical port of Espíritu Santo so often and so variously described by the ancient mariners.[17] Yet it was not now so glorious as had been pictured in earlier days. A further, more complete examination was made in the summer of 1693 by Francisco Milán Tapia whose detailed report included six sketches of the shoreline as well as descriptions of the islands and measurements of the bay depths.[18]

As a result of the findings of Rivas and Milán Tapia, Spanish interest had focused on a bay farther east which the Mexican cosmographer Sigüenza y Góngora hailed as the "finest jewel in possession of His Majesty," and which he rightly reckoned as Soto's "Ochuse" and Luna's "Santa María de Filipina."

Iberville had for the most part been unaware of the details of the recent Spanish explorations when he was chosen in the winter of 1698 to explore the northcentral gulf (in effect, to continue the work of La Salle) and to secure the mouth of the Mississippi by establishing an outpost at the most strategic location.[1] In January 1699 (after finding the Spanish firmly lodged at Pensacola) he had sounded the entrance to Mobile Bay in blustering winds and torrential rains, conditions which prevented him from discovering adequate anchorage. Had weather allowed, he would surely have discovered the harbor between Pelican and Massacre Islands (which, though lacking the depth of Pensacola's bay, would have been sufficient to his purpose), would have gone thence to the Île des vaisseaux from where he would have discovered entrance to the Mississippi before returning to Mobile Bay to erect his initial outpost. Failing to discover suitable anchorage at Massacre Island, however, (nor suspecting he was at the harbor which the Spanish

17. Andrés de Pez y Martín de Rivas al Conde de Monclova, July 24, 1688, AGI, *México*, L. 616.

18. Diario de Francisco Milán Tapia, Aug. 1, 1693, AGI, *México*, L. 616.

1. Mémoire, BN, Ms. Clairambault, 495, f. 485–92. Iberville to min., June 18, 1698, AC, C13A, 1, f. 83–89. Iberville to min., AM, B4, 19, f. 370–76. Min. to Iberville, June 25, 1698, AC, B 20, f. 102–05. Iberville had access, however, to at least one Spanish chart, a copy of which had been sent to him by Nicolas de La Salle, through Pontchartrain, in Sept., 1698. The original map had been taken from a Spanish ship captured by Pierre Patoulet de Mazy of the *Bon* in 1697. Min. to La Salle, Aug. 27, 1698, AC, B 21, f. 173–74.

were now calling Espíritu Santo), Iberville had moved on to Biloxi Bay where he established Fort Maurepas, then sailed back to France. Since that time he had returned to Louisiana only once (in early 1700), the only products of that expedition being the construction of a small outpost on the lower Mississippi and the acquisition of more data concerning the topography of the coast and of the interior.[2]

Returning now on the third of his strategic missions, Iberville had a much better grasp of the Louisiana landscape as well as of political aims in both Europe and North America. Although the minister of marine, Jérôme Phélypeaux, Comte de Pontchartrain, was keeping close rein on his own personal feelings, Iberville felt confident of Pontchartrain's sincere interest in the establishment and development of a colony that would grow and endure.[3] Conversely, Pontchartrain felt assurance in Iberville's general strategy to secure and develop Louisiana: Mobile Bay had been recommended by the commander as the location to establish a colony (in the event the Spanish refused to cede Pensacola) as early as the spring of 1700. Iberville's reasons for preferring this location were mainly two in number: first of all, in view of the fact that an adequate harbor had been discovered at Massacre Island (and that the timber and water resources were considered superior) it offered much better material advantages than either Biloxi Bay or the lower Mississippi. Secondly, though he well realized the necessity of maintaining the security of the Mississippi (and planned colonization as well as continued development of its fortifications), the Alabama-Tombigbee river system seemed of more immediate strategic value. Because of its closer proximity to the line of English advance, it offered greater opportunities to communicate with the principal nations of the interior—the Choctaw, the Chickasaw and the Alabama—nations which Iberville must win over if he were to stem the tide of the numerically superior Carolinians and

2. Journal du *Marin*, BN, FF, 9097, f. 21–38. *Journal Historique*, pp. 6–29. Journal d'Iberville, BN, FF, NA, 9296, f. 9–26. Martínez al gobernador de la Habana, Feb. 21, 1699, AGI, *México*, L. 618. Andrés de Arriola al rey, May 9, 1699, AGI, *México*, L. 618. Arriola al virrey, Feb. 20, 1699, AGI, *México*, L. 618.

3. While Louis XIV's view of Louisiana at this juncture was essentially pragmatic, Pontchartrain's attitude appears more subjective. Though retaining a basic practicality, the minister seems at times like a proud philatelist surveying his collection while trying to forget its possible cost-value ratio. Min. to Bégon, April 22, 1699, AM, B2, 140, f. 115–16. Min. to Iberville, Aug. 26, 1699, AC, B 20, f. 267–69.

Virginians who would eventually, he was certain, begin to flood the southern frontier. If communication, then, with the interior tribes were the paramount consideration of Iberville's colonial policy in 1701 (and if the Spanish remained adamant in their determination to hold Pensacola), the bay of Mobile seemed not only a preferred choice but the only real alternative as the location for the new (and hopefully permanent) establishment.[4]

Nearing landfall on the coast of Florida in the second week of December, 1701, his body still racked with pain as a result of Clavery's incision, Iberville's brain was trying desperately to focus on some unnamed and unfixed point in the massive area between Massacre Island's harbor at the entrance of the bay and the village of the Mobile Indians some 73 miles upstream. Where in that ungentle scrubland, in that vast expanse of bayous, bogs and bluffs would the ailing commander begin his new establishment? By what logistics would he transfer a decadent outpost on the bay of Biloxi and build a thriving village in the wilderness?

The details of his tactics were not yet certain but his scheme had already been set.

4. Bégon to Villermont, June 12, 1700, BN, FF, 22809, f. 254–57. Iberville to min., Sept. 7, 1700, AM, B4, 20, f. 422–37. Mémoire par Iberville [1701], AC, C13A, 1, f. 334–38.

I

Confrontment at Pensacola

IBERVILLE'S ships made their landfall on the fifteenth of December at three o'clock in the afternoon five and a half miles to the east of the bay of Pensacola. By early evening the commander's pilots had moved the four ships (the *Renommée*, the *Palmier* and two smaller vessels) to the entrance of the port, where they anchored in six fathoms of water. After sending an officer to Fort San Carlos to ask permission of the Spanish governor [1] to enter the harbor, Iberville, still flushed with fever and barely able to move about, retired for the night, not anticipating a reply until morning.[2]

As to whether or not the governor (whom the French thought to be Andrés de Arriola) would allow him entrance, Iberville could only guess. It had been nearly three years since he had first anchored at the approach to Pensacola. On that occasion, he had been refused entrance to the harbor by this same Andrés de Arriola, a brilliant but sometimes erratic officer and engineer whose exploits in the field of exploration rivaled those of Iberville, culminating in his founding of Pensacola in 1698.[3] Although Arriola

1. Junta de Guerra de Indias, August 1, 1702, AGI, *México*, L. 618. Although Bienville's title, as king's lieutenant, would be simply "commandant" for the years 1702–1711, the Spanish authority at Pensacola was known as "gobernador." AC, F1A, 10, f. 282; 13, f. 113. ADM, A, Jan. 19, 1710. El gobernador de Panzacola al rey, July 12, 1713, AGI, *México*, L. 632. Louisiana had no titled governor living at Mobile until the arrival of Cadillac in 1713. Both Iberville (appointed in 1703) and Daneau de Muy (named in 1707) died before arriving. Cadillac to min., Oct. 26, 1713, AC, C13A, 3, f. 48. Min. to Brisacier, May 25, 1707, AC, B 29, f. 262–62v.

2. Journal d'Iberville, Dec. 15, 1701—April 27, 1702, AM, B4, 23, f. 315–17.

3. Consulta del Consejo de las Indias, March 12, 1705, AGI, *Santo Domingo*, L. 851. Relación de servicios, Oct. 25, 1695, AGI, *México*, L. 615. Arriola al rey, Nov. 15, 1699, AGI, *México*, L. 618.

had never been enthusiastic about the value of his fortress, he had nonetheless been diligent in carrying out orders to defend it. Yet in the three years that had elapsed since the fort's establishment, European politics had changed drastically. Since 1700 France and Spain had been moving closer together against an expanding English foe and while the court in Madrid had remained adamant in refusing to cede Pensacola to the French, Iberville had good reason to expect closer co-operation in Louisiana by virtue of both nations' distrust of their common adversary.[4]

Early the following morning Iberville's messenger returned, bringing with him a pilot sent by the Spanish governor to aid the French in entering the harbor. Only a single pilot was sent, however, and Iberville had requested two. Did this mean the Spanish were but half-heartedly offering to co-operate, hoping perhaps that one of Iberville's ships might run aground? Annoyed, but slightly more alert after his only good night's rest since leaving Cap-français, Iberville sent the Spanish pilot on to the *Palmier*, then supervised one of his own pilots in steering the *Renommée* into the harbor where after some difficulty she was eventually anchored. After a seven-gun salute had been offered by the French (which the guns of San Carlos answered equally), the Spanish governor, "a well-built man, possessing the manners of a Frenchman," came aboard the flagship along with several of his officers. The Spanish commander, however, was not the one whom Iberville expected. He was in reality only the acting governor, Sergeant-Major Francisco de Córcoles y Martínez, replacing for the time being the absent Andrés de Arriola who had recently sailed for the port of Veracruz in search of food and supplies.[5]

Martínez, then, would be the authority with whom Iberville would have to treat. Actually, Iberville knew the acting governor well, both personally and by reputation; for Martínez had been active on the Gulf Coast since 1685 when he had played a significant role in the Spanish search for the colony of Cavelier de La Salle. Martínez had risen through the ranks from cadet to captain; he had campaigned in Ceuta and Catalonia, in Palermos and Gibraltar. He had been a prisoner of war in France and counted wounds in his left arm and right leg among his battle scars. Arrogant on

4. Min. to Harcourt, July 27, 1701, AM, B2, 155, f. 179–82.

5. Para despachar una carta de Martínez, April 14, 1702, AGI, *México*, L. 618. Consulta del Junta de Guerra, Aug. 1, 1702, AGI, *México*, L. 633. Arriola al Consejo de las Indias, Nov. 15, 1701, AGI, *México*, L. 618. Journal de Le Sueur, Feb. 1, 1702, AM, 2 JJ 56, 9.

occasion, even recalcitrant, as when he later refused to conduct the *residencia* of a former St. Augustine governor's administration because he said he was "too busy fighting Indians," Martínez was nevertheless an uncompromising patriot as well as a zealous administrator.[6]

In contrast to earlier meetings between Iberville and Spanish officials, this December confrontation could not have started on more amicable terms, especially when Iberville confirmed the news of the elevation of the grandson of Louis XIV, Philippe de Bourbon, to the crown of Spain. Martínez offered Iberville "his services" and Iberville offered Martínez the same. Yet Iberville must have wondered at the governor's apparently excessive cordiality. What, in fact, did the French have to offer the Spanish? Was not Martínez firmly established at the most coveted harbor on the Gulf Coast? Was not Iberville once again treading on territory that the Spanish government was claiming as its exclusive domain? Even a cursory examination of the fort of San Carlos, however, would have given a clue to Martínez's hospitality. For the three-year-old *fuerte* was in fearful straits, and had been so practically from its establishment in November, 1698 by Andrés de Arriola and Juan Jordán de Reina.[7] Not only was the fort itself already beginning to rot at the bastions, but leaky roofs and fires (at least one of which had been ignited by a member of the garrison) had helped keep the settlement in a pitiable condition. Added to this was the almost constant threat of desertion and mutiny and the continual lack of food and supplies, all of which resulted in a decidedly thin morale. On previous expeditions, Iberville had been quick to recognize that the harbor of Pensacola, though adorned

6. Memorial de Don Francisco Córcoles y Martínez, April 20, 1705, AGI, *Santo Domingo*, L. 833. Although this Spanish officer is variously listed in Spanish and French documents as Martínez, Córcoles, or Córcoles y Martínez, his signature is generally Martínez. Martínez a Guzmán, Feb. 1, 1702, AGI, *México*, L. 618. Consulta del Consejo de las Indias, Sept. 13, 1713, AGI, *Santo Domingo*, L. 836.

7. Andrés de Arriola al rey, Dec. 1, 1698, AGI, *México*, L. 618. The fort had been named San Carlos for Archduke Karl of Austria. Designed and constructed by the Austrian engineer Jakob Franck, it was similar in size and shape to Fort Maurepas and the first Fort Louis. Although the site has not yet been rediscovered by archaeologists, my investigation indicates it must have been located several hundred yards east of where the ruins of Fort Barrancas now stand. Plano de Santa María de Galve, 1698, AGI, *México*, L. 617. Notes de Claude Delisle sur la géographie de la Louisiane, AM, 2 JJ, 56, 17.

with a well-designed fort, was not really immune to invasion because the eight and ten pounder cannons were effective up to a range of only five hundred yards and the entrance to the harbor covered a breadth of nearly one and a half miles (from the *presidio* to the tip of Santa Rosa Island across the bay).[8]

In a private conference with Martínez Iberville disclosed his plans to establish a fort and colony at Mobile Bay. Martínez, while taken aback, only listened attentively (for the time being). The governor, however, had some disturbing news himself: Ensign Sauvole, commandant of Fort Maurepas, had died the previous August 22 of the same malady that he had described in his journal. Unknown to Iberville, the commander's brother, Bienville, was now in charge at the Biloxi fort, leaving Louis Juchereau de Saint-Denis in command of Fort La Boulaye on the Mississippi. Moreover, neither Bienville nor the majority of the garrison had fully recovered from the effects of that late-summer epidemic. Having relayed this information, Martínez returned to Fort San Carlos and Iberville retired for the evening.[9]

The next morning, December 17, Iberville dispatched Desjordy-Moreau and Le Moyne de Châteaugué in a felucca to Fort Maurepas with orders for Bienville to begin the establishment of Mobile: Bienville was to proceed at once to Massacre (now Dauphin) Island in the longboats and the smack with everything necessary for the new establishment. Jousselin de Marigny, whom Iberville had earlier sent from Cap-français, was to load the guns and other effects of the garrison, while *aide-major* Dugué de Boisbriant was, with 20 soldiers, to guard what remained at the fort. All the officers, laborers and craftsmen were to proceed with Marigny and Bienville to begin work on a warehouse at Massacre

8. Jakob Franck a Martín de Sierra Alta, Feb. 19, 1699, AGI, *México*, L. 618. Although maximum range of these pieces was nearly a mile their effective range was closer to 1500 feet. In any case it was clear to Iberville (though he misjudged the guns to be only 6 and 8-pounders) that Pensacola Bay was not adequately defended. Andrés de Arriola al rey, Dec. 1, 1698, AGI, *México*, L. 618. Fort Barrancas Quadrangle, 1970, U.S. Dept. of the Interior Geological Survey Map (7.5 minute series), N3015–W8715/7.5. Auttos fechos sobre las providentias dadas sobre la preocupación y fortificación de Santa María de Galve, año de 1703, AGI, *México*, L. 618.

9. Journal de Sauvole, Aug. 4, 1701, AC, F3, 24, f. 35–35v. Apparently Iberville kept this information secret for the time being, for other officials aboard the *Renommée* did not learn of Sauvole's death until the return of Desjordy-Moreau from Biloxi on December 31. La Salle to min., April 1, 1702, AC, C13C, 2, f. 35.

Island where Iberville would join them when he had sufficiently recuperated.[10]

The activities of Iberville's men in beginning the fortification of Mobile were keenly observed by Martínez during the next few weeks. They were in fact taking place with the Spanish governor's private blessing; for Martínez well realized that the Spanish garrison, far from the authority of Mexico City, had a good deal to gain at this point by French presence at Mobile, one advantage of which had sharply come home to him the previous week when a French longboat, on its way to seek corn from the village of the Little Tomeh, delivered up five of sixteen Spanish deserters.[11]

For the record, nevertheless, Martínez penned an official request to Iberville on the night of December 31, which he had delivered the next day by his captain of infantry, Joseph de Robles y Morales:

> As you have informed me of your orders from His Very Christian Majesty to take possession of the Mobile River . . . and to erect fortifications there . . . I will tell you, as I am bound to do, that my orders from the Viceroy and Captain-General of this country . . . point to maintaining good relations with you . . . and that I should ask of you, or give you, whatever may be necessary in any emergency which may arise, that I should befriend and support the natives of the Mobila, Tome and La Grande Chacta . . . I nevertheless request you to suspend the execution of your intention of proceeding to take possession of the Mobile, until I have reported it to the Viceroy; and, as I have no vessel here, nor a pilot, I am obliged to request you to lend me one of those which you have with you here, even if it be the smallest, as long as it is equipped with what is necessary to sail to New Spain, whence my orders are to come to me.
>
> As for us, you may feel confident that I am very much aware of the close alliance of the two Crowns, and that the

10. Journal d'Iberville, April 27, 1702, AM, B4, 23, f. 316–21. Iberville himself had named the island "Massacre" after having discovered on Feb. 1, 1699 "sixty skeletons at the southwest extremity of the island, skulls as well as bones three or four years old with household effects." Journal d'Iberville, 1698–99, AM, 2 JJ 56, 4.

11. Martínez a Guzmán, Feb. 1, 1702, AGI, *México*, L. 618. Two days later, Iberville notified Martínez of his intentions in writing. Para despachar una carta de Francisco Martínez, April 14, 1702, AGI, *México*, L. 618. Journal de Le Sueur, Nov. 30, 1702, AM, 2 JJ 56, 9.

> object with which His Very Christian Majesty has determined about this matter is of great advantage to our monarchy . . . This inquiry is made by me only in the course of duty. Meanwhile I am always ready to carry out what you may be pleased to order, promising to accomplish it with hearty goodwill in return for whatever I owe you. May God guard and protect you for many years.[12]

Iberville must have been struck by the irony of the Spanish governor's message. Martínez was in one breath begging Iberville to suspend plans for fortifying Mobile Bay (which Iberville knew was what the governor actually desired) and with the other was pleading for a ship to send to Veracruz to ask what the viceroy's orders on the matter would be. Iberville knew too, from reports he received on the condition of the Pensacola *presidio*, that advice from the viceroy was not the only reason Martínez sought a vessel to send to Veracruz.

Receiving Martínez's missive in much the same spirit in which it was sent, Iberville dispatched the following reply two days later:

> . . . I will lend you one of my vessels with pleasure, Monsieur . . . if you have a pilot to put on board, or one of your officers who knows that country; for I have no one on my ship who has been on that coast. I will have it readied for that objective, but as I have orders to form a settlement on the Mobile, and have but two months to remain on this coast, I cannot put it off and must set to work immediately . . .[13]

Iberville went on to explain that he had no other objective than to stop the advance of the English by supporting the natives of the districts which were allied to France and Spain. His intention was not only to befriend the natives but to arm them as well and to supply them with the necessary ammunition to defend themselves against the savages in concert with the English. Having emphasized this, he added:

> . . . it appears to me, Monsieur, that in view of the smallness of your force at Pensacola, it would be to the interest of Spain to induce the Appalache to oppose the raids which are made daily by the allies of the English in the vicinity of your

12. Martínez to Iberville, January 1, 1702, AC, F3, 24, f. 37. AC, C13A, 1, f. 361–62. This dispatch was written in Spanish by the bilingual Martínez. A copy under the same date is in AGI, *México*, L. 618.

13. Iberville to Martínez, Jan. 3, 1702, AC, C13A, 1, f. 357–58.

> district. This is a nation which is at your disposal yet you leave them at rest while the English and their allies are destroying the other tribes which are allied to us. This smooths the way for the English at the posts which they already have among over twenty tribes in this vicinity. It is most important in the interests of the two Crowns to prevent such activity for it is an evil to which a remedy should be applied before it gets worse.
>
> . . . I will not omit anything whatever which should be done to thwart the schemes of the English and their allies. I am supplied with everything that is needed for that purpose, and it would be advantageous that we should take steps to succeed in this together. I am certain that if you were in a position to do what I am doing you would do the same thing, but I understand that, destitute as you now are of everything, it is not possible for you to assist me in this undertaking.
>
> I have already had the pleasure of offering you, Monsieur, everything I have here, whether men, provisions or stores, and in general all that is in my power. You will oblige me by making use of them as if they were entirely at your disposal.[14]

By the time Martínez received Iberville's reply, Desjordy-Moreau and Châteaugué had already returned from Fort Maurepas with news that Jousselin de Marigny's smack (which Iberville had sent from Cap-français) had never arrived. This indeed was alarming, for supposedly Marigny had plenty of time in which to complete the voyage. Commandant Bienville, nevertheless, sent news that he had fully recovered from his illness and that he was proceeding to Mobile Bay, though more than half his men were still sick or convalescent. For better or for worse, the establishment of Mobile was about to begin.

14. *Ibid.*, f. 358–60.

II

Transfer to Massacre Island

BIENVILLE began his move from the bay of Biloxi on January 4, 1702, sending out a freighter and two feluccas loaded with Fort Maurepas' belongings. The next day, the fifth of January, he departed the fort himself, bringing with him the majority of the garrison as well as the remainder of the Canadians and a small number of French artisans.[1]

On the third of January, Iberville had dispatched a Canadian merchant-sailor named François Pillet, commander of the forty-five ton ketch *Dauphine*, to Massacre Island, laden with the bulk of new supplies brought to Louisiana on the *Renommée* and the *Palmier*, including three exceptionally large tents which were to protect the colony's goods until the warehouse could be built.[2]

1. *Journal Historique*, pp. 36–37. The portion of the foregoing journal used as reference in this work was assembled either by the royal geographer, Jean de Beaurain (1696–1772) or, more likely, by Jean-Baptiste Bénard de La Harpe (1686–1765) from incoming reports of Bienville, La Salle *et al.* A close study of the *Journal's* early entries (particularly those of the years 1703–1705) indicates that much of the information came from letters now missing from Vol. 1 of C13A in the Archives des Colonies, letters known to have been received by Pontchartrain. Min. to Bienville, Nov. 4, 1705, AC, B 27, f. 188–88v. Min. to La Salle, July 23, 1707, AC, B 29, f. 29. *Cf.* Wedel, "The Bénard de La Harpe Historiography on French Colonial Louisiana," *Louisiana Studies*, XIII, No. 1, pp. 5–67. Where there are differences in the various manuscripts and editions I have followed the Chicago Historical Society Manuscript.

2. Pillet, *dit* Lajeunesse, 37-year-old native of Paris, had formerly commanded the *Saint-François Xavier*, *DGFC*, *I*, p. 484. AJTR, Greffe de Cusson, March 10, 1691. AJQ, Greffe de Rageot, April 24, 30, 1691. Estat de la Depense qui a esté faite par M. d'Iberville pour les Marchandises et autres choses nécessaires pour l'établissement de la Rivière de la Mobille depuis le premier janvier au 31 Mars, 1702, AC, F1A, 10, f. 288–90v. Compare with La Salle's report signed aboard the *Renommée* just before Iberville's return to France. La Salle, April 20, 1702, AC, C13A, 1, f. 371–76.

Pillet's ketch, however (hired at seven *livres* per ton), was only spacious enough to transport a small portion of the goods brought by the *Renommée* and the *Palmier*. The transference of equipment and supplies loaded at Rochefort and La Rochelle (as well as the livestock taken on at Cap-français) would require innumerable trips, especially as Iberville intended keeping the *Renommée* anchored in Pensacola Bay for the duration of the expedition. Nor did Iberville have on hand the diversity of craft he needed to accomplish the various voyages between Pensacola and Massacre Island and from Massacre Island to the Mobile River.

To aid him in establishing the new settlement, Iberville appealed to Governor Martínez, who was only too willing to deliver the French four of his own boats in return for the traversier he hoped Iberville would lend him for a voyage to Veracruz. Following Martínez's delivery of a medium-sized launch, two of Iberville's brothers, Joseph Le Moyne de Sérigny and Antoine Le Moyne de Châteaugué (both of whom were to play vital roles in the founding of Mobile), set out on the first of several voyages to Massacre Island.[3]

The primary order of business, it seemed to Iberville, was the completion of the king's warehouse to protect the colony's most valuable supplies (not only from the vicissitudes of weather but also from the sometimes furtive hands of his own men). To help supervise the construction of the warehouse as well as to take charge of the unloading of supplies, Iberville sent a middle-aged Frenchman, Nicolas de La Salle, with Pillet on the *Dauphine's* initial trip to Massacre Island. La Salle, whose career was to span the whole of Old Mobile's history (excepting the last five months) had come highly recommended by Iberville himself. Born of a Parisian family long in the civil service of France, Nicolas had, as a younger man, accompanied Cavelier de La Salle and Henri de Tonti on their historic voyage to the mouth of the Mississippi in 1682. Subsequently recalled to France after seven years of service in Canada, La Salle had been employed as a purser in the navy at the port of Toulon when Iberville's Louisiana enterprise was launched in 1698.[4] When Pontchartrain sought him out the fol-

3. Martínez a Guzmán, Feb. 1, 1702, AGI, *México*, L. 618. Para despachar una carta de Francisco Martínez, April 14, 1702, AGI, *México*, L. 618.

4. Nicolas, son of Nicolas de La Salle and Marie Harot, had two brothers who died while serving France. Charles, commissary-general of the galleys at Marseille died in 1695 and another brother died in 1690 while serving as commissary of the Marine and Intendant in Siam. La Salle to min., July

lowing year in connection with some *mémoires* he had reputedly written concerning his Mississippi experiences, La Salle thought he saw unusual opportunity in the land he had long ago departed. After all, was he not now one of a dwindling clan of survivors of Cavelier de La Salle's epic journey? Would not his willingness to serve in a not-too-promising enterprise neatly coincide with the minister's search for experienced personnel? Applying to Pontchartrain in July of 1700, La Salle asked for "a better post than that which I now fill, in which it is almost impossible for me to live, burdened as I am with a large family." [5] Pontchartrain, mindful of the immediate need in Louisiana for a more efficient clerk, suggested La Salle's name to Iberville who, anxious to enlist both capable servants and large families for his colony-to-be, saw a double advantage in La Salle's recruitment.[6] Though at first more interested in the fact that La Salle would be bringing along his wife and three young sons (Nicolas, Simon and François), Iberville was quickly impressed with La Salle's work at La Rochelle in the summer of 1701, describing the *écrivain* as "a most worthy man, capable of discharging the duties of his appointment well." [7] After further observing La Salle's work, Iberville had personally requested for his new recruit a higher salary than the fifty *livres* per month allotted him, which eventually resulted in La Salle's raise in pay (a favor that Iberville would not fail to remind him of several years later).[8]

On the fifth of January, 1702, La Salle and his family approached Massacre Island, along with Sérigny and Châteaugué. The heavy northwest winds were unfavorable for entering the

---

22, 1700, AC, C13B, 1, No. 4, f. 2. Min. to La Salle, Aug. 27, 1698, AC, B 21, f. 173–74. Min. to Bégon, June 1, 1701, AM, B2, 154, f. 523–24.

5. La Salle to min., July 28, 1700, AC, C13B, 1, No. 5, f. 1–2. La Salle had married Madelaine Chartroux on June 24, 1692 in Toulon. Madelaine, daughter of Antoine Chartroux and Anne Le Vray, was of an old Toulon family, one branch of which traced their ancestral roots to fifteenth century Paris. By 1699 she had borne La Salle at least three sons. Archives Municipales de Toulon, Mariages (Paroisse de Sainte-Marie), June 16, 1699; Feb. 5, 1640; March 27, 1663. État civil, GG 85, f. 32v; 87, f. 224; 92, f. 13. Archives département du Var, ville de Toulon, 7 E État civil, 24 juin, 1692.

6. Min. to Bégon, June 1, 1701, AM, B2, 154 f. 524. Min. to Bégon, June 22, 1701, AM, B2, 154, f. 641–43. Ordre royal, May 29, 1701, AM, B2, 152, f. 121.

7. Iberville to min., July 30, 1701, AM, B4, 21, f. 532.

8. Compare AC, Fonds des colonies, F1A, 10, f. 281–82 and F1A, 13, f. 113. La Salle's salary had by 1706 increased to 800 *livres* per year.

harbor inside Pelican Island, which forced the vessel to anchor outside the inlet and which necessitated the supplies to be unloaded by the remainder of the boats loaned the French by Martínez which were manned by members of the *Renommée's* crew. Later, when the winds subsided, the Spanish launch was able to enter the inner harbor, near enough to the shoreline for the remaining cargo to be unloaded in rowboats. Sérigny found a depth of twenty-one feet at low tide, which prompted La Salle to report:

> There is a good bottom at all parts of this roadstead . . . it is one of the best harbors on all this coast, and vessels of forty and fifty guns would be completely safe here. There will always be water and wood for ships. If the great drought in summer should dry up the water, they could take it in by means of long-boats a league within the bay of Mobile.[9]

Late in the afternoon of the fifth of January, Bienville arrived at Massacre Island with Charles Levasseur, a veteran Canadian lieutenant, and forty men of the Fort Maurepas garrison. Bienville's cousin, aide-major Dugué de Boisbriant, had remained at Fort Maurepas with the garrison's residue of twenty soldiers.

It was at Massacre Island that La Salle and Bienville first came into personal contact. Neither of the two officials on that cool January evening could foresee the tempests that would shatter their future relationship. La Salle knew Bienville only by reputation, most of his information coming from Bienville's relatives—Iberville, Châteaugué and one of the Le Moyne's two brothers-in-law, Pierre-Jacques Payen de Noyan—all of whom La Salle at this point held in the highest regard. Yet even at this early juncture La Salle must have questioned the wisdom of placing so much responsibility on a young man half his own age. Brash though engaging, given to frequent illness though his stocky frame possessed unusual stamina, Bienville was experienced far beyond his twenty-one years. While adept enough at the simpler native languages and possessed of an exceptional single-mindedness, Bienville's most conspicuous advantage at this point in his career was his family name—Le Moyne. Orphaned at the age of ten (his father had been among Montreal's most wealthy merchants), the young Canadian had been reared by his already renowned brothers

9. La Salle to min., April 1, 1702, AC, C13C, 2, f. 35.

—Charles, Pierre and Joseph. His considerable native ability had been tempered by the stark realities of Indian massacres and combats at sea and by the instruction of kinsmen more able and mature than he. His father's name was a memory commanding respect if not affection among all Canadians and since the *Québecois* constituted the most numerous and most influential group in the colony, his family connections gave him greater advantage at this stage in his service than perhaps his qualifications warranted.[10]

In any event, after a cordial meeting, the next day (the sixth of January) the two officials began in earnest to pursue their separate tasks. While Bienville, with Sérigny and Charles Levasseur, was making preparations for beginning the principal establishment at some as-yet-undetermined bluff on the Mobile River, La Salle and Châteaugué set to work on their respective responsibilities: Châteaugué's chief assignment as the official in charge of the Massacre Island post, was to see the warehouse to its completion, while La Salle busied himself with signing the artisans to contracts for the construction work and with recording the items being unloaded from the incoming craft.

Among the goods La Salle and his assistant (the Sieur Gerard) checked off at Massacre Island as they were delivered by the ketch and the four small Spanish boats were 13 large barrels of wine with a capacity of 225 *litres* each at 100 *livres* per barrel, 4 casks of flour at 66 *livres* per cask and 1 large barrel of lard at 180 *livres*. François Pillet had delivered from the *Dauphine* 7 casks of lard costing the king 560 *livres*, 24 casks of flour at 1584 *livres*, 5 casks of meat at 250 *livres* and 5,000 wooden shingles at 40 *livres* per thousand. Besides the foregoing items were large quantities of molasses, wheat, barley and 220 *litres* of sugar Iberville had purchased at Cap-français.[11]

In addition to the provisions brought for the new establishment, the ships unloaded goods for a special expedition into the interior: for Henri de Tonti's proposed peace mission to the Choctaw and Chickasaw country La Salle checked off cooking pots, axes, guns, butcher knives, red stockings (for red was the color the natives preferred), and above all, hand bells and glass beads. The merchandise for the native villages, carefully selected, had been fur-

10. Journal d'Iberville, April 27, 1702, AM, B4, 23, f. 316–29.

11. La Salle to min., March 4, 1708, AC, C13B, 1, No. 8, f. 2–3v. Estat de la Depense, March 31, 1702, AC, F1A, 10, f. 288–90v. La Salle, April 20, 1702, AC, C13A, 1, f. 371–76.

nished by the French merchant La Gresse at a total cost of 552 *livres.*[12]

There were other diverse items checked off by La Salle and his assistants: small tools, such as tack hammers, planes, chisels, pliers, iron punches, two-handled saws, as well as heavier implements, such as the sledge hammers furnished by Michel Beaussier, the gunsmith-merchant from La Flèche. Finally, such articles as half-hour sand glasses and a large clock (priced at 160 *livres*) were unloaded and, like the rest, placed on the shore near the site where the warehouse was being constructed. While the warehouse was being completed by the craftsmen and laborers from Fort Maurepas (among them carpenters Pierre Ardouin and Pierre Gasque of La Rochelle, calkers Jacques Le Compte and Jean La Salle and masons and roofers such as Pierre La Brie, and Pierre Bloquien of Bordeaux), the unloaded merchandise was housed in the three large tents sold to the colony by the Montreal merchant Charleville, while the soldiers and Canadians, even La Salle's family, were forced to seek shelter under the pines just back from the sand beaches and under small make-shift lean-tos.[13]

By the tenth of January, five days after Bienville's arrival, the basic structure of the wooden warehouse had been erected. Only the roof lacked completion. The building was over fifty feet long and had a width of some twenty-five feet, standing twelve feet in height between two sheds—not a monumental structure but a good deal more spacious than either of the two *magasins* to be built upriver.[14]

The port at Massacre Island, while at this point only in an embryonic stage, was the beginning of what was to be the most strategic location the French would make on the Gulf Coast and one which would remain so as long as Old (and later New) Mobile remained the capital of Louisiana. For only at Massacre Island (at least, within the confines of what the French then claimed as

12. AC, F1A, 10, f. 288v. AC, C13A, 1, f. 371–73. For comparison of supplies requested by Iberville with those he actually received, contrast the preceding documents with the following: Iberville to min., July 9, 1701, AM, B4, 21, f. 514–35. Mémoire sur le Mississipi, July 12, 1701, AM, B4, 21, f. 544–46. Min. to Bégon, July 6, 1701, AM, B2, 155, f. 1–12.

13. Depenses de l'Entretien et sub.[ee] de la garnison et ouvriers du fort Louis de la Louisiane pendant l'année derniere 1702, Nov. 24, 1703, AC, F1A, 11, f. 87–91.

14. Dénombrement du 31 aoust 1704, AC, C13A, 1, f. 468. This warehouse was only slightly smaller than the one built to replace it in 1707. Dartaguiette to min., Feb. 26, 1708, AC, C13A, 2, f. 57–58.

Louisiana) could the large ocean-going ships both conveniently and safely anchor. Supplies transported from Rochefort, La Rochelle and other foreign ports, would henceforth be unloaded at Port Massacre before being transported to smaller vessels going upriver to the establishment.[15] Commissary La Salle saw, even at this early stage, the necessity of fortifications to protect the vital harbor. "It will be necessary," he reckoned, "to build a fort here with [at least] twelve guns; and a garrison of thirty or forty men will be sufficient for its protection . . ."[16] It was a recommendation that Bienville was later to regret not having the persistence or wherewithal to see fulfilled.[17]

As Bienville, Levasseur and Sérigny made ready to leave on the eleventh of January to investigate possible locations for building the new establishment, Châteaugué was given a task force of ten men to finish shingling the warehouse roof and to transfer the supplies from the tents to the warehouse once the roof had been completed. At this point La Salle seemed highly optimistic at prospects for the colony's success; at least he was strongly encouraged by the natural habitat and by what thus far had been achieved. "The harbor of Mobile," he wrote the minister, "is an excellent one for the anchorage of ships . . . it will ultimately be superior to that of Pensacola as far as defense is concerned as well as for the ships' safety when we have a fort with a garrison . . . The harbor will serve as an *entrepôt* for all the trade we shall do both on the great river Mississippi and on all the other neighboring streams . . ."[18]

Despite his meager salary and the present discomforts being suffered by himself and his family, the eager commissary could look forward to a promising future and a more pleasant situation on the bluffs of the Mobile which Bienville, Sérigny and Lavasseur were preparing now to survey. The supplies on hand seemed abundant enough (enough, in fact, to keep the settlement well-provisioned for fourteen months) and thus far the work of transference had proceeded in advance of schedule.

15. Mémoire sur les establissements à faire à l'embouchure du Misisipi et à la Mobile, AM, 3 JJ 277, 4. The Île des vaisseaux, outside the Bay of Biloxi, would of course no longer be as useful since Fort Maurepas was being abandoned.

16. La Salle to min., April 1, 1702, AC, C13C, 2, f. 35–38.

17. Dartaguiette to min., Jan. 10, 1711, AC, C13A, 2, f. 633–34.

18. La Salle to min., April 1, 1702, AC, C13C, 2, f. 41–43.

III

Beginning the Establishment

CHARLES LEVASSEUR, *dit* Ruessavel, was of an ancient Parisian (Saint-Nicolas-des-Champs) family long distinguished in the carpentry and woodcarving professions. Son of Jean Levasseur, *dit* Lavigne, a master joiner who had migrated to Canada in the middle 1600's, Charles had been reared in the shadow of the parish church of Quebec where his father was one of the founders of the Confrérie de Sainte-Anne. His family connections (among others, the renowned Dugués de Boisbriand), along with his native gifts, enabled him to rise rapidly in the Canadian army as an officer-engineer. Aside from his serious pursuits, Levasseur showed a sense of the jocular, as evidenced in the sobriquet he no doubt chose for himself (Ruessavel is Levasseur spelled backwards!). He was particularly valuable to Iberville's colonial designs because of his abilities as a draftsman and because, as a younger man, he had seen service with Cavelier de La Salle.[1]

Levasseur had, however, been chosen for the strategic mission of beginning the establishment on the Mobile River not only because of his technical skills but because more than any officer of the garrison, he had acquired an expert knowledge of the Mobile River basin. As early as June 19, 1700 Levasseur, in com-

1. AJQ, Greffe de Audouart, Aug. 13, 1654; Greffe de Duquet, 1663–84, *passim;* Greffe de Rageot, 1666–1702, *passim. DGFC, I,* p. 391. Compte et Transport, Sept. 28, 1717, AN, MC, E XX, l. 455. Levasseur's surname has at least seven variant spellings in contemporary letters and documents; "Ruessavel," however, is the spelling used by Levasseur himself. The "Bageret" listed in the Laffilard index (AC, D2C, 222) is, like a number of other names in that list, simply the result of faulty transcription. *Cf.* AC, F1A, 10, f. 197, 282; 11, f. 218. Contrat de mariage entre Jean Levasseur et Marguerite Richard, Paris, April 23, 1645, Greffes de Philippe Le Cat et Jean Le Semelier, notaires au Châtelet, AN, Y, 184, f. 236.

pany with four Canadians, had been dispatched from Fort Maurepas by Commandant Sauvole (on the recommendation of Iberville) to explore the almost unknown "rivière des Alibamons," to solidify relations with the Mobile Indians and surrounding villages, to bargain for much-needed Indian corn and to concretely lay claim to the entire river system for France.[2]

Levasseur's mission of 1700 was not the first instance in which he had come into contact with the Indians of the Mobile River. During the several years the French had been stationed at Fort Maurepas the Mobilians had made numerous missions to the bay of Biloxi, Sauvole having more than once credited them with supplying the grain that kept starvation at bay. By the summer of 1700, however, the Mobile River basin (though visited briefly once by Bienville) had not yet been thoroughly explored or surveyed and Pontchartrain, through Iberville, had been adamant in his requests for more details. Reaching the main village of the Mobilians just above what is now Promised Land landing (some thirty-nine miles upstream from the river's mouth), Levasseur had gained valuable intelligence from a savage of the Mougoulacha temporarily living with the Mobilians. The Mougoulacha had given Levasseur an oral list of some thirty-six small nations that lived along the banks of the Mobile-Alabama river from the Mobile village to as far northeast as the confluence of the present-day Coosa and Tallapoosa rivers. "The English are every day in those nations," the Mougoulacha assured Levasseur. "They bring packhorses loaded with all the apparatus of guns, muskets, powder, lead and a great deal of other merchandise for which the natives exchange cured buckskins or ox hides, green and with the wool still on them . . . but the greatest traffic that the English have had with the natives

2. Mémoire de ce qu'il est du bien du service du roy que M. de Sauvole fasse après mon départ de ce pays, May 26, 1700, AC, C13A, 1, f. 248–51. Journal de Levasseur-Russouelle [sic] du fort des Billochies, 1700, BN, FF, 21690, f. 310–21v. Voyage de M. de Sauvolle . . . June 19, 1701 to Nov., 1701, Extrait de Claude Delisle, AM, 2 JJ 56, 16 (formerly classified under ASH, 115X, 16). The date should be 1700. Sauvole, of course, was dead by Aug. 22, 1701. AM, B4, 23, f. 315–16. Min. to Polastron, July 5, 1702, AM, B2, 162, f. 41. Min. to Luscançay, Aug. 8, 1702, AM, B2, 169, f. 336–37. Min. to Iberville, Sept. 14, 1701, AM, B2, 155, f. 458. Levasseur's journal (the same listed as Delisle's "Voyage de M. de Sauvolle") can be dated 1700 with certainty by the fact that the eclipse of the moon mentioned by Levasseur took place on Aug. 29, 1700. Furthermore, Andrés de Arriola's ship, reported by Levasseur as having been lost "the previous spring," was wrecked on the night of March 31, 1700. Arriola al virrey, June 4, 1700, AGI, *México*, L. 618. Franck al rey, June 4, 1700, AGI, *México*, L. 618.

is the trade of slaves which the natives go and make of their neighbors with whom they engage in continual war, killing the men, carrying away the women and children whom they sell to the English, each one for a gun, the practice of which has brought great destruction in the neighboring nations, among them being the Pensacola and the Mobile." [3]

Levasseur found nearly five hundred inhabitants, including women and children, in the five Mobilian villages. He also discovered (in the first village) a cross, which the natives told him had been planted by the Spanish, and two hogs which the natives reported also came from the Spanish.[4] The fact that the Spanish were courting the Mobilians was not as surprising as it was disconcerting. For Pensacola's governor, Andrés de Arriola, had repeatedly claimed the Mobile River as a part of Spanish domain, a claim Iberville had on various occasions seemed to accept before he realized the river's strategic value.[5] Moving farther upriver, Levasseur had reached the village of the Little Tomeh on the lower Tombigbee before coming back down the eastern arm of the Mobile known now as the Tensaw near the mouth of which he spent the night (at the village of the Pensacola Indians). The next morning, he crossed Mobile Bay to the present site of downtown Mobile where he planted a cross eight feet tall on a conspicuous bluff near the edge of the woods, giving the Spanish notice that the French were reserving the right to occupy the bay at some future date.[6]

None of Levasseur's exploratory missions (nor any of the voyages of his fellow Canadians) had revealed a suitable site for an establishment. In fact, when Levasseur first learned of Iberville's

3. Journal de Sauvole, 1699–1700, AC, F3, 24, f. 25–26v, 27v–30v. Journal de Sauvole, Aug. 4, 1701, AC, C13A, 1, f. 315–18. A number of *voyageurs* from Fort Maurepas had, however, lived at the several villages of the Mobile during the years 1700–01. Min. to Iberville, Sept. 14, 1701, AM, B2, 155, f. 457. Journal de Levasseur, *loc. cit.*, f. 311v–12, 313–14v. U.S. Army Corps of Engineers, Mobile, *Black Warrior-Tombigbee Navigation Charts*, April, 1972, pp. 8–9.

4. Journal de Levasseur, *loc. cit.*, f. 313–14v.

5. Iberville to min., July 9, 1701, AM, B4, 21, f. 519–21.

6. Journal de Levasseur, *loc. cit.*, f. 315–16v. In 1700, the Spanish had little interest in Mobile Bay, believing it to be a harbor of scant potential. Martínez a su magestad, April 14, 1702, AGI, *México*, L. 618. The Pensacola had abandoned Santa María de Galve for Mobile Bay in the early 1690's. Diario de Torres y Ayala, 1692, AGI, *México*, L. 616.

orders to transfer the fort, he had no particular location to recommend. While he had passed the present Courtauld dock site on eleven separate occasions, that elevation had never been noted by him as an acceptable location for an establishment. There was, in truth, nothing of extraordinary importance to recommend the bay area for a permanent settlement, except the strategic value of its river system and the plenitude of fish and small game. The delta was approximately eight miles wide at its southern extremity, extending (and tapering slightly inward) from the head of the bay some thirty-five miles northward to the confluence of the Alabama and Tombigbee rivers. It was swampy, laced with lakes, creeks and bayous, and cut north to south by the Mobile, Tensaw and Middle rivers—all created by the merger and subsequent dispersion of the Alabama and Tombigbee. Once (sometimes twice) a year the pattern changed—the rivers rose and the delta flooded. The game moved to the highlands east and west of the swamp, and even the banks became covered, before the waters slowly subsided, leaving a thin overburden of alluvium.[7]

Like Charles Levasseur, Joseph Le Moyne de Sérigny was of a notable Canadian family, well-established in the province of Quebec. Born in Ville Marie de Montréal in 1668, Sérigny was the sixth son of Charles Le Moyne and Catherine Thierry. After beginning his service as a midshipman at Rochefort, Sérigny rose rapidly as an officer and interpreter, once having escorted a band of Iroquois Indians from Quebec to Marseille and back. By 1694, he had assumed command of the frigate *Salamandre* and together with Iberville captured York Fort from the English at Hudson's Bay (though with the loss of his brother Louis Le Moyne de Châteaugué, killed in the siege). It was in 1696 that Sérigny assumed command of the *Palmier*, having met many of the Canadians now under his command at Plaisance, before his success in the recapture of Fort Bourbon made him, as the highest ranking officer, commander of Hudson's Bay at the age of twenty-eight. More recently, he had married Marie-Élisabeth Héron, twenty-year-old daughter of Antoine Héron, merchant and king's councillor at La Rochelle, and sister of Marc-Antoine Héron, civil and criminal judge at Cap-français. Already well-to-do (by illegitimate com-

7. Trickey & Holmes, "A Chronological Framework for the Mobile Bay Region, revised, 1970," *Journal of Alabama Archaeology*, Vol. XVII, No. 2, Dec. 1971, pp. 115–28. Notes de Claude Delisle sur la géographie de la Louisiane, AM, 2 JJ 56, 17.

merce in furs), Sérigny was on his first voyage to Louisiana, soon to profit further by additional illicit trade.[8]

Sérigny, Levasseur and Bienville left Massacre Island on the morning of January 11 and arrived at the main village of the Mobilians on the evening of the 13th, making notes and observing closely the terrain on the west bank of the river. Passing the night at the Mobile village, the trio left early the next morning to go back downstream to re-investigate possible sites for the establishment, accompanied by one of the Mobilian chiefs. Since the natives were more familiar with the terrain, the tides and water levels (and over longer periods of time) it seemed practical to take advantage of their experience. Bienville must have looked carefully at the site inhabited by the Mobilians themselves; the land they occupied at the fork of the Mobile and the Spanish (now Tensaw) rivers was the most strategically located site in the vicinity. The ground was not greatly elevated, but judging from the length of time the Mobilians had remained there, the danger of flooding seemed scant, a fact which did little to alert the three Canadians to the dangers of nearby, more elevated locations.[9]

There were other potential sites to the north of the Mobilian village. Farther upstream, however, would place the settlement too far from Massacre Island and there were no bluffs of sufficient height near the mouth of the river. The choice narrowed finally to two bluffs on the western bank (the eastern bank consisted almost entirely of low, marshy terrain), one 21 miles above the river's mouth, and the other 25.7 miles. Each bluff had its distinct advantages. The second bluff (Courtauld's dock) was higher, had a more natural landing for boats and was closer to the site of the Mobilian village. The first bluff (21-Mile Bluff) was broader and more level and commanded a better view of the river. Moreover, it was closer to the harbor at Massacre Island.[10]

8. *DGFC, I,* p. 379. APR, 1 E 340. Min. to Bégon, April 22, 1699, AM, B2, 140, f. 115. Rolle des Canadiens . . . May 5, 1699, AC, C13C, 2, f. 15–17v. Châteaurenault to min., May 11, 1705, AM, B3, 132, f. 287–90. ACM, Rivière & Soullard, 1715, f. 11. Min. to Naurois, May 17, 1707, AM, B2, 197, f. 841. Min. to Héron, May 9, 1708, AM, B2, 207, f. 538–39. Min. to Sérigny, Jan. 12, 1707, AM, B2, 196, f. 216. ACM, baptêmes, paroisse de Saint-Jean, Dec. 2, 1700; paroisse de Saint-Barthélémi, Feb. 13, 1705.

9. Iberville, Mémoire sur l'établissement de la Mobile, 1702, AC, C13C, 2, f. 46–49. Journal de Levasseur, 1700–01, BN, FF, 21690, f. 311–18v.

10. Bay Minette, Ala. Quadrangle, 1941. U.S. Geological Survey Map (15-minute series) N3045–W8745/15. In computing distances, the present Bankhead Tunnel at the foot of Government St. (only several hundred feet

After Levasseur made several sketches of the bluffs, Bienville dispatched two men to Iberville at Pensacola with Levasseur's drawings and his own notes on the two sites, along with a report of the opinion of the Mobilian chief. This accomplished, Bienville and the two officers returned to the village of the Mobilians to await Iberville's instructions.[11]

Meanwhile, Iberville, though his health was rapidly improving, was still too weak and too much in pain to leave Pensacola. Other matters, as well, compelled him to remain at Santa María de Galve. Acting Governor Martínez and his officers were afoot night and day, fearing a revolt of their men, all discontent because of the lack of food and supplies, a reality which bade no good either for Martínez or Iberville. Martínez, fearing for his garrison as well as for his life, came on board the *Renommée* to request that Iberville deliver the vessel he had mentioned some weeks prior. Iberville, seeing the state of destitution Pensacola was in, promised Martínez the *Précieuse*,[12] a traversier that had been in use in Louisiana since the establishment of Fort Maurepas. "The Spaniards have no provisions, no clothing and no money," Iberville later wrote

---

from the New Fort Louis-Fort Condé site) is used by engineers to designate the "mouth of the river." Using engineering landmarks the site of Old Fort Louis was at Courtauld's dock (25.7 miles from the tunnel) rather than at 27-Mile Bluff which presently refers also to a bluff nearly a mile upstream. *Cf. Black Warrior-Tombigbee Navigation Charts, op. cit.*, p. 8. The minimum distance from the Massacre Island port to the site of Old Fort Louis, when the shorter route (followed by canoes and lighter craft) was used was approximately 59.7 miles. Larger and more heavily laden craft were forced to sail a few miles farther, making a greater arc around the Pointe à Guillory.

11. Of the 1702 sketches and plans only two have survived, both of which are preserved "sans nom d'auteur" at the Archives Nationales. Plan de la Ville et du Fort de la Maubille, 1702, AN, DFC, Louisiane, No. 119A. Relation ou annale veritable, de ce qui s'est passé dans Le païs de La Loüisiane . . . (Relation de Pénigault), BN, FF, 14613, f. 82–86. *FLC*, pp. 56–59. The spelling "Pénigault" is used because this is the way he signed his name, in his engagement to Le Sueur as well as in the Mobile parish records. ACM, Rivière & Soullard, 1699–1700, f. 72. ADM, A, April 7, Oct. 27, 1708; March 20, 1710. Moreover, it is the form generally followed by his own family in La Rochelle. BMLR, Registres des familles protestantes, Mariages, July 20, 1670; Baptêmes, Jan. 5, 1678.

12. The *Précieuse* had been on the Gulf Coast since 1698, captained by Jean-François Levasseur, older brother of Charles Levasseur, *dit* Ruessavel. *DGFC, I*, p. 391. Rolle de la garnison laissée au Fort Maurepas, Aug. 25, 1699, AC, C13A, 1, 209–11. Rolle de la garnison du fort de Biloxy, May 26, 1700, AC, C13A, 1, 255–57.

Pontchartrain. "And out of 180 men, 60 are convicts, who are their best men." [13] The *Précieuse*, being careened for the first time in four years, was not yet ready for sailing, but Iberville hastened the task, for he well realized that Martínez would soon be pleading for flour and provisions from the Massacre Island warehouse and he did not wish to draw from that supply if it could be avoided. By the 28th of January, the *Précieuse* was prepared to sail. Immediately upon being notified of her readiness, Iberville dispatched the traversier to Veracruz by his cousin, Jean-Sidrac Dugué de Sainte-Thérèse (older brother of *aide-major* Boisbriant), and a Pensacola captain of infantry in command of sixteen men.[14]

Meanwhile, the Canadians sent by Bienville arrived at Pensacola on the 16th of January with Levasseur's sketches and Bienville's notes. Iberville, though he had previously examined the lower portion of Mobile Bay, was not personally familiar with either of the sites described by his brother. Furthermore, he was reluctant to place too much weight on the recommendations of the natives; for Bienville, he remembered, had once before been misled by them when the site for Fort La Boulaye on the lower Mississippi had been chosen.[15] Yet, though he preferred postponing judgment until he could personally examine the locations, the pressure of time forced Iberville to reach a decision. Apparently, he considered it slightly more advantageous to be nearer the main Mobilian village than to Massacre Island. Too, the more northerly bluff was somewhat more elevated, though narrower, than the one downstream and he wished to avoid the mistake Bienville had made with the Mississippi fort in selecting too vulnerable a site (as far as the river waters were concerned). Accordingly, on the seventeenth of January, he wrote to Bienville to "form the settlement at the second steep part of the bank," an order which would later be the cause of unanimous regret.[16] As ordered by Iberville, the fort was

13. Journal d'Iberville, Dec. 15, 1701–April 27, 1702, AM, B4, 23, f. 318–21; AC, F3, 24, f. 41–47.

14. Journal d'Iberville, f. 317–19. *Journal Historique*, p. 38. AM, C1, 161, f. 276. AC, E 150, Nos. 22, 118.

15. Iberville to min., Feb. 26, 1700, AC, C13A, 1, f. 229–31. Pénigault, BN, FF, 14163, f. 31–33, 42. Journal de Gravier, Feb. 16, 1701, *JR*, *LXV*, pp. 160–61.

16. Journal d'Iberville, *loc. cit.*, f. 317–19. Iberville's intention to establish settlers along the banks of the Mobile as far up river as what is now Old St. Stephens (in much the same manner as the banks of the St. Lawrence had been settled) was another reason for locating at Courtauld's dock. A site farther down river would have placed the fort too far from

to be of four bastions, similar in size and shape to the presently-being-abandoned Fort Maurepas.[17]

Along with the Canadians dispatched to the Mobile River with Iberville's instructions, Iberville sent Pillet's ketch back to Massacre Island, laden with more of the colony's provisions from the *Renommée*. Soon after Pillet departed, Robinau de Bécancour followed in the *Palmier's* longboat accompanied by two pinnaces with twenty of Iberville's crewmen to assist in conveying the goods from Massacre Island to the Mobile River. The problem of transporting the colony's supplies to the new establishment was to be a major difficulty, for the entrance of the river showed a depth of only six-and-a-half feet. Realizing that the shallowness at the river's base would be an everpresent obstacle, Iberville commissioned Jacques Le Roux, a thirty-six-year-old master carpenter from Rochefort, and all the ship's carpenters and caulkers to set to work to build a pinnace of some 45 tons. The vessel was to be distinctly designed for use on the Gulf Coast. It was to be built with a sharp bow but with a flat bottom, so that it could sail the gulf as well as navigate the rivers and bayous, while drawing not more than four-and-a-half feet of water when loaded.[18]

The Canadians sent with Iberville's instructions arrived at the village of the Mobilians on January 19th. The next day, Bienville, Sérigny and Levasseur brought their small labor force downstream and began "brushing" the area on the bluff selected by Iberville. Using bill-hooks, a kind of axe with a long blade curved down at the end to form an arc (in fact, a slightly heavier version of the sickle), the laborers quickly removed the underbrush and small trees in order to give the axemen room to wield their blades and to remove impediments to the free fall of the larger trees. A few

---

the projected plantations, dissuading settlers from venturing great distances from their base of security. Bienville to min., Feb. 25, 1708, AC, C13A, 2, f. 102.

17. Fort Maurepas was shortly to be demolished. Though in time it would have decayed, Iberville had no intention of leaving an uninhabited fort standing. No longer interested in Biloxi Bay, he nevertheless planned to leave several settlers in the area to grow food and raise cattle for support of the Île des vaisseaux in which he still saw possible value as an anchorage point. Bégon to Villermont, June 27, 1702, BN, FF, 22811, f. 172–73. Mémoire pour servir d'instruction au Sieur de Bienville . . . , April 25, 1702, AC, F3, 68, f. iv. BN, FF, 9097, f. 125.

18. AC, F1A, 10, f. 282v. Journal d'Iberville, *loc. cit.*, f. 317–21. Relation de la rivière de la Mobile, AM, 3 JJ 277,8. La Salle to min., April 1, 1702, AC, C13C, 2, f. 37–39.

days later, La Salle arrived in company with a larger force of laborers—men of the garrison and crewmen from the ships—and began negotiating agreements for their work on the fort and on the pinnace to be built by Le Roux. The contracts completed, La Salle, Bienville and Sérigny prepared to return to Massacre Island on the Spanish vessel, leaving Levasseur in charge of the construction of the fort.[19]

The bluff Iberville had chosen (on the basis of Bienville's and Levasseur's information) was surely high enough (21 feet at its maximum height with an average elevation of approximately 18 feet); somewhat long and narrow, irregularly shaped, it hugged the west bank of the river for perhaps a quarter-mile. At the point where the fort was being erected it was steep enough to be fully protected from the highest river waters even during the flooding season. No doubt the Mobilian who accompanied Levasseur was correct in reporting that the top levels had never been inundated during his lifetime. Yet, the bluff sloped gently back and down, to a creek at its northern extremity and to a miry bog on its western edge, so that even Bienville's residence, which was to be built on the highest land excepting Fort Louis, would at times be subjected to the poor drainage.[20]

After Levasseur completed his final plans for the fort (the general specifications of which had already been approved by Bienville and Sérigny) the construction was begun in earnest. When the bluff and surrounding area had been thoroughly brushed, the refuse was piled in heaps or rows so that when the large trees were felled their upper branches settled on the piles, after which the trunks were chopped into ten and fifteen-foot lengths to be used in the fort itself or as stakes in the palisades surrounding it. As the work progressed, additional laborers from Massacre Island began arriving daily, signed on by La Salle before he and Bienville left for the port. The new laborers joined in

19. Journal d'Iberville, *loc. cit.*, f. 318–19. La Salle to min., *loc. cit.*, f. 38–41. Iberville, Mémoire sur les establissements à faire a l'embouchure du Misisipi et à la Mobile, AM, 3 JJ 277,4.

20. Plan de la Ville et du Fort de la Maubille, 1702, *loc. cit.*, No. 119A. Bay Minette, Ala. Quadrangle, *op. cit.*, N3045–W8745/15. Iberville was correct in assuming the bluff would never flood, the river showing at most a tide differential of 12–18 inches. He failed to take into account, however, the larger area's inability to discharge its rainwater and creek overflow. Extrait d'une lettre du neveu de M. Lefevre, March 15, 1702, BN, FF, 9097, f. 123–23v.

clearing the rest of the area with their short crude axes. Two men were set digging a powder magazine which measured six feet to a side and slightly more than ten feet deep, unsupported at the sides by either wood or brick and with a capacity of 360 cubic feet. When the bulk of the bluff's trees had been felled, the task of removing the stumps was begun. This operation proved so laborious that only the stumps that were unusually obstructive were removed; the rest were left standing.[21]

According to Levasseur's plan, the fort was to be of four bastions with a staked palisade encircling the fort all the way to the river, enclosing also the powder magazine at the highest point of the bluff near the river bank. The fort, though later described as "very small" was nevertheless to be slightly larger than Fort Maurepas, capable of containing at least 200–300 people in times of emergency.[22]

The logs gained in clearing the area were, the most suitable of them, squared into timbers twelve to eighteen inches thick (dovetailed at the corners) and used for the double *pièce-sur-pièce* construction of the bastions and curtains. Inside the double wall was a space of several feet which was to be filled with earth. Most of the wood being used in the construction was red pine, the most common variety in the vicinity, which was taken from the bluff area and from the endless forests to the west of the fort.[23]

When the walls and bastion foundations were set, Levasseur began the construction of four buildings within the fort, a layout carefully designed by Bienville to give himself certain advantages that the unsuspecting La Salle (now on his way back to Massacre Island) could not anticipate and which later would pique the suspicion of Minister Pontchartrain. Against the western curtain, with a small double-doored entrance facing the town, the framework of a building to be used as a chapel was begun. Since no provision had yet been made for a church, nor even a pastor, the

21. Dénombrement de l'état de la colonie de La Louisiane . . . par Nicolas de La Salle, Aug. 31, 1704, AC, C13A, 1, f. 468–69.

22. *Ibid.*, f. 468. Dartaguiette to min., Feb. 26, 1708, AC, C13A, 2, f. 63–67. Dartaguiette to min., Oct. 1, 1708, AC, C13A, 2, f. 346–47.

23. Dénombrement . . . *loc. cit.*, f. 469. Plan du fort De Maurepats a la coste meridionale de la Florida, AM, 4044C, No. 81. Plan de la ville et du fort de la Maubille, 1702, AN, DFC, Louisiane, No. 119A. *Cf.* "Colonial Fortifications and Military Architecture in the Mississippi Valley" by Samuel Wilson, Jr., in McDermott, ed., *The French in the Mississippi Valley*, pp. 104–110.

chapel, a long narrow building measuring sixty-two by sixteen feet, was to serve as the center of what religious activity would be practiced for the next several years.[24]

Against the southern curtain a smaller building, the king's storehouse, was begun. Forty feet in length by sixteen feet wide, the storehouse was the first fully completed building, necessary as it was to store the goods now being transported in small boats from the warehouses at Massacre Island and Dog River.[25]

Facing the river and attached to the front curtain was the most elaborate of the four structures inside the fort. Sixty-eight feet long by sixteen feet wide, this building was designed as alternate lodging for the highest officials as well as an orderly room where the administrative affairs of the colony would be transacted. Bienville's office was in the center of the building, his living quarters just to the south and his kitchen at the extreme southeastern corner, providing the commandant and his servants easy access to the entrance of the storehouse. Contrary to what La Salle would later wish, the commissary's office and quarters were located at the southwestern corner of the building to serve as a chapel, leaving Bienville's quarters equally near as those of La Salle to the storehouse entrance, an arrangement that was to assume greater significance as the years progressed. Bordering the front of the administrative building was a long narrow gallery six feet wide facing the river just above the curtain,[26] and attached to the northwestern curtain was a forty-by-sixteen foot construction, divided into two medium-sized chambers: on the river side, a compartment twenty-five feet long set aside for the storing of guns and ammunition, and toward the western curtain a small fifteen-by-sixteen foot guardhouse.

The roofs of the buildings inside the fort were steep, as in the Canadian manner, covered with large oak shingles one-half yard in length and one-third in width. Although the detailed work of the fort was carried out chiefly by the carpenters and craftsmen of the western ports of France, such as Jean-Baptiste La Croix, *dit* Grimauld of Havre de Grâce and Pierre Gasque of La Rochelle,

24. La Salle to min., Sept. 7, 1706, AC, C13A, 1, f. 474–77. Min. to La Salle, June 30, 1707, AC, B 29, f. 265–66.

25. Dénombrement . . . *loc. cit.*, f. 469. Dartaguiette to min., *loc. cit.*, f. 61–68.

26. Dénombrement . . . *loc. cit.*, f. 469. La Salle to min., *loc. cit.*, f. 473–78. Min. to La Salle, *loc. cit.*, f. 264–67.

the general plan of construction followed the conceptions of the Canadians Levasseur, Bienville and Iberville.[27]

As the buildings inside the fort were being erected, the bastions on the outside were nearing completion. The lumber brought in from the fields where the townsite was now being cleared was squared into planks three inches thick for use in flooring the bastions. On these pine and oak floors the cannons from Fort Maurepas (as well as the two additional pieces brought by Iberville) were shortly to be placed; ten feet above the ground they would peer through the gun holes beneath the four-foot parapets.[28]

Meanwhile, the laborers were busy digging three-foot trenches around the fort into which were being placed twelve-foot pine stakes of medium thickness, pointed at the ends. The palisade stakes (bound temporarily by heavy cords two feet from the top), when placed in the trenches and stood upright, would reach a height of over nine feet, high enough to prevent the enemy from hurdling them but low enough for the cannons to fire above them.[29]

By the middle of February the work on the fort was progressing at a more than reasonable rate. The northern portion of the bluff was fully cleared, except for the stumps that dotted the area, and the bastions were virtually completed. Even the four buildings inside the fort were beginning to assume final proportions, enough to provide the workmen a modicum of shelter from the brisk February nights.[30]

Behind the bluff on which the fort was situated, where a village of some seventy houses would shortly rise, Levasseur watched

27. Dénombrement . . . *loc. cit.*, f. 468–69. Pérez a Zúñiga, May 25, 1703, AGI, *Santo Domingo*, L. 858. Depenses de l'Entretien . . . de la garnison et ouvriers du Fort Louis de la Louisiane pendant l'année derniere, 1702, AC, F1A, 10, f. 283.

28. Pérez a Zúñiga, May 25, 1703, AGI, *Santo Domingo*, L. 858. Pénigault, *Relation*, BN, FF, 14613, f. 84–86. Plan de la Ville et du Fort Louis sur la Mobile, 1711, AN, DFC, Louisiane, No. 120B. Only one of the Fort Maurepas-Fort Louis guns has been found. In 1712 all of the Old Fort's cannons were moved to the present site of Mobile. When the British gained control of Fort Condé in the 1760's, the French guns were dumped into the marsh along the river bank; during the 1973 dredging for the George Wallace Tunnel one of the twelve-pounders was recovered and donated to the Museum of the City of Mobile.

29. Harris, *An Archaeological Survey of Fort Louis de La Mobile, Final Report*, figure 2.

30. Journal d'Iberville, *loc. cit.*, f. 329–34.

the once-thick growth of trees and underbrush becoming daily thinner by dint of the axe and bill-hook. The low, gently sloping terrain, though somewhat damp, was free of standing water (due to a relatively dry winter). Observing the apparently fertile countryside, the progress his men were making, Levasseur had good reason to feel a tinge of optimism about the future of the establishment as well as a glow of satisfaction in the dischargement of his own responsibilities.[31]

Bienville, meanwhile, after having led a party of five Canadians in blazing an overland trail to Pensacola (and after having conferred briefly with Iberville aboard the *Renommée*), was now on his way back to the river establishment, accompanied by Sérigny and by additional men and supplies.

31. *Ibid.*, f. 327–29. Extrait d'une lettre du neveu de M. Lefevre, March 15, 1702, BN, FF, 9097, f. 123–23v. Martínez a Guzmán, Feb. 1, 1702, AGI, *México*, L. 618.

IV

Tonti and the *Pax Gallica*

IBERVILLE, in the late winter of 1702, though still shaky from the effects of his illness, was confident that the transfer of fortifications to the Mobile River was going well. Most of the supplies had been conveyed to Massacre Island with little difficulty or loss and the development of the proposed establishment was proceeding approximately according to schedule. At last report he had learned that the building of the fort was already in progress at the location he had specified.[1] The first stage of his overall scheme was in full swing; it was now time to begin the second phase: the pacification and unification of the principal Indian nations.[2]

Although Iberville recognized the defensive value of the small coastal tribes—the Mobile, the Tomeh and the Pascagoula—and was careful to locate in close proximity to their village sites in order to make use of their food resources and navigational services, his mind was preoccupied with the larger, more strategically located nations—the Choctaw, the Chickasaw, and the Alabama.[3] All of these nations, located on or near the several upper branches of the Mobile River, inhabited positions capable of obstructing the line of English advance from Carolina: the Choctaw in what is now eastcentral Mississippi and the Chickasaw some one hundred and twenty miles farther north, near the headwaters of the Tombigbee.[4] The Choctaw, the largest of the three nations,

1. *Journal Historique*, pp. 37–38, 71.

2. Mémoire sur les establissements à faire à l'embouchure du Misisipi et à la Maubile, par Iberville, AM, 3 JJ 277, 4.

3. Relation de la rivière de la Mobile, AM, 3 JJ 277, 8. Carte de la Louisiane, par le Sr. d'Anville, 1732, BN, Cartes et plans, Collection Danville.

4. Mémoire sur l'etablissement de la Mobile et du Misisipi, 1704, AC, C13C, 2, f. 46–53.

numbered (according to Iberville's figures) several thousand effective men. The Chickasaw, he guessed (though surely an overestimate), totalled at least twelve hundred to two thousand families. The Alabama, while numerically inferior to both the Choctaw and the Chickasaw, occupied the most strategic location —a magnificent bluff near the junction of the present day Coosa and Tallapoosa rivers.[5]

Yet these large important nations had for centuries been at war with one another, a fact that Carolina tradesmen were playing to full advantage.[6] By promoting conflict between the various villages the English were making a premium of such articles as the musket and the slave, reaping high profits from the trade of both and gradually extending their influence and control toward the Mississippi.[7]

To prevent the Carolina traders from gaining further domination of the interior, Iberville planned to send his most able and experienced Indian agent to the grand village of the Choctaw in an attempt to persuade that tribe to make peace with the war-like Chickasaw. The pacification of these two nations, whom Iberville would court with bells, beads, priests and muskets, would, he hoped, insure a general peace among all the villages, would stifle the expansion of slave-trading and bring all the smaller tribes close under the wing of the French. To head the most important mission Iberville had yet undertaken in the back country the French commander pinned his hopes on a half-pay captain of Canadian infantry, a man who once held aspirations of commanding the entire Louisiana enterprise but who now was merely biding his time in camp, watching the twenty-two-year-old Bienville direct the building of a fortress he thought should rightfully be under his own command.[8]

Born Enrico di Tonti (of Neapolitan parents who had lost a considerable fortune after participating in an abortive revolt against the Spanish viceroy, the Duque de Arcos), the infantry

5. Résumé d'Iberville, June 20, 1702, AC, C13C, 2, f. 43–46. Mémorandum par d'Iberville, June 20, 1702, AC, F3, 24, f. 38–47. For the Choctaw Iberville listed 38 villages totalling 1,146 cabins and for the Chickasaw 18 villages totalling 588 cabins. Delisle [1702], AM, 2 JJ 56, 24.

6. Delgado a Cabrera, Sept. 19, 1686, AGI, *México*, L. 616.

7. Iberville to min., July 30, 1701, AM, B4, 21, f. 532–34. Thomas Nairne [to Lords Proprietors], July 10, 1708, PRO, CO 5, 382, f. 23–26. Journal de Le Sueur [1702], AM, 2 JJ 56,9. Mémoire pour servir d'instruction au Sieur de Bienville . . . du 25 avril 1702, AC, F3, 68, f. 2–2v.

8. Journal d'Iberville, April 27, 1702, AM, B4, 23, f. 317–21.

captain Iberville had chosen (a native-born Italian) had been reared in northcentral France where his parents had sought refuge soon after his birth. Following entrance into the military as a young man, Tonti was sent to Sicily where during a Spanish attack his right hand was mutilated by a grenade, eventually necessitating its amputation. Yet it was the loss of his hand, replaced by a conspicuous iron hook, that eventually helped secure Tonti's endearment to the North American Indians while he was pursuing a new career as a fur trader on the Mississippi and in the Great Lakes region (following his voyage with La Salle to Quebec in 1678).[9]

Over the next twenty years Tonti became a legend to the Indians of North America, as much by his endurance in braving the wildernesses of the South and Midwest for long periods of time as by the metal hook which so fascinated them. Yet if his influence with the Indians had steadily increased and if he had been successful in constructing a string of small forts from the Great Lakes region to the lower Mississippi, his major commercial enterprises failed to prosper despite auspicious beginnings. After borrowing a substantial amount of capital to expand his beaver trade, Tonti found himself effectively opposed by the merchants and officials of Montreal. In addition the limitations placed by Louis XIV on the extension of the beaver commerce brought him toward increasing desperation. To combat the government's controls, Tonti began promoting the development of the Mississippi Valley, not only as a positive commercial venture, but also as a defensive measure against England. In support of his recommendations, Tonti authorized the publication of his memoirs in 1697; yet the *mémoires* had been highly romanticized by his publishers (much to his dismay and humiliation), the distortions making him the object of much ridicule by those who were familiar with the wilds of the Mississippi first-hand.[10]

9. Tonti's date and place of birth are not presently known. Information concerning his early life and ancestry must be gleaned from related documents. Mariage de Alphonse de Tonty et Marie-Anne Picoté de Belestre, ANDM, Feb. 17, 1689. *DGFC, I,* p. 568; *VII,* pp. 318–19*n.* AC, D2, 47–48 (1695). Tonti to min., 1700, AC, C11A, 18, f. 49. Mémoire du Roy de M. de Tonti, Oct. 27, 1698, AN, G7, 535. Bibliothèque de l'Arsenal, Manuscrits Bastille, No. 12472, f. 142–42v. Tonti was called "le Bras Coupé" as well as "la Main de Fer."

10. Mémoire de M. de Tonti, Nov. 14, 1684, BN, Clairambault, 1016, f. 220–79. Concession aux Pères Jésuites de la rivière des Arkanzas, Nov. 26, 1689, ASQ, Polygraphie, 13, 33. Lettre de Tonti, July 23, 1682, BN,

Despite Tonti's hopes of commanding the defense and development of the land described in his book, all seemed to work against him: the hostility of the Jesuits, his enemies among the merchants in Montreal, his lack of support at court. Despite his renown among the natives and New World *voyageurs*, his reputation as an explorer was not quite so widespread in Europe as he would have liked to believe. When the leadership of the Louisiana enterprise was conferred upon Iberville, a pro-Jesuit whose father had been among the most influential of the Montreal merchants, Tonti's dismay was deeply felt if not plainly seen.[11]

Yet Tonti, somewhat reticent in nature, seldom inclined to open resentment, could at least hope to play a minor (perhaps even a major) role in an enterprise led by a man he greatly admired and respected. He was not prepared for the ill treatment he received from Iberville in subsequent years. Relegated to punitive expeditions, passed over for the trade and command of the proposed Ohio concession in favor of Iberville's close associate, Charles Juchereau de Saint-Denis, Tonti had been brought to financial desolation. Now in 1702, at the age of fifty-two, the "Iron Hand" was merely sulking in camp, bankrupt, dejected, watching the beginnings of a colony on the Mobile under direction of a man who had a few years before humiliated him but who now desperately needed his services.[12]

Soon after François Pillet returned to Pensacola from the Dog River warehouse in late January, Iberville dispatched two Canadians from Pensacola to Mobile Bay (to follow the same trail Bienville had blazed the previous week). The two Canadians, following Iberville's directive, were to travel by foot to the edge of the bay (where a pirogue which Bienville had left behind would await them near the mouth of the Spanish River), then to cross the bay and paddle upriver to the fort with special orders for the commandant who by that time would have returned from Pensa-

---

Clairambault, 1016, f. 165–68v. Mémoire de Tonti [1691?], AC, C13C, 3, f. 128–41v; BN, FF, NA, 7485, f. 103–18. Paul Du Ru Journal [1700], Newberry Library, Ayer Collection, 262.

11. Saint-Cosme à l'évêque de Québec, Jan. 2, 1699, ASQ, Lettres, R 26. Gravier [to Laval], Sept. 20, 1698, ASQ, Lettres, N 132; *JR, LXV*, pp. 57–62. Mémoire pour servir d'instruction au Sieur d'Iberville, July 23, 1698, AC, B 20, f. 111–14.

12. Iberville to min., July 9, 1701, AM, B4, 21, f. 515–26. Min. to Iberville, July 20, 1701, AM, B2, 155, f. 108–09. Tonti à son frére, Feb. 28, 1700, AM, 3 JJ 387, 14. Tonti à son frére, March 4, 1700, AM, 3 JJ 387, 14.

cola. Six days later, the Canadians arrived at the fort, handing over Iberville's orders to Bienville to provide Tonti with ten hand-picked men to accompany him to the village of the Choctaw and "from there to the Chickasaw to persuade them to make peace with one another, and to escort the chiefs of their two tribes to Mobile in order to make a solid alliance between them." [13]

Tonti, with his valet and eight Canadians, left Mobile on the morning of the eighth of February for the village of the Little Tomeh,[14] carrying several packloads of presents for the natives. Though optimistic about his chances of success Tonti was nonetheless apprehensive over the relatively small supply of gifts which he carried. While Bienville was able to spare nine small cooking pots, eight axes and six large compasses, he was able to give Tonti only a small supply of guns (what the natives most desired) and several pairs of bright red stockings. The lack of an ample amount of presents greatly concerned Tonti at this point, for he well realized that while the natives might be wooed with priests, pluck and promises, they could not (in the long run) be permanently won from the English except on a competitive economic basis.[15] Perhaps, however, they could be temporarily satisfied by an adequate supply of knives, beads, and bells. Bienville, watching Tonti and his small force disappear into the early morning, could only wonder at the irony of so consequential a mission being placed in the hands of so few men with such empty hands in an attempt to win the largest and most powerful nations on the southern frontier.

Meanwhile, back at Pensacola, Iberville was sufficiently recovered, he felt, to make an inspection of Massacre Island before going on to the site of the new establishment. On the last day of January, he was cheered by a visit from his old friend and associate, Pierre-Charles Le Sueur, who had been living at Fort Maurepas since his return from the upper Mississippi, and by Jesuit Paul Du Ru who had come from the fort to return to France on the

13. Journal d'Iberville, *loc. cit.*, Jan. 28, 1702. Danville, Carte de la Louisiane, 1732, BN, Cartes et plans.

14. Journal de Le Sueur [1702], AM, 2 JJ 56, 9. The French had not yet established a close relationship with the Grand Tomeh. Before the year 1702, they use Tomeh to mean Little Tomeh, a village half the size of the Grand Tomeh, living on Nannahubba Bluff. Journal de Levasseur, 1700, AM, 2 JJ 56, 16.

15. La Mobille, Estat de la Depense . . . , March 31, 1702, AC, F1A, 10, f. 288–90v.

Renommée.[16] On the morning of February 15, Iberville embarked on the *Palmier*, on which he had loaded all the remaining goods of the colony; but, despite the short distance, he was three days in finding anchorage for the vessel in the harbor at Massacre Island due to the stiff northwest winds. When he finally anchored (in thirty feet of water), he found Ensign Jousselin de Marigny and pilot Nicolas La Voyé grounded against the sands in their smack.[17]

Despite strenuous efforts to get the smack afloat, Marigny's vessel would not budge. Anxious for a boat to transport Illinois Jesuit Jacques Gravier and a large number of Canadian *voyageurs* (whom Iberville could not economically support at Mobile) back to the Mississippi, the commander (through La Salle) was forced to hire François Pillet's ketch (for a sum of 500 *livres*) to transfer them for the time being to Fort La Boulaye.[18] Iberville had been highly frustrated by the presence of these *voyageurs* on the Gulf Coast: he could use them, but he could not support them; yet he dared not offend them, for they were threatening to take their deerskins and oxhides to the English should Iberville be unable to provide a market for their wares. In the face of this dilemma, Iberville acted with characteristic diplomacy: the Canadians could come back to Mobile the following year; in the meantime they would return to the Mississippi to carry on their trapping until Iberville could negotiate viable trade agreements with the authorities in France.[19]

Meanwhile, Bécancour and Châteaugué arrived from the Mobile River with the two *feluccas* and the two pinnaces and loaded more goods from the Massacre Island warehouse. The next day, as Le Sueur was leaving on his pirogue for the Mississippi, an unusually heavy sea rose and freed Marigny's smack from the sands. Iberville immediately sent the smack back to the bay of Biloxi to help transfer a number of the items still remaining at Fort Maurepas.[20] The following morning the commander set out from Massacre

16. Journal d'Iberville, *loc. cit.*, Feb. 15, 1702. Journal de Le Sueur [1702], AM, 2 JJ 56, 9.

17. Journal d'Iberville, *loc. cit.*, Feb. 18.

18. Journal de Sauvole, Aug. 4, 1701, AC, C13A, 1, f. 317–21. AC, F1A, 10, f. 289v–90v. Pillet had already been paid 574 *livres* for the use of the *Dauphine* (a brigantine of 45 tons) in transporting supplies from Pensacola. *Ibid.*, f. 289v.

19. Journal d'Iberville, *loc. cit.*, Feb. 22, 1702.

20. *Ibid.* Journal de Le Sueur, Feb. 23, 1702, AM, 2 JJ 56,9.

Island with Châteaugué and Bécancour for the new settlement, but contrary winds and heavy rains drove them back to port. Sérigny, in the meantime, had arrived from the fort with an order for supplies that Commissary La Salle, after some hesitation, declined to fill. Already the new *commissaire* was beginning to be wary of approving orders for merchandise for which he knew not the why and wherefore. On Sérigny's complaint to Iberville, the commander intervened by gently but firmly defining for La Salle the limits of his authority.[21]

The order Sérigny brought had come directly from Commandant Bienville, but La Salle's reluctance to fill it was not so astounding. Conflict between commandant and commissary was nothing novel in the annals of French colonial administration.[22] Ensign Sauvole had his difficulties over the same question with his scrivener Crassé. Was the commissary to bend blindly to the will of the commandant in opening His Majesty's storehouse? Or should the commissary exercise discretionary powers in addition to his ministerial duties? Was he an executive or a mere clerk? Crassé had seen more to his position than filling orders and keeping records and apparently so did La Salle. For the moment Iberville's intervention quieted the dispute: La Salle's storekeeper (Sieur Gerard) would issue nothing intended for presents to the Indians, nor any other goods in fact, without an order from the commandant to La Salle (who in turn would present the order to Gerard). Iberville's solution seemed simple enough, given the good will of two reasonable officials. But this temporary resolution in late February of 1702 scarcely settled what would be a central area of conflict for the duration of Old Mobile's history.[23]

On the last day of the month the rains stopped; the winds changed. Iberville set out once more for the river fort, leaving a longboat behind to transport La Salle and his family to their new quarters. By nightfall Iberville had reached the mouth of Dog

21. Journal d'Iberville, Feb. 25, 1702.

22. Min. to Bégon, Oct. 28, 1699, AM, B2, 142, f. 107–08. Min. to Duguay, Oct. 13, 1699, AC, B 20, f. 268. Iberville to min., May 7, 1700, BN, FF, NA, 9295, f. 211v. La Salle to min., April 1, 1702, AC, C13C, 2, f. 41–49.

23. AC, F1A, 10, f. 197–98, 282. Journal d'Iberville, *loc. cit.*, Feb. 25. What constituted a legitimate order was not strictly defined by Iberville. Must the order be always in writing? How were emergencies to be treated in the event La Salle could not be reached? Must La Salle give his approval of the bill? Could the commandant empty the king's storehouse at his own discretion?

River where he camped for the night, noting in particular the excellent position of the warehouse on the bluff of the stream's southern bank. The next day he entered the mouth of the Mobile River and spent the night five miles upstream. After camping the next night at Twenty-One Mile Bluff, Iberville rose early and began his approach to the new settlement on the morning of the third of March. Just beyond the bend, some four miles in the distance, the carpenters and woodsmen were busy with their hammers and axes.[24] Meanwhile Henri de Tonti and his small contingent of Canadians and natives were moving through the back country several hundred miles away in the distant forests.

Tonti and his expeditionary force had spent several days at the village of the Little Tomeh, just above the river's fork, before heading northwest to the Choctaw country.[25] The Little Tomeh, whose village site was located at the lower end of the great *écor* today known as Nannahubba Bluff, had been visited often by Charles Levasseur and other Canadians during the years 1700–01. The Little Tomeh were well-known to the French and had taken in a number of the Canadians during the time when food supplies had been especially low at Fort Maurepas. Like the Mobilians and the Alabama these natives occupied a highly strategic site which allowed them a wide measure of control over a principal branch of the Mobile River system. Furthermore, the chief overland trading path from the Choctaw country to the Mobile Bay area led directly through their village.[26]

It was this main path that Tonti and his men had taken on their

24. Journal d'Iberville, *loc. cit.*, March 3.

25. The village of the Little Tomeh was located at that portion of Nannahubba Bluff known as Calvert's Landing (and nearby Seaboard Landing). Tensaw Quadrangle, 1943. AMS 3446 III-Series V744. *Ala. River Navigation Charts*, 1972, p. 12. The village of the Tomeh (or Grand Tomeh) was located 12.7 miles farther upstream just below McIntosh Landing. *Black Warrior-Tombigbee Navigation Charts*, 1960, p. 15. Field Survey of the River Mobile and Part of the Rivers Alabama and Tensaw [without date or author], PRO, CO 700/Florida 40. Map of Mobile River [without title or date], PRO, CO 700/Florida 28 (Part). The Little Tomeh had at this time about 300 people while the Tomeh were 600. Journal de Levasseur, 1700, AM, 2 JJ 56, 16. Mémoire sur la Louisiane, vers 1725, AC, C13C, 1, f. 371v–72.

26. Journal de Lavasseur, *loc. cit.*, 16. *Journal Historique*, Aug. 8, 1699. Tonti and his men had journeyed to the Little Tomeh in Tonti's large pirogue. AC, F1A, 10, f. 289. Field Survey of River Mobile . . . , *loc. cit.*, Florida 40.

way northward. On the morning of February 14 they had departed the Little Tomeh village (after Tonti had dispatched a message to Iberville advising the commander of his departure) with two Mobilians and two of the Little Tomeh in return for whose services Tonti had promised each of them "a gun, a little powder and some bullets." [27] Moving in a westerly direction, then veering to the northwest, Tonti's party crossed several small streams that first day, making camp only three leagues from the Little Tomeh village. The next day the party made seven leagues and the next day, nine. Continuing over what Tonti called "mountains and large, never-ending hills, pure forests mixed with oak and chestnut," the expedition reached (on the third day) the Buckatunna River several miles from where that stream fell into the Pascagoula.[28] "All the streams," Tonti noted, "have banks which must be forded in water up to the armpits. We found no animals except two squirrels. We were reduced to a porridge of flour without any seasoning." [29]

By the twentieth of February, having switched to a more northerly direction, Tonti and his contingent reached the first village of the Choctaw nation, and the next day reached the cabin of the "chief of the loyal settlement," four leagues distant. The French, though they had made prior contact with the chief of this village on his visit to Fort Maurepas several years before, had never visited this locality themselves.[30] Tonti, however, was more anxious to reach the final Choctaw village whose chief had not yet made any contact with the French at all. Without delay (the time factor was important here, for Tonti hoped to return to Mobile with the chief of this village before Iberville embarked

27. Tonti to Iberville, Du Village des Chacta, Feb. 23, 1702, AM, 2 JJ 56, 20.

28. *Ibid.* By "rivière des Pascagoulas," Tonti meant what is now called the Chickasahay River. He was using the "North American post league" (2,000 *toises* = one *lieue*), which equalled 2.423 English statute miles. Danville, *Carte de la Louisiane*, 1732. However, Tonti had no accurate way to measure his leagues; in practice they might vary from 1.8 to 4.0 miles.

29. Tonti to Iberville, Feb. 23, *loc. cit.*, 20.

30. *Journal Historique*, *op. cit.*, Aug. 8, 1702. This was probably Couéchitou (village du grand-chef) which was situated in present-day Kemper County, Mississippi 3 miles northeast of Old Bloomfield at the headwaters of Sucarnoochee Creek. Meridian Strategic Map, 1953. NI 16–10, Series V501. Tonti by-passed the villages of Yowani and Chickasahay for a more northerly route.

for France), Tonti went on to the next village where he presented its chief with a gun and some small presents. Here, having covered a distance of over one hundred and fifty miles in nine days through difficult terrain, Tonti spent all of the day of the twenty-third, in order to stock up on provisions and get some well-deserved rest.[31]

Having traversed the entire Choctaw country, Tonti was favorably impressed, not only with the number of people and cabins in the nation but also with the vigorous quality of the warriors. "This nation is numerous," he reported to Iberville, "and I judge this by what I have been able to see of the people and [their] widely separated cabins, some on mountains and hills. They carry on farming in the lowlands. The men are strongly made and I can compare this nation very favorably to the Natchez." [32]

The Choctaw were no less impressed with the French, despite their small party and lack of presents. "They are very pleased that you wish them to make peace with the Chickasaw," Tonti added. "They have received us very well." [33]

Having successfully completed the first of his objectives (to convince the Choctaw of the desirability of peace with the Chickasaw), Tonti prepared to tackle the second, more difficult part of his assignment—to convince the Chickasaw to make peace with the Choctaw.[34] February 24th dawned extremely cold. Tonti quickly finished a letter to Iberville, asking him for an extension of five days ("for the time you gave me to return on March 20th is too short"), then dispatched two Choctaw to Mobile with his missive, promising each of the two runners "six knives, two hatchets and two necklaces of large beads." Leaving the Choctaw village

31. This would seem to be the village of Scanapa (a town of some thirty cabins) located near the Kemper-Noxubee county line in present day Mississippi. *Cf.* Journals of Régis and Lusser, 1729–30, AC, C13A, 12, f. 67–99, 100–34. Few of these Choctaw village sites have been precisely identified. Carte de la Louisiane et du cours du Mississipi . . . par Guillaume Delisle, [1718?], AM, cartes et plans, 4040B. Delisle notes, 1702, AM, 2 JJ 56, 24.

32. Tonti to Iberville, Feb. 23, *loc. cit.*, 20.

33. *Ibid.*

34. The mission to the Chickasaw was doubly important. The agreement with the three principal Choctaw chiefs was that they would accompany Tonti to Mobile only if Tonti were successful in persuading the chief of the Chickasaw to come also.

with a leading chief and several headmen, Tonti marched to the north-northeast, taking "the most easterly of the two routes to the Chickasaw towns by way of the village of Chachouma." [35]

Three days later, traveling more rapidly than before, Tonti and his forces found evidences of a Chickasaw war party apparently on its way to attack the Choctaw. This discovery caused some of the Choctaw and even some of Tonti's Tomeh guides "to take other routes which prolonged our trip and which caused me to cover 56 leagues from one village to the other."

A few days later, nearing the Chickasaw village, Tonti heard a gunshot in the distance. Startled, he immediately sent a scouting party to determine the nature of the disturbance but his scouts soon returned without finding the source of the gunfire. Sometime afterwards, a Chickasaw warrior appeared through the brush ahead, seeming to want to make communication. Questioned, the warrior reported two advance parties nearby—one smaller force (of which he was the leader) and another of four hundred men being led against the Choctaw by an Englishman. At this point Tonti felt his entire mission threatened. One rash act by the Chickasaw could irreparably defeat the expedition's principal objective.[36]

Nevertheless, Tonti and his men continued on their course, arriving at the village of the Chickasaw without further incident on the third of March, having passed by a nearby village of the Chakchiuma "on a small hill three *arpents* from the town." [37] The Chickasaw response at this initial confrontation with the Frenchmen was surprising enough. Several of the natives came to greet them on very cordial terms and conducted them to the entrance of the chief's cabin where a somber Englishman named

35. Tonti to Iberville, Feb. 23, *loc. cit.*, 20. Judging by a comparison of Tonti's narrative with modern charts, his route would seem to have been the most westerly of the two roads.

36. Tonti to Iberville, March 14, 1702, AM, 2 JJ 56, 20. The heading for this document in the Archives de la Marine is "Extrait d'une au [tre] lettre du meme au meme [Tonti to Iberville] Des Chacta le 14 Mars 1702." Like the preceding letter (Feb. 23), it seems to be not an extract but a full copy by Delisle of the original letter by Tonti. Delisle, however, did later make abstracts of both letters. AM, 2 JJ 56, 10.

37. The Chakchiuma, at this time very near the principal village of the Chickasaw, were later moved by Bienville to a location near the mouth of the Yazoo. Bienville to min., April 14, 1735, AC, C13A, 20, f. 45.

Ajean[38] faced them outside the door. Tonti described that first crucial meeting in some detail:

> They had us sit on piles of reeds facing the cabin. The chief was seated there along with an Englishman [Ajean] whom I had trouble recognizing as such. He was seated, holding a gun in his hands and a sword beside him. He had a very dirty blue shirt, no pants or stockings or shoes, a red blanket and necklaces around his throat like a savage. Our leading Choctaw made a speech and then the Englishman, on whom I had looked only with indignation, approached me and asked me if I knew how to speak Chaounon.[39] I told him no, and that I had come to win over the chief at your [Iberville's] insistence, that as I knew him by reputation as a wretch he should keep from making any speech against us; that if I became aware of it he would have a hard time. He [Ajean] asked me what reason I had to believe him so evil. I told him that he had tried to kill M. Davion[40] when he was at the Chicacha [Chickasaw] which he [Davion] had told me himself and that he was causing the destruction of these nations in order to acquire slaves and that he ought to be surfeited with human flesh, to which he answered that it was only the savages who were given to making war; but when I asked him how it happened that his comrade was at the head of four hundred warriors he had no answer for me.[41]

After this encounter, Tonti and his men retired for the evening toward the outskirts of the village. The next day Tonti presented the Chickasaw chief with a gun, some powder, bullets and knives and attempted to make him understand the far-reaching purposes of his mission.[42] The Chickasaw chief, able to comprehend only

38. This is Delisle's spelling of the Englishman's name. It is possible Tonti meant Johnson, as there were several Carolina traders of that name in the Chickasaw country in the early and middle 18th century.

39. Chaouanon, or as the Carolinians referred to it, Shawnee, a prevalent language in the early upper Southeast. Journal de Sauvole, Aug. 4, 1701, AC, C13A, 1, f. 319–20. Bienville to min., Aug. 20, 1735, AC, C13A, 20, f. 154. Bienville and Salmon to min., [*s.d.*], AC, C13A, 21, f. 21v.

40. Albert Davion, later to return to the Gulf Coast, had founded a mission among the Tunica in 1699 on the borders of the Chickasaw country. St.-Cosme à l'évêque de Québec, Jan. 2, 1699, ASQ, Lettres, R 26. Montigny à l'évêque de Québec, March 3, 1699, AN, K 1374, 82.

41. Tonti to Iberville, March 14, 1702, *loc. cit.*, 20.

42. Tonti noticed that when the presents were distributed Ajean wound up with the lion's share of the goods. *Ibid.*, 20. AC, F1A, 10 f. 288v.

that Tonti wanted him to accompany the French to Mobile Bay, was unconvinced of the necessity of leaving his village. To go with the French meant only that he would have to pass through the hostile territory of the Choctaw, a risk he was unwilling to take. At Tonti's prodding, the Choctaw chief attempted to convince the Chickasaw that the Choctaw came only in peace; but the Chickasaw had apparently heard that story before. The evening passed with neither Tonti nor the Choctaw chief being able to convince the Chickasaw of the ultimate purpose of the French mission.

The next day Tonti located a native who spoke the language of the Illinois (in which Tonti was more adept) through which he was able to express his intentions more clearly. The Chickasaw chief, though still not fully comprehending[43] the French plan, decided nevertheless to allow five of his most influential townsmen to accompany the expedition to Mobile.

On the morning of the sixth of March, the combined party, consisting of Tonti, his Canadians and Choctaw allies, five Chickasaw leaders, two paid warriors and three Chickasaw women, left the main village of the Chickasaw and took up the road to the Choctaw country.[44] Four miles from town a heavy rain obliged the party to seek shelter, whereupon it was discovered that a young Choctaw had been left behind in the village. Tonti, suspecting that the Choctaw had been forcibly detained, saw quickly the possible consequences of this pass: if the Choctaw youth were murdered or sold into slavery the Choctaw nation might consider its confidence betrayed and the success of the entire mission would be jeopardized. Upon short reflection, Tonti demanded that one of the Chickasaw leaders return to town to rescue the lost youth. Tonti's fears were well justified: when the Chickasaw warrior returned to town, he found Ajean in a desperate effort to sabotage the peace by attempting to carry the young Choctaw back to Carolina. Shortly after the expeditioners had left town, the Englishman had the Choctaw bound, then started on his way out of the village. Just out of town he decided to release his prisoner's legs and place him on a packhorse, but just as he began cutting the bonds the Chickasaw chief overtook him and snatched the would-be slave from his grasp. This incident precipitated a violent

43. Tonti's remark, "apparemm. dans l'esper^{ee} de recevoir des presens" suggests the chief's failure to fully grasp the reason for the journey. Tonti to Iberville, March 14, *loc. cit.*, 20.

44. *Ibid.*

quarrel between Ajean and the principal Chickasaw chief who had hastened upon the scene. Ajean, in a fit of temper, not only threatened to permanently break commercial relations with the main village, but to incite the Alabama and Coweta against the entire nation, a threat which prompted the Chickasaw chief to reply, "Take your leave, then, and go. The French have only one mouth but you have two . . . the French desire only furs and peace with all the nations, but you have your head between your legs." [45]

When the young Choctaw was returned to the campsite, the party continued down the path toward the Choctaw country, Tonti more optimistic now than ever. Not only had he succeeded in bringing the Chickasaw with him, but the Englishman had apparently lost his influence at the village. Only two factors now stood between Tonti and the successful completion of his mission: time, and a possible incident between the rival nations farther down the road.

The incident Tonti feared was not long in coming. On the third day's march, only eighteen miles from the northernmost Choctaw village, the party came to the banks of a large river, a swollen stream which appeared uncrossable. "The savages told us we must encamp," Tonti reported, "that it would only take one night for the waters to fall, and that after then it would only be up to our waists." The party encamped. Two hours after noon a courier arrived from the Chickasaw village with a distressing report: the Chakchiuma (for what reason no one understood) had two nights before dispatched a party of warriors to the Choctaw country, had attacked a small village and murdered three men before seizing the women and children from a large cabin. Hearing this news, the Chickasaw chieftains, sensing the probability of reprisal, notified Tonti they wished to turn back to their village.[46]

Tonti, fearing his labors may all have been in vain, conferred with his lieutenants: the use of force was out of the question, yet if he allowed the chiefs to return to their village, the peace would surely be lost. After one of the chiefs fled camp, he called the remaining ones together in a last-ditch effort to placate their fears. "I made the others understand," he later reported, "that I was employed to come and save them, that if they did not come with me to see the great chief [Iberville], their wars would continue forever, that the French would not go among them any more, while

45. *Ibid.*
46. *Ibid.*

there would always be a great number of us among the Choctaw, that the Choctaw would have much powder and guns and that the two nations would soon destroy each other, while the English would then come to seize the rest; that if they came with me, you [Iberville] would give them presents and Frenchmen to escort them to their village, that you would send them canoes loaded with merchandise by the Mobile River, which passes within a day and a half of their village, that they would have nothing to fear for themselves."[47]

Apparently Tonti's speech reassured the Chickasaw; even the chief who had fled camp was overtaken and persuaded to return. Once again the "Iron Hand" had averted disaster. The party succeeded the next day in crossing the river "in water higher than our waists," although it took more than an hour and a half to reach the other side. Once across, the expedition proceeded in a southeasterly direction, crossing another large river the next day. By the eleventh of March, the expedition had reached an ancient repository of shells that the natives told Tonti had been deposited "when the great chief was angry and flooded all the earth."[48]

After crossing several more rivers, then making their way across the lowlands, plains, and hills of the back country, Tonti and his party arrived on the thirteenth of March at Scanapa, the outermost village of the Choctaw, where the Chickasaw chiefs were surprised at the friendly reception they were given. Tonti, however, concerned about this aspect of the return trip, had sent his most trusted lieutenant, François Danbourné, and the Choctaw chief to the village the day before in order to ensure that the reception would not be hostile. The Choctaw, seemingly eager for peace, had met the French-Chickasaw party on the outskirts of Scanapa with food and presents. In the village now they were unusually hospitable to their erstwhile enemies.[49]

47. *Ibid.* Tonti's words, given in desperate circumstances, were a preview to Iberville's later speech at Fort Louis. Journal d'Iberville, *loc. cit.*, March 26, 1702.

48. Tonti assumed, as did James Adair half a century later, that the natives had some pre-historic idea of the deluge. *Cf.* Adair, *The History of the American Indians*, pp. 3–97. The Chickasaw, however, probably got this idea from their early contacts with the Carolinians in the late seventeenth century.

49. Tonti to Iberville, *loc. cit.*, 20. Danbourné appears on the roster of Canadians for 1702 at 360 *livres* per year. AC, F1A, 10, f. 284. He appears neither on the 1700 nor the 1703 list. AC, C13A, 1, f. 255–60; AC, F1A, 11, f. 71–73.

Tonti, still uneasy about the time schedule (the alliance would more firmly be sealed if the chiefs could meet the "Great Chief" in person and be personally assured of the promises Tonti had made), took advantage of the stopover at the Choctaw village to draft a letter urging Iberville not to depart for France until his return. Furthermore, he wanted to make certain that the presents he had promised the various chiefs would be readily available upon their arrival at the fort:

> Permit me, Monsieur, to tell you that these nations wish to be won over by numerous presents, and in making allies of these people all the others will not dare rebel; and if they are not happy with the French, one should not be surprised that the English will do all they can to attract them in order to destroy all your neighboring savages; that they will strike while the iron is hot.
>
> The Chickasaw want trade, which is very easy to accomplish by the Mobile River which comes within thirty-six hours of their village. The Choctaw, as they are located nearer, can bring their business to the fort . . .[50]

Tonti went on to remind Iberville that in case he were forced to leave before the party arrived to be certain that Bienville could have the presents delivered, for the success of the mission would hinge on the complete fulfillment of this promise. His message ended on a humble, even chauvinistic note:

> If the discoveries in the West of which I have spoken do not please you and if you find me useful somewhere else, you know what my brother told you in France and what I have also told you. Use me without hesitation and be confident that I will always find pleasure in doing what you would like.[51]

Dispatching the letter by Danbourné, Tonti readied his forces to leave the Choctaw villages by the sixteenth of March. By the seventeenth, he and his party of Canadians, Chickasaw and Choctaw chiefs and three Chickasaw women began to emerge from the last villages of the Choctaw, moving through the barren wilds of forest and swamps that bordered the rich farmlands of the upper Pascagoula and the lower Tombigbee. As the first day of spring neared, Tonti's mission to the interior powers seemed assured of fulfillment.

50. Tonti to Iberville, *loc. cit.*, 20.
51. *Ibid.*

V

Iberville at Fort Louis

ON the same day that Tonti entered the principal village of the Chickasaw, Iberville landed his small vessel at the budding river settlement. La Salle, his wife and sons were still on Massacre Island with Châteaugué and Robinau de Bécancour. When he arrived at the location Iberville found his brother Bienville occupied in completing the fort, clearing the trees from the proposed town site and overseeing the work on the pinnace which was nearly ready for the timbers to be bent. The commander was elated at the progress of construction, as well as with the appearance of the site chosen for the establishment. "This settlement," he noted in his journal, "is on a bluff over twenty feet high, covered with trees of various kinds, white and scarlet oaks, laurels, sassafras, white-wood trees, hard walnut trees, in particular, a large number of pines suitable for making masts." [1]

With the work progressing smoothly on the fort and interior buildings, Iberville took up lodging in the almost-completed administrative quarters, leaving most of the immediate decision-making to Charles Levasseur. Tonti, he reckoned, would be back at the fort in two weeks, hopefully accompanied by the Chickasaw and Choctaw chiefs. In the meantime, Iberville would occupy himself with a number of other tasks, foremost among them the directing of a thorough reconnaissance of the area surrounding Fort Louis, with particular attention to the several native villages. The day after his arrival, he had a mainmast cut for Sérigny's *Palmier*,[2]

1. Journal d'Iberville, April 27, 1702, AM, B4, 23, f. 321–27. Tonti to Iberville, March 14, 1702, AM, 2 JJ 56, 20.

2. The *Palmier's* mainmast, severely damaged by lightning off the coast of Saint-Domingue, had been only temporarily repaired at Cap-français. Iberville to min., Nov. 14, 1701, AM, B4, 21, f. 541–43.

then dispatched Bienville to investigate the islands in the marshlands north and east of the fort.

Bienville set out on the morning of March 4, guided by natives from the village of the Mobilians. Moving upstream he cut through a narrow bayou and made his way to the northeast, noticing a number of deserted village sites which the natives told him had been abandoned during past wars against the Alabama and the Apalachicola. The former settlements were on numerous islands in the Mobile delta, many of them apparently under water at flood times. Curiosity about the location of the natives' idols (about which he had heard so many tales) compelled Bienville to ask one of the Mobilians to direct him to the house of the god-heads where the natives often went to offer sacrifices. The Mobilian, afraid for his own life and claiming that no man could touch such figures without dying, declined at first to lead Bienville to their location; upon delivery of a much-coveted gun, however, he acquiesced, guiding Bienville through what is now Bayou Matche to the still-intact mound on Bottle Creek.[3] Once on the mound the Mobilian refused to go closer than ten paces to the idols' location; even then he would only approach them stepping backwards. After a short search, Bienville found some crude sculptures in the canes near an old village site which had been destroyed. The idols consisted of five figures: a bear, an owl, a man, woman and child, molded of some type of plaster-like material.

Later that evening, Bienville brought the idols back to the fort and showed them to Iberville and a few of the officers. The commander thought they were the work of some Spaniard who in the time of Soto had made images of some of the local Indians in clay.[4] The idols were kept at the fort; the Mobile and the Little Tomeh who came to see them were astonished at the boldness of the French and were surprised that Bienville was not dead as a result of the act of retrieving them. Although he later described them as "not very remarkable," Iberville kept them on display for a few

3. The large Bottle Creek mound was only four miles overland from Fort Louis. Bienville's route, no doubt, took him from Bayou Matche up Middle River, down Tensaw River into Bottle Creek, from whence he had to walk about 500 yards. Tensaw Quadrangle, 1943. AMS 3446 III-Series V744.

4. While Luna's expedition passed within 900 yards of the Bottle Creek mound, Soto's line of march took him nowhere near the vicinity. Los capitanes al campo del Sargento Mayor, 1560, AGI, *Justicia*, L. 1013. The figures were very likely made by area natives of a much earlier period.

days; then when the mainmast for the *Palmier* was completed, he sent them on to Massacre Island to be transported back to France.[5]

Two days after Bienville's return from the Mobile delta, Iberville went to reconnoiter the vicinity himself in search of an adequate stream where a sawmill could be built. He found nothing suitable, and three days later set out in a long-boat for the village of the Little Tomeh from which Tonti had departed for the lands of the Choctaw nearly a month before. On the way to the Little Tomeh, Iberville observed numerous deserted settlements along both sides of the river, indicating that perhaps this part of the Mobile had once supported an unusually large native population.[6] He reached the village of the Little Tomeh on the tenth of March and spent the day observing the area around Nannahubba Bluff and the lowlands near the confluence of the two arms of the Mobile. After passing the night at the Little Tomeh village, he ascended the Alabama for a few leagues before returning to the fort the next day.[7]

On his return to Fort Louis, Iberville found La Salle and his family (who had been transported by Desjordy-Moreau) waiting for him, as well as some recent letters from Francisco Martínez. The Pensacola governor was short of provisions again and was asking for additional aid. Iberville, though he had recently supplied Martínez with fifty barrels of flour, was not unsympathetic to the needs of the Spanish. The well-being of Fort San Carlos, he knew, would be beneficial to the success of Fort Louis during the early stages. Over the next few years, supply ships from Veracruz would be coming regularly to Pensacola. No doubt they would arrive on numerous occasions when Fort Louis was lacking in supplies.[8]

The next day, Iberville, in an attempt to fill Martínez's request, sent Desjordy-Moreau upriver to purchase some maize from the natives. That evening Châteaugué and Robineau de Bécancour arrived from Massacre Island with another load of provisions and the next day were sent back again just before Desjordy-Moreau descended the river with two *feluccas* filled with corn, one of

5. Journal d'Iberville, *loc. cit.*, March 4.

6. Iberville was trying to determine if the bluffs along the river were capable of supporting the plantations he envisioned. Journal d'Iberville, *loc. cit.*, March 10.

7. *Ibid.*

8. La Salle to min., April 1, 1702, AC, C13C, 2, f. 37–39. BN, FF, NA, 9295, f. 239–41.

which was sent on to Martínez at Pensacola. The following day, as two pinnaces arrived from Île Massacre, Iberville sent one of the longboats back to the Little Tomeh village to purchase more maize.

All of these movements had been carried out in spite of unusually heavy rains. The downpours had begun on the eleventh of March, had fallen almost continuously for nearly a week, resulting finally in the cave-in of the powder magazine—a loss of over seven hundred man-hours of labor.[9]

On the nineteenth, in the midst of the rains, François Danbourné returned from the Choctaw country, the night before Tonti was originally scheduled to arrive at the fort. Iberville, upon receiving Tonti's letter, was elated that his emissary had succeeded in convincing the Choctaw and Chickasaw chiefs to return with him to Mobile. According to his letter Tonti would arrive at Fort Louis on the twenty-fifth of the month, which gave Iberville five days to prepare for the approaching conference.[10]

As Tonti's party was moving down the backroads of the forests, Iberville took advantage of the time to lay out more concretely plans for the town behind the fort. While Charles Levasseur was busy drawing a sketch of the town as it was progressing and as it was to eventually appear, Iberville was at work marking out the lines of the streets and assigning plots of ground within the town to the Canadians and French artisans.[11] The four families that Iberville had brought over on the *Renommée* and the *Palmier* were by this time already housed and were hard at work trying to clear the ground around their establishments in time for a spring planting. La Salle and his family had been temporarily located in his unfinished quarters in the fort while his house on the riverfront next to Bienville's and that of Pierre Poudrier, was being completed.[12] The commissary's corner lot measured 160 feet along the river bank with a side of 256 feet which ran along the rue des

9. Extrait d'une lettre du neveu de M. Lefevre, March 15, 1702, BN, FF, 9097, f. 123v–24. Journal d'Iberville, *loc. cit.*, March 19. For safety measure, this temporary magazine had been dug on high ground near the edge of the bluff; it was to be used only until a permanent magazine within the fort was completed. Plan de la Ville et du fort de la Maubille, AN, Section Outre-mer, DFC, 119A.

10. Tonti to Iberville, March 14, 1702, *loc. cit.*, 20.

11. Gravier to Lamberville [postscript of March, 1702], *JR*, *LXV*, p. 179. Plan de la Ville et du fort de la Maubille, *loc. cit.*, 119A.

12. *Ibid.*

Jésuites.[13] It was a generous assignment that Iberville had given to La Salle; except for the lots given to François Lemay and Jean-Baptiste Joussette, *dit* La Loire, it was the largest of all the designated plots, totalling nearly 41,000 square feet, which La Salle and his young sons, Nicolas and Simon, would shortly begin to cultivate.[14] Though La Salle's lot was considerably larger than that given to Bienville (which totalled less than 26,000 square feet), Iberville took pains to locate his brother between La Salle and the fort where the king's storehouse was situated.[15]

In general, Iberville and Levasseur blocked off the town in large square blocks measuring three hundred and twenty feet by three hundred and twenty feet (or about 102,400 square feet). Each block was then subdivided into lots of various shapes and sizes, the most predominant being (like those of surgeon Pierre Clavery and Canadians Mathurin Moquin and Zacharie Drapeau) rectangular-shaped, measuring approximately eighty by one hundred and sixty feet. Many of the plots within the blocks were, however, irregularly shaped, such as some of the plots of the block on the rue Saint-Joseph between the rue d'Iberville and the rue de La Salle. Four of these lots, two of which were given to Canadians Joseph Simon, *dit* La Pointe, and Gilbert Dardenne, were rectangular in shape, while another four, two of which were assigned to Denis Durbois and Philippe Minette, were square-shaped, measuring a mere eighty by eighty feet (among the smallest of the lots granted by Iberville). The remaining four, like those given Jacques Simon, *dit* La Pointe (older brother of Joseph), and Claude Charland, *dit* Francoeur, were "L-shaped," each containing some 9,600 square feet.[16]

One of the four colonists given a small square lot within this block (occupied mostly by Canadians) was Frenchman Jean Le Caën, a metal worker and master locksmith. Artisan Le Caën, recruited three years before in Rochefort, had been serving at Fort Maurepas since 1700, one of the few married men in the colony.

13. *Ibid.* Journal d'Iberville, *loc. cit.*, March 23. Plan de la ville et du Fort Louis, sur la Mobile, 1711, AN, Section Outre-mer, DFC, 120B.

14. La Salle to min., July 28, 1700, AC, C13B, 1, No. 5, f.4. AMT, État Civil, GG 85, f. 32v; 87, f. 224; 92, f. 13.

15. Plan de la ville et du Fort Louis . . . , *loc. cit.*, 120B.

16. *Ibid.* Plan de la Ville et du fort de la Maubille, *loc. cit.*, 119A. AC, F1A, 10, f. 282v–85. *FLC*, pp. 58–60. BN, FF, 14613, f. 81–86. Lettre, Sept. 10, 1704, BN, FF, 9097, f. 140–43. Dénombrement, Aug. 31, 1704, AC, C13A, 1, f. 468–70.

His wife, Madelaine Robert, had arrived on the *Renommée* after receiving permission the previous summer to join him.[17]

François-Xavier Lemay, *dit* Poudrier, a twenty-eight-year-old Canadian powdermaker, was granted a large lot between Jean-Baptiste Joussette, *dit* La Loire, and land that Levasseur had wanted set aside for a hospital but which would later become a brickyard. Lemay's plot, though it was some distance from the fort, was the largest in the colony assigned to a private individual. Though Lemay was on the payroll at only thirty *livres* per month, Iberville had good reason to grant him so substantial a lot; Lemay, son of Michel Lemay and Marie-Michelle Dutost, had grown up in Quebec where his family had been neighbors and close friends of the Rivard de La Vigne clan. Young Lemay had early learned the profession of "powdermaking" from his father; he had won Iberville's respect as a young man of twenty-two by ably serving in Iberville's Hudson's Bay campaign against the English. Sent to Rochefort after that engagement, Lemay married a French girl, Angela Orsseau, had sired two children by her by the time he left his new family to come to Louisiana on Iberville's second expedition. Thus, when it became known that Iberville was searching for families to bring to Louisiana in 1701, it was only natural that Lemay (then at Fort Maurepas) should request the commander to bring his wife and family on the next voyage from France.[18]

Aside from the foregoing assignments, Iberville made a grant to Jacques Leméry, a volatile, hard-drinking ex-freebooter, whose wife had also come with Iberville on the *Renommée;* to Charles Juchereau de Saint-Denis (in absentia) the commander assigned a lot between Pierre Dugué de Boisbriant and Charles Levasseur; to Pierre-Charles Le Sueur, who was already making plans to return the next year with his large family, Iberville granted a lot 96 feet by 160 next to François Sainte-Marie on the rue de Ruessavel.[19]

The Jesuits, being in Iberville's favor (more for their potential in aiding the commander's enterprise than for theological reasons),

17. AC, F1A, 10, f. 283. ADM, A, Oct. 4, 1704; March 13, 1709; March 20, 1710. LSMA, DCS, July 23, 1725.

18. *DGFC, I*, p. 376. Liste des Canadiens engagés par M. d' Iberville pour l'entreprise du Nord, July 6, 1697, AC, C13A, 1, f. 256–58. AC, F1A, 10, f. 283v. ADM, A, Sept. 18, Oct. 22, 1704; March 9, 1709; March 19, 1710.

19. AC, C13A, 1, f. 257–59. AC, F1A, 10, f. 283. ADM, A, April 11, 1705. Plan de la Ville et du fort de la Maubille, *loc. cit.*, 119A. Leméry is often listed as Humery in the documents. *Cf.* Mémoire par Dartaguiette, Feb. 25, 1708, AC, C13A, 2, f. 73.

received a large, choice lot fronting the river, between Nicolas de La Salle and Canadian Guillaume Boutin. The seminary priests, though they were not yet a force in the settlement, were granted an entire block (though the most distant location from the fort), bounded by the rue du Séminaire and the rue Saint-Joseph.[20] In general, the plots were assigned to the inhabitants according to their particular profession or station in the colony. The carpenters, for example, were grouped together in a district on the northwest side of town; the *voyageurs* and Canadians, such as Joseph Guillet de Bellefeuille, Pierre Sauton and Pierre de Launay were toward the western outskirts of town, while the administrative personnel and officers, such as Gerard, La Salle, Tonti and Bécancour were grouped in close proximity to the fort and administrative quarters.[21] The choicest ground (the highest and flattest part of the bluff, consisting of nearly three acres and bounded by the rue de Bienville and rue de Châteaugué), was reserved for the future use of the king.[22] All of the blocks were bounded by straight and wide streets which were named after high-ranking officers (Saint-Denis, Châteaugué, Bécancour), particular saints (Saint-François, Sainte-Marie, Sainte-Anne) as well as for one of the religious present, Balthazar-Michel de Boutteville. Except for the avenues named for the Le Moyne brothers—Sérigny, Châteaugué, Bienville and Iberville—none of the streets retained the same name for a distance longer than one block, following the custom in France.[23]

Shortly after Iberville and Levasseur completed laying out the streets and the basic design of the town, five of Tonti's men arrived at the fort with a message from their captain: Tonti was now at the village of the Little Tomeh, only twenty-two miles upstream. He would enter Mobile on the next day, with the chiefs of the Choctaw and Chickasaw.

20. Originally most of the plot granted to the seminary priests was near the center of the marshiest portion of the town site. After Boutteville objected, the seminary priests were assigned higher ground; the old site was subdivided and later distributed to Charles Dumont and the Chauvin brothers.

21. Plan de la Ville et du fort de la Maubille, *loc. cit.*, 119A. Lettre, Sept. 10, 1704, BN, FF, 9097, f. 141–43.

22. This land reserved for the king was never put to any use. Plan de la ville et du Fort Louis, sur la Mobile, 1711, *loc. cit.*, 120B.

23. *Ibid.* Gravier to Lamberville [postscript of March, 1702], *JR*, *LXV*, p. 179. Mémoire pour servir d'instruction au Sieur de Bienville, Lieutenant de Roy du fort de Bilocchy au fort de la Mobile donnés par d'Iberville, April 25, 1702, AC, F3, 68, f. 7v–8.

Early the next morning, Tonti and the Choctaw and Chickasaw chiefs left the village of the Little Tomeh in Tonti's pirogue, accompanied by several other dugouts carrying the chiefs of the Mobilians and Little Tomeh. It was Sunday, the twenty-sixth of March. At eleven o'clock, Tonti arrived at the landing place just north of town. Iberville, Levasseur, Bienville and most of the other officers were in the recently completed fort chapel where the new chaplain, Jesuit Pierre Dongé, was conducting one of the first masses. When the services were completed, Iberville went out to meet Tonti and the "three chiefs and four men of importance belonging to the Chickasaw, and the four chiefs of the Choctaw." Iberville gave all of them the "best welcome I could" but deferred assembling them for the planned conference until the next day.[24]

The scheme to bring the chiefs of the various nations to the site of Mobile had been drawn from three considerations. First of all, Iberville had not been strong enough to make the demanding trip to the back country himself and he had wanted to meet with them personally. Secondly, the possibility of securing consent from the Choctaw and Chickasaw to meet together was infinitely greater if the meeting were to take place on neutral ground. Thirdly, Iberville wanted to impress the natives with the appearance of the fort and town itself. If the French were able to lay out a goodly sized town and erect a formidable fort in the short time they had been present, Iberville was confident the savages would be sufficiently infixed with French potential. Too, the size and appearance of the ten and twelve-pounder cannons in the fort would surely make their effect on the native chieftains, most of whom had never before seen such awful weapons.[25]

By eight o'clock the following morning, Iberville had the gifts he intended to present to each of the two nations laid out around the fort's plaza: four hundred *livres* worth of bullets and powder; two hundred *livres* worth of shot for game; twelve rifles; one hundred hatchets; one hundred and fifty knives; a supply of cook-

24. Journal d'Iberville, *loc. cit.*, March 25. Both La Salle and Tonti reported five Chickasaw chiefs. Obviously, two of those Tonti considered "chiefs" were two of Iberville's "important men." La Salle to min., April 1, 1702, AC, C13C, 2, f. 37–41. Tonti to Iberville, March 14, 1702, AM, 2 JJ 56, 20.

25. Tonti to Iberville, March 14, 1702, *loc. cit.*, 20. La Salle to min., April 1, 1702, *loc. cit.*, f. 36–40. Min. to Bégon, Sept. 14, 1701, AM, B2, 155, f. 459–59v. Journal de Le Sueur, 1702, AM, 2 JJ 56, 9; AM, 4 JJ 14, 4. Extrait d'une lettre de Rochefort . . . , July 10, 1702, BN, FF, 9097, f. 125–26.

ing pots, glass beads, gun flints, awls and various other articles of hardware, all of which created an imposing display for the savages. When the presents were all set out, Iberville had the various leaders assembled in the plaza where with his brother Bienville acting as interpreter he addressed the chiefs.[26] After expressing his pleasure at seeing they were disposed to live at peace with one another and with the other villages in the country and after emphasizing that it was in their interest to do so instead of destroying one another as they had been doing, Iberville warned the Chickasaw that they had been ill-advised in following the counsel of the English whose only object was to cause their destruction by inciting them to war only in order to obtain slaves. "Have not the English themselves," Iberville reminded the Chickasaw, "purchased some of your own brothers when your enemies have taken them prisoner? Have not they sold them into slavery to the Islands [English possessions in the West Indies] just as they have traded the Choctaw? Have not the English over the last eight or ten years been responsible for the deaths of over eighteen hundred Choctaw and eight hundred Chickasaw? The Choctaw see clearly what has been happening and the Chickasaw likewise ought to see it; the English, after weakening both your nations, will come with other nations from the east and carry off what few people remain in your villages to be sold elsewhere, into far-off lands from which your people will never return." [27]

Iberville went on to warn the chiefs that in order to prevent these misfortunes, "you must not listen to the English anymore, you must drive them away from you." Then, having proposed what course the two nations should follow, the commander shifted to a more threatening tone: in the event the Chickasaw should fail to heed his warning, "We could never be friends with one another and I would carry on no trade with you. I would arm all the Choctaw, Tomeh and Mobilians with guns, as I have already begun to arm the Natchez and other tribes who are our allies, and far from preventing the Illinois from making war on you, I would even incite them to do so; so you can plainly see that you would not be able to hold your own against so many tribes, and you would have the grief of seeing your men slaughtered at the gates of your own village with your women and children." [28]

26. AC, F1A, 10, f. 288v. La Salle to min., April 1, 1702, *loc. cit.*, f. 36–39.
27. Iberville to min., *loc. cit.*, March 26, 1702.
28. *Ibid.*

"However," Iberville continued, returning to his original plea, "if you should drive the English (who long for nothing but blood and slaves) away from your country, I will have a village built between the Choctaw and Chickasaw villages, as you have wished, where you will be able to find goods of all kinds in exchange for your ox hides, deerskins, and bearskins—these are the only slaves I ask for, and you can feed yourselves and all your families on the meat you kill in hunting. And this will be a trade that will never cost you your lives to carry on." [29]

When Iberville's speech was concluded, the Choctaw and Chickasaw chiefs came forward, smoked the calumet of peace with the officers,[30] then swore to expel the English, as Iberville had advocated, on the promise that the French would live up to the trade agreements the commander had proposed. After the prices were agreed on for the skins the Chickasaw had promised to deliver, Iberville, in a generous gesture, presented one of the Chickasaw chiefs a gun, a blanket, a cloak, a hatchet, two knives, and powder and bullets in order to compensate the chief for the Choctaw slave he had rescued from Ajean as Tonti and his party were leaving the Chickasaw village three weeks earlier.[31] Iberville, moreover, armed all of the chiefs of the two nations who had come to Mobile with additional guns and gave each of them a shirt and a number of small presents. He then promised the Chickasaw he would immediately inform all the nations who were allies of the French not to make further war against them; in return, the Chickasaw were to induce the Alabama and Apalachicola to make peace with the Choctaw, Mobilians and Tomeh and to attempt to persuade the former two nations to visit Fort Louis as soon as possible.[32]

With the agreements thus set, Iberville, Bienville and Tonti sat down with the chieftains to draw up an accurate census of their separate villages and to reckon the various distances between each one. The Chickasaw, enumerating their villages family by family, listed 580 cabins. Counting three or four men per hut, the Chickasaw claimed at least two thousand men, of whom seven to eight hundred were armed with guns. The Choctaw, counting their

29. *Ibid.*

30. *Cf. FLC*, pp. 5–7, 61. BN, FF, 14613, f. 20–27.

31. AC, F1A, 10, f. 288–90v. Tonti to Iberville, March 14, 1702, *loc. cit.*, 20. Journal d'Iberville, *loc. cit.*, March 26.

32. *Ibid. Journal Historique*, pp. 71–72. Pénigault, *Relation*, BN, FF, 14613, f. 88–89. *FLC*, p. 61. Journal de Le Sueur, *loc. cit.*, f. 71–75. Lettre de Bergier, Nov. 17, 1702, ASQ, Lettres, R 58.

three main villages, claimed 1090 cabins totalling thirty-eight hundred to four thousand men.[33]

As the Chickasaw and Choctaw chiefs prepared to return to their village, Iberville retired to the fort to begin preparations for his return to Pensacola. Towards the afternoon, Robinau de Bécancour arrived in a pinnace loaded with supplies from the Massacre Island warehouse, having left Châteaugué to unload more supplies at the small warehouse Iberville had ordered built at the mouth of Dog River. Inside the fort, the commander sat down to pen some important letters: to Louis-Marc Bergier, vicar-general at the Tamaroa, Iberville wrote asking him to send four missionaries to the Chickasaw and Choctaw as soon as possible in order to assist the French in keeping their hold on those nations;[34] to Albert Davion, seminary priest at the Tunica, he wrote informing him of the new alliance and asking him to persuade some of the Chakchiuma who had removed to that district to return to their village near the Chickasaw; to Nicolas Foucault, missionary at the Arkansas, and to Jean-François Buisson de Saint-Cosme,[35] missionary at the Natchez, Iberville wrote asking them to relay the news of the alliance to all the surrounding villages so as to prevent them from provoking unnecessary wars which would endanger the peace.[36]

Finishing these dispatches, Iberville retired for the night. Early the next morning, he sent Bécancour back to Massacre Island, along with men from his crew who were to board the *Palmier;* he then handed over the letters[37] he had written the night before to the Choctaw and Chickasaw couriers (who would carry them by

33. Journal d'Iberville, *loc. cit.*, March 26. Iberville notes, "They [the Choctaw] are the handsomest men in these lands. They have the Iroquois style, and the manner of warriors." Relation de la rivière de la Mobile, AM, 3 JJ 277, 8. Mémoire d'Iberville, 1701, AM, 3 JJ 277, 4. Despite the concerted efforts of Tonti and Iberville, no strictly accurate census was achieved (during these early years). From first-hand observation, Davion swore there were only 311 cabins at the Chickasaw. Davion [to SME Dirs.], Dec. 12, 1702, ASME, 344.

34. Lettre de Marc Bergier, Nov. 17, 1702, *loc. cit.*, R 58.

35. Saint-Cosme the younger (1667–1706), distant cousin of the burser of the Séminaire de Québec. ASQ, Polygraphie, IX, 24–25. AJQ, Greffe de Duquet, May 24, 1671.

36. Journal d'Iberville, *loc. cit.*, March 27.

37. The natives, regarding written messages with profound respect, were generally found to be highly trustworthy as postal agents, often risking their lives to see that the letters were delivered.

horseback to the various villages where the missionaries were located), then directed François Danbourné and four other Canadians to prepare to escort the Chickasaw chiefs back upriver to the vicinity where Iberville had promised a post would be established.[38]

Danbourné and two of the Canadians were to proceed from the site of the proposed post with two Chickasaw warriors to the Illinois to ask for the return of all Chickasaw prisoners (as per the agreement) and to notify the Illinois to discontinue aggression; the two remaining Canadians were to return to Mobile in Tonti's canoe, gathering intelligence about the river and the surrounding countryside.[39]

With the supply of presents ready to be transported back to their villages, the Choctaw and Chickasaw chiefs departed Fort Louis on the twenty-seventh of March, carrying with them a French youth named Saint-Michel who was to remain in the Chickasaw village to learn the Chickasaw language so as to be able to serve as an interpreter.[40] After a last conference with Bienville, Levasseur, Boisbriant and Tonti, during which Iberville discussed the difficulties the new establishment would likely encounter (shortage of food would be a central problem in six months time, according to the memorandum La Salle presented), the commander set out in his felucca later in the afternoon to return to Massacre Island.[41] Iberville had been present at Fort Louis only twenty-five days, but despite the short stay, despite the minor setbacks he had encountered, he had thus far succeeded in accomplishing all his major objectives. The fort had been duly constructed, lacked, in fact, only some finishing touches; most of the houses planned (over fifty, so far) had either been completed or were nearing completion. Most important of all, the two most powerful nations on the southern frontier had been successfully

38. The proposed fort was to be located in the vicinity where later Fort Tombecbé would be constructed. Danville, Carte de la Louisiane, 1732, BN, Cartes et plans, Collection Danville.

39. Relation de la rivière de la Mobile, *loc. cit.*, 8. AC, F1A, 10, f. 289v.

40. Saint-Michel was possibly the son of Jean-Baptiste Legardeur de Saint-Michel, "capitaine des vaisseaux du roi du port de Rochefort." He had been in Louisiana for several years where he had already learned the language of the Houma, a tongue similar to the Chickasaw. AC, C13A, 1, f. 216–18, 257–59. *FLC*, pp. 68, 73–76.

41. Mémoire pour servir d'instruction au sieur de Bienville . . . par d'Iberville, AC, F3, 68, f. 1–9v. AC, F1A, 10, f. 282–90v.

reconciled.[42] Rounding the first bend south of Fort Louis, Iberville caught a last glimpse of his infant settlement, as well as of his younger brother Bienville whom he had left in command of the fort. Though he was planning to return the following year, the commander could not foresee the tumultous events in Europe that would soon divert his attention.

Bienville, now commandant of the new Fort Louis, went back to the work of the establishment as Iberville continued downstream toward Massacre Island. Three leagues down Iberville passed Châteaugué on his way to the fort with eighty barrels of flour. After passing the night at what is now Magazine Point, Iberville resumed his voyage down river, met by heavy winds and rains from the southwest,[43] then spent the next night at the warehouse on Dog River where he found his ship's ensign, Bécart de Granville, with the *Palmier's* longboat, occupied in unloading the smack.[44]

The following morning, Iberville sent the smack back to the *Palmier*, then followed with all of the longboats and pinnaces. Hoping to find the *Précieuse* (under Dugué de Sainte-Thérèse) back from Veracruz and François Pillet's ketch returned from Fort La Boulaye, the commander was disappointed to find neither of them. Boarding the *Palmier*, Iberville attempted to leave the harbor at Massacre Island to return to Pensacola, but unfavorable winds prevented his departure. While waiting for a change in winds, Iberville had the smack loaded with supplies from the warehouse to take to the Dog River depot, but as the master of the smack, Jousselin de Marigny, seemed incapable of negotiating the narrow channel, Iberville gave the responsibility to his sub-lieutenant on the *Renommée*, Robinau de Bécancour "who is most capable and highly skilled in his profession, and [who] has taken great pains with all the labor that is to be done."[45]

On the last day of March, Bécancour left for the Dog River warehouse and Iberville managed to get the *Palmier* out of the

42. Mémoire de Le Sueur, 1702, BN, FF, NA, 9301, f. 127–28. Min. to Iberville, June 17, 1703, AC, B 23, f. 192–94.

43. Journal d'Iberville, *loc. cit.*, March 27.

44. *Ibid.*, March 28.

45. AC, F1A, 10, f. 282v, 289v–90. Journal d'Iberville, *loc. cit.*, Feb. 4, 18, March 29. Apparently Iberville was irked at the past performance of Jousselin de Marigny.

harbor; by the end of the next day, the first of April, Iberville had anchored in the roadstead of Santa María de Galve.[46]

At Pensacola, Iberville had hoped to find news of the traversier he had sent to Veracruz under Ensign Sainte-Thérèse, but Governor Martínez had received no report of the vessel. Martínez, even more anxious than Iberville for the return of Sainte-Thérèse's ship, had not even received word of the launch he had sent to Apalache in search of provisions. "This governor," Iberville noted, observing the sad state of affairs at Pensacola, "could not have subsisted except for my efforts during the past two months." [47]

For the next two weeks, Iberville impatiently whiled away the time at Pensacola. Disgruntled, anxious to embark for France, he nonetheless felt it important to wait for the ship from Veracruz (in order to determine how his vessels would subsequently be received in that port). Equally important, he felt it necessary to await the arrival of François Pillet's ketch, which supposedly was transporting the furs and beaverskins Iberville had promised the Canadian *voyageurs* on the Mississippi he would carry to France in hopes of arranging a market.[48]

On the tenth of April the Spanish launch returned from Apalache, but without any provisions.[49] Three days later Sainte-Thérèse's traversier arrived from Veracruz but with only a month's provisions for Fort San Carlos. Both Iberville and Martínez were distraught, not only because the authorities at Veracruz had not promised to fit out a supply ship until the following month but because (according to Sainte-Thérèse) the royal officials at that port did not appear overly concerned that the Pensacola garrison was in such dire straits.[50]

Six days later François Pillet arrived from the Mississippi in the

46. Journal d'Iberville, *loc. cit.*, April 1, 1702.

47. Martínez to Guzmán, Feb. 1, 1702, AGI, *México*, L. 618. Journal d'Iberville, *loc. cit.*, April 1. Para despachar una carta de Martínez, April 14, 1702, AGI, *México*, L. 618.

48. *Journal Historique*, pp. 71–72. La Salle to min., April 1, 1702, *loc. cit.*, f. 38–39.

49. There were only eight Spanish families at Apalache in 1702, most of whom supported themselves by raising cattle. Manuel Solana and Jacinto Roque Pérez headed a garrison of only twenty-five soldiers. El gobernador de la Florida al rey, June 22, 1701, AGI, *Santo Domingo*, L. 840.

50. Journal d'Iberville, *loc. cit.*, April 13. Andrés de Arriola al Consejo de las Indias, June 2, 1702, AGI, *México*, L. 618. Viceroy Juan de Ortega y Montañés was to be officially replaced on the very day (April 28) Iberville was to leave Pensacola, although he did not relinquish the seals of office until Nov. 25.

Dauphine with the beaverskins and small furs of the *voyageurs*. Iberville spent the next three days unloading the furs from the *Dauphine* and transferring them to the *Palmier* and the *Renommée*, then set about preparing for his return voyage to France. Henri de Tonti who had come with Iberville from Fort Louis handed over to Iberville a letter he had written to Pontchartrain, while Pierre-Charles Le Sueur, retiring commissary Crassé, and erstwhile Jesuit Chaplain Paul Du Ru boarded ship for the return voyage.[51] Weeks behind schedule, Iberville was finally ready to weigh anchor. There remained only one last chore: penning final instructions to his brother Bienville.

Reviewing La Salle's memorandum concerning provisions for the garrison, Iberville was perturbed at the rapidity with which the supplies he had brought had been consumed. According to La Salle's report, there was only a six-month supply of flour left and but a three-month supply of meat, including what the Spaniards were to repay. Martínez cautioned the commander, however, that he did not believe he would be able to repay what the Spanish had borrowed until at least the first of the year. Iberville therefore emphasized in his last instructions to Bienville the necessity for sending the traversier *Espérance*[52] under Bécancour to Veracruz to attempt to purchase further provisions. The commander, in an elaborate memorandum, set forth a number of additional reminders: as soon as the fort was finished and the cannons mounted, Bienville was to have Jacques Le Roux's bark finished and launched; he was to punish debauchery and "establish religion throughout the land," he was to prevent slave-trading, insofar as possible, among all nations and was not to allow any slaves to be brought to Mobile. On the contrary, if he were presented slaves or should he even hear of the existence of any, he was to seize them, even purchase them if necessary, and send them back to their homes. "By this practice," Iberville noted, "we will gain the good will of the families and friends of those captured and of all the nations."[53]

51. La Salle to min., April, 1702, *loc. cit.*, f. 39. Tonti to min., April 15, 1702, AC, C11A, 20, f. 149v–50.

52. Bécancour's *Espérance* had sailed with the *Renommée* in 1701, but the *Précieuse* had been in service on the Gulf Coast since Iberville's first voyage in 1698–99. Dugué de Sainte-Thérèse, *ensign de vaisseau* for the *Renommée*, had been reimbursed 400 *livres* for supplies and expenses covering his trip to Veracruz. AC, F1A, 10, f. 282v, 292v.

53. Mémoire pour servir d'instruction au Sieur de Bienville . . . par d'Iberville, April 25, 1702, AC, F3, 68, f. 1, 6v–7.

As far as communications with Pensacola were concerned, Iberville reminded Bienville of the necessity for developing an overland trail, "the straightest path possible," to Santa María de Galve, in order "to be able to come and go as quickly as possible in times of need." Bienville was to secure the aid of the savages for this task and was to appeal to Martínez for any additional labor that might be needed. When the road was completed, he was to persuade some of the inhabitants to settle near the mouth of the Spanish River (the Tensaw), where the road would meet the bay.[54]

After Fort Maurepas was destroyed and the few remaining men (those in charge of the livestock and cannon) were brought to Fort Louis, Bienville was to journey to Bayou Saint-Jean with Boisbriant and three men to begin a new establishment on the Mississippi, the old one (Fort La Boulaye) not being considered in the most desirable location. The proposed establishment (which years later would be realized as "Nouvelle-Orléans") was even at this early stage considered a paramount necessity for the defense of the Mississippi, especially as Tapiscania, chief of the important Bayougoula nation, had been pleading with the French to establish near his village between Lake Pontchartrain and the Mississippi.[55]

One of the most significant points of the *Pax Gallica*, Iberville felt, was the French promise to build a fort on the upper western branch of the Mobile River (the Tombigbee), between the Choctaw and Chickasaw nations. According to Iberville's instructions, Henri de Tonti, as soon as the fort and bark were finished, was to depart with twenty men to a suitable location, "as near as possible to the Chicasas." Tonti was to have the fort built with "four small bastions, about four feet on the sides, the curtains about forty feet long following the terrain . . . situated on the west side of the river and as close as possible to the bank, where sloops will be able to anchor." He was to carry eight *pierriers* (weapons which cast large stones), until the arrival of some "little cannon suitable for this fort." The fort completed, Tonti was to remain as commandant with twelve men, sending the remaining eight back to Fort Louis. "This fort," Iberville noted, "being near the two largest nations in this land, we will become their masters entirely,

54. *Ibid.*, f. 8. In support of this order, Bienville later persuaded the veteran Canadian Philippe Minette to settle on the bay now bearing Minette's name. *DGFC*, I, pp. 434–35. AC, F1A, 10, f. 284.

55. Mémoire pour servir d'instruction . . . April 25, 1702, AC, F3, 68, f. 1v, 3–3v, 8v–9. Journal de Sauvole, 1699–1700, AC, F3, 24, f. 25v–26v, 27v–29.

and [by this advantage] we will ultimately win over the Conchaques [here meaning what would later be called the upper and lower Creeks] . . . because we are nearer to them than the English."[56]

Completing his instructions to Bienville, Iberville handed the orders over to Tonti, bade farewell to Martínez and boarded the *Renommée*, his brother Sérigny resuming command of the *Palmier*. On the twenty-eighth of April, under unusually favorable winds, the commander set sail for Havana where he hoped to be able to confer with veteran squadron commander Châteaurenault regarding prospects for improved trade with Veracruz and other Spanish ports. By the time he reached Havana, however, Châteaurenault was already on his way to Veracruz. Iberville remained in Havana for the next ten days, toying with the idea of waiting for the squadron leader's return, but after an outbreak of Yellow fever in the Cuban port, Iberville cut his visit short; on the seventeenth of May he once again set sail, this time for France.[57]

Moving through the old Bahama Channel and out to the open sea, Iberville could look back on the most significant of the three voyages he had made to Louisiana with no small satisfaction. His first mission had resulted in the mere building of a temporary fort and the establishment of a small garrison; his second, only the building of a crude blockhouse and the gathering of certain additional details of the land and its peoples. In this, the third of his Gulf Coast expeditions, he had established a fort and town, a promising settlement consisting of men, women (at least four) and children (at least seven) that he felt confident would grow and endure.[58] Not of lesser importance, he had managed (thanks to Henri de Tonti) to woo and apparently win from the English the two most powerful and influential aboriginal nations to what he hoped would be a firm and permanent alliance. He had not by any means solved all his difficulties: Fort Louis, while seemingly on solid footing, was admittedly no Charles-Town nor even a St. Augustine; the natural resources of the area the French controlled,

56. Mémoire pour servir d'instruction . . . , *loc. cit.*, f. 1v–2v, 4v, 7v.

57. *Ibid.*, f. 1–1v, 9. Journal d'Iberville, *loc. cit.*, April 27, May 10, 17. Journal de Le Sueur, 1702, AM, 2 JJ 56, 9. Both Lieutenant-general André Nesmond and *chef d'escadre* Marc Rosmadec died during this epidemic, Rosmadec three days before Iberville weighed anchor. Archivo de la Catedral de San Cristóbal de la Habana, Registro de las sepulturas, May 14, 1702.

58. Dénombrement du 31 août 1704, AC, C13A, 1, f. 468–70.

though abundant enough, seemed limited in diversity, and, to be sure, were as yet unexploited; shortage of food, supplies and personnel promised to be a certain and continuing vexation. Yet even the dour, unimaginative commissary, Nicolas de La Salle, was in those early spring days of 1702, compelled to describe the new settlement as "that which promises to be one of the most notable colonies the king possesses."[59]

Reaching France in late June, Iberville planned to become thoroughly and energetically involved in promoting his newly-founded colony, in seeking assistance of all who would lend a receptive ear or extend a helping hand.[60]

59. La Salle to min., April 1, 1702, *loc. cit.*, f. 37.

60. Résumé d'Iberville, June 20, 1702, AC, C13C, 2, f. 43–44. Journal de Le Sueur, 1702, AM, 2 JJ 56, 9. Mémoire sur les etablissements à faire à l'embouchure du Misisipi et à la Mobille, [1704], AM, 3 JJ 277, 4.

VI

Early Dissensions

WITHIN two weeks of Iberville's departure from Fort Louis, the Chickasaw chiefs had fulfilled one part of their agreement with the Canadian commander: they had sent couriers to the villages of the Alabama, relaying Iberville's invitation to those towns to come to Mobile to receive presents and smoke the calumet of peace. Shortly thereafter, several of the Alabama chieftains, ostensibly receptive to the idea of peace, visited Fort Louis and were received cordially by Bienville and his officers. Presented with a number of gifts, the Alabama were apparently persuaded to quit their intended aggressions against the Mobilians, the Tomeh and the Little Tomeh and, after a few days at the fort, returned quietly to their villages.[1]

Bienville, believing he had set the stage for a future alliance with the Alabama, went back to his more pressing labors, foremost of which was the completion of the public buildings and private houses of the settlement. The most important structures—the administrative quarters, the guardhouse, the king's storehouse and the chapel (all within the fort)—were, by late spring, virtually completed (except for the windows and "mortaring"), as were the warehouses on Dog River and Massacre Island. Concerted efforts were now being made toward the completion of private residences. As late as the end of March many of those craftsmen who had been laboring on the fort and public buildings were themselves

1. *Journal Historique*, pp. 75–76. Pénigault, *Relation*, BN, FF, 14613, f. 173–79. *FLC*, pp. 64–69. "Tomeh" seems a preferable standardization and closer to the way the name was actually pronounced. French spelling of these tribes' names was generally "Tomé" or "Thomes," which indicates the "s" sound was not used.

without places to live, but by mid-April they were actively engaged in building their own private homes.[2]

It was perhaps fortunate that the late winter and early spring of 1702 had brought unusually heavy rains (after a particularly dry December and January). The downpours forced the inhabitants to plan their residences with a knowledge of what for the next nine years would be a distressing condition: while the buildings within the fort would never be subject to flooding, perhaps eighty percent of the private sites were now, and would continue to be, plagued with standing waters of from two to eighteen inches during the rainy seasons. Ignace La Valle and François Hayot, whose lots were among the most poorly drained, were forced, as were at least thirty other residents, to build their houses on wooden pilings some eighteen to twenty-four inches above the ground to protect their floors from the especially high spring waters overflowing from the nearby creek.[3]

Others, like Canadians Guillaume Boutin and Jean-Baptiste Joussette, *dit* La Loire, were able to build their homes practically on ground level which, nonetheless, subjected them as much as the others to the ravages of termites and "wood rot." The majority of houses, both large and small, were constructed of young pine. Had the builders been more selective in their choice of materials they could have warded off much of the difficulty; there was an abundance of cypress, cedar and "heart pine" in the vicinity—enough to construct all of the buildings within the town. Yet the use of these presented certain problems: the cypress trees, more impervious to rot, grew in swampy, inaccessible areas, while the large virgin pines were too bulky for the lightweight saws and axes to easily shape into usable timbers. As a result the builders chose the smaller and younger pines whose original sizes and shapes were more similar to those they would use in actual construction.[4]

2. Dénombrement du 31 août 1704, AC, C13A, 1, f. 468–70. Journal d'Iberville, April 27, 1702, AM, B4, 23, f. 321–29. La Salle to min., April 1, 1702, AC, C13C, 2, f. 36–41. BN, FF, NA, 9295, f. 240–41.

3. *Alabama River Navigation Charts*, 1972, p. 8. Plan de la Ville et du Fort Louis, sur la Mobile, 1711, AN, Section Outre-mer, DFC, 120B. Although the undated, unsigned map is dated in the DFC inventory as 1711, it would appear from a close study of the nomenclature that it was completed early in 1705. *Inventaire des archives du Dépot des fortifications des Colonies, anciennes archives de la France d'Outre-mer conservées au dépot de la rue Oudinot* (Unpublished inventory at the AN in Paris).

4. Plan de la ville et du Fort Louis, *loc. cit.*, 120B. Pénigault, *Relation, loc. cit.*, f. 79–87. Lettre, Sept. 10, 1704, BN, FF, 9097, f. 140–44. Darta-

Too, in these early days, the carpenters were not experienced enough to know precisely how the various woods would withstand the onslaught of the area's weather and insects.

The residences were constructed in much the same fashion as houses in the homeland of the individual builder. Jean Le Caën, for example, followed the method he had learned in the vicinity around Rochefort and La Rochelle, while Charles Aigron, *dit* Lamothe's home was constructed in the Canadian manner. In many cases there was a good deal of similarity in the methods, as a large percentage of the Canadians (such as Lamothe) were of families originally from the Rochefort-La Rochelle area.[5] Yet, even when French and Canadian methods of construction were followed, the differences in the native materials of Louisiana themselves influenced the architecture. Suitable quantities of stone and brick were not readily available in these early days, which meant chimneys had to be constructed of planks, covered by a sort of provincial mortar or pitch, rather than of materials normally used in France or Quebec.[6]

The largest of these private homes, such as the ones built by the more well-to-do Canadians, Baudreau de Graveline, Robinau de Bécancour and Charles Levasseur, were approximately fifty feet long by twenty feet wide.[7] Many of the residences, like Fort Maurepas and Fort Louis, were of *pièce-sur-pièce* construction, but the majority consisted of verticle posts set upright in the ground with timbers notched and nailed between the framework; between the spaces in the timberwork was packed a makeshift mortar composed of damp clay, sand and oyster shells which dried into a barely adequate filling to keep out winter drafts.[8]

---

guiette to min., Feb. 12, 1710, AC, C13A, 2, f. 545. La Vente [to Brisacier], July 4, 1708, ASQ, Lettres, R 83. Dartaguiette to min., June 20, 1711, AC, C13A, 2, f. 644–45. Cadillac to min., Aug. 6, 1712, AC, C13A, 2, f. 651.

5. Mémoire par Le Maire, Jan. 15, 1714, AC, C13C, 2, f. 131–34. Charles' father, Pierre Aigron, *dit* La Mothe, had emigrated from Saint-Étienne d'Estrées in the mid-seventeenth century. *DGFC*, I, p. 2.

6. Mémoire par Le Maire, *loc. cit.*, f. 132–33. Pénigault, *Relation*, *loc. cit.*, f. 195–97.

7. Plan de la ville et du fort de la Maubille, AN, Section Outre-mer, DFC, 119A. Min. to Beauharnois, Oct. 6, 1712, AC, B 34, f. 127v–28. Min. to Crozat, Oct. 24, 1712, AC, B 34, f. 131. Min. to Demuy, July 6, 1707, AC, B 29, f. 291. Testament de Levasseur, 1717, AN, MC, XX–455.

8. La Vente [to Brisacier], July 4, 1708, *loc. cit.*, R 83. A partially preserved construction similar to one of these early Mobile houses survives

Around the more elaborate houses, all of which were one-storey structures, were placed covered galleries, where, during the excessive temperatures of the summer, the residents could comfortably spend their late afternoons. The more modest houses had no galleries while the crudest of the homes, such as those owned by Denis Liénard-Durbois and Antoine Roussin, were no more than cabins composed simply of stakes posted in the ground and roofed with canes and palmetto leaves similar to the roofing of the Mobilians and Little Tomeh. Most of the houses had only two rooms (a kitchen, which doubled as a living room, and a bedroom), while a small number, among them those built by François Lemay, Jean Le Caën, and Jacques Leméry, had at least two bedrooms.[9]

The houses were situated near the edge of their respective plots, facing the streets which fronted their lots. Thus, Liénard-Durbois' house faced the rue Saint-Joseph while Claude Trépanier's house was close upon the rue de Ruessavel. In the case of corner lots, such as those owned by Canadians Philippe Minette and François Montreuil, the houses here faced the rue d'Iberville and the rue de Boisbriant respectively. In any case, all of the lots were sufficiently large for their intended purpose. Attempts at agriculture consisted at this time only of private gardening. Bienville encouraged planting, of course, but at this early date (without benefit of either black or Indian slaves) the amount of land the inhabitants were assigned was already more than they were willing to cultivate.[10]

By the middle of June nearly sixty private residences, most of which belonged to Canadians, had been completed. But since the settlement at Fort Louis totalled just over one hundred and thirty men, there were still a large number of people, mostly soldiers and a few *voyageurs*, without adequate shelter. For the moment

---

in the old La Pointe house in nearby Pascagoula, which though repaired and modified many times, retains the flavor and many materials of the original. La Pointe, a resident of Old Mobile in 1702, built this modest dwelling in 1715–16 to be used as a residence-workshop while he was completing his elaborate plantation home several hundred yards away. Dartaguiette to min., June 20, 1711, AC, C13A, 2, f. 644–45. Carte de la Rivière des Pascagoula . . . 1726, par Dumont de Montigny, BN, Cartes et plans, Ge. DD 2987, 24.

9. Cadillac to min., *loc. cit.*, f. 651. La Vente [to Tremblay], Sept. 10, 1704, ASQ, Lettres, R 75. La Vente [to SME Dirs.], Sept. 20, 1704, ASQ, Lettres, R 77. *DGFC, I*, p. 394. AC, F1A, 10, f. 283–84v, 289.

10. Plan de la ville et du Fort Louis, sur la Mobile, 1711, *loc. cit.*, 120B. Bienville to min., Feb. 20, 1707, AC, C13A, 2, f. 22–24. BN, FF, NA, 9097, f. 140.

these unfortunates must content themselves with sleeping in the guardhouse and in the tents brought by the *Renommée*.[11]

By early summer, Bienville had not yet found a suitable site for a sawmill, nor had he been successful in completing the vessel that La Roux had begun. Despite such failures, the commandant would later look back to the beginnings of a successful administration. He had practically finished the construction of the town (and in record time), he had taken a first step in making an alliance with the Alabama, and his supplies, managed carefully, were holding out well enough. At least Fort Louis was faring much better than Fort San Carlos on the bay of Pensacola.[12]

Bienville discovered the status of the Pensacola garrison on the twenty-fifth of June, by virtue of a letter from Francisco Martínez brought via launch by a young infantry captain, Joseph de Robles y Morales. According to Martínez, Fort San Carlos was yet in extreme want of meat and flour. The Spanish supply vessel, due from Veracruz in late May or early June, had still not arrived and the Pensacola garrison was in dire straits. Soldiers Juan Domínguez, Alonso López and Francisco Velasco had recently died and many more deaths were feared imminent due to the almost non-existent food supply and the seemingly constant presence of disease brought by occasional ships from Havana. The garrison had suffered a disastrous conflagration two years before in which many of the main buildings had been lost and small fires had recently broken out in the private huts surrounding the fort.[13]

There was in truth not much to the defenses at Santa María de Galve. Martínez commanded a garrison of less than two hundred officers, soldiers and laborers, many of whom were servants and convicts. There were no families at Pensacola and only a few craftsmen and Franciscan fathers. Furthermore, there were no natural resources, large rivers or native allies in the immediate vicinity. Even the considerable forests nearby could not supply lumber suitable for constructing ships, although it was hoped that

11. La Salle to min., April 1, 1702, AC, C13C, 2, f. 41–43. AC, F1A, 10, f. 282–86. Bienville to min., Sept. 6, 1704, AC, C13A, 1, f. 462–63.

12. *Journal Historique*, pp. 75–76. Martínez to Guzmán, Santa María de Galve, Feb. 1, 1702, AGI, *México*, L. 618. Pérez al gobernador de la Florida, May 25, 1703, AGI, *Santo Domingo*, L. 858. Consulta del Junta de Guerra, Aug. 1, 1702, AGI, *México*, L. 633.

13. *Journal Historique*, p. 76. Consulta del Junta de Guerra, Aug. 1, 1702, *loc. cit.*, L. 633. Arriola al consejo de las Indias, Nov. 15, 1701, AGI, *México*, L. 618.

the straight, limber pines would eventually provide Veracruz with poles appropriate for making masts. The only conceivable value of Pensacola, with its fine port for harboring large ships, was its potential for defense.[14]

Yet Bienville was keenly interested in Pensacola's welfare, had in fact been ordered by Pontchartrain (through Iberville) to aid the floundering settlement in any way not deleterious to Fort Louis. For security reasons, it was to Bienville's advantage to have a friendly post nearby, at least until the French fort was more permanently established. Then too, despite the recent breakdown in communication, Pensacola had a much closer source of supply. In future emergencies, Martínez could possibly look to Havana, Apalache, and St. Augustine as well as to Veracruz for supplies. Bienville, far from Quebec and Rochefort and even from Cap-français, hoped that by befriending Pensacola when his storehouse was full, he could depend on Spanish authorities to return the favor when his own *magasin* was lacking. Moreover, as he had recently learned, Francisco Fernández de la Cueva y Enríquez, Duque de Alburquerque, had on April 28 been nominated to succeed the interim viceroy Ortega y Montañés. Bienville, realizing at this early stage that trade with Veracruz was to be a key factor in Mobile's economic well-being, was anxious to get in the good graces of the new viceroy who would be taking office in the fall. He therefore did not hesitate, though his own stores were low, to provide Robles y Morales with food sufficient to support the Pensacola garrison until the vessel from Veracruz arrived.[15]

Soon after Bienville provisioned Martínez with a generous supply of flour, the Spanish vessel from Veracruz reached Pensacola with supplies sufficient to repay Mobile. A few weeks later, Robinau de Bécancour, who had been sent to the same port shortly after Iberville had sailed for Havana, returned to Massacre Island, his ship (the *Espérance*) loaded with meat and flour. Fort

14. Franck al rey, June 4, 1700, AGI, *México*, L. 618. Martínez al gobernador de Habana, Feb. 21, 1699, AGI, *México*, L. 618. Para despachar una carta de Martínez, April 14, 1702, AGI, *México*, L. 618.

15. Pérez al gobernador de la Florida, May 25, 1703, AGI, *Santo Domingo*, L. 858. Para despachar una carta de Martínez, April 14, 1702, *loc. cit.*, L. 618. Besides supplying Pensacola with food and armaments, both Bienville and Boisbriant periodically sent the latest intelligence about the natives and such maps as they could persuade the natives to help construct. Copia de carta escrita a Andrés de Arriola por Boisbriant, May 23, 1704, AGI, *México*, L. 618. Copia de carta escrita a Andrés de Arriola por M. de Bienbilla, May 13, 1704, AGI, *México*, L. 618.

Louis, with the loan repaid by Martínez and the new supplies brought by Bécancour, appeared well set as far as foodstuffs were concerned by mid-summer of 1702.[16]

If the problem of food was for the moment apparently solved, ominous sounds were beginning to be heard on the lower Mississippi. Bienville knew that one of his chief responsibilities—to maintain the *Pax Gallica* among the aboriginal nations of the back country—would be a task that would tax his diplomatic skills. His objective, however, was not merely to maintain what Iberville and Tonti had achieved with the Choctaw and Chickasaw, but to extend their accomplishments to other nations as well. He did not expect a crisis to arise so soon.[17]

A year earlier, Bienville, after succeeding Sauvole as commandant of Fort Maurepas, had selected a young Canadian, Louis Juchereau de Saint-Denis, to fill his position as commandant at the Mississippi fort. Saint-Denis, now in his twenty-seventh year, with two distinguished older brothers (Charles and François) in the service of France, had come to Louisiana with Iberville on his second voyage in 1699–1700, and had served with distinction since that time. Born of one of Canada's most distinguished families, Saint-Denis, a vibrant man of undoubted abilities, was in mid-1702 champing at the bit at being, in effect, exiled to such a barren post as Fort La Boulaye.[18]

Restless in the midst of a long, dull summer, Saint-Denis, on his own initiative, undertook an exploratory mission (with a handful of soldiers and Canadians who had been hunting on the lower Mississippi) in search of a river route to New Spain. Heading up the present Bayou La Fourche, Saint-Denis' forces were attacked without warning by a band of roving Chitimacha whose village site was farther upstream. Retaliating, Saint-Denis, in company with the Canadians, a few soldiers from his Mississippi garrison and a number of Colapissa Indians, vigorously pursued the fleeing Chitimacha, managing to capture a number of prisoners whom he had ideas of later selling into slavery.[19]

16. *Journal Historique*, pp. 75–77. Para despachar una carta de Martínez, April 14, 1702, *loc. cit.*, L. 618. AC, F1A, 10, f. 282v. La Salle to min., May 20, 1703, AC, C13A, 1, f. 387–88.

17. Mémoire pour servir d'instruction au Sieur de Bienville . . . , April 25, 1702, AC, F3, 68, f. 1–9v.

18. AC, F1A, 10, f. 282. *DGFC, I*, pp. 328, 379.

19. *Journal Historique*, pp. 76–78. Pénigault, *Relation, loc. cit.*, f. 29–31, 97–113. Davion à l'évêque de Québec, Feb. 14, 1703, ASME, 344.

When news of this incident reached Bienville, the commandant was extremely distressed. Iberville's instructions to him had been specific about maintaining peace. One small incident such as this could ignite flames that would consume his entire Indian policy. He had taken great pains to spread the word among the scattered missions and villages of the Mississippi of the new peace treaty between the Choctaw and Chickasaw, had issued specific orders that no wars were to be promoted by one nation against the other. Now, only four months later, one of his own officers was guilty not only of waging war, but of taking slaves. To make matters worse, the responsible officer was of a family closely allied to the Le Moyne clan.[20]

Saint-Denis' contention that the Chitimacha had been the aggressors had little effect on the commandant. Despite Bienville's high regard for the Canadian, he severely upbraided him for his lack of discretion in taking the sword against a nation that had until now been friendly to the French. Intentional or not, it was clear that the commandant of Fort La Boulaye had committed a grievous blunder. Bienville's demand that Saint-Denis return the prisoners immediately was met with haughty indignation; but the dressing-down was a necessary chastisement and one that would leave strained relations between the two young Canadians for several years to come.[21]

The confrontation between Bienville and Saint-Denis was, of course, one the commandant would have wished to avoid. Except for the brief squabble with La Salle it was as yet the only divisive incident arising between himself and his staff. Thus far, Bienville had managed to maintain the smooth flow of communication between himself and his officers that Iberville had set in motion. All of the men in a position of military command stood firmly behind him—Boisbriant, Levasseur, Henri de Tonti, Robinau de Bécancour, even those of lesser authority, such as Antoine Siré, Sergeant Pierre Dubreuil, *dit* Lafleur, Corporals Jean Arnet, *dit* La Roche, and Jérôme Broüen, *dit* La Forest. The Canadians, totalling seventy-one, sixty-four of whom were in the pay of the king, had been almost to a man in support of the commandant. Bienville's

20. Mémoire pour servir d'instruction au Sieur de Bienville, April 25, 1702, *loc. cit.*, f. 1–2v, 6–9v. Journal d'Iberville, April 27, 1702, AM, B4, 23, f. 323–31. *DGFC, I*, pp. 328, 379.

21. Pénigault, *Relation, loc. cit.*, f. 269–78. Although Saint-Denis would be slow to forget his dispute with the commandant, Bienville would soon afterwards seek a reconciliation. Bienville to min., Sept. 6, 1704, AC, C13A, 1, f. 460–61.

older brothers, Iberville and Sérigny were now returned to France, yet their reputations, their prestige seemed to hang over the young lieutenant, lending an aura of expertise to his inexperience, and clothing him with added authority. Besides his departed brothers (including Châteaugué, who had gone back to raise a company of soldiers) numerous other individuals who had played prominent roles in the founding of Mobile were in some way related to him, either by blood or through marriage—Charleville, Dugué de Sainte-Thérèse, Le Sueur, Boisbriant, Saint-Denis, Denis de La Ronde, Denis Liénard-Durbois. The list of relatives in the colony was long and would increase through the years as more of his cousins and nephews would make their way to Louisiana.[22]

Perhaps Bienville's staunchest ally in these early days was his strong, silent cousin, Pierre Dugué de Boisbriant, occupying the position of *aide-major*. Boisbriant, son of famed Canadian soldier, Michel-Sidrac Dugué de Boisbriand, and younger brother of Dugué de Sainte-Thérese, had grown up on the Île de Montréal near where Bienville was to be born five years after Boisbriant's birth. Attaining the rank of ensign when only nineteen years of age, Boisbriant had risen steadily in the Canadian military. He had served with Iberville in the latter's attack on Newfoundland, then participated in the battle to recapture Fort York at Hudson's Bay. When Iberville returned to Fort Maurepas in early 1700 on the *Renommée*, Boisbriant had made the voyage with him, having been assigned the position of *aide-major* at Fort Maurepas the previous August. For a brief period, after Sauvole's death in August 1701, Boisbriant had been acting commandant of the Biloxi fort.[23] The need for Bienville to maintain the loyalty of his fellow officers was especially important during these early years. As a colonial administrator he was obviously unqualified by virtue of training or experience. His family prestige, his predilection to lead, did not

22. AC, F1A, 10, f. 282–82v, 283v, 285. La Salle to min., April 1, 1702, AC, C13C, 2, f. 40–41; BN, FF, NA, 9295, f. 240–41. *DGFC, I*, pp. 180–81, 209–10, 379, 389, 394.

23. Estat des Appointemens . . . pour L'Année 1702, AC, F1A, 10, f. 282. *DGFC, I*, p. 210. Years later Père Raphael de Luxembourg would describe Boisbriant as "a man against whom no reproach can be brought with reference to his personal conduct; if he does wrong it is through a kindliness that often goes to the extent of being silent when he ought to express himself." Père Raphael to Abbé Raguet, May 15, 1725, AC, C13A, 13, f. 405. Although the family signature in Canada was predominantly "Boisbriand," Pierre's autograph was "Boisbriant." AJM, Greffe de Basset, Nov. 1, 1667. Induction de La Vente, Sept. 28, 1704, ADM, Miscellaneous French Papers, 1704–1764. AC, E 150, No. 118. AM, C1, 161, f. 276.

nearly begin to compensate for his youth, his small education or his lack of executive skills. Nor was there any administrative machinery present upon which he could rely. In these early days, Louisiana had no *Conseil superiéur*, no legislative body, not even a governor in absentia, in fact. Iberville, as *capitaine de frégate*, had merely been the officer in charge of a particular enterprise who, having had to absent himself, had delegated his authority to a subordinate. Subordinate Bienville was merely a "lieutenant du roi faisant les functions de commandant" until Iberville's return. His authority at this time came to him through Iberville whose authority flowed ultimately (though sometimes through indirect channels) from the minister of the marine.[24]

In theory, Mobile was governed in accordance with the *Ordonnance de la Marine* of 1681, by which the then minister, Jean-Baptiste Colbert, had shaped the French marine into a military-commercial instrument. In civil affairs the local residents were supposedly to be governed in accordance with the rather comprehensive *Coutumier de Paris*. In practice, however, there was no one in Mobile, certainly not Bienville, who had more than a vague understanding of the specific provisions of either the *Ordonnance* or the *Coutumier* or how to apply them. True, Pierre-Charles Le Sueur was shortly to be given authority to exercise judicial authority in the colony, but even Le Sueur had little knowledge of the law; moreover, he was not scheduled to return until 1703.[25]

Bienville, then, with considerable power and numerous disadvantages, was pressed by the exigencies of the moment to make the best of his situation. With the exception of Tonti and Levasseur, there were in fact few available men whom Iberville could have better chosen. Under an established government, the young Le Moyne might have been an excellent administrator. Engaging, energetic, capable of bold, often percipient decision-making, he could have effectively dealt with the number of non-military problems had he been able to lean on a small core of specialists to aid him with the difficulties that would shortly arise. In cases

24. Liste des officiers . . . , June 22, 1701, AM, B2, 152, f. 133. AC, F1A, 10, f. 282; 11, f. 69. Min. to Iberville, June 17, 1703, AC, B 23, f. 192–94.

25. *Ordonnance de la Marine du mois d'Aoust, 1681, II*, p. 2. Valin, *Nouveau commentaire sur l'ordonnance de la marine, I*, pp. 46–47. Min. to Iberville, June 17, 1703, *loc. cit.*, f. 193. Mémoire de Le Sueur, 1702, BN, FF, NA, 9301, f. 128–29. In recommending Le Sueur for the judicial post at a salary of 500 crowns per year, Iberville suggested there would not be a great number of private suits for a long while. Iberville to min., 1702, AC, C13A, 1, f. 380–81.

requiring discipline, such as the recent dispute with Saint-Denis, he alone, calling perhaps on the counsel of Boisbriant, Levasseur and Tonti, must make the ultimate judgments, relying principally on his own common sense and intuition.[26]

Bienville's foremost policy objective at the moment was the maintenance and extension of the *Pax Gallica*. The achievement of this goal would test to the limit not only his proficiency in dealing with the natives but his ability to ply the religious (of whom was expected a vital role) as an effective political force. In early 1702, there had been four Jesuits on the Gulf Coast—Jacques Gravier, Paul Du Ru, Joseph Limoges and the newly arrived Pierre Dongé. Farther west and north, scattered in villages on or near the Mississippi, were seminary priests Albert Davion, Balthazar-Michel de Boutteville, Nicolas Foucault, Marc Bergier and Jean-François Buisson de Saint-Cosme.[27]

For the past two years, Bienville had been pleased to have as chaplain the reverend Jesuit father Paul Du Ru, whom Iberville had been successful in bringing to Louisiana in 1700 to replace the Franciscan Anastase Douay. The fact that Du Ru had been sent (with Pontchartrain's approval) at a time when the seminary priests were beginning to move into the Mississippi Valley was considered by the Le Moyne brothers to be a mild victory, in harmony with their program to win the natives. The small prejudices the Le Moynes had thus far shown against the seminary priests were neither innate nor deeply-rooted in religion; they were much more pragmatic. The Jesuits, as the Le Moynes had known them, were simply better equipped than the "white collars" to aid in carrying out the twin objectives of colonization and defense. They seemed more dedicated, more able (particularly as far as mastery of the native languages was concerned); equally as important, they were backed by the greater resources of their order.[28]

26. Bienville to min., Feb. 25, 1708, AC, C13A, 2, f. 103–04. Dartaguiette to min., May 12, 1712, AC, C13A, 2, f. 809. Bienville to min., Oct. 27, 1711, AC, C13A, 2, f. 593–96. Information faite par Dartaguiette, February, 1708, AC, C13A, 2, f. 249–57.

27. Davion [to SME Dirs.], Dec. 12, 1702, ASME, 344, f. 56–63. Saint-Cosme [to Tremblay], Oct. 21, 1702, ASQ, Lettres, R 36. Davion [to SME Dirs.], Sept. 23, 1703, ASME, 344. Saint-Cosme [to Ango Des Maizerets], April 19, 1702, ASQ, Lettres, R 35. Passeport, July 17, 1698, ASQ, Missions, 60.

28. Journal de *Marin*, 1699, BN, FF, 9097, f. 70–71. Mémoire, par Pontchartrain, Sept. 22, 1699, AC, B 20, f. 280–81. Min. to Duguay, Sept. 29,

Du Ru, in particular, seemed to fit the role that the Le Moynes had envisioned for their missionaries. Young (36), spirited, anxious to master the aboriginal tongues, Du Ru was willing to work assiduously with the Bayougoula and Houma as well as to minister to the soldiers and Canadians of the garrison.[29] Like so many other of the religious, however, Du Ru's enthusiasm varied in proportion to his success. His early optimism was dimmed by the irreverence and "spirit of presumption" of the Canadians "which often degenerates into brutality."[30] Insofar as the natives were concerned, he had high hopes for their souls' future as long as they assented to his destruction of the phallic symbols they kept in their village squares, as long as they reverently listened to his sermons and sedulously labored to construct his chapel. When all was going well, Du Ru was confident he had made the natives understand that "all men shall appear before the Great Nanboulou [the Holy Spirit], the good to dwell with Him in heaven, and the evil to go under the earth where they shall burn in everlasting fire." When they behaved as Du Ru wished, the savages were "intelligent and comprehending of the good" Du Ru was trying to do for them:

> . . . they understand that they are not making this building for me but for the great Nanboulou and that it is in it [the church] that He will speak to me. They understand that the great Nanboulou is not seen, because He has no body like a man, that He has made all things, that He acts without hands, talks without a tongue, and walks everywhere without feet. They know that every man is composed of body and soul, that the body dies, but the soul does not, that after a long period souls will rejoin the dead bodies and that the bones in their temples will come to life.[31]

Yet when the savages' interest waned, Du Ru complained that, in directing the construction of the church, he could not even

---

1699, AM, B2, 141, f. 355–56. Min. to Duguay, Oct. 13, 1699, AM, B2, 142, f. 40v. Tremblay [to Laval], May 28, 1701, ASQ, Lettres, N 114. Tremblay [to Ango Des Maizerets], April 2, 1701, ASQ, Lettres, O 31. Iberville to min., Feb. 15, 1703, AC, C13C, 2, f. 62–62v.

29. *JR, LXXI*, p. 160.

30. Journal de Du Ru, 1700, Newberry Library, Ayer MS, 262. Despite differences, Du Ru and Sauvole had been equally incensed by the Canadians' irreverence and lack of regard for authority. Journal de Sauvole, Aug. 4, 1701, AC, C13A, 1, f. 316–19, 322.

31. Journal de Du Ru, *loc. cit.*, 262. The manuscript is not folioed.

make them understand the correct place to lay the planks. He was delighted to see "the symbol of our faith become an object of veneration to the savages," but at the same time, "I cannot help but groan on seeing that it is all really futile, for even within sight of this salutory cross, many of these poor blind people will perish miserably through lack of knowing its virtue . . . if I were to ask a miracle from God for their benefit, it would be the gift of tongues." [32]

Du Ru's early dismay (and pity) gave way eventually to admitted displays of temper and finally to disdain. The savages were "lazy, and I find that their whole desire is to get from everyone what they want." [33]

Jesuit Du Ru, then, by early 1702, was hopelessly discouraged with his Louisiana mission. He had labored diligently, no doubt, but his successes with both the natives and the French garrison were meager indeed. Despite his failures, however, he might have been convinced to stay on at Mobile but for another cause of dismay: the movement of the seminary priests into the missions of central and lower Louisiana and the persistent rumors that the "white collars" would eventually gain full control of the field that the Jesuits had pioneered. Du Ru did not object to the presence of an occasional seminary missioner, especially one of the caliber of François de Montigny. ". . . it was a great relief," he wrote in his journal, "to meet the missionary to the Taensas [Montigny] and to know him personally. He is a saintly man and I hope that we shall co-operate to promote religion and show by our actions that, though wearing different habits, we have the same purpose." [34] It was only that he did not wish to see his narrow but hard-earned accomplishments overshadowed by a rival order. He had, therefore, sometime before decided to return to France with Iberville on the commander's next return voyage to present his observations on the Louisiana mission in person to the proper authorities.[35]

32. *Ibid.*

33. Du Ru seems to forget his own admission that ". . . it took a little display of temper to assemble the savages for the work they had begun." The natives no doubt wondered about Du Ru's "whole desire." Journal de Du Ru, *loc. cit.*, 262.

34. *Ibid.* Montigny returned to France in 1700. Tonti to Villermont, Oct. 13, 1700, BN, FF, 9097, f. 111.

35. Père Goüye to min., Feb. 23, 1703, AC, C13A, 1, f. 397–401. Min. to Bégon, March 8, 1703, AM, B2, 167, f. 689–91, 693–96. Père Goüye to min., March 9, 1703, BN, FF, NA, 9295, f. 265–67. AC, C13A, 1, f. 403–09.

In early 1702, Du Ru had been one of three Jesuits present at Mobile Bay. With Jacques Gravier going to the Illinois and Du Ru returning to France, the chaplainship fell to the newly-arrived Pierre Dongé. In his thirty-second year, Dongé was even younger than Du Ru. Less assuming, more tolerant than the forceful Du Ru, he was much more suited to the post of chaplain than to the role of missioner; furthermore, he had neither the taste nor the temperament for dealing with the natives in the way that Bienville envisioned for his missionary agents.[36]

A more likely candidate to help execute Bienville's policies was the thirty-two-year-old native of Vannes in Brittany, Joseph Limoges. After entering the Jesuit order in 1686, Limoges had studied in Paris for five years, had served as an instructor at Amiens before arriving in Quebec in 1698. From Canada the young missionary had been sent to the upper Mississippi, where he had worked among the Sioux and the Osage before continuing downstream to the village of the Houma from whence he joined Du Ru at Fort La Boulaye in 1700. By the summer of 1702, Limoges had already gained considerable experience in dealing with the natives; moreover, he had become somewhat hardened to the wilderness, having descended the Mississippi in the severe winter of 1700, nearly losing his life in the process. Now in lower Louisiana, Limoges was one of a handful of missionaries for whom Bienville had high aspirations.[37]

With seminary missioner Albert Davion at the Tunica, and Buisson de Saint-Cosme, Nicolas Foucault and Boutteville scattered among missions on the Mississippi, Bienville had little hope (from only five possibilities—one Jesuit and four seminary priests) of soon fulfilling his promise to begin missions at the Chickasaw and Choctaw. Unfortunately even that slim hope was to dim in late 1702 by the abandonment of all but one of the lower Mississippi missions.[38]

By mid-summer of 1702, Bienville had reason to be better satis-

36. Journal d'Iberville, *loc. cit.*, Feb. 18. Père Saint-Gilles to min., July 11, 1701, AC, C13A, 1, f. 313–14. BN, FF, NA, 9295, f. 224–25. Min. to Père Saint-Gilles, July 27, 1701, AM, B2, 155, f. 186. *JR*, *LXXI*, pp. 130, 161.

37. Journal de Levasseur, 1700, AM, 2 JJ 56, 16. *JR*, *LXV*, pp. 153–55. Limoges had arrived at the village of the Houma (just south of present-day Natchez) about three days before Gravier came in late November of 1700. Journal de Du Ru, 1700, *loc. cit.*, 262. Lettre, May 28, 1700, BN, FF, 21690, f. 310–18v. *JR*, *LXV*, pp. 102, 162.

38. Davion [to SME Dirs.], Dec. 12, 1702; Feb. 14, Sept. 23, 1703, *loc. cit.*, 344.

fied with the work of the seminary priests than with the labor of the Jesuits. Limoges (as it turned out) and Dongé were clearly not made of the stuff of a Gabriel Marest or even a Jacques Gravier. While the two Jesuits were serving "without especial distinction" in their respective posts, it was the seminary missioners at this time who most capably (and who, alone in their separate villages) were struggling to expand the mission field.[39]

Nicolas Foucault, a Parisian by birth, had been ordained a priest in 1689, a year after his arrival in Quebec. After a brief service with Abbé Marc Bergier at the Tamaroa mission in the Illinois country, Foucault, assenting to Iberville's request (through Bergier) went south to establish a mission at the Arkansas. The Arkansas, barbarous and indifferent, proved less than willing receptors of the gospel. When François Danbourné, sent out by Iberville at the end of March with two Canadian companions to help settle differences between the Chickasaw and the Illinois, arrived at the Arkansas village in July, Foucault decided to travel downstream with him to confer with Albert Davion. Perhaps with Davion's encouragement he would go on to establish the mission at the Chickasaw. Danbourné and his Canadian companions being ill, the party stopped at the village of the Koroa to hire two warriors to row the group down to the mouth of the Yazoo from where Foucault could easily reach Davion's mission.[40]

On July 29, on the way downstream, the two Koroa, coveting the missionary's goods and tiring of manning the oars, murdered Foucault, Danbourné and the two other Canadians as they lay sleeping on the river bank where they had stopped to rest. Several days later, Davion, on his way to visit Foucault, came upon the murder scene.[41]

Horrified, Davion lost little time in retreating from his Tunica mission. On his way back down river, he stopped at the village of the Houma where Joseph Limoges was ministering and together the two missionaries came on to Mobile to report the murder of

39. *Ibid.* AC, F1A, 10, f. 282. Saint-Cosme [to Tremblay], Oct. 21, 1702, ASQ, Lettres, R 36. La Vente [to SME Dirs.], Sept. 20, 1704, ASQ, Lettres, R 77.

40. Bergier [to Ango Des Maizerets], March 19, 1702, ASQ, Lettres, R 51. AAQ, Registres d'insinuation, A, 235, 281. AC, F1A, 10, f. 283–84. Journal d'Iberville, *loc. cit.*, March 28–29. Tonti to Iberville, March 14, 1702, AM, 2 JJ 56, 20. Bergier [to Tremblay], July 3, 1703, ASQ, Lettres, R 62.

41. *Journal Historique*, p. 73. Davion [to SME Dirs.], Dec. 12, 1702, *loc. cit.*, 344. Bergier [to Tremblay], July 3, 1703, *loc. cit.*, R 62.

Foucault and Danbourné, followed shortly by a frightened Boutteville.[42]

It was the bitterest news the commandant had yet received since taking command. Danbourné, as one of Tonti's most able lieutenants, had been a valuable and trustworthy aide; moreover, Bienville could ill afford to lose three such stalwart Canadians from his garrison. Even more serious was the loss of the seminary missioner Foucault; his murder meant not only his own removal: discovery of the slaughter had brought Davion, Limoges and Boutteville scurrying to the safety of Mobile. Only Saint-Cosme at the Natchez remained in the field. Perhaps the most distressing facet of the massacre to Bienville was his realization that the most likely prospect for fulfilling the promise of the Chickasaw mission was gone; with Foucault's loss the peace that Iberville and Tonti had struggled so patiently to achieve would be ever more difficult to hold.[43]

The presence of four *religieux* at Mobile gave rise to new tensions, not so much between Jesuit and seminary priest as between commandant and religious. The two black robes (Dongé and Limoges) and the two white collars (Davion and Boutteville) seemed on friendly enough terms in these early days. Crisis and threat of life had brought about a modicum of unity and respect, at least for the moment.[44] Bienville had reason to be disappointed in his Jesuits—Dongé was too inexperienced, Limoges too meek and ineffectual. How he longed for more vigorous, dedicated and able men of the black cloth, men like Pierre-Gabriel Marest (a zealous, hardened master of the native tongues now serving on the upper Mississippi at Kaskaskia) or even Paul Du Ru (now returned to France). Yet Dongé could be useful enough by serving Fort Louis as chaplain; Limoges at least could be used to minister to the nearby Mobilians and Little Tomeh. Too, Bienville felt confident he could eventually persuade Limoges to return to his mission on the Mississippi.[45]

42. *Journal Historique*, p. 73. Davion [to SME Dirs.], Feb. 14, 1703, ASME, 344, f. 65–67.

43. Tonti to Iberville, March 14, 1702, *loc. cit.*, 20. Mémoire d'Iberville, 1704, AC, C13C, 2, f. 42–43. Mémoire sur les establissments à faire à l'embouchure du Misisipi et à la Mobile . . . par d'Iberville, AM, 3 JJ 277, 4.

44. Davion à l'évêque de Québec, Sept. 23, 1703, ASME, 344.

45. *JR*, *LXV*, pp. 153–55. AC, F1A, 10, f. 282. Marest to Iberville, July 10, 1700, AM, 2 JJ 56, 15. Marest [to La Vente], April 25, 1709, ASQ, Missions, 48. Min. to Bégon, March 8, 1703, AM, B2, 167, f. 689–95.

It was Davion and Boutteville (thirty-one-year-old native of Saint-Germaine-le-Vieux) who as the months passed began to draw the fire of the restive young commandant. Why, when his whole program was being jeopardized, when the native villages needed missionaries so desperately, were these shrinking servants of God huddled in the town, personal safety their only apparent consideration? If they would not risk their lives for France, would they not at least trust in the Lord for protection in fulfilling His missions? Apparently the memory of Foucault's crushed skull was all too recent. If God were offering to use Davion and Boutteville in the way in which He had used Foucault, the two missioners had just as soon decline the opportunity. After all, a missionary could be as useful by living as by dying.[46]

It was not only fear, however, that kept Davion and Boutteville at Mobile. Boutteville felt that by serving the local residents in somewhat the same capacity as a parish priest he was performing necessary functions that would be sanctioned by Bishop Saint-Vallier himself. For Davion's part, he wanted desperately to be heard in the counsels on Indian affairs, a desire more likely to be fulfilled by his continued presence. Yet Bienville failed to even consult the missioner, which aroused Davion's indignation: the commandant's haughtiness in believing his own judgment on such matters beyond question (beyond even Davion's opinion) was perhaps unwarranted. After all, had not Davion served in Louisiana equally as long as Bienville? Moreover, had not the elder missioner gained more first-hand experience with the natives than the commandant, having served *in* the villages on a day-to-day basis? In any case, what gave Bienville the right to treat so offhandedly with the lives of seminary missioners? Was this part of the Le Moynes' scheme for gaining lower Louisiana for their precious Jesuits, by subjecting the seminary priests to the axe and sword of the native?[47]

Davion further reproved Bienville's attitude by pricking at a highly tender spot: as Davion knew, there was no mystery about

46. Before returning to Mobile after Foucault's death, Davion had himself been attacked by the savages, his companion, Charles Dumont, having lost a finger in defending him. Davion [to SME Dirs.], Dec. 12, 1702; Feb. 14, Sept. 23, 1703, *loc. cit.*, 344. Davion's life had earlier been threatened by the Chickasaw and Yazoo at the instigation of the English. Tonti to Iberville, March 14, 1702, AM 2 JJ 56, 20.

47. Davion [to SME Dirs.], Dec. 12, 1702; Feb. 14, Sept. 23, 1703, *loc. cit.*, 344.

who had struck down Foucault and Danbourné; the Koroa had boasted of the act to Davion's own Tunica villagers shortly after the murders took place. The proper course of action seemed simple enough to the generally meek but now ruffled missionary: if Bienville wished Davion to return to his mission field (as Davion himself desired) he should send a punitive expedition to the Mississippi to find the murderers and bring them to the fort for execution. The principle of "a head for a head" was one Davion well knew Bienville accepted. Yet six months after the murder of Foucault and Danbourné, Bienville had taken no action. Was the commandant squeamish about venturing into a country (at the head of a well-armed detachment of soldiers) to which he was recommending Davion return alone? The question was an affront not only to Bienville's initiative but to his manhood as well.[48]

On hearing Davion's complaints, Bienville merely grumbled, claiming that the solution was not that simple. He did not expect a mere missionary to comprehend the complexities of frontier diplomacy. Without confiding to Davion his future plans, he announced he could not at the moment spare enough men for such an expedition. Meanwhile, Davion, Boutteville and the two Jesuits remained in Mobile, trying to be as useful as they could. There was no parish church for the moment, only a small chapel inside the fort served by Chaplain Dongé. Amicably enough, Dongé applied no restrictions on the use of the chapel to the seminary priests, and the four religious, according to Davion himself, were living in perfect accord:

> I can assuredly say that it would be desirable that everywhere such pure harmony be maintained between the Jesuits and us as is now maintained here. We have been in Mobile for almost a year now, four in all, and we are working together as if we were all members of one community.[49]

If, however, the religious were serving with no appreciable discord in Mobile, there was, and had been, considerable contention in Europe and Quebec over which order should have rights to missionize lower Louisiana, a controversy coming on the heels of

48. *Ibid.* Min. to Bienville, Jan. 30, 1704, AC, B 25, f. 4. Bienville to min., Sept. 6, 1704, AC, C13A, 1, f. 450–51. Bienville to min., Feb. 20, 1707, AC, C13A, 2, f. 11–12.

49. Davion à l'évêque de Québec, Sept. 23, 1703, ASME, 344, f. 69.

a similar dispute in the Illinois country concerning the village of Tamaroa.[50]

In early 1703, Jesuit Thomas Goüye, former mathematics tutor to Minister Pontchartrain and now Parisian agent for his order's foreign missions, pleaded with Bishop Saint-Vallier (in Paris since 1700) to grant the Jesuits a separate sector in Louisiana, to be governed in Saint-Vallier's name by a Jesuit vicar-general. Saint-Vallier turned a deaf ear to the proposal. Irritated at the heated objections made by the Jesuits in the Tamaroa affair, Saint-Vallier seemed pleased that the Jesuits were threatening to remove themselves from further missionary activity in lower Louisiana should the request for a separate sector not be granted. When Goüye took his appeal to his old student Pontchartrain, the minister assured Goüye that although the proposal had the sympathy of both minister and king (both of whom had in the past shown decided Jesuit leanings), neither would attempt to encroach on the bishop's domain.[51] To make the matter final and to avoid offending his former professor's sensitivity, Pontchartrain put the situation to Goüye in euphemistic but unalterable terms:

> His Majesty will allow you to withdraw what religious you have there at present, and not feel obligated to send any more, leaving to the bishop the responsibility of providing missionaries for that country, at his sole discretion.[52]

Jesuit protest did not end with the refusal of king and minister to intervene, though further action would have seemed to be futile. Goüye appealed to Clement XI through Fabrizio Paolucci, the pope's secretary of state, but the pontiff only referred the matter to the cardinals of the Sacrae Congregazione who but

50. Tremblay [to Glandelet], May 28, 1701, ASQ, Lettres, O 34. Bergier [to Laval], March 13, 1702, ASQ, Lettres R 50. Delanglez, in *The French Jesuits in Lower Louisiana* (pp. 38–47), and Giraud in *Histoire de la Louisiane*, Vol. I. (pp. 24–28,), describe the early rivalry of the two orders; but the most incisive commentary is made by O'Neill in *Church and State in French Colonial Louisiana* (pp. 15–45).

51. Père Goüye to min., Feb. 23, 1703, AC, C13A, 1, f. 397–401. Tremblay [to Ango Des Maizerets], June 15, 1703, ASQ, Lettres, O 39. Père Goüye to min., March 9, 1703, AC, C13A, 1, f. 403–11. Min. to Goüye, April 18, 1703, AM, B2, 168, f. 178v. La Chaize [to Laval], May 22, 1702, ASQ, Polygraphie, 7, f. 65.

52. Min. to Goüye, April 11, 1703, AM, B2, 168, f. 116v. Min. to Goüye, April 18, 1703, AM, B2, 168, f. 178–78v.

meekly backed the Jesuits.[53] Bishop Saint-Vallier remained unmoved in the face of such intrigue. Indirectly he had the assent, if not the spiritual blessing, of pope, king and minister to do as he pleased, and it would please him, for the moment at least, to exclude the Jesuits from the Mobile parish.[54]

On July 20, 1703, therefore, Jean-Baptiste de La Croix de Chevrières de Saint-Vallier, Bishop of Quebec, formally added a new parish to his North American diocese:

> . . . informed that His Most Christian Majesty has founded a new French colony in North America on the banks of the river called Mobile, and that His same Royal Majesty has sent there many French families by whose arrival this colony has indeed so greatly increased, that gathered together in one place, they founded a town with its own governor, its peculiar magistrates and other similar things required for political order, we have decided it necessary to appoint over that people a pastor by whom they will be helped by the support of the sacraments, and at the same time nourished by word and example and fashioned to share in divine worship.
>
> Therefore . . . we have decreed to erect a parish in that place, and we hope that by the King's piety and the zeal of those who are there in charge by his authority, a church will be built outside the royal citadel . . . the inhabitants should gather together for prayer in this church and chapel which we have authorized and do erect as a parish church subject to our jurisdiction and that of our successors, the bishops of Quebec.[55]

In his proclamation, Saint-Vallier went beyond merely erecting a parish; he proceeded to nominate a pastor whose service and career had for several months prior been under close consideration:

> By virtue of this grant, we appoint as first pastor of the parish church in the place called Mobile (outside the royal citadel), M. Henri Roulleaux de La Vente, a priest from the diocese of Bayeux, who has been nominated and presented to

53. Mémoire de Fabrizio Paolucci, card., 1703, AGPF, SOCG, 546, f. 154v–57v. Act of Sept. 24, 1703, AGPF, Acta, 73, f. 211v–12.

54. Min. to Père Goüye, April 11, 18, 1703, AM, B2, 168, f. 168, 178v. Min. à l'évêque de Quebéc, Dec. 5, 1703, AC, B 23, f. 195–95v.

55. Lettre de Mgr. de Saint-Vallier au sujet des missions du Missisipi, July 20, 1703, ASS, Section Canada, Dossier IX, No. 3. ASQ, Missions, 65.

> us, and who for a long time has already done praiseworthy work both in France and in the missions in the Indies, and who can and may perform all the functions of pastor among this Christian people.[56]

Although it would be a full year before the instructions embodied in Saint-Vallier's decree would be made manifest, the bishop hoped that he had firmly set the scene for the establishment of an orderly and active parish. Iberville and Bienville, upon hearing of the bishop's decision, could only look with skepticism upon the conferral of spiritual powers to an order that in other mission fields had failed to prove they could achieve the goals the Le Moynes had set forth as their colonial objectives.[57] In any case, since neither commander nor commandant knew the pastor-select, they would adopt a wait-and-see attitude. It remained to be seen whether Bienville would seek to reduce the new pastor to the status of chaplain as he seemed to be doing in the case of Davion and Boutteville.[58]

As the months wore on, the missionary situation at Mobile changed very little. The two seminary priests remained near the fort. Saint-Cosme, at the Natchez, remained the sole missioner in the lower Louisiana field. At least there was one missioner not afraid to do his duty, Bienville was not above pointing out. Davion's retort to this barb was that even Saint-Cosme ought to seek refuge at the fort since the commandant was not going to insure his safety by seeking out the murderers of Foucault and the Canadians. It would not be long, Davion gloomily predicted, before the colony would be minus still another missionary as the natives grew confident they could purge as they pleased.[59]

Aside from the friction between Bienville and the seminary priests (and occasional incidents between the commandant and his subordinates), a relative harmony prevailed in the colony. In February the colonists celebrated Mardi Gras for the first time in two years. The previous season, during the transference from Fort Maurepas to the Mobile River, there had been little time for

56. *Ibid.*

57. Ordre du Roy pour servir d'instruction à M. de Bienville, Feb. 6, 1704, AC, B 25, f. 23–23v.

58. Davion [to SME Dirs.], Dec. 12, 1702, *loc. cit.*, 344.

59. Saint-Cosme [to Tremblay], Oct. 21, 1702, ASQ, Lettres, R 36. Saint-Cosme [to Bergier], Oct. 31, 1704, ASQ, Lettres, R 38. Bergier à l'évêque de Québec, April 15, 1705, ASQ, Lettres, R 73.

such frolicking, but by February of 1703, the inhabitants had resumed the festivities they carried on in 1700 and 1701. The merrymaking, of course, was nowhere near as elaborate as that which they had enjoyed in France. Dancing would not become a part of the occasion until 1705 and except for a few exuberant souls who donned masks and painted their faces red, the merriment consisted primarily of group singing and excessive eating and drinking.[60]

By the spring of 1703, however, food and supplies in Mobile had grown noticeably thin. It had been nearly a year since the *Renommée* and the *Palmier* had returned to France. Bienville had expected a supply ship from Rochefort by the first of the year but the vessel had not yet arrived. Pressed for flour, the commandant was forced to send Canadians to live in the villages of the Mobilians and Little Tomeh. Lacking in meat, he sent hunters down the coast toward the Baye de Saint-Louis. Robinau de Bécancour, recently returned from Veracruz on a voyage requested by Martínez, was dispatched again to the Mexican port, this time not in relief of Pensacola but of Mobile. He left on the twenty-first of May in the *Précieuse*, having been furnished with 5,497 *livres* by several residents in the colony.[61] The want of food and supplies, of course, had its effect on relations between Bienville and the inhabitants of Mobile, the commandant receiving more than his share of the blame for the lack of relief. The first rumblings of discontent were now being heard among the townfolk. Bienville, providing for the needy as best he could and never one to suffer criticism gladly, reacted irritably and in a high-handed manner to the grumblings of the inhabitants; in particular was he annoyed by the imputations of Commissary La Salle whose

60. In 1700 Du Ru had bemoaned the fact that "Sagamité was the only [Mardi Gras] dish . . . while the people of France satiate themselves." Du Ru Journal, 1700, Newberry Library, Ayer Collection, Ms. 262. *FLC*, p. 23. *Cf. JR, V*, p. 23; *XLI*, pp. 30–31; *XLVIII*, pp. 192–93; *LXVIII*, pp. 314–15. The first Mardi Gras in lower Louisiana was celebrated on Tuesday, March 3, 1699, at which time Mardi Gras Bayou on the lower Mississippi was named.

61. *Journal Historique*, pp. 73–76. Iberville to min., June 20, 1702, AC, C13C, 2, f. 44–45v. Lettre, Sept. 10, 1704, BN, FF, 9097, f. 140–45. AC, F1A, 10, f. 282v. Reponse de M. Duclos au mémoire des officiers Royaux de la Veracrux . . . du 13 août 1714, AC, C13A, 3, f. 609–13. Procès-verbal du 21 mai de 1703, AC, F3, 24, f. 46. Autos hechos de 28 de Abril, 1703, AGI, *México*, L. 618.

petulance and hairsplitting in his management of the king's storehouse was becoming hard to bear.[62] As far as Bienville was concerned, La Salle's responsibilities were to "keep accurate records" and to deliver merchandise at Bienville's command, not, as La Salle would have it, to quibble over the advisability of each expenditure. The "dual responsibility" La Salle kept harping about was, Bienville felt, damaging his effectiveness as a leader. While his leadership was not in the least threatened (at this early date), the commandant was plainly irritated at La Salle's criticism of his use of the storehouse. Nevertheless, he felt confident that by pushing his authority and influence vigorously enough he would eventually break the resistance of this French-born upstart.[63]

La Salle, though alone through most of 1702 in his opposition to Bienville's manner of operation, was not cowed by the reputation of the Le Moyne clan. Who were these Canadian ruffians, he asked, but a coterie of backwoodsmen who only recently had risen to levels of power and influence by brow-beating their opposition with profuse energy and superior numbers? Why should a more civilized continental Frenchman whose family had long served the king in responsible places be humbled by those beneath him both intellectually and socially. Had not his two older brothers, one *commissaire-ordonnateur* at Bangkok and the other *commissaire-général* at Marseille, both died in the service of France? Had not he himself descended the Mississippi with Tonti and the great Cavelier de La Salle? Had not he been present on that day in 1682 when Louisiana had first been claimed for France (while Bienville was but an infant of two years)? [64]

La Salle's difficulties had increased in early 1703 when *garde-magasin* Gerard (like himself, a native-born Frenchman) died on February 22. Gerard, though appointed by Iberville, had generally been sympathetic to, and supportive of, La Salle's policy of keep-

62. La Salle to min., May 20, 1703, AC, C13A, 1, f. 387–89v. Davion [to SME Dirs.], Dec. 12, 1702; Feb. 14, Sept. 23, 1703, *loc. cit.*, 344. AC, F1A, 10, f. 282, 288–290v.

63. La Salle to min., April 1, 1702, AC, C13C, 2, f. 38–43. Bienville to min., April 10, 1706, AC, C13A, 1, f. 505–08. Bienville to min., Oct. 10, 1706, AC, C13B, 1, No. 6, f. 1v–9. La Salle to min., Sept. 7, 1706, AC, C13A, 1, f. 472–83.

64. Min. to Iberville, Aug. 10, 1701, AM, B2, 155, f. 240–41. Min. to Bégon, Aug. 24, 1701, AM, B2, 155, f. 319–22. La Salle to min., July 22, 1700, AC, C13B, 1, No. 4, f. 2. La Salle to min., July 28, 1700, AC, C13B, 1, No. 5, f.1. Min. to Bégon, June 1, 22, 1701, AM, B2, 154, f. 524, 642.

ing tight rein on the colony's storehouse. At Gerard's death, however, La Salle's support was somewhat weakened. Since La Salle had no powers of appointment, Bienville managed to increase his hold on the storehouse by elevating one of his Canadians, Jacques Leméry, to succeed Gerard as *garde-magasin.* This action further threatened La Salle; the scrivener felt that the frequently drunk, former freebooter was no fit replacement for Gerard and certainly not a proper associate for a sensitive and conscientious civil servant such as himself.[65]

If La Salle were practically alone in his opposition to Bienville through most of the year of 1702, the lean months of 1703 saw a small coterie of malcontents drawing slowly together in opposition to the established authority. René Boyer, a hot-headed, twenty-seven-year-old gunsmith from Rochefort, began to openly side with La Salle after several displays of violence (including the manslaughter of an aged corporal) had caused Bienville to shackle him (Boyer) for several weeks in irons.[66] Somewhat later, a ship's carpenter, Pierre Ardouin of La Rochelle, joined Boyer and La Salle after a dispute with the commandant over wages. With the added support of Davion and Boutteville, the opposition began to be more outspoken. Even a few of the Canadians, Clement Bégon and Gilbert Dardenne, and, in particular, Guillaume Boutin, a volatile native of Quebec who would later prove a thorn in Bienville's side, began to voice their discontent.[67] This group of reactionists, small as it was, would constitute the only vocal opposition to the Le Moyne regime until the crisis of the late summer of 1704. For the present, the motley band was an inef-

65. La Salle to min., March 4, 1708, AC, C13B, 1, No. 8, f. 3–7v. AC, F1A, 10, f. 282; 11, f. 69–69v. Gerard had earned 72 *livres* for the year 1703. AC, F1A, 11, f. 69v. Canadian Pierre Couillard, *dit* La Fontaine, was suggested as a possible permanent replacement for Gerard. Min. to Bégon, Oct. 21, 1705, AC, B 27, f. 183. Min. to Iberville, Oct. 21, 1705, AC, B 27, f. 184. AC, F1A, 10, f. 283; 11, f. 72. Jacques Leméry received the temporary appointment, also serving occasionally in the capacity of notary. AC, F1A, 13, f. 114. Extrait de Testament de Charles Levasseur, Sept. 28, 1717, AN, Fonds Particuliers, MC, Étude XX–455.

66. AC, F1A, 10, f. 283; 11, f. 70. AC, C13A, 2, f. 250–53, 303–12. ADM, A, June 19, 1707.

67. AC, F1A, 10, f. 283v–84; 11, f. 72–73. Davion [to SME Dirs.], Dec. 12, 1702, ASME, 344. *DGFC, I,* p. 82. Min. to Demuy, Sept. 27, 1707, AC, B 29, f. 288. ADM, A, April 2, July 26, Aug. 4, 1710. La Salle had served as godfather at the baptism of Boutin's son, Nicolas. ADM, A, Dec. 23, 1707.

fectual element, serving only to criticize but not to alter any of Bienville's procedures or policies.

Three days before Bécancour sailed on his third[68] voyage to Veracruz (in May of 1703), La Salle, critical of the commandant's ability to arrange effective trade agreements, appealed to Pontchartrain with a suggestion of his own:

> It seems to me that it would be in the King's interest that His Majesty arrange an agreement with the viceroy of Mexico whereby necessary provisions for this garrison at Mobile would be on accounts which would be presented and paid off in France; for without this precaution we will always be in danger of lacking for them, until there are enough people to cultivate the land.[69]

Although La Salle knew that Bienville would be displeased at his initiative in making the suggestion embodied in his letter (provided he became aware of it), the commissary felt that such an arrangement with the Mexican authorities was desperately needed in view of the fact that the administrators of the colony had been forced to borrow heavily from the officers and inhabitants in order for Bécancour to have sufficient funds to pay for the goods he planned to purchase at Veracruz.[70]

As the summer of 1703 approached, the garrison of Fort L'Huillier which Le Sueur had left on the upper Mississippi under Commandant Daraque, arrived at Fort Louis, having been driven from the area by a band of Mascouten warriors. The increased personnel at the fort now made the lack of provisions an even more pressing problem. As the officers and inhabitants waited impatiently for a ship from France, Davion and four Canadians prepared to leave for the village of the Natchez, the report by Daraque of Indian attack having further reminded the missioner of the jeopardy his *confrère* Buisson de Saint-Cosme was in. He would go and fetch the lone priest to Mobile where his return

68. Bécancour to Alburquerque, Jan. 21, 1703, AGI, *México,* L. 618. Bienville to Alburquerque, Dec. 11, 1702, AGI, *México,* L. 618. Procès-verbal du 21 mai de 1703, AC, F3, 24, f. 46.

69. La Salle to min., May 20, 1703, *loc. cit.,* f. 395–96.

70. *Ibid.,* f. 389–90. *Journal Historique,* pp. 74–81. Bienville would later be accused of intercepting those letters of La Salle that he suspected of casting him in unfavorable light. Tremblay [to SQ Dirs.], June 25, 1707, ASQ, Lettres, M 38. AC, F 68, f. 46.

might serve a double objective: it would save Saint-Cosme from possible massacre and it would further remind the haughty commandant that if he would have missionaries in the field it would behoove him to see to their protection.[71]

71. *Journal Historique,* p. 76. Pénigault, *Relation,* BN, FF, 14613, f. 176–77. AC, F1A, 13, f. 113–14. Journal de Le Sueur, 1702, AM, 2 JJ 56, 9. Davion [to SME Dirs.], Sept. 23, 1703, *loc. cit.,* 344. Saint-Cosme [to Bergier], Oct. 31, 1704, ASQ, Lettres, R 38.

VII

Perfidy and Reprisal

WHILE Iberville had been recuperating at Pensacola in early 1702 he had expressed to Francisco Martínez in no indefinite terms his distrust of Anglican activity in the West:

> The English, on their part, have no other aim in their raids than to destroy the tribes which are allied to us, by carrying them away, as they continually do, to make slaves of them or compel them to put themselves under their control, and afterwards to seize upon all these districts, which they can easily enough do, as they are already masters of most of the tribes on the upper part of the Mobile River where I know they intend to remain.[1]

Back in France later the same year Iberville, in a memorandum concerning Florida, added:

> It surely behooves Spain to concentrate her attention on the territory of Florida where it has only the fort of St. Augustine, which is very meager in comparison with the English in that vicinity, who have strong settlements there and gain over all the Indians by means of the trade they carry on with them; if they [the English] should take possession of that fort, all the natives will be at once on their side.[2]

1. Iberville to Martínez, Jan. 3, 1702, AC, C13A, 1, f. 358–59.

2. Mémoire d'Iberville, Nov., 1702, AC, C13A, 1, f. 327. Iberville was deeply concerned about the relatively large population of Carolina which was almost daily increasing. At this time Carolina consisted of 2,010 dissenters (mostly Presbyterians), 1,809 Anglicans, and approximately 400 French Huguenots. Added to these Europeans were 3,250 Negroes and 800 Indian slaves for a total population of 8,270. By contrast there were less than 240 Frenchmen and Canadians in lower Louisiana and only 208 soldiers under Zúñiga's command at St. Augustine. La Salle to min., April 1, 1702, AC, C13C, 2, f.40. El gobernador de la Florida al rey, March 25, 1702, AGI, *Santo Domingo*, L. 840.

Iberville's fears of English aggression proved wholly justified. Carolina Governor James Moore, a Barbadian of Irish descent, typified more than any other the objects of Iberville's disdain and distrust. Moore had come into the colony about 1675 and later married Margaret Foster, widow of Sir John Yeamans (a previous governor of the province). After managing Dame Yeamans' plantations for a time, he made his fortune in the very enterprise which Iberville so detested: slave-trading. Elected governor on Sept. 11, 1700 (succeeding Joseph Blake who had died on Sept. 7), Moore, a political realist and self-made ruffian, began planning an offensive which he hoped would break the strength of the Franco-Spanish hold on the Gulf Coast.[3] Even before the outbreak of general war in Europe, Moore had engineered the destruction of the Timuquan mission of San Tomás de Santa Fe as early as May, 1702. By September of the same year the Carolina Assembly had approved legislation to equip an expedition to attack St. Augustine; by Oct. 29, Moore and Colonel Robert Daniel, with a force of 500 English volunteers and 450 Yamasee, Tallapoosa and Alabama warriors, were laying siege to Governor Zúñiga y Cerda and his much smaller forces huddled in the Castillo de San Marcos.[4]

Zúñiga, however, had the foresight to anticipate an attack from Carolina. Upon hearing of the assault of the missions north of San Juan, he dispatched pleas for assistance to Havana, Apalache, Pensacola and Mobile. Ensign Diego de Florencia arrived in Pensacola on Nov. 24, where Governor Martínez gave him ten men under command of Francisco Montes and sent him on to Mobile. The French, Martínez assured Florencia, were equally concerned about Carolinian aggression, and Commandant Bienville would do everything in his power to help save San Marcos.[5]

3. Records of the Lords Proprietors, PRO, CO 5, 286, pp. 164–65; CO 5, 288, pp. 52, 287–88; CO 5, 1311, D 56, 9–10; CO 5, 1311, D 56; CO 5, 1258, C 22, 172–73.

4. El gobernador de la Florida al rey, June 6, 1703, AGI, *Santo Domingo*, L. 840. Michael Cole to William Blathwate, Dec. 22, 1702, PRO, CO 5, 306, 2. As far as Moore's contingent is concerned it is probably better to believe English figures than Spanish estimates though neither is quite accurate. James Moore and Robert Daniel to the council, St. Augustine, Nov. 9, 1702, PRO, CO 5, 382, 8, i. Quary to Board of Trade, Dec. 7, 1702, PRO, CO 323, 3, E 54. Council to the Secretary, Nov. 26, 1702, PRO, CO 5, 382, 8.

5. Consulta del Consejo de las Indias, May 22, 1703, AGI, *Santo Domingo*, L. 836. Martínez had returned from Mobile several weeks before, having brought news to Bienville that France and Spain were officially at war

When Diego de Florencia arrived in Mobile on November 28, 1702, he found a settlement which somewhat surprised him. Though less than ten months old, Mobile was already far superior to Pensacola, containing a well-built if not-quite-completed fort and some seventy houses. Bienville invited the young ensign to lodge at the officers' quarters inside Fort Louis and expressed his willingness to offer immediate aid to Zúñiga. The lending of any militia, however, would at this time be out of the question, despite the contingency. The influenza Florencia had found in Pensacola had reached almost epidemic proportions in Mobile, resulting in a severe shortage of man power. "Besides," Bienville added, "we still have the work of the fort before us."

The truth was, nonetheless, that Fort Louis was not in great need of additional work, as Florencia could easily see. Had Iberville been present he would no doubt have sent Zúñiga at least 15 men which with some sacrifice he could have afforded. Bienville, however, lacking a governor's authority as well as prestige, was unwilling to place himself on such a limb at this stage in his administration. He did, nevertheless, supply Florencia with what he could reasonably spare, which, generously enough, amounted to "one hundred new and servicable guns, one thousand pounds of powder—five hundred in fine powder for the smaller weapons, and the other five hundred coarse for the cannons, but all good—and one thousand gun flints . . . plus two hundred cartridge belts."[6] Moreover, Bienville promised to dispatch (and did, four weeks later) his traversier to Veracruz to ask the Duque de Alburquerque for further support.[7]

In addition, as Florencia was departing Mobile, Bienville at-

---

with England. He had asked for and received a generous loan of arms and powder. *Journal Historique*, p. 74. Martínez a Manuel Solana, Dec. 2, 1702, AGI, *México*, L. 618. Carta de Francisco Martínez, Nov. 25, 1702, AGI, *México*, L. 618.

6. Zúñiga y Cerda a Martínez, Nov. 1, 1702, AGI, *México*, L. 618. Diego de Florencia a Zúñiga, Jan. 25, 1703, AGI, *Santo Domingo*, L. 858. *Journal Historique*, pp. 74–75. Procès-verbal, Nov. 29, 1702, AC, F3, 25, f. 279–80. Bienville understandably had some doubts regarding the amount of the loan, especially considering La Salle's scrutiny. To cover himself, he brought together the most respected men of the town—Boisbriant, Tonti, and Charles Levasseur—all of whom signed the order with him. Tonti personally delivered the merchandise to Pensacola. Carta de Francisco Martínez, Dec. 2, 1702, AGI, *México*, L. 618.

7. La Salle to min., May 20, 1703, AC, C13A, 1, f. 387. El rey al virrey, Nov. 24, 1703, AGN, *Historia*, 298. M. de Bienbilla al Virrey, Dec. 11, 1702, AGI, *México*, L. 618.

tempted to compensate for his inability (or unwillingness) to provide soldiers by contriving a scheme (one he would repeat to Roque Pérez a few months later) to further aid the Spanish settlements: his brother Iberville would be returning in the spring with two ships-of-the-line and two of more moderate size. While Iberville used the ships to help bolster Spanish coastal defenses, Bienville would (assuming the Spanish could repay the weapons and supplies lent) persuade the Chickasaw to raid the villages of the Apalachicola in the same vicinity where Spanish forces under Romo de Uriza had met defeat the previous spring.[8]

By the time Florencia had left Mobile and returned to Florida, however, four relief galleons sent by the governor of Cuba, Benítez de Lugo, appeared off the bar of the Castillo de San Marcos, trapping Moore's ships inside the harbor. The frustrated governor hastily burned his vessels on the nearby beaches and slowly retreated to Carolina, after setting fire to the abandoned village of St. Augustine.[9]

Although the Carolinians had failed to capture the Castillo de San Marcos, they had inflicted serious damage on the defenses of Spanish Florida. Zúñiga was left with a wrecked and demoralized town. The church and convent were in ruins and most of the settlers were homeless.[10] Yet Zúñiga's wretched situation was of little consolation to Moore. Having returned to Charles-Town in keen disgrace (he had failed to take the castle, had lost most of his ships and supplies, had squandered £26,000 in military expenses), the ruthless governor set out again ten months later, this time at the head of 1,500 Yamasee and Tallapoosa Indians and 48 Carolinians. Ravaging the countryside, Moore and his unholy warriors swept through the district of Apalache, burning villages and butchering hapless natives, slaying even those who carried a flag of surrender. After a massacre at Ayubale, Moore marched through practically every village in the province, through Bacuqua and Escambe, Patale, and Aspalaga, demanding and receiving one unconditional surrender after another. When the ruthless marauders returned to Carolina the next year they had for all

8. Diego de Florencia a Zúñiga, *loc. cit.*, L. 858. Roque Pérez a Zúñiga, May 25, 1703, AGI, *Santo Domingo*, L. 858.

9. El gobernador de la Florida al rey, Jan. 6, 1703, AGI, *Santo Domingo*, L. 840. *Idem.*, Jan. 8, 1703. Moore and Daniel to the council, *loc. cit.*, 8, i.

10. Martín de Alcano al rey, June 30, 1703, AGI, *Santo Domingo*, L. 864. El gobernador de la Florida al rey, Jan. 6, 1703, *loc. cit.*, L. 840.

practical purposes destroyed the province of Apalache as a useful Spanish zone of defense and Moore was able to boast that he had done it all with the loss of four whites and fifteen Indians. "Before this expedition," he loudly proclaimed, "we were more afraid of the Spaniards of Apalatchee . . . and the French of Mississippi and their Indians doing us harm by land than of any forces of the enemy by sea. This has wholly disabled them from attempting anything against us by land." [11]

In truth it appeared to Bienville that his brother's worst fears were rapidly coming to pass and Governor Zúñiga in St. Augustine lamented that "over six hundred Christian Indians have shifted allegiances to Carolina." [12] Yet, despite the awful destruction in Apalache, Bienville wondered how serious was the threat to the immediate security of his village on the Mobile. The Choctaw nation seemed safe enough and the Chickasaw, though wavering slightly, were still loyal. Regardless of the setbacks, there was not yet cause for panic.

One nation occupied Bienville's thoughts more than any other during events of the past year and a half—the Alabama. If the Choctaw were the most numerous of the southern aborigines and the Chickasaw the most ferocious, the Alabama were certainly the most strategically located.[13] Grouped around a relatively small area at the junction of the Coosa and Tallapoosa rivers (which together formed the "rivière des Alibamons"), the nation of the Alabama was composed of seven or eight stray and heterogeneous villages. The first and largest of these Alabama towns (ascending river) was Koasati, a village of some 200 warriors, followed by Culasa with 150 headmen and Tawasa with barely a hundred.

11. El gobernador de la Florida al rey, March 30, 1704, AGI, *Santo Domingo*, L. 840. El rey al gobernador de Florida, Aug. 22, 1704, AGI, *Santo Domingo*, L. 836. Lucas Álvarez de Toledo al rey, Aug. 22, 1704, AGI, *Santo Domingo*, L. 840. Although Moore made no direct attack on Fort San Luis de Apalache, that last remaining stronghold was abandoned in the summer of 1704 and the garrison withdrew to Pensacola. El gobernador de la Florida al rey, Oct. 6, 1704, AGI, *Santo Domingo*, L. 858. Thomas Nairne memoir, July 10, 1708, PRO, CO 5, 382, 24–26. Moore to the Lords Proprietors, April 16, 1704, Library of Congress, "Spanish Papers," VI, 888.

12. Iberville au gouverneur de Pensacola, Jan. 3, 1702, *loc. cit.*, f. 358–59. El gobernador de la Florida al rey, March 30, 1704, AGI, *Santo Domingo*, L. 840.

13. PRO, CO, Maps, NAC, General, No. 7. Carte de la Louisiane par Le Sr. D'Anville, 1732, BN, Ge. DD, 2987, No. 88006. Notes de Claude Delisle sur la Géographie de la Louisiane, 1703, AM, 2 JJ 56, 17.

These three refugee villages had only recently become part of the nation called Alabama, having fled from the Cherokee country in 1680 after relentless persecution from a coalition of English traders and Chuchumeco braves.[14] Arriving at the rivers' junction in 1681 they allied themselves with four smaller villages speaking a Choctaw dialect, who themselves had sought refuge at the junction in the late sixteenth century after numerous wars in the Choctaw-Chickasaw country had reduced their numbers considerably. The most numerous of these latter four peoples, the original Alabama, were the first of the Muskogean tribes to drift into the area in the years after Soto's expedition had passed through their location west of the Chickasaw country. Settling near what is now Selma, the Alabama maintained dominance over that vicinity for nearly a century, but after several decades of war with the Mobilians, moved upriver to their present (1702) location, followed by the Tuskegee, the Wetumpka, and the Pacana.[15] Sometime after 1687, the village of Alabama, numbering then only 30 warriors, crossed to the east side of the Coosa and joined with the village of Okchai, thus losing their identity as a distinct town. A few years later they separated from the Okchai and retreated back to the west side of the Coosa where they (the original Alabama) became known as the Okchaiutci or "Little Okchai."[16]

Iberville, as did the Mobile Indians, knew these diverse villages only as the nation of "Alibamons." He had no personal contact with any of them, for, by the time the Alabama first visited Fort

14. Adair, *History of the American Indians*, pp. 267–68. PRO, CO 5, 286, 165–66. Delgado a Cabrera, Sept. 19, 1686, AGI, *México*, L. 616. The Alabama villages at this time numbered less than 600 men. Iberville had estimated 400 families in 1701. Mémoire d'Iberville, 1701, AM, 3 JJ 277. Relation de la rivière de la Mobile, AM, 3 JJ 277. PRO, CO, Maps, NAC, General, 7. Boisbriant reported "400 men who live in the nation." Dugué de Boisbriant a Andrés de Arriola, May 23, 1704, AGI, *México*, L. 618.

15. The Muklasa had migrated originally with the Alabama but by 1702 could no longer be considered part of the Alabama nation. *Relaçam verdadeira . . . feida per hũ fidalgo Delvas*, pp. *lxxxix–xci*. Delgado a Cabrera, *loc. cit.*, L. 616. Domingo de la Anunciación y otros a Luna, Aug. 1, 1560, AGI, *Justicia*, L. 1013. Rand, "The Structural Phonology of Alabaman, a Muskogean Language." *IJAL*, Vol. XXXIV, pp. 94–103.

16. Informe de Marcos Delgado, Tuave, Provincia de Cosate, Oct. 30, 1686, AGI, *México*, L. 616. Adair, *op. cit.*, pp. 257, 266–67. Delgado a Cabrera, *loc. cit.*, L. 616. Milfort, *Mémoire ou coup-d'oeil rapide . . .* pp. 266–68. Le Cours de la Riviere des Alibamons, *n.d.*, BN, Ge. DD,2987, C 7963. Ressensement des Villages Sauvages de la Forte des Alybamons, Jan. 24, 1764, PRO, WO 1, 49.

Louis in the spring of 1702, Iberville had already departed for France. Soon after his return, Iberville recorded what little he knew of the nation in a memoir to Pontchartrain. ". . . the Alibamons," he reported, "whose first villages are 35–40 leagues NE by E of the Tohomés are on the banks of a stream which falls into the Mobile . . . most of them have guns; they are friends of the English [at present], but will very soon be our allies." [17]

Iberville had, in fact, good reason to be optimistic. For the Alabama, though a few would several months later join in the siege of St. Augustine, had as yet (at least as far as Iberville knew) no permanent allegiance to either the English or the Spanish.[18] Iberville had, in his speech to the Choctaw-Chickasaw delegation, exhorted those nations "to induce the Conchaques and the Alibamons to make peace with the Chactas, the Tohomés, and the Mobiliens, to visit the French fort and not to listen to the English any more." And in his instructions to Bienville in April he had reminded the young commandant to entice the Alabama to Mobile by whatever means necessary.[19]

Bienville and his officers had known of the existence as well as the influence of the Alabama as early as the spring of 1699 when the French had first made contact with the Mobilians; and an Alabama chieftain had visited Fort Maurepas in October of 1701. Moreover, when Charles Levasseur explored the Mobile River in the spring and summer of 1700 that lieutenant was able to gather a good deal of information about them from the Mobilians and the Little Tomeh. Even before Iberville had returned to Pensacola in early April, Chickasaw couriers were on their way to the villages of the Alabama to invite them to Fort Louis.[20]

It was May 12, 1702 when eight of the leading chiefs of the Alabama villages arrived in Mobile.[21] The Alabama had come to

17. Mémoire d'Iberville, June 20, 1702, AC, F3, 24, f. 38.

18. Years later an Alabama chief informed Bienville that in the year 1702 some of his nation had joined Moore in the siege of St. Augustine, but only with the understanding that the English would thenceforth offer a one-third reduction in their prices of trade goods. Even then only a small number had participated. Bienville to min., March 7, 1741, AC, C13A, 26, f.58v–59.

19. Journal d'Iberville, June 20, 1702, AM, B4, 23, f. 337. Mémoire pour servir d'instruction au Sieur de Bienville, April 25, 1702, AC, F3, 68, f. 2–9v.

20. Journal de Sauvole, April 1, 1700, AC, F3, f. 25. Journal de Levasseur-Ruessavel du fort des Billochies, 1700, BN, FF, 21690, f. 310–13v.

21. *Journal Historique*, pp. 76–77. Mémoire pour servir d'instruction au Sieur de Bienville, *loc. cit.*, 68, f.2. Pénigault, *Relation*, BN, FF, 14613, f. 178.

the fort out of no idle curiosity nor chiefly for the presents the Chickasaw (by Bienville's directions) had promised them they would receive. They came to enhance their bargaining position. For the Alabama, even at this early stage in wilderness diplomacy, well understood the diplomatic maneuver of "flirting" among frontier rivals. By consorting with the enemy of the English, they would apprise themselves of what the English could not know and would place themselves in better position to force concessions from Charles-Town officials apprehensive of the possibility of new directions on the western frontier.

On this initial visit to Fort Louis the Alabama chieftains were visibly impressed with what they saw: the infant town was rapidly developing, the Canadians and artisans were preoccupied in building, in planting, and more significantly, the storehouse was full.[22] Bienville supplied the Alabama generously with blankets, beads, and bells. Moreover, he showed them (though he did not issue them any) a reservoir of guns and ammunition. When the chiefs asked (somewhat deferentially) whether they should continue their wars against the Choctaw and the Tomeh, Bienville abjured them to desist from *all* wars which they (predictably) promised to do. When they left a few days later with an abundance of goods and kind words (something the English had yet to give them), Bienville had reason to believe he was on the road to an important diplomatic victory; he was even more optimistic when on October 1 some forty of the Alabama returned, smoked the calumet of peace and promised to live in harmony with the Chickasaw, Pensacola and Apalache.[23]

The Alabama did not return for nearly seven months. When they came again in early May, 1703, led by a principal chief named Deerfoot, they saw a somewhat different situation. The optimisim on the faces of the residents was considerably lessened, the large store of guns and ammunition was nearly depleted (lent to the Spanish the previous autumn). More serious was the low supply of food in the settlement, Bécancour's three-month supply brought from Veracruz in February almost consumed.[24]

22. Depenses de l'Entretien et subee de la garnison et ouvriers du Fort Louis de la Louisiane pendant l'année derniere 1702, AC, F1A, 10, f. 281–90v. *Journal Historique*, pp. 75–76.

23. *Ibid.*, p. 77. The Oct., 1702 visit is mentioned only in the Chicago Historical Society manuscript of the *Journal Historique*.

24. Thomas Nairne memoir, July 10, 1708, PRO, CO 5, 382, 25–27. *Journal Historique*, pp. 76–77.

Deerfoot had an answer to Bienville's problem of food shortage: the Alabama had an abundant supply of corn in their villages and would be happy to supply it to the French for a reasonable price. When Bienville expressed concern about the presence of Englishmen in the Alabama villages, Deerfoot replied that the English had all withdrawn to the east, to the Coweta and Conchaque villages. Without Anglican interference, the French could now carry on a safe and profitable trade with the Alabama. In view of the special French predicament, would it not be worth an experiment?[25]

Reluctantly but somewhat hopefully Bienville agreed. A five-man party could easily journey to the Alabama villages and return to Mobile in less than five weeks.[26] The mission would not only help ward off starvation but could gather much-needed intelligence of the Alabama country and perhaps seal an economic alliance that seemed ripe for the closing. Moreover, were not the Alabama making a concrete gesture which, if refused, might prevent any future and meaningful relationship? Considered in this light the commandant of Fort Louis saw little alternative.

For this strategic mission, Bienville chose five sturdy Canadians experienced in the ways of natives and travel: among the members of the expedition were François Dumesnil, Étienne La Chambre (a Fort Maurepas veteran), and a cousin of Dumesnil named Pierre Charly, *dit* Saint-Ange. To head the detachment Bienville chose Jacques-Philippe Matou, *dit* La Brie, twenty-eight-year-old son of Philippe Matou and Marguerite Doussinet of Sainte-Famille, Île d'Orléans in Quebec. La Brie had been on the Gulf Coast since 1699, having departed France with Iberville in 1698. An experienced woodsman, he was no stranger to savage behavior,

25. Pénigault, *Relation*, *loc. cit.*, f. 178–79. *Journal Historique*, p. 77.

26. In 1759, Jean-Bernard Bossu made a more leisurely trip up the Alabama River during the late winter and early spring, covering a distance of 366 miles(Fort Condé to Fort Toulouse) in 50 days. Bossu, *Nouveaux Voygages aux Indies Occidentales . . .* , April 28, 1759, Lettre XV. U.S. Army Corps of Engineers, *Alabama River Navigation Charts*, Sept., 1972, pp. 2, 66. This was an average of only 7.32 miles per day but it occured at the height of the rainy season, against unusually strong currents. Beauchamps once made 21 miles in a single day up the same river (Journal de Beauchamps, Aug. 28, 1746, AC, F3, 24, f. 422) and Régis Duroullet covered 48 miles in three days (Duroullet to min., Nov. 11, 1729, AC, C13A, 12, f. 69–71). The distance the five Canadians planned to travel (Fort Louis to Koasati) was 331 miles. *Alabama River Navigation Charts*, *op. cit.*, pp. 8, 65. In calculating these distances allowances must be made for river changes and, in particular, for the Fort Mimms cut-off. *Ibid.*, pp. 2, 4.

several members of his family having been massacred by Indians in Quebec.[27]

On the fourth of May, 1703, La Brie and the four Canadians left Mobile with Deerfoot and the Alabama. After spending the evening at the village of the Mobilians, the party continued its journey up the Alabama River in three large pirogues. Swift currents caused by the spring rains made ascending the river a difficult task and the contingent was able to average but a mere sixteen miles per day. By mid-morning of the twentieth day's journey they had reached a bluff at the present city of Montgomery fifteen miles below Koasati, the first village of the Alabama. Unknown to the Canadians, Deerfoot had sent news of the whereabouts of the party to Koasati the night before and later that afternoon, the 24th of May, a group of young warriors arrived at the campsite, welcoming the visitors with calumets.[28]

At nightfall Deerfoot dispatched the warriors back to Koasati under pretext of preparing the villages for the arrival of the Canadians the next day. Presumably satisfied with this explanation for the warriors' sudden departure, the Canadians fell asleep. In the early morning hours, however, the Alabama returned, swooping down on their sleeping victims with English muskets and lances. La Brie, Dumesnil, and La Chambre were killed outright, but Charly and an unidentified comrade awakened in time to offer resistance. Unarmed and outnumbered, they managed to roll down the bluff where they frantically pushed one of the pirogues into the river and fell inside, shots of the Alabama whizzing over their heads.[29]

27. Donation par Marie Dumesnil à Jean-Baptiste et Pierre Charly, AJM, Greffe de Adhémar, May 28, 1690. *DGFC, I*, pp. 117, 163, 420. *Journal Historique*, pp. 76–77. Pénigault, *Relation*, *loc. cit.*, f. 179. Role de la garnison, August 25, 1699, AC, C13C, 2, f. 18–20V. Role de la garnison du fort du Biloxy, May 26, 1700, AC, C13A, 1, f. 255–60. AC, F1A, 10, f. 283v, 284v. Jacques-Philippe Matou, *dit* La Brie is not to be confused with Jean Labrière, *taillandier*, who came from France on the *Pélican* in 1704 (AC, F1A, 11, f. 219), or Jacques La Bierre, *Canadien* (AC, F1A, 11, f. 73). The parents-in-law of Marie-Madelaine (La Brie's sister) had been massacred by the Iroquois in 1695 at Boucherville. *DGFC, I*, p. 179.

28. *Alabama River Navigation Charts*, *op. cit.*, pp. 8, 63–65. *Journal Historique*, p. 79. Cf. notes 26 above and 29 below. The campsite was at the top of the bluff near the present L & N Railroad Depot. Montgomery North, Quadrangle, 7.5 minute series, 1958 (photorevised, 1972), AMS 3748 IV NE-Series V844. Le Cours de la Rivière des Alibamons, *n. d.*, BN, Ge. DD, 2987, C 7963.

29. Pénigault, *Relation*, *loc. cit.*, f. 178–79. Min. to Iberville, Nov. 28, 1703, AM, B2, 170, f. 465–66. There is some dispute concerning the date of

Fortunately for the two survivors, the Alabama (believing the Canadians to be mortally wounded) chose not to pursue them; for Charly had received a near-fatal wound which a Châteaugué halberdier later described as "a sabre blow on his shoulder having a depth of three fingers." It was a gruelling journey home for Charly and his companion. Drifting slowly down the Alabama, barely able to maneuver the paddles, the badly wounded men were compelled to stop at short intervals along the river to dress their wounds with pine resin which they chewed before applying.[30]

When the two Canadians arrived back at the fort in early June, Bienville was incensed at the news of the Alabama treachery. Not only had the colony lost three potential *habitants* (men it could ill afford to lose) but Bienville had failed to get the corn or the intelligence he expected. Instead of being able to gloat over diplomatic inroads against the English he was now reduced to planning a punitive expedition, a type of mission he detested but which he nonetheless felt necessary to the long-range success of his Indian policy.[31]

The turn of events was a bitter blow to Bienville, yet the cause of the Alabama turn-around lay not in Bienville's miscalculations but in a sequence of incidents initiated by two uncommon Carolinians, Stephen Bull and Thomas Nairne. Before 1699 the English exercised a near monopoly on the interior Indian trade; the

---

the Alabama massacre. The *Journal Historique* (pp. 76–77, 79) would have it about May 15, 1703, but other sources warrant the above conclusion. The account registers list death dates as accurately as possible for the purpose of paying next-of-kin the exact amount earned by the deceased while in service. Estat du payment qui a eté fait aux officiers majors, mariniers, matelots, ouvriers, Canadiens et Mousses . . . pendant L'Année 1703, AC, F1A, 11, f. 71v, 72v. La Chambre, La Brie, and Dumesnil each earned 144 *livres* for the 4 months and 24 days they served during the year 1703. *Cf.* notes 26 and 28 above. Balthazar-Michel de Boutteville (quoted by Delisle) in Notes de Claude Delisle sur la géographie sur la Louisiane, vers 1703, AM, 2 JJ 56, 17. Lettre, Sept. 10, 1704, BN, FF, 9097, f. 140–42. The letters Bienville and La Salle wrote to Pontchartrain in June and October of 1703 would shed additional light on this incident but apparently they are not extant. Min. to Bienville, Jan. 30, 1704, AC, B 25, f. 4. Min. to La Salle, Jan. 30, 1704, AC, B 25, f. 3. Min. to Iberville, Nov. 28, 1703, AM, B2, 170, f. 465–65v.

30. Lettre, *loc. cit.*, f. 140–42. Pénigault, *Relation*, *loc. cit.*, pp. 178–79. Deerfoot later reported to Thomas Nairne that he believed all five Canadians had perished. Thomas Nairne memoir, *loc. cit.*, f. 24–25. The unidentified comrade may have been Joseph Bonhomme, a thirty-one-year-old Canadian who died at Fort Louis on July 19, 1703 of wounds inflicted by the natives. AC, F1A, 11, f. 72.

31. Min. to Bienville, Jan. 30, 1704, *loc. cit.*, f. 4.

Spanish in Florida offered no formidable competition. Mistreatment of the natives by Carolina traders caused no great concern in Charles-Town. When news of the French establishments on the gulf reached Carolina, however, prescient Englishmen (aware of French tactics in Canada) realized they could no longer be so casual in their trade policies. They could not let abuses by unconscionable traders jeopardize their Indian alliances.[32]

In 1701 Colonel Bull, former surveyor-general and a man noted for fair play with the natives, was dispatched to the Alabama to lay groundwork for an improved relationship with that nation by informing them of new directions in Anglican policy. The next year Thomas Nairne, a frontier Scotsman employed by the Assembly to regulate trading practices, visited the Alabama and encouraged some of them to join the English in the siege of St. Augustine in which he (Nairne) served as a company captain under James Moore. Nairne, in accordance with the actions of a conference committee on Indian affairs which recommended that the Alabama not be discouraged from making war on "those Indians that are our enemies," returned the next year just before the Alabama departed for Fort Louis. During a conference with several important chiefs Nairne emphasized what he considered crucial questions. Did the Alabama not wish to be in permanent league with a proven victor, on the side of those who had stopped coldly the advance of the Spaniard Uriza from Apalache the year before and who had destroyed the town of St. Augustine? Were not presents from Carolina superior and more numerous than those from Mobile? Could the quality of the red woolen blankets (those of French origin made in Languedoc) compare with those supplied from Charles-Town? Finally, Nairne remonstrated, were not the French arming their allies, the Choctaw and Chickasaw, with firearms which these tribes were using to spill Alabama blood? Strike a blow against these Gallic intruders, he implored the natives, and avenge that blood which has already been shed.[33]

32. *JCHA*, Jan. 14–16, 20–21, 24, April 2, Aug. 14–15, 20–22, 27, 1702. Proprietors to Joseph Blake, Dec., 1697, PRO, CO 5, 289, 38. Board of Trade Memorial, April 7, 1702, PRO, CO 323, 3, E 32. Gravier to Lamberville, Feb. 16, 1701, *JR, LXV*, pp. 116–18. Montigny à l'évêque de Québec, Aug. 25, 1699, ASQ, Missions, 41. Min. to Desmaretz, Jan. 29, 1714, AN, G7, 535.

33. Iberville au gouveneur de Pensacola, *loc. cit.*, f. 358–59. *JCHA*, Aug. 14–16, 27, 1701; Jan. 14, April 2, Aug. 20, 1702. El gobernador de la Florida al rey, Sept. 30, 1702, AGI, *Santo Domingo*, L. 840. Romo de Uriza al gobernador de la Florida, Oct. 22, 1702, AGI, *Santo Domingo*, L. 858.

Thomas Nairne knew, of course, that the Alabama were not of sufficient strength to launch an attack against Fort Louis. But he also realized that a direct assault against the French was unnecessary at the present time. The promotion of a single sanguinary incident would suffice to foil any immediate plans that Bienville might have for winning over the Alabama. For Nairne well knew that the French were adequately educated in the savage law that "blood must be avenged by blood," the execution of which would precipitate a flow that could not easily be checked. Returning to Charles-Town in April, 1703 Nairne could report to the provincial governor that the scheme was set, that the Alabama had asked for "a drum, a stand of colors, and the right to buy ammunition to be used against the French . . ."[34]

Bienville was now aroused enough to lead an immediate attack on the Alabama villages. Yet he realized that, for the moment, an attempt at reprisal would be foolhardy. The Alabama, near harvest time, were now concentrated in their villages, no doubt prepared for a French assault. Would it not be wiser to wait until hunting season when the warriors would be more dispersed, more vulnerable to surprise? Too, Bienville was sorely lacking in supplies, a state which he hoped would soon be remedied by a ship from France. More importantly, he felt wanting in authority for such a full-scale mission. Pontchartrain's sentiments about reprisal were sometimes conservative indeed and Bienville had some doubts about the minister's blessings in such an enterprise. Nevertheless, Bienville dispatched a report to Pontchartrain concerning the Alabama incident (which he sent in June via a small ship to Havana), asking his permission to lead a punitive mission, describing as well the squalid condition of his colony.[35]

On August 20, 1703, a supply ship, the *Loire*, arrived at Massacre Island, loaded with provisions and seventeen passengers. The *Loire* had sailed from La Rochelle the preceding March 16, a month and a half before the visit of the Alabama chieftains. By the time the *Loire* departed Île Massacre in mid-October, however, Bienville had already reached a decision; if he waited for a reply

34. *JCHA*, Feb. 3, April 17, 1703. Thomas Nairne Memoir, *loc. cit.*, f. 25–27. Min. to Desmaretz, *loc. cit.*, f. 535. Min. to Gayot and Néret, Feb. 9, 1714, AC, B 36, f. 55–55v. Min. to Ramezay and Bégon, Nov. 7, 1715, AC, C11A, 35, f. 30–31.

35. Bienville to min., Feb. 20, 1707, AC, C13A, 2, f. 9–16. Bergier lettre, March 30, 1704, ASQ, Lettres, R 64. Min. to Bienville, June 30, 1707, AC, B 29, f. 279–80. Min. to Bienville, Jan. 30, 1704, *loc. cit.*, f. 4.

from Pontchartrain his advantage might be lost; he therefore informed the minister (by the *Loire*) that he was proceeding with the expedition immediately.[36]

By the end of October, Bienville had issued invitations to four nations—the Mobilians, the Pascagoula, the Little Tomeh and the Choctaw—to gather at the main village of the Mobilians during the first week of November for an event of major importance. The precise nature of the expedition was not revealed (except to the Mobilians, without whose co-operation the mission could not succeed), Bienville believing he could more successfully arouse the various tribesmen when they were assembled together. On this point, Bienville's judgment was not lacking. When he arrived at the rendezvous point with a detachment of sixty soldiers, sailors and Canadians headed by Louis Juchereau de Saint-Denis and Henri de Tonti, festivities had already begun. Huge fires crackled in the November night; the brisk autumn air was rent with war whoops and laughter as a procession of warriors danced through the grand square in the town's center. The entire village was present, as well as warriors from Pascagoula and Yowani. Medicine men, covered with animal skins, burst from their magic-huts, shrieking in unknown tongues. Youths were flogged until their blood ran, the chiefs and old men exhorting them to bear their pain gracefully, as the warriors would do on the forthcoming expedition. The French and Canadian onlookers were so caught up in the spectacle, they joined in the rites themselves, Bienville allowing his chest to be tatooed with figures of snakes, in the manner of the natives.[37]

Amid the furor Bienville spoke to the assembled chiefs and warriors, reminding them of the recent murderous acts committed by the Alabama and that by helping to avenge the blood of the three dead Canadians they could prove their attachment to the French and gain the blessing of their father beyond the seas (Louis XIV). Bienville's oration was received with unrestrained approval. "One would have said," the commandant later reported, "that they were one and the same nation their feelings were so much in accord." [38]

36. Min. to Bienville, Jan. 30, 1704, *loc. cit.*, f. 4. Estat du payment . . . , *loc. cit.*, 1703, f. 67–73v.

37. Estat du payment . . . 1703, AC, F1A, 11, f. 69. Pénigault, *Relation*, *loc. cit.*, f. 181–83. Journal de Bertet de La Clue, 1720, MCM, manuscripts, I.

38. Pénigault, *loc. cit.*, f. 182. Bienville to min., Sept. 6, 1704, AC, C13A, 1, f. 450–51.

After distributing guns and swords to the principal chiefs and warriors, Bienville embarked his forces from the village of the Mobilians in pirogues and shallops, leading a combined force of 280 French and Indians. The plan developed by Bienville, Tonti, and Saint-Denis entailed paddling upstream to a landing place on the Alabama River some fifteen miles above the Mobilian village, thence to debark and march overland toward the Alabama villages, some 170 miles distant. The expedition moved slowly, the Mobilians lagging behind under pretext of "hurrying on the provisions." In reality the Mobilians were already beginning to have second thoughts about guiding an expedition against a nation that exerted such powerful influence on a river system which they themselves must regularly employ. Although the Mobilians had at various times during the preceding century been at war with the Alabama, they did not wish to needlessly antagonize them. Moreover, they realized that in any retaliatory war their village location was more vulnerable to raiding parties than was Fort Louis. Nonetheless they proceeded to advance with Bienville, however slowly.[39]

Reaching the landing place eight miles up from the Alabama-Tombigbee junction just past what is now Holley Creek, Bienville distributed powder and bullets to those Indians who had been given muskets, cautioning them not to approach the campfires too closely. The warning went unheeded by two of the Mobilians who, when the powder exploded in their faces, suffered a slow, agonizing death. This incident proved calamitous to the success of the expedition, the natives seeing in it an omen of more perilous events to come. Three days later Bienville began to wonder at the sincerity of his guides. The expedition seemed to be moving in circles, advancing toward its destination only slightly. Despite the suspected sabotage, however, Bienville was at the mercy of the Mobilians were he to surprise the Alabama by a land route. For not one Frenchman on the expedition was familiar with the backwoods trails leading to the Coosa-Tallapoosa junction.[40]

Two days later Bienville began to sense that the country of the Alabama was somewhat farther than the estimate made by the Mobilians. The detachment had only advanced as far as present-day Frisco City when Bienville's surgeon, Pierre Clavery, and his

39. *Journal Historique*, p. 82. Bienville to min., *loc. cit.*, f. 451–54. Delgado al gobernador de la Florida, Sept. 19, 1686, AGI, *México*, L. 616.

40. Bienville to min., *loc. cit.*, f. 452–53. *Alabama River Navigation Charts*, *op. cit.*, p. 2.

chaplain, Pierre Dongé, fell ill, along with twelve of his infantry. As if this were not sufficient, the chief of the Little Tomeh took sick and abandoned the expedition entirely, returning to his village on the Tombigbee with all his warriors.[41]

Just beyond present-day Monroeville, Bienville took stock of his remaining troops. Still over a hundred miles from Koasati, the nearest Alabama village, Bienville could count less than a hundred and twenty fit men of his original force of nearly three hundred. Moreover, the few remaining Indians were becoming increasingly fearful and daily threatened to abandon the expedition, a warning which, if carried out, would leave the small French force in an unfamiliar wilderness without guides.[42]

A conference between Bienville, Tonti and Saint-Denis produced the following determination: the French force, small as it was, represented the nucleus of the colony's defense. If by chance it were surprised and massacred, the fortunes of France in Louisiana would be in severe jeopardy. Fort Louis might never recover from such a debacle. There was, in this tenuous condition, only one reasonable course of action. The following day, Bienville ordered the expedition to return to Fort Louis and the long journey home was begun, a march completed by late November.[43]

Bienville, however, was nothing if not persistent. Even before he returned to the fort he had formulated a plan for a second expedition. The new strategy called for an entirely French mission, without the Mobilians who "we felt certain . . . had warned the Alabama of our approach toward them," and who, if again taken into confidence, "would warn them of our return." It was a plan which, once formulated, Bienville "thought of nothing but executing . . . vigorously." [44]

In the early weeks of December, Bienville ordered six large pirogues to be constructed by the Canadians. By the twenty-second day of December the pirogues were completed, but most of the men who had fallen ill on the first expedition were not yet

41. Estat du payment . . . *loc. cit.*, f. 69–69v. Bienville to min., *loc. cit.*, f. 453. The Mobilians were following the old Indian paths which in the twentieth century were developed into Highway 59 and Highway 21.

42. Bienville to min., *loc. cit.*, f. 451–53.

43. Lettre, Sept. 10, 1704, *loc. cit.*, f. 140–41. In Jan., 1704, Fort Louis was capable of putting only 95 effective men in the field including sailors and artisans. Estat du payment . . . *loc. cit.*, f. 69–73. Estat des depenses . . . 1704, AC, F1A, 11, f. 218–22v.

44. Bienville to min., *loc. cit.*, f. 453–54.

recovered (or claimed they weren't). Bienville left without them, taking with him only forty-eight men. Since the entire expedition was to be made by water, Bienville took along the Canadian named Charly whose services as a guide would now be indispensable.[45]

The voyage upstream (difficult but not as strenuous as a journey during the rainy season) was made in record time. Gliding past the village of the Mobilians at night to conceal its movements from that tribe (who it was feared might try to warn the Alabama), the French party reached the junction of the Alabama-Tombigbee early the following morning. The next portion of the journey was made by light of day, with overnight stops on the banks of the river. By the end of the sixth day (December 28), the expeditioners had reached the present Selma, where they camped for the night. The next morning they slept late, waiting until dusk before continuing their course. The remainder of the voyage was made by night in order to avoid being detected by hunting parties. By New Year's Eve they had reached Tallawassee Bar and on the night of January 1, 1704 they saw a large fire in the distance just beyond a place called "Quatre Isles." Creeping closer, Bienville's scouts detected nine pirogues secured near the water's edge, further reconnaissance revealing a large hunting party, including women and children.[46]

When the scouts returned, Bienville made camp for the night. The next day was spent in gathering additional intelligence regarding the size and movements of the Alabama party. According to Pierre Charly they were stationed near the same bluff where La Brie, La Chambre and Dumesnil had been murdered, a supposition later confirmed by the discovery of those Canadians' ghastly remains. An impetuous Bienville wanted to attack that very day, January 2, but Tonti and Saint-Denis convinced him a more perfect thrust should be made at night (as the savages themselves might do) if the most were to be made of their advantage.[47]

By midnight the French were ready to attack but the Indian campfires still burned brightly. They waited, watching the fires closely. It was a few hours before dawn before the flames had

45. *Ibid.*, f. 454. *Journal Historique*, pp. 81–82. Although the distance by water was nearly twice the distance by land, Bienville had little choice. Charly was familiar with the water route; no one knew the overland course.

46. Le cours de la Rivière des Alibamons, *n. d.*, BN, Ge. DD, 2987, C 7963. Montgomery North Quadrangle, *op. cit. Alabama River Navigation Charts, op. cit.*, pp. 46–47, 59, 64.

47. Pénigault, *Relation*, f. 183. Bienville to min., *loc. cit.*, f. 454.

spent themselves. Bienville, hoping for a massacre but still not certain of the exact number of the hunting party, ordered ten men to ascend the bluff where the Alabama lay sleeping, the main body of French troops to follow closely. Advancing through a web of thorns and blackberry bushes, the front guard moved stealthily up the bluff until a lead Frenchman snapped a dry cane with his boot. One of the dozing Alabama sentinels heard the noise and asked who was there. The advance men, playing for time while the main body of troops struggled up the bluff, made no answer. The sentinel, growing impatient, alarmed the other warriors who after some moments' hesitation began firing into the brush. One of the advance men, Raymond Saintot, a veteran sailor from La Marque (Île de Ré) who had sailed with Iberville in 1698, fell dead. Bienville ordered the attack to begin and heavy firing from both sides ensued.[48]

The French, however, failed to get their full force into action in time. The Alabama women and children retreated, covered by their warriors who continued firing as they fell back. Bienville wanted to pursue them but the darkness and the unfamiliar landscape made this too risky a maneuver. He contented himself with firing into the darkness, hoping to impress the retreating party with French power. The French remained at the Alabama campsite until daybreak, at which time they discovered they had killed two Alabama hunters and wounded two others. Bienville allowed the wounded Alabama to return to their villages, taking full advantage of his opportunity to convince the natives that any further Alabama aggression against the French would be returned with even greater reprisal.[49]

After hacking the nine Alabama pirogues to pieces and dumping their supplies into the river, Bienville, with his expeditionary force, began the long journey back to Fort Louis, confident he had achieved his purpose. If his mission had not been as destructive

48. *Ibid.*, f. 455. Pénigault, *Relation, loc. cit.*, f. 182–84. Role de la garnison, Aug. 25, 1699, AC, C13A, 1, f. 211–13. Estat de depenses, *loc. cit.*, 1704, f. 218–19. *Journal Historique*, pp. 81–82. Bienville mentions two Frenchmen killed, as does the *Journal Historique*. However the official statements (cited above), drawn up by La Salle, list only one, as does Pénigault. Although Pénigault's figures are generally inaccurate he is seemingly correct in this instance. A close study of this portion of his relation indicates he was probably a member of the expedition.

49. Lettre, Sept. 10, 1704, *loc. cit.*, f. 141. Bienville to min., Sept. 6, 1704, *loc. cit.*, f. 454–55.

as he had hoped, he was able to later report "it had spread terror among our enemies," an accomplishment that made the Alabama more discreet if no less antagonistic. Arriving back at Fort Louis on January 11, Bienville immediately sent couriers to his Indian allies, the Chickasaw, Choctaw, Tomeh and Mobilians, informing them of his achievement, a feat which seemed to place the French in a nobler light, especially among the smaller nations: the Mobilians, the Little Tomeh and the Pascagoula, who now perceived that the French alone could accomplish what the French in conjunction with their allies could not. By the middle of March, the Chickasaw were bringing Alabama scalps to Fort Louis in exchange for guns, bullets and powder, taking advantage of an earlier offer Bienville had made to the natives but which had gone unaccepted until Bienville's retaliation had been accomplished.[50]

50. *Ibid.*, f. 453–55. *Journal Historique*, pp. 82–83.

VIII

Recruitment in Paris

EVEN before Bienville had completed his punitive mission against the Alabama, he had been anticipating a certain supply ship from France, though he did not expect her arrival until October or November of 1704.[1] The promised vessel, which Iberville (on his departure two years before) had informed him would surely be arriving, however late or soon, was to be no ordinary supply ship. It would contain what officials in Versailles and Rochefort hoped would be the female progenitors of an eventually populous colony.

Iberville, as early as 1702, had recommended to Pontchartrain that the sending of "a hundred girls" to Mobile would accomplish two vital objectives: first of all, it would increase the birth rate (until 1704 there had been only two or three Caucasian births in Mobile), thus providing a basis for population growth other than by emigration (which was costly); secondly, it would furnish incentive for the restless Canadians to settle down and become permanent residents.[2]

Iberville had arrived at the ambitious figure of "one hundred" because he hoped by the time the girls arrived that the number of Canadians on the king's rolls would approximate that total. Although the minister had originally shown some sympathy with this figure, the recent outbreak of war in Europe and the difficulty of convincing "young and well-bred" girls of the advantages of life in Louisiana made a less ambitious number more feasible. A hundred girls could, of course, have been procured (provided funds were approved), but the ministry was interested only in

1. Bergier [to Brisacier], March 30, 1704, ASQ, Lettres, R 64.

2. Min. to Bégon, Feb. 13, 1704, AC, B 25, f. 22v. Min. to La Salle, Jan. 30, 1704, AC, B 25, f. 14–15v. ADM, A, Sept. 18, Oct. 4, 22, 1704. AC, F1A, 11, f. 217–19. Dénombrement du 31 août 1704, AC, C13A, 1, f. 468–69.

women of high moral character, as the lack of that quality in female immigrants had recently created substantial unrest in such French colonies as Martinique and Saint-Domingue.[3]

But where would the future mothers of Louisiana be found in the France of 1703? In the hospitals of Paris, Rochefort or La Rochelle? Pontchartrain rejected these possibilities for the most part, believing that more favorable sources could be found elsewhere (in the local orphanages and convents, such as the Couvent des Filles de Saint-Joseph at No. 10–12 rue Saint-Dominique) though his own office lacked the time and personnel to launch more than a cursory search. Instead he responded to a suggestion by Iberville that Monseigneur Saint-Vallier, Bishop of Quebec, be entrusted with the responsibility of selecting the prospects. After all, had not the bishop only recently erected the new church of Mobile as part of the diocese of Quebec? Did not the bishop himself have a vested interest in who populated his parish? [4]

The bishop could certainly be trusted to act with discretion in the judgment of moral character. Too, his prestige might be instrumental in convincing favored individuals to co-operate in such a venture. If the bishop described life in Louisiana as a wholesome opportunity, would it not carry greater force than the promises of a military officer or bureaucrat? [5]

Saint-Vallier accepted the responsibility with some misgivings but with the realization that no one in Paris was more ideally suited for the task. Screening the prospects in the summer of 1703, the bishop approved twenty girls "reared in virtue and piety . . . who are accustomed [also] to labor and diligence . . ." Some of the girls had been locally connected with Parisian religious communities, such as the "filles du Reverend Père Barré" (a charitable and educational order closely associated with the Séminaire des

3. Min. to Desclouzeaux, June 2, 1700, AM, B2, 147, f. 255–56. Min. to Puis-Martin, Oct. 27, 1706, AC, B 28, f. 301–02. Min. to Le Page, April 5, 1702, AC, B 24, f. 71. Min. to Bégon, Oct. 3, 1703, APR. 1 E 50, f. 41.

4. Plan manuscrit du couvent de Saint-Joseph, BHVP, B, 601. This community, founded by Marie Delpech de L'Etang in 1641, sought to prepare young girls between the ages of ten and twenty for a career with the church or state, in case they failed to marry. Madame de Montespan built the convent while still in Louis XIV's favor and resided there after her departure from court in 1691. Min. to Bégon, Feb. 27, 1703, AC, B 23, f. 188–89v. Érection et nomination, July 20, 1703, ASQ, Missions, 65. Min. à l'évêque de Québec, Aug. 15, 1703, AM, B2, 169, f. 433–33v. Min. to Desclouzeaux, *loc. cit.*, f. 255.

5. Min. à l'évêque de Québec, *loc. cit.*, f. 433v. AM, B2, 175, f. 192–92v.

Missions Étrangères), the Communauté de l'Annonciation on the rue du Bac and the Couvent de Notre-Dame de la victoire de Lépante à Picpus.[6] Others, among them Louise-Marguerite Housseau and Renée Gilbert, had come from towns outside of Paris—Tours and Chantilly, respectively. The girls were indeed young and respectable, most of them between the ages of fourteen and eighteen. At the time of her selection by Saint-Vallier, for example, Marie-Catherine Philippe was sixteen years of age, daughter of Charles Philippe, a respected resident of Meaux-en-Brie whose close friend, Charles Huguier, an *advocat en parlement*, had been a witness to Marie-Catherine's baptism at Notre-Dame de Chaague à Meaux. Gabrielle Savary, daughter of Pierre Savary and Jeanne Fautisse, had been born the 28th of January, 1684, in the parish of Saint-Denis where her godfather, Plomier Deseluse, had been an important merchant. Marie-Marguerite Dufresne, aged fourteen, was a daughter of Charles Dufresne, Sieur Dumotel, a squire of the parish of Saint-Germain. Others of the group, such as Marie-Thérèse Brochon and Angélique Drouin, were not as well-born, perhaps, but of no less piety.[7]

Three other girls, sisters Jeanne-Louise, Geneviève and Marguerite Burelle, aged twenty, seventeen and fifteen respectively, needed no endorsement by Saint-Vallier, for they were to be accompanied by their parents, Étienne Burelle and Marguerite Rousseau, as well as by their younger brother Louis. The elder Burelle, by profession a pastry cook, was no stranger to the New World. Born in Paris (Saint-Sévérin, Île-de-France) in 1656, he had emigrated to Cap Saint-Ignace in Canada at an early age where he married Marguerite, widow of Mathurin Ducheron, *dit* Deslauriers, on Nov. 10, 1682. Siring four children, Burelle migrated to Quebec from Cap Saint-Ignace, where a son, Vital, was born, after which he returned to Paris with his family about the turn of the century. Eager to return to the New World, the pastry cook

6. *Ibid.*, f. 192. Collinet to Villermont, May 22, July 10, 1703, BN, FF, 22812, f. 125–27, 237. Collinet to Villermont, Sept. 27, 29, 1703, BN, FF, 22813, f. 85–86v, 88–89. Min. to Bienville, Jan. 30, 1704, AC, B 25, f. 15v.

7. ADM, A, Aug. 16, 1705, Feb. 23, July 28, 1707. AVP, Extrait du registre des actes de Naissance de la Paroisse St.-Sulpice, April 25, 1702. ADM, B, 1732. Marie-Marguerite, however, had been born out of wedlock on July 28, 1689. Her parents had been married in 1690 and she was legitimated in 1702 in the parish of Saint-Sulpice. Archives de Seine-et-Marne, N.-D. de Chaage à Meaux, July 11, 1687. ADM, C, March 14, 1726. Archives de la ville de Saint-Denis, RB, Jan. 30, 1684, No. 8896. ADM, A, Aug. 16, 1705, June 11, 1707. *DGFC, I*, p. 96. AC, F1A, 11, f. 223–23v.

seized the opportunity for free passage after learning of Saint-Vallier's search for colonists.[8]

Three of the girls, Jeanne-Élisabeth Le Pinteaux, Jeanne-Catherine de Berenhardt and Marie-Françoise de Boisrenaud ("la fille supérieure"), acted with some authority over the slightly younger girls, in concert with Sister Marie Malbécq (chosen by Saint-Vallier himself) and "Monsieur Le Roux," a staff assistant of the "Compagnie du Guet" located in the Châtelet on the right bank of the Seine. Saint-Vallier had relayed Pontchartrain's promise that the ministry would provide sufficient goods and support for the girls for a period not to exceed one year. The total subsidies, in fact, came to some 7,000 *livres*, a substantial portion of the colony's budget for that year. Included in the appropriations was a sum for certain supplies and "niceties" for the girls, of which the responsibility for purchase fell to the wife of the man who was to captain the ship carrying them to Louisiana, Madame Guymont Ducoudray.[9]

By the first week in October, arrangements for the voyage were apparently nearing completion, the group's supplies having been purchased by Madame Ducoudray and by a certain Mademoiselle Séguier. The girls no doubt expected to make a quick trip to Rochefort, where a ship would be waiting, freshen up for a few days, and be on their way to Louisiana by the last week in October. Perhaps they would be married and living in some condition of luxury by New Year's Eve.[10]

The convoy did not leave Paris, however, until the second week

8. *DGFC, I*, p. 96. AC, F1A, 11, 222, 223v. Étienne was the son of Pierre Burelle and Jeanne Vanier of Saint-Sévérin. The majority of family signatures show "Burelle," rather than "Burel." ADM, A, June 11, Nov. 27, 1707; March 17, April 7, 1708. Apparently Marguerite Rousseau, native of Rouen, was born in 1656. After emigrating to Cap Saint-Ignace in 1670 with her parents, Jean-Baptiste Rousseau and Louise Meni, she married Deslauriers on Sept. 28, 1673. *DGFC, I*, pp. 96, 207. LSMA, DCS, May 14, 1737.

9. In 1703, the allotment for the "filles" totaled 24,950 *livres* but this was anticipatory to having considerably more girls. AC, F1A, 11, 66v, 223. Min. à l'évêque de Québec, Aug. 15, 1703, AM, B2, 169 f. 433v. Min. to Bégon, Oct. 1, 1703, AM, B2, 170, f. 2. BN, FF, 22813, f. 133–34, 141. La Vente [to Tremblay], Sept. 10, 1704, ASQ, Lettres, R 75. La Vente [to Tremblay], Sept. 25, 1704, ASQ, Lettres, R 76. Conseil de Marine, Dec. 10, 1718, AM, B1, 30, f. 429–29v. Min. to Madame Ducoudray, Sept. 12, 1703, AM, B2, 169, f. 710.

10. *Ibid.*, f. 710. Min. à l'évêque de Québec, Versailles, Sept. 12, 1703, AM, B2, 169, f. 703–04.

in October. After an arduous journey of nearly three hundred miles, its horse-drawn carts having wobbled over the dusty highways that led through the towns of Étampes, Blois and Amboise, the party arrived (during the last week of the month) at Rochefort, a small port ten miles from the mouth of the Charente River. At Rochefort the girls found that the ship that was to transport them was not yet readied, had not, in fact, even been selected. The court's September plans had called for Iberville to head a sizable squadron of vessels, including the *Renommée*, the *Charente* and the *Pélican*, one of which was to transport the girls; but the vagaries of war were causing an almost daily shift in schedules.[11]

The girls, with their chaperon, were temporarily lodged in the local orphanage (located a few blocks from the river near the spacious Jardin du Roy) while preparations for the embarkation were finalized. During the month of November they were allowed, within rather stringent limits, to go about the town. They began then to hear strange conversation, lurid descriptions of the new land which began to stir their latent fears: Mobile was a desert in the wilderness, a wasteland inhabited only by boy soldiers and Canadian barbarians; there was little in that barren swamp but poverty and disease and one had constantly to fear the inclemencies of weather as well as attacks by savages and wild animals; reports of the murder of at least four of their prospective husbands had recently reached the port city.[12]

In fact, the inhabitants of Rochefort were much more familiar with the seamier side of Louisiana than either Pontchartrain or Saint-Vallier. The local taverns and cafes were filled with truths

11. *Ibid.*, f. 703v. AC, F1A, 12, f. 109v. Collinet to Villermont, Sept. 1, 1703, BN, FF, 22813, f. 53–54v. Min. to Villette, Sept. 12, 1703, AM, B2, 169, f. 662. Min. to Duval, Sept. 12, 1703, AM, B2, 169, f. 710. A typical stage journey from Paris to Rochefort required 8–9 days. Relation du Voyage . . . 1737, ASS, Fonds Canada, Dossier CII, No. 1. Min. to Duguay, Sept. 12, 1703, AM, B2, 169, f. 657–59v. Mémoire du Roy . . . à M. Le Roux, Oct. 3, 1703, AM, B2, 166, f. 110. Min. à l'évêque de Québec, Oct. 17, 1703, AM, B2, 170, f. 142. Min. to La Peigné, Oct. 17, 1703, AM, B2, 170, f. 208. Min. to Bégon, Oct. 17, 1703, APR, 1 E 50, f. 80.

12. Bégon to Villermont, Feb. 14, 1704, BN, FF, 22814, f. 44. Collinet to Villermont, April 8, 1704, BN, FF, 22814, f. 130. Extrait du 3 jan. 1704, BN, FF, NA, 21399, f. 32. Min. to Bégon, Nov. 7, 1703, AM, B2, 170, f. 342–43v. The hospice des orphelines de la marine, a Recollet orphanage founded by Madame Bégon (Madelaine Druillon) in 1694 and later administered by the Soeurs de Saint-Vincent de Paul and the Daughters of Charity, was destroyed in 1841. The original site is now occupied by the Armée de l'air at the corner of rue Bégon and rue Chanzy.

and half-truths alike brought back by Canadians and French sailors who had experienced Louisiana's woes first-hand and who delighted in exaggerating its dangers. When such talk began to reach the ears of the young Parisians they were understandably alarmed. Had they been duped by the ministry of the marine? Had Bishop Saint-Vallier not told them the full truth about prospects for a more affluent life? Even the more optimistic of the girls began to doubt the wisdom of continuing, the least confident requesting permission to return to Paris. All of them were, quite conceivably, apprehensive.[13]

To counteract this development, Intendant Bégon, in charge of the operation since it reached Rochefort, instituted several emergency measures. First of all, he confined the girls more strictly to the orphanage, discontinuing past privileges to come and go (even within narrow limits) so that their heads would not be further filled with "irresponsible gossip." What is not repeated soon loses its force, Bégon reasoned. Secondly, the girls were soothed with occasional gifts and social get-togethers, were given an allowance of 15 *sols* per day (an extravagance severely criticized by Pontchartrain when news of it reached him). Furthermore, they were promised private quarters (apart from the rest of the crew and ship personnel) once they arrived on board, a policy however that Bégon (by Pontchartrain's directive) had intended anyway.[14]

In this manner the girls were somewhat quieted, at least enough to dissuade them from openly disavowing their agreements. Yet as the weeks wore on, then the months, their ship was still not ready to sail. Though it was now certain that the convoy itself would be traveling on a large, recently captured Dutch vessel of some 600 tons burden called the *Pélican*, commanded by René-Hervé Guymont Ducoudray, the ships that were necessary to escort the *Pélican* to the open seas (due to the threat of English aggression on the western coast of France) were not yet prepared to embark. Iberville, fallen ill in the autumn, was still not recovered; there was grave doubt as to whether or not he would be able to accompany the *Pélican* in the *Renommée* (or any other ship, for that matter). Pontchartrain, anxious about the continued delays, was by the month of January ordering Iberville to leave

13. Bégon to Villermont, *loc. cit.*, f. 44. Collinet to Villermont, *loc. cit.*, f. 130.

14. Collinet to Villermont, May 22, 1703, BN, FF, 22812, f. 126–27. Min. to Iberville, Feb. 13, 1704, AM, B2, 174, f. 374–74v. Min. to Bégon, Mar. 19, 1704, AM, B2, 174, f. 709–12v.

as soon as possible, the latest plans calling for three vessels under the Canadian commander to leave for Louisiana by February 1, 1704.[15]

The first of February, however, came and went; still the vessels remained, the anxiety of the girls as well as that of the officials daily increasing. Meanwhile, additional changes were taking place in the personnel who were to depart on the *Pélican.* The twenty girls that had left Paris in October (excluding the Burelle sisters), were supplemented by additional recruits, some of whom were from Rochefort and nearby La Rochelle: Marie Linant and Marie Grissot, nursing sisters from the local orphanage, hired by Saint-Vallier to help compensate for the loss of Le Roux and Marie-Jeanne Malbécq who had returned to Paris; [16] a midwife, Catherine Moulois (hired at the substantial salary of 400 *livres* per year) and her husband Laurent Cloquinet; an edge-tool maker, and a carpenter; two companies of soldiers recruited by Châteaugué and François Juchereau de Vaulezard, and a frail, lisping seminary priest named Alexandre Huvé who, suffering from the infirmities of myopia and a weak constitution, was an unlikely choice to serve in so indelicate a parish as Louisiana.[17]

Huvé's immediate superior, approved by Bishop Saint-Vallier to serve as *curé* of the new church at Mobile, was also awaiting

15. Min. to Bégon, Oct. 17, 1703, APR, 1 E 50, f. 77, 85. Bégon to Villermont, Oct. 30, 1703, BN, FF, 22813, f. 140–40v. Iberville fell seriously ill in late October. By Nov. 13 he was off the critical list but the effects of his illness lingered until mid-winter. Bégon to Villermont, Nov. 7, 1703, BN, FF, 22813, f. 158v. *Ibid.*, Nov. 18, f. 184–84v. Extrait du 3 jan., *loc. cit.*, f. 32. Min. to Iberville, Dec. 26, 1703, AM, B2, 170, f. 705. Min. to Bégon, Jan. 2, 1704, AM, B2, 174, f. 2. Min. to Bégon, Oct. 3, 1703, APR, 1 E 50, f. 41, 48–49. The *Pélican* had been captured from the Dutch in 1702, renamed the *Saint-Jean-de-la-Chine*, then later that same year renamed the *Pélican*, no doubt by Iberville in honor of his flagship sunk in the battle of Hudson's Bay. Collinet to Villermont, Aug. 18, 1703, BN, FF, 22813, f. 26.

16. Liste des filles et des deux familles qui seront envoyées de Paris à Rochefort, Oct. 3, 1704, AC, B 25, f. 9–10. AC, F1A, 11, f. 223–23v. Iberville had been given permission to secure ten girls from the Rochefort-La Rochelle vicinity but none were taken aboard. Min. to Bégon, Oct. 1, 1703, AM, B2, 170, f. 1–3v. The number of women aboard the *Pélican* totaled twenty-seven (23 marriageable girls, 2 wives and 2 nursing sisters), a sum conforming exactly to the count mentioned in Bienville's September report. Bienville to min., Sept. 6, 1704, AC, C13A, 1, f. 458.

17. Liste des filles et des familles . . . *loc. cit.*, f. 10v. AC, F1A, 11, f. 223–23v. *DGFC, I*, pp. 328, 379, 494. BN, FF, 22813, f. 133–34, 141. Bienville to min., Oct. 10, 1706, AC, C13B, 1, No. 6, f. 5–6v. AC, C13A, 1, f. 542; 2, f. 16. La Vente [to SME Dirs.], June 27, 1708, ASQ, Lettres, R 82. Tremblay [to Ango Des Maizerets], June 12, 1712, ASQ, Lettres, O 54.

passage, having helped escort the convoy from Paris to Rochefort. Henri Roulleaux de La Vente, former priest from the village of Beauchêne (diocese of Bayeux) in Calvados, was already (in 1704) nearing fifty years of age. Ordained as a priest towards the year 1688, he had only six years previously (in the spring of 1698) been leaving for another mission, for the Île-de-Bourbon (now Réunion) just east of Madagascar, with another seminary priest, Goulven Calvarin of the diocese of Léon. Calvarin (who was later to labor and perish in upper Louisiana) and La Vente had served well together; they ministered at the mission of Saint-Paul (near present Saint-Denis) for over three years, La Vente performing his last act of baptism on July 24, 1701. La Vente had served his parishioners beyond duty's call, manifesting unusual interest in their public as well as private affairs. He was remembered long after he departed as "a good man and a noble priest." [18]

La Vente, in truth, cut a grand figure among a largely bland personnel. Dynamic, forthright, he came highly recommended by the archbishop of Paris, Louis-Antoine de Noailles, as well as by Abbé Henri-Jean Tremblay, agent in Paris of the Séminaire de Québec. Tremblay, who had known La Vente casually for nearly fifteen years, had some reservations about his age, his health (even now La Vente was beginning to walk with a limp, early manifestations of a paralysis that would totally disable him by the year 1716), his unlikelihood of mastering the native languages. Yet the abbé considered him "wise, a hard worker, perfectly capable of ministering to the needs of the people . . . who, however, is quite independent." By his latter reference, Tremblay was no doubt remembering La Vente's report of August, 1700 when the pastor not only lodged protests against a civil official at Bourbon but presented a written complaint to the colony's governor, Lacour de La Soulaye, signed by twenty-eight witnesses (the signatures of which La Vente had solicited himself). Such activism led later to a complete break with the governor, resulting in La Vente's leaving Bourbon.[19]

18. Min. to Brisacier, Jan. 9, 1704, AC, B 25, f. iv. La Vente [to SME Dirs.], April 6, 1700, ASME, 958, f. 56–61. *Idem.* [to *Idem.*], Aug. 13, 1700, 966, f. 187–89. AAQ, Registres d'insinuation B, 189, 244. Tremblay à l'évêque de Québec [and Mssrs.?], March 12, 1704, ASQ, Lettres, M 30. Calvarin, a native of Brittany (Vannes), died in 1719, shortly after his arrival at the Tamaroa. ASQ, Chapitre, 40; Missions, 43, 73c.

19. Tremblay [to Laval], June 15, 1703, ASQ, Lettres, N 121. Pénigault, *Relation*, BN, FF, 14613, f. 165. Bienville to min., Oct. 10, 1706, AC, C13B, 1, No. 6, f. 4–9. Tremblay [to ?], March 12–15, 1704, ASQ, Lettres,

Yet La Vente was not in this instance recalled or removed. He had himself requested (along with colleague Calvarin) to be replaced. He furthermore had offered to donate monies coming from his salary at Bourbon toward the new mission in Louisiana (funds, however, that neither La Vente nor the Louisiana mission ever received). Despite any shortcoming of personality, then, this zealous servant had the blessings of the authorities in Paris. He was capable, he was willing, and, more decisive in his selection, there was no flock of God's sheep nudging the seminary door for a chance to serve in Louisiana.[20]

By the end of January it was apparent that Iberville would not be able to meet his embarkation deadline. The minister therefore ordered the *Pélican*, under Ducoudray, to depart as soon as possible. "The king," Pontchartrain wrote Bienville on January 30, "is sending to Louisiana the vessel *Pélican* . . . [which] is bringing you the scheduled supplies for the colony . . . He [the king] had [previously] decided to send M. d'Iberville . . . with two frigates to accompany the said *Pélican*, but the poor condition of his [Iberville's] health and other matters that have arisen have prevented the carrying out of this plan." [21]

Despite the note of immediacy in Pontchartrain's missive to Bienville, however, delays continued to impede the *Pélican's* embarkation. Soldiers were constantly deserting from Châteaugué's and Vaulezard's companies; a concerted attempt to replace them, requiring time and effort, was not fully successful. The spoilage of wine and food supplies, the vicissitudes of weather—all acted to further delay the operation. Moreover, reports of English warships on the horizon were constantly recurring.[22]

In the meantime an attempt was made to load the girls on board

---

M 30. La Vente [to SME Dirs.], Aug. 13, 1700, ASME, 966, f. 187–89. *Idem.* [to *Idem.*], Sept. 5, 1700, ASME, 865, f. 121–33. Brisacier [to a missionary of the Mississippi], Oct. 31, 1716, ASQ, Missions, 45.

20. La Vente [to SME Dirs.], Aug. 13, 1700, *loc. cit.*, f. 188–90. Tremblay [to Laval], June 15, 1703, *loc. cit.*, f. 6. Tremblay à l'évêque de Québec, March 12, 1704, *loc. cit.*, f. 7–9.

21. Min. to Bienville, Jan. 30, 1704, AC, B 25, f. 4–5. The *Pélican*, a "vaisseau de 3ème rang," measured 116 French feet from bow to stern with a breadth of "29 pieds 4 pouces" and a depth of "11 pieds 6 pouces." Before her departure from Rochefort she was judged in good-to-mediocre condition. AM, G, 13 *bis*.

22. Min. to Bégon, Dec. 12, 1703, AM, B2, 170, f. 578–79. Min. to Iberville, March 5, 1704, AM, B2, 174, f. 572–73.

the *Pélican*. In late March a launch left Rochefort, making its way downriver then across the large harbor where the *Pélican* lay anchored in deep water. The unusually rough seas made it impossible for the small vessel to reach its destination. After three or four days the launch was forced to return to port. A few days later, it made another attempt. This time the launch was successful in reaching ship, followed by a trail of other launches.[23] Once on board, however, the convoy suffered additional delays. Since the *Pélican* was now to be the only ship to sail to Louisiana, all possible supplies were loaded, almost to the danger point. Furthermore, new reports of English warships in the area (a clear and present danger made more manifest a few months later when Bishop Saint-Vallier's ship was captured between La Rochelle and the Azores) made it mandatory for more armed escorts to be readied.[24]

In early April, the *Pélican*, already carrying a full load, departed Rochefort and moved up to La Rochelle where Ducoudray boarded additional merchandise that he hoped to sell at Havana.

Finally, after the convoy had endured several weeks of severe discomfort, of rolling and tossing in the outer harbor of La Rochelle, Commander Ducoudray weighed anchor on the nineteenth of April and headed for the open sea, escorted by a squadron of twelve gunboats. Unknown to Ducoudray a fleet of "twenty-two large English vessels was on its way from Lisbon," to seek the squadron out. The English ships were two or three days too late, however, and Ducoudray was untroubled by them. They did nonetheless futilely pursue one of the *Pélican's* rear guard vessels and several days later Ducoudray caught sight of one of them in the distance. Some time later, a few smaller English ships were sighted and the *Pélican* gave chase to one of them, only to be outrun.[25]

After their precarious April departure, the *Pélican's* passengers settled back, able now, even in their crowded conditions to relax

23. Bégon to Villermont, March 25, 1704, BN, FF, 22814, f. 85. Collinet to Villermont, April 8, 1704, *loc. cit.*, f. 130–30v. It was surely a shrewd, if callous maneuver to board the passengers before the supplies.

24. *Ibid.*, f. 130. Min. à l'évêque de Québec, June 29, 1707, AC, B 29, f. 30–30v.

25. Joseph de Guzmán al virrey, Sept. 22, 1704, AGI, *Santo Domingo*, L. 857. La Vente [to Brisacier], Baracoa, June 25, 1704, ASQ, Letters, R 74. If La Vente's dates (as first kept in his daily journal and later incorporated into his letter of Sept. 20) are correct, the *Pélican* must have left the outer harbor of La Rochelle on the evening of April 19. La Vente [to SME Dirs.], Sept. 20, 1704, ASQ, Lettres, R 77. The journal, however, is not extant.

somewhat. The open sea lay ahead, the skies unclouded. The Atlantic was unusually warm and serene for that time of year. Perhaps the worst was over, the passengers hoped. Perhaps, after all, there had been some modicum of truth in the bishop's comforting promises . . .

IX

Robinau de Bécancour

WHILE Bishop Saint-Vallier was recruiting in the convents of Paris during the summer of 1703, Bienville and the majority of inhabitants of Mobile remained close to the fort, their food supplies rapidly dwindling. The expected supply ship from France was long overdue; Bienville was forced to dispatch five or six hunters to the Baye de Saint-Louis to search for small game, not to mention the some twenty or thirty volunteers he was compelled to send to the villages of the Natchez, the Bayougoula and the Biloxi.[1]

By mid-summer, the crisis in food had temporarily ended. Andrés de Arriola, back at Santa María de Galve after a long absence, notified Bienville of the arrival of three ships from Veracruz which had brought substantial relief to the Pensacola garrison. At Arriola's invitation, Bienville sent Boisbriant to Fort San Carlos to receive the provisions owed the French by the Spanish which Arriola was now able to repay. Four weeks later Robinau de Bécancour returned from Veracruz with supplies Bienville had authorized him to purchase (with monies borrowed from the officers and inhabitants), along with a letter from the Duque de Alburquerque thanking Bienville for the aid he had given to St. Augustine and Pensacola.[2]

1. Bienville to min., Sept. 6, 1704, AC, C13A, 1, f. 457–65. Pénigault, *Relation*, BN, FF, 14613, f. 116–23. *Journal Historique*, pp. 77–82. Lettre, Sept. 10, 1704, BN, FF, 9097, f. 140–44. La Salle's assessment of the state of the storehouse was generally more reliable than Bienville's. The commandant, looking ahead, was inclined to "poor-mouth" in hopes of gaining a surplus of supplies, a tactic which failed to influence the minister's judgment. La Salle to min., May 20, 1703, AC, C13A, 1, f. 387–88.

2. Alburquerque had sent six months of provisions (including flour, pastries and meats) by a captured English vessel, a packet-boat and a small fishing smack. El Virrey a su Majestad, April 20, 1703, AGI, *México*, L. 618. Bécancour had embarked for Veracruz on May 21, several weeks after

In August, the long-awaited supply ship, the *Loire*, arrived at Massacre Island under command of Dugué de Sainte-Thérèse who the year before had made the first relief trip to Veracruz in one of the colony's traversiers, the *Précieuse*. The *Loire*, a 500-ton *flûte* built at Brest in 1684 by the *constructeur* Louis Hubac, had left France in the spring of 1703 without Châteaugué, Vaulezard or Le Sueur (all of whom had been scheduled to embark along with two companies of soldiers and a large number of artisans and families). In addition, after it had become apparent that Iberville (due to his involvement in the war in Europe) would not be able to sail with the *Loire* himself, a number of excellent recruits from Limoges, which the commander had chosen with great care, deserted. Moreover, Le Sueur lost at least twelve laborers who had planned to sail on the *Loire* but who changed their minds when they discovered that Le Sueur would not be traveling with them.[3]

As suggested by Pontchartrain, the *Loire*, after stopping at Cap-français where she took on some much needed livestock, followed the route of the old Bahama Channel in order to more directly reach the harbor at Havana. During the layover at the Spanish port, Iberville's clerk, Lagresse, sold nearly two hundred barrels of flour to Jean-Baptiste Jonchée, director of the Royal Trading Company at Havana. When the *Loire* reached Massacre Island in August, Bienville was highly disappointed to learn that neither his brothers nor Vaulezard and Le Sueur, nor any large numbers of workmen or colonists, nor the two companies of soldiers he had requested were among the passengers. He was, however, elated to receive a relatively sufficient amount of supplies, including all the necessary stones to build the already planned and greatly needed mill. He was also pleased to receive into the colony brick-makers Pierre Brossard, Charles Miré and Pierre Barteau of Poitou as well as *armurier* Gabriel Martineau and Jean-Baptiste Alexandre of Dieppe.[4]

La Brie and the Canadians had departed for Koasati. *Journal Historique*, pp. 76–82. Procès-verbal, May 21, 1703, AC, F3, 24, f. 46.

3. AC, F1A, 10, f. 290v; 11, f. 64v–69, 71. ACM, Minutes Rivière & Soullard (1709–10), f. 67–68. The *Loire* was 110 *pieds* on her keel and 28 *pieds* 8 *pouces* in width. AM, G, 13 *bis*. Min. to Chaulnes, March 28, 1703, AM, G, 13 *bis*. Min. to Chaulnes, March 28, 1703, AM, B2, 167, f. 698. Min. to Bégon, Feb. 27, 1703, AC, B 23, f. 189–90. Min. to Bégon, Dec. 12, 1703, AM, B2, 170, f. 578–79. Min. to Iberville, Feb. 15, 1703, AM, B4, 25, f. 370–71. Min. to Bégon, March 7, 1703, AM, B2, 167, f. 519–19v.

4. Min. to Blécourt, Jan. 24, 1703, AM, B2, 167, f. 197–203. Min. to Bégon, Feb. 27, 1703, AC, B 23, 172 ff. Dartaguiette to min., Aug. 18, 1708,

The *Loire* anchored at Massacre Island for nearly two months, the supplies she brought enabling Bienville to plan his long-delayed punitive mission against the Alabama. When the *flûte* left on October 16, she had a new commander, Nicolas Perrot, who had come to investigate commercial possibilities and to captain the return voyage home. Dugué de Sainte-Thérèse, who had commanded the voyage from France, sailed only as far as Havana, where he was given command of a fireship. Limoges and Boutteville both departed with Perrot on the *Loire*. Bienville, though he now had little regard for Jesuit Limoges and had suffered his differences with seminary priest Boutteville, was regretful to see them leave, for their absence meant that only Davion and Dongé remained to carry on the essential tasks the commandant envisioned for his religious. Bienville could only hope that the next ship would bring a heartier lot of missioners.[5]

The supplies brought by the *Loire* enabled the colony to abide in good style until the late winter of 1704. By the end of March, however, the food rations had begun to diminish alarmingly, especially after Bienville was compelled to send over six thousand pounds of flour to Pensacola on March 10 to enable that garrison to survive until the next Spanish ship from Veracruz.

The constant demands made by Pensacola on Mobile's commissariat were at this point causing Bienville to question whether the maintenance of good relations with that port was actually worth the price. Yet the commandant had good reason to be generous, both from official and private considerations. The Spanish had cash; the French did not. On certain occasions the Spanish had been equally as generous: their provisioning of the Mobile settlement in June of the previous year came at a time when the French colonists most needed assistance. Further, the food and sup-

---

AC, C13A, 2, f. 338–39. *Journal Historique*, pp. 79–81. Min. to Iberville, March 5, 1704, AM, B2, 174, f. 572–73. Bienville to min., Sept. 6, 1704, *loc. cit.*, f. 461–64. AC, F1A, 11, f. 71. The *Journal Historique* has Jacques Barbazant de Pailloux arriving with these men but although recruited by Châteaugué as a sergeant in 1703, he apparently did not reach the colony until 1704 on the *Pélican*. *Journal Historique*, p. 80. AC, F1A, 11, f. 221v.

5. *Journal Historique*, pp. 79–81. Davion [to SME Dirs.], Sept. 23, 1703, ASME, 344. Limoges returned to Vannes, France where he died on January 30, 1704. Boutteville went on to Paris where he provided Claude Delisle with valuable information on the geography of Louisiana; at this time in 1704, he was planning to return to Quebec from La Rochelle with Bishop Saint-Vallier. Notes de Claude Delisle sur la géographie sur la Louisiane, vers 1703, AM, 2 JJ 56, 17.

plies that Dugué de Sainte-Thérèse and Bécancour had been able to purchase (not without inconvenience, however) at Veracruz had on at least two occasions enabled the French to ward off starvation. Nonetheless, it was becoming increasingly apparent, as time wore on, that the French were being forced to assume the lion's share of what La Salle felt should be a mutual burden.[6]

In truth, events beyond the control of Arriola, Martínez and the Duque de Alburquerque were largely responsible for the woes of the Pensacola garrison during the early years of the decade. The attack on St. Augustine and English aggression in Apalache had depleted Spanish resources in those areas, drawing on what meager reserves had been present in Pensacola and claiming some measure of support even from Mobile. If Bienville had contributed guns and ammunition to the defense of St. Augustine, so had Pensacola; but in late 1702, Mobile, short-supplied as it was, could still afford to lend aid with less sacrifice than could Pensacola. The following year the Carolinians had attacked the Spanish *doctrinas* in Apalache. Bienville had once more contributed to the cause against English aggression; but again, so had Pensacola (not only with supplies but with valued personnel as well).[7]

In the spring of 1704, then, the English were still threatening Apalache, and Pensacola was again appealed to for help. Martínez, after dispatching what aid he could, turned once more to Mobile. Bienville did not hesitate to lend his support; he not only sent the Spanish seventy-five sacks of flour but he also dispatched Henri de Tonti to aid in preparing defenses in case the English should extend their invasion to the *presidio* at Santa María de Galve. Moreover, in recent months, Andrés de Arriola had asked Boisbriant for intelligence concerning English activity that he felt

6. El virrey a su Majestad, April 20, 1703, AGI, *México*, L. 618. AC, F1A, 10, f. 290v. La Salle to min., May 20, 1703, AC, C13A, 1, f. 387–89. *Journal Historique*, pp. 78–80. Pérez a Zúñiga, May 25, 1703, AGI, *Santo Domingo*, L. 858. Diego de Florencia al gobernador de la Florida, Jan. 25, 1703, AGI, *Santo Domingo*, L. 858. Alburquerque had thus far been unsuccessful in locating more than a few families to settle in Pensacola. El rey al virrey, Nov. 24, 1703, AGN, *Historia*, 298.

7. El rey al virrey, Dec. 10, 1704, AGN, Historia, 298. Solana al gobernador de la Florida, July 8, 1704, AGI, *Santo Domingo*, L. 856. Solana a Andrés de Arriola, April 26, 1704, AGI, *México*, L. 618. Consulta de la Junta de Guerra, July 18, 1704, AGI, *Santo Domingo*, L. 852. Gobernador de la Florida al rey, March 29, 1706, AGI, *Santo Domingo*, L. 840. Carta de Monsiur Bienebille, Dec. 11, 1702, AGI, *México*, L. 618.

certain the French had gathered in their communications with the interior natives.[8] Boisbriant was prompt in responding to the request. On May 23, the aide-major of Mobile briefed the Pensacola governor:

> Having been questioned about the English forces in this land, I wish to give you information which I have acquired from these natives, especially those from the Chicacha who have always traded with this nation; they assure me that at the Alabama there are two Englishmen who provide this village with sufficient ammunition for the four hundred men who live in the nation; the Conchaque [Apalachicola] natives neighbor the Alabama, about six leagues away, and they have two Englishmen; the Chicacha are at four days' journey from the Conchaques and they have six Englishmen. Among the Englishmen there is one who indoctrinates the natives in their religion, and according to the opinion of our natives, there are two thousand men at the Chicacha and five hundred at the Conchaques.[9]

The note from Boisbriant to Arriola was indicative of the support the French were willing to lend insofar as the imparting of highly confidential and hard-earned intelligence was concerned. Ten days before, Bienville had himself written to Arriola:

> I send my sloop again to remit the twenty-five rifles which you had asked for, and to let you know that I received your two letters in which you show your gratitude about the small benefit I have been to Pensacola. I was not able before to convey how pleased I am to be of service to you, but I am persuaded by your incoming correspondence to do so now. Fulfilling the request I received from you eight days ago about the power which the natives and Englishmen have in this province, I am remitting to you a map which was made by the natives and according to a number of persons this map is very precise; at the same time I remit a barked sloop. If it is agreeable to you, I trust you will send the sloop to His Ex-

8. Carta de Andrés de Arriola, June 9, 1704, AGI, *México* L. 618. Duque de Alburquerque al Rey, May 30, 1704, AGI, *México*, L. 618.

9. Copia de Carta escrita a Andrés de Arriola por Boisbriant, May 23, 1704, AGI, *México*, L. 618.

cellency the Viceroy, an action which I will very much appreciate . . .[10]

When Bienville offered the sloop to Arriola to send to Alburquerque, he was unaware that Pensacola was shortly to be in better stead food-wise than was Mobile. Joseph de Robles y Morales had arrived at the fort on April 6 to plead with Bienville to send the *Espérance* to notify Alburquerque of the deprivation being suffered at Pensacola.[11] Six weeks later, however, before Bienville could come to a final decision, Andrés de Arriola (having left Veracruz on April 30) arrived at Fort San Carlos with an abundance of food supplies, enough in fact to pay back with ease the seventy-five sacks of flour due Mobile. Boisbriant was hastily dispatched to Santa María de Galve to bring back the repayment. News of Arriola's presence on the Gulf Coast, however, had arrived a little late: anchoring in Pensacola Bay on May 16, Arriola had immediately begun unloading his ships; the task completed, he sent word on to Mobile. In the meantime, Bienville, anxious about his dwindling food supply, had been taking steps to head off what appeared to be certain famine, still assuming that the next supply ship from France would not arrive until mid-autumn at the earliest. In this dilemma there seemed but one course of action to pursue: send Robinau de Bécancour back to Veracruz in the *Précieuse* to obtain the supplies that would sustain the colony until aid from France arrived.[12]

François-Alexandre Robinau de Bécancour had been for nearly three years Iberville's most able, most respected and most highly salaried associate in the defense and development of Louisiana.[13] Although his father René Robinau de Bécancour, Baron de Portneuf, and Chevalier of the Ordre de Saint-Michel, had been active in Quebec since 1645, François-Alexandre (now in his forty-first year) had been born in Paris (Saint-Nicolas-des-Champs) on

10. Copia de Carta escrita a Dn. Andrés de Arriola por Sn. de Buenvilla, May 13, 1704, AGI, *México*, L. 618.

11. *Journal Historique*, pp. 82–83. Bienville to min., Sept. 6, 1704, *loc. cit.*, f. 463. Carta de Andrés de Arriola, June 9, 1704, AGI, *México*, L. 618.

12. Testimonios de Cartas escritas al Señor el duque de Alburquerque, año de 1704, AGI, *México*, L. 618. Bienville to min., Sept. 6, 1704, *loc. cit.*, f. 463–64. Carta de Andrés de Arriola, June 9, 1704, *loc. cit.*, L. 618. *Journal Historique*, p. 82–85. AC, F1A, 10, f. 290v.

13. Journal d'Iberville, Dec. 15, 1701–April 27, 1702, AM, B4, 23, f. 339–41. AJQ, Succession d'Iberville, Greffe de Chambalon, Nov. 8, 1707. AC, F1A, 10, f. 290v.

February 13, 1664 during one of the family's numerous sojourns in France. His grandfather, Pierre Robinau, secretary in the king's privy chamber, had once been presented to Louis XIV as a candidate for the position of governor of New France.[14]

One of Bécancour's brothers, Joseph Robinau de Villebon, had served as governor of Acadia and another brother, Daniel Robinau de Neuvillette, a naval officer, had been killed during his ship's combat with an English brigantine out of Boston. His family connections included the clans of Leneuf de La Poterie, Legardeur and Ailleboust Des Muceaux, associations which added to his influence with the class-conscious Le Moynes. Nevertheless, the Robinau family fortunes had suffered immeasurably in recent years due to the deaths of Bécancour's father and his two aforementioned brothers, all between the years 1699–1702.[15]

Bécancour, himself, after coming to Quebec with his father on one of his return trips from Paris, had been reared by his family at the manor house of Portneuf, from where he enviously watched his older brothers enter into the service of France. After beginning his own career as a *garde-marine* in Canada, Bécancour continued his service at the port of Rochefort, eventually attaining the rank of *ensigne de vaisseau*, after which Iberville convinced him to sail to Louisiana to replace François Guyon, late master of the traversier *Voyageur*.[16]

While the colony's first voyage to Veracruz had been made in the *Précieuse* by Dugué de Sainte-Thérèse in early 1702 (during which time Bécancour had been helping transport the colony's supplies from Biloxi, Pensacola and Massacre Island to the Mobile River), Bécancour had commanded every mission since then, not

14. *DGFC, I*, pp. 381, 523. AJM, Greffe de Basset, July 7, 1671. AJQ, Greffe de Genaple, April 4, 1699. ASQ, Documents Faribault, 112, 122. ASQ, Polygraphie, III, 141. Godbout, "Les Robinau de Bécancour," *Mémoires* (SGCF), Vol. IV (1951), pp. 158–62. BN, FF, NA, f. 783–85.

15. *DGFC, I*, pp. 152–53, 369–70, 381. AJQ, Greffe de Genaple, Oct. 23, 1693. ASQ, Documents Faribault, 57, 125. ASQ, Polygraphie, IV, 8. *JR, VIII*, p. 220; *XVIII*, p. 90; *LXXIII*, p. 79. AC, D2C, 221, f. 36. AC, F3, 4, f. 493–94.

16. AJM, Greffe de Basset, July 7, 1671. Bécancour, having been born in Paris, is missing from the *DGFC* (I, p. 523) and (as well as his family) from the Recensement de 1666. *Cf.* Aveu et dénombremont de Messire René Robineau, seigneur de Bécancour, grand voyer de la Nouvelle-France, pour le fief et Seigneurie de Portneuf, Sept. 3, 1677, APQ *Rapport, 1925–26*, pp. 340–42.

always with complete success.[17] Soon after Sainte-Thérèse's return, Iberville had sent Bécancour on to the Mexican port in the *Espérance*. Back in France, Iberville complained to Pontchartrain:

> I have received a letter from M. de Bécancour from Veracruz, dated the sixteenth of last June, brought by M. de Surgères, which informs me he had arrived at Veracruz. As I had the honor of reporting to you, I gave him orders to go there in search of provisions for the garrison of Pensacola and that of the fort of Mobile; I directed him to buy from twenty to thirty ewes there, to stock the settlement at Mobile. He [Bécancour] informs me that they told him this would not be allowed, but he could have as many males as he wishes, and also oxen, but not cows. That shows clearly that they have no desire that we should be able to continue at Mobile.[18]

When Bécancour made his initial voyage to Veracruz, the Duque de Alburquerque, though already appointed, had not yet taken office as viceroy of New Spain. Spanish authorities in Mexico, under the interim *virrey*, Archbishop Juan Ortega y Montañés, were still smarting from France's presumption in building forts on the Mississippi and the Gulf Coast.[19] Now in the spring of 1704, policies had somewhat changed regarding relations between French and Spanish colonies. The war in Europe, the English attacks on St. Augustine and Apalache had for the moment brought French and Spanish possessions closer together, especially since Bienville had demonstrated his good faith in aiding Pensacola and the more eastern Spanish outposts in times of need. Moreover, Alburquerque himself displayed a certain proclivity for things French. Unlike his predecessor, the stale and stuffy *arzobispo*, the new viceroy relished the pomp and delicate artistry that characterized the court of Louis XIV. His inherent fondness for Gallic style was not diluted by the grand manner in which he and his entourage were escorted from Saint-Domingue (via Havana)

17. AC, F1A, 10, f. 290v. La Salle to min., May 20, 1703, *loc. cit.*, f. 387–89. AC, F1A, 11, f. 218–18v, 224v–25, 228. Señor el Beccancourt al virrey, Jan. 21, 1703, AGI, *México*, L. 618.

18. Iberville to min. [1702], AC, C13A, 1, f. 381–82.

19. *Ibid.* AC, F1A, 10, f. 282v. Arriola to Iberville, March 23, 1700, AC, C13A, 1, f. 243–46. Min. to Comte de Marcin, March 15, 1702, AM, B2, 160, f. 536–36v. Min. to Marquis de Blécourt, June 1, 1701, AM, B2, 154, f. 552–53. BN, FF, 9097, f. 42–43. Carta de Francisco Martínez, Oct. 22, 1702, AGI, *México*, L. 618.

to Veracruz in 1702 by the celebrated French buccaneer Jean-Baptiste Ducasse.[20]

The change in Spanish sentiment was further indicated in Bienville's report to Pontchartrain in September of that year:

> . . . four months ago the governor of Pensacola sent to request me to dispatch a small vessel to Veracruz to inform the viceroy of the distress that he and the Apalache country were in at that time due to English aggression. I was pleased to have this excuse to send our small vessel [the traversier] since I was on the verge of sending it out anyway to hunt provisions for us since we were in low supply because of having to lend Pensacola so much. I did myself the honor of writing to the viceroy of New Spain to ask him to send me on the return voyage of this small vessel supplies of flour for five months and for three months of pork and vegetables . . .[21]

So it was with higher expectations that Bécancour in the spring of 1704 prepared to make his fourth voyage to Veracruz. There were two traversiers operating on the Gulf Coast in 1704: the *Espérance*, generally commanded by Bécancour, and the *Précieuse*, alternately captained by Ignace La Valle, a former coastal pilot who had been elevated in 1703 to succeed Charles Levasseur's brother, Jean-François (who had commanded her from 1698–1701), and Pierre Cheviteau of La Rochelle who had succeeded François Guyon.[22] To man the two traversiers Bienville maintained a staff of some fifteen *matelots* and crewmen. Over half of these, François Mathé, Raymond Trias, *dit* Beldent of Bordeaux and Jean Roy of La Rochelle among others, boarded the *Précieuse* on May 26 and the next morning Bécancour, the assigned commander, weighed anchor and departed Massacre Island in a southwesterly direction.[23]

20. El virrey al rey, April 20, 1703, AGI, *México*, L. 618. Auto del virrey, Oct. 29, 1703, AGN, *Historia*, 394. Diego de Florencia al gobernador de la Florida, Jan. 25, 1703, AGI, *Santo Domingo*, L. 858. Junta de Guerra de Indias, May 26, 1705, AGI, *México*, L. 618. Arriola al virrey, Sept. 20, 1704, AGI, *México*, L. 618. Real cédula, May 8, 1702, AGN, *Historia*, 298.

21. Bienville to min., Sept. 6, 1704, AC, C13A, 1, f. 463.

22. Role de la garnison, Aug. 25, 1699, AC, C13A, 1, f. 211–12. François Guyon, master of an earlier traversier, the *Voyageur*, apparently died about 1701. AJM, Greffe de Laferté, Jan. 19, 1702. AC, F1A, 10, f. 282–82v; 11, f. 69v.

23. *Journal Historique*, pp. 82–83. AC, F1A, 11, f. 218–19v. Bienville to min., Sept. 6, 1704, *loc. cit.*, f. 463.

The favorable gulf breezes pushed the *Précieuse* along in unusually good time. The late spring was generally an auspicious time to sail; the season of storms was not yet upon the gulf and if the winds were not exceptionally strong, at least they were not as erratic as they might have been during the winter or during the hurricane months of August and September. From Massacre Island to Veracruz was a distance of some eight hundred miles, a typical voyage requiring at least two weeks.[24]

By the third day of June, the *Précieuse*, carrying only some ten or eleven crewmen and a small cargo of articles belonging to a few of the officers and private settlers of Mobile (such as Charles Rochon, Jacques Chauvin, Baudreau de Graveline and Rivard de La Vigne) which they hoped to sell unobtrusively to the inhabitants of Veracruz, was passing to the west of the port of Tampico. By the next day she was approaching Antigua Veracruz (or Veracruz Vieja) near the harbor where Fernando Cortés had landed his warriors nearly two hundred years before. And the following afternoon Bécancour was slowly guiding his ship across the Bahía de Vergara and through the channel between the large marsh bank just north of the town and the island fortress of San Juan de Ulúa just out from the walled city. Bécancour dropped anchor on the fifth of June and the next morning he and his men debarked from the *Précieuse* and went into town.[25]

The port of Nueva Veracruz was actually over a hundred years old in 1704. Founded in 1600, it had been thoroughly sacked by pirates twenty years before Bécancour first arrived, an act which shortly thereafter persuaded Spanish authorities to augment de-

24. Andrés de Arriola's recent voyage from Veracruz to Pensacola required sixteen days. Carta de Andrés de Arriola, Aug. 9, 1704, AGI, *México*, L. 618. The *Baron de La Fauche* sailed from Pensacola on Aug. 2, 1713 and arrived at Veracruz on Aug. 23, while Bazares in 1558 required 11 days to sail from Antigua Veracruz to Mobile Bay. *Cf.* Duclos to min., Oct., 1713, AC, C13A, 3, f. 149–95. La Jonquière et Dirigoin à Crozat, Oct., 1713, AC, C13A, 3, f. 351–61. El virrey al oficiales de Veracruz, Aug. 28, 1713, AGI, *México*, L. 632. Andrés de Arriola, however, required 28 days to reach Pensacola from Veracruz in the fall of 1698. Arriola al rey, Dec. 1, 1698, AGI, *México*, L. 618.

25. Abrégé de témoignage, Feb., 1708, AC, C13A, 2, f. 295–96. AC, F1A, 10, f. 29; 11, 218 ff. Veracruz, 1715. In Ottens, *Atlas sive geographia compendiosa* . . . Vol. II, 401. Plan de la rade et ville de la Vèra-Cruz, *ca.* 1764; La Vera-Cruz ville du Mexique, *ca.* 1764. In Bellin, *Le Petit Atlas Maritime*, 261–62. La Salle to min., May 20, 1703, *loc. cit.*, 387 ff. Dartaguiette to min., May 12, 1712, AC, C13A, 2, f. 803.

fenses and improve the fortress of San Juan de Ulúa.[26] Surrounding the now rebuilt town was a thick, irregularly shaped wall with a number of bastions at strategic points; outside the walls to the south stood the Capilla del Santo Cristo, enclosed by a large cemetery. Though Veracruz was the principal western terminus of the trade between New Spain and the mother country, the population of the city was only some two to three thousand persons, many of whom were Negroes and mulattoes.[27]

Bécancour lost no time in making his way to the administrative headquarters to make arrangements for receiving the needed supplies. After paying his respects to the *castillano* of San Juan de Ulúa, Juan Fernández de Velasco, and Veracruz Governor Francisco Manzo y Zúñiga,[28] Bécancour laid down his request to the royal port officials in the form of a letter from Bienville to the viceroy, written three weeks prior:

> I have dispatched a notification to Veracruz, as the governor of Pensacola asked me to do, to inform Your Excellency about the poverty in which he and the inhabitants of Apalache find themselves. I have given him all aid as regards maintenance and merchandise that I could afford, including corn for the subsistence of his garrison. At present, however, I find myself in the same need as Pensacola, and seeing that the assistance I am expecting from Europe is delayed, I beg that Your Excellency may be pleased to send, according to the enclosed list, provisions for five months . . .[29]

The enclosed list had been drawn up on May 19 by Nicolas de La Salle. Entitled "Report of the necessary supply of provisions to maintain one hundred and thirty men . . ." it included 150 barrels of flour, 24 quintals of bacon, 57 quintals of vegetables and 15 quintals of salt.[30] On being presented Bienville's letter and the list

26. The Austrian engineer, Jakob Franck, who had designed Fort San Carlos de Austria in 1698, had some years before planned the improvement of San Juan de Ulúa. Arriola al rey, Dec. 1, 1698, AGI, *México*, L. 618. Franck al Sierra Alta, Feb. 19, 1699, AGI, *México*, L. 618. Plan de Vera-Cruz, port du Mexique [*incl.* Isle de St. Jean d'Ulúa] *ca.* 1740. In Ottens, *Atlas sive geographia compendiosa* . . . Vol. I, 261.

27. Plan de la Veracruz, 1715; a map of the West Indies, 1715. In Moll, [Atlas], pls. 46, 48.

28. Junta de 25 de enero de 1703, AGI, *México*, L. 618.

29. Bienville [to Alburquerque], May 18, 1704, AGI, *México*, L. 618.

30. Memoria de los abastecimientos necessarios . . . May 19, 1704, AGI, *México*, L. 618.

of needs, the Veracruz officials hesitated. The requested cargo, though not exorbitant, represented a substantial amount of supplies. How were the French going to pay for such merchandise? On being informed by Bécancour that the French had no specie on hand, that they expected to receive the necessary supplies purely on the basis that they had lent Pensacola and Apalache similar amounts only two months before, the officials showed little sympathy to the proposal. As merchants, they were not accustomed to dealing with colonial outposts except on a cash basis. Besides, where was the evidence that the French had actually handed over such merchandise to Pensacola? [31]

Bienville, La Salle and Bécancour had, of course, anticipated the demand for proof. Bécancour promptly presented a letter from Pensacola's commissary, Joseph Félix Franco, written six weeks before, which demonstrated conclusively how the French had come to that *presidio's* relief:

> In complaisance to my obligation, I must inform Your Excellency how from the fourth day of March, we have been without provisions, having been given a ration of only a pound of biscuit following the order of the sergeant-major, from the first of February to the aforementioned day . . . at which time we were aided by the governor of the fort of Mobile with six thousand and seventy-six pounds of flour . . .[32]

Receipt of the Pensacola commissary's testimonial was not sufficient to convince the officials at Veracruz to follow through with Bécancour's request. The officials, not personally sympathetic to the French, could never have issued the merchandise on their own authority anyway, at least not on the terms Bécancour had proposed. Approval of large exchanges with a foreign power based exclusively on prior loans must come from the central government which alone could guarantee payment. Thus, the local officials referred the matter to the viceroy in Mexico City. The appropriate

31. Consulta de la Junta de Guerra, May 26, 1705, AGI, *México,* L. 618. Veracruz merchants and officials were generally reluctant to accept any payment except cash, prices being unusually high while the galleons were in port. Bienville to min., Feb. 25, 1708, AC, C13A, 2, f. 647–49. M. d'Artaguiette au vice-roi de la Nouvelle-Espagne, 23 fév., 1711, AC, C13A, 2, f. 647–49. Dartaguiette to min., June 20, 1711, AC, C13A, 2, f. 641–43. Bienville to min., June 20, 1711, AC, C13B, 1, No. 11, f. 1–3v. Vice-roi Linares à M. de Bienville, 27 mars, 1711, AC, C13B, 1, No. 10, f. 1–1v.

32. Carta de Joseph Félix Franco, May 6, 1704, AGI, *México,* L. 618.

letters and documents were sent on to Alburquerque and the General Council, and Bécancour was notified he would have to await their decision.[33]

By this time nearly a week had gone by since Bécancour and his men had disembarked from the *Précieuse* on June 6. Two of Bécancour's sailors, Raymond Trias, *dit* Beldent and François Mathé, had not been seen since that time, nor were several other crewmen who had apparently lost themselves in the town.[34] The city of Veracruz, while squalid and sultry, was, after all, a bustling port, with all its attendant opportunities for amusement and distraction. If it could not be compared to the more elegant French ports of Bordeaux or La Rochelle, it still represented more civilization than most of Bécancour's pleasure-starved crewman had seen in several years, certainly more than they had enjoyed on Louisiana's barren coast. There were things to do: there was music and dancing in the taverns; there were women in the brothels, a fact that also no doubt diverted Bécancour's attention during some of the long, sweltering nights.

By the end of the third week in June, however, Bécancour was becoming increasingly edgy. It was not that the French officer had expected action on his petition any sooner; yet he could not fail to feel a certain degree of helplessness as he was forced to while away the days. On June 20, he took up his pen and drafted a personal note to Alburquerque:

> The garrison of Mobile presently finds itself without provisions or specie which has forced me to come to this port to plead to Your Excellency that he order that I be forwarded, on His Christian Majesty's account, the credit that I will need to obtain the necessary supplies. This will be a service that I hope Your Excellency will do for the King, my Lord, and it will surely be fully acknowledged . . . I am waiting for Your Excellency's orders so that I can leave this port [as soon as possible] . . .[35]

33. Alburquerque al rey, Sept. 22, 1704, AGI, *Santo Domingo,* L. 377. El Rey al virrey, Dec. 10, 1704, AGN, *Historia,* 298. Testimonios de cartas escritas al Señor Duque de Alburquerque, año de 1704, AGI, *México,* L. 618. El Rey a Señor Duque de Alburquerque, Aug. 12, 1705, AGN, *Historia,* 298.

34. AC, F1A, 11, f. 218–19v, 224v–25, 228.

35. Carta de S. de Becancourt, June 20, 1704, AGI, *México,* L. 618.

The note was forwarded immediately to Alburquerque. When the viceroy received it (on June 24), he ordered one of his secretaries, Juan de Estacasolo y Otalora, to make translations of all the French letters and documents and to turn them over to his *fiscal* and most trusted advisor, Joseph Antonio de Espinosa. Espinosa was to study the requests and to make recommendations to the General Council which Alburquerque ordered to convene the following afternoon (Wednesday, June 25) at four o'clock.[36]

By the time the council convened the next day, Espinosa had studied the French request and had drafted a recommendation to Alburquerque which he hoped the council would approve: "The fiscal feels that the merchandise should be given them, not only because the French garrison asks for it . . . nor merely as a reward for the previous assistance given to Pensacola, but because the French are in dire need of provisions; because the crowns of Spain and France are united in spirit and His Majesty orders that there not be any differences between them." [37]

There were questions raised by members of the council, particularly by Joseph de Luna and Miguel Calderón de la Barcas, but the chief issues related primarily to the ways and means by which the goods would be transferred (Would a separate account be set up? Would the Treasury hand over specie to be used in purchasing from the Royal Estates?), especially to the most prompt method by which the request could be fulfilled. As to whether or not consent would be granted there was no question whatever. Approval was unanimous, Espinosa's proposal being signed by all seven members of the council.[38] After the council prepared a dispatch for the viceroy to sign and forward to the officials at Veracruz ("ordering those officers to provide all the merchandise from the Royal Estates, and it may be even more prompt to provide goods from the boxes of cargo and deliver these . . ."), the meeting was concluded.[39] Alburquerque's order was sent on to Veracruz the next day.

By the twenty-ninth of June, the Veracruz officials had com-

36. Testimonios de cartas escritas al Señor Duque de Alburquerque, año de 1704, AGI, *México*, L. 618. El virrey al rey, Sept. 22, 1704, AGI, *Santo Domingo*, L. 377.

37. Memoria de Joseph de Espinosa, June 25, 1704, AGI, *México*, L. 618.

38. Junta general, June 25, 1704, AGI, *México*, L. 618. Junta de Guerra de Indias, May 26, 1705, AGI, *México*, L. 618.

39. *Ibid.* The plan at this time was to deduct the expenses of the shipment from the allowance for Pensacola. Alburquerque al rey, Sept. 22, 1704, AGI, *Santo Domingo*, L. 377. El Rey a Señor Duque de Alburquerque, Aug. 12, 1705, AGN, *Historia*, 298.

menced loading the goods onto the *Précieuse*. Bécancour, disgruntled at the poor quality of some of the foodstuffs, was further annoyed by the fact that crewmen Trias and Mathé had apparently deserted.[40] He would probably have been even more chagrined had he been able to give such matters their due concern; but by late June the French captain had come down with a debilitating fever which even after a short while had already driven him to bed.[41]

It was not astonishing that Bécancour had been taken ill in Veracruz; there was little to commend the port city for human habitation. Situated in a dreary low-lying area segmented by small, sluggish creeks, swamps and stagnant pools, the swarms of gnats and mosquitoes created an atmosphere that was singularly unsalutary. The frequent downpours of the long rainy season left a dank humidity that was almost suffocating, in which every sort of pest and noxious insect seemed to proliferate.

Bécancour's condition did not seem to improve as the first day of July passed. The local inhabitants and officials were certain he was taken with what they called the *vómito negro*. The loading of the *Précieuse* was temporarily discontinued. Bécancour, having earlier spotted some of the faulty flour, ordered the cessation until he recovered so as to be in a position to examine the goods more thoroughly. His crew stood patiently by, waiting for him to regain his health. The fevered captain was not to recover, however. On the second and third of July, his condition grew steadily worse; and the next day, Friday, July 4, 1704, Bécancour succumbed at the local hospital.[42]

The death of Robinau de Bécancour left the expedition thoroughly disorganized. There was no high ranking officer left to take command of the *Précieuse*; the loading had only been partially concluded. Moreover, the desertions of Mathé and Trias left the vessel's crew (which even before had been inadequate) critically

40. AC, F1A, 11, f. 218–19v, 224v–25. The Spanish also complained of the poor quality of the flour. Carta del rey al gobernador de la Florida, May 22, 1702, AGI, *Santo Domingo*, L. 836.

41. AC, F1A, 11, f. 219–19v, 232v. Bienville to min., Sept. 6, 1704, AC, C13A, 1, f. 463–64. *Journal Historique*, pp. 82–85. Consulta de la Junta de Guerra, May 26, 1705, AGI, *México*, L. 618.

42. Bienville to min., Sept. 6, 1704, AC, C13A, 1, f. 463–64. Autos fechos sobre la providencia dadas sobre la preocupación y fortificación de Santa María de Galve, Año de 1703, AGI, *México*, L. 618. AC, F1A, 11, f. 218–18v, 224v, 228, 232. Consulta de la Junta de Guerra, May 26, 1705, AGI, *México*, L. 618. *Journal Historique*, pp. 84–85.

shorthanded. Fortunately, however, a French transport from Cap-français was presently in port. The captain of the French vessel graciously lent the *Précieuse* two of his crewmen—François L'Espére and Marcial Monerie—to replace the two deserters, while François Léon, who had served Bécancour as chief pilot, succeeded to the *Précieuse's* command.[43]

As far as the transactions with the port authorities were concerned, the man to whom the crewmen looked for leadership was Jacques Allemand, a barely literate steward, a strong Bienvillist (at this point in his career) and a man whom the commandant had sent along to act as special scrivener for the traversier. After Bécancour was buried (probably in the large cemetery near the Capilla del Santo Cristo outside the walls of Veracruz), Allemand ordered the lading resumed. The loading proceeded slowly, however, Allemand individually examining each barrel of flour as well as each of the other containers of foodstuffs as they were placed aboard. Six days later, after twenty-five hundred and one *piastres* and four *reales* had been transferred from the royal treasury to purchase the supplies, the packing and loading were completed. On July 11, Allemand signed the receipt. At last the *Précieuse* appeared ready to return to Mobile.[44]

The vessel, however, was not quite prepared to weigh anchor. Bereft of a commander and carrying new crewmen, it was not until after the third week in July that the *Précieuse* finally set sail, just after Andrés de Arriola's ships had returned to the Veracruz harbor. Even then the voyage back to Mobile was to be longer than usual. After ten days at sea, the demoralized crew, struggling in a northeasterly direction against highly unfavorable winds, was far off course, and still well out into the Gulf of Mexico. Dismayed by their lack of progress, the crewmen were not more heartened by the realization they were bringing home news of the death of the colony's most able sea captain.[45]

43. Consulta de la Junta de Guerra, May 26, 1705, AGI, *México*, L. 618. AC, F1A, 11, f. 232v.

44. Extrait du mémoire des officiers royaux de la Veracrux des avances faites à la colonie de la Louisiane . . . depuis le 11 juillet 1704 jusques au 13 aoust 1714, AC, C13A, 3, f. 675–78. AC, F1A, 11, f. 232–32v. *Journal Historique*, pp. 82–85. The burial records for Veracruz are extant only from 1742.

45. Extrait du mémoire . . . , AC, C13A, 3, f. 675–77. Alburquerque al rey, Sept. 20, 1704, AGI, *Santo Domingo*, L. 377. It was only after Arriola returned to Veracruz on July 11 that the officials in Mexico City found that Pensacola had already repaid the French. Carta de Andrés de Arriola, Aug. 9, 1704, AGI, *México*, L. 618.

Meanwhile, Bienville, back at the fort, was growing increasingly impatient waiting for the return of the *Précieuse*. Even with Arriola's repayment of flour there was a scarcity of foodstuffs (notably bacon, vegetables and salt) in the warehouse; the Canadians who had volunteered to go to the several Indian villages to subsist were still with the Natchez, the Bayougoula and the Biloxi.[46]

As if the shortage of food were not enough to trouble him, Bienville shortly began to receive ominous reports of Indian activity in the interior. Two natives from Pensacola brought a letter from Joseph de Guzmán, acting governor of Fort San Carlos, reporting that a coalition of natives allied to the English had attacked several of the *doctrinas* in Apalache, killing twenty-eight of the forces that Guzmán and Andrés de Arriola had sent there by launch. Guzmán was pleading with Bienville for immediate assistance.[47]

Sometime later, two Choctaw Indians arrived at the fort reporting that four Carolinians had come to the Chickasaw nation with eight packhorses loaded with merchandise to try to offset the advantage the French had gained in aiding the Chickasaw two years before. This was indeed unbidden news; for, if true, it indicated that the English intended to challenge the French every inch of the way for the favor of the Chickasaw. Bienville, though plainly disconcerted, was somewhat skeptical of the Choctaw report. He nevertheless dispatched a party of the Little Tomeh to the Chickasaw villages to learn what the truth was. "I very much doubt that the Chickasaw will receive the English," he later confided to Pontchartrain, "since they have always seemed to me to be very anxious to maintain friendship with the French." The report, however, increased the commandant's disdain for Albert Davion. A single missioner in the Chickasaw village might serve to offset any advances that the English might make to that nation; yet Davion, while others were making unusual sacrifices for the colony, remained safe and inactive at Mobile, jeopardizing, Bienville felt, the entire colonial enterprise.[48]

In mid-July of 1704, Bienville could only wait and hope: Bécancour would soon be mooring at Massacre Island with the

46. Pénigault, *Relation, loc. cit.*, f. 116–23.

47. *Journal Historique*, pp. 83–85. Manuel Solana al gobernador de la Florida, July 8, 1704, AGI, *Santo Domingo*, L. 856. Joseph de Guzmán al virrey, Aug. 22, 1704, AGI, *Santo Domingo*, L. 857. Alburquerque al rey, Sept. 20, 1704, AGI, *Santo Domingo*, L. 377.

48. Bienville to min., Sept. 6, 1704, AC, C13A, 1, f. 460. *Journal Historique*, pp. 84–85.

provisions from Veracruz that would partially relieve the colony's sufferings; and, after that, the supply ship from France would arrive in the fall with an ample supply of women, missionaries and soldiers. Perhaps the inhabitants could hold out until then; possibly the vessel from France would arrive sooner than expected.

X

The Voyage of the *Pélican*

THE *Pélican* moved easily over the still calm North Atlantic waters, her fifty-six guns basking in the warm sunlight, the western skies, however, beginning to darken over the far horizon. It was the first week of June, 1704; the ship's first port-of-call, Cap-français on the northwestern coast of the island of Saint-Domingue (now Haïti's Cap-Haïtien), lay some one hundred and fifty miles in the distance.[1]

It had been, for most, a fairly pleasant if uneventful voyage (forgetting its inauspicious beginnings). The seas had been unusually pacific, fortunate, in view of the fact that the *Pélican* had been shipping a good deal of water and was "exorbitantly overloaded" which caused a number of crewmen to be without a place to sleep. True, there had been some mild cases of seasickness. Alexandre Huvé had "paid his tribute to the ocean" on several occasions and the young girls, experiencing their first voyage at sea, were equally beset with chronic cases of nausea. But, for the most part, the voyage had thus far been as favorable as could be expected. While at least one man of the crew had perished (and was quickly buried at sea), the *Pélican*, according to La Vente, was proving to be "the most easy-riding ship in the world."[2]

One of the men who helped to make the long voyage more endurable was the profane, hale-and-hearty explorer-trader Pierre-Charles Le Sueur. A skilled raconteur, full of energy and optimism, Le Sueur had kept most of the officers and crewmen (if not Huvé,

1. Joseph de Guzmán al virrey, Aug. 22, 1704, AGI, *Santo Domingo*, L. 857. U.S. Navy Hydrographic Map 5244. (North Atlantic Ocean—Southern Sheet). 1st Ed. August, 1941. The *Pélican*, a "moitié-en-guerre," was described by Collinet as having "60 canons holendois." BN, FF, 22813, f. 65.

2. La Vente [to SME Dirs.], Sept. 20, 1704, ASQ, Lettres, R 77. La Vente [to Tremblay], Sept. 25, 1704, ASQ, Lettres, R 76.

La Vente and the several Calvinists aboard) in higher spirits by recounting his varied and earthy experiences among the natives of upper and lower Louisiana. He was exuberant, too, in pointing out commercial opportunities for Louisiana's development. Le Sueur had good reason to promote the colony: now in his forty-eighth year, a native of Artois in France, he had been early and thoroughly involved in the fur trade on the upper Mississippi where his knowledge of the Sioux and Chippewa Indians had made him an important ally and business associate of Canadian Governor Buade de Frontenac.[3] Eager to advance the trade in furs, Le Sueur had made two trips to France in the last decade of the seventeenth century in an attempt to gain commercial privileges under the pretext of exploiting mines for the king. He was finally successful in forming a "Compagnie des Sioux" in 1699 by involving farmer-general Rémy-François L'Huillier as well as his close friend, Le Moyne d'Iberville. Recruiting a group of artisans at La Rochelle in September of 1699 (which included Jean Bon and André-Joseph Pénigault, current inhabitants at Mobile), Le Sueur ascended the Mississippi in 1700 where he built Fort L'Huillier on the Rivière Bleue (now Blue Earth River near St. Paul, Minnesota). Leaving a detachment at the new fort under the Canadian officer Daraque, Le Sueur returned to Mobile Bay in the late winter of 1702 (with a load of minerals and furs) in time to make the return voyage to France with Iberville in June.[4]

Back in France, Le Sueur came under heavy criticism for his flagrant disregard of the prohibition on the beaver trade. His minerals, moreover, failed to provoke official excitement. Although Pontchartrain denounced his new commercial proposals, Iberville, interested in making the most of Le Sueur's services in exploiting the Mississippi trade (for their own mutual advantage as well as

3. Bergier [to Laval], March 13, 1702, ASQ, Lettres, R 50. Gravier to Lamberville, March 25, 1702, *JR, LXVI*, pp. 32–34. Marest to Lamberville, Nov. 26, 1702, *JR, LXVI*, pp. 38–40. Marest à l'évêque de Québec, Nov. 18, 1702, ASQ, Fonds Verreau, 13, 31. Le Sueur was born ca. 1657 near Notre-Dame de Heudin in Pas-de-Calais, the son of Victor Le Sueur and Anne Honneur. *DGFC, I*, p. 389.

4. Journal de Le Sueur, BN, FF, NA, 21395. Min. to Iberville, Aug. 26, 1699, AC, B 20, f. 268–69. Marest à l'évêque de Québec, *loc. cit.*, *pièce* 31. Le Sueur had married Iberville's first cousin, Marguerite Messier, in 1690, five days after her fourteenth birthday. *DGFC, I*, p. 389, 427. ACM, Rivière et Soullard, 1699–1700, f. 72 *bis*. Journal de Le Sueur, 1702, AM, 2 JJ 56, 9. Mémoires de Le Sueur, BN, FF, NA, 9296, 47.

for Louisiana's development), interceded in his behalf. As a result of Iberville's intervention, the two Canadians were able to win considerable concessions and privileges from the court. Le Sueur was to return to Mobile on the *Loire* in 1703 to act as judicial officer of the new colony (at a moderate salary). Now that Mobile seemed more likely to become a flourishing establishment it was not difficult to convince the ministry that an official was needed to adjudicate the numerous civil disputes that were certain to arise. Moreover, Le Sueur was to be granted privileges to recruit men for exploratory purposes—a richly deserved prerogative, considering the contributions that Le Sueur had already made (as witnessed by the reports and narratives he turned over to Guillaume Delisle) toward a fuller understanding of the king's Mississippi geography. Le Sueur would, moreover, move his wife and large family (four young daughters and a son) from Canada to Louisiana to help further populate the colony.[5]

Due to illness and the failure to conclude commercial agreements, Le Sueur had been unable to embark on the *Loire* in 1703. He had, however, reached Rochefort in time to join the passengers of the *Pélican*, even as his wife, Marguerite Messier, was making arrangements to gain permission from Governor Rigaud de Vaudreuil to leave Montreal. Now in early June, as the *Pélican* neared the port of Cap-français, Le Sueur could look forward to a position of high influence in the new colony, surrounded by his wife and children and a coterie of effectual relatives and friends.[6]

Le Sueur was no doubt the most entertaining, the most lionized passenger aboard ship. Even the young Parisian girls took every small advantage of engaging him in conversation. For who better than Le Sueur (excepting possibly the young Châteaugué) could give them a preview of their establishments, of their future situations? Had he not actually been present at Mobile Bay during the late winter and early spring of 1702 when Mobile was founded? Did he not already know the sizes and shapes of their waiting homes, the nature and appearance of their husbands-to-be? Perhaps he would tell them of Jean Bon, of François Trudeau and

5. Min. to Bégon, March 7, 1703, AM, B2, 167, f. 519v. Min. to Bégon, Feb. 27, 1703, AC, B 23, f. 189–90. Journal de Le Sueur, *loc. cit.*, 9. Carte de la Rivière de Missisipi, 1702 [by Delisle], BN, Cartes et Plans, 138, 3, 2. *DGFC, I*, p. 389.

6. Min. to Bégon, March 7, 1703, *loc. cit.*, f. 519v. Mémoire du Roy à MM. Vaudreuil et Beauharnois, June 14, 1704, AC, B 25, f. 101–01v.

René Boyer, with whom he lived and toiled in the wilds of Louisiana?[7]

If Le Sueur was a favorite with the officers and young girls, however, he was no object of adulation to pastor-to-be Roulleaux de La Vente. La Vente, usually at odds with civilian officials, showed little but disdain for the rough Canadian backwoodsman, not merely because of Le Sueur's former Jesuit associations, but because La Vente, proud and haughty, felt uncomfortable in the presence of a man who, at this point, seemed more authoritative than he. As the voyage progressed, La Vente, generally no model of amiability except to those who deferred to him, grew increasingly cranky. As the ship neared its first port-of-call, the clouds overhead loomed heavier and darker. A thunderstorm appeared imminent. Though La Vente felt well enough to make daily entries in his journal, to spend the long idle hours trying to convert a number of Calvinists aboard ("two of which we have already instructed and [who are now] desirous of embracing the Catholic religion which they had not [before] thought of professing"), the fever and chest inflammation that had plagued him since the embarkation were not improving, his leg beginning to pain him more.[8]

Then, too, there was the task of safeguarding the girls' virginity, a duty more vexing to La Vente the longer the voyage lasted. "I had always envisaged the responsibility of the young girls," La Vente wrote the seminary in Paris, "as a very onerous work, not only because it was contrary to my inclinations and dangerous to my health but even more so because it was a question of reconciling two very different things—to wit—on the one hand the will of God, and on the other, the affection and the esteem of the officers. Here I must render glory to God, confessing that on these occasions Providence gave us good favor well beyond our hopes. We succeeded in the first, and if we do not dare presume thus for the second, our consciences reproached us for many failings."[9]

7. Journal de Sauvole, Aug. 4, 1701, AC, C13A, 1, f. 318–19. From his days at Fort Maurepas and Fort La Boulaye Le Sueur knew many of the men who would become husbands of these girls. Although he was present at Massacre Island during the time Fort Louis was being constructed he had not seen the new establishment himself. Journal de Le Sueur, 1702, AM, 2 JJ 56, 9. *Journal Historique*, pp. 38–39. Journal d'Iberville, April 27, 1702, AM, B4, 23, f. 321–24.

8. La Vente [to Brisacier], June 25, 1704, ASQ, Lettres, R 74.

9. La Vente [to SME Dirs.], *loc. cit.*, R 77.

In point of fact, it was a difficult responsibility for La Vente to carry out. Sailors on the high seas could become accustomed to sexual deprivation far more easily when the means to satisfy their appetites were not so close at hand. The proximity of such "well-made girls" made it difficult indeed for the officers and men to keep their distances. La Vente blamed his poor health for his inability to more diligently perform his duty; but he also lashed out at nursing sisters Marie Grissot and Marie Linant, whom he claimed were not only "incapable of serving, but who . . . exhausted the greatest patience." [10]

Nevertheless, there was not as much mingling between officers and girls as might have been expected. Pontchartrain and Bégon had given strict orders to keep the girls in their private quarters and La Vente was thankful for "Monsieur Ducoudray, who has supported with his authority that which I could not do myself." [11]

By the seventh of June the *Pélican* was nearing Puerto Plata, a small but ancient Spanish port on the northeastern coast of Saint-Domingue, some one hundred and thirty miles from Cap-français. In the distance Ducoudray could see an armed bark moving menacingly toward him. As the *Pélican* followed the northern coastline of Saint-Domingue, the bark continued her course, Ducoudray observing with surprise that the vessel was Spanish. A battle alert was sounded; the crewmen scrambled to their positions. At the last moment the Spanish ship seemed desperate in trying to shift her course, finally hoisted full sail, and with a mighty effort avoided a direct collision. Ducoudray, puzzled, changed his course only slightly before continuing down the coastline, while the Spanish ship sprang a leak and struggled back to Puerto Plata where it eventually sank.[12]

10. *Ibid.*

11. *Ibid.* La Vente [to Brisacier], *loc. cit.*, R 74. Ducoudray, son of Hervé Guymont de Chaumont and Madelaine Le Normant, was, by marriage, related to the notable Bégon family. His sister Catherine had married the marine commissioner Michel Bégon de Montfermeil (1655–1728), sometimes confused with the Rochefort Intendant Michel Bégon (1638–1710). BN, FF, 22815, f. 100. Bézard, *Fonctionnaires maritimes et coloniaux* . . . , pp. 3–127. Min. to Bégon, Oct. 3, 1703, APR, 1 E 50, f. 48–49.

12. Auger to min., Sept. 17, 1704, AC, C9A, 7, No. 24. Only upon his arrival at Cap-français did Ducoudray discover that the Spanish bark had been commissioned by authorities in Saint-Domingue to prey on English privateers who were threatening French ships in the Caribbean. The Spanish captain observed too late (for his own ship's survival) that the *Pélican* was a French vessel. La Vente [to Brisacier], *loc. cit.*, R 74.

The next morning, the *Pélican* rounded Montecristi (Punta de la Granja), still thirty miles from Cap-français. A violent thunderstorm broke, the winds rocking the ship so violently that La Vente reported, "we almost perished." Though the *Pélican* was now quite near Cap-français (near enough to pull into port that very evening), the foul weather necessitated waiting in the outer waters most of the night, due to the excessive danger of the narrow passage into the roadstead.[13]

By dawn the storm had subsided; the seas, however, were still choppy. Slowly Ducoudray moved the *Pélican* through the close passage between Fort La Pointe on the channel's western shore and the two large sandbanks to the east. The harbor was filled with some fifteen vessels when the *Pélican* pulled in on the morning of June the tenth. As the surrounding ships fired their salutes, Ducoudray anchored in twelve fathoms of water due east of the old Spanish fort and one mile northeast of the town. The long oceanic voyage of "52–53 days" was over. Ducoudray placed a light at the head of the *Pélican's* mizzenmast to signal some of the vessels' captains and a few of the local officials to ship while Ducoudray and his officers prepared to debark.[14]

Ashore, Ducoudray delivered to the authorities a letter for Governor Charles Auger from Pontchartrain (which had been written on Sept. 26, 1703) and an important order from the king relative to Cap-français' religious controversy, a directive about which La Vente apparently knew and had become quite curious as to its contents.[15]

If, however, the reaching of Cap-français was welcomed as a rest stop by Ducoudray and the male passengers and crewmen, there was no such rejoicing for the young girls and the two nursing sisters. They were to remain aboard ship, much to the consternation of some of the *Pélican's* officers. "One cannot imagine," La Vente later wrote, "more requests than were made in this place to put these girls ashore, but as M. Ducoudray did not wish to undertake it, and since . . . I knew that they [the men] wanted to take some of the girls and since it was against the in-

13. La Vente [to SME Dirs.], *loc. cit.*, R 77. U.S. Naval Oceanographic Map 848 (Hispaniola with Windward and Mona Passages), 20th Ed., Dec. 1, 1969.

14. Journal de Bertet de La Clüe, Cap-français, May 27, 1720, MCM, Manuscripts I, *n.p.* La Vente [to SME Dirs.], *loc. cit.*, R 77. Plan du Cap François, in Laval, *Voyage de la Louisiane*, p. 68.

15. Auger to min., Sept. 17, 1704, *loc. cit.*, No. 24.

tentions of the court which did not intend them for that place but rather for here [Fort Louis], I remained obdurate."[16]

Once ashore the officers and crewmen amused themselves at the local taverns, especially at those in the old Spanish quarter, trying to forget the girls left aboard. La Vente was aghast at the status of his Lord's missions in the town. "I shall not linger to tell you of the state of religion," he wrote Jacques-Charles de Brisacier, director of the Foreign Mission Seminary in Paris. "It would necessitate not only just a letter, but a complete revelation."[17] As the disturbed *curé* had discovered, the young missions in and around Cap-français were still shaking from a series of recent scandals: Father Hubert, a Carmelite, had viciously attacked a brother-in-Christ, doing violence to his person after an argument during which both had been heavily drinking; an apparently innocuous monk had recently raped an eleven-year-old Negress; a Benedictine priest, former procurer of the Couvent de Saint-Ouin in France, had emigrated to the cape under the alias of "Launcelot" after having signed a contract of marriage with a young girl at La Rochelle whom he brought with him (procuring a position as notary, he had lived with the unsuspecting damsel for three years before being discovered and deported, having in the meantime fathered two children by her); a priest named Labat, *curé* of Morin near Cap-français, was shot dead by a sentinel while trying to escape after having been arrested for fathering an illegitimate child, which he freely acknowledged.[18]

La Vente was understandably disconcerted by these manifestations of spiritual corrosion. Was this a preview of situations that would confront his own mission in Louisiana? Certainly the failings of his fellow laborers in Cap-français had disastrous results for the Capuchin effort in Saint-Domingue. In consequence, the order's authorities in Normandy were forced to abandon their field. Moreover, Father Paullin, the Carmelite superior with whom La Vente was to become intimately acquainted, had received the king's order (delivered him by Ducoudray) to immediately dispense with all property on the island belonging to the Carmelites and to embark on the *Pélican* with Ducoudray with whom he was

16. La Vente [to SME Dirs.], *loc. cit.*, R 77.

17. La Vente [to Brisacier], *loc. cit.*, R 74.

18. Mémoire des affaires des Capuchins du Cap-français, par Auger, gouverneur, Sept. 15, 1704, AC, C9A, 7, No. 22. This Labat was not, of course, the celebrated Jacobin Père Jean-Baptiste Labat (1663–1738). *Cf.* Labat, *Nouveau Voyage aux Isles de l'Amérique.*

to sail to Louisiana before making the return voyage to France. The *ordre du roi* precipitated a good deal of confusion, since Governor Auger, who was to supervise the sale, was presently at Léogane on the other side of the island, and the *Pélican* was scheduled to remain in port only a few days longer. Unless Auger returned quickly, Paullin would be forced either to abandon the Carmelite property without conducting its sale or to ignore the king's directive to embark on the *Pélican*.[19]

Apparently Paullin decided the king's order to sail was the more imperative. After seven days wait, Auger had still not returned. Ducoudray and his officers boarded the *Pélican* along with their Carmelite passenger and departed Cap-français the seventeenth day of June. Ducoudray had orders to call at the port of Havana on his way to Mobile; he was therefore compelled to take the route through the old Bahama Channel between the northern coastline of Cuba and the Bahama Islands rather than the southern route around Cabo San Antonio which Iberville had followed three years before. Ducoudray, however, had no experienced pilot to guide him through the treacherous channel. No one aboard, not even the veteran Le Sueur, was familiar with the ordered route.[20]

Leaving Cap-français, the *Pélican* headed in a west-northwesterly direction. Shortly thereafter, two armed vessels appeared on the horizon, moving toward the French ship. As they neared, Ducoudray gave another battle alert (the third such alert given since the departure from La Rochelle), seeing now that the ships were English. As the ships moved closer, however, Ducoudray could discern that although the vessels were each sporting forty cannon, they had but few men on board to man the guns. Furthermore, the English apparently judged from the size of the *Pélican* that she must be carrying "some 60–70 guns," an observation (though faulty) which caused the pursuing ships to retire before firing a shot.[21]

The crisis having passed, Ducoudray continued on his way

19. Mémoire des affaires . . . *loc. cit.* Auger reported to Pontchartrain that Paullin "has discarded all ambition for his order." The Carmelite mission was succeeded in 1704 by the Jesuits, headed by Père Girard.

20. La Vente [to Brisacier], *loc. cit.*, R 74.

21. *Ibid.* U.S. Oceanographic Map 848 (Hispaniola with Windward and Mona Passages), 20th Ed. Dec. 1, 1969. The *Pélican* was actually carrying fifty-six guns, as Sergeant-Major Joseph de Guzmán later reported to the Duque de Alburquerque. Guzmán al virrey, Aug. 22, 1704, AGI, *Santo Domingo*, L. 857.

toward Havana. After crossing the Windward Passage between Cuba and Hispaniola the *Pélican* stopped for a few days at Baracoa, an old Spanish port on the eastern tip of Cuba, from which La Vente penned a hasty note to Brisacier and where Ducoudray employed a Spanish pilot to guide him through the Bahama Channel. At Cap-français there had been rumors that the English had driven the French from Louisiana. At Baracoa these rumors were dispelled: according to the Spanish, the English were merely threatening St. Augustine again (after having been rebuffed two years before). Only if they captured St. Augustine would they be in a position to attack Mobile and Pensacola. To prevent this possibility Havana had recently dispatched over five hundred men to Florida. Mobile for the moment was safe, still in French hands.[22]

Leaving Baracoa during the last days of June, the *Pélican*, guided by her Spanish pilot, moved slowly through the old Bahama Channel, past Punta Santa Juana and Cayo de Lobos. Storm clouds were forming over the distant peaks of Santo Ladro in the fastnesses beyond the shoreline. By the third of July the *Pélican* was moving through the most perilous narrows of the old pass between Anguilla and the Isla del Buey. Overhead the dark clouds which seemingly had pursued the ship for several days, began finally to break, "the storms and thunderbolts as continual as they were extraordinary." Ducoudray pulled to the north, barely missing the small but treacherous Cayo del Americano. Rocking and tossing through the narrow channel, the young girls becoming increasingly nauseated, the *Pélican*, suffering "recurring dangers," rounded Boca del Padre, barely able to see her chief landmark, Punta de Ycacos, through the rain and the mist. The ship was in great distress at this point, perhaps in the greatest peril of her voyage. The seas were thrashing against her starboard side, the sails nearly tearing from the mast. For most of the night the distressed ship floundered in the jolting waters, barely holding her own.[23]

22. La Vente [to Brisacier], *loc. cit.*, R 74. El gobernador de la Florida al rey, March 30, 1704, AGI, *Santo Domingo*, L. 840. Claudio de Florencia al rey, June 9, 1707, AGI, *Santo Domingo*, L. 840.

23. La Vente [to SME Dirs.], *loc. cit.*, R 77. U.S. Coast and Geodetic Survey Map 1007 (Gulf of Mexico), 24th Ed., Nov. 8, 1969. Bahama's and Windward Passage, by John Seller, 1689, in *The English Pilot*, 1689–1789. A chart of the Gulf of Florida or New Bahama Channel . . . by Charles Roberts, 1794, in [West India Atlas], 1741–1807.

By mid-morning of the next day, however, the winds and waves began to subside. The Pan de Matanzas, a high peak and important landmark, was plainly visible in the distant south. Moving past the picturesque Iron Hills just back from the coastline, the ship began to approach her last port-of-call (before her final leg across the Gulf of Mexico), the sunlight dappling the still choppy waters between Cuba and the Florida Keys. On the afternoon of the seventh of July, Ducoudray moved past the splendid Castillo del Morro at the entrance of the harbor and anchored near the town in fifty feet of water.[24]

All aboard the *Pélican* were imbued with the magnificence of this old Spanish seaport. It was, even then, nearly two centuries old, its channel showing depths of over forty feet well into the innermost reaches of the harbor. The walled city, buttressed by a staggering of fortifications (including the Fuerte de la Punta near the harbor's entrance, and the Fuerte anciano at the head of the town), was not only well protected but elegant as well, its great number of churches and convents dotting the town. La Vente was particularly impressed by what he later learned was a "seminary for girls," which was plainly visible from the harbor.[25]

The stay in Havana began as the bright spot of the voyage, especially for the girls and nursing sisters who were allowed to leave their cramped quarters on ship for the first time since departing Rochefort over three months before. La Vente and Huvé were particularly elated by the "kindness and cordiality" of the Havana religious, chiefly Diego Evelino de Compostela, Bishop of Cuba, who in part relieved the French clergy for nearly a week of their responsibility of watching over the girls. After receiving them with "charity and magnificence," the bishop "refreshed our young ladies to perfection in a house which adjoins the Episcopal establishment which he calls the Collegium Virginium," a generous gesture which La Vente thought appropriate in view of the fact that "several of the girls are of high birth and are awaiting their settlements." The gracious bishop not only received the girls "as if in a convent" but entertained them as well, "at his own expense." For four or five days he conducted

24. La Vente [to SME Dirs.], *loc. cit.*, R 77. U.S. Coast and Geodetic Survey Map 1007, *op. cit.* Plan der . . . hafens Havana, 1739, in Homann, *Grosser Atlas über die gantze welt* . . . , 1737–53.

25. La Vente [to SME Dirs.], *loc. cit.*, R 77. Carte Nouvelle de la Mer du Sud (with inset of Havana Harbor ca. 1700), in Ottens, [Atlas sive geographia compendiosa . . .] *n.d.*

them on what amounted to a guided tour of the many shrines, convents and gardens in Havana, while La Vente was being entertained by some of the local religious, particularly by Juan de Pedraza and Francisco de Sayas. With the aid of Sayas the pastor was able to purchase a milch cow which was immediately loaded onto the already overcrowded *Pélican*.[26]

While the Havana religious were hosting La Vente, Huvé and the young girls, Ducoudray had been conferring with the local officials, especially Luis Chacón, "alcaide y castellano del Castillo del Morro," and Nicolás Chirino Vandevall, "gobernador de la Habana." Ducoudray informed Chirino Vandevall that his only purpose in stopping at Havana was to take on fresh water for the *Pélican*. In reality, Ducoudray had been specifically ordered by Pontchartrain to call at the Spanish port: in addition to delivering a number of packages to Jean-Baptiste Jonchée, director of the Company of the Assiento at Havana, Ducoudray was to take on board as prisoner a certain Artur, employee of a ship supplier who had been accused of wasting and mismanaging food supplies sent the squadron of Châteaurenault. However, Ducoudray, himself, had even further reasons for calling at Havana. On board he was carrying an excess of flour, as well as merchandise of his own, that he hoped to sell to Spanish merchants. Moreover, there were sixteen or seventeen packages belonging to Iberville that the commander had asked him to exchange for hard cash.[27]

Unloading goods at Havana, however, presented certain difficulties: the Spanish had strict regulations against the buying or selling of contraband merchandise. Under the restrictions of a royal *cedula* of July 23, 1690, no foreign goods could be purchased by Spanish merchants. In fact no Spanish official was to board French ships in port, even to inspect merchandise. Nonetheless, a

26. La Vente [to SME Dirs.], *loc cit.*, R 77. El gobernador de la Florida al rey, March 10, 1701, AGI, *Santo Domingo*, L. 840. Consulta del consejo de las Indias, July 23, 1704, AGI, *Santo Domingo*, L. 836. La Vente [to Tremblay], Sept. 10, 1704, ASQ, Lettres, R 75. Archivo de la Catedral de San Cristóbal de la Habana, Registro de las sepulturas, Libro IV, f. 65, No. 69. La Vente, Mémoire general des marchandises, 1707, ASQ, Lettres, R 78.

27. Oficiales reales al rey, July 16, 1704, AGI, *México*, L. 618. Luis Chacón al virrey, May 4, 1704, AGI, *Santo Domingo*, L. 377. Min. to Bégon, Jan. 30, 1704, AC, B 25, f. 1–2v. Mémoire pour servir d'instruction au capitaine Ducoudray . . . Jan. 30, 1704, AC, B 25, f. 7–9. Dartaguiette to min., Aug. 18, 1708, AC, C13A, 2, f. 337–38. Oficiales reales al rey, Aug. 29, 1704, AGI, *Santo Domingo*, L. 409.

cedula of June 8, 1700 provided that in certain cases flour could be sold from the visiting ships up to an amount of 150 pounds. Relying on this exception, two Havana merchants, Bartolomé de Burgos and Francisco Jorge convinced Ducoudray to sell them a supply of flour from the *Pélican.* Unfortunately for Burgos and Jorge, Ducoudray allowed the two merchants to purchase fifty-three barrels above the limit. After losing part of the flour during the unloading, Burgos and Jorge were caught *in flagrante delicto* by the port officials and thrown into prison. Governor Vandevall then confiscated the remaining flour and used it to replace losses of the Windward Squadron. While the French were allowed to keep the hard cash paid them by Burgos and Jorge, a coolness developed between Ducoudray and the Havana officials which persuaded the French captain that the time for departure from Havana was drawing nigh.[28]

Although the stopover at Havana had been a welcomed break from the tedious voyage at sea, it had not been entirely pleasant (even aside from the brush with Havana's commercial regulations). The passengers had noticed the change in climate almost immediately upon debarking. The cool, salty, ocean breezes were replaced by a dank, stuffy atmosphere. Beyond the elegant Spanish architecture in the town, patches of low swamp-like areas surrounded the several stagnant ditches that even during the rainy season but trickled into the harbor. The narrow streets, no more than twelve feet in width, appeared to steam in the high humidity.[29]

The sultriness showed little sign of remission during the long sweltering nights. Though it was perhaps more pleasant to sleep on solid ground than on the deck of a tossing ship, the soldiers from France were annoyed by the unpleasant humming of mosquitoes around them; all too often the mosquitoes would flit down during the nights to prick their victims' uncovered areas of flesh. The girls, too, were piqued by the *moustiques;* one in particular,

28. Carta de Luis Chacón, May 4, 1704, AGI, *Santo Domingo,* L. 377. Carta de Nicolás Chirino, Aug. 29, 1704, AGI, *Santo Domingo,* L. 377. Oficiales reales al rey, July 16, 1704, AGI, *México,* L. 618. Alburquerque al rey, Sept. 20, 1704, AGI, *México,* L. 618. Burgos and Jorge were processed and fined one hundred *reales* each. Autos contra Bartolomé de Burgos, 1704, AGI, *México,* L. 618. Oficiales reales al rey, Dec. 2, 1704, AGI, *Santo Domingo,* L. 409. Oficiales reales al rey, Dec. 9, 1704, AGI, *México,* L. 618.

29. La Roche, *Yellow Fever . . .* Vol. II, p. 391. Carte Hydrographique de La Baye de La Havane . . . par le S. Bellin, 1762, in *Hydrographie Françoise,* 1756–1802.

Louise-Françoise Lefevre de Malpalu, complained several times of being bitten.[30]

Finally, on the fourteenth of July (the eighth day in port), the passengers, in high spirits despite their occasional discomforts, returned to the *Pélican* where the crewmen quickly hoisted sail. All seemed well at this point: there were few clouds in the sky; the winds were strong and predictable. Most of the men were in good health, and Massacre Island, the *Pélican's* final port-of-call, lay just over the Gulf of Mexico, perhaps only a week's voyage away. True, one of the officers and some of the soldiers had come down with a fever toward the last day's stay in Havana. True, also, the iron-man Le Sueur had fallen "dangerously ill" just before embarkation and had to be left behind, but with a few exceptions, none of these cases were judged to be anything more than incidents of ordinary sickness, to be expected at this time of year.[31]

The *Pélican* had only been a few hours gone from the port of Havana when a general alarm was sounded: so much water was being shipped (due perhaps to the several tons extra burden taken on at Havana) that it was feared the ship was sinking. The decision was quickly made to return to port. The *Pélican* had already turned sail, was heading back to Havana when it was discovered that by shifting a few tons of supplies from near the bow to the stern the vessel then shipped no more than an ordinary amount of water.[32]

Shifting sail once more the *Pélican* slowly turned and resumed her northward course. Shortly thereafter, some of the crewmen began to complain of chills and headaches. Fevers among the soldiers and sailors were increasing with alarming rapidity. The next morning, a "very fine officer and ensign" died and was hastily buried at sea, after complaining of thirst and severe pains in the back and joints. Among the soldiers in particular, a slightly yellowish cast was being observed by the officers, along with some unusual cases of muscular debility.[33]

The distressed ship sailed on, moving swiftly across the untroubled gulf waters, the symptoms of the disease which La Vente and some of the officers were now calling "the tavardille" con-

30. La Vente [to SME Dirs.], *loc. cit.*, R 77. Estat des depenses, 1704, AC, F1A, 11, f. 223.

31. La Vente [to SME Dirs.], *loc. cit.*, R 77.

32. *Ibid.*

33. *Ibid.*

tinuing to spread. The fevers and chills, though most prevalent among the soldiers and crewmen, had touched all quarters of the ship. Even one of the girls, Louise-Françoise Lefevre, was now complaining of fever and headache.[34]

Meanwhile back in Havana, Le Sueur had gone from bad to worse, having been removed to the hospital behind Governor Chirino Vandevall's quarters. On the day the *Pélican* had sailed for Massacre Island the explorer had apparently sensed the inevitable. Sinking fast, he called for the Havana notary, Bartolomé Nuñez, and drew up his will in the presence of Jean-Baptiste Jonchée and Diego Bondas (who agreed to serve as his testamentary executors), naming his five children as his heirs. During the early morning hours of the seventeenth of July, Le Sueur drew his last breath, having received the holy sacraments from Juan de Pedraza. Later that same morning he was laid to rest in the parish church of San Cristóbal.[35]

By the twentieth of July, the *Pélican* had made landfall near Pensacola where she anchored briefly in the outer harbor to take on fresh water. The next morning, after a short communication with Pensacola's acting governor, Joseph de Guzmán, Ducoudray pulled anchor once more and headed west where at last, on the twenty-second of July, the *Pélican* entered the harbor of Massacre Island.[36]

34. Although La Vente uses "tavardille," a French corruption of the Spanish "tabardillo" (a term widely used in Havana and Santo Domingo to denote a prevalent fever generally considered to have been Typhus) to describe the sickness, the affliction was not Typhus but Yellow fever. Chambolle, "Observations sur la Fièvre Jaune . . ." *Annales de la Médecine Physiologique*, Vol. X, pp. 391–92. Chatard, "Notice Succincte du Typhus . . . ," *Observateur des Sciences Médicales de Marseille*, Vol. V, p. 333. Had the disease been Typhus, it would have had to have been contracted at Baracoa rather than at Havana.

35. Archivo de la Catedral de San Cristóbal de la Habana, Registro de las sepulturas, July 17, 1704, Libro IV, f. 70v, No. 37. Owing to an attack by the English on Cuba, news of Le Sueur's death did not reach Mobile until some months later, probably from Pensacola via a ship from Veracruz. Bienville to min., Sept. 6, 1704, AC, C13A, 1, f. 449–65. AC, F1A, 11, f. 217–34. Carta de Luis Chacón, Dec. 14, 1704, AGI, *Santo Domingo*, L. 377. Bishop Evelino de Compostela also died during this epidemic. Oficiales reales al rey, Aug. 29, 1704, AGI, *Santo Domingo*, L. 409.

36. The governor of Pensacola, Andrés de Arriola, was absent when the *Pélican* anchored at Santa María de Galve. Guzmán al virrey, Aug. 22, 1704, AGI, *Santo Domingo*, L. 857.

If the passengers aboard the *Pélican* were expecting any elaborate situation at Louisiana's chief port they were sorely disappointed. Even as the vessel drifted up the narrow channel just west of the Île-aux-Espagnols, the newcomers could see but long rows of lonely pines behind a seemingly endless plain of flat, sandy beaches. As the *Pélican* moved toward the center of the island then turned back sharply to the east and glided through the narrow passage between Île Massacre and the northern tip of the Île-aux-Espagnols, the situation appeared even more desolate. There was, in reality, little on the island to observe: only a small warehouse surrounded by a few crudely built cabins, with five or six men mingling about —a vivid contrast to the magnificence of the port they had departed the week before.[37]

Despite the barrenness of Massacre Island, however, the sight of land was exceedingly welcome. The passengers were far more concerned with the state of their own health than with the poorness of the port. Nearly sixty of the *Pélican's* soldiers and crewmen were already feverish, some succumbing to a mysterious delirium, and the number was increasing almost hourly. No sooner had the passengers disembarked than the sick began to die: four from Châteaugué's company, followed by two from Vaulezard's. La Vente officiated at the hasty burials, assisted by Huvé, while a few small vessels began to take on some of the *Pélican's* supplies for the trip upriver to Fort Louis.[38]

Confusion at the port was rampant at this point: the few boats available at Massacre Island were not nearly sufficient to transport all of the passengers and supplies to Fort Louis. A few days before, Governor Guzmán had sent word to Bienville from Pensacola of the *Pélican's* arrival at Santa María de Galve, but the message only reached the commandant at approximately the same time the *Pélican* was approaching Île Massacre. Then, too, there were only two available barks at Fort Louis to be used as transports. It was the twenty-seventh day of July before Bienville's barks reached Massacre Island. By that time six more soldiers from Vaulezard's company had died and at least two from Châteaugué's. La Vente

37. Carte de L'Isle Dauphine, faite par le Sr. Vermale, 1717, BN, 138, 10, 7^2, D. Veue de L'Isle Dauphine, 1717, BN, 138, 10, 6, D. Dénombrement . . . par La Salle, Aug. 31, 1704, AC, C13A, 1, f. 468–70. Plan du Fort Dauphin et de la Rivière de la Mobile, 1712, BN, Ge C65735.

38. La Vente [to SME Dirs.], *loc. cit.*, R 77. AC, F1A, 11, f. 221v–23v. Bienville to min., *loc. cit.*, f. 458–63.

had so far escaped the fever but several of the young girls had been afflicted; one, Louise-Françoise Lefevre, was nearly delirious. The day of the twenty-eighth was spent in loading the boats, but few of the *Pélican's* crew were in condition to work and the transfer of goods progressed slowly. The next day two boats, loaded to the hilt with passengers, left Massacre Island and began to move sluggishly up the bay of Mobile.[39]

After two days of laborious travel, the overloaded vessels entered the mouth of the Mobile River and by the end of the next day, August 1, 1704, the passengers came upon the settlement, which sight they had for nearly a year been anticipating. Situated on the highest part of a twenty foot bluff the relatively small wooden fort stood out from the rest of the town, more from its position on the bluff than because of any vast superiority of size or construction. (Upon landing, La Vente noticed that although the fort was not yet three years old it was already beginning to rot around the bastions).[40]

As the boats moved past the fort and circled back toward the creek to the northwest of the town, the rows of crude wooden dwellings (numbering nearly eighty in all) could be seen extending upward from the damp streets and water-soaked gardens surrounding them. Near the landing point the low bluffs were crowded with curious soldiers and Canadians who stood waiting to help with the unloading and for their first glimpses of the long-awaited passengers.[41]

It was not, however, the glorious occasion that either the inhabitants of Mobile or the young girls from Paris had envisioned. The girls were obviously in a debilitated condition, their drawn, feverous cheeks barely able to form even the faintest of smiles. Bienville was there to greet them, as were officers Charles Levasseur and Henri de Tonti, the commandant aghast at their feeble responses. Bienville was appalled too at the ages and physical condition of the soldiers who had accompanied the girls in the two barks. "The soldiers are nothing but boys," he noted, "all

39. Guzmán al virrey, *loc. cit.*, L. 857. Bienville to min., *loc. cit.*, f. 458–59. AC, F1A, 11, f. 223. La Vente [to SME Dirs.], *loc. cit.*, R 77. Dénombrement . . . par La Salle, Aug. 31, 1704, AC, C13A, 1, f. 469–70.

40. La Vente [to SME Dirs.], *loc. cit.*, R 77. Plan de la ville et du fort de la Maubille, 1702, AN, DFC, 119A. *FLC*, pp. 96–97. *Journal Historique*, pp. 84–85.

41. Dénombrement du 31 août 1704, AC, C13A, 1, f. 468–70. Plan de la ville . . . *loc. cit.*, 119A.

aged about 14–15 years," and they were all in a woeful state of health.[42]

If Mobile, however, was not what the passengers on the *Pélican* had envisioned, they were surely too tired and sick to care at this point. They had reached their destination (despite the threats of battle, storm and disease)—this was what mattered at the moment. They would be given habitable quarters for the night, for the succeeding nights. They could stop living like cattle. They would rest and recover. They could stop traveling at last . . .

42. Bienville to min., *loc. cit.*, f. 458–65. Lettre, Sept. 10, 1704, BN, FF, 9097, f. 141v. *FLC*, pp. 96–97.

XI

Summer Scourge

AUGUST in Mobile was not radically different from what July had been in Havana. The air was a little less saline perhaps, the humidity not quite as high; but the heat was no less uncomfortable and the familiar hum of mosquitoes could be heard in the fervid nights.

Of the several girls who had fallen ill aboard ship all seemed to be recovering except one: Louise-Françoise Lefevre. Upon her arrival at Fort Louis, she was immediately taken to the seminary quarters on the rue Sainte-Anne where after a night of delerium and vomiting she succumbed the following morning. Albert Davion officiated at the burial ceremonies that same afternoon (August 2), and by the next week it was widely believed (after the demise of a few more soldiers who had arrived at Mobile at the point of death) that the disease which had thus far claimed over twenty lives had died out.[1]

Meanwhile, some of the girls had found temporary lodging with several families in the town—in the households of François Lemay, Jean-Baptiste Joussette, Jean Le Caën and Jacques Leméry. The Burelle sisters, of course, remained with their own family for the time being. Bienville, hard-pressed to find space, managed to locate provisional shelter for the remaining girls in the houses of those Canadians who had sailed to Veracruz or who were hunting at the Baye de Saint-Louis. The commandant, however, was not anxious to make the girls excessively comfortable at this

1. La Vente [to SME Dirs.], Sept. 20, 1704, ASQ, Lettres, R 77. Although dated Sept. 20, this was La Vente's second letter to his superiors; begun soon after his arrival at Mobile, it was not completed until the third week in September. His first letter was mailed at Baracoa. AC, F1A, 11, f. 223. ADM, A, Sept. 19, Oct. 4, 22, 1704; April 11, 1705.

point. They had been brought to Mobile, he reasoned, for the primary purpose of being married to the incontinent Canadians and the most attractive thing about most of the Canadians was that each had a private home (however modest) to offer to a homeless girl.[2]

The courtships began soon after the debarkation on the first of August. If the girls were in no condition to socialize that first day, they no doubt remembered some of the faces and gestures of assistance that had met them on landing. Renée Gilbert no doubt caught a fleeting glimpse of the young cannoneer from La Rochelle, Jean-Baptiste Roy. Marie Briard was perhaps assisted in some way by the enterprising merchant from Batiscan, Antoine Rivard de La Vigne. Perhaps even on the day of landing Marie-Thérèse Brochon at least made acquaintance with Pierre Brossard.[3]

One thing was certain on that initial afternoon: the Canadian and French-artisan bachelors were more than anxious to become acquainted with the young Parisian Mademoiselles. If the girls had arrived sick and exhausted, the Canadians were restless and eager for personal contact. There had been no widespread illness at Fort Louis as yet and the men of Mobile were at this moment all in excellent health. Having lived in long expectation of the arrival of their prospective brides, the Canadians could not be expected to repress their enthusiasm, regardless of the languor of the girls.[4]

The arrangements for the marriages of the girls were not left entirely to chance. While the Canadians knew nothing beforehand of their brides-to-be, the girls had already learned a good deal about their prospective husbands. From Louisiana veterans at the port of Rochefort, from Châteaugué and the now-deceased Le Sueur they had gleaned a number of solid portraits. Moreover, their "governess," Marie-Françoise de Boisrenaud, had seriously taken upon herself the responsibility for seeing that her *filles* were well-matched. The earnest mademoiselle made it her business, both

2. AC, F1A, 11, f. 218–23v. Plan de la ville et du fort de la Maubille, AC, DFC, Louisiane, 119A. It is probable that some of the girls were lodged in the houses of Bécancour, Baudreau de Graveline, Louis Juchereau de Saint-Denis and André Pénigault, all of whom were absent during the month of August. AC, F1A, 11, f. 69–72, 218–23. Lettre, Sept. 10, 1704, BN, FF, 9097, f. 141.

3. La Vente [to SME Dirs.], *loc. cit.*, R 77. ADM, A, Sept. 19, 1704; Aug. 16, 1705; Feb. 23, 1707. Recensement de Canada, 1681, AC, G1, 460.

4. François Montreuil had died on July 21 of a "maladie," the only inhabitant to perish for several months before the ship's arrival. His death, however, had no connection with Yellow fever. AC, F1A, 11, f. 220.

before and after the landing, to become well-informed of the backgrounds and present situations of the bachelors. From a group of some fifty or sixty eligible men in the town, only about forty would be seriously considered, and of these, perhaps twenty-five would be regarded as good prospects. Highest on the list of qualifications, of course, was "ability to provide." Next came "position" or "rank" in the colony, followed by such factors as age, health, physical attractiveness and congeniality.[5]

Intelligence concerning the bachelors spread quickly among the girls, being passed on to them by "Governess" Boisrenaud, Pastor La Vente and Commandant Bienville, as well as by the local townfolk. As far as position and rank in the colony was concerned, Charles Levasseur, Canadian infantry officer, and Pierre Dugué de Boisbriant, *aide-major*, both ranked as prime prospects. Henri de Tonti (though some may have winced at his age and his crude metal hand) was also a man of stature, as was Louis Juchereau de Saint-Denis, commandant of Fort La Boulaye. Perhaps considered the most eligible man in the colony, though he was presently thought to be in Veracruz, was François-Alexandre Robinau de Bécancour, a man of esteemed background, high position and relative wealth.[6]

As far as the group known as "les Canadiens" was concerned, there were no affluent men, but some were better established than others: Guillaume Boutin, Joseph Simon, *dit* La Pointe, Jean-Baptiste Saucier, François Trudeau and Antoine Rivard de La Vigne were all men of above average means. A few of the French artisans—Jean Alexandre, a master-joiner from Dieppe, and Jean-Baptiste La Croix, *dit* Grimauld, a carpenter from Havre de Grâce—could at least be expected to support a wife and family in comfortable circumstances. The name of André Pénigault, the young carpenter from La Rochelle, had been mentioned, but he was, along with several Canadians, away on a hunt during these early days of August. Even had he been present his Protestant back-

5. AC, F1A, 11, f. 69–70v. Min. to Bégon, Sept. 5, 1705, AM, B2, 182, f. 470–71. Min. to Iberville, Nov. 4, 1705, AC, B 27, f. 187. Min. to Bégon, Oct. 21, 1705, AM, B 27, f. 183v.

6. Bécancour's pay in 1702 was listed at 150 *livres* per month, compared to Bienville's 100, Tonti's 50, and Levasseur's 50. AC, F1A, 11, f. 282–82v. By 1704, Bécancour was earning 1800 *livres* per year. AC, F1A, 11, f. 69v. Saint-Denis, as commandant of Fort La Boulaye, was on the lower Mississippi in August of 1704. AC, F1A, 11, f. 218–18v. Lettre, Sept. 10, 1704, *loc. cit.*, 9097, f. 141.

ground may have somewhat weighed against him, at least as far as the recommendation of Mlle. Boisrenaud was concerned.[7]

But what of the commandant himself? Could the independent, impetuous Bienville be persuaded to take a wife? Perhaps. He was surely high on the list of eligibles. Young, on occasion charming, he was a man of position and (by Canadian standards, at least) of family. Next to Bécancour, he was the highest man on the payroll at twelve hundred *livres* per year.[8] He had so far shown little interest in the girls, although he had been seen on several occasions conversing with Françoise de Boisrenaud. Perhaps he would seek the hand of the "governess."

Among the twenty-one girls then seeking husbands there were some, quite naturally, who were considered more desirable than others by standards of comeliness, vivacity and family background. Having been reared in more delicate and refined circumstances, however, even the least desirable of the girls felt somewhat superior to the majority of Canadian ruffians most of whom seemed to regard them as so many "pieces of merchandise." In addition, the girls were keenly sensitive to the fact that both the Canadians and the townfolk were aware that they had, in effect, signed contracts to "throw themselves blindly into marriage." Recognition of this community awareness that they had voluntarily chosen exile in an unknown land, agreeing to marriage with men whom they had no prior contact, was enough to make the girls a little haughtier and perhaps more distant than they might otherwise have been.[9]

Despite the girls' sensitivity to their situation, however, there was the practical matter to consider: they must find husbands, if for no other reason than simple survival. Then too if their options were small, were they not greater than the alternatives left behind in France? They could not quite forget the rather dismal life they had endured in the convents of Paris. Had they remained in France the majority of girls would have eventually married; but being for the most part of the middle and upper-middle classes

7. AC, F1A, 11, f. 71–73, 220–20v. Lettre, Sept. 10, 1704, *loc. cit.*, f. 141. Pénigault, *Relation*, BN, FF, 14613, f. 181–94. Graveline, while listed with the Canadians during the early years of the colony, was by this time an independent merchant. AC, C13A, 1, f. 256–57. AC, F1A, 10, f. 280–84v, 290.

8. AC, F1A, 11, f. 217–18.

9. La Vente [to SME Dirs.], *loc. cit.*, R 77. Min. to Bienville, Jan. 30, 1704, AC, B 25, f. 15v. Bienville to min., Sept. 14, 1706, AC, C13A, 1, f. 503. Bienville to min., July 28, 1706, AC, C13A, 1, f. 540. Min. to Bégon, March 5, 1704, AM, B2, 174, f. 568v–69.

they would no more have been able to follow the pure dictates of their hearts than in Louisiana. They would have married according to the arrangements of their parents or faced returning to the dreary existence of the convent. Here in Mobile, while their choices were somewhat limited, they had at least a little more control of their individual destinies; if their sensibilities were slightly offended by their present situation, they were surely in greater demand.[10]

Excluding a few exceptions, the least desirable, the least "well-made" of the girls married early, the remainder holding out "because they were more ambitious and because they did not want to seem too eager." [11] Louise-Marguerite Housseau from Chantilly was early courted by merchant-cannoneer Guillaume Boutin, a twenty-nine-year-old Canadian from Dombourg in upper Quebec. Marie-Catherine Christophe was sought by a master gunsmith of Rochefort named René Boyer, and two of the Burelle sisters, Marguerite and Geneviève, were being wooed by Claude Trépanier and Gilbert Dardenne, respectively, two Canadians of some means.[12]

Marie Briard was being pursued by the Canadian from Batiscan, Antoine Rivard de La Vigne, son of Nicolas Rivard (a native of Tourouvre, France) and Catherine Saint-Père from Saint-Jean-d'Angély. The Rivard family was fairly well-connected in Quebec; Antoine could count among his cousins and in-laws the families of Moreau, Dufresne, Préville and Guillet. Rivard's father, Nicolas, had been closely associated in business with Pierre Juchereau, Sieur Des Moulineaux, back in Tourouvre, and the Rivard family had been close to the notable Juchereaux ever since Nicolas had emigrated to Quebec in the mid-seventeenth century. Aside from its immediate importance, this courtship between Rivard and Marie Briard was to have far-reaching repercussions in the political and social history of Louisiana.[13]

10. La Vente [to SME Dirs.], *loc. cit.*, R 77. Min. à l'évêque de Québec, Sept. 12, 1703, AM, B2, 169, f. 703v–04.

11. La Vente [to SME Dirs.], *loc. cit.*, R 77. AC, F1A, 11, f. 220–20v, 223–23v.

12. *Ibid.*, f. 223. ADM, A, June 19, Dec. 23, 1707; April 8, Dec. 8, 1708; Feb. 5, 1709. *DGFC, I*, pp. 82, 158, 193.

13. Rivard was, like Graveline, an independant merchant by 1704; yet he was still in the pay of the king. AC, F1A, 11, f. 220–20v. ADM, A, Sept. 19, 1704; Oct. 4, 1707. Antoine was the eleventh child of Nicolas Rivard de La Vigne and Catherine Saint-Père. *DGFC, I*, p. 519. Recensement de Canada, 1681, AC, G1, 460.

By the beginning of the second week in August, the aforementioned girls, as well as Marie-Catherine Philippe, Catherine Tournant, Marguerite Tavernier, Marguerite Guichard, Jeanne-Élisabeth Le Pinteaux, Marie-Madelaine Oüanet, Marie-Thérèse Brochon and Renée Gilbert, were presumably satisfied with the men who had been paying them court, enough to consent to enter into marriage contracts with them. During the next few days (in the presence of the couples' friends and neighbors), the execution and signing of the agreements took place inside Fort Louis where Davion and La Vente, acting as notaries, drew up the contracts after which the parties signed or made their marks. A few of the girls, such as Marie Philippe and Marie-Magdelaine Oüanet were illiterate. Françoise de Boisrenaud, overseeing the proceedings, made certain that they understood the provisions of the agreements they were signing, that the contracts contained mutual donation clauses (so that in the event of the death of the husband, the wife would retain full rights to the property of the deceased, providing there were no children).[14]

Afterwards, formally betrothed, the engaged couples returned to their separate residences, now entering into a period of more concentrated courtship: they saw each other more often now, became more familiar with each other's habits and idiosyncrasies. Even marriages undertaken in such unusual circumstances were not taken lightly. It was a serious matter, involving not only the lives of the separate parties but their material possessions as well. Rivard de La Vigne, in agreeing to his contract with Marie Briard, was assigning future rights to his estate, as well as relinquishing some portion of his personal liberty.[15]

Although the engagement period was more brief (out of necessity) than would have been the case were the couples being married in Paris or La Rochelle, there were several days during which a number of festivities took place. The "families" (those

14. AC, F1A, 11, f. 223. La Vente [to SME Dirs.], *loc. cit.*, R. 77. ADM, A, June 18, 1708; Feb. 24, 1709. These marriage contracts, carefully worded in accordance with article 180 of the *Coutume de Paris*, often had far-reaching effects stretching over several generations. Thomas Desercy vs. Marie-Anne Artus, LSMA, DCS, May 3, July 17, 21, 23–24, Aug. 6, 1725. The contracts themselves were valued documents; duplicates were generally requested of the notary at the time of signing in order to insure the preservation of evidence. LSMA, DCS, Feb. 15, 1725.

15. Glasson, *Histoire du Droit et des Institution de la France*, Vol. VIII, pp. 433–35. LSMA, DCS, July 21, 23–24, 1725. Ferrière, *Dictionnaire de Droit et de Pratique*, Vol. II, pp. 203–05.

temporarily lodging the girls) hosted small celebrations which their friends and acquaintances attended. Though the affairs were modest, there was nevertheless a good deal of socializing; there was plenty of food and drink (supplies from the *Pélican* were daily being delivered to the settlement and purchased by the inhabitants) and there was dancing: the *minuet* of the *habitant* and *petit bourgeois*, with its graceful steps, its vigorous improvisions, backed by cheery hand-clapping and the strains of an amateur "fiddler," with his instrument pushed against his waist. The dancing went on into the early hours of the morning; the feasting was heavy and the inhabitants consumed large amounts of wine and "hard liquor," often to the point of inebriation.[16]

Practically every day during the middle of August, one or more marriage ceremonies were held at the small, unadorned chapel inside Fort Louis. By the seventeenth of August, 1704 thirteen marriages had been consecrated by Davion and La Vente. The new brides went with their grooms to their new homes in the town: Jean-Baptiste Roy and Renée Gilbert to Roy's house on the corner of the rue de Pontchartrain and the rue d'Iberville, next to Marc Berrichon; Antoine Rivard and Marie Briard to the outskirts of town on the rue Dugué, next to Canadian Mathurin Moquin. Geneviève Burelle, Marie-Catherine Philippe and Marguerite Burelle would all be living on the same block, between the rue Saint-Joseph and the rue de Ruessavel.[17]

There were still eight girls without husbands, not including Françoise de Boisrenaud: Marie-Noël Dumesnil, Gabrielle Savary, Angélique Drouin, Marie-Marguerite Dufresne, Jeanne Burelle, Gabrielle Bonnet, Marie-Élisabeth Des Hayes and Jeanne-Catherine de Berenhardt. A number of these *filles* were perhaps more ambitious than the girls who had already agreed to be married. For the most eligible of the bachelors had not yet made their selections: Robinau de Bécancour, Henri de Tonti, Charles Levasseur, Dugué de Boisbriant, Juchereau de Saint-Denis, Bienville and Nicolas de La Salle. The girls seeking the favor of these men were quite naturally more coy. By holding themselves aloof they hoped to strike a certain chord in the sensibilities of those

16. Douville et Casanova, *La Vie Quotidienne en Nouvelle France*, pp. 23–39.

17. Plan de la ville et du fort de la Maubille, *loc. cit.*, 119A. ADM, A, Aug. 16, 1705; Oct. 4, 1707. Plan de la ville et du Fort Louis, sur la Mobile, 1711, AN, Section Outre-mer, DFC, 120B. AC, F1A, 11, f. 223–23v.

officers who may have equated early consent with coquetry. As La Vente put it, "They did not wish to hurry." [18]

By the twentieth of August, however, the mood of the establishment had begun to change. News had recently come (by the vessel returning from Veracruz) that Robinau de Bécancour had taken sick and died on July 4th at the Mexican port. With Bécancour eliminated and Bienville apparently not interested, the core of officers eligible for marriage narrowed; the more so when Nicolas de La Salle signed his engagement with Jeanne-Catherine de Berenhardt during the third week in August.[19]

The La Salle-Berenhardt engagement had, for the most part, been "prearranged." Shortly after La Salle arrived in the colony in 1702 with his three sons, his wife, Madelaine Chartroux, died. Spouseless, his young sons in need of a stepmother, La Salle had written to France by a vessel to Veracruz requesting that one from the shipload of girls which he knew would eventually arrive be carefully selected and set aside for him. Who more than a widowered father of three with high responsibilities needed a suitable wife, he had pleaded.[20]

La Salle's need was not ignored by the authorities in France. Reports of his request eventually reached Marguerite-Louise d'Orléans, wayward Grand Duchess of Tuscany then *pensionnaire* at the Couvent de Notre-Dame de la victoire de Lépante à Picpus, who selected a proper maiden from her establishment. When the *Pélican* arrived at Massacre Island in July, a message to La Salle espoused the virtues of Jeanne-Catherine: ". . . a young lady of quality . . . much recommended by Madame la Grande Duchesse . . . whose refinements are known also to Madame Ducoudray." The prolonging of the engagement, however, was apparently not entirely due to Jeanne-Catherine. La Salle himself seems less than fully smitten by the young *Parisienne* since, as he later reported, "I became married in order to completely satisfy the king's intentions." [21]

18. AC, F1A, 11, f. 220–23v. La Vente [to SME Dirs.], Sept. 20, 1704, *loc. cit.*, R. 77.

19. *Journal Historique*, pp. 84–86. AC, F1A, 11, f. 223–23v. According to La Harpe, Bécancour's vessel returned to Mobile on Aug. 12. Junta de Guerra, May 26, 1705, AGI, *México*, L. 618. Alburquerque al rey, Sept. 22, 1704, AGI, *México*, L. 618.

20. Iberville to min., July 30, 1701, BN, FF, NA, 9295, f. 228. AC, F1A, 10, f. 197–98. *Journal Historique*, pp. 80–81. Dartaguiette to min., Jan. 10, 1711, AC, C13A, 2, f. 636–39.

21. La Salle to min., Sept. 7, 1706, AC, C13A, 1, f. 490.

There was further reason why La Salle (by the third week in August) was still only engaged and why but thirteen marriages had yet been consecrated: the return of the dreaded Yellow fever. When the supply boats landed the passengers from the *Pélican* at Fort Louis on August 1, there was no sickness among the inhabitants already there. The soldiers and crewmen who had been infected at Havana were either dead, in the last stages of death, or beginning to recover. During the early weeks of August, therefore, the disease had apparently died out.[22]

Unknown to the residents of Mobile, however, the mosquitoes at Fort Louis were already beginning to pick up the virus from the slowly-recovering passengers. From the last of the diseased victims, the native *moustiques* began to draw the potent virus during the first nights of August. Some weeks later, now able to transfer the deadly organism, the mosquitoes began infecting the unsuspecting residents of the town.[23] Henri de Tonti and Charles Levasseur, officers sleeping within a hundred and fifty feet of each another (and near locations where some of the diseased soldiers had been lodged), were infected toward the third week in August. By the beginning of the next week both Tonti and Levasseur had come down with the fever; they were soon confined to their quarters, complaining of weariness, their faces appearing excessively red. Already engaged, the ailing officers were too weak to undergo their marriage ceremonies.[24]

By this time most of the other girls were formally betrothed: Gabrielle Savary to Jean-Baptiste Saucier; Jeanne Burelle to François Trudeau; Marie-Élisabeth Des Hayes to Jean Bourbonnois;

22. La Vente [to SME Dirs.], Sept. 20, 1704, *loc. cit.*, R 77.

23. The female of the species *Ædes Ægypti* is the vector in the transfer of Yellow fever (urban, epidemic). The insect ingests the virus as it draws the blood of an infected victim. From the intestine of the mosquito the virus migrates in about twelve days to the insect's salivary glands at which point she is capable of infecting anyone she bites (unless they are immune). Yellow fever is non-contagious and there is yet (1974) no treatment. Bugher, "The pathology of Yellow fever," in Strode, G. K. (ed.), *Yellow Fever*, pp. 137–63. Elton, Romero and Trejos, "Clinical pathology of Yellow fever," *Amer. J. Clin. Path.*, vol. 25, pp. 135–46.

24. Bienville to min., Sept. 6, 1704, AC, C13A, 1, f. 458–65. The deduction is made that Levasseur and Tonti were "engaged" from La Vente's statement that "two of the girls would have been well-established had it not been for the death of two officers present." Since Levasseur and Tonti (a widower) were the only two officers to die at Mobile, it follows that they were the men to whom the pastor referred. La Vente [to SME Dirs.], *loc. cit.*, R 77. AC, F1A, 11, f. 217–18, 224, 228, 232.

Marie-Marguerite Dufresne to Jean-Baptiste Alexandre; Angélique Drouin to Jean-Baptiste La Croix. By late August, however, the Yellow fever had attacked over half of the town's inhabitants and several other of the marriage ceremonies had to be postponed. There were few inhabitants who felt up to entertaining or dancing or even attending a consecration. The greater part of activity in Mobile came to an abrupt halt. Two of the newly-wed girls, Catherine Tournant and Jeanne-Élisabeth Le Pinteaux soon came down with the fever, attended by the nursing "soeurs" Marie Grissot and Marie Linant. Moreover, the fever finally appeared in the clerics Roulleaux de La Vente and Albert Davion, who had been consecrating most of the marriages.[25]

When *Curé* La Vente and his assistant Alexandre Huvé first arrived at Fort Louis, they had been met by Jesuit chaplain Pierre Dongé and their fellow seminary priest Davion. Dongé, who was reported by La Vente as having "received us with a perfect affection and . . . who is as accomodating as he is meritorious," was quick to offer his assistance. From his quarters near the fort, the genial Jesuit was preparing to return to France on the *Pélican* which Ducoudray had informed him would be leaving by August 31. Dongé was only too willing to render aid to the seminary priests; he was by nature cordial and helpful; too, his approaching departure made unmeaning any rivalry of sect (since he was the last remaining Jesuit in Mobile). With cheerful disposition, he lent La Vente a sum of seven hundred *livres* to pay for past debts that Davion had incurred in building the house where La Vente, Huvé and their two servants would dwell during their tenure at Fort Louis.[26]

The house where Davion had been living and where La Vente and Huvé would reside was only half completed when the two missioners arrived. Situated just beyond a low-lying area on the outskirts of town (at the corner of the rue du Séminaire and the rue d'Iberville), "where we are subject to being set afire by the

25. ADM, A, Oct. 17, Nov. 27, 1707; March 17, April 18, 1708. La Vente [to Tremblay], Sept. 25, 1704, ASQ, Lettres, R 76. Min. to Dartaguiette, May 10, 1710, AC, B 32, f. 324v. ADM, A, April 7, 1708; March 29, 1710. Pierre Charly married one of the girls but it is not known which.

26. La Vente [to Tremblay], Sept. 10, 1704, ASQ, Lettres, R 75. Plan de la ville et du Fort Louis, sur la Mobile, 1711, *loc. cit.*, 120B. Guzmán al virrey, Aug. 22, 1704, AGI, *Santo Domingo*, L. 857. Ordre du Roy . . . au Sieur de Bienville, Feb. 6, 1704, AC, B 25, f. 23–23v. Tremblay [to Laval], April 4, 1705, ASQ, Lettres, N 122.

smallest attack of the enemy savages," the house measured forty-two by sixteen feet and consisted of "a living room, a little salon and two studies which can scarcely lodge two ecclesiastics without an additional building and without being able to store the small number of provisions we have nor provide sleeping room for our two servants . . ." Davion, lacking funds, had been able to contract only for a make-shift "thatched" roof which constantly leaked. The doors and windows had not yet been hung; the whole construction appeared to the meticulous La Vente as "nothing but a barn." [27]

Davion himself was enduring a Spartan existence. Reduced to sleeping on the bare ground for lack of a bed, he was surviving on bacon, drinking water and the "fruits of his mission," none of which was overly nutritious. If Davion, however, could manage on such deprivations, La Vente could not. Incensed at his private situation, the pastor fired off a letter to Henri-Jean Tremblay complaining of his lack of brandy, flour, tools and nails, as well as of the exorbitant price of labor. Making a detailed list of items needed, he listed everything from barley for his cow to hatchets, gunflints and glassware for trade with the Indians. "I am still chiding myself," he added, "for having failed to bring a carpenter from France . . . at whatever price necessary, since no *curé* is obliged to build for himself . . . it is perfectly possible that we could expend more than two thousand *livres* and nevertheless still live a bit crowded." [28]

After his lengthy memorandum of needs and complaints to Tremblay, La Vente had somewhat piously added, ". . . I may assure you that my plan is, if God does not withdraw me, to die as poor as when I came and all my small works will have no other purpose but the church and this establishment . . ." [29]

While La Vente's conception as to what constituted poverty would later be subjected by Bienville to more stringent examination,[30] the pastor had little time at the moment to indulge himself

27. *Ibid.*, N 122. La Vente [to Tremblay], Sept. 10, 1704, *loc. cit.*, R 75. La Vente [to SME Dirs.], Sept. 20, 1704, *loc. cit.*, R 77. Plan de la Ville et du Fort Louis, sur la Mobile, 1711, *loc. cit.*, 120B. La Vente's house was approximately one-quarter of a mile from the entrance of the fort.

28. La Vente [to SME Dirs.], Sept. 20, 1704, *loc. cit.*, R 77. It was characteristic of La Vente that his first letter sent out from Mobile dealt almost entirely with his material needs. La Vente [to Tremblay], Sept. 10, 1704, *loc. cit.*, R 75.

29. *Ibid.*, R 75.

30. Bienville to min., Oct. 10, 1706, AC, C13B, 1, No. 6, f. 3–9. Bienville to min., Aug. 20, 1709, AC, C13A, 2, f. 411–13.

in self-pity. The present crisis had not yet allowed his being formally inducted as *curé* of his parish (had not, in fact, even permitted him to conduct the Holy Mass). Events during the first three weeks in August had demanded his constant attention: tending the sick and burying the dead (during the first week or so) and consecrating marriages (during the second and third weeks). True, he was assisted by Davion, Huvé and for a short time by Père Dongé; but Davion was merely initiating La Vente to his duties before his planned departure in October or November for his Tunica mission.[31]

During the third week of August the now-infected mosquitoes began to spread the virus rapidly. La Vente and Huvé were infected about the fifteenth of the month; on the twentieth the symptoms began to appear. The two missioners, as well as Davion, began to come down with the fever which in a few days had all but incapacitated the three of them.[32] La Vente and Huvé gave in to their afflictions and remained in their quarters while Davion, more accustomed to pain, less slave to his feelings, struggled valiantly to minister to the victims in the town (which by the end of August included the larger portion of the establishment). The tables were now turned, even though the turnabout went at first unnoticed by the townfolk: those who had come afflicted on the *Pélican* were now all recovered, while those who had been healthy at the *Pélican's* arrival were now all (or most all) diseased. The fever, the dizziness, the muscular debility were daily increasing and the dread of the dark vomit was prevalent indeed. Étienne Cantinteau, a valuable carpenter from France, took sick on the 21st of August and was dead by the 28th. Ducoudray, unable to secure enough healthy men from Bienville to man his return to France, was forced to delay his embarkation.[33]

In the midst of these catastrophic August days, Bienville and his officers were taken aback by a visit from the Franciscan father of Pensacola and a number of Indian leaders from the villages of the Talimali and the Chato in Apalache. While Bienville was not uninformed as to what had been transpiring in the country between Pensacola and St. Augustine during the sanguinous months of June and July of 1704, he was apparently surprised that the refugees from the principal *doctrina* of San Luis de Apalache, so long and so closely connected to the Spanish, had accepted his

31. La Vente [to SME Dirs.], Sept. 20, 1704, *loc. cit.*, R 77.

32. *Ibid.*

33. *Ibid.* Bienville to min., Sept. 6, 1704, *loc. cit.*, f. 458–65. AC, F1A, 11, f. 219–33v. *Journal Historique*, pp. 84–85.

offer to settle near the French rather than under the wing of Pensacola.[34]

The Christianized villages of the district of Apalache had for three-quarters of a century been under the influence of Franciscan fathers and Spanish military administrators. Even the Chato, a warlike, multi-villaged nation farther north had, after numerous wars with the Yamasee, drifted southward where they accepted missionaries Miguel de Valverde and Rodrigo de la Barreda among them in 1674. The Chato had not been easy converts, however; the year after accepting the Franciscans, they turned on Friar Rodrigo, wounding him severely and driving him to the new mission of Santa Cruz nearby. After Hernández de Florencia, with a command of twenty-five soldiers, backed Rodrigo's cross with the threat of the sword, the Chato were quieted, moved nearer, in fact, to the central *doctrina* of San Luis where they formed two villages—San Pedro de los Chines and San Carlos de los Chato. Here, enveloped by the twelve other Christian villages near San Luis they began to absorb the new religion more thoroughly.[35]

The Chato in the late seventeenth century numbered only four or five hundred in their several villages. The much larger village of Talimali, the most populous in Apalache, where the chief Spanish fortification was located, boasted some fourteen hundred natives. The population had been considerably scattered, however, by the early summer of 1704, and after Moore's attacks on the villages of Escambe and Patale in June, the numbers in the remaining villages decreased rapidly.[36]

The fourth of July, the same day Bécancour was dying in Veracruz and the same night the *Pélican* was floundering in a

34. Bienville to min., Sept. 6, 1704, *loc. cit.*, f. 461–62. ADM, A, Sept. 6, 1704. As late as 1704 the Apalache villages numbered fourteen, but there were other smaller villages in the district—some pagan, some partly Christian, lacking established missions or missionaries. Francisco de Florencia y Juan de Pueyo al virrey, Aug. 18, 1704, AGI, *Santo Domingo*, L. 856.

35. Francisco Gutiérrez de Vera al rey, May 19, 1681, AGI, *Santo Domingo*, L. 226. Carta de Miguel Abengojar, July 3, 1681, AGI, *Santo Domingo*, L. 226. Diego de Quiroga al rey, Aug. 26, 1690, AGI, *Santo Domingo*, L. 228. Laureano de Torres Ayala al rey, March 11, 1695, AGI, *Santo Domingo*, L. 839. El gobernador de la Florida al rey, March 30, 1704, AGI, *Santo Domingo*, L. 840.

36. Relación de los Religiosos existentes en las conversiones de la Florida y pueblos donde estan las Doctrinas, Dec. 8, 1680, AGI, *Santo Domingo*, L. 226. Declaración de Bartolomé Ruiz de Cuenca, Jan. 20, 1705, AGI, *Santo Domingo*, L. 856.

storm near Havana, was the turning point in the struggle for Apalache: the Spanish garrison, striving to maintain control of San Luis, was rallying its few militia and natives from Ocuia, Ivitachuco and Talimali for a desperate counteroffensive when rumors began circulating among the natives that a massacre was about to ensue, that the English, backed by thousands of Alabama, Yamasee and Apalachicola warriors, were silently encircling their prey and in a few hours' time they would crush all resistance and subject their hapless captives to the sword and the torch. Such fears had little basis in fact. The Apalache and Chato, had they united, were perfectly capable (even with their scarcity of weapons) of blocking the English advance. Yet the rumors, once started, were difficult to repress: the Apalache could not forget past defeats, nor the repeated failures of the Spanish to produce needed arms and reinforcements. Slowly at first, then frantically, they began to retreat, some into the woods, others into the camps of the British and the remainder back to the blockhouse at San Luis. But by this time the blockhouse was filled with refugees; none of the fleeing Indians was permitted entrance. Again the Spaniards had failed them. Turned away, the remnant Apalache saw but two alternatives: they would flee to the woods with those who were already scattering or they would head west where the faraway *presidio* of Pensacola would shield them.[37]

Toward the middle of July, some eight hundred natives (Christians from Talimali, Chato and Escambe, and a few pagans from a refugee Yamasee village) were moving across western Apalache, followed by bands of Alabama and Apalachicola raiders who at random were attacking the rear guards and slaying the small herds of cattle the Apalache natives were driving along with them. Arriving at Pensacola later that month, the refugees were welcomed by Governor Guzmán, who, prophesying the day when renewed Spanish strength would enable the Apalache to return to their villages, pleaded with them to remain at Santa María de Galve. Over the next several weeks, Guzmán did what he could to please them but he was singularly short of both food and arms; he could offer them little but promises. Except for the Escambe and a few of the Talimali, the Apalache would have none

37. Francisco de Florencia y Juan de Pueyo al virrey, Aug. 18, 1704, *loc. cit.*, L. 856. Guzmán al virrey, Aug. 22, 1704, AGI, *Santo Domingo*, L. 857. El gobernador de la Florida al virrey, Sept. 10, 1704, AGI, *Santo Domingo*, L. 852. El gobernador de la Florida al rey, Sept. 15, 1704, AGI, *Santo Domingo*, L. 852.

of Guzmán's promises. Had the governor not already reduced their flour supply within four days of their arrival? Was he not even now refusing them arms with which to protect themselves? [38]

Weary of being slaughtered (trying to defend themselves with stone-age weapons against English rifles), the Talimali and Chato could see perhaps a worthier friend farther west. As described to them by their Canadian comrade, Joseph Belinde (whom Bienville had sent in 1703 to persuade them to emigrate to Mobile Bay and who had suffered and been tortured with them), the lands surrounding Fort Louis were abundant and fertile. The French, too, were Roman Catholic. Moreover, the Frenchmen had guns as well as God; no English Indians had dared attack the Mobile stronghold. There they would find refuge for themselves and their families.

By the middle of August, the Chato and half of the Talimali had made their camps on the eastern side of Mobile Bay, having sent their chiefs, along with the Franciscan father from Pensacola, to confer with Bienville.

Bienville received these emissaries with mixed emotions. His difficulties in Mobile were at the present vexing enough. Moreover, though the storehouse was filled, another supply ship was not expected for nearly a year; certainly he could not arm them all. Yet it was no small opportunity for the French, a chance for an alliance that Bienville had actively sought. The Apalache were known to be diligent workers and farmers. The fact that they were already Christian might aid in furthering the gospel among the still-pagan Choctaw, Chickasaw and Tomeh. Furthermore, since the English were their proven antagonists, in war as well as in religious faith, Bienville could be certain of their continued loyalty.[39]

After short consultation with his officers the commandant agreed to assign the Apalache lands and to help them form a village.[40] Juan, chief of the Chato, was alloted territory at the

38. Guzmán al virrey, *loc. cit.*, L. 857. Francisco de Florencia y Juan de Pueyo, Aug. 18, 1704, *loc. cit.*, L. 856. El gobernador de la Florida al rey, Oct. 6, 1704, AGI, *Santo Domingo*, L. 840. Manuel Solana al gobernador de la Florida, July 8, 1704, AGI, *Santo Domingo*, L. 856. Alburquerque a su Majestad, Sept. 20, 1704, AGI, *México*, L. 618.

39. Declaración de Bartolomé Ruiz de Cuenca, Jan. 20, 1705, *loc. cit.*, L. 856.

40. Years later Bienville boasted, "I made them [the Chato] abandon the bay of St.-Joseph in 1703. They had 250 men then, very brave and very industrious." Mémoire sur la Louisiane, par Bienville, vers 1725, AC, C13C, 1, f. 370.

mouth of the river where his mother Jacinta and two hundred of his villagers moved to the site called the *Oignonets*, location of present-day Mobile. The Talimali were consigned lands farther upriver between the village of the Mobilians and the confluence of the Alabama-Tombigbee rivers, at the present Mount Vernon Landing. Only two hundred Talimali actually settled on the new site assigned the chiefs and an additional two hundred remained camped across the bay (on present-day Baptizing Creek).[41]

If Bienville was elated with his new alliances, La Vente was less than exhilarated by the presence of so many new Christian brothers. "You cannot believe the trouble the Apalache are causing us . . . ," he wrote to Tremblay on September 25. "They are constantly asking us for sacraments and we cannot understand them anymore than we can make ourselves understood." [42] La Vente's frustrations in being called upon to minister to hundreds of new natives at a time when his parish was in such distress (and while his own body was so racked with fever) was underscored by his letter five days earlier to the directors of the seminary in Paris. "At least two hundred Apalache savages have fled here who have all been Christians for a long time and who give us proof every day of this by coming here when they are ill and bringing their children for baptism. There are still two hundred more of them to come . . ." [43]

The problem of the Apalache was not merely one of numbers at this point. By the first week in September the Yellow fever had spread to their village site sixteen miles upriver (nine miles by the foot-path). Shortly thereafter they began bringing their fevered children (who were at the point of death) to the fort to be baptized, but La Vente and Huvé were too sick to minister to them. Davion baptized a little Apalache girl (who died shortly after) on

41. Dartaguiette to min., June 20, 1711, AC, C13A, 2, f. 643–44. Lettre de Davion, Oct. 20, 1711, ASQ, Missions, 46. Pénigault, *Relation*, BN, FF, 14613, f. 185–86. Pénigault says only that the Apalache were located between the Mobilians and the Tomeh. Pénigault, *loc. cit.*, f. 194–95. La Vente gives their distance from Fort Louis as "4 or 5 leagues" in 1704. La Vente [to SME Dirs.], *loc. cit.*, R 77. Gravier in 1708 estimates 4 leagues. Lettre du P. Jacques Gravier, Feb. 23, 1708, *JR, LXVI*, pp. 130–31. Bienville gives the most accurate description of their location: "one league below the confluence of the rivers [Alabama-Tombigbee]." Mémoire sur la Louisiane, *loc. cit.*, f. 370v–71. ADM, A, Jan. 14, 1709. *Ala. River Navigation Charts*, 1972, p. 11.

42. La Vente [to Tremblay], Sept. 25, 1704, *loc. cit.*, R 76.

43. La Vente [to SME Dirs.], Sept. 20, 1704, *loc. cit.*, R 77.

Sept. 6, and judging by La Vente's cursory entry, the pastor was extremely weak when he inscribed it.[44]

As if the problems of sickness and excessive numbers were not enough, the difficulties of the language barrier became increasingly more apparent as the days progressed. Both the Chato and the Talimali (though each spoke in a different dialect) belonged to what has been broadly described as the "Muskhogean linguistic family." Each of the two villages understood Spanish fairly well, however, and even their own dialects had absorbed a good deal of the Spanish language. The Franciscans at Pensacola were able to communicate with them easily enough, but there were very few besides Châteaugué at Fort Louis who understood Spanish, and none of the three seminary priests knew even a smattering of that language. The Talimali had early begun to use Spanish nomenclature to identify themselves—Juan, Joseph, Lucía, Sánchez, Juana—even their fallen chief (tortured and burned by the English) had been named Antonio Feliciano. No wonder then La Vente was exasperated by the new villages about which Bienville was so elated.[45]

If Yellow fever were wreaking havoc among the newly-established Talimali (apparently the Chato were isolated enough or far enough away from stagnant water to escape the infected mosquitoes), the nearby villages of the Tomeh were suffering even more. The Little Tomeh, located at Nannahubba Bluff, numbered some 300 people, while the Grand Tomeh, some fifteen miles farther upstream near the present Three Rivers Lake, numbered nearly five hundred villagers. The nearest village, that of the Mobilians, was also hard-hit, but according to Bienville, the two villages of the Tomeh suffered more than any other native towns and he blamed the disease of that year as being the chief cause of their population decline from a combined total of eight hundred in 1704 to only eighty by 1724.[46]

44. *Ibid. Alabama River Navigation Charts*, 1972, pp. 8–11. This baptism by Davion is the first of the extant baptismal records of Old Mobile. ADM, A, Sept. 6, 1704. Although Davion performed it, La Vente recorded it in the register.

45. Pénigault described their language as "a mixture of Spanish and Alabama." Pénigault, *Relation*, *loc. cit.*, f. 193–95. ADM, A, Jan. 14, 1705; July 5, 1710; Jan. 29, 1711. Huvé phonetically listed Juan, chief of the Chato, as "Ouan," as did later François Le Maire. ADM, A, Jan. 14, 1709; Nov. 22, 1711. Manuel Solana al gobernador de la Florida, July 8, 1704, AGI, *Santo Domingo*, L. 856.

46. Mémoire sur la Louisiane, 1725, *loc. cit.*, f. 371v–72.

Life on the rue du Séminaire was in early September indeed chaotic. The sickness that had plagued La Vente, Huvé and Davion spread not only to La Vente's two servants but also to Davion's faithful servant-helper Charles-François Dumont (living just down the street on the rue de Boutteville). With the influx of others who were ill, the house of the seminary priests became a veritable hospital. Even their chickens suffered a high mortality rate during August and September. It was well that the missionaries were in such close proximity to the cemetery (just across the street at the corner of the rue du Séminaire and the rue Sainte-Anne). Though the cemetery encompassed an area of over 25,000 square feet, it was rapidly being filled. It was about to receive two of the colony's most illustrious officers, each engaged to one of the so-called "*Pélican* girls." [47]

Henri de Tonti had been sick now for nearly two weeks, having come down with the fever during the third week in August. By the third of September, he began to expel the black vomit, which was characteristic of the disease in its most severe stage, and his neighbors on the rue de Tonti, Canadian Antoine Roussin and surgeon Pierre Clavery, were beginning to prepare themselves for the inevitable. It would be a heavy loss for the colony, not only for the young girl to whom Tonti was betrothed (who now must face the prospect of finding another husband) but also for the seminary priests who, in Tonti, had found a measure of sympathy they would fail to find in the other officers of the garrison.[48] In this instance (though it was to be one among few) La Vente's loss was also Bienville's loss. For if Tonti did not occupy the position of importance he once sought for himself, he was nevertheless a valuable knight backing many of Bienville's policies. Commander of the Canadians, he had been instrumental in the founding of Mobile, in the reconciliation of the Indian nations (a principal factor in Bienville's continuing strategy) and in the leadership of necessary though inglorious punitive missions. Too, his mere presence among the personnel of the colony lent a certain prestige

47. Plan de la ville et du Fort Louis, sur la Mobile, 1711, *loc. cit.*, 120B. La Vente [to SME Dirs.], Sept. 20, 1704, *loc. cit.*, R 77.

48. *Ibid.*, R 77. Plan de la ville et du Fort Louis, sur la Mobile, 1711, *loc. cit.*, 120B. Tonti [to his brother], March 4, 1700, AM, 3 JJ 387, 14. "B[v]ómito prieto" (dark vomit) and vómito negro" (black vomit) were frequently-used Spanish terms for Yellow fever. Autos fechos sobre la Providencias dadas sobre la preocupación y fortificación de Santa María de Galve, año de 1703, AGI, *México*, L. 618.

to the settlement, not only among the natives but among the unruly Canadians as well. On the morning of September 4, 1704, Tonti's gritty resistance which for a full quarter-century had enabled him to withstand the severest onslaughts of climate and disease finally broke and the "Iron Hand" expended his last breath. After a solemn and simple ceremony (conducted by Davion) Tonti's haggard corpse was laid to rest in the cemetery across from the house of La Vente and Huvé.[49]

Even as Tonti was being interred his fellow officer and neighbor, Charles Levasseur, *dit* Ruessavel, lay near death. Levasseur, named Charles by his godfather Charles Aubert de La Chesnaye (an ally of Bienville's father and perhaps the most powerful businessman in seventeenth century New France), had, like Tonti, been a member of La Salle's epic exploration of the Mississippi, had been instrumental in the founding of Mobile. It was Levasseur who had first explored the Mobile River basin for France, who had helped gain the friendship of the local Indians, who had, in 1700, planted the cross at the base of the river (now the present site of Mobile). Also, like Tonti, he had been engaged to one of the young girls whom he was now leaving unestablished.[50]

Levasseur had been struck with the fever at about the same time as Tonti. When the black vomit first began to discharge, he had called for Jacques Leméry, assistant clerk of the king's storehouse and one of those authorized to act as a notary, who recorded his last desires. Levasseur's final wishes included: the donation of two hundred *livres* to have prayers uttered in behalf of his soul; two hundred *livres* to be given to the poor; one hundred and fifty *livres* worth of nails to be used in finishing La Vente's house and for use in building the new church; two hundred *livres* to Madame Charly; a total of twelve *livres* and twenty *sols* to compatriots

49. AC, F1A, 10, f. 282, 289; 11, f. 69, 217–18, 224, 228, 232. Bienville to min., Sept. 6, 1704, *loc. cit.*, f. 465. Since Tonti's death occurred in the summer his body was no doubt quickly sealed in its coffin, carried to the fort's chapel by his neighbors, and after brief rites, rolled to the cemetery up the rue d'Iberville. His burial record is not extant; neither are any of the other burials to the year 1726. *Cf.* ADM, Registres mortuaire, C, 1726–1830.

50. *DGFC, I*, p. 391. Journal de Levasseur, 1700, AM, 2 JJ 56, 16. Levasseur's godmother had been Marie-Barbe de Boullongne, widow of Louis d'Ailleboust, governor of New France. ANDM, Notre-Dame de Montréal (1665), Registres des baptêmes, April 7, 1665. La Vente [to SME Dirs.], Sept. 20, 1704, *loc. cit.*, R 77. AC, F1A, 10, f. 282; 11, f. 69, 217–18. In 1680, Aubert had married Marie-Angélique Denis, sister of Louis Denis de La Ronde (commander of the *Enflammé*). *DGFC, I*, p. 14, 180.

Lespérance, Beaupré, Brindamour and Bourguignon to whom Levasseur owed small debts.[51]

The remainder of the dying Canadian's possessions, consisting of a house, animals and poultry, clothes, tools and numerous smaller articles, were to be sold at auction and the proceeds (along with his overdue salary) distributed to his family, to wit: one half to his brother who was at Versailles (who in turn would give one hundred *écus* to another brother in Paris), the other half to his mother in Quebec if she be living (if not it would be equally divided between another brother named Noël Levasseur and his four sisters).[52]

After listing the thirty *livres* owed Levasseur by soldiers Des Daniels and Lafleur, Leméry obtained the Canadian's feeble signature; the next day, September 5, Levasseur died and was inhumed near his old comrade, Tonti. Two days later, an inventory was made by Leméry of Levasseur's household effects (in the presence of Boisbriant, Châteaugué and Philippe Blondel) and the recorded merchandise was shortly sold to the highest bidder.

With the passing of Tonti and Levasseur, Bienville had lost his two most experienced army officers. Within a period of only sixty days he had lost (not forgetting Bécancour in Veracruz) fully fifty percent of his high-ranking command.[53] The three officers who had witnessed Leméry's inventory of Levasseur's property were all that were left to him. Jacques Barbazant was but a relative newcomer to the colony and Juchereau de Saint-Denis was still at the Mississippi. Looking ahead, Bienville would shortly begin to groom a core of young replacements—Gabriel Philippe de Saint-Lambert and his brother François-Philippe Philippe de Mandeville, both Canadians of good family; Antoine Siré, who had been in the colony since the earliest days, and the Sieur Daraque who would eventually succeed to Tonti's old position as

51. Extrait de testament de Charles Levasseur, Sept. 28, 1717, AN, Fonds particuliers, Minutier central: Étude XX-455. The influence of La Vente can be felt in Levasseur's provision for nails to be used in roofing La Vente's house and the proposed parish church. La Vente [to Tremblay], Sept. 10, 1704, *loc. cit.*, R 75.

52. *Ibid.* The back salary due Levasseur for 1704 was 490 *livres*. AC, F1A, 11, f. 218. His cash assets amounted to slightly less than 768 *livres*. Extrait de Testament, *loc. cit.* Levasseur's widowed mother, Marguerite Richard, lived for four years after her son's death. She died at Lorette in 1708. *DGFC, I*, p. 391. AJQ, Greffe de Gilles Rageot, 1666–1691.

53. AC, F1A, 11, f. 217–32.

"Commander of the Canadians."[54] Furthermore, back in France there were others yet to come: François Juchereau de Vaulezard, Saint-Denis' older brother; and the most capable young officer who expressed a desire for service in Louisiana—Antoine-François Ruette d'Auteuil de Monceaux, Saint-Denis's nephew and son of the attorney general to the Conseil Souverain de Québec. Mulling over prospective replacements, Bienville's reflections took on a more optimistic tone: all of these men could loosely be described as "Bienvillists" and three were, in fact, closely allied to his family.[55]

Nevertheless, the immediate situation at Fort Louis was all too bleak. The disease continued to spread through the colony. Two of the recently married girls, Catherine Tournant and Jeanne-Élisabeth Le Pinteaux had come down with the fever during the second week in September.[56] Their husbands, ecstatic with the joys of new marriage, were suddenly inconsolable. Bienville, himself despondent, found a new source to blame for the colony's sufferings. "I take the liberty," he wrote to Pontchartrain, "of directing your attention to the distress in which this establishment will remain so long as there is no fresh meat at all to nourish the ill who are reduced to soup made of salt pork. It seems to me that if the king incurred the expense of maintaining a boat for one year to transport livestock from Havana here where they could be purchased by the settlers, the king would not only profit from it but the colony would become much better off . . . I am convinced that if there were fresh food here, people would be as healthy as they are in France."[57]

Bienville's complaint of the lack of fresh meat was echoed by the townfolk. In reality there was plenty of flour and vegetables in the fort in mid-September of 1704. The *Pélican* had brought a substantial amount of supplies in early August, and Bécancour's vessel had returned with another load from Veracruz two weeks

54. *Ibid.*, 12, f. 103; 13, f. 113–14v. Bienville to min., Oct. 27, 1711, AC, C13A, 2, f. 569. In the late autumn of 1704 Saint-Lambert and Mandeville were still in the Wabash, preparing to leave for Mobile. *Journal Historique*, pp. 88–89.

55. Ruette's father was François-Madelaine-Fortuné Ruette d'Auteuil de Monceaux. *DGFC, I*, p. 159. His mother was Marie-Anne Juchereau, widow of François Pollet de La Combe-Pocatière, Iberville's father-in-law. *DGFC, I*, pp. 379, 494.

56. Le Vente [to Tremblay], Sept. 25, 1704, *loc. cit.*, R 76.

57. Bienville to min., Sept. 6, 1704, *loc. cit.*, f. 459.

later.[58] But the lack of meat, not the general food supply, was what the authorities were concerned about. "We need bacon . . . in greater quantity," La Vente complained to Tremblay, like Bienville seeming to think the lack of meat was the root of the colonists' inability to resist the fever.[59]

Meanwhile, Ducoudray was preparing the *Pélican* to leave for France via Havana. Originally scheduled to depart by the end of August, the preparations were slowed almost to a standstill by the lingering epidemic. Not only had he lost a substantial number of his crewmen to the disease but the fever, still raging, prevented many of the replacements with which Bienville had supplied him from energetically carrying out their duties.[60] Nevertheless, Ducoudray went ahead with his plans to leave as soon as possible. On September 9, one of the barks at Fort Louis was loaded with pelts, packets of letters (among them reports from La Vente and Bienville) and a number of other small items to be taken on board the *Pélican*. In addition, there were numerous passengers planning to return to France. The first bark left that morning, making its way downriver to Massacre Island with one of Bécancour's old pilots, Jacques Bernard, *dit* Matagon, aboard. Two days later another bark left Fort Louis for the port, carrying Canadians Antoine Damedieu, Joseph Simon, *dit* La Pointe, François Bonvalet and Antoine Fort. The following day (the twelvth of September), a third boat left for Massacre Island, carrying the retiring chaplain of Fort Louis, Pierre Dongé, and two sailors, François Leboeuf and Gaspard Thomas.[61]

Despite all of this activity, Ducoudray had little hope for an immediate weighing of anchor. Bienville's replacements were too inexperienced, too sluggish in preparing the *Pélican* for departure. The captain assured La Vente that the pastor would have ample time to finish his principal letter in time to have it sent by the ship to France. Towards the third week in September, vessels were constantly traveling back and forth between Fort Louis and Massacre Island. One of the last left the fort on September 26, carrying the third of La Vente's letters, which he had hastily written the night before.[62]

58. *Journal Historique*, pp. 84–85.
59. La Vente [to Tremblay], Sept. 10, 1704, *loc. cit.*, R 75.
60. Guzmán al virrey, Aug. 22, 1704, AGI, *Santo Domingo*, L. 857. Bienville to min., Sept. 6, 1704, *loc. cit.*, f. 464.
61. AC, F1A, 11, f. 218–220, 222, 225–28v.
62. La Vente [to Tremblay], Sept. 25, 1704, *loc. cit.*, R 76.

Three days after La Vente penned his last letter, the colony, slowly beginning to recover (although several of the inhabitants were still near death), managed to assemble itself at the fort for an impressive but overdue ceremony. The induction of Roulleaux de La Vente, whom Bishop Saint-Vallier had from Paris in 1703 named "first pastor of the parish church . . . (outside the royal citadel)," had been delayed for nearly two months due to the colony's severe distress.[63] Furthermore, when Saint-Vallier made his nomination he assumed a parish church would be physically erected by the time La Vente arrived; yet even by this date the building was still not begun.[64]

When Jesuit Dongé left Fort Louis on September 12, he relinquished his ministry of the chapel inside the fort, the chaplainship now to fall to Alexandre Huvé, one of the seminary priests.[65] As soon as it was convenient, Davion, lacking a more suitable location, arranged for the induction of the new clerical authority "outside the fort" to take place *within* Fort Louis' curtains. On the day of the twenty-eighth, the little chapel, capable of seating comfortably only forty-eight parishioners, was packed.[66] The ceremony began, Davion officiating. Bienville, Boisbriant, Châteaugué and La Salle sat on the front benches watching La Vente's entrance into the chapel, after which followed the dispersion of holy water, the kissing of the main altar, the touching of the book of the mass, the approaching of the "très Sainct-Sacrement de l'autel," and finally the ringing of the bells.[67]

The rituals completed, Davion had the proceedings recorded by La Vente in the parish register and the formality was capped by the signing of the induction, as witnessed by Davion, La Salle, Bienville and Boisbriant.[68] Despite the humble surroundings, the act of induction engendered a certain feeling of pride among the colonists, as was generally the case when a new village on the

63. Lettre de Mgr. de Saint-Vallier au sujet des missions du Mississippi, July 20, 1703, ASS, Section Canada, Dossier IX, No. 3. ASQ, Missions, 65.

64. The parish church was not built that year (1704), nor the next. Bienville to min., Feb. 20, 1707, AC, C13A, 2, f. 28–29.

65. AC, F1A, 11, f. 218, 224, 232.

66. Dénombrement du 31 août 1704, AC, C13A, 1, f. 468–69. "Comfortably" refers only to space. The chapel had no permanent pews at this early date.

67. Induction de Roulleaux de La Vente, Sept. 28, 1704, ADM, Miscellaneous French papers, 1704–1764 [formerly bound as the second page of baptismal register A (1704–1778)].

68. *Ibid.* The record of induction is unmistakably in La Vente's hand.

frontier officially received its *curé*. Saint-Vallier's "erection and nomination" was now sealed by actuality. Even Bienville, despite his lack of favor toward the seminary priests, seemed pleased. It was one further step fulfilled in his plan to create a solid colony and a formidable base of operations at Mobile.

Toward the first week in October, the *Pélican* finally managed to depart from Massacre Island. Ducoudray weighed anchor and sailed toward Havana where Father Dongé died either shortly before or after the ship's layover in the Spanish port.[69] During her sojourn at Mobile Bay, the *Pélican* had brought both good fortune and catastrophe to Louisiana. While calamity outweighed benefit as far as the Tomeh, Talimali and other victims of the scourge were concerned, the same could not be said for the colony as a whole. As valuable as had been the lives and services of Tonti, Levasseur and the some forty-odd other casualties of the epidemic (excluding natives), the far-reaching effects of the young girls' entrance into the colony would be incalculable.

If the *Pélican's* personnel, however, had seen the last of the widespread mortality, the epidemic was dying hard in the land they left behind. While La Vente, Huvé and Davion had almost completely recovered by the last week in September, death was still taking its toll among a number of the inhabitants. Catherine Tournant and Jeanne-Élisabeth Le Pinteaux, both of whom had been married in mid-August and had taken sick in September, died in those early days of autumn, Catherine on September 23 and Jeanne-Élisabeth two days later.[70] The epidemic continued to menace the establishment during the early days of October, its toll gradually diminishing until it disappeared completely when the first frost of November destroyed the mosquito larvae.

69. Tremblay [to Laval], April 4, 1705, ASQ, Lettres, N 122. ARSI, Francia, 45, 426. *JR*, *LXXI*, p. 161. Havana burial records show only one Frenchman (a certain "Juan, frances nat. de Bourdeu" interred during the time the *Pélican* was anchored at the Spanish port. Archivo de la Catedral de la Habana, Registro de las Sepulturas, Nov., 1704, Tomo IV, f. 65, No. 69.

70. La Vente [to Tremblay], Sept. 25, 1704, *loc. cit.*, R 76. AC, F1A, 11, f. 223.

XII

Continuing Crises

AFTER the departure of the *Pélican* and with the appearance of the first autumn frost, a degree of normality returned to Mobile. The mosquitoes vanished, and with them the dreaded Yellow fever that had precipitated the horrors of the late summer of 1704. It had been a summer which those who had lived through it would not easily forget (engendering more painful memories than any epidemic that would take place during the French occupation of Louisiana); but the cool nip in the air now seemed to bring renewed health and energy to the colony, and those who had been taken with the fever (which included practically everyone) must have felt as if they had awakened from an extended nightmare.[1]

As far as personnel were concerned the situation at the fort was radically different than it had been before the arrival of the *Pélican.* Tonti, Levasseur and Bécancour were gone; twenty-three new women were present (from the twenty-seven who had come on the *Pélican*) and most were now married. One of the still-single women was André-Joseph Pénigault's sister-in-law, Marie Grissot, who with the widow Duman (Marie Linant) had helped escort the girls of the *Pélican* from Rochefort the previous spring. These *soeurs du orphelinat* had not found favor with Roulleaux de La Vente on the voyage over, the priest having chided them for their laxity and ineptitude; they were in no higher esteem now that most of the girls were married.[2]

1. Decades later Bienville would recall the harrowing losses of August and September. Mémoire sur la Louisiane, par Bienville, vers 1726, AC, C13C, 1, f. 371–72.

2. Four of the *Pélican*'s twenty-seven women had died of Yellow fever. AC, F1A, 11, f. 223. La Vente [to Tremblay], Sept. 25, 1704, ASQ, Lettres, R 76. APR, 1 E 50, f. 39, 47, 80, 113, 194. LSMA, DCS, Dec. 22, 1718. La Vente [to Brisacier], June 25, 1704, ASQ, Lettres, R 74. La Harpe

Maire Grissot, however, found quick opportunity for employment upon the death of *sage-femme* Catherine Moulois (who, after receiving specialized training at the Hôtel Dieu in Paris, had come on the *Pélican* to serve as midwife at the respectable salary of 400 *livres* per year; soon after Dame Catherine's arrival, however, she had died, leaving her husband Laurent Cloquinet and her young son Henri, Marie Grissot succeeding her as *sage-femme*). Since Pontchartrain, at Iberville's request, had ordered a midwife sent to Mobile to aid in what was hoped would be numerous births, Bienville had felt obliged to seek a replacement; Marie Grissot, being single and impoverished, was eager to fill the vacancy, though she had little experience in that capacity.[3]

The need for a midwife was considered questionable by Bienville; it was not so held by Iberville and Pontchartrain. Nor did the surgeon Pierre Clavery, the husbands or the women of the town object to the idea. The *sage-femme* was very much in vogue in early eighteenth century France and the women of Fort Louis considered themselves fortunate not to have to brave the then dangerous act of childbirth alone.[4]

The new midwife was very soon to have an opportunity to perform her function; for in the autumn of 1704 there were two women in the latter stages of pregnancy at Mobile—Madelaine Robert, wife of carpenter Jean Le Caën and Angela Orsseau, wife of François Lemay, *dit* Poudrier. The imminent birth of Madelaine Robert's child had made her the object of much attention among the townfolk; at that time there were but ten children in the settlement (seven boys and three girls), ranging in age from one to ten years.[5]

On the fourth of October, Marie Grissot was summoned to Le

---

referred to the two nurses as "soeurs grises." *Journal Historique*, pp. 84–85. ADM, A, March, April, May, June, July, 1709 (following entry of May 30, 1709), Feb. 16, 1710. Collinet to Villermont, May 22, 1703, BN, FF, 22812, f. 126. Bégon to Mme. Durand, Nov. 21, 1703, AM, B2, 170, f. 470. While Grissot and Linant were not "Grey Sisters" themselves, they had been employed at an orphanage administered by the Daughters of Charity.

3. AC, F1A, 11, f. 218, 223. BN, FF, 22813, f. 133–34, 141–42. AM, B2, 166, f. 110. Min. to Bégon, Jan. 30, 1704, AC, B 25, f. 1. Dénombrement des familles et habitants . . . Aug. 1, 1706, AC, G1, 464.

4. Min. to Bienville, May 10, 1710, AC, B 32, f. 39v. AC, F1A, 12, f. 103v. Bienville to min., Oct. 27, 1711, AC, C13A, 2, f. 583–84.

5. ADM, A, Oct. 4, 22, 1704. Dénombrement du 31 août 1704, AC, C13A, 1, f. 468–70.

Caën's house at the corner of the rue Saint-Joseph and the rue de La Salle where Dame Madelaine was in the midst of labor, surrounded by several women of the settlement. By dusk, the selected godparents, François Lemay and Marguerite Burelle, had arrived at Le Caën's house, along with surgeon Pierre Clavery (who was to be more of a witness or spectator than an active participant). Sometime during the evening, Dame Madelaine, with Marie Grissot attending, gave birth to an apparently robust male child. Since the child was healthy and no complications were present, Grissot retired for the night to her own dwelling, the child being handed over to his mother. The next day, the fifth of October, the newborn infant was taken to the fort where during an impressive ceremony in the chapel (attended by a large number of the inhabitants) the young child was christened by Alexandre Huvé and named Jean-François by François Lemay.[6]

The fanfare surrounding this delivery was understandable considering that it was among the first births to take place at Mobile. The celebration of a baptism was in marked contrast to the numerous funeral rites which had been conducted over the past several months. Such a notable *naissance* seemed to momentarily lift the spirits of the inhabitants, for it signalled the promise that there could be life, as well as death, in the nascent colony.[7] Moreover,

6. ADM, A, Oct. 4, 1704. Plan de la Ville et du Fort de la Maubile, 1702, AC, DFC, Louisiane, 119A. AC, F1A, 11, f. 217, 220, 223. Neither Marguerite Burelle nor François Lemay signed the entry in the register. ADM, *loc. cit.*, Oct. 4.

7. *Ibid.* Jean-François' birth raised the total of young children at Mobile to eleven (eight boys and three girls). Dénombrement, Aug. 31, 1704, *loc. cit.*, f. 469–70. While Jean-François was not the first *créole* to be born at Mobile, his birth did predate that of Claude Joussette, *dit* La Loire. La Salle's entry, "Jean Le Camp [Le Caën] a le premier enfant masle [mâle] né a La Louisiane," in the 1706 census must be accepted as the best evidence, contrasted to Claude Joussette's later claim [*Cf.* note 54 below], since La Salle was closer to the fact and presumably had no axe to grind. Dénombrement, 1706, AC, G1, 464. Jean-François was dead by 1708, when his father remarried. LSMA, DCS, April 27, May 3, July 21, 23, 28, 1725. Excepting half-breeds the first *créole* born at Mobile was a female, although Robert Talon, a later resident of Mobile, had been born in late 1684 on board Robert Cavelier de La Salle's ship before the expedition had reached Galveston Bay. La Salle himself was Talon's godfather. *DGFC, I*, p. 558. Léon al virrey, July 12, 1690, AGI, *México*, L. 617. Relation de Joutel, July 24, 1684, Margry, III, p. 257. Interrogations faites à Pierre et Jean Talon, Sept. 14, 1698, Margry, III, p. 617. ADM, A, Jan. 5, 1719; Oct. 4, 1721; April 6, 1722. ADM, C, May 23, 1745.

the successful delivery of young Le Caën seemed a sort of communal victory; for the act of childbirth, although an honored and blessed occasion, was the most hazardous event in a woman's life, even in civilized France, but especially so in the wildernesses of America. Not so happy an occasion transpired several weeks later when Marie Grissot was again summoned, this time to the house of Jean-François' godfather, François Lemay, near the brickyard on the river front. Lemay's wife, Angela Orsseau, had been expecting the birth of her baby at roughly the same time as had her close friend Madelaine Robert. Already the mother of at least one child (who had been born in France) Angela began labor on the evening of October 21. At four o'clock the next morning she bore an infant male who immediately upon birth, as midwife Grissot could see, was at the point of death. On such occasions (when a newborn's chances for survival seemed in question), the midwife in charge was empowered to baptize the child immediately by applying a sprinkling of holy water along with the words "I baptize you in the name of the Father, the Son and the Holy Ghost" until a priest could perform the function more officially. Marie Grissot accordingly performed the emergency baptism and awaited the priest, but by daylight the unnamed Lemay infant had died and by the time Alexandre Huvé reached the scene a few hours later there were only the burial rites to perform.[8]

The loss of their infant son was not the only tragedy the Lemay family had suffered that autumn. Barely a month before, they had lost a little Indian "slave" who had been living with them and serving them for the past several years. It had been the custom of the local natives—the Mobilians and the Tomeh, in particular—to offer their children to live with those Frenchmen whom they admired and who had the desire and means to support young servants. By October of 1704 there were nearly fifteen such "slaves" living with French officers and inhabitants of some means. The custom was not opposed by the French. Besides cheap labor it was hoped by this practice to gain the good will of the savages, to keep closer contact with the villages and to help break the language barrier.[9]

8. ADM, A, Oct. 22, 1704. Plan de la Ville et du Fort de la Maubile, 1702, AC, DFC, Louisiane, 119A.

9. Dénombrement, Aug. 31, 1704, *loc. cit.*, f. 469–70. ADM, A, Sept. 18, 19, Oct. 1, 1704. It was by the aid of his "slaves," notably Jeanne-Louise and Jean-Baptiste, that Bienville absorbed the Mobilian tongue, the only native language he thoroughly mastered (though he was reasonably proficient in at least seven others). ADM, A, April 11, 1705; June 11, 1707.

But the Yellow fever that wreaked havoc with the Europeans was no less destructive of the young savages in French households. The day after La Vente performed the rites of burial for the Lemays' slave, Huvé conducted a funeral for a slave of Antoine Rivard who had been living in Rivard's household for more than a year. A few weeks later, Huvé was further called on to bury a slave of Canadian Philippe Minette and (with Albert Davion) to bury two slaves of the recently arrived Le Moyne de Châteaugué.[10]

Davion, who buried Châteaugué's slaves on the last day of October, had for nearly two months been waiting impatiently to return to his Tunica mission on the Yazoo River. Now that La Vente had assumed his duties as pastor, Davion felt useless in the town. Furthermore he was still annoyed at Commandant Bienville, as much for Bienville's failure to finance the building of the parish church as for his refusal to consult him on Indian policy. At the moment, however, Davion's chief concern was that after two years Bienville had still failed to send a detachment to punish the Koroa and the Yazoo for the murder of Foucault, which alone Davion felt would make the way safe for renewed missionary effort.[11]

In reality, Bienville felt as strongly as Davion about the need for punishing native aggression. The commandant had, in fact, already persuaded the Arkansas to launch an attack on the Koroa; yet he did not quite believe them when (no doubt, in order to receive more presents) they reported they had annihilated the Koroa. This suspicion on Bienville's part later proved correct. However, even if the commandant had given full credence to the Arkansas claim, he probably would not have informed Davion that the way was clear; for Bienville still had hopes at that time of persuading the missioner to transfer to the Chickasaw country rather than return to the village of the Tunica. By late 1704, however, Bienville had nearly given up on Davion as a possibility for the Chickasaw villages. Aged and not consistently healthy, the *abbé* could no longer be expected to pick up a new language with any facility and the more Bienville observed him in action the less he was convinced that Davion could fulfill such an assignment.[12]

10. ADM, A, Sept. 18, 19, Oct. 1, 28, 1704. AC, F1A, 11, f. 217–18v.

11. Davion [to SME Dirs.], Sept. 23, 1703, ASME, 344, 70. ADM, A, Oct. 28, 1704. Min. to Bienville, Nov. 4, 1705, AC, B 27, f. 192–94.

12. Min. to Bienville, Jan. 30, 1704, AC, B 25, f. 4–5. Davion [to SME Dirs.], Sept. 23, 1703, *loc. cit.*, 70. Bienville to min., Sept. 6, 1704, AC,

Perhaps Bienville was wiser on the question of a French reprisal mission than Davion. His experience in the Alabama campaign had taught him something: for all his impetuosity, the commandant retained a certain caution, especially when it concerned the security of his troops. He was confident an opportunity for reprisal would arise if he could await the initiative of the natives. The commandant's hopes were realized on December 21, 1704 when several chiefs of the Tunica came to the fort to plead for Davion's return to their village. Bienville took advantage of the chiefs' request to propose a bargain: if the Tunica hoped to see Davion return to his mission let them assume responsibility for making the way secure; let the Tunica strike at the Koroa and the Yazoo and bring to the fort the heads of Foucault's murderers as well as the Englishmen responsible for fomenting the aggression. For his part, Bienville agreed to provide a small detachment of Canadians from Fort La Boulaye under Louis Juchereau de Saint-Denis and to provision the Tunica with sufficient weapons and ammunition. Moreover, Bienville had recently received word that Gabriel Philippe de Saint-Lambert (commandant of Charles Juchereau de Saint-Denis' old establishment on the Wabash since Charles' death in 1703) was on his way down the Mississippi to Mobile with a detachment of forty Canadians. Saint-Lambert was to be intercepted on the Mississippi and persuaded to join Saint-Denis and the Tunica in a joint attack on the Koroa and the Yazoo.[13]

The agreement having been made with the Tunica, Bienville supplied them with a modicum of war materials and sent the chieftains on their way, Davion to follow in a few weeks with the Canadians who were preparing their pirogues at the fort.[14]

When Saint-Denis received his orders from Bienville, however, he balked: apparently the commandant of Fort Louis had been misinformed or, at least, he was not correlating what intelligence he had received. Saint-Denis, still smarting from the dressing down he had received a few years before from Bienville, saw a chance

---

C13A, 1, f. 456. La Vente no doubt got his information on the affair from Bienville. La Vente [to SME Dirs.], Sept. 20, 1704, ASQ, Lettres, R 77.

13. Davion [to SME Dirs.], Dec. 12, 1702, Sept. 23, 1703, ASME, 344, 57–70. *FLC*, pp. 98–99. *Journal Historique*, pp. 86–88. Charles Juchereau de Saint-Denis who died on Aug. 27, 1703 is generally referred to in the documents as Juchereau (Jusserot, Jucherot, etc.), while his brother Louis is usually called Saint-Denis (St.-Denys). AC, C11A, 36, f. 402–03, 411. AC, C13A, 1, f. 241, 457, 460–61. *FLC*, pp. 62, 76, 81, 107, 253.

14. *Journal Historique*, pp. 87–88.

to forestall an explosive situation and at the same time give tit for the upstart Le Moyne's tat. Ordering the Tunica chiefs (with a few Canadians) to tarry at Fort La Boulaye, Saint-Denis made a quick trip to Mobile in the early weeks of January 1705.[15]

Arriving while the Canadians were still busy preparing their pirogues for the retaliatory mission, Saint-Denis smugly asked Bienville if he were not himself promoting the sort of activity for which he (Saint-Denis) had previously been reprimanded: the unnecessary stirring up of an otherwise halcyon state of affairs. Continuing, Saint-Denis gave his own appraisal of the situation on the Mississippi: the murder of Foucault had not been the result of English promotion. In fact, it was not an act of the Koroa (as a nation) at all, but a non-political, spontaneous assault by a few greedy Koroa underlings who had apparently been abused by François Danbourné and his Canadian companions. The two Koroa had, on their own initiative, seized an opportunity to gain coveted possessions by retaliating for mistreatment by their employers. This appraisal was further indicated by the fact that the young Koroa murderers had dumped the bodies of Foucault and Danbourné into the river in an effort to hide their acts not only from the French but from their own Koroa chieftains. Furthermore, the Koroa chiefs themselves had discovered who the murderers were and had them executed shortly before Bienville had turned the Arkansas against them. In conspiring with the Arkansas to attack the Koroa, Bienville had done the latter nation a great injustice by punishing an entire village for the irresponsible acts of a few. According to Saint-Denis' recommendation, Bienville's proposed mission should be terminated immediately: since there was no need for punishment, any further reprisal would serve only to promote more incidents. Davion could return to his mission without fear for his life.[16]

Perceiving his mistake, Bienville quietly called off the expedition, although somewhat miffed by his error in judgment. No

15. *FLC*, p. 71. *Journal Historique*, pp. 87–88. Mémoire de . . . Richebourg, *s.d.*, AC, F3, 24, f. 73v–79. Pénigault jumbles the murders of Foucault and Saint-Cosme; nevertheless a good deal can be gleaned from a close comparison of his accounts when compared to other data. *FLC*, pp. 70–72, 98–99.

16. Mémoire de . . . Richebourg, *s.d.*, AC, F3, 24, f. 73–79. *Journal Historique*, pp. 87–88. AC, F1A, 10, f. 284. Davion [to SME Dirs.], Dec. 12, 1702, Feb. 14, 1703. ASME, 344, f. 57–65.

doubt he ascribed his misreckoning to not being properly informed. In any case, Saint-Denis returned to Fort La Boulaye and informed the Tunica that orders for the expedition had been revoked. To allay any disappointment to the aroused Tunica, he brought with him their beloved Davion who could now return with them to their village on the Yazoo. Thus, by late February of 1705, Albert Davion was back at his Tunica mission; Indian affairs on the Mississippi remained in good stead, thanks to the actions of the commandant of Fort La Boulaye.[17]

If stability on the Mississippi had been re-established, however, the tenuous Choctaw-Chickasaw alliance was in grave danger. Bienville, through no fault of his own, had been unable to fulfill his earlier promises to the Chickasaw: to send missionaries to their villages; to establish a thriving trade; to build a fort in their province. Sensing Bienville's inability to fix his relations with the Chickasaw on a firmer foundation, the English were now making renewed efforts to regain that nation's favor, a policy which was causing Bienville great concern and which was creating suspicion on the part of the Choctaw. With English backing, could the Chickasaw be persuaded to launch an attack on the scattered Choctaw villages? With Carolinian rifles, would the Chickasaw be soon capable of overwhelming their numerically superior rivals? [18]

Yet the Chickasaw were still hopeful of maintaining close relations with the French: from previous dealings with the French they instinctively inclined towards them, especially since they felt the French could keep their powerful and close neighbors (the Choctaw) at bay. Still, if the French deserted them (as Bienville's failure to live up to his promises seemed to indicate), the Chickasaw would have little defense against English-backed aggressions from the east. In the absence of full French support, they must maintain an open door to Carolina.[19]

The English took full advantage of this open door, which their greater resources permitted them to do. By the late fall of 1704 they were again trading in slaves with the Chickasaw and by

17. *FLC,* p. 71. *Journal Historique,* pp. 86–88.

18. Mémoire de Le Maire, Jan. 15, 1714, AC, C13C, 2, f. 125–26. Bienville to min., Oct. 10, 1706, AC, C13B, 1, No. 6, f. 2–8v. Bienville to min., July 28, 1706, AC, C13A, 1, f. 523–26, 529.

19. Dartaguiette to min., Feb. 26, 1708, AC, C13A, 2, f. 144. Bienville to min., Oct. 12, 1708, AC, C13A, 2, f. 183–84. Bienville to min., Feb. 20, 1707, AC, C13A, 2, f. 9.

February of 1705, the French had learned that the English had persuaded a number of Chickasaw warriors to seize several Choctaw families who were visiting Chickasaw villages. The English slipped away with their Choctaw prisoners to Carolina, confident they had caused a breach of good faith.[20]

When the Chickasaw chiefs (who were not directly involved in the complicity) realized the seriousness of the affair, they deemed it a proper time to approach the French (on this and several matters). Perhaps they could use the incident to persuade the commandant to live up to his unfulfilled promises. Aside from these considerations, the Chickasaw chiefs genuinely feared retaliation by the Choctaw. In early February, 1705, some seventy Chickasaw arrived at Fort Louis, having taken a round-about way to reach Mobile so as not to pass through the Choctaw country. On hearing news of the slave raid, Bienville was furious, as much at the renegade Chickasaw as at the English. He was no less bitter at authorities in France, both religious and secular, for their failure to provide him with a minimum of support. "The small assistance I have so far received," he wrote Pontchartrain, in subdued anger, "has prevented me from having the fort built that I had promised the Chickasaw; but since it is absolutely necessary to have one constructed in order to maintain peace between these natives and the Choctaw and to prevent them from turning to the English, I am going to go myself to have this fort built at which place I will leave an officer and a few chosen men. . . . I am convinced that the English will do everything they can to drive out the French from this post because they realize the importance of it, but I hope I will be given the means to sustain myself." [21]

What was at stake at the villages of the Chickasaw, Bienville felt, was the eventual dominance of the frontier. Was the court, he moaned, willing to jeopardize control of the interior for failure to provide a few soldiers, a few missionaries, a few thousand *livres* worth of presents? Nonetheless, a more immediate difficulty was at hand, salient enough in itself: the large group of Chickasaw warriors, women and children must be returned to their villages safely; somehow confidence must be restored between the distrustful antagonists. At the risk of inciting retaliation, the French must escort the Chickasaw delegation directly through the Choctaw country, in order to demonstrate to both nations that the French

20. *Ibid. Journal Historique*, pp. 88–91.
21. Bienville to min., July 28, 1706, *loc. cit.*, f. 523–24.

still supported their wayward ally (despite the breach of conduct).[22]

For this crucial mission Bienville chose his *aide-major* Pierre Dugué de Boisbriant, who, with twenty-five Canadians and the seventy Chickasaw, departed Fort Louis on February 9. By the twentieth of the month the French-Chickasaw party had arrived at the principal Choctaw village where the grand chief expressed surprise at seeing Frenchmen escorting a "band of traitors." While the chief promised Boisbriant not to molest the Chickasaw for the time being (acquiescing to Bienville's request), he wondered aloud whether the Chickasaw were leading the French into a trap? The Choctaw chief had good reason to be concerned over such a possibility, for if Boisbriant and the twenty-five Canadians were massacred, the Choctaw's chief ally against the Chickasaw and the English would be severely weakened. The Choctaw chief's reason for suspecting Chickasaw treachery (other than the recent seizure of the Choctaw families) jolted Boisbriant's confidence in his own safety. The chief put the matter bluntly: were the French going to be burned at the stake as young Saint-Michel, the French adolescent Iberville sent to the Chickasaw in 1702, had been burnt? [23]

Confronting the Chickasaw chiefs with this accusation, Boisbriant received a flat denial: the Choctaw were promoting this rumor to divide the French and the Chickasaw. Saint-Michel was alive and well.[24]

When Boisbriant conveyed the denial to the Choctaw chief, the Choctaw proposed a test: let the Chickasaw send two runners to their home camp to bring Saint-Michel back to the Choctaw village. The deliverance of an alive-and-well interpreter would prove whether the accusation were false.[25]

The Chickasaw chiefs had no objection to this demonstration, nor to Choctaw insistence that they be held hostage until the French boy could be delivered. Accordingly, the Chickasaw chiefs and warriors were confined to a large cabin, while Boisbriant and

22. *Ibid.*

23. AC, F1A, 10, f. 282; 11, f. 217; 13, f. 112. *Journal Historique*, pp. 88–90. Saint-Michel, who had left Brest with Iberville in 1698, had been in Louisiana continuously since 1699. AC, C13A, 1, f. 218, 258. After 1700, however, he is listed with the Canadians at a salary of 360 *livres* per year. AC, F1A, 10, f. 284v; 11, f. 220v.

24. *FLC*, p. 73.

25. *Ibid.*, p. 74.

his Canadians settled back to await the return of the Chickasaw couriers.[26]

A week elapsed with no word from the interior; understandably, since nine days at the very least would be required to make the round trip. Yet the silence began to weigh heavy on all concerned. The Chickasaw began to grow anxious, as did Boisbriant and the Canadians. Unknown to either Boisbriant or the Chickasaw, the Choctaw chiefs had dispatched a small party to follow the Chickasaw couriers, to murder them before they reached their villages. Yet the Choctaw had not heard from their own runners: had the Chickasaw couriers eluded their trackers? Perhaps the trackers had gone too far; perhaps they had been led too deeply into Chickasaw territory where they themselves had been slain?[27]

The chief of the Choctaw was unwilling to wait any longer. If the Chickasaw runners had somehow safely reached their villages, they would soon be returning to the Choctaw village with Saint-Michel, and the opportunity for revenge would be lost.

Boisbriant's position grew increasingly more awkward. He had been commissioned by Bienville to maintain the peace, but though he had every confidence the Chickasaw were telling the truth about Saint-Michel's safety, he had no evidence to lay before the Choctaw. Realizing he had been outmaneuvered, Boisbriant pressed for more time, but on the last day of February, the Choctaw chiefs assembled several thousand warriors, together with the Canadians and Chickasaw prisoners. After a bitter speech against the Chickasaw, attacking their villagers for permitting Choctaw families to be sold into slavery to the English, the Choctaw chieftain began to advance his warriors against the Chickasaw. The hapless Chickasaw defended themselves with ferocity, managing to strike dead numerous of their Choctaw assailants; but hopelessly outnumbered they were finally massacred (except for the women and children) almost to a man. The Canadian detachment, after first attempting to intervene, retreated from the scene of slaughter; but Boisbriant, in the resulting *melée*, was inadvertently wounded by Choctaw gunfire.[28]

The escort mission thus ended in miserable failure. The Choc-

26. *Ibid.* According to Pénigault, the principal Choctaw chief at this time was Le Dos Grillé. *FLC*, p. 130.

27. Tonti to Iberville, Feb. 23, 1702, AM, 2 JJ 56, 20. *FLC*, pp. 74–75. Tonti to Iberville, March 14, 1702, AM, 2 JJ 56, 20.

28. *Journal Historique*, pp. 88–91. *FLC*, pp. 75–76, 78.

taw had gotten their revenge, but afraid that in the wounding of Boisbriant they had permanently alienated the French, the chiefs began to try to make amends. The *aide-major* was placed on a stretcher and, escorted by three hundred Choctaw warriors, carried back to Mobile, where the contingent arrived on the tenth of March.[29]

When the Choctaw arrived at Fort Louis with the seriously wounded Boisbriant, Bienville received them in no good temper. Yet his anger was not reserved for the Choctaw alone. It was still another instance he felt that could have been prevented with but a minimum of aid from France. Had he been able to maintain missionaries in the Chickasaw villages the incident could have been avoided. As matters stood (in the late winter of 1705), Bienville feared that the carefully laid out Choctaw-Chickasaw alliance had been permanently damaged, that the French could henceforth rely only on the support of the loyal but erratic Choctaw.[30]

If Bienville's difficulties in the country to the northwest had multiplied, however, there was also increasing concern for the eastern lands from whence Bienville had recently received word that the English were planning an assault on Mobile and Pensacola. As a consequence of those rumors the commandant was awaiting impatiently the return of his brother, Le Moyne de Châteaugué, supposedly now somewhere between Mobile and Veracruz.[31]

Back in November, Pensacola had been practically consumed by a disastrous fire which had swept through the houses and barracks of the post. Andrés de Arriola and his sergeant-major, Joseph de Guzmán, had lost considerable amounts of supplies. When four days after the November 23 conflagration a relief mission appealed to Bienville for help, the commandant felt he could not refuse the request. In the event of English aggression a stable Pensacola would form an important bastion of defense. Three weeks after receiving Arriola's plea for assistance, Bienville sent Châteaugué in the *Précieuse* to provision the Pensacola garrison

29. *Journal Historique*, pp. 90–91.

30. Bienville to min., July 28, 1706, *loc. cit.*, f. 523–24. It was, after all, the Choctaw who were bringing back Alabama scalps. *Journal Historique*, pp. 82–86.

31. Hervé Guymont Ducoudray had relayed this news (which was current in Havana in November 1704) by a French brigantine. *Journal Historique*, pp. 85–86. Carta de Luis Chacón, Dec. 14, 1704, AGI, *Santo Domingo*, L. 377.

with a large supply of bacon, a hundred barrels of flour and all the arms and ammunition he could spare.[32]

Châteaugué, upon his return to Louisiana on the *Pélican*, had been given command of the *Précieuse*, the late Bécancour's ship. During the fall of 1704 Châteaugué had been using the vessel for occasional voyages to Pensacola. Thus when Arriola requested a ship be sent to Veracruz to inform authorities in New Spain of the catastrophe, Bienville commissioned his younger brother to make this voyage also. Châteaugué, who three years prior had played a significant role in the founding of Mobile, departed Massacre Island on January 21, 1705, reaching Veracruz during the first week of February.[33]

Having lent Guzmán and Arriola such a generous amount of supplies, Bienville was becoming increasingly concerned about his own provisions. Always farsighted where supplies were concerned, Bienville had instructed Châteaugué to petition the authorities at Veracruz for immediate replacement of the supplies lent Pensacola. When Châteaugué returned to Massacre Island on March 20, ten days after Boisbriant had been returned to Mobile from the Choctaw country Bienville was gratified to hear that not only had the authorities at Veracruz replaced the one hundred barrels of flour that had been lent to Pensacola but that Viceroy Alburquerque had sent orders to the governor of Pensacola "to reckon with him for all that had been reciprocally furnished." [34]

In any case, Châteaugué brought the welcome news to Pensacola that Alburquerque was sending aid "as soon as possible" which assistance was all the more needed since Pensacola had suffered yet another fire while Châteaugué had been at sea in February. "As soon as possible," however, proved to be "considerably overdue" as far as Andrés de Arriola was concerned. Although a *bergantín* of the Armada de Barlovento, carrying emergency supplies, followed closely on the sails of Châteaugué in the spring, it was not

32. El virrey a su magestad, Dec. 10, 1706, AGI, *México*, L. 477. Junta de Guerra de Indias, Dec. 2, 1707, AGI, *México*, L. 377. Bienville to min., July 28, 1706, AC, C13A, 1, f. 515–16.

33. AC, F1A, 10, f. 282; 11, f. 216–18, 221v. El virrey a su magestad, Dec. 10, 1706, *loc. cit.*, L. 477. Extrait du mémoire des officiers Royaux de la Veracrux des avances faites a la colonie de la Louisianne tant en argent, vivres qu'en autres effets depuis le 11 juillet 1704 jusque au 13 aoust 1714, AC, C13A, 3, f. 675–86.

34. *Journal Historique*, pp. 88–89. Bienville to min., July 28, 1706, *loc. cit.*, f. 515–16. Junta de Guerra de Indias, May 26, 1705, AGI, *México*, L. 618.

until late August that the *Nuestra Señora del Rosario* under Vice-admiral Antonio Landeche arrived at Santa María de Galve with a six months supply of provisions for the garrison, with arms and ammunition to repay the French, and with more than two hundred men to rebuild Fort San Carlos. Depositing the men and supplies, Landeche made a quick trip to Havana, but on his return to Pensacola to take aboard masts for the shipyard at Veracruz, the *Nuestra Señora del Rosario*, after anchoring at Pensacola Bay, was wrecked by a September hurricane.[35]

Apprised of the fate of Landeche's capital ship, Bienville sent La Salle and Châteaugué (in response to Guzmán's request for the loan of a freighter) to Pensacola on the *Précieuse* to make arrangements for the loan of that ship to transport Landeche back to Veracruz to inform Alburquerque of the misfortune. Bienville had two conditions for the loan of the *Précieuse:* first, that Châteaugué be permitted to command the ship; and secondly that the *Précieuse* whose hull was in need of extensive repairs be restored at Spanish expense. When La Salle secured this agreement, Châteaugué, with a number of his crewmen, set out in a Spanish felucca for Massacre Island to await the *Précieuse's* repair.[36]

Thus another helping hand had been lent the Spanish by the French. Bienville was later to report that "the Spaniards of Pensacola have fortified themselves perfectly well since their recent fires. They have even managed to increase their garrison by fifty men." Bienville was particularly generous at this stage in his relations with Pensacola because of his immediate fear of the English and because he was certain that in time he would find it necessary to call on the Spanish for similar assistance. Had the same disasters struck Mobile as had befallen Pensacola, Bienville would have been even more dependent on the Spanish than Pensacola had been on the French.[37]

Surface relations had been unusually amicable between the two establishments; there was nevertheless an undercurrent of Spanish resentment born of the supposition that the French were somehow intruding on a land that had long been regarded by Spain as her

35. Junta de Guerra de Indias, Dec. 2, 1707, *loc. cit.*, L. 377. El virrey al rey, June 6, 1706, *loc. cit.*, L. 477. El virrey a su magestad, Dec. 10, 1706, *loc. cit.*, L. 477.

36. La Salle to min., Sept. 7, 1706, AC, C13A, 1, f. 483–85. Bienville to min., April 10, 1706, *loc. cit.*, f. 502–03. *Journal Historique*, pp. 90–92. Junta de Guerra de Indias, Dec. 2, 1707, *loc. cit.*, L. 377.

37. Bienville to min., July 28, 1706, *loc. cit.*, f. 517–18.

exclusive domain.[38] Moreover, the Spanish had been somewhat resentful that the French with a minimum of effort had gained the loyalty of so many Spanish Indians from Apalache merely because of the presence of Fort Louis: had the French not been established at Mobile, the Apalache refugees who now resided on Mobile Bay would have been forced to remain under the Spanish (who needed them for their hoped-for repossession of the province). Guzmán had persuaded at least several of the Apalache village groups (among them the Escambe) to remain near Pensacola when the majority had drifted to Mobile in August of 1704, but by late 1705, even most of these remnants had deserted Pensacola for Mobile.[39] Bienville was thence able to report to Pontchartrain:

> I have acquired the remainder of those Apalache and Chatonatives who were established near the Spaniards. The governor of Pensacola [Guzmán] offered very considerable presents to the leaders of these two nations to make them return to the Escambia River but they refused, claiming that the French assisted their allies better than did the Spanish, the French furnishing more arms, in addition to the fact that the natives were not masters of their own wives while among the Spaniards and that among the French they had no fear on that point.[40]

Aside from the sensitive issue over the refugees from Apalache, the question of exact boundaries had frequently arisen in communications between the commandants of the two posts. Bienville had maintained that since the French occupied Mobile Bay that this quite naturally included both banks of the river and bay; whereas Guzmán (and before him Martínez and Arriola) maintained that since a natural boundary must, of necessity, exist somewhere, what more natural dividing line was there than the river and bay itself (especially in view of the fact that the Spanish

38. El rey al virrey, Aug. 22, 1704, AGN, *Historia*, 298. Min. to Rémonville, Feb. 4, 1711, AM, B2, 226, f. 441. Min. to Demuy, June 30, 1707, AC, B 29, f. 265–66. Dartaguiette to min., Feb. 26, 1708, AC, C13A, 2, f. 145. Bienville to min., Oct. 27, 1711, AC, C13A, 2, f. 583.

39. La Vente [to SME Dirs.], June 27, 1708, ASQ, Lettres, R 82. Bienville to min., Sept. 6, 1704, AC, C13A, 1, f. 461–62. Lettre de Jacques Gravier, 1706, AC, C13A, 1, f. 575–76. Guzmán al virrey, Aug. 22, 1704, AGI, *Santo Domingo*, L. 857.

40. Bienville to min., July 28, 1706, *loc. cit.*, f. 530–31.

under Luna had in 1560 actually colonized the bay's eastern shore).[41]

Until the fall of 1705 the question was strictly academic, but as Châteaugué was returning to Massacre Island in September in the felucca loaned him by the Spanish the issue suddenly came to the forefront. Lodged on the easternmost rises of the Îles-aux-grand gosier (a part of which was later called Île de Sable or Sand Island) just south-southwest of Mobile Point was a small brigantine. Supposing the vessel to be English, Châteaugué approached the ship cautiously, but soon began to hear voices calling out for help in French. From her commander, a certain Captain Maurice, a privateer from Martinique, Châteaugué soon learned how the *Saint-Antoine*, as the ship was known, came to be lodged on the bar: she had been returning from a trading voyage to Havana and Veracruz, was heading back to Martinique when near the Cabo San Antonio (the western tip of Cuba) a storm had broken off her mainmast and crushed her prow. During the tempest the huge waves had carried off eight men with her forecastle and had flooded a part of the bridge. Set adrift, the *Saint-Antoine* was washed across the gulf where she finally ran aground along the sands below Mobile Point.[42]

Châteaugué, after anchoring the ship as firmly as he could, had Captain Maurice and his some ninety survivors transported as quickly as possible to Massacre Island, where after a short rest they were taken on to Fort Louis. Châteaugué then set about the task of recovering the brigantine's booty. In the meantime acting governor Guzmán had received word of the stranded ship; with little delay the Pensacola captain dispatched "sixty men in two ship's boats to take possession of the vessel," maintaining that since the ship was permanently lodged on the eastern side of the river channel that the Spanish could exercise salvage rights. Châteaugué, with his twenty-five Canadians, challenged Guzmán's forces, re-

41. Bienville to min., April 10, 1706, *loc. cit.*, f. 510–11. Min. to Bienville, May 10, 1710, AC, B 32, f. 40v. François Le Maire à son oncle, Oct. 10, 1711, AM, 2 JJ 56, 22. Los Capitánes al campo del sargento mayor, 1560, AGI, *Justicia*, L. 1013.

42. Bienville to min., Oct. 27, 1711, AC, C13A, 2, f. 583. Carte de L'Isle Dauphine, 1717, BN, 138, 10, 72, D. Preliminary Chart (No. 26) of the Seacoast of the United States from Mobile Bay, Ala. to Lake Borgue, La., 1857, Dept. of the Gulf, Map. No. 11, Mobile and vicinity, July, 1863, LC, G&M Div., Group RMR. *Journal Historique*, pp. 92–93. *FLC*, pp. 117–18.

minding them that the French claimed both banks of the Mobile River; the feisty Le Moyne had no intention of allowing the Spanish to haul away any loot, or even to board the vessel. Guzmán's actions, which in effect forced the boundary issue, came at an extremely inopportune moment for him, for Pensacola was possibly at her lowest ebb: Guzmán desperately needed loan of the *Précieuse;* he did not know the value of the cargo aboard the *Saint-Antoine.*[43]

The Spanish grudgingly retreated, Châteaugué proceeding to transfer the ship's plunder to his feluccas. The salvage proved considerable. Châteaugué recovered at least seventy-two thousand *piastres* in gold and silver from the ship's hold, which he promptly carried with him back to the fort and delivered to Bienville. The commandant used a portion (two thousand *piastres*) of the spoilage to pay back some of the colony's debts to Guzmán, but what became of the residue was never known. Bienville later attempted to have Captain Maurice reimbursed for at least the two thousand *piastres* he had used to repay Guzmán.[44]

A few weeks later, the *Saint-Antoine* was washed off the sand islands and drifted out to sea where it eventually sank. Châteaugué returned with his crew in the felucca to Pensacola. The *Précieuse's* hull was repaired and the younger Le Moyne set sail for Veracruz, carrying Vice-admiral Landeche and his officers and part of the crew of the *Nuestra Señora del Rosario.*[45]

Meanwhile, back at the fort, Bienville was still very much concerned over the state of Choctaw-Chickasaw relations. Two weeks after Boisbriant had been returned to Mobile by the Choctaw, a group of ten Chickasaw headmen arrived in a pirogue at the village of the Tunica. Encouraged by Davion, the Chickasaw then continued on to Mobile where they assured Bienville that despite the recent massacre by the Choctaw they still desired peace. Moreover, they expressed surprise that Bienville and Boisbriant should question them about the well-being of young Saint-Michel, by

43. La Salle to min., Sept. 7, 1706, AC, C13A, 1, f. 481–85. *FLC*, pp. 118–19. Bienville to min., April 10, 1706, *loc. cit.*, f. 510–11. El virrey a su magestad, June 6, 1706, *loc. cit.*, L. 477.

44. La Salle to min., Sept. 7, 1706, *loc. cit.*, f. 481–85. *FLC*, pp. 118–19. *Journal Historique*, pp. 91–93. Min. to Bégon, May 25, 1707, AC, B 29, f. 242–43.

45. *Ibid.*, pp. 92–93. Junta de Guerra de Indias, Dec. 2, 1707, *loc. cit.*, L. 377.

which response Boisbriant then knew for certain that the Chickasaw couriers who had been sent to fetch the interpreter had been murdered before they reached their homeland. Bienville's hopes for a restoration of peace were thus brightened, but he wanted Saint-Michel to be brought to Mobile first so he could confront the Choctaw with the hard evidence. Promising to bring back Saint-Michel, the Chickasaw departed Mobile in mid-April, 1705.[46]

Confrontations between the smaller nations Bienville was able to keep under control by the sheer force of his personality. When a villager from the Little Tomeh killed a Mobilian woman, Bienville was able to restore peace by his personal intervention before hostilities erupted on a larger scale. However, at the same time the commandant was desperately trying to maintain peace among the nations allied to the French, he was actively promoting aggression against the Alabama villages. At Bienville's instigation the Choctaw arrived regularly at the fort to present their Alabama scalps for each of which they were awarded a rifle.[47]

Unknown to Bienville at the time, a treaty (in the form of a letter of intentions) was being finalized in the Indian village of Coweta in August of 1705 declaring all of the natives allied to the French as "enemies to be attacked and annihilated." The proclamation was drawn up by Carolina Indian agents Daniel Henchman, John Jones and John Musgrove and was signed by (among others) chiefs of the villages of the Alabama, Coweta, Kasihta and Okmulgee (practically all the nations that would in later years be referred to collectively as the Upper and Lower Creeks).[48]

The chiefs of the aforementioned villages apparently meant what they signed. In the autumn of 1705, three thousand of the natives bound by the declaration launched an assault against the "villages of the Choctaw who, having been warned, abandoned their cabins and retreated to the woods." The "Creeks," spurred on

46. *FLC*, pp. 78–79. *Journal Historique*, pp. 92–93. AC, F1A, 11, f. 220v.

47. Bienville to min., July 28, 1706, *loc. cit.*, f. 530. Mémoire de . . . Richebourg, *s.d.*, AC, F3, 24, f. 73–79. A gun for a scalp was an exchange long established in Canada; Pontchartrain, though he reluctantly consented to the idea, thought the practice too costly for Louisiana. Bienville to min., July 28, 1706, *loc. cit.*, 526. Twenty-seven scalps were brought to Fort Louis in 1705, mostly by the Choctaw. Bienville to min., April 10, 1706, *loc. cit.*, f. 508–09.

48. The Humble Submission of Several Kings, Princes, Generals, & c., to the Crown of England, Aug. 15, 1705, British Museum, London, 1707 broadside. Lettre de François Le Maire, Jan. 15, 1714, AC, C13C, 2, f. 125–26.

by the English, ravaged and burned the Choctaw's cabins and crops, before making a hasty retreat. On the English Indians' withdrawal, the Choctaw emerged from the woods, launching a heated counter-offensive which resulted in the destruction of several hundred of the English coalition. According to Bienville, the Choctaw "returned to their lands very proud of their deeds, attributing their advantage to the arms that we have given them." The eastern savages temporarily disheartened, the inhabitants of Fort Louis were for the moment freed from the anxiety of being attacked, although the invasion of the Choctaw by the Alabama was surely foreboding.[49]

The year 1705 witnessed a number of new arrivals at Mobile. On January 28, Gabriel Philippe de Saint-Lambert and his brother Mandeville arrived at the fort with a small force of renegade Canadians after being forced to abandon their post on the Wabash. Saint-Lambert, whose younger brother, Jean-François Philippe de Hautmesnil, was already serving at Mobile, was a welcome addition to the colony where Bienville was needful of capable, robust officers; Saint-Lambert was quickly assigned the command of Vaulezard's company at 480 *livres* per year in which post he would prove extremely useful for the next year and a half.[50]

Later that year, fifty *voyageurs* arrived from the Illinois country, among them Pierre Sauton and another named Saint-Laurent. Sauton had served at Fort Louis before, along with his traveling companion Joseph Guillet de Bellefeuille. He had in fact been assigned a lot by Iberville on the rue de Boutteville (which later had been given to Charles Dumont and his son when those servant-helpers had followed Albert Davion down to Mobile after Foucault's murder). Saint-Laurent and Sauton had for two years been traveling through the Missouri country, trading with the Indians. "The Missouri," they reported, "where the Spanish come to trade, is the finest [country] in the world." To prove it, the explorers brought three samples of mineral deposits which Bienville judged to be mostly "copper and a metal that is quite unknown." Bienville, however, remembering the disappointing results of past

49. *Journal Historique*, pp. 94–95. Bienville to min., April 10, 1706, *loc. cit.*, f. 509–10.

50. AC, F1A, 11, f. 71v, 113v. *Journal Historique*, p. 95. *DGFC, I*, p. 300. AC, F1A, 10, f. 284; 11, f. 71v, 220; 13, f. 118. Among those arriving with Saint-Lambert were Michel Philippe, Nicolas La Berge and Alexis Guay (whom Bienville was shortly to appoint as *garde-magasin* of the Massacre Island warehouse).

mineral tests, was only mildly interested in Sauton's samples, as was Pontchartrain when the news reached him.[51]

Towards the end of summer, a large canoe filled with a family of Bienville's relatives arrived at the fort. On April 30 of the previous year, Marguerite Messier, slender blond wife of Pierre-Charles Le Sueur, had engaged François Benoît, *dit* Livernois of Longueuil to escort her and her family down the Mississippi from Montreal to a rendevous at Mobile with her husband (who was thought to be arriving from Rochefort on the *Pélican*). Besides Dame Marguerite and Livernois, the party had consisted of Marguerite's brother, Jean-Michel Messier de Saint-Michel; her young son Jean-Paul Le Sueur, and daughters Marie-Anne, Louise-Marguerite, Marie and Marguerite.[52]

Upon arrival at Mobile, Le Sueur's family was crestfallen to learn that the explorer had been dead for over a year. Yet this news was but the crowning blow of a tragic summer. Two months after the party had passed through Kaskaskia in April (and two months before it reached Mobile), Dame Marguerite's brother, Jean-Michel, and one of her daughters, Louise-Marguerite, had also died. Despite what she might have preferred, however, Widow Le Sueur was compelled to remain at the fort. The voyage down the Mississippi had been a long and arduous journey; a return trip would be doubly difficult. Then too, at Mobile she *was* among family and friends. Fortunately her late husband already had a house constructed on the rue de Ruessavel across the street from fellow Canadians Claude Trépanier and Philippe Minette. Practically destitute (aside from the house and property Le Sueur had left her) she wrote back to Maurice Blondeau, a Montreal merchant, to dispose of her Canadian home and lands and to send her the proceeds.[53]

51. *Journal Historique*, p. 93. Bienville to min., April 10, 1706, *loc. cit.*, f. 504–06. Plan de la ville et du fort de la Maubile, 1702, AC, DFC, Louisiane, 119A. Davion [to SME Dirs.], Dec. 12, 1702, ASME, 344. ADM, A, Sept. 22, 25, 1707. *DGFC, I*, p. 291.

52. AJM, Greffe de Adhémar, April 30, 1704. Mémoire du Roy à Mssrs. Vaudreuil et Beauharnois, June 14, 1704, AC, B 25, f. 101–03. ADM, C, March 5, 1741. *DGFC, I*, pp. 41–42, 389. Madame Le Sueur was further described as "very tall, with a well-shaped face . . . though not beautiful . . ." Mémoire de Gannes, Oct. 21, 1720 [in reality, a letter of Pierre di Lieto, ca. 1711], Newberry Library, Ayer Collection, Vol. 4.

53. *DGFC*, I, pp. 291, 379, 427. Lettre de Marguerite Messier, Veuve Le Sueur, May 21, 1706, Chicago Historical Society, Schmidt Collection, I, p. 173. Plan de la ville et du fort de la Maubile, *loc. cit.*, 119A. It is possible

Aside from immigrations, Mobile's population also increased as a result of the births which took place in the summer and fall of 1705 (as may have been expected from the number of marriages performed in 1704). Marie Rivard, daughter of Antoine Rivard de La Vigne and Marie Briard, was born in the autumn of 1705. Soon thereafter followed a daughter of Gilbert Dardenne and Marguerite Burelle as well as children of André Renaud, Pierre Brossard, Claude Trépanier and Jean Brunet, *dit* Bourbonnois. And sometime during the year 1705 Claude Joussette was born. Young Claude's father, Jean-Baptiste Joussette, *dit* La Loire had come to Louisiana three years before on the *Renommée*, without his wife Marie-Anne Nadeau whom he had married at La Rochelle. The next year his young wife had come alone on the *Loire* and by that time Jean-Baptiste had completed their house on the riverfront, next to that of François Lemay, *dit* Poudrier in the northwestern sector of town. The young couple (Jean-Baptiste was twenty-seven when his wife arrived) had barely become accustomed to their new home when Marie-Anne became pregnant. The next year their first child, Claude, was born, a birth which was to become in later years a subject of considerable controversy.[54]

On the morning of August 16, 1705 midwife Marie Grissot was summoned to the house of Jean Roy, a master cannoneer from La Rochelle, who had constructed a modest home on a large lot next to Canadian Pierre de Launay on the rue de Pontchartrain. Roy's wife, Renée Gilbert of Tours, whom he had married the previous August shortly after she had arrived on the *Pélican*, was in the latter stages of labor. At noon she delivered a son. *Sage-femme*

---

that the Le Sueur party was accompanied to Mobile by Gabriel Marest although no presently known document records his arrival. Bergier [to SQ Dirs.], April 15, 1705, ASQ, Lettres, R 73.

54. Gabrielle Savary, who had been one of the last of the so-called "*Pélican* girls" to marry, had two children by her husband Jean-Baptiste Saucier during a fourteen-month period, a fact which indicates she either had twins or employed a wet-nurse. Dénombrement . . . Aug. 1, 1706, AC, G1, 464. ADM, A, Nov. 27, 1707. In later years Claude, hoping to receive a subsidy, petitioned the government to declare him the first male child born in Louisiana. After nearly a decade of appeals, he was allowed a small stipend, thanks to testimony by Jean-Baptiste Baudreau de Graveline and Joseph Girardy. However, neither Graveline nor Girardy had been present at Mobile at the time of Claude's birth and Claude's own testimony indicates he was born in 1705. LSMA, DCS, Jan. 16, 1720; March 3, 4, 1731. Bienville and Salmon to min., May 6, 1733, AC, C13A, 16, f. 25–26. Claude died in New Orleans in 1781, having amassed a considerable estate. LSMA, Spanish Judicial Records, Nov. 19, 1781.

Grissot sent for La Vente but he was nowhere to be found. Alexandre Huvé had removed to the village of the Talimali some sixteen miles distant. Thus the child was not baptized on the day of his birth. The next morning at eleven o'clock, still unable to locate La Vente, Jean Roy had the infant privately baptized (by Grissot), having decided not to wait for Huvé's return from the Apalache village. When Huvé returned the following week, the infant was taken to the fort's chapel where the missioner performed the "cérémonies ordinaires" necessary to give full validity to the sacraments of baptism. This time the child's godparents, carpenter Jacques Le Compte and Gabrielle Savary, were present and the child was christened Jacques.[55]

If the aforementioned births were occasions for rejoicing, there were numerous others which brought nothing but anguish. Many of the infants born that year, particularly in the late fall and early winter of 1705, suffered early deaths. Bienville was to censure La Vente for the premature demise of most of them, citing the *curé's* practice of baptizing the infants naked during the winter months. On the other hand, René Boyer, a master gunsmith who had married Marie-Catherine Christophe, blamed Bienville for the early death of *his* child, charging that the commandant had refused him milk during the child's illness. Whatever the reasons for the mortality, a number of infants *did* perish, a fact that was as disconcerting to Bienville, who hoped to see the colony increase, as it was to the distraught parents.[56]

The infant mortality rate was not the only disconcerting pass in these last days of 1705. The fort, less than three years old, was beginning to decay rapidly; Bienville was seeking Pontchartrain's permission to have it rebuilt, of bricks this time, and hopefully

55. ADM, A, Aug. 16, 1705. AC, F1A, 10, f. 282v; 11, f. 69v. Dénombrement des familles et habitants . . . Aug. 1, 1706, AC, G1, 464. ADM, B, May 25, 1734.

56. Interrogatoire des habitants . . . Feb. 26, 1708, AC, C13A, 2, f. 306. There are no recorded baptisms in the Mobile baptismal register from Aug. 16, 1705 until February 23, 1707 (the period covering Bienville's accusations), although at least seventeen births took place during that time. While Bienville charged that nine consecutive baptisms resulted in deaths, only Guillaume Boutin, François Dupré and Jean-Baptiste La Croix, *dit* Grimauld are known to have lost children during this period. Perhaps Bienville was also including Indian baptisms in his charges, although the natives were not usually baptized at birth during this time. ADM, A, Aug. 16, 1705; Feb. 23, 1707. Bienville to min., Feb. 20, 1707, AC, C13A, 2, f. 26. Dénombrement . . . Aug. 1, 1706, AC, G1, 464.

within the next two years. Already the townfolk were beginning to grumble about the specific location of the settlement: it was too far upriver; the lands where the houses stood were poorly drained; after each rain several weeks were required for the standing water to drain. Nicolas de La Salle wanted to move the principal establishment to Massacre Island (to eliminate the long delays of goods reaching the fort after having been brought by the ships from France), a suggestion that irked Bienville since it reflected on the judgment of both himself and his brother Iberville.[57]

The flooding around Fort Louis also interfered with what little agriculture was being attempted. The majority of residents had but simple gardens around their dwellings (which served only to supplement the general food supply), but many of the inhabitants were more ambitious—Rivard, La Loire, Graveline, Saucier, the Chauvin brothers. Such men of higher than average means and aspirations envisioned large plantations by which they could gradually become wealthy by supplying their excess produce to markets in Pensacola, Havana and Veracruz as well as to the king's storehouse at Mobile. To expand on any large scale, however, the entrepreneurs needed slaves to work the land and they were constantly pressing Bienville to import blacks from Martinique and Saint-Domingue. The few Indian slaves present were put to good use, but they were not sufficient in number and there was always the possibility, frequently realized, that the natives would run away if pushed too severely.[58]

The requests for black slaves from these would-be planters were not received unsympathetically by Bienville. In fact, the commandant, as did Iberville, heartily endorsed the idea, both leaders having previously pressed for such importations. Pontchartrain, however, had considerable reservations. Owing to the war in Europe (and the resulting curtailment of oceanic voyages), the slave trade in the West Indies had been severely reduced. Besides, the minister reasoned, how would the colonists pay for such slaves? Only a few merchants would have the capital to purchase them outright; the majority would have to resort to slave-trading—

57. Bienville to min., April 10, 1706, *loc. cit.*, f. 506. La Salle to min., Sept. 7, 1706, *loc. cit.*, f. 477–91. Gravier to min., 1706, AC, C13A, 1, f. 570–72.

58. Bienville to min., Sept. 6, 1704, AC, C13A, 1, f. 459–60. Interrogatoire des habitants . . . Feb. 26, 1708, *loc. cit.*, f. 256–57, 273, 296. Mémoire du Roy . . . June 30, 1707, AC, B 29, f. 251–51v. Gravier to min., 1706, *loc. cit.*, f. 570–72.

Indian for black—an alternative which would be certain to stimulate the very practice the French were trying to eliminate.[59]

Aside from slaves to work the land, the colonists lacked tools and oxen. In late 1705 there were but thirteen oxen (only five of which were privately owned) and seven bulls in the colony. Not a single horse was present, although hogs and hens numbered in the hundreds, and the some twenty or thirty cows made dairy farming a promising venture.[60]

Aside from other disadvantages, another factor that dissuaded the colonists from planting was the lack of a mill to grind their grain. Although stones for a mill, furnished by a merchant from Rochefort, had been brought over on the *Loire* two years earlier, the mill had never been completed due to the death of the only man thought capable of assembling the parts. As a result, the residents were forced to grind their grain in wooden mortars, a tedious process. Bienville still hoped to have the mill built, a task which he reckoned might be accomplished by the few skilled carpenters present for the sum of three thousand *livres*. Aside from the meager amounts of grain they grew themselves and the occasional quantities received from Veracruz, the colonists subsisted on the maize of the natives, always a last resort. "The men who are in Louisiana are accustoming themselves to maize," Bienville reported, "but the women, who for the most part are natives of Paris, are very reluctant to consume it. This makes them grumble a great deal against the Bishop of Quebec who had made them understand they would be coming to the Promised Land." [61]

In the last days of 1705 Bienville's expectations for the colony were less than soaring. He was, in fact, thinking seriously of returning to France. His sturdy constitution had withstood the onslaughts of disease but not without ill effects. He was already complaining of sciatic gout and inflammation of the chest; he thought perhaps if he could return to the continent he could not only

59. Mémoire du Roy . . . June 30, 1707, *loc. cit.*, f. 251v. Bienville to min., July 28, 1706, *loc. cit.*, f. 522. Dartaguiette to min., June 20, 1711, AC, C13A, 2, f. 640. Min. to Bienville, May 10, 1710, AC, B 32, f. 39. Robert to min., Nov. 26, 1708, AC, C13A, 2, f. 359–62.

60. AC, F1A, 10, f. 200, 288–89v; 11, 64v–68v. Min. to Dartaguiette, June 30, 1707, AC, B 29, f. 286. Dénombrement . . . Aug. 31, 1704, AC, C13A, 1, f. 468–70. Bienville to min., Feb. 20, 1707, *loc. cit.*, f. 6.

61. AC, F1A, 13, f. 109–10. Bienville to min., Sept. 6, 1704, *loc. cit.*, f. 463. La Salle to min., Sept. 7, 1706, *loc. cit.*, f. 492. Bienville to min., April 10, 1706, *loc. cit.*, f. 503.

regain his health but could convince authorities in Rochefort and Versailles to meet what he considered critical requests.[62]

One of these requests would certainly be the more regular sending of supply ships from France. It had been nearly a year and a half since the *Pélican* had landed at Massacre Island; since that time no other large ship had arrived, although the colony had anticipated an additional vessel the previous summer. While the colony had been able to survive by sending occasional traversiers to Veracruz and Havana, the voyages had been both costly and hazardous: Spanish prices for supplies were exorbitant even for inferior merchandise and the French had lost one of their most capable officers (as well as several deserters) at Veracruz.[63]

On Christmas Eve of 1705, the colony was to suffer a further blow as a result of these emergency voyages. Châteaugué, who had sailed from Pensacola on October 16 on the *Précieuse*, had reached Veracruz safely with Vice-admiral Landeche. On his return trip, however, he had been caught in a storm below the harbor of Massacre Island. Although Châteaugué was able to salvage the food he had obtained at Veracruz (as well as the sails and equipment) the *Précieuse* was dashed aground on the sand bars south of Massacre Island and split assunder by the oncoming waves. It was another catastrophe for the colony. When Châteaugué arrived at the fort in a felucca a few days after Christmas, Bienville could but hang his head in despair. Only the *Espérance* was now left to transport goods from Massacre Island to the fort, to supply the garrison on the Mississippi and to connect Mobile with Havana and Veracruz.[64]

62. Bienville to min., Oct. 10, 1706, *loc. cit.*, f. 1–7v. Bienville to min., Feb. 20, 1707, *loc. cit.*, f. 29.

63. Bienville to min., July 28, 1706, *loc. cit.*, f. 514–16, 518–19, 523, 528. Bienville to min., Feb. 25, 1708, AC, C13A, 2, f. 92.

64. Réponse de M. Duclos au mémoire des officiers Royaux de la Vera crux en datte du 13 aoust 1714, AC, C13A, 3, f. 611–12. Mémoire des officiers Royaux de la Vera crux . . . 1714, AC, C13A, 3, f. 681–86. La Salle to min., Sept. 7, 1706, AC, C13A, 1, f. 489. *Journal Historique*, p. 94. La Salle to Bégon, Aug. 10, 1706, AC, C13A, 1, f. 566.

XIII

Bienville and La Salle

THE abundance of food and supplies at Mobile in the late summer of 1704 (as a result of Spanish repayments, the arrival of the *Pélican* and the return of the *Précieuse* from Veracruz) was by the spring of 1706 nearly depleted. No supply ship from France had arrived at Massacre Island for nearly two years. Moreover, the colony's principal transport had been lost by Châteaugué during a storm the preceding December. Although the inhabitants had for some time been expecting relief (by virtue of a new ship from France under command of Iberville), they waited in vain for its arrival.[1]

The results of the lack of supplies from France were a crippling poverty and a soaring inflation. Even in good times prices of goods in the colony were twenty-five to fifty percent above prices in France, but the severe shortages made the differences much more marked. A jug of milk rose from twelve to twenty *sols* and the price of a pound of beef more than doubled. Practically everything was affected. Jean-Baptiste Joussette, for example, paid an outrageous price of two hundred *livres* for a cask of wine. Skilled craftsmen, such as carpenter Jacques Le Compte and cooper Pierre Gagné, who plied invaluable trades (Le Compte, for example, was soon to be contracting to work on the parish church for three *livres* per diem), were able to increase their charges to combat the inflation, but the soldiers and most of the Canadians on the king's payroll had no way of increasing their incomes. Even the few merchants such as baker Dominique Julien and tavern-owner Étienne Burelle could not raise their prices at will, for they too

1. Min. to Iberville, Dec. 30, 1705, AM, B2, 183, f. 863–64. Bienville to min., July 28, 1706, AC, C13A, 1, f. 527. Min. to Bégon, Nov. 4, 1705, AC, B 27, f. 186–87. El rey a Señor Duque de Alburquerque, Aug. 12, 1705, AGN, *Historia*, 298.

would suffer—for lack of paying customers. Among the officers, only Bienville and Châteaugué had comfortable cash reserves (although technically they were heavily in debt), but the most destitute were the soldiers such as Denis Lafleur and Nicolas L'Anglois whose allowances totaled only 108 *livres* per year.[2]

As if the low wages were not enough, none of the town's personnel had actually received any specie since the arrival of the *Pélican.* In the absence of hard cash, nearly eighty percent of Mobile's residents were heavily in debt to the king's treasury, a situation Bienville often made worse by ordering the issuance of goods and supplies to the inhabitants on too easy credit. By this practice, the commandant felt he was easing the colonists' suffering as well as strengthening his political support. La Salle, however, himself with six mouths to feed on a salary of only 800 *livres* per year, took issue with what he felt was Bienville's too casual attitude about His Majesty's *magasin* (though he himself was heavily in debt to the king).[3]

It was in these unprosperous circumstances that the rivalry between commandant and commissary, for years simmering beneath the surface, began finally to erupt. In better times the personal differences between Bienville and La Salle might have remained in the background, but in the midst of the poverty of early 1706, new angers flared and old prejudices were renewed.[4]

Four years before, on Massacre Island, La Salle had objected to what he considered to be the Le Moyne brothers' high-handed commandeering of the newly constructed warehouse. The commissary let it be known he did not consider himself a mere clerk sent to sign out goods on whatever whim happened to strike Bienville, Sérigny or Châteaugué. Such presumption was, however, quickly put down by the overpowering figure of Iberville who had been present at the scene of contention. La Salle had been alone at the time and the times were relatively good. During those early months, with no support from either colonists or officials, the

2. La Vente [to Tremblay], Sept. 10, 1704, ASQ, Lettres, R 75. Interrogatoire des habitants . . . Feb. 25, 1708, AC, C13A, 2, f. 272. Iberville to min., AM, B4, 35, f. 370–71. Mémoire de la Louisiane, par Mandeville, April 29, 1709, AC, C13A, 2, f. 471–79. La Vente [to Brisacier], July 4, 1708, ASQ, Lettres, R 83. After deductions the soldiers were due only 18 *livres* for the entire year. AC, F1A, 13, f. 115–16v.

3. La Salle to min., Sept. 7, 1706, AC, C13A, 1, f. 487–91. Bienville to min., April 10, 1706, AC, C13A, 1, f. 502–11. AC, F1A, 13, f. 113. Bienville to min., Feb. 20, 1707, AC, C13A, 2, f. 18–20.

4. Bienville to min., Oct. 10, 1706, AC, C13B, 1, No. 6, f. 1–8v.

commissary realized the futility of objecting to any practice of the Le Moyne clan, though the methods and manners of the commandant must have chafed him severely. By early 1706, however, the Le Moynes seemed not quite so invincible as previously. Iberville and Sérigny had been absent from the colony since April of 1702 and Châteaugué was at sea a good portion of the time. The ship that had brought Châteaugué back to Louisiana a year and a half before had also brought Huvé and the outspoken La Vente, the now-disgruntled girls from Paris and the young soldiers from La Rochelle and Rochefort: the continental Frenchmen (of whom La Salle was one) now outnumbered the *Québecois* at Mobile. La Salle was no longer a lone lamb in the midst of Canadian wolves.[5]

The preceding September (1705), La Salle had gone with Châteaugué to Pensacola to make arrangements for the loan of the *Précieuse* to carry Vice-admiral Landeche back to Veracruz (after the loss of the *Nuestra Señora del Rosario*). According to La Salle, while he was absent a warder at the hospital approached his wife, Jeanne-Catherine de Berenhardt, pleading for a mattress and a blanket for a needy soldier. Jeanne-Catherine declined to fulfill the request, claiming she had no authority to issue provisions in her husband's name. Finally, out of compassion, she wrote a note to one of Bienville's warehousekeepers, Jacques Leméry, asking him to deliver the mattress and blanket. The warehousekeeper refused to accept the order, claiming he would have to get Bienville's approval.[6]

A few days later this same Jacques Leméry approached Madame La Salle with a request similar to her own: another soldier had been received in the hospital. This soldier also needed a mattress and blanket. Leméry had approved *this* request but he needed La Salle's signature (for which he asked that Madame La Salle sign for him).[7]

Jeanne-Catherine's answer was that she was in want of the same authority that Leméry claimed he lacked, that this matter would

5. La Salle to min., April 1, 1702, AC, C13C, 2, f. 35–41. Journal d'Iberville, Dec. 15, 1701, AM, B4, 23, f. 317–29. Bienville to min., Sept. 6, 1704, AC, C13A, 1, f. 459–65. AC, F1A, 13, f. 113–120v.

6. *Journal Historique*, pp. 91–93. Junta de Guerra de Indias, Dec. 2, 1707, AGI, *México*, L. 377. La Salle to min., Sept. 7, 1706, AC, C13A, 1, f. 481–84. AC, F1A, 11, f. 223; 13, f. 114–14v.

7. La Salle to min., Sept. 8, 1706, AC, C13A, 1, f. 557–58. Jacques Leméry (Humery) was the *garde-magasin en second* appointed by Bienville to serve at 360 *livres* per year. AC, F1A, 13, f. 114–14v. AC, C13A, 2, f. 310. La Salle to min., Aug. 10, 1706, AC, C13A, 1, f. 566–69.

also have to be taken to Bienville for approval. Leméry replied that Bienville would not approve it: the commandant had found out about his refusal to honor Madame La Salle's request and was angry with him for not acceding to her wishes. Moreover, Bienville was eating lunch and did not like to be interrupted, and the matter was very pressing. Madame La Salle took Leméry's note and had it submitted to Bienville who after writing some ungracious words on the back of it returned it to Jeanne-Catherine unapproved.[8]

Jeanne-Catherine wondered why, if Bienville had chastised Leméry for refusing to honor her request, would he deny a similar entreaty *himself* when she had appealed to him directly? Meeting neighbor Geneviève Burelle on the rue de Ruessavel, Jeanne-Catherine complained loudly about Bienville's behavior: the commandant had deliberately tried to trick her into signing her husband's signature, in order to obtain written evidence that she and her husband were conspiring to arbitrarily have goods leave the warehouse. How dare this skulking Canadian treat an honorable woman in such fashion while her husband was away? [9]

Bienville, overhearing her charge (according to La Salle, he was hiding in the bushes), confronted her with the accusation, demanding that she come to his office and apologize. When she refused, Bienville gave orders to the sentinels posted at the gates of the fort to refuse her admission to the chapel.[10]

When La Salle returned from Pensacola in October, he was outraged at the commandant, not only for having tried to use his wife to gain evidence against him but for refusing Jeanne-Catherine's entry into the chapel at a time when she was in the latter stages of pregnancy. Going directly to Bienville with his complaints, La Salle found the commandant in no mood to be criticized. Jeanne-Catherine was an impudent woman, Bienville retorted. She had conducted herself in most unladylike fashion. La Salle replied that his wife was not in the least to blame and that Bienville was deceiving no one, to which Bienville replied that since La Salle was assuming such a haughty attitude he would now be forced to prevent Jeanne-Catherine from *ever* entering the chapel. When La Salle threatened to escort her past the sentinels himself, Bienville

8. La Salle to min., Sept. 8, 1706, *loc. cit.*, f. 556–59. La Salle to min., May 12, 1709, AC, C13A, 2, f. 445–46.

9. ADM, A, April 8, 1708; Feb. 5, 1709. La Salle to min., Sept. 8, 1706, *loc. cit.*, f. 558.

10. *Ibid.*, f. 555–59.

assured La Salle he would use whatever force was necessary to prevent her from entering.[11]

With this, La Salle stomped away, but a few days later he returned: as Jeanne-Catherine was on the point of giving birth and quite anxious to receive the ordinary sacraments, he himself would apologize for her, reserving the right to demand future justice for this outrageous conduct. Bienville, realizing he was treading on dangerous ground, accepted the formal "apology" and in a few days Jeanne-Catherine was attending church once more.[12]

If Bienville was able to shrug off the incident after due time (he had, after all, received an apology), La Salle was not to forget so easily. It was the incident that would forever block a workable relationship between the commissary and his commandant. From this point on, La Salle would be diligent in gathering the data which he would ultimately use in more formal, written accusations.[13]

La Salle's wrath was not reserved for the commandant alone, but extended to his brothers and Canadian relatives as well. It was against Sérigny (sent by Bienville from Fort Louis) that he had first asserted himself. It was from Iberville that he had received his first rebuff. Prior to the aforementioned Massacre Island incident of 1702, La Salle had maintained good relations with Iberville. La Salle's high regard for the Canadian commander had been duly returned. Iberville considered himself fortunate to have on his expedition a man of experience and ability, had gone out of his way to recommend for the commissary a raise in pay. Yet the years between 1702 and 1705 saw a gradual decline in mutual respect. From his brothers Iberville received increasingly onerous reports of a *provocateur* on the scene: the mischief-maker from Toulon was, like Crassé before him, a meddler. His was to take orders, not to give them. He was a "clerk attempting to perform the functions of a commandant." [14]

Iberville, though far from Louisiana, had in recent years ap-

11. Mémoire du Roy, June 30, 1707, AC, B 29, f. 255v. Min. to La Salle, June 30, 1707, AC, B 29, f. 266v.

12. *Ibid.* La Salle to min., Sept. 8, 1706, *loc. cit.*, f. 557–59.

13. *Ibid.*, f. 545–65. La Salle to min., July 25, 1707, AC, C13B, 1, No. 7, f. 1–3v. La Salle to min., March 4, 1708, AC, C13A, 2, f. 154–58. La Salle to min., Sept. 12, 1708, AC, C13A, 2, f. 193–211.

14. La Salle to min., April 1, 1702, *loc. cit.*, f. 36–43. Journal d'Iberville, Dec. 15, 1701, AM, B4, 23, f. 316–29. Iberville to min., July 30, 1701, AM, B4, 21, f. 539–41. Bienville to min., Feb. 20, 1707, AC, C13A, 2, f. 17–22.

parently taken great pains to have Bienville keep him informed on La Salle's activities. Reported the commissary to his minister:

> M. d'Iberville writes me in a very menacing tone, finding fault with the good faith in which I perform the king's service. Among other things he tells me that it would be very easy for me to fabricate in my own false expense accounts and to counterfeit the signature of the late Sieur de Beccancourt [Bécancour] who died three years ago. I leave it to your highness to judge the character of a man who passes for something entirely different in your estimation.[15]

According to La Salle, Iberville, in several recent letters to him, was continually threatening him with the loss of his position as commissary by leveling charges of incompetence and incapacity. Moreover, he had been constantly urging La Salle to enter into questionable agreements, to sign certain orders that would tend to incriminate him, a charge Bienville was to later partially admit was true.[16]

La Salle's charges against the Le Moyne brothers, petty as they sometimes were, more often centered on an exceedingly volatile issue. His Majesty's storehouse was held to be sacrosanct by the court. Commerce on the part of colonial governors was not generally viewed with enthusiasm; but aside from that, dipping from the royal till at the expense of the colony was a heinous offense.[17] It was at this violation that La Salle in his early letters more than hinted. Though he lacked hard evidence, La Salle did not fail to accuse:

> In vain do I labor from morning till night to attempt to establish order as things are done in France. M. de Bienville only orders the contrary, in addition to which the proximity of his kitchen renders this storehouse his own, where his servants live and take away merchandise at all hours of the day, and sometimes the night, which is setting a bad example for all the garrison. I must also inform your highness that M. de Bienville takes for his own use the meats and other

15. La Salle to min., Sept. 7, 1706, *loc. cit.*, f. 500–01.

16. *Ibid.*, f. 499–501. La Salle to min., Sept. 8, 1706, *loc. cit.*, f. 553–56. La Salle to min., March 4, 1708, AC, C13A, 2, f. 156. Dartaguiette to min., Oct. 1, 1708, AC, C13A, 2, f. 341–49.

17. Min. to Demuy, June 23, 1707, AC, B 29, f. 278–78v. Mémoire du Roy, June 30, 1707, AC, B 29, f. 280v.

> foods brought by the savages, and lives on them whereas they could be used to cure the sick and for distribution as rations for the people of the garrison, which would prolong the supplies for some time, and by that means the presents which he makes us give to the savages would be repaid for the king. He sells a deer for eighty *francs*, to his own profit.[18]

Indeed Bienville did have his kitchen next to the storehouse. With Charles Levasseur's assistance (and no doubt on Iberville's advice) Bienville had the proximity so arranged from the outset. To what extent he planned beforehand to use its facilities for his own personal advantage is not clear but it is certain (and perhaps understandable) that as commandant he wished to make sure he was as near to the source of supplies as the *officier de plume*. As for the charge of engaging in private commerce, evidence was not lacking. Bienville was operating a small warehouse near the waterfront which had been built by (and was owned by) Iberville and which was tended by Jacques Allemand, a temperamental clerk from La Rochelle, brother of Claude (Iberville's confidant). Bienville was using this warehouse to store articles he received from the natives as well as goods purchased from the king until he could sell them to the more affluent of the inhabitants. On occasion (although La Salle overestimated the number of the instances) Bienville would (through agents) purchase certain goods from the storehouse at twenty-five percent above prices in France then sell the same goods to the inhabitants at increases ranging from fifty to as much as three hundred percent. In prosperous times Bienville may have realized huge profits from these practices but in Mobile at this time there were not enough buyers to purchase the inflated merchandise. While Bienville was surely guilty of some of the charges La Salle was bringing against him, his profits were scarcely what the commissary imagined.[19]

The charges La Salle in 1706 felt bold enough to openly circulate among the inhabitants brought Bienville into increased conflict with certain other personages, some of whom began to openly

18. La Salle to min., Sept. 7, 1706, *loc. cit.*, f. 483–85.

19. Dartaguiette to min., Feb. 26, 1708, AC, C13A, 2, f. 57–65. La Salle to min., Sept. 7, 1706, *loc. cit.*, f. 472–98. Mémoire du Roy, June 30, 1707, AC, B 29, f. 266v–72. Mémoire du Roy, June 30, 1707, *loc. cit.*, f. 248v–58v. Min. to Demuy, July 23, 1707, AC, B 29, f. 277v–78v. Interrogatoire des habitants . . . Feb., 1708, AC, C13A, 2, f. 249–312. Mémoire de Dartaguiette, Feb. 25, 1708, AC, C13A, 2, f. 72–75.

side with the *commissaire*. Étienne Burelle, an ex-Canadian originally from Paris (who in his fiftieth year was the only grandfather in Mobile) operated a tavern in the center of town where he sold mostly wine, brandy and pastries. After having bought a hundred and fifty *livres* worth of goods that had been stolen from the king's storehouse by a soldier, Burelle was accused by the soldier (after the goods had been traced to him) of having knowingly purchased stolen articles. Despite Burelle's claims of innocence, Bienville had presided over an inquiry by the officers of the garrison (and which included La Salle) by which Burelle was found guilty. Bienville fined Burelle twice the amount he was accused of buying and closed down his tavern for six months, a sentence which endeared the commandant no more to the inhabitants than to Burelle. When Burelle took his complaints to Roulleaux de La Vente, the pastor insisted Burelle was innocent and persuaded La Salle not to accept Burelle's payment of the fine.[20]

Jacques Allemand, who had supervised the Le Moyne's warehouse on the river, had lately fallen out with Bienville over a matter involving missing supplies. Later when Bienville caught him in a "crying injustice" that he had committed against an inhabitant, the commandant clamped him in irons, whereupon Allemand, with insults and threats, ridiculed the judgment Bienville had made and shouted from the guardhouse that the commandant would perish from his hand.[21]

Bienville had put gunsmith René Boyer in irons more than once: for mortally wounding an old corporal and for refusing to clean and assemble a musket that Ensign Daraque, an officer of the Canadians, had brought to him on the commandant's orders. After Boyer's refusal and Daraque's insistence, the two had almost come to blows, whereupon Bienville cast Boyer into the guardhouse for twenty days. Aside from these imprisonments, Boyer was furious at Bienville for the commandant's refusal to lend him free-of-charge the king's oxen to haul some timbers to support his house which was in danger of falling.[22]

20. *DGFC, I*, p. 96. LSMA, DCS, May 14, 1737. ADM, A, Nov. 27, 1707. Dénombrement des familles et habitants . . . Aug. 1, 1706, AC, G1, 464. Plan de la ville et du fort de la Maubile, 1702, AC, DFC, Louisiane, 119A. Interrogatoire des habitants . . . Feb. 26, 1708, AC, C13A, 2, f. 252, 288–93. Bienville to min., Feb. 25, 1708, AC, C13A, 2, f. 104.

21. *Ibid.*, f. 106. Interrogatoire . . . Feb. 24, 1708, *loc. cit.*, f. 252.

22. Bienville to min., Feb. 28, 1708, *loc. cit.*, f. 106. Interrogatoire . . . Feb. 27, 1708, *loc. cit.*, f. 304–312. ADM, A, June 19, 1707. AC, F1A, 13, f. 119v.

Burelle, Boyer and Allemand were native-born Frenchmen who may have been expected to side against Bienville in the erupting *démêlé*. But Guillaume Boutin, husband of Louise-Marguerite Housseau, was, like Bienville, a Canadian.[23] Shortly after the burning of Pensacola, Governor Guzmán had requested Bienville to lend him a few craftsmen to help rebuild his fort. Bienville responded by sending two unmarried workers, *armurier* Jean Bon and *taillandier* Jean Labrière. Eyeing the relatively abundant currency in Pensacola, Boutin, with Bienville's knowledge but without his specific permission, took passage on the pirogue with Bon and Labrière. After several months time Bienville had second thoughts about allowing Boutin to work on the project: other potential *habitants*, married men with families, were asking to follow Bon, Boutin and Labrière. If Bienville acceded to these requests, it might spur a mass exodus to Pensacola where it was believed by many that living conditions were vastly improving. At least there was hard cash to be earned at that post. Upon Bienville's refusal of these requests, those not receiving permission loudly objected to Boutin's being allowed to go, which prompted the commandant to order Boutin home.[24]

When Boutin returned to Fort Louis, Bienville gave him his reasons for having him returned. Boutin, after mild objections, asked Bienville for permission to return to Pensacola to retrieve his tools (which after some consideration Bienville allowed him to do). Two months passed, however, and Boutin failed to return to the fort, despite several warnings to do so.[25]

Realizing Boutin intended to stay indefinitely, Bienville sent soldiers to Pensacola to have him arrested. Governor Guzmán, though he had become somewhat attached to his Canadian friend, had no choice but to order him to leave with the French soldiers.[26]

Back at Fort Louis, Bienville put Boutin under arrest and lodged him in the guardhouse. A week later he released him. Free, Boutin cursed Bienville repeatedly, claiming the commandant had cost him nearly a year's wages. When Bienville threatened him with im-

23. *DGFC, I*, p. 82. La Salle and his wife served as godparents for the birth of Boutin's son, Nicolas, in 1707. ADM, A, Dec. 23, 1707; July 26, 1710. AC, F1A, 10, f. 284.

24. ACM, Rivière et Soullard, 1699–1700, 72ff. AC, F1A, 10, f. 284–84v. Bienville had already struck Boutin from the payroll by late 1704. AC, F1A, 11, f. 220–20v.

25. Bienville to min., Feb. 25, 1708, *loc. cit.*, f. 104–05.

26. *Ibid.*, f. 105.

prisonment, Boutin lost his temper completely, threatened Bienville's life and when a young guard attempted to restrain him, Boutin overpowered the guard and fled to his house on the rue Sainte-Marie. After calming himself somewhat, Bienville sent Sergeant Clement Bégon and four soldiers from Vaulezard's company to order Boutin to surrender himself without violence. When at length the Canadian returned to the fort, Bienville, ignoring Boutin's plea for mercy, shackled him in chains where he remained until the commandant, at the request of Guzmán, released him a few weeks later.[27]

If La Salle and certain of the inhabitants of Mobile had good reason to be critical of Bienville's arrogance and sometimes tyrannical management of the colony's affairs, the commandant also had reason to find fault with La Salle and the rising coalition of anti-Le Moynists. Too many of the inhabitants (women as well as men) were shiftless, Bienville complained, and would apparently as soon starve as do a good day's work. The land was "not the richest in the world," he admitted, but certain crops would surely thrive (as proved by the natives) if idle hands were put to the plow. He was especially critical of the young wives from Paris whose lofty attitudes not only prevented them from working themselves, but "poisoned" the attitudes of their husbands as well. Moreover, there were many among the French soldiers and even among the Canadians whose conduct could only be described as "seditious," who, far from being mistreated, deserved worse punishment than he was meting out to them.[28]

Of La Salle, whom Bienville labled an "obstructionist," the commandant complained that he was doing everything possible to create dissension among the ranks: while the commissary complained of Bienville's having two private manservants and a little lackey cabin-boy on the company payroll (each of whom, according to Bienville, was serving the king admirably), La Salle had, for the four years he had been in Mobile, allotted himself five such servants who were rendering no service to anyone.[29] On

27. Interrogatoire . . . Feb. 25, 1708, *loc. cit.*, f. 282. Bienville to min., Feb. 25, 1708, *loc. cit.*, f. 104. AC, F1A, 13, f. 116v.

28. Bienville to min., Oct. 10, 1706, AC, C13B, 1, No. 6, f. 2–6v. Bienville to min., July 28, 1706, *loc. cit.*, f. 516–544. Bienville to min., Feb. 20, 1707, *loc. cit.*, f. 6–31.

29. Bienville to min., Oct. 12, 1708, AC, C13A, 2, f. 187–88. On another occasion, however, Bienville accused La Salle of lowering the dignity of his office by having no servant at all. Bienville to min., April 10, 1706, *loc. cit.*, f. 512.

La Salle's charge that Bienville was bypassing standard procedure in the issuance of merchandise, Bienville retorted:

> The Sieur de La Salle, king's scrivener serving here as commissary, complains to your highness that for two years I have stopped giving him the [written] order. It is true, monseigneur, that having learned that he made light of it, giving it to the first comer as soon as he received it, even to his wife, in the presence of two infantry officers who advised me of it, I made him return it. He is a man to be watched closely in his duties and the more I trouble him to report on everything he does and not to deliver the smallest trifle without orders from me, the more likely will the king be served.[30]

As late as the spring of 1705, the rumblings of the Bienville-La Salle feud had not yet reached Pontchartrain's ears. The Le Moyne family was still in the highest graces of the king. Iberville and Sérigny were still in France, preparing for the next voyage to Louisiana, but their plans had suffered innumerable delays. The viccissitudes of war had caused several shifts in plans. Ships that Iberville and Sérigny had arranged for the new Louisiana expedition were taken from them at the last moment for use in emergency coastal defense. Moreover, Iberville's failing health, due to repeated attacks of malaria, further delayed his departure.[31]

In January 1706 Iberville and Sérigny finally departed La Rochelle. By this time, however, Iberville's orders had been changed drastically. With a squadron of twelve ships the commander was to harass the English in the West Indies; after that his brother Sérigny was to transport to Mobile by the *Coventry* (a 48-gun English vessel captured by Duguay-Trouin in 1704) the abundant supplies loaded at Rochefort for Louisiana, while Iberville would continue the offensive against the English, this time in Carolina.[32]

30. Bienville to min., Oct. 10, 1706, *loc. cit.*, f. 7–8v.

31. Châteaurenault to Pontchartrain, May 11, 1705, AM, B3, 132, f. 287–90. Bégon to Villermont, Nov. 7, 1703, BN, FF, 22813, f. 141–42. Min. to Iberville, Aug. 22, 1703, AM, B2, 169, f. 447. Min. to Iberville, March 5, 1704, AM, B2, 174, f. 572–73.

32. Min. to Sérigny, Nov. 25, 1705, AM, B2, 183, f. 557v. The *Coventry*, a 4th rate of 670 tons built in 1695 at Deptford, was captured off the Scillies on July 24, 1704 by René Duguay-Trouin in circumstances which led to the dismissal of her captain, Henry Lawrence, from the service. She was 106 ft. long on her keel, 34 ft. 5 in. in width and had 13.5 ft. depth in hold. Recap-

Arriving at Martinique in March, Iberville, along with his brother-in-law, Pierre-Jacques Payen de Noyan (commander of the 300-ton *Aigle*), began immediate preparations for an attack against Nevis, a prosperous but ill-defended island under English dominion. By the first week in April, Iberville had succeeded in capturing the island *in toto*, making prisoners of nearly two thousand men, women and children and some six thousand black slaves. Moreover, twenty-four English-made vessels (one of which, the *Aventurier*, was sent on to Mobile for use as a transport) were apprehended in Nevis' principal harbor, as well as considerable prizes from the plantations and public buildings of the island. Iberville was unable to prevent (if indeed he had made the effort) the violence and uncontrolled looting which followed.[33]

After the sacking of Nevis, Iberville divided the spoils of conquest among the several officers and groups involved, then disbanded his squadron. The *Apollon*, *Brillant*, *Glorieux* and *Phénix* were dispatched to France; Sérigny sailed the *Coventry* for Veracruz (instead of Louisiana), and Payen de Noyan set out for Massacre Island by way of Cuba. Iberville himself sailed for Saint-Domingue, first stopping at Cap-français, then Léogane, where he furthered preparations for a general assault on English colonies on the Atlantic coast. After several weeks at Saint-Domingue, his newly organized squadron sailed for Havana, where for the first part of the summer, he busied himself in illicit commerce (selling several tons of iron goods to the Cubans) while seeking to involve the Spanish more directly in his forthcoming enterprise.[34]

Even as Iberville, Sérigny and Payen de Noyan were sailing for the West Indies, Pontchartrain began receiving reports of fraudulent operations in the outfitting of the squadron at Rochefort and later at La Rochelle. Uncertain at first that any wrongdoing had taken place (as the silent partners of the expedition had complained) the minister finally became convinced by the number and specificity of the charges and appointed a special commission

---

tured by the 50-gun *Portland* on May 5, 1709, she was broken up immediately after. PRO, Admiralty Dimensions Books,B. Clowes, *The Royal Navy . . . II*, p. 506*n*.

33. LSMA, DCS, May 1, 1735. *DGCF, I*, pp. 379, 468. Iberville to min., April 10, 1706, AM, B4, 31, f. 149–150v. Journal de Maupeou, *s.d.*, AM, B4, 31, f. 153–55.

34. Iberville to min., April 10, 1706, *loc. cit.*, f. 149v–151v. Guérin, *Histoire Maritime . . . IV*, p. 476. Carta de Álvarez de Villarín, May 30, 1706, AGI, *Santo Domingo*, L. 377. Carta de Luis Chacón, May 26, 1706, AGI, *Santo Domingo*, L. 377.

to investigate the alleged misconduct. Before the summer of 1706 was over, the minister's investigators were assured of at least one fact: Iberville and a number of officers and private investors had conspired to substitute other merchandise for the supplies needed to relieve Louisiana. Tools of iron and large barrels of merchandise which Iberville intended to sell at Martinique and Havana had been substituted for flour, dry vegetables and other items needed desperately by the colony. Moreover, it soon became apparent that Iberville had defrauded the shipowners by shorting food supplies needed for the campaign while pocketing for himself much of the money allotted for that purpose, a manuever that more than any other caused the inquirers to realize they had opened a can of worms.[35]

While investigations were underway in France, Sérigny (on Iberville's instructions) had switched the *Coventry's* destination from Louisiana to Veracruz. The *Coventry*, a ship with over twice the tonnage of the *Aigle*, transferred her supplies intended for the colony to the smaller ship and took on board some of the booty from the sacking of Nevis and Saint-Christophe. Reaching Veracruz, Sérigny set about trading slaves, captured merchandise and a Portuguese vessel seized at Saint-Christophe for sundry Mexican goods which included tobacco, indigo, cochineal and Spanish specie amounting in value to thirty thousand *livres*. Overall, to the detriment of the colony and despite the complaints to the Spanish crown of the merchants and royal officers of Veracruz, Sérigny was leaving that port with a cargo that would net him and his brother Iberville over a quarter-million *livres* in profits.[36]

While Sérigny was enriching himself at Veracruz, the colonists in Mobile were eagerly awaiting the arrival of a French ship at Port Massacre, Bienville having received word from Pensacola that Iberville had landed in the West Indies and would soon supply the colony by way of Havana. Impatient for supplies, Bienville had sent Châteaugué in the *Espérance* to Havana on April 4, along

35. Min. to Bégon, May 25, 1707, AC, B 29, f. 241. Min. to L'Hostellier, May 25, 1707, AC, B 29, f. 243–44v. Min. to Bégon, June 23, 1706, AM, B2, 189, f. 973–74. Commissions extraordinaires du Conseil, 1707, AN, V7, 214. Min. to Robert, June 30, 1706, AM, B2, 189, f. 1091. Min. to Mithon, Sept. 19, 1710, AC, B 32, f. 172–76.

36. Min. to Bienville, Nov. 4, 1705, AC, B 27, f. 188. Min. to Sérigny, Jan. 12, 1707, AM, B2, 196, f. 216. Bienville to min., Feb. 20, 1707, AC, C13A, 2, f. 17–18. Min. to L'Hostellier, Feb. 29, 1708, AM, B2, 206, f. 697–98. Min. to Bégon, May 25, 1707, AC, B 29, f. 241–42. *Cf.* Giraud, *Histoire de la Louisiane Française, I*, pp. 100–03, 110–11.

with the survivors of the *Saint-Antoine* who had become a drain on the food supply. By early June, however, Châteaugué had not returned.[37]

Meanwhile, Bienville was beset with further unrest at Mobile. The colonists, especially the women from Paris, were becoming increasingly difficult to manage in view of the widespread poverty. Caught up in the now open controversy between Bienville and La Salle, the inhabitants were beginning to split more incisively into two factions, one supporting Commandant Bienville and the other Commissary La Salle. One such partisan was Marie-Françoise de Boisrenaud, the former *supérieure des filles* who had come on the *Pélican* in 1704.[38]

Back in France, Marie-Françoise had first been associated with the Abbaye de Fontevrault near Saumur, an ancient and wealthy establishment directed by the brilliant and perhaps most stable of the remarkable Rochechouart sisters, Marie-Madelaine. While at Fontevrault she had become acquainted with Louis XIV's favorite and most prolific mistress, Françoise-Athénaïs de Rochechouart, known to history as Madame de Montespan. The once flamboyant Madame, no longer in the king's favor, had by 1690 begun devoting her life to more pious endeavors, in particular, to her favorite institution, the Couvent de Saint-Joseph to which she enticed Marie-Françoise following a visit to Fontevrault. After a long association at Saint-Joseph with Madame de Montespan, Mlle. Boisrenaud had become a member of the Communauté de l'Annonciation. It was from this community that she had been withdrawn in 1703 to conduct nineteen other unmarried girls to Louisiana.[39]

Within two months after the convoy's arrival in Mobile all of the surviving girls had married except Marie-Françoise. Understandably, in view of her past high associations, Mlle. Boisrenaud was not especially attracted to the coarse Canadian backwoodsmen. Perhaps she would have accepted a union with Charles Levasseur or Robinau de Bécancour but fate had prevented that. So she refused to marry, a decision temporarily tolerated by Bienville

37. Bienville to min., Feb. 20, 1707, *loc. cit.*, f. 17–18. *Journal Historique*, pp. 95–97. *FLC*, p. 118–19. Carta de Luis Chacón, May 26, 1706, AGI, *Santo Domingo*, L. 377.

38. Boisbriant to min., Oct. 1, 1706, AC, C13A, 1, f. 585–88. La Salle to min., Aug. 10, 1706, AC, C13A, 1, f. 566–68. AC, F1A, 11, f. 223. La Vente [to Brisacier], March 4, 1708, ASQ, Lettres, R 79.

39. Conseil de Marine, Dec. 10, 1718, AM, B1, 30, f. 429–29v.

because she was at least performing certain useful functions if not helping to people the colony: after the girls under her supervision had married, she had devoted herself to instructing the native women and children, attending to their baptisms and "giving lessons to the *habitants*' daughters, showing them what they are capable of learning." [40]

Bienville's relationship with Mlle. Boisrenaud was tenuous, to say the least. While he approved of her humanitarian activities, he was constantly prodding her to marry and help settle down yet another of the rambunctious Canadians, several of whom were "sighing for her" and who were "incessantly urging" Bienville to force her to a decision. As time passed, it began to irritate Bienville that she would not accept any of her suitors, the more so since the excuse she gave was that the Canadians (of which Bienville was one) were unsuitable to a woman of her noble background. Yet she had a large following, was popular in fact with several heterogeneous groups, and Bienville, in this time of civil discord, did not wish to antagonize her. In April of 1705, the commandant (in order to flatter her) had asked her to serve as a godparent (along with officer Antoine Siré) at the baptism of one of his young Indian slaves, Jeanne-Louise, a request she finally accepted.[41]

There was one Canadian towards whom Marie-Françoise showed no prejudice. When the wounded Pierre Dugué de Boisbriant had been brought back from the Choctaw country in March of 1705, Mlle. Boisrenaud had accepted the responsibility for nursing him back to full health.[42] During the several months of Boisbriant's convalescence a romance began to blossom between the *aide-major* and the haughty spinster, culminating in Boisbriant's proposal of marriage. By the time of Boisbriant's recovery, however, Bienville's relationship with Marie-Françoise had deteriorated drastically due to her vocal criticisms of the colony's administration and her close association with La Salle's wife and the seminary priests. Bienville would have none of such a potentionally damaging liason between his chief supporter and the La Salle sympathizer. After repeated remonstrations by Bienville and Châteaugué, Boisbriant agreed to forego the union, a decision which

40. AC, F1A, 11, f. 217–19, 223–23v. Conseil de Marine, Dec. 10, 1718, *loc. cit.*, f. 429v. Liste des filles . . . Oct. 31, 1704, AC, B 25, f. 9v–10v. Min. to Brisacier, June 15, 1707, AC, B 29, f. 264v–65.

41. Bienville to min., Oct. 10, 1706, AC, C13B, 1, No. 6, f. 2–9v. ADM, A, April 11, 1705. Min. to Brisacier, June 15, 1707, *loc. cit.*, f. 265v.

42. *Journal Historique*, pp. 90–91.

forever alienated Mlle. Boisrenaud and the commandant. Henceforth, she would be one of La Salle's most vigorous supporters and would complain bitterly that Bienville did not have the necessary qualities to govern the colony.[43]

In late 1705, the Chickasaw chiefs returned to Fort Louis (as they had promised the previous spring).[44] Boisbriant, in particular, was relieved to see the interpreter Saint-Michel brought with them. Here was concrete evidence of Choctaw guile, yet at the same time hope for the reinstatement of the Choctaw-Chickasaw alliance (since the Chickasaw were now asking for a re-establishment of the peace). In pursuit of this peace Bienville sent Gabriel Philippe de Saint-Lambert, with two Canadians and two Tomeh as guides, to the village of the Choctaw to bring back the principal Choctaw chief to discuss terms. On January 7, 1706 Saint-Lambert returned with the chief of the Choctaw; two weeks later three more chiefs followed, bringing with them nine Alabama scalps which the Choctaw hoped would help atone for their massacre of the Chickasaw and for the accidental wounding of Boisbriant. By late January, Bienville felt that the Choctaw-Chickasaw alliance had been successfully re-established. The chiefs of the two nations had smoked the calumet and, Bienville witnessing, had also faithfully vowed to forget the past. On these dulcet notes the two groups returned to their separate nations, while Saint-Michel remained at Mobile.[45]

Two months later, the Choctaw returned to Fort Louis, bringing reports that the Chickasaw had broken the truce: in spite of their avowals the Chickasaw (or at least a portion of them) had attacked a Choctaw village and during a single night had carried off more than one hundred and fifty captives which they proceeded to sell to the English as slaves. Bienville could only hang his head in despair: without sufficient presents, without missionaries or close surveillance of the villages, it was impossible to place any reliance on the conduct of the natives. When the Choctaw asked for powder and bullets with which to defend themselves, Bienville

43. Lettre de Mlle. Boisrenaud (extrait), *s.d.*, AC, C13A, 1, f. 582–83. Bienville refused to supply her with the rations she requested from the storehouse. AC, F1A, 13, f. 113–21. Lettre de Père Lamberville, March 1, 1707, AC, C13A, 1, f. 582.

44. The previous April Bienville had kept six of the ten Chickasaw chiefs at Fort Louis as security for the life of Saint-Michel. *Journal Historique*, pp. 90–95.

45. *Ibid.*, f. 94–96. *FLC*, pp. 72–73. AC, F1A, 13, f. 113v, 114v.

reluctantly granted the request. The Choctaw, after all, despite their occassional lapses, had proven themselves his most valuable and powerful ally and he could ill afford to lose their confidence.[46]

Part of the January peace terms at Fort Louis included a French promise to make an attack on the Alabama villages in reprisal for Alabama participation in the invasion of the Choctaw the previous fall. Accordingly, toward the latter part of January, 1706, Bienville sent Boisbriant (now completely recovered) and Saint-Lambert, with some fifty Canadians, up the Alabama river in six pirogues to assault the Alabama in their villages. Just below present-day Selma, however, Boisbriant was surprised by an Alabama war party on its way to assail a Choctaw village. After a brief skirmish, during which two Alabama warriors were seized, then bludgeoned to death, and one prisoner (a woman) was taken alive, the Alabama retreated to their villages. Boisbriant, seeing his chance for a surprise attack lost, returned to Mobile, bringing with him the female prisoner. Back in Mobile, Boisbriant reported the aborting of the mission to Bienville, and turned the captive over to him. Bienville sold the prisoner to one of the colony's families and the woman went quietly to serve her owners (with whom she remained for many years). The failure of the expedition, resulting in only two scalps and one slave, was not a strategic loss since it was made only to fulfill a promise, but La Salle took advantage of the lack of success to bring new charges that Bienville had further emptied the storehouse specifically to supply his own supporters (beyond the needs of the expedition).[47]

His Indian policies fraught with failure, his food supplies almost gone, Bienville's morale (like that of the majority of the colonists) was now at its lowest ebb. La Vente and Huvé, as had Davion and Boutteville before them, were clamoring for the long overdue building of the parish church. Moreover, Fort Louis, like the warehouse on Massacre Island, had rotted so badly that the cannons could not be fired without risking collapse of the bastions. When Bienville mentioned repairing the fort, even building an entirely new one, La Salle was loud in his protests against the proposal,

46. *Journal Historique*, pp. 93–96. *FLC*, p. 73. Bienville to min., Oct. 10, 1706, *loc. cit.*, f. 1–1v. Bienville to min., July 28, 1706, *loc. cit.*, f. 523–25.

47. Mémoire de Dartaguiette, Feb. 26, 1708, AC, C13A, 2, f. 65–66. *FLC*, pp. 72–73. *Journal Historique*, pp. 95–96. Mémoire du Roy, June 30, 1707, AC, B 29, f. 253–53v. Mémoire du Roy, June 30, 1707, AC, B 29, f. 270. Interrogatoire . . . par Dartaguiette, Feb. 24, 1708, AC, C13A, 2, f. 257–58, 281, 289. La Salle to min., Sept. 7, 1706, *loc. cit.*, f. 475–76.

blaming the Le Moyne brothers for their lack of foresight in locating it "in the midst of the woods." [48] The scrivener was still recommending the abandonment of the site altogether and relocating either at the base of the river (where Bienville had established one of the Chato villages) or at Massacre Island where at this time only the small, decaying warehouse stood guarded by a few ragged soldiers. Owing to the economic distress, the shortage of food and the discord, both Bienville and Châteaugué were planning (and would in a few months officially request) to return to France, pleading ill health, but in reality, hoping to present the colony's difficulties to high authorities in person.[49] Such was Bienville's assessment of the situation: that unless Louisiana were supplied with more merchandise as well as with more capable personnel, the eventual triumph of the English would be assured. News from Europe (which Bienville occasionally received from Spanish ports) was also discouraging. Recently, he had learned that Bishop Saint-Vallier, along with two Canadians prominent in the early years of Mobile (seminary priest Boutteville and Denis de La Ronde) had been captured off the coast of France and were now in English prisons.[50]

Aside from the colony's long range problems, the immediate one was the shortage of food. Already some of the Canadians had left the town itself to try raising crops near the mouth of the river where the land was reportedly more fertile. Pierre Leboeuf, longtime veteran from Quebec, Claude Parent, a tool-maker from Beauport and Charles Rochon, a thirty-two-year-old *voyageur* who had first come to Louisiana with Henri de Tonti, settled in the area called the *Oignonets* (near the village of the Chato) and were gamely trying to grow wheat and vegetables.[51]

48. La Vente [to SME Dirs.], June 27, 1708, ASQ, Lettres, R 83. La Salle to min., Sept. 7, 1706, *loc. cit.*, f. 476–79. Bienville wanted to build a new fort (at the same location) of bricks. Bienville to min., April 10, 1706, *loc. cit.*, f. 506.

49. Châteaugué to min., Sept. 30, 1706, AC, C13A, 1, f. 589–90. Bienville to min., July 28, 1706, *loc. cit.*, f. 528–29.

50. Min. à l'évêque de Québec, June 29, 1707, AC, B 29, f. 30–30v. Tremblay [to Des Maizerets], April 12, 1706, ASQ, Lettres, O 45.

51. AC, F1A, 10, f. 285. Charles, progenitor of the large and later prosperous Rochon family of colonial Louisiana, had been born in Boucherville in 1673, descendant of ancestors from Saint-Côme-le-vert in the bishopric of Mans. His mother, Mathurine Buisson, was a sister of Jean-François Buisson de Saint-Cosme (1660–1712) of the Séminaire de Québec. *DGFC, I*, pp. 54, 525. AC, F1A, 11, f. 73; 13, f. 118. AJQ, Greffe de Duquet, May 24, 1671. [Montigny to Tremblay], 1700, ASQ, Missions, 107, 1. ADM, A, entry following May 30, 1709; Aug. 4, 1710.

For the most part, however, Bienville was forced to look to Guzmán for aid. Such reliance on Pensacola weighed heavily on the commandant, for Spanish prices were exorbitant. Besides, Bienville had just recently settled accounts with Guzmán's commissary for past supplies: on February 27, a launch had arrived from Pensacola, commanded by Pedro García y Vinuesa, a royal paymaster who had come to square accounts between the two posts. After several days' reckoning, García y Vinuesa presented Bienville with a bill for the three thousand *livres* by which the French were in debt to Pensacola plus statements for several large supplies of corn and flour. Bienville used part of the considerable amount of coinage salvaged from the wreck of the *Saint-Antoine* a few months before to settle the account and made arrangements with the Spanish to borrow more Indian corn and flour should he run short before the arrival of a supply ship. By the middle of May no ship had yet arrived and Bienville was forced once again to appeal to Pensacola for relief. Guzmán responded by shipping forty hundredweight of corn and a large quantity of flour, the bulk of which arrived on May 28.[52]

The first of June came and went; still Chateaugué had not returned from Havana. Bienville grew increasingly concerned with each passing day. Had the *Espérance* met the same fate as the *Précieuse?* He did not want to dwell on the possibility, for unless Châteaugué soon returned, the probability would be great that his ship was lost; extreme famine would be the result. Thus, by the second week in June the eyes of the soldiers guarding the Massacre Island warehouse were every moment searching the southeastern horizon, casting eagerly about for a *fleur-de-lys* in the wind.[53]

52. La Salle to min., Sept. 7, 1706, *loc. cit.*, f. 491–96. Bienville to min., April 10, 1706, *loc. cit.*, f. 502–03. The debt was otherwise recorded as 988 *piastres*, 2 *reales*. *Journal Historique*, pp. 94–96. Bienville to min., July 28, 1706, *loc. cit.*, f. 514–18. Mémoire du Roy, June 30, 1707, AC, B 29, f. 267–67v. Junta de Guerra de Indias, Dec. 2, 1707, AGI, *México*, L. 377.

53. *Journal Historique*, pp. 95–96. Châteaugué to min., Sept. 30, 1706, *loc. cit.*, f. 589–90.

XIV

Gravier and La Vente

IF the months before the arrival of a relief ship from France witnessed an outbreak of hostility between commandant and commissary which radiated among the inhabitants, the period saw also the deterioration of an even more tenuous relationship—that between commandant and *curé*—between the brash young Bienville (now twenty-six years old) and the equally headstrong Roulleaux de La Vente (nearly twice the commandant's age). If there were one individual Bienville was growing to despise even more than Nicolas de La Salle, it was the pastor from Beauchêne.[1]

During the years 1704 and 1705, Bienville and La Vente had kept their distance from one another, only occasionally coming into direct conflict. From the outset, however, it was clear that there would be no personal affection lost between the two leaders. For both private and practical reasons, Bienville had been highly disappointed by La Vente's appointment to the nascent settlement. The commandant, interested in the advancement of the colony even more than in his own material gain, had wanted a younger, more zealous clergyman for the position of parish priest, and preferably a Jesuit. He was interested in seeing the Jesuits missionize Louisiana because of that order's greater resources, their superior personnel, their fervor and diligence, their reputation for mastering native languages and because of their intrepidity in the face of difficult and hazardous situations. Hoping for a Gabriel Marest or a mature Paul Du Ru, he received instead a weakling (Alexandre Huvé) and a stuffy, petulant materialist (La Vente).[2]

1. Bienville to min., Oct. 10, 1706, AC, C13B, 1, No.6, f.3–8v. La Vente to min., March 2, 1708, AC, C13A, 2, f. 160–64.

2. The early letters of Bienville and La Vente give little indication of the approaching storm. Bienville to min., Sept. 6, 1704, AC, C13A, 1, f. 449–65. La Vente [to Tremblay], Sept. 25, 1704, ASQ, Lettres, R 76. La Vente [to

Bienville had not been overly impressed with La Vente's labors during the catastrophic days of August and September of 1704. La Vente had too easily given way to his sufferings, the commandant felt, while he (Bienville) had continued performing his own functions without complaint. Even old Davion, decrepit and ill, had borne up better under adversity than La Vente. While the Jesuits, Bienville felt, would have gloried in suffering and taking risks for "the cause," La Vente contented himself with constant carping about the state of the colony, his own discomforts and the lack of earthly pleasures.[3]

There was no doubt a good deal of justification for the charge of materialism made against the pastor. La Vente was no sooner in the colony than he began firing off letters to the seminary's agent in Paris requesting more supplies for himself. "Please notice," he beckoned to Tremblay, "that in this letter I speak only of business. The most important point is to determine in what manner our salaries will be adjusted in France or with M. D'Iberville . . . moreover, we need guns, axes, glassware . . . but of better quality than what M. Fleury has sent." [4]

Later the pastor would dispatch a memorandum of four long pages in request of such items as lead, vermeil, musket powder, fabrics of all sorts, hatchets, spades, pocket knives, long rifles, millstones, silver basins, a large copper water container, a milch cow (in addition to the one he already possessed) and large amounts of some twenty smaller articles. Only on the next-to-last page of his memorandum did he mention items needed for the church.[5]

In his list of requests, La Vente was careful to specify the types and qualities of merchandise. For example, he did not want mere shirts, but "let them always be made for cultivated people, even a bit expensive." Not "ordinary millstones such as those in Paris of quite modern construction," but "a set of two stones which curve inwards at the head of the hammer, such as one finds at Port Louis or even at La Rochelle, provided they are two or two-

SME Dirs.], Sept. 20, 1704, ASQ, Lettres, R 77. However, several of Bienville's letters from this period are missing, as are a few by La Vente and La Salle. Min. to Bienville, Jan. 30, 1704, AC, B 25, f. 4. Min. to Iberville, Nov. 28, 1703, AM, B2, 170, f. 465–65v.

3. La Vente [to SME Dirs.], Sept. 20, 1704, *loc. cit.*, R 77. Bienville to min., Oct. 10, 1706, *loc. cit.*, f. 8v–9v. In the extant baptismal records of 1704–05, La Vente managed only two entries. ADM, A, Sept. 18, 1704; Aug. 11, 1705.

4. La Vente [to Tremblay], Sept. 10, 1704, ASQ, Lettres, R 75.

5. Mémoire général des Marchandises . . . 1707, ASQ, Lettres, R 78.

and-a half feet in diameter."[6] Of the merchandise La Vente requested, only a portion of it was to be utilized personally by himself or Huvé (or by the church). The larger part was to be used for trading with the natives and inhabitants for profit:

> The long rifles should be embellished with copper. That is what makes them valuable to the savages . . . glass beads should have the shape of the olives of France and the color should always be a milky white; the largest and lightest is the best; if the needed amount of this quality is not to be found, which over here surpasses all others in every way, then in place of it send the same size but of a sky-blue color, not just blue; this color of sky-blue has its own price whether it is all of this color or streaked with milky white. After these two varieties, the glazed ones, somewhat similar to those we received this year, are not to be scorned . . .[7]

La Vente's purpose in requesting such supplies was to increase the wealth of his mission by trading with the savages and carrying on as much commerce with the inhabitants as he could manage. The church, he felt, could function better if it were not reduced to beggary. Better to have his own *magasin* than to be dependent on the goods of the king, especially in view of his relationship with the commandant and the usual state of the storehouse. Also, unlike his ascetic colleague, Marc Bergier, vicar-general in the Illinois country, La Vente liked his temporal pleasures—his brandy and his billiards.[8] More than once he asked the directors of the seminary in Paris for a billiard table or at least the means to construct one: "You will please use the funds [I am sending you] to help in purchasing a billiard cloth the length of one *aune* such as are used for the excellent tables from La Rochelle, with all the necessary nails, both copper and iron, to make the said table here. I shall not ask you to pay for the woodworking, which will be done here, but we need, if you please, three or four sets of billiard balls and even a few more. If possible you must please not forget certain necessary directions and screws, nor the balls, nor the printed books of rules for this game. I have written about it to M. Tremblay and

6. *Ibid.*
7. *Ibid.*
8. La Vente [to SME Dirs.], Sept. 20, 1704, *loc. cit.*, R 77. La Vente [to Brisacier], Oct. 6, 1708, ASQ, Lettres, R 85. La Vente [to Brisacier], Oct. 4, 1708, ASQ, Lettres, R 84. ASQ, Polygraphie, IX, 26, 27.

this necessary sum to be spent for these billiards will be deducted from what I am giving as wages to the domestic." [9]

In truth, La Vente had greater resources than anyone in the colony not excepting Bienville and the more affluent of the inhabitants such as Rivard, Graveline and Joussette. Although he could hardly depend on tithes for much support, his salary amounted to one thousand *livres* per year, a rate only slightly lower than Bienville's and Châteaugué's earnings.[10] In addition to the commerce he was carrying on, La Vente, frequently acting as notary, took in tidy fees for his service in that capacity. Moreover, he could count on receiving sizable bequests from the estates of many of those who died in the colony, who, far from their next-of-kin, often gave their entire estate to the church (persuaded to do so no doubt by him who heard their last confessions).[11] For example, La Vente drew up a will in 1706 for the expiring Sebastien Pourchasse, *dit* Le Breton, a Frenchman from Trégnerard in Vannes. Le Breton's estate amounted to 1,200 *livres*, one-fourth of which was bequeathed to the parish church.[12] Similarly, on the death of a certain Lajeunesse, La Vente was able to report to Brisacier, ". . . this Lajeunesse when he died made me and the church heirs to whatever might be left." [13]

Although Bienville tolerated La Vente's limited commerce (who was he to raise such objections?) in earlier days, he was soon offended by the pastor's insistence that the colony bear full expense for the building of the parish church (especially when he knew full well that La Vente could better afford to have it built himself).[14] Some months after the seminary priest's arrival, a heated discussion had arisen between Bienville, La Vente and Davion concerning Pontchartrain's instructions about sending soldiers to the Indian villages to protect the missionaries and to assist them in "assembling" the tribes into larger villages. Bienville claimed the minister had given him wide discretionary powers

9. La Vente [to Brisacier], Oct. 6, 1708, *loc. cit.*, R 85.

10. AC, F1A, 11, f. 218; 13, f. 113–14. On his arrival, however, La Vente discovered that his salary had not yet been provided for, an omission soon corrected. La Vente [to SME Dirs.], Sept. 20, 1704, *loc. cit.*, R 77.

11. Bienville to min., Oct. 10, 1706, *loc. cit.*, f. 3–4.

12. La Vente [to Brisacier], Oct. 6, 1708, *loc. cit.*, R 85.

13. *Ibid.*

14. Soon after arriving, La Vente, expecting work on the church to begin, sent back a list of needed supplies to Tremblay which included "a banner of the Holy Virgin and one or two bells from Rochefort." La Vente [to Tremblay], Sept. 10, 1704, ASQ, Lettres R 75.

concerning such policies and to prove it he produced Pontchartrain's letter of January 30, 1704. In allowing Davion and La Vente to read for themselves the minister's instructions, Bienville won this point. But in doing so, he gave La Vente additional ammunition concerning the issue of the church. For just above Pontchartrain's directions on the Indian question, La Vente noticed the minister's words:

> . . . in his expenses His Majesty has allocated a sum of six hundred *livres* for the construction and support of the parish church of Mobile. You must also induce the inhabitants to give on their part several days for building it and see to it that divine worship is conducted with as much decency as the place can afford; that the impious blasphemers and persons who provoke scandal are repressed according to His Majesty's wishes.[15]

These were instructions La Vente would not allow Bienville to forget. Over the next two years the *curé* needled Bienville at every opportunity for his failure to abide by his minister's directions:

> . . . M. de Bienville had orders from the court as soon as we arrived here, by instructions which he allowed me to read several times, to have a church built for the parish, and the king promised 200 *écus* for the construction and upkeep of this edifice. M. de Bienville has refused to listen to our entreaties and demands at court nor has he paid by the voucher the promised sum for this place.[16]

Despite La Vente's best efforts, by early 1706 the church had not been built, Bienville pointing out to La Vente that survival of the colony came before even the building of a church and complaining to the court that La Vente himself possessed over and above the necessary funds for construction, since:

> . . . most of those who die here, finding themselves a long way from their relatives, make their testaments in his [La Vente's] favor—probably as he coerced them to do—and that just from one man he got up to seven or eight hundred *livres*, without counting a thousand other enterprises, but he does not hurry because he even hopes for further funds from Your Highness . . .[17]

15. Min. to Bienville, Jan. 30, 1704, AC, B 25, f. 6v.
16. La Vente [to Brisacier], July 4, 1708, ASQ, Lettres, R 83.
17. Bienville to min., Oct. 10, 1706, *loc. cit.*, f. 3–4.

Lacking Bienville's support in building the church, La Vente found occasion to retaliate in mean and petty ways. Noticing for several months the commandant conversing in public with Catherine Moulois, the first *sage-femme* and wife of Laurent Cloquinet, La Vente took the opportunity to warn Bienville about his "too great a familiarity" with the woman, which he claimed was causing scandalous gossip.[18] Bienville, knowing his conversation with Madame Cloquinet to be purely casual and concerning only business, dismissed La Vente's warning with little thought. Some months later, however, Bienville was invited by Jean-Baptiste Saucier to act as godfather at the birth of Saucier's first daughter. After the birth had taken place, La Vente refused to baptize the child so long as Bienville was to act as godparent. While refraining from publicly charging Bienville with adultery, La Vente nonetheless claimed he would be doing the child an injustice by baptizing her under the sponsorship of one so tainted in the public mind with debauchery. Irate, the commandant presented witnesses to La Vente, including the woman's widower (Catherine Moulois had died in the meantime), who testified to the falsity of charges. Confronted with this evidence and by a demand from Bienville that he offer a public apology, the *curé* haughtily replied that he was not obliged to apologize for any error in public opinion, that if the rumors were false it was the commandant's responsibility to avoid even the appearance of evil. Bienville was left fuming, but there was little he could do to controvert such malice.[19]

It was not only Bienville, however, who came under the fire of La Vente and with whom the pastor was becoming increasingly unpopular. Many of the unmarried officers and Canadians had found a regular and rather convenient outlet for their sexual energies: taking young Indian girls into their dwellings as housekeepers, the salacious bachelors found the servant girls doubly useful. It was a practice La Vente from the beginning frowned upon; later, as Bienville seemed unwilling to take measures to stop it, the *curé* became more outspoken on the matter: these libertines were not only living in sin, they were setting a standard

18. La Vente to min., March 2, 1708, *loc. cit.*, f. 163.

19. Tremblay [to SQ], March 18, 1707, ASQ, Lettres, M 35. Bienville to min., April 10, 1706, *loc. cit.*, f. 507–08. Dénombrement, Aug. 1, 1706, AC, G1, 464. Tremblay [to Laval?], June 25, 1707, ASQ, Lettres, M 38. Bienville was not quite confident enough to accuse La Vente (whom he surely suspected) of initiating the rumors himself.

that could have serious diplomatic consequences and the commandant was but winking at the arrangements.[20]

Thus, La Vente and Bienville moved farther apart. During the early years, their differences were primarily personal, La Vente calling Bienville to task for his independence, his general lack of judgment and respect, while Bienville upbraided La Vente for his pettiness, his haughty and quarrelsome nature. As the colony drifted deeper into poverty, the charges the two leaders brought against each other related more to the concrete issues at hand: La Vente and his assistant Huvé were too much concerned with their own commerce; as missionaries, they were plainly ineffective, neither being willing to learn the languages of the Indians Bienville hoped they could convert. Bienville, on the other hand, was, according to La Vente, at the root of the settlement's sorry state. By his chicanery and his sloppy administration, he was bringing the colony closer to the verge of ruin.[21]

Shortly, however, the conflict would take on a more political and idealogical tone. An old and bitter feud was to be renewed in January of 1706 with the appearance on the scene of Jesuit Jacques Gravier. Gravier, a veteran missionary from the Illinois country, now in his fifty-fifth year, was no stranger to the Louisiana wilderness. After some six years of theological and philosophical studies at the Collège Louis-le-Grand à Paris, the ordained priest had sailed for Quebec in 1684, from where after a year or so, he set out for the western country, serving among the Ottawa, then at Starved Rock on the river Illinois. For fully a decade Père Jacques served among the Illinois villages, and at Michilimackinac as "Superior of the Missions among the Ottawa, the Illinois, the Miami and others," before journeying downriver in 1700 to the infant defense posts at Fort La Boulaye and Fort Maurepas.[22]

Gravier remained on the Gulf Coast for nearly two years where he won the admiration and loyalty of the young Bienville. Shortly

20. La Vente to min., March 2, 1708, *loc. cit.*, f. 163–64. La Vente [to Brisacier], July 4, 1708, *loc. cit.*, R 83. Min. to Bienville, May 10, 1710, AC, B 32, f. 39–39v. La Vente [to Brisacier], March 4, 1708, ASQ, Lettres, R 79. Marc Bergier had earlier complained of debauchery at Mobile. Lettre de Bergier, March 30, 1704, ASQ, Lettres, R 64.

21. Bienville to min., Oct. 10, 1706, *loc. cit.*, f. 3v–8. Boisbriant to min., Oct. 1, 1706, AC, C13A, 1, f. 586.

22. Tremblay [to SQ], March 18, 1707, *loc. cit.*, M 35. ARSI, Gallia, 110 II, f. 269–72v, 273v. Gravier [to Laval], Sept. 20, 1698, ASQ, Lettres, N 132. *JR, LXV*, pp. 58–62. Lettre du Père Jacques Gravier . . . Feb. 15, 1694, BN, FF, 6453, f. 30–43v. SLUA, Mission des Illinois, March 20, 1692.

after the founding of Mobile (which he had visited briefly), Gravier, in February of 1702, returned to his post among the Illinois where he served for the next three years, having been named superior of that mission.[23]

As a missionary, Gravier was singularly dedicated to converting the natives. Like Bienville he was adept at learning savage languages (unlike La Vente, refusing to use age as an excuse for not doing so), was thereby unusually successful in winning the natives to his own faith. Perhaps he was too successful. In the late summer of 1705 a young Peoria warrior, convinced of the sanctity of Gravier's god, approached the priest with his dead relative whom he wanted buried in the most holy church. When Gravier refused to allow it, the Peoria, thinking Gravier's refusal might mean exclusion from the heavenly kingdom, went beserk. He attacked the astounded priest with bow and arrows, one projectile tearing through Gravier's ear, another piercing his forearm, its point lodging just below the elbow. With streams of blood pouring from his wounds, in particular from a severed artery, Gravier "plucked the arrow stem from his arm but the stonehead stuck in the sinews near the joint of the elbow." [24]

Over the next several months Gravier was wracked with pain and fever. Attempting to leave his mission he was prevented from doing so by the natives themselves. With the aid of a servant named Deman and a loyal blacksmith called Saint-Michel, Gravier escaped eventually to the village of the Kaskaskia where Père Jean Mermet, a fellow Jesuit recently arrived from the Miami, attempted to reduce the swelling by having the wound lanced. Unable to remove the arrowhead, however, Mermet convinced Gravier to journey to Mobile "where there are surgeons . . . who know their trade." [25]

23. Relation . . de r.p. Jacques Gravier, 1700, *JR, LXV*, pp. 100–09. Journal de Le Sueur, 1702, AM, 2 JJ 56, 9. Gravier to Père Lamberville, Feb. 16, 1701, *JR, LXV*, pp. 120–43. SLUA, mission des Illinois, April 13, 1703.

24. Lettre du P. Mermet, March 2, 1706, *JR, LXVI*, pp. 50–63. Bienville to min., Oct. 10, 1706, *loc. cit.*, f. 8–9v. Gravier described the Peoria as "a barbarbian who shot at me *in odium fidei.*" Epistola Patris Jacobi Gravier ad Reverendissium Patrem Michaelem Angelum Tamburini . . . , *JR, LXVI*, pp. 120–21. Lettre du Père Gabriel Marest, Nov. 9, 1712, *JR, LXVI*, pp. 246–47.

25. Mermet, March 2, 1706, *op. cit.*, pp. 57–61. ARSI, Gallia, 15 I, f. 66–8; 110 II, f. 261–64; Francia, 25 II, f. 298v–99. *JR, LXVI*, pp. 38–40, 51–55. SLUA, mission des Illinois, I, Jan. 19, 1707.

Heeding Mermet's advice the suffering priest left Kaskaskia on the sixth of November with famed Canadian guide François-Marie Bouat and a *donné* called Jacques Largillier, *dit* Le Castor. After a fairly rapid journey downriver, Gravier and his small party arrived at Fort Louis during the third week of January, 1706.[26]

Commandant Bienville, elated at Gravier's presence (if not at the cause for his coming), settled the weakened missionary at the house of the departed Pierre Dongé on the riverfront across from Commissary La Salle on the rue des Jésuites. Once recovered from his strenuous journey, Gravier sought to have the stonehead removed from his elbow. But if he expected expert treatment (as Father Mermet had led him to believe), he was quickly disappointed: there were no skilled surgeons in Mobile—only Pierre Clavery (who, at a salary of thirty *livres* per month, was little more than a medic) and his aide, Mathurin Meunier. Neither could perform the operation Gravier needed. The Jesuit's only consolation was the hope that Bienville held out to him that the next ship from France would bring a bona fide surgeon. Meanwhile, Gravier, now more chronically annoyed than acutely in pain, must bear the imbedded stone as best he could.[27]

Insofar as the state of religion in the colony was concerned, there was little to cheer the beleaguered missionary. Even by the kindest standards, La Vente and Huvé were ineffectual; and Gravier's standards were not generally charitable. It did not take the wilderness-hardened priest long to conclude that the pastor was "a strange man . . . who is hated by nearly everyone. In all truth it is impossible to conceive how boldly he advances and maintains deceptions. His character, his age, his devout and imposing air, give him authority, and shield him from everything; and when he is convicted of impostures and falsehoods, he denies them as brazenly as he uttered them." [28]

If La Vente quickly became an object of Gravier's contempt, the *curé's* colleague Alexandre Huvé was viewed by the Jesuit

26. As to the gravity of Gravier's wound, Mermet added, "I greatly fear he will die of his wound or be crippled by it for the remainder of his life." Mermet, *op. cit.*, pp. 62–63.

27. AJM, Greffe de Raimbault, Oct. 1, 1718; Sept. 12, 1720. Mermet, *op. cit.*, pp. 61–63. AJQ, Greffes de Rageot, Duquet, Becquet, Oct. 1, 1672; March 17, 1673; July 30, 1675. *JR, LXVI*, pp. 124–27, 134–35, 340. AC, F1A, 10, f. 282; 11, f. 69v, 73, 217–18; 13, f. 114v.

28. Lettre du P. Jacques Gravier, February 23, 1708, *JR, LXVI*, pp. 129, 131–33.

father with pity as well as with disdain. It was patently obvious that Huvé, a slightly built man, frequently ill, was not fashioned for the rugged life. Moreover, he suffered from both a speech impediment and severe myopia. Even the Indians derided him for his infirmities and weak constitution. As if this were not enough, his attitude and service record were not indicative of intense religious fervor.[29] Observed Gravier of the misfit:

> Monsieur Huvé knows not a single word in the savage tongue, although he has been here several years. He has, it is true, served for some time in the village of the Apalache, four leagues from here; but he knows nothing of their language, and he hears confessions, baptizes, marries and administers communion and extreme unction, without understanding the savages at all. What would be said if a Jesuit were to do as much? The Apalache have driven him away twice—both because he does not learn their language and because he is very particular about his food; for they have given him a house and a chapel and they feed him.[30]

In conversations between Bienville and Gravier the question of Huvé's service received unusual attention. How was Huvé's position to be defined, anyway? Was he assistant pastor, or chaplain of the fort? If assistant pastor, could he also properly serve as chaplain? If chaplain, was he not subject to orders of the commandant? There was little doubt over the latter question, but had not Huvé himself protested bitterly (when Bienville ordered him not to leave town without authorization) that he was not like a servant, having to ask permission to go to his own mission; that, as assistant pastor, he intended taking orders from no one but the pastor. If this were Huvé's attitude, then he could not properly serve as chaplain for it was well established that a fort's *aumônier* must be subject to orders from the commandant.[31]

In truth, instructions from the court were not current regarding

29. Bienville to min., Oct. 10, 1706, *loc. cit.*, f. 6. Bienville to min., Résumé, Oct. 10, 1706, AC, C13A, 1, f. 537–38. La Vente [to SME Dirs.], June 27, 1708, ASQ, Lettres, R 82. La Vente [to Brisacier], July 4, 1708, *loc. cit.*, R 83. Tremblay [to Des Maizerets], June 5, 1712, ASQ, Lettres, O 54.

30. Lettre du P. Jacques Gravier, Feb. 23, 1708, *JR*, *LXVI*, p. 131.

31. Tremblay [to SQ Dirs.], June 25, 1707, ASQ, Lettres, M 38. Bienville to min., Oct. 10, 1706, *loc. cit.*, f. 5–8v. AC, F5A, 3, f. 36–38v. Bienville to min., Résumé, Oct. 10, 1706, *loc.*, *cit.*, f. 536–40.

the chaplaincy of Fort Louis. When Huvé arrived with La Vente, Jesuit Dongé had been serving as chaplain. After Dongé's departure on the *Pélican* there was no one available to take his place (except temporarily Albert Davion) and the court had not taken steps to provide for a permanent replacement. Moreover, Jesuits in the Illinois country, unclear on orders from their provincial, had for several years been discussing plans for locating a Jesuit chaplain at Mobile which, stretching Saint-Vallier's meaning, could conceivably be worked into the fabric of the bishop's pronouncements. Despite the resentment of seminary missioner Marc Bergier, the bishop's vicar-general in the Illinois country who got wind of the plan, Gravier was still in 1706 planning such a move.[32]

The situation was complicated, however, by the lack of a parish church which had yet not been constructed. Since there was no public place of worship, La Vente must of necessity perform his services in the fort chapel, which he had been doing since his arrival. Would La Vente be willing to share the chapel with a Jesuit? Bienville, of course, knew La Vente too well to expect anything but high indignation at such a proposal. After lengthy consultation with Gravier, he and the Jesuit priest reached a decision: in order to get La Vente out of the fort Bienville would proceed with plans to build the parish church at the king's expense. Gravier would become Bienville's private chaplain (and would be entered on the payroll as such), while Huvé would continue serving as assistant pastor and missionary to the Apalache.[33]

The scheme as such was not mentioned to the seminary priest; it was merely put quietly into action. Gravier began his duties as chaplain and work was begun on the church. For some time now, La Vente, in an attempt to gain sympathy and to demonstrate to the inhabitants that he was being forced to build the church "from scratch," had been collecting pieces of lumber which he had

32. AC, F1A, 11, f. 224v. On the 1704 list of accounts Huvé is listed as "prestre servant" at 500 *livres* per year, while Albert Davion served as chaplain at 360 *livres*. By the time Gravier arrived, however, Davion had returned to his mission. AC, F1A, 11, f. 217–18, 224v, 228. In the accounts of 1705 Huvé is listed as "aumosnier du fort Louis de La Louisiane" at 600 *livres* per year. AC, F1A, 12, f. 92v.

33. Bienville to min., Feb. 20, 1707, AC, C13A, 2, f. 522–30. Lettre du P. Jacques Gravier, Feb. 23, 1708, *op. cit.*, pp. 124–41. Lettre de Gravier (extrait), 1706, AC, C13A, 1, f. 570–77; *Idem.*, Feb. 27, 1707, AC, C13A, 1, f. 578–79. La Salle to min., Sept. 7, 1706, AC, C13A, 1, f. 485–89. Bienville to min., April 10, 1706, *loc. cit.*, f. 507 (and Pontchartrain's marginal note).

stacked near the location where the proposed church was to be built.[34] Only a portion of the wood was usable but when Bienville ordered construction of the church, he utilized those timbers which had not yet rotted and which were of sufficient size. Not to be satisfied at the least action of the commandant, La Vente grumbled:

> He [Bienville] pretended he was being obliging on this occasion, but that was far from his thoughts. However, the hope I had that sooner or later the court would see to it that I had a proper place to worship I placed on the same level as my hope of being reimbursed for the expenses incurred in providing the wood. M. de Bienville, seeing the timbers prepared and by the advice of the Reverend Jesuit father, decided to build the church. He took my wood by his own authority and commenced the task without even having notified me.[35]

Work on the church proceeded rapidly; Bienville was anxious to have La Vente out of the fort as soon as possible. When finished (or at least completed as far as Bienville intended), the church was forty feet long by twenty-six feet wide, only slightly larger than the fort's chapel. When La Vente complained of its meager size, Bienville merely replied that the pastor had wanted a larger place of worship and that he had given it to him. He did not rub in the fact that "larger" meant only "an increase of 368 square feet." After all, next to the headquarters, the new church was now the largest building in the settlement.[36]

La Vente's criticisms of the church, however, were not limited to its small size. This "framework of a house," as he referred to it, "is what in France one would call half-timbered, that is to say, open on all sides without having either windows or roofing and which, because of the location of the place where the foundation is, necessarily needs a floor to be habitable." [37]

34. La Vente [to Brisacier], July 4, 1708, ASQ, Lettres, R 83. *FLC*, p. 116.

35. La Vente [to Brisacier], July 4, 1708, *loc. cit.*, R 83.

36. The chapel totalled 672 square feet (French), while the new church encompassed 1040 square feet (the headquarters covering 1088). Dénombrement, Aug. 31, 1704, AC, C13A, 1, f. 468. Bienville to min, Feb. 20, 1707, *loc. cit.*, f. 28–29.

37. La Vente [to Brisacier], July 4, 1708, *loc. cit.*, R 83. La Vente further complained that the construction was "not very secure" and supposed that it might "fall in ruins in a few months." *Ibid.*

In point of fact, Bienville had given the church a roof only of beams crossed by rounded poles which still required shingles to keep the water from pouring in when it rained. Having spent seven hundred *livres* above the amount the court allotted for the construction (which he had been obliged to pay in goods from the king's storehouse at 100% above prices in France), the commandant claimed his responsibility was ended, that the trimmings (doors, windows and shingles) were up to La Vente, depending on how comfortable he wanted himself and his parishioners to be.[38] As for Bienville, his officers and his Jesuit chaplain, they would retain use of the fort's chapel.

La Vente, in a huff, temporarily resigned himself to the church's sorry condition. "In this skirmish," he wrote Brisacier, "we have recourse only to our divine ointment—patience—which is the most universal and most specific remedy for all our ills." [39]

Whatever patience La Vente was able to muster for the time being, he was shortly to lose. Bienville not only ignored his continued requests to pay for the church's shingling, but, according to the *curé*, in order to generate ill feeling he spread rumors among the inhabitants that La Vente had received 15,000 *livres* from the court to cover the cost for numerous buildings, which funds the pastor was keeping in his private possession. "In this [character assassination]," La Vente admitted, "M. de Bienville is not a little successful." [40] Closely observing affairs at the fort, however, La Vente shortly saw a chance to launch an attack of his own. His opening came when Jacques Gravier exceeded the narrow range of his duties as Bienville's personal chaplain. As long as Gravier performed services strictly of a private nature for Bienville, the commandant was perfectly within his rights to appoint the Jesuit. Even La Vente conceded this. Bienville and Gravier no doubt felt certain that once La Vente was away from the fort and involved with his parishioners in the town, Gravier's position

38. Bienville to min., July 28, 1706, *loc. cit.*, f. 527–28. According to La Vente's pre-inflation estimates, costs for the shingles, excluding labor, would amount to 20 *livres* per thousand (in 1704). Since the wooden shingles measured 1 x 1½ French feet, the total cost for roofing the church (including labor) would not have reached 250 *livres*, well within either La Vente's or Bienville's budget. La Vente [to Tremblay], Sept. 10, 1704, ASQ, Lettres, R 75. AC, F1A, 10, f. 290v. Pérez a Zúñiga, May 25, 1703, AGI, *Santo Domingo*, L. 858.

39. La Vente [to Brisacier], July 4, 1708, *loc. cit.*, R 83.

40. *Ibid.*

could gradually be extended to fort chaplain without restrictions. The Jesuit was soon conducting mass not only for the commandant but for Bienville's servants as well. When one day La Vente heard the bells of the fort's chapel (which were calling the servants to mass), the *curé* lodged a protest: if Gravier could ring the bells (for a mass other than for Bienville), his duties were more than merely private. He would next be ringing for the officers and soldiers, most of whom were lodged in the town. If Gravier were allowed to extend his functions in this manner he could soon be ministering to significant numbers of the townfolk. Envisioning a *de facto* reinstatement of the Jesuits, La Vente became more alarmed. Was there a possibility the rival order could become permanently restored should the *curé* and his assistant (both past middle age and neither in optimal health) suddenly expire?[41]

Pastor La Vente demanded that Gravier desist immediately from performing any functions not directly related to his position as Bienville's chaplain. On hearing of the *curé's* order, Bienville asserted himself on the issue. As a matter of fact, he saw no good reason why Gravier could not perform the full functions of fort chaplain in addition to his private duties. The court had never been clear on such a point; in the absence of a court-appointed chaplain, the commandant was well within his rights to appoint one. At this juncture La Vente announced that he was coming back to the fort to perform all his functions as *curé* since the church Bienville had built was obviously insufficient. When Bienville asked him by what authority he was returning, La Vente answered "by the authority vested in me by Bishop Saint-Vallier as his vicar-general." Implied in this authority was the *curé's* power of deciding where to hold his services if there was reasonable question of the adequacy of his place of worship.[42]

With this announcement Bienville could not knowledgeably quarrel. Though he questioned La Vente's claim of being vicar-general, it was not an unreasonable assertion. La Vente, after all, had enjoyed an intimate if brief association with Saint-Vallier in mid-1703. It was barely possible that such a commission had been made. On the advice of Gravier, Bienville retreated. In view of the commandant's ambition, he must move cautiously, being careful

41. Bienville to min., July 28, 1706, AC, C13A, 1, f. 533–36. La Vente to min., March 2, 1708, *loc. cit.*, f. 161–64. Bergier à l'évêque de Québec, April 15, 1705, ASQ, Lettres, R 73.

42. Bienville to min., Oct. 10, 1706, *loc. cit.*, f. 2v–9v. Tremblay [to SQ Dirs.], March 18, 1707, *loc. cit.*, M 35.

not to leave himself open. Judicial and canonical disputes were decided impartially and precisely by the court. It was one thing to engage in personal disputes with the clergy; it would be quite another to openly bar the court's approved pastor from performing his functions, a specific and easily proven offense. Having been outmaneuvered by La Vente, Bienville arranged a temporary compromise: both the chaplain *and* the pastor would be allowed to use the chapel. Perhaps this arrangement would suffice until the next ship from France could bring more precise instructions.[43]

The "truce" was not long-lived. La Vente, suspicious of both Gravier and Bienville, attempted to insure that Gravier would not often use the chapel for any type of service by squeezing his services so tightly together that there was little time left for the Jesuit. Bienville, fully cognizant of the ploy, later described the pastor's actions to the minister:

> He [La Vente] says a full mass with long sermons, not to mention three low masses which take all morning, feast days and Sundays which are the days set aside for the services. I told him that this did not suit me and that he was going to force me to send him back to his church to perform his functions, upon which he threatened that if I was audacious enough to keep him from performing his functions in the fort he would excommunicate me.[44]

After several weeks, the patience of the generally restrained Gravier began to wear thin. Père Jacques publicly announced he would hold a "special" Easter service in the chapel at which time he would give communion to the soldiers. On hearing this news, La Vente put his foot down solidly: such a service would be a formal and obvious violation of the wishes of both the court and the bishop. The troops (most of whom lived in the town because there were no lodgings in the fort) belonged spiritually to the *curé;* the pastor was not about to lose half of his flock to "a wandering Jesuit, pretending to perform the functions of a chaplain." If Gravier insisted on carrying out such a contrivance, La Vente would have no alternative but to interdict the Jesuit father.[45]

43. Bienville described La Vente to Pontchartrain as "acting under the pretext of being vicar-general." Bienville to min., Oct. 10, 1706, *loc. cit.*, f. 4v–5v.

44. *Ibid.*, f. 3v–4.

45. Lettre du P. Jacques Gravier, Feb. 23, 1708, *op. cit.*, pp. 129–41. La Vente to min., March 2, 1708, *loc. cit.*, f. 160–64. La Vente [to Brisacier],

Furious at La Vente's threat, Bienville retaliated in a devious manner: with premeditated spite, the pastor had been dragging out the Sabbath services; but since Sundays were the regular days for review of the troops, Bienville accused La Vente of interferring with the fort's schedule of operations. If the commandant's authority in matters of religion were limited, surely he had the right to control the functions of his fort. Apparently on solid ground, Bienville began fixing the hours that La Vente could use the fort to hold his services. When La Vente refused to abide by these hours, Bienville began locking the two entrances to the fort to prevent the *curé* from entering. La Vente attacked this gambit by charging that while Bienville had the right to lock the main gate, he had no authority to bar the western gate, since by this entrance the pastor and his parishioners could both enter and leave the chapel without disturbing the military order of the day. When Bienville answered that as commandant *he* would decide what constituted interference, it was then that La Vente threatened Bienville with excommunication.[46]

At this threat, Bienville, again on the advice of Gravier, withdrew his restrictions: he was still young, with a long future ahead of him, while La Vente's days were surely numbered. The ambitious commandant did not need excommunication on his record. When La Vente, in a fit of temper, entered Bienville's house and bellowed that within a year one of the two of them would be gone from the colony, Bienville could reasonably hope that the pastor's prediction would ultimately turn in his favor. For the rest of the spring of 1706 the commandant would tread more softly, keeping his guard up, but not allowing himself to be inveigled into rash actions. Though he could not know precisely the feelings of the court on the pastor's record of service, he was confident that the headstrong *curé* would eventually undo himself. The greater number of reports reaching officials in Paris and Versailles would inevitably bear out the fact that La Vente was old, destructive and useless. Though he would control his actions, however, Bienville could moderate neither his tongue nor his pen.

March 4, 1708, ASQ, Lettres, R 79. Bienville to min., Oct. 10, 1706, *loc. cit.*, f. 3–9v. Pontchartrain, however, seems to have disapproved of La Vente's blocking Gravier's plans for an Easter service. *Cf.* Pontchartrain's note to Bienville's April 10 letter (AC, C13A, 1, f. 507).

46. Bienville to min., Oct. 10, 1706, *loc. cit.*, f. 4v–10. La Vente [to Brisacier], July 4, 1708, *loc. cit.*, R 83. Bienville to min. (Résumé), Oct. 10, 1706, *loc. cit.*, f. 532–37.

In his correspondence with Pontchartrain, he was unable to restrain his pent-up anger. "I do not believe, Monseigneur," he wrote, "that there could be found a man on the face of this earth more violent, more hot-headed, more two-faced or one who has a blacker soul." [47]

For his own part, La Vente made his virulences more public, blasting Bienville even from the chapel in the fort, charging the commandant with obstruction of religion and—what from the colonists' point of view was infinitely more relevant to them—the responsibility for the widespread poverty in the colony. Both the pastor and Bienville were preoccupied with this latter situation, and, as the spring of 1706 moved to a close, each hoped that the anticipated ship from France would bring nourishment for the flesh as well as resolution (in the form of additional missionaries and more specific instructions) for the needs of the spirit.[48]

47. Bienville to min., July 28, 1706, *loc. cit.*, f. 527–41. Bienville to min., Feb. 20, 1707, *loc. cit.*, f. 23–30.

48. *Ibid.*, f. 24–29.

XV

The *Aigle* Arrives

ON the morning of the thirteenth of June, 1706, the few soldiers and workmen remaining at Massacre Island espied on the far southeastern horizon the sails of two ships moving slowly toward them. Later, as the ships neared the channel entrance just beyond Pelican Island, the enthralled men could see two white flags in the wind. One ship (the *Aigle*), which appeared to be heavily laden, they recognized as a French-made vessel. The other (the *Bienvenu*, a small boat captured at the siege of Nevis and recently placed under the command of Châteaugué) appeared to be of English make. Closer observation of the vessels as they began drifting up the narrow channel, however, must have evoked more than a tinge of disappointment. Even from a distance of a quarter-mile, the men on the island could estimate the ships' relative sizes (in comparison with the *Renommée* and the *Loire*) and they found them both inadequate. For it had been expected that the next supply ship from France would be the largest yet sent to Mobile.[1]

In truth, the ship originally designated to supply Mobile, the *Coventry*, was the largest vessel the ministry had yet outfitted for Louisiana. At 670 tons burden, the captured English ship was 70 tons heavier than the *Pélican* and 170 tons greater than the *Loire*. Moreover, since she had been carrying fewer personnel than either the *Pélican* or the *Renommée*, there had been even more room available for supplies. Iberville and Sérigny, however, having switched ships after the sacking of Nevis, had transferred (with considerable loss and damage) the bulk of the merchandise bound for Louisiana from the *Coventry* to the *Aigle*. Sérigny was at this

1. *Journal Historique*, p. 96. Min. to Martinet, Oct. 21, 1705, AM, B2, 183, f. 117. AC, F1A, 12, f. 182. Min. to Iberville, Dec. 30, 1706, AM, B2, 183, f. 863–64. Dartaguiette to min., Feb. 26, 1708, AC, C13A, 2, f. 62–67.

very hour at the port of Veracruz with the *Coventry*, trading some of the remaining merchandise to the Spanish for his and Iberville's profit.[2]

The ship that now carried the greater portion of the supplies for Mobile (the *Bienvenu* carried perhaps only one-tenth) had been built by the shipbuilder Félix Arnaud at Bayonne in 1692. A "vaisseau de 5ème rang," the *Aigle*, of three hundred tons burden, was capable of carrying less than half the weight the *Coventry* could bear, and, though in good condition, she carried but thirty-four guns, none larger than eight-pounders. Her captain, Payen de Noyan, now in his forty-third year, was negotiating his second entrance of the harbor at Île Massacre. Four years before, as a sub-lieutenant under his brother-in-law, Sérigny, Payen had helmed the much larger *Palmier* from Pensacola to the Massacre Island port. Now in June of 1706, commanding his own vessel, he slowly brought the *Aigle* to anchor in the mid-morning sun.[3]

Massacre Island had changed very little in the years since Payen had helped found Mobile. There was one difference he could not but notice, however. The warehouse he and Châteaugué had helped erect in 1702 showed a decided lean; small, inadequate to its purpose, it now stood rotting, nearly dilapidated, just back of the lagoon in front of the large sand dunes. Except for a few additional huts surrounding the decaying depot, the island seemed as bare and desolate as when the French first came. As the unloading of the *Aigle* began and some of the passengers began disembarking, a courier was hastily dispatched to Fort Louis to notify the authorities that the ship had arrived.[4]

One of the first men off the ship was Claude Allemand, Iberville's agent and brother of erstwhile traversier scrivener Jacques Allemand (now serving as a warehousekeeper at Fort Louis). Claude, entrusted by Iberville to manage his personal commodities (of which Iberville hoped to quite profitably dispose), began im-

2. Min. to Bégon, Nov. 4, 1704, AC, B 27, f. 183–84. *Cf.* Chapter XIII, note 32. Min. to Sérigny, Dec. 29, 1706, AM, B2, 192, f. 962–65. Interrogatoire de Claude L'Allemand, Nov. 4, 1707, ACM, Cours et jurisdictions, B 5921.

3. Min. to Bégon, Oct. 28, 1705, AM, B2, 183, f. 148–51. Arnoul de Vaucresson to min., June 21, 1706, AC, C8A, 16, *n.p.* AM, G, 13, 13 *bis*, 14, 18. *DGFC, I*, pp. 379, 468. LSMA, DCS, May 1, 1735. Journal d'Iberville, Dec. 15, 1701, AM, B4, 23, f. 321–39. Clairambault to min., May 9, 1707, AM, B3, 147, f. 335–43.

4. Journal d'Iberville, Dec. 15, 1701, *loc. cit.*, f. 323–38. La Salle to min., April 1, 1702, AC, C13C, 2, f. 36–45. La Salle to min., Sept. 8, 1706, AC, C13A, 1, f. 545–49.

mediate preparations to safeguard his cargo, investigating the capability of the warehouse to temporarily store it.[5]

The unloading and disembarking, however, did not proceed in earnest until the following day. The next morning Valentin Barraud,[6] the long-awaited surgeon from France, stepped onto Massacre Island, as did the new seminary missioner from Paris, François Le Maire. Le Maire, a hulking young man of thirty-one, had recently served as vicar of Saint-Jacques de la Boucherie. Somewhat of a scholar and poet and also interested in geography, he had been seized by the romantic notion of ministering to the natives of Louisiana. The long, gruelling voyage in the *Coventry*, however, had severely tested his appetite for the rugged life and the sight of the barren island before him now did nothing to lift his spirits.[7]

Within twenty-four hours, Bienville had received word of the *Aigle's* arrival. Some of the merchandise, mostly flour and bacon, was already being transported to the fort, the majority being temporarily stored in the warehouse. Bienville, along with some of the Canadians, hastened to Île Massacre where they found Captain Payen de Noyan directing the unloading while at the same time selling merchandise on his own account. Châteaugué was not long present after the commandant and the Canadians arrived. Bienville had already arranged with him that as soon as he reached port he was to transfer a portion of the merchandise from the *Aigle* to the *Aventurier* and make haste to Pensacola, there to sell what he could to the Spanish who as usual were loaded with cash. Later, when La Salle questioned this act, Bienville had a ready reply: the French were in debt to the Spanish for a hundred quintals of flour; before further spoilage occurred, it would be wise to get the flour to Pensacola as soon as possible to eliminate the debt. A plausible explanation, perhaps, but to La Salle (who had been forced to remain at the fort because Bienville ordered his assistant to accompany him to Massacre Island) it was only an excuse to carry on commerce without the commissary being able to audit it.[8]

5. Clairambault to min., March 7, 1707, AM, B3, 147, f. 180–84. La Salle to min., Aug. 10, 1706, AC, C13A, 1, f. 567–69.

6. AC, F1A, 13, f. 114. ADM, A, July 20, 1707; Jan. 29, 1708. Dartaguiette to min., May 25, 1708, AC, C13A, 2, f. 322–23.

7. *FLC*, p. 115. Min. to Bienville, Nov. 4, 1705, AC, B 27, f. 188–89. Lettre du P. Jacques Gravier, Feb. 23, 1708, *JR, LXVI*, pp. 130–31.

8. Bienville to min., Oct. 10, 1706, AC, C13B, 1, No. 6, f. 1v–2v. La Salle to min., Sept. 8, 1706, *loc. cit.*, f. 545–56. La Salle to min., Aug. 10, 1706, *loc. cit.*, f. 566–69.

At this point, La Salle was in an almost hopeless situation. Responsible for recording the reception of supplies, it was impossible for him to effectively carry out his duty. With some of the merchandise on the way to Fort Louis, with an unspecified amount bound for Pensacola, with part in the warehouse and part still on the *Aigle*, the commissary was at a loss as to how to reconcile amounts actually received with the bill of lading made out by Rochefort Intendent Michel Bégon. Questionable commerce was taking place almost before his eyes and he was powerless to check it: François Trudeau purchased a barrel of brandy, some shoes and stockings and linen from one of the *Aigle's* officers, while Jean-Baptiste Joussette, *dit* La Loire bought a large amount of clothes and twelve quarts of brandy at thirty-two *piastres* a quart from the first pilot of the *Aigle*. Étienne Burelle purchased twenty-one pieces of Brittany linen for four *piastres* each, eight to nine pounds of thread at twelve *livres* a pound and four quarts of brandy at forty *piastres* a quart.[9]

To aid him in combatting such confusion, La Salle received precious little in the way of records or instructions. Besides Bégon's bill of lading, the commissary was presented by Payen de Noyan with but two letters. One from Iberville, written at Nevis, seemed veiled with threats: it ordered him to record reception of only those goods listed on the original bill of lading and to send him receipts following precisely the form he was remitting.[10] The other was a short letter from Pontchartrain instructing him to "take great care of the foodstuffs and munitions and to take the necessary measures to have them used according to His Majesty's intentions." [11]

The instructions from Pontchartrain seemed to La Salle to be strangely vague and out-dated:

> It is necessary that you confer with M. d'Iberville in case he visits you personally or with the Sieur de Sérigny to whom he will explain his news on what he is to propose to you re-

9. La Salle to min., Sept. 7, 1706, AC, C13A, 1, f. 472–73. Interrogatoire des habitants, Feb. 25, 1708, AC, C13A, 2, f. 267–68, 275–77. *Id.*, Feb. 26, 1708, *loc. cit.*, f. 291–92. La Salle to min., March 4, 1708, AC, C13B, 1, No. 8, f. 4–5v.

10. *Ibid.*, f. 2v–3. This letter was later forwarded to Pontchartrain, but it was too vaguely worded to count for much as evidence against Iberville. Min. to Dartaguiette, May 10, 1710, AC, B 32, f. 4.

11. Min. to La Salle, Nov. 4, 1705, AC, B 27, f. 7.

garding the execution of the orders which he has received from His Majesty . . .[12]

However, neither Iberville nor Sérigny were present at the *Aigle's* landing and as far as Pontchartrain's instruction to "take great care" was concerned, this seemed for the moment to be almost ludicrous.

In reality, Commandant Bienville was himself displeased with the turn of events. Reading over the bill of lading La Salle had received, Bienville was at a loss to explain the obvious and decided difference in merchandise sent and merchandise received. He knew far better than La Salle what the actual differences were and it made him angry that his brothers had gone to such great lengths for their personal gain when it meant that he too would suffer as well as the colony. Expecting this to be the largest amount of supplies yet received, he saw only an amount similar to that which had been brought by the *Loire* three years before. And that shipment had been barely adequate. Hoping for enough merchandise to reap sizable profits himself as well as enough to support the colony in good style he saw quickly that the supplies were sufficient for neither objective. All of the bacon was completely spoiled and most of the vegetables intended for Louisiana had apparently never left Rochefort. Especially in the number of military reinforcements was he disappointed. Hoping for enough recruits to fill out the companies of Châteaugué and Vaulezard (which should have had fifty men each but which at present totaled less than sixty together) Bienville winced to see what he had received: "Only sixteen young soldiers [among them Guillaume Bélon, Étienne Chaprat and Louis Foussé] who are a very poor lot and not at all capable of doing battle." The soldiers, moreover, were ill (as were many others on the ship) due to widespread fever picked up in Havana.[13]

Bienville was further disappointed by the lack of missionaries sent. Opening his instructions from Pontchartrain his eyes quickly fell on the minister's words:

12. *Ibid.*, f. 7–8.

13. AC, F1A, 11, f. 64v–68v; 13, f. 115v, 116–16v. Bienville to min., July 28, 1706, AC, C13A, 1, f. 519–20. Min. to Bégon, May 25, 1707, AC, B 29, f. 241–43. Vaulezard, himself, remained in La Rochelle, having recently married Marguerite Gaigmeur, daughter of the principal recruiter for Canada. ACM, Greffe de Soullard, June 22, 1705. Relations were not always harmonious between Bienville and his brothers; especially was there dissension between him and Sérigny.

> The gentlemen of the Foreign Missions are sending two priests to Louisiana who are to go and serve with the Choctaw and Chickasaw so as to preach there the propagation of the faith. You should do everything in your power to assist them in the accomplishment of this objective by inducing these savage nations to assemble [into larger villages] in order to have them in better position to be instructed. Inform these priests of the instructions I am giving you and confer with them about everything there is to do in order to attain this good end.[14]

But there was only one missionary on Massacre Island at the moment. Confronting François Le Maire, Bienville (who had hoped for at least two or three missioners) asked where the other priest mentioned by Pontchartrain was. Le Maire, noting that the minister's letter was dated November 4 (over two months before Iberville's squadron had sailed), informed Bienville that another missionary, the young and capable Nicolas Gervaise, provost of Saint-Martin's church at Tours, had made plans to come with him, but that at the last moment his family and superiors had pressured the court to prevent his departure. Bienville almost wished he had not asked; his disappointment was even keener as he listened to Le Maire describe Gervaise as "a young, wealthy and dedicated servant of God" who had wished to spend his fortune as well as his considerable talents and energy in Louisiana.[15]

Stifling his disappointment, Bienville returned to Fort Louis, determined to make the most of what men and supplies had been sent. He had not yet given up hope that he would receive more merchandise before Iberville's squadron went back to France. From what Châteaugué had told him, Sérigny was still at Veracruz or somewhere in the gulf region and Iberville was still at Havana, making plans to attack English settlements on the Atlantic Coast. Perhaps the commander would be successful in gaining large

14. Min. to Bienville, Nov. 4, 1705, AC, B 27, f. 189. This should have been the answer to Bienville's entreaties. With one missioner at the Chickasaw and another at the Choctaw, he could have reasonably hoped to keep his allies in check and at peace with one another.

15. Lettre de M. Tremblay, April 12, 1706, ASQ, Lettres, O 45. *Id.*, June 18, 1706, ASQ, Lettres, N 124. Tremblay à l'évêque de Québec, Jan. 20, 1706, ASQ, Lettres, P 8. Extrait mortuaire, Jan. 23, 1724, AN, Fonds particuliers, MC-Étude LII-225. Certificat de décès de M. Gervaise, May 14, 1731, AN, Fonds particuliers, MC-Étude LII-246. Min. to Bégon, Nov. 25, 1705, AM, B2, 183, f. 55v. Min. to Brisacier, Dec. 16, 1705, AM, B2, 183, f. 728. Min. to d'Iberville, Dec. 16, 1705, AM, B2, 183, f. 727v.

amounts of booty from the Carolina offensive and, unable to manage it all, would convey a large portion to Massacre Island where Bienville and Châteaugué could use it for the colony or sell it at Pensacola or Veracruz. At any rate, there was presently little else for which to hope. Before Châteaugué left for Pensacola, Bienville ordered him to send the *Bienvenu* back to Havana to try to pick up more merchandise as well as the Negro slaves that Iberville had promised the inhabitants who could afford to purchase them.[16]

Back at Mobile, Payen de Noyan was given lodging in Châteaugué's quarters near the fort and François Le Maire went to live with La Vente and Huvé. Surgeon Barraud was given a lot on the south side of town where he began hiring workers to construct a house while he lodged temporarily at the fort with some of the officers of the *Aigle*. The commerce that was begun at Massacre Island was continued at Fort Louis, the inhabitants as eager to make purchases as the Canadians who had gone with Bienville had been. All this early buying and selling was done over the strenuous objections of La Salle who had wanted to gather a precise record of all goods (both private and royal) as they came off the *Aigle* and as they were delivered to Fort Louis *before* any private commerce began. Working with Jacques Leméry and Christophe Poirier, the warehousekeepers at Fort Louis, La Salle found himself in a losing battle. Without an accurate inventory of the merchandise unloaded at Massacre Island he was unable to keep anything straight. In fact, he had only two records to guide him. The bill of lading sent by Bégon which supposedly showed that supplies were loaded at Rochefort on the *Coventry*, and his own record of what was actually being delivered to Fort Louis.[17]

As the days progressed, La Salle could see that these were nowhere near conformity. Like Bienville, he concluded that in all probability not everything on the bill of lading had left Rochefort. Furthermore, though La Salle was unaware of it, not everything on the *Coventry* had been transferred to the *Aigle* and many goods had been damaged and destroyed. How much was being taken to Pensacola by Châteaugué and Claude Allemand would never be known. Even large amounts of merchandise, particularly foodstuffs and munitions, that Poirier and Alexis Guay (under Bien-

16. Bienville to min., Oct. 10, 1706, AC, C13B, 1, No. 6, f. 1–2v. Bienville to min., July 28, 1706, *loc. cit.*, f. 514–19. Dartaguiette to min., Feb. 26, 1708, AC, C13A, 2, f. 63–66.

17. Bienville to min., Oct. 10, 1706, *loc. cit.*, f. 1–8v. AC, F1A, 13, f. 114. ADM, A, Jan. 29, 1708. La Salle to min., Sept. 8, 1706, *loc. cit.*, f. 545–65.

ville's supervision) had checked off at Massacre Island never reached Fort Louis. La Salle complained to Bienville that the supply boats transporting the goods to the fort were abnormally slow and that much of the merchandise was being stolen by the Canadians who were responsible for its transportation. Bienville's reply, that he "was doing the best he could to prevent it," was unsatisfactory to the commissary but there was little that La Salle could do but throw up his hands in despair. "You cannot imagine," he wrote Pontchartrain, "the waste which occurs in transporting [the goods] from Massacre Island to the place on the Mobile River where Fort Louis is situated, as well as the expenses which His Majesty's ships incur while having to wait in port for all the merchandise to be carried to the fort." [18]

Bienville, angry at La Salle's accusations, responded by refusing to sign the order for payment of La Salle's five servants, which effectively removed them from La Salle's employ. La Salle replied by challenging Bienville to also remove the Canadians from the payroll, which he knew Bienville had been ordered by Pontchartrain to do. Bienville antagonized not only La Salle but Pontchartrain as well by refusing to carry out the minister's instructions on this point. Admitting he had received orders to "no longer support the Canadians who are at Mobile," he nevertheless wrote Pontchartrain on July 28 that he "could not carry out such an order this year because I must re-establish the fort which is falling into ruins and because the garrison is very feeble, being composed of only sixty young men instead of a hundred." [19]

There were several reasons for Bienville's going out on a limb for the Canadians: their credit line on the colony's accounts gave him additional leeway in controlling the storehouse; he needed their support against the growing opposition to his leadership. But the principal reason was the truth he wrote to the minister: that the Canadians could possibly survive without the colony, but the colony absolutely needed the Canadians at this point to see it through these early and difficult years. "I don't know what I would do without the Canadians," he later wrote and it was perfectly true. Men like Claude Charland, *dit* Francoeur, Pierre La Boulaye, *dit* Ramezay, Marc Berrichon, and Charles Aigron, *dit* Lamothe

18. Min. to Bégon, May 25, 1707, AC, B 29, f. 241. Min. to L'Hostellier, May 25, 1707, AC, B 29, f. 243v–44. La Salle to min., Sept. 7, 1706, *loc. cit.*, f. 475–76.

19. La Salle to min., Sept. 8, 1706, *loc. cit.*, f. 545–46. Bienville to min., July 28, 1706, *loc. cit.*, f. 519–20.

had served under Bienville since the days of Fort Maurepas; for seven years they had rendered the colony every service imaginable: in reconnaissance missions and in conflicts with the natives as well as in construction tasks and in manning the traversiers. True, some of them, like Jean La Barre and Mathieu Sajean, had been unusually irresponsible, but for the most part the Canadians were the backbone of the colony. And they had proven they could settle down: André Renaud, Pierre Brossard and Jean Brunet, *dit* Bourbonnois, among many others, had all taken wives and were supporting families. Taken as a whole, the Canadians were the colony's most valuable asset and, as far as Bienville was concerned, the colony should support them as far as possible.[20]

Yet Bienville did not refuse Pontchartrain's orders wholesale. Bowing (after constant reminders by La Salle) to the necessity of gradually removing the Canadians from dependence on the king, he agreed to thin the lists piecemeal. Some who he especially feared might leave the colony or whom he personally favored, men such as Zacharie Drapeau and Antoine Rivard, he left on the roll, but others, including Alexis François, Pierre de Launay and Jean-Baptiste Saucier, he removed, along with eleven more. Some of those, like Saucier and Joussette, he removed because they were more affluent than most of the others. Yet he also added a few names to the list, those like François Guillory who had recently come to Fort Louis from Canada and Pierre Sauton (who had returned after a lengthy absence). The men he added to the rolls were mostly newcomers who had no other means of support, who in fact had not yet even had the opportunity to begin planting.[21]

One of those Bienville removed from the list was François Philippe de Hautmesnil, a twenty-three-year-old Montreal trader, better known in the colony as "Mandeville." Brother of Gabriel Philippe de Saint-Lambert who was now serving Bienville as ensign in Vaulezard's company, Mandeville had been for several years on the colony's payroll as a Canadian at 360 *livres* per year, after having spent a short time in the Wabash country with Saint-Lambert and Charles Juchereau de Saint-Denis. Mandeville had never been an admirer of Bienville; he was greatly angered when Bienville removed him from the payroll in mid-June. A few weeks later,

20. Bienville to min., July 28, 1706, *loc. cit.*, f. 519–24. Bienville to min., Feb. 20, 1707, AC, C13A, 2, f. 8–9, 12–13. AC, F1A, 10, f. 284. La Salle to min., May 12, 1709, AC, C13A, 2 f. 441–43. Dénombrement, Aug. 1, 1706, AC, G1, 464.

21. AC, F1A, 12, f. 92–93; 13, f. 108–09, 117v–18v.

however, Saint-Lambert died (on July 15, 1706), one of the few fatalities stemming from the fever brought by the *Aigle* from Havana. Bienville, looking for a replacement, appointed Mandeville, describing him to Pontchartrain as "a man very suitable for such a position." [22]

The appointment of Mandeville caused La Salle to raise bitter objections (as Pontchartrain did later). La Salle charged Bienville with arbitrarily filling the position without approval from the court. The commissary had wanted the appointment for his oldest son, Nicolas, who at the time of Saint-Lambert's death was a bare thirteen years of age but who, according to La Salle, was capable of bearing arms, was fluent in native languages and was skilled in the ways of the wilds. Bienville, of course, refused to consider the La Salle adolescent, and the youth's father took his pleas to the court. [23]

If La Salle was not successful in convincing Bienville to implicitly obey Pontchartrain's instructions to remove all of the Canadians from the payroll, he was at least able to remove a part of the drain on the storehouse by badgering Bienville into finally dismissing some of them. Not only had the number of subsidized Canadians been reduced from a high of sixty-five in early 1702 to thirty by midsummer of 1706 but Bienville had at last begun plans to eventually remove them entirely. Despite this, relations between Bienville and La Salle were to deteriorate still further, La Salle becoming even more diligent in gathering information that he would shortly use to cast doubt on Bienville's credibility and which when presented to the court would ultimately help to block Bienville's bid for the governorship of Louisiana.[24]

22. *DGFC, I*, pp. 233, 300. AC, F1A, 13, f. 113v, 118–18v. AC, C13A, 3, f. 685–87. Mémoire sur la Louisiane par Mandeville, April 29, 1709, AC, C13A, 2, f. 471–80. Mandeville's younger brother, Jean-François, aged 21, was also at Mobile, having come in 1702. *DGFC, I*, p. 300. AC, F1A, 10, f. 284; 11, f. 72v, 220; 13, f. 118. AC, D2C, 222. Bienville to min., July 28, 1706, *loc. cit.*, f. 544.

23. La Salle to min., Sept. 8, 1706, *loc. cit.*, f. 563–65. Mandeville completed his brother's term at the same salary of 40 *livres* per month, or 220 *livres* for the 5½ months he served in 1706. AC, F1A, 13, f. 113v. La Salle had claimed his son (large for his age) was sixteen, but the scrivener had not married until June 24, 1692 and Nicolas was not born until Aug. 30, 1693. AMT, État civil, GG 85, f. 32v; 87, f. 224.

24. AC, F1A, f. 117v–18v; 14, f. 58–61; 15, f. 62–70. Bienville to min., Feb. 25, 1708, AC, C13A, 2, f. 92–93.

Unable to do much else, La Salle busied himself with this activity and with trying to reconstruct the record of what had happened to the goods in the colony. Also, on the first day of August, he completed a census on which he had been working since the arrival of the *Aigle* in accordance with instructions sent him by Pontchartrain. This census, as recorded by La Salle, showed twenty-four families, including thirty-four children, in Mobile. The total of eighty-five persons excluding unmarried Canadians, naval officers, sailors, soldiers, slaves and priests, was not much different than it had been the year before. The few new people were barely sufficient to replace the ones who had died since the previous summer. Among the recently deceased was a forty-eight-year-old carpenter named Jean Preau from Saint-Jean d'Angély near Rochefort. Preau had attempted to immigrate to Louisiana previously, but was turned down because both Bienville and Iberville felt that his five young daughters (of which only Élisabeth and Marguerite were near maturity) were too much of a liability. In the three years since his first application was turned down, however, two of his other daughters, Jeanne and Marie, had reached marriagable ages. Moreover, the colony was still in need of skilled craftsmen. He was finally allowed to take passage with his wife, Anne Prévost, whom he married in Saint-Jean d'Angély in 1685, his four daughters (the fifth had died) and his brother, Antoine. Soon after his arrival on the *Aigle*, however, Jean Preau had died, leaving his forty-three-year-old widow to care for the daughters, one of whom, Marie, shortly thereafter was married to Vincent Alexandre.[25]

Aside from the Alexandre-Preau union, one other marriage took place in the summer of 1706. Valentin Barraud, the newly arrived *chirurgien-major*, on the rolls at six hundred *livres* per year, married Hippolyte Mercier of La Rochelle who along with her sister, Marie, had recently entered the colony. Apart from such occasional marriages, however, the colony was showing few signs of change or growth. La Salle had not been encouraged, either, by

25. LSMA, DCS, Oct. 22, 1736. Dénombrement, Aug. 1, 1706, AC, G1, 464. Bibliothèque Municipale, St.-Jean d'Angély, RM, July 16, 1685; RB, July 31, 1686; Sept. 18, 1687. It is possible that included in this carpenter's family was Marguerite-Catherine Prévost (who shortly after arrival married André Pénigault), perhaps a younger sister or relative of Anne Prévost. ADM, A, Oct. 27, 1708; March 12, 1709; March 20, 1710; B, Sept. 18, 1724; C, Aug. 26, 1739.

Pontchartrain's hint in his most recent letter that the ships bringing additional passengers and supplies would be even fewer and farther between.[26]

Now, in the early days of August, after two months in port, Payen de Noyan was ready to return to Havana to confer once more with Iberville concerning commercial matters and the proposed attack on Carolina. Châteaugué, commanding the *Aventurier,* planned to accompany Noyan to bring back his traversier, the *Espérance,* as well as the *Bienvenu* which had not yet returned and which was long overdue. A few of the Canadians who were dissatisfied at being taken off the rolls boarded the *Aigle,* as well as some of the craftsmen (such as Gabriel Martineau and Jacques Goulard), to return to France.[27]

On August 10, La Salle went down to Massacre Island to oversee the departure of the ships and to try to ensure that nothing was taken from the warehouse and reloaded on the *Aigle* for sale at Havana and that nothing else left the colony without authorization. In this, he was only partially successful. Claude Allemand succeeded in boarding the *Aigle* (according to La Salle) with 15,000 *piastres* gained by selling the colony's goods at Pensacola and Mobile. La Salle sent a short letter on the *Aigle* giving his version of what had taken place that summer, along with numerous reports and lists of missing merchandise.[28] It was only after he returned to Fort Louis that he had time to draft two detailed letters by which he was determined to set the record straight concerning the conduct of Bienville and his relatives. In heated complaints to Pontchartrain, La Salle first of all criticized Bienville for launching unnecessary expeditions as an excuse for having supplies delivered from the warehouse:

> I must warn your highness that although the savage Alibamons are not making any threat against us, M. de Bienville sent a party of fifty Frenchmen into the country to attempt a decisive blow. But being only two-thirds of the way, they satisfied themselves with killing one man and taking one woman a prisoner who was put to death by a slow fire at the gate of Fort Louis. When the Canadians are equipped for this sort of

26. Dénombrement, Aug. 1, 1706, AC, G1, 464. ADM, A, July 20, 1707; A, Jan. 29, 1708. Dartaguiette to min., May 25, 1708, AC, C13A, 2, f. 322–23.

27. *Journal Historique,* pp. 96–97. Bienville to min., July 28, 1706, *loc. cit.,* f. 521–22. AC, F1A, 13, f. 119v.

28. La Salle to min., Aug. 10, 1706, *loc. cit.,* f. 566–69.

> detachment they do not faithfully bring back the things with which they are armed from the King's warehouse, alleging that those should remain with them, and I am not upheld by the commandant when I bring him my complaints about all this.[29]

Having leveled this charge, La Salle then moved more directly to the disastrous unloading of the *Aigle* and to Bienville's conduct at the fort:

> . . . it is impossible to avoid the theft of half of everything during the transportation [of goods] to Fort Louis, as it seems to us from the receipts which we draw up. Besides this great loss, the distribution of everything is in terrible confusion . . . It is not possible, Monseigneur, to halt the exorbitant flow of daily expenses which occurs here. This arises from the fact that this commandant tries to govern also as commissary and in order to vex us furnishes supplies illegally and on various pretexts and when I object strongly he receives back these orders in a fit of temper and doubles them, so that in order to economize the king's property I dare say nothing. A roebuck used to cost us thirty to forty *sols* from the savages; he receives it then sells it to Frenchmen for eighty *livres* in order to favor the tavern-keepers who are charged with selling him his wine at two hundred *piastres* the barrel. He makes use of almost everyone here although they are in the service of the king. His warehouse is still here, although under another name than his own. He takes the king's goods at 25% and sells them at 400% profit for his own personal benefit.[30]

Shifting his charges to Iberville and his other brothers and officers, La Salle charged that the commander had some months before tried to entice him via letter to forge the signature of Robinau de Bécancour (dead now for two years), then when that wasn't successful had threatened him with loss of his position. He then returned to the theme of conflict of interest.

> I am giving notice that the ships' crews have almost always been employed for the benefit of M. d'Iberville and his brothers, carrying their goods to Veracruz and the furs from the

29. La Salle to min., Sept. 7, 1706, *loc. cit.*, f. 474–75.
30. *Ibid.*, f. 479–83, 499–500.

> *coureurs-de-bois* to the port of Mobile, where they have been loaded on the king's vessels to be carried to France. The cost of this will have to be charged to His Majesty's account . . . I see here great squandering of all things to the point where at Massacre Island everything was used up while the crews of the ships of the king were occupied in transporting the property of M. de Bienville, which was considerable, and likewise that all the officers of this vessel, which they sold at exorbitant prices, which ruins all the people who have planned to establish themselves . . .[31]

La Salle ended his charges on a curt note: "I have the proof at hand of what I state."[32] This letter completed, La Salle composed another the following morning, very similar in content, and tucked them both away. The *Aigle* having departed, there was no immediate way to send them. The next day, however, Bienville sent another transport back to Havana. La Salle deposited his original letter on the transport and sent the duplicate to Pensacola where Spanish ships took it on to France via Spain. A few weeks later, La Salle took time to draft an additional letter leveling even more specific and detailed charges. This letter, dated October 1, was transported to France later that same month by a merchant ship from Martinique which had stopped at Mobile because of inclement weather.[33]

The reason La Salle took pains to send more than one letter covering the same subjects was not rooted entirely in his own misgivings about the possible fate of his correspondence. A day or so before the *Aigle* weighed anchor, Bienville hastily sent a pirogue from Fort Louis with some last-minute items to load aboard a launch which had just left the fort. The haste with which Bienville had dispatched the pirogue had aroused the suspicion of Roulleaux de La Vente who had been watching from the river bank. Almost casually, La Vente mentioned to La Salle that Bienville was probably sending a man to retrieve the letters he had written

31. *Ibid.*, f. 481–85, 500–01.

32. *Ibid.*, f. 501.

33. Of the four letters La Salle wrote between Aug. 10 and Oct. 1, 1706, only the letter of Sept. 7 has survived in the original. AC, C13A, 1, f. 472–501. Extracts of two others have survived (AC, C13A, 1, f. 545–65, 566–69) while the letter of Oct. 1 is apparently not extant, although there are numerous references to its contents. AC, C13A, 2, f. 71–72, 250, 258, 265, 289, 297. Pontchartrain acknowledged receipt of La Salle's letters of Sept. 7 and 8. AC, B 29, f. 264.

to the seminary which had been put aboard the launch. Over the next few weeks, La Vente reinforced this suspicion in La Salle (that is, the notion that Bienville would go so far as to prevent the mails from being carried through). La Salle, who had for some time been suspecting the same thing, had dashed off a paragraph on August 10, accusing Bienville of intercepting the mails, a charge he was to repeat in his letters of September 7 and 8 (as well as in several subsequent reports).[34]

La Vente's conflict with Bienville had reached a peak during August of 1706. For one thing, with the arrival of François Le Maire, La Vente had expected Jacques Gravier to be boarding the ship back for France. But now in late August the *Aigle* had already departed and Gravier was still in Mobile. When would he be rid of this thorn in his flesh, La Vente asked himself, wondering if Bienville were going to further flout the desires of court and bishop by trying to reinstate the Jesuit as chaplain.[35]

Bienville assumed that La Vente would have been satisfied by recent actions while the *Aigle* was still in port. Having received favorable reports from the court concerning the capability of Le Maire and believing that Le Maire would soon be on his way to the Choctaw, Bienville had officially announced on July 14 that henceforth Alexandre Huvé would be the chaplain of the fort. In a compromise witnessed by Payen de Noyan in which La Vente was to quit harrassing Gravier and desist from publicly blaming Bienville for the economic situation, Bienville had made that concession in view of what he suspected was probably the will of the court anyway. By trying to appear as a peacemaker—one willing to sacrifice his own desires for the sake of harmony in the colony—Bienville hoped to enhance his standing with Pontchartrain.[36]

34. Min. to Bégon, May 25, 1707, AC, B 29, f. 241–42v. Tremblay [to SQ Dirs.], June 25, 1707, ASQ, Lettres, M 38. While it is demonstrable that none of La Salle's letters were held up, with the possible exception of a statement he sent Bégon in Aug., 1706 (La Salle extract, Aug. 10, 1706, AC, C13A, 1, f. 569), there is a large gap in La Vente's extant correspondence from Sept. 25, 1704 until March 2, 1708 (except for a brief 1707 memoir and a letter of Aug. 1, 1706). ASQ, Lettres, R 78. Is it likely that the headstrong and verbose pastor would have refrained from writing for so long merely to create the impression that his letters were being intercepted? There also remains the possibility that any such letters written were lost.

35. La Vente [to Brisacier], March 4, 1708, ASQ, Lettres, R 79. Lettre de Gravier [extract], Feb. 27, 1707, AC, C13A, 1, f. 578.

36. *Ibid.*, f. 578–79. Min. to Bienville, Nov. 4, 1705, AC, B 27, f. 188–89. Bienville to min., Oct. 10, 1706, *loc. cit.*, f. 6–7v.

Le Maire, however, declined to leave the vicinity of Mobile. Without a companion, he had no intention of venturing into the backwoods, a refusal that aroused the ire of Bienville and Gravier alike. "Monsieur Le Maire," wrote Gravier, "neither chants, nor preaches, nor visits a single soldier . . . [he is a man] who thinks of nothing but eating, and for whom nothing but contempt is felt." [37] Huvé, on the other hand, spent little time in the fort. His physical limitations, his weak constitution and stammering speech made him feel uneasy around the officers and soldiers who looked upon him with scorn. He went to the nearby Indian villages for days and weeks at a time to avoid assuming the responsibilities he abhorred. Even the chidings by La Vente, who realized what Bienville would attempt to make of Huvé's conduct, were unsuccessful in making him serve more diligently.[38]

Secretly Bienville had been conniving with Noyan and some of the Canadians to circulate a statement pointing to the ineptitude of La Vente and his seminary missioners. The petition of grievances, widely circulated and signed by a large number of inhabitants, was subsequently taken aboard the *Aigle* to be delivered to Pontchartrain. When news of the petition reached La Vente, he was infuriated. In conjunction with La Salle, the pastor then took it upon himself to set up a temporary court of inquiry. Drawing up a statement against Bienville and his officers, La Vente, in his capacity as "judge" (having been "appointed" by La Salle), received a number of signatures for his own petition. Moreover, he vigorously interrogated numerous inhabitants who had signed Noyan's statement, warning them that it was "no less than a hanging matter to testify against their priest." In the face of such intimidation many of the inhabitants retracted their signatures (or marks); but when La Vente presented their names to Bienville, demanding that they be removed from the list, the commandant turned the names over to Noyan and the officers, who then approached the persons in question. Even more fearful of the officers than they were of La Vente, the hapless villagers, "far from disavowing their attestations, confirmed them anew." [39]

37. Lettre du P. Jacques Gravier, Feb. 23, 1708, *JR*, *LXVI*, p. 130.

38. Bienville to min., Oct. 10, 1706, *loc. cit.*, f. 5v–7. Boisbriant to min., Oct. 1, 1706, AC, C13A, 1, f. 588.

39. La Vente to min., March 2, 1708, *loc. cit.*, f. 160–64. Bienville to min., Oct. 10, 1706, *loc. cit.*, f. 4–5v. Tremblay [to SQ Dirs.], June 25, 1707, ASQ, Lettres, M 38. SME Dirs. (extraits), 1708, AC, C13A, 2, f. 161. Boisbriant to min., Oct. 1, 1706, *loc. cit.*, f. 588–89. Bienville to min., Feb. 20, 1707, AC, C13A, 2, f. 22–23.

A few weeks later, Bienville, furious at Huvé's refusal to remain in the fort, threatened to return Gravier to the chaplainship. Incensed at Bienville's and Gravier's persistence in trying to reestablish the Jesuits in what he considered a settled matter, La Vente launched a new attack on the "Black Robes." At Bienville's contention that the presence of Jesuits was beneficial to the colony and that the inhabitants themselves were pleading for them, La Vente scoffed that their "benefit to the establishment" had always been overrated. ". . . actually no Jesuit was ever on good terms with him [Bienville]," the pastor wrote Brisacier, "except those that hoped to be promoted to chaplain and maybe even to *curé*. They have always fought among themselves; the complaints of Père Limoges against Paul Du Ru, which openly circulated, are living proof of it, and Père Dongé protested to me that he was going to lodge official charges when he returned to France, but death prevented it." [40]

In one respect, La Vente was eminently correct: not all Jesuits, particularly the ones who had served at Fort Louis, were Gabriel Marests. Even Gravier, had he been placed in a position of authority, could not have worked miracles, either with the natives or with the French. At age fifty-five, his powers and enthusiasm were surely waning. A few years earlier, frustrated by his lack of success at Fort Maurepas, Gravier had written, "Unless God grants me His sure aid for my conversion, I shall no longer have anything of the religious about me except the habit." [41] In fact, he seemed almost on the verge of a breakdown, having lived for most of "the last nineteen years without a companion, often without even a servant." [42] Now, having been severely wounded by one of his own converts, Gravier was reduced to using such irreligious epithets as "barbarians" and "brutes" when describing the natives.

Furthermore, Gravier's arm was still giving him pain. If he had hoped that the new surgeon, Valentin Barraud, would relieve his suffering, he was keenly disappointed. Barraud, ignorant and incompetent, at least knew his own limitations as a surgeon. Like Clavery before him, he advised Gravier that he could not remove the arrowhead, now permanently grown over by muscle and skin.

40. Bienville to min., Oct. 10, 1706, *loc. cit.*, f. 5v–7. La Vente [to Brisacier], March 4, 1708, ASQ, Lettres, R 79.

41. Gravier to Lamberville, March 25, 1702, *JR, LXVI*, p. 35.

42. Gravier to Tamburini, March 6, 1707, *JR, LXVI*, p. 123.

To make the attempt, Barraud warned him, would probably result in the loss of his arm.[43]

In view of the limitations to Gravier for further service at Fort Louis, there seemed to him but one course of action. He would journey to France by the next available ship. At Versailles and at Paris he could present to the authorities a definitive picture of the situation in Louisiana. He could lobby for certain concessions to be made at Mobile and at Massacre Island. Perhaps he could even get the stonehead removed from his elbow by expert Parisian surgeons (although he denied that this was one of his purposes in returning). In mid-October, he boarded the ship from Martinique that had anchored at Massacre Island and two months later he was crossing the Atlantic, carrying a letter from Bienville to the court extolling his virtues beyond justice:

> The good that the Jesuit Father had done here has gained him the hearts of everyone to such an extent that as soon as they knew of the resolution he had been forced to make, all the garrison and the inhabitants begged me not to let him go; and to instruct Monsieur La Vente that he was to leave in peace the father in whom alone they have confidence. I allowed him to go to France, seeing that he was going to become useless because of the interdiction. If he presents himself to Your Highness I beg you to give full credence to what he will tell you of the state of the colony, as he is perfectly well informed on that subject.[44]

Even with Gravier's absence, relations between Bienville and La Vente did not improve. While La Vente may have rejoiced to see that Jesuit leave Mobile, he was not pleased to see him go to France where the pastor knew only too well what mischief an "arch-plotter" could make. La Vente took out his frustrations on Bienville over an issue that had come to the forefront some months before: the question of sexual relationships between the French and the natives, in particular where the Canadians were concerned.

For some time now a large number of the Canadians and a few of the officers had been living in concubinage with their Indian

43. Bienville to min., Oct. 10, 1706, *loc. cit.*, f. 8v–9v. It perhaps did not occur to Bienville or Gravier to journey to Pensacola where a more able surgeon, the Reverend Felipe Arboloes, acted as superior of the Hospital de San Juan de Dios de San Carlos. Junta, July 24, 1708, AGI, *México*, L. 633.

44. Bienville to min., Oct. 10, 1706, *loc. cit.*, f. 9–10.

slaves, and also with Indian women in some of the native villages. It was a practice well known in the colony. La Vente, of course, had loudly condemned such actions. Bienville's attitude was more complicated. As for the cohabitation of officers and Canadians with their Indian slaves, the commandant was willing to overlook these arrangements. While he probably did not personally approve, he well understood the natural urges of his men. When La Vente openly attacked the practice, Bienville, at the supplication of his officers and men, backed his subordinates against the pastor's outcries. To maintain female slaves to do housework is understandable, La Vente claimed, but when the servants' duties are done, let them spend the night elsewhere, in the private homes of some of the families, if necessary. To this proposal Bienville weakly answered that such a procedure would be too inconvenient; it would work hardship not only on the officers but also on the townfolk required to lodge the native servants. Yet La Vente was to eventually have his way. After the pastor complained to the court, and the court agreed, Bienville was forced to acquiesce: henceforth (officially, at least) the young slave girls were to perform their household chores only by day; at night they were to lodge with appointed families.[45] The problem of concubinage went further, however. Many of the Canadians, in search of sex as well as food, went to live in the nearby villages of the Tomeh and the Pascagoula and in the more distant Natchez, Biloxi and Tunica nations. Cohabitation with the natives in their own villages, Bienville felt, was of much greater danger than concubinage within the town. The majority of Canadians were too difficult to control as it was, he reasoned, and this continued activity would lead to only two things: first of all, it would tend to make the Canadians even wilder, even less dependent on the fort for protection and sustenance, which undermined the commandant's control over them and which hindered orderly growth of the colony; secondly, there was always the peril that an "incident" arising over sex would result in the breaking of peace.[46]

La Vente, too, descried cohabitation in the native villages. But seeing it as a moral problem, he offered but a moral solution. Let

45. Bienville to min., Oct. 10, 1706, *loc. cit.*, f. 4v–6. La Vente [to Brisacier], March 4, 1708, *loc. cit.*, R 79. La Vente [to Brisacier], July 4, 1708, ASQ, Lettres, R 83. Bienville to min., Feb. 25, 1708, AC, C13A, 2, f. 116–17.

46. La Salle to min., May 12, 1709, AC, C13A, 2, f. 397–401. Dartaguiette to min., Sept. 8, 1712, AC, C13A, 2, f. 798–801.

the Canadians marry the Indians, he urged. Once the practice is established, concubinage will be gradually eliminated, numerous baptisms will result and the extension of Christianity among the natives will follow. To objections of miscegenation, he observed that there wasn't a great deal of difference in the skin-coloration of the natives and that of numerous of the Frenchmen.[47]

Bienville hotly disputed the claims of any beneficial results from French marriages with the natives. The Canadians will become more like the savages rather than the savages becoming Christian, he argued. Besides, the excessive mingling of French among savage women would endanger harmony between the native villages and the French. Was not Spanish co-mingling with the savages one of the primary reasons that the villages of Apalache had deserted Pensacola? [48]

La Vente replied that while at the same time Bienville was praising the good judgment of the Jesuits at the Illinois, had not Jacques Gravier himself been active in promoting such unions? Had not Père Jacques himself baptized numerous of the offspring of interracial marriages? Furthermore, was not one of the respected inhabitants of Mobile, Jean Colon, *dit* La Violette (living at Mobile now with his Indian wife, Catherine Exipakinoea, and two children) living proof of how such unions could prosper? Had not two of Bienville's esteemed Jesuits, Gabriel Marest and Julien Binneteau, baptized several of Colon's infants while Colon was still at Kaskaskia? [49]

With implicit faith in his own judgment, La Vente hastened to authorize Davion and Saint-Cosme to perform several marriages at their villages on the Mississippi, which were shortly consummated. Furious, Bienville denounced La Vente for his impudence and lack of foresight:

> The fact is, that under pretext of being vicar-general of Monseigneur de Québec, he made the missionary to the Tunica perform a marriage of a Frenchman to a young female savage and three among those with the Natchez, where there is no Christian nor any adult who wants to become one

47. La Vente [to Brisacier], July 4, 1708, *loc. cit.*, R 83.

48. Bienville to min., July 28, 1706, *loc. cit.*, f. 536–37. Bienville to min., Oct. 10, 1706, *loc. cit.*, f. 1v–2.

49. Bienville to min., Aug. 20, 1709, AC, C13A, 2, f. 412–13. Lettre du P. Jacques Gravier, Feb. 15, 1694, BN, FF, 6453, f. 33–43v. SLUA, mission des Illinois, I, March 20, Oct. 4, 1692; May 13, 1697; Nov. 27, 1698. Dénombrement, Aug. 1, 1706, AC, G1, 464. ADM, A, Nov. 4, 1707; A, Sept. 19, 1709.

> and who have been little instructed during the seven years that the missionary has been among them, so greatly does their lubricity separate them from Christianity. I had written to these missionaries that the intention of the king was that no Frenchman be married to a native girl in the villages of this new colony (I do not know by what reasoning the Sieur de La Vente was not satisfied with what I had told him); that I did not think it fit for the good of the colony that there should be any such marriages, and that those who performed them would not be upheld until it should be explained to the court that the *coureurs-de-bois* should all be concentrated in Mobile and in French dwellings and not be dispersed among the savage villages to live like libertines and under no authority, under the pretext that they have married among the savages. These sorts of marriages should be declared null. If the court does not permit them, it seems to me that the Sieur de La Vente and all his *confrères* should have more respect for that which a commandant who is in the king's service tells them.[50]

The question brought to the surface by La Vente's action, however, was not to be settled as a result of local confrontation between the pastor and Bienville. The issue would be discussed and debated for years to come, both in the colony and in France. Meanwhile (although Bienville was presently on solid ground), it was merely another issue to quibble about. On a recent occasion La Vente had boasted that he had higher authority on his side that would eventually bear him out while Bienville had only "Monsieur" d'Iberville as a patron. The way in which La Vente sneered the term "Monsieur," repeating it several times, infuriated Bienville; but for the moment the commandant felt secure in his brother's patronage; "Monsieur" d'Iberville was still the most prestigious name in the colony short of Pontchartrain and Louis XIV, and as long as the commander backed him, Bienville feared not the likes of La Vente and his supporters at the seminaries in Quebec and Paris.[51]

The situation in the colony was shortly to change, however. Noyan had left Massacre Island in the *Aigle* on August 14, carry-

50. Bienville to min., Oct. 10, 1706, *loc. cit.*, f. 5v–6.

51. Min. to Rémonville, Sept. 14, 1710, AC, B 32, f. 208–09. La Vente [to Brisacier], July 4, 1708, *loc. cit.*, R 83. Bienville to min., Oct. 10, 1706, *loc. cit.*, f. 6v–7v.

ing forty to fifty thousand *livres* worth of pelts brought down the Mississippi by Canadian traders. Accompanying him was Châteaugué, commanding the *Aventurier*, the brigantine captured from the English and sent to Mobile by Sérigny to help replace the loss of the *Précieuse*. Châteaugué was returning to Havana at Bienville's insistence to bring back the *Espérance* and the *Bienvenu* (which by all estimates should have returned to Massacre Island by the first of August).[52]

In the meantime, back in July, Iberville had been preparing to launch his attack on Carolina. However, Yellow fever had been rampant in Havana for weeks, felling several hundred of the local population. Pedro Álvarez de Villarín, newly appointed governor and captain-general of Havana, had been in Havana less than two months when he was stricken. On July 8, at two o'clock in the afternoon, Villarín had died. Iberville, who had been in Havana nearly as long as Villarín and who had spent considerable time in his company discussing the planned Carolina campaign, was stricken with the fever at about the same time as the Spanish governor. At the time of Villarín's demise, Iberville was also near death. Two days before, sensing the inevitable, he had drawn up his will in the presence of a Spanish notary. Then, late in the evening of the eighth of July, 1706, the commander-general of Louisiana yielded his last breath, after being administered holy sacraments by Spanish priest Dionisio Rezino.[53]

The deaths of two such important and respected personages (not to mention several other, subordinate officers) coming on the same date threw a blanket of gloom over Havana officialdom. Shortly after Álvarez de Villarín passed away, a group of Spanish officials composing the municipal council somberly met in the office of

52. Châteaugué to min., Sept. 30, 1706, AC, C13A, 1, f. 589–90. La Salle to min., July 25, 1707, AC, C13B, 1, No. 7, f. 1v–5v. *Journal Historique*, pp. 96–97. Bienville to min., Feb. 20, 1707, AC, C13A, 2, f. 17–18. Dartaguiette to min. Feb. 26, 1708, *AC*, C13A, 2, f. 58–59, 66–69. Cadillac to min., Oct. 26, 1713, AC, C13A, 3, f. 63–64.

53. Carta de Luis Chacón, July 15, 1706, AGI, *Santo Domingo*, L. 377. Álvarez de Villarín had arrived in Havana on May 13 on the *Nuestra Señora de Guadalupe y Santa Teresa*, commanded by Bartolomé Antonio Garrote. Nicolás Chirino Vandevall a su magesdad, July 15, 1706, AGI, *Santo Domingo*, L. 377. Archivo de la Catedral de San Cristóbal de la Habana, Registro de las Sepulturas, July 9, 1706, Libro IV, f. 78, No. 26. Testimonio de Juan de Uribe, July 8, 1706, AGI, *Santo Domingo*, L. 377. Min. to Madame d'Iberville, Sept. 22, 1706, AM, B2, 191, f. 358. Min. to Bégon, May 25, 1707, AC, B 29, f. 241–43v.

Notary Juan de la Berrera. After Juan de Uribe, Villarín's notary, testified as to the fact and exact time of the governor's death, the Royal Mandate of January 19, 1656 was read and the authority passed jointly to Lieutenant General Nicolás Chirino Vandevall and Luis Chacón, commandant of the Castillo del Morro. Villarín's funeral was set for the next day, July 9. When later that evening news came of the death of Iberville, funeral services for the French commander were also scheduled for the following day.[54]

The next morning, July 9, both burials were carried out at the parish church. Soon after the interment of Villarín, Iberville's body was taken to the "Holy Parochial Church of San Cristóbal" and after a somber ceremony conducted by Dionisio Rezino and attended by a host of both French and Spanish officers, Iberville's body was laid to rest near the remains of his close friend and associate Pierre-Charles Le Sueur who had died of the same disease and in the same city nearly two years before.[55]

Almost immediately after Iberville's burial, his squadron, consisting of thirteen ships, began to scatter. At least one went on to Veracruz, several returned to the Antilles and the rest sailed for Europe.[56] Iberville's death considerably weakened the planned assault on Carolina, a scheme for which the commander had ardently but not too successfully been seeking support from the Spanish. Nicolás Chirino Vandevall and Luis Chacón, now civil and military governors, respectively, of Havana, were unable to promise more than token aid and Viceroy Alburquerque refused to support the effort at all. Before Iberville died, he had transferred authority to Jacques Lefebvre who with a considerably weakened French force continued Iberville's plans for attack. On September 7, Lefebvre, who had sailed for St. Augustine shortly after Iberville's death and enlisted the support of Francisco Martínez (recently appointed Governor of Florida), reached Charles-Town's harbor and launched an attack two days later. The assault and subsequent engagements proved disastrous for the French. The

54. Nicolás Chirino Vandevall a su magesdad, July 15, 1706, AGI, *Santo Domingo*, L. 377. Testimonio de Juan de la Barrera, July 12, 1706, AGI, *Santo Domingo*, L. 377.

55. Entierro del gen.l Dn. Pedro Berbila, July 9, 1706, Archivo de la Catedral de San Cristóbal, Registro de las Sepulturas, Libro IV, f. 78, No. 26. Nicolás Chirino Vandevall a su magesdad, July 15, 1706, AGI, *Santo Domingo*, L. 377.

56. Luis Chacón a su magesdad, July 15, 1706, AGI, *Santo Domingo*, L. 377.

Carolinians killed thirty and captured over three hundred French, Spanish and Indian troops. Moreover, one of Lefebvre's ships, the seventy-two gun *Brilliant*, was captured by the English during a battle just out from Holybush Plantation.[57]

Towards the end of August, Châteaugué and Payen de Noyan arrived in Havana, shocked to learn that Iberville had been dead for nearly two months. They were further astonished at the absence of French ships in port. Only the *Espérance* and the *Bienvenu* remained, yet the latter vessel no longer belonged to the French. The *Bienvenu*, having reached Havana three days after Iberville's death, found herself stranded for several weeks, the majority of her crew deserting. In the meantime, Sérigny had arrived from Veracruz, but having few sailors with which to man the vessel, had sold her to the Spanish three weeks before leaving for Saint-Domingue to carry on further trade. As for Châteaugué's mission, he was unable to procure the slaves (except for a few domestics) that Iberville had privately promised to hold for Bienville; he nevertheless spent the month of September in Havana loading what few supplies he could gather, which amounted to only forty quintals of bacon and some additional foodstuffs. Towards the end of September he received word from Sérigny that since the *Bienvenu* had been sold, the colony could retain possession of the *Aventurier*. Accordingly, during the second week of October, he divided his crew among the *Aventurier* and the *Espérance* and set sail for Mobile, Noyan departing for Léogane in the *Aigle*.[58]

Châteaugué arrived at Massacre Island on October 19, bringing news of the failure of the French expedition against Carolina and the death of Iberville at Havana. The report of the commander's loss struck the colony hard. Unaware for the most part of Iberville's and Sérigny's fraudulent commerce which had acted to the detriment of the colony, the inhabitants deeply mourned his passing. Despite his long absence, he had still been considered by the majority of officers and townfolk as being their chief voice in

57. El rey al virrey, May 22, 1705, AGI, *Santo Domingo*, L. 836. El gobernador de la Florida al rey, Sept. 30, 1706, AGI, *Santo Domingo*, L. 840. Projet sur la Caroline, 1702, AC, C11A, 20, f. 224–29. Account of the invasion of Carolina, 1706, PRO, CO 5, 382, I. Auto para llamar a junta . . . Sept. 23, 1706, AGI, *Santo Domingo*, L. 840.

58. Dartaguiette to min., Feb. 26, 1708, *loc. cit.*, f. 65–68. *Journal Historique*, pp. 96–97. Bienville to min., Feb. 20, 1707, AC, C13A, 2, f. 17–18. Châteaugué to min., Sept. 30, 1706, AC, C13A, 1, f. 589–90.

Europe, who more than any other had been responsible for what concessions were wrung from the purse of the court.[59]

There was little grief shown, however, by La Salle or La Vente, both of whom no doubt felt a surge of hope that events were beginning to turn in their favor. As for Bienville, his "chief and only patron" (as La Vente referred to Iberville) was no more. Bracing himself to his situation, the commandant could but hope that he, young as he was, would be elevated to the position of governor, replacing his dead brother as the chief authority in Louisiana. He had, in fact, only nine days before (knowing Iberville's lack of interest in the governorship) petitioned Pontchartrain "that for seven years I have had the honor of commanding in this colony, and I beg you to grant me the governorship of this land." [60] Little did he know of the inquiries already begun in Rochefort, Paris and Versailles that were moving to discredit the service of the Le Moyne family.[61]

59. *Journal Historique*, pp. 96–97. Bienville to min., Feb. 20, 1707, *loc. cit.*, f. 17–18.

60. Bienville to min., Oct. 10, 1706, *loc. cit.*, f. 6v–7v, 9v.

61. Min. to Bégon, Sept. 15, 1706, AM, B2, 191, f. 171–72. Bégon to Desmarets, Sept. 11, 1706, AN, G7, 340.

XVI

Embroilments Old and New

SCARCELY a month after the departure of Jacques Gravier for France relations between the native villages of lower Louisiana began to smoulder and flame. The eruptions were not entirely unexpected, however. The smaller nations—the Houma, the Bayougoula, the Tunica—though they were uniformly loyal to the French, were not infrequently at each other's throats, generally over a minor incident: a theft, the rape of a squaw, etc. In the late summer of 1706, the Tensa, a small village located temporarily some ten miles from the west bank of the Mississippi, about thirty miles above the Natchez, abandoned their village site (due to English-spurred harrassment by the Chickasaw and the Yazoo) and withdrew downriver to the village of the Bayougoula who received them graciously. No sooner had the Tensa settled in the Bayougoula village than they betrayed the trust of their hosts: wishing to appropriate the site, they slaughtered a majority of the Bayougoula, then quickly drove the survivors into the forests.[1]

When the remnant Bayougoula escaped to the nearby villages of the Houma and Colapissa in the neighborhood of Fort La Boulaye, the Tensa began to fear reprisal by those nations friendly to the Bayougoula. After hasty deliberation, the Tensa decided to shift to yet another location; before they moved on, however, they invited several families from the nearby Chitimacha villages to feast with them at the former Bayougoula village. When only a small

1. Bienville to min., Feb. 20, 1707, AC, C13A, 2, f. 7–9, 11–13, 16. *Journal Historique*, pp. 101–03. *FLC*, pp. 70–72. Mémoire de Bienville, 1726, AC, C13C, 1, f. 363–63v, 370–70v. Bienville received the Tawasa, recent refugees from the country between Pensacola and Apalache, in September of 1706 and located them at 21 Mile Bluff.

number of the Chitimacha accepted the invitation, the Tensa took them prisoner and moved quickly to a new village site.[2]

When the Chitimacha chiefs received word of the Tensa duplicity, they were enraged. It was surely the French who were behind this treachery: were not the white men daily in the small villages along the Mississippi, attempting to procure slaves by whatever means they could conceive? Apparently the ruthless Canadians and *voyageurs* were not content to merely sleep with the wives of Chitimacha warriors. Now they were resorting to murder, to kidnapping as well as adultery, to satisfy their fiendish purposes. Remembering how the hapless Koroa had been unjustly accused and punished a few years before for the murder of the missionary Foucault, the chiefs of the Chitimacha began to view French presence on the lower Mississippi with increasing anger and distrust.[3]

In late November, Jean-François Buisson de Saint-Cosme, missionary at the Natchez, was on his way to Mobile to confer with his superior, La Vente.[4] Saint-Cosme, on the Mississippi since 1699 (originally at the Tamaroa to act as a link between the Tensa and the seminary at Quebec; then, since 1700 at the Natchez), had not been particularly successful in his missionary efforts with the Natchez. In his six years at the mission, he had won precious few converts or friends; he had even failed to master the language of the Natchez, and, judging by his numerous letters, he was not even kindly disposed toward his "brothers-in-Christ" against whom he more than once resorted to physical force to protect his person. "Send me servants who are able to stand up to these wicked brutes," he once wrote, "for it is awkward for a missionary to have to strike them." Nevertheless, in spite of his failures, Saint-Cosme had shown unusual perseverance in remaining at his mission (where he was well-known to all the villagers between Fort La Boulaye and the Tunica). His fear and distrust of the natives, however, proved wholly justified, for on this occasion, two days' journey downstream from his mission, Saint-Cosme and the several Canadians who were escorting him to Mobile were attacked

2. *Journal Historique*, pp. 101–02. The Chitimacha at this time numbered six hundred men. Mémoire de Bienville, 1726, *loc. cit.*, f. 363v.

3. La Salle to min., May 12, 1709, AC, C13A, 2, f. 441–43. La Salle to min., July 25, 1707, AC, C13B, 1, No. 7, f. 6v–7v. Davion à l'évêque de Québec, Feb. 14, 1703, ASME, 344, f. 61–65.

4. La Vente [to SME Dirs.], June 27, 1708, ASQ, Lettres, R 82.

by a band of Chitimacha and hacked to death while they slept on the banks of the Mississippi. Only a young Natchez slave escaped to bring the news to Saint-Denis at the Mississippi fort.[5]

At the time the report of Saint-Cosme's murder reached Saint-Denis, Marc Bergier, vicar-general of the bishop of Quebec for the Mississippi Valley missions, was resting at Fort La Boulaye, having passed through the village of the Natchez a few weeks earlier. Saint-Denis drafted a note to Bienville, informing him of the tragedy, and since Bergier was on his way to Mobile in search of supplies for his mission, Saint-Denis turned the message over to the seminary priest and his party for delivery.[6]

It was the first of January, 1707, when Bergier arrived in Mobile, accompanied by a "young, handsome and well-built Indian domestic who can read and write and who is well-educated."[7] Bienville was heartened to see the vicar-general (whom by reputation he admired) but he was also distraught to hear of the loss of four more invaluable men. Writing Pontchartrain a few weeks later, he moaned:

> I have learned recently of the death of M. de Saint-Cosme, missionary to the Natchez, who was killed by savages of the Chitimacha nation established on the southern part of the Mississippi two days' inland as he was descending the Mississippi with three Frenchmen. Although this nation had already killed four *voyageurs* twelve years ago, we did not in the least distrust them.[8]

After this forthright announcement, Bienville took advantage of the occasion of Saint-Cosme's death by pointing to the causes of such incidents, which he hoped, with minimal aid from the court, he could soon eliminate:

> All the savages of these lands are throughly treacherous. They have already committed many assassinations and there is reason to believe they may commit more because of the small

5. Lettre de Buisson de Saint-Cosme, Jan. 8, 1706, ASQ, Lettres, R 40. ASQ, Polygraphie, IX, 13, 17, 25. Document de 1728, BN, FF, NA, 2550, f. 115–18. *FLC*, pp. 70–71. *JR*, *LXVII*, p. 303. Bienville to min., Feb. 20, 1707, AC, C13A, 2, f. 11. La Salle to min., July 25, 1707, AC, C13B, 1, No. 7, f. 6v–7. Mémoire de Bienville, 1726, *loc. cit.*, f. 363v–64.

6. *FLC*, pp. 70–72. Bergier [to Tremblay], July 14, 1704, ASQ, Lettres, R 67.

7. La Vente, Feb. 5, 1709, ASQ, Lettres, R 86.

8. Bienville to min., Feb. 20, 1707, AC, C13A, 2, f. 11–12.

> fear that they have of the French. They have such a low opinion of us that recently the Choctaw and Chickasaw chiefs asked me in great seriousness if there were really as many people in France as there were here or whether there were very many more. I tried to make them see the truth of the matter by striking comparisons, but it was impossible for me to make them understand although I know their language very well. They retorted that if there were really as many people as I claimed, some of them would come here to avenge the deaths of the Frenchmen, "else you have no courage at all," they said to me: "You have been here for six years. Instead of increasing, you are diminishing. The strong men are dying and only children come in their places." [9]

Bienville's assessment was not idle complaint; he was, with good reason, unusually concerned about the impression the French were creating on the Indians. The chiefs of the Choctaw and Chickasaw had spent most of the winter of 1706–07 at Fort Louis; they were returning to their villages unmoved by French potential. Bienville had still been unable to fulfill his promises to the Chickasaw to build a fort on the upper Mobile, or to supply the Choctaw with a missionary. He knew that when those nations heard of the most recent Mississippi murders they would once again be watching closely to see by what dispatch Frenchmen punished their assailants. Despite Bienville's lack of manpower, there seemed but one alternative to follow: if the French wished to maintain any measure of respect among the natives, another punitive mission would have to be executed. Yet how could the commandant send mere boys (of which the majority of Châteaugué's and Vaulezard's company was composed) to combat lusty savage cutthroats in the savages' own domain? There were, in fact, only forty-five soldiers (some twenty-three had died or deserted during the past two years) remaining at Fort Louis and neither Châteaugué (who was more often than not at sea) nor Vaulezard (who had never arrived from France) was present to lead them. Once again Bienville would be forced to call on the group which he had been ordered to dismiss from the king's payroll.[10]

In early January, Bienville sent the *Espérance* with twenty Canadians and a shipment of guns, munitions and presents to Saint-

9. *Ibid.*, f. 12–13.

10. Bienville to min., Feb. 20, 1707, *loc. cit.*, f. 7–8, 10–13. AC, F1A, 13, f. 113v–21.

Denis at Fort La Boulaye. The presents were designated for the villages near Lake Pontchartrain—the Biloxi, the Houma, the Chawasha and the remnants of the Bayougoula—to entice them to make war upon the Chitimacha. Saint-Denis, successful in recruiting some eighty warriors, including four of the Natchitoche, moved shortly afterwards up the Mississippi in pirogues. Two days later, with his combined force of Canadians and savages, he reached the entrance of the rivière des Chitimacha. Ascending this small tributary to within three leagues of one of the Chitimacha villages, the party rested all day, then as night fell, attacked the unsuspecting savages. The small village of about forty Chitimacha was quickly scattered. Four or five warriors were killed; several men and women were taken prisoner, along with twelve or thirteen young children, and quickly escorted back to Fort Louis. To Bienville's delight, one of the Chitimacha prisoners brought in irons was the very one who had boasted of having put six arrows through the missionary Saint-Cosme. On Bienville's order, this prisoner was taken to the fort and tied to a stake in the center of the square. After conferring with his officers, Bienville decided the mode of execution for the confessed murderer: he was forthwith bludgeoned to death with a heavy stone weapon. His skull broken, he was then scalped and his body thrown in the river. "I did not do it," Bienville later wrote Pontchartrain, "without knowing the good effect that it would produce in the villages of the other nations. It is the custom in all these nations, not only of this province but also of those of Canada to kill as many of the men of their enemies as they have lost on their side; otherwise it is disgraceful among them to speak of reconciliation if they have not got vengeance man for man." [11]

As a punitive expedition, Saint-Denis' mission had been wholly successful; for a number of the inhabitants of Mobile it had also been profitable. Bienville had 800 *livres* in merchandise paid to the Canadians for their services. Moreover, the young Chitimacha slaves brought back from the mission were sold to some of the inhabitants (among them Pierre Charly and René Boyer) for 200 *livres* each. However, if the expedition had been successful (and profitable), it had also been costly. There had been no casualties on the French side; but on her return from the Mississippi, the

11. Bienville to min., Feb. 20, 1707, *loc. cit.*, f. 9–10. Bienville to min., Feb. 25, 1708, AC, C13A, 2, f. 101–02. *Journal Historique*, p. 102. *FLC*, pp. 70–72. La Salle to min., July 25, 1707, AC, C13B, 1, No. 7, f. 7v. AC, F1A, 13, f. 117v–18.

Espérance had run aground and was destroyed by a squall in the Massacre Island port. Since Bienville had no transport available (the *Aventurier*, now in poor condition, was preparing to leave for Veracruz) to supply Fort La Boulaye, and because of the scarcity of soldiers, Bienville was forced to abandon the post, though he hoped to later rebuild it near the vicinity of present-day New Orleans, a move he had been contemplating for nearly six years. Commandant Saint-Denis, however, remained on the Mississippi, where he took up residence near the village of the Biloxi on Bayou Saint-Jean.[12]

The presence of Marc Bergier at Mobile precipitated a change in conduct (if not in attitude) among the officers and clergy. Gaunt and gangly, Bergier cut a striking figure in contrast to the more full-bodied La Vente and Le Maire. The dedicated missioner had been serving the Tamaroa since the late winter of 1700, having arrived there with the murdered Saint-Cosme's younger brother, Michel. His ministry had not been overly productive (yet by his Spartan manner he had managed to gain the respect of the natives). Moreover, he had early become involved in disputes with the Jesuits over authority to missionize the Tamaroa district, one result of which was his scathing indictment of what he considered a pernicious Jesuit plot to monopolize the mission field. A particular object of his wrath had been the now departed Jacques Gravier.[13]

Despite his ideological and political conflicts with the Jesuits, however, Bergier was greatly admired by Bienville for his zeal and dedication. How different might things be at Mobile, the commandant wondered, if such a man had been appointed parish priest. Ironically, both Bienville and La Vente expected to gain from the missioner's presence, each anticipating Bergier to put the other "in his place." Bergier went immediately to lodge with La Vente, Huvé and Le Maire; the pastor, expecting to gain the

12. La Salle to min., July 25, 1707, *loc. cit.*, f. 7–7v. ADM, A, March 23, 30, 1709. Bienville to min., Feb. 20, 1707, *loc. cit.*, f. 9–10. Dartaguiette to min., Feb. 26, 1708, AC, C13A, 2, f. 58–60. Carta al virrey, March 14, 1707, AGI, *México*, L. 479. Mémoire pour servir d'instruction au Sieur de Bienville . . . , April 25, 1702, AC, F3, 68, f. 2–9v.

13. Mémoire général des marchandises . . . , [1707], ASQ, Lettres, R 78. Tremblay [to SQ Dirs.], June 25, 1707, ASQ, Lettres, M 38. ASQ, Polygraphie, IX, 11, 26, 27. Tremblay [to Ango Des Maizerets], Jan. 14, 1708, ASQ, Lettres, O 49. Bienville to min., Feb. 20, 1707, *loc. cit.*, f. 24–25. *Journal Historique*, p. 101. Bienville to min., Feb. 25, 1708, *loc. cit.*, f. 109–10.

vicar-general's ear, stuck closely to his superior's side and was startled by what he observed:

> M. Bergier lives in a manner we cannot imitate . . . he commits himself to an avowed war against his body . . . for many years he has sentenced himself to continued abstinence from meat, fish and eggs, and as he believes that does not suffice, he limits himself to just one meal a day which he usually takes in the evening . . . and on fast days he has only a little Indian corn and grain boiled in water . . . he sleeps on the ground for only three or four hours a night; the rest he spends in prayer . . .[14]

Although La Vente was shocked by what he saw first-hand, Bergier's propensity for self-denial was not unknown to him. For some time they had been corresponding. "It has been three years," La Vente later wrote, "since I first learned of his manner of living, which caused me to write to him to desist, since it was almost certain to kill him . . . that although it was good to indulge in self-mortification, it was not permissible to kill oneself, that neither our lives nor our bodies belonged to us, but to Jesus Christ." Despite La Vente's remonstrations, however, Bergier's only answer was that La Vente did not understand him, nor did he know the savages he had in his charge—"that for him such a life was necessary, that the savages were possessed of a demon which the Saviour assures us is expelled only through fasting and prayer." [15]

Bergier and La Vente conversed intimately and confidentially during the long winter nights. Bergier confided to the pastor that he was compiling a dictionary of the Tamaroa language (a project made necessary by the fact that a few years prior the Jesuits had tried to prevent seminary priests from learning the Illinois languages). La Vente brought Bergier up to date on happenings at the fort, his reasons for interdicting the chapel, and especially on a recent incident which was uppermost in the pastor's mind. According to La Vente, several months after the departure of the *Aigle*, he had asked Bienville on three separate occasions for enough flour to ward off starvation, but Bienville refused to supply him any from the storehouse. In desperation he had written to the departing governor at Pensacola: "He [Joseph de Guzmán] sent me

14. La Vente [to Brisacier], Feb. 5, 1709, ASQ, Lettres, R 86.
15. *Ibid.*

a very courteous reply in which he promised to send me what I asked for, but M. de Bienville, having some inkling of the favor M. the governor of Pensacola was granting us, wrote to him not to send any, that it was false, that we had plenty and had even refused some. Nevertheless, M. de Châteaugué, to whom M. Le Maire lodged complaints of this affair for us, far from justifying his brother, stated to him coldly that they would like to be able to cause us to expire from hunger." [16] As evidence that he had not refused any flour, La Vente showed Bergier the letter from Guzmán and added that "since I made my complaint in public everyone knew that I had no excesses." [17]

Confronting Bienville with La Vente's account, Bergier received a somewhat different version: yes, M. La Vente had asked for flour, but Bienville refused to give him any because he already had more than anyone else in the colony. "Nothing is more malicious," Bienville retorted, "than for the Sieur La Vente to write to strangers that I am killing him with starvation and ask them for flour. Three months ago some Spaniards [the father superior of the convent, the commissary, the treasurer and the ad-interim governor, sergeant-major Sebastián de Moscoso] came here and went to the house of La Vente themselves only to find a twelve hundredweight surplus of flour in six barrels." [18] Embarrassed, La Vente confessed that the extra flour for which he was asking was actually for workmen who he claimed were starving.

Bienville took the occasion of La Vente's complaints to lodge charges of his own. "What impudence," he exclaimed, "on the part of M. La Vente to complain to foreigners of such things and to make them acquainted with the dissension that exists here. He dissuades the inhabitants from establishing themselves as much as he can by assuring them that [this place] will be abandoned if the war [in Europe] continues, that the king is not now in a position to support this post." [19]

Other matters were brought by the commandant to Bergier's attention. The action which interested the vicar-general most was the interdiction of the fort's chapel. According to Bienville, La Vente had interdicted the chapel without any justifiable reason,

16. La Vente [to Brisacier], July 4, 1708, *loc. cit.*, R 83.

17. *Ibid.*

18. Bienville to min., Feb. 20, 1707, *loc. cit.*, f. 23–24, 26–27. The chaplain of Fort San Carlos at this time was Tiburcio Osario. Junta de 24 de Julio de 1708, AGI, *México*, L. 633.

19. Bienville to min., Feb. 20, 1707, *loc. cit.*, f. 27–28.

solely on the pretexts that too much noise was made in the fort and that the chapel was not decent. After proscribing the chapel, La Vente had begun performing pastoral functions in his own kitchen which was far removed from town (at a time when the water in the vicinity of his house was half-way up to one's knees), because he was unwilling to accept a private home that the inhabitants had offered him. "His sole motive was to annoy everyone," Bienville charged. "My soldiers on guard at the fort did not hear mass at all since they were quite unable to leave their guard-house unprotected. In vain did I call his attention several times to how little piety there was, two-thirds of the families missing mass on account of the flooded streets. What mortified me most was that the Sieur La Vente used the occasion when the Spaniards were present . . . who witnessed the pastor's ridiculous manners." [20]

La Vente countercharged that Bienville had set the drills for the soldiers, contrary to all past practices, in the courtyard of the fort (which was only about 3,000 square feet) on Sundays and on the mornings of feast days when it was customary to have the parochial services: "M. Huvé and I went to see M. de Bienville and said we couldn't administer the sacraments nor perform the priestly functions while all sorts of activities were going on. M. de Bienville replied that we may do as we wish but that is the way it was going to be. When M. Huvé replied that he didn't think the court would approve, M. de Bienville answered that in this place *he* was the court and that he desired a low mass at nine o'clock and as to a high mass we could say that one at eleven-thirty, else he would have the gate to the fort closed." [21]

The following Sunday, La Vente had appeared at his customary time to celebrate the low mass. He was no sooner in the fort than Bienville locked him in. The bells were rung; some of the inhabitants came for the mass, others for confession. But neither group of parishioners could get in, and La Vente could not get out. Finally the pastor found a small door that was left ajar. He slipped through the opening, then led his parishioners inside, where mass was finally said. The next Sunday La Vente and Huvé returned to the fort, this time early in the morning, to administer the last sacrament to a dying inhabitant. On this occasion, all the doors to the fort were locked tight, and La Vente and Huvé could carry on no service at all.[22]

20. *Ibid.*, f. 22–24.
21. La Vente [to Brisacier], July 4, 1708, ASQ, Lettres, R 83.
22. *Ibid.*

After that rebuff, La Vente had interdicted the chapel of the fort and began conducting his services at the new, but now almost dilapidated church. On one occasion, however, a drift of hogs found their way into the church and left such a stench that services had to be postponed for a full week. A month later, during a violent wind squall, the new church, already weakened by rot though barely a year old, collapsed. According to La Vente, he then tried to rent, at his own expense, a house in the middle of town to conduct his services, but none of the inhabitants, out of fear of Bienville, would offer to make one available. He therefore proceeded to hold services in his kitchen.[23]

Vicar-general Bergier, occupied by loftier matters, viewed these local squabbles with obliging disgust. He nonetheless took measures to settle them, first by lifting the interdict La Vente had placed on the chapel, then by persuading Bienville to instate François Le Maire as chaplain. But the chapel in the fort had been damaged by the same stormwinds which had destroyed the new church. Although it was propped up again and nailed (with no door, however), the chapel was practically inoperable as a site for regular worship services. At the instigation of Bergier, Bienville obtained a house from one of the inhabitants to which La Vente moved his altar; it was in this house that most of the worship services were to be held for the next four years.[24]

If La Vente had believed Bergier would sustain him in his act of interdiction, he was sorely disappointed. Several years before, Bergier himself had placed Père Pierre-François Pinet under interdict in the Illinois country, an act that he had soon come to regret: Pinet refused to abide by it and even Bergier had second thoughts about its validity. Under the circumstances it was understandable that he did not now view interdiction as a useful or proper instrument. Nor did he uphold La Vente in any of the other contentions in the colony. If by his presence he was able to hear first-hand La Vente's judgments of Bienville, he was also able to hear the telling complaints of the inhabitants against La Vente. In vain did he labor to convince the pastor to renounce his policy of baptizing newly-born infants in the nude (a practice which many

23. Bienville to min., Feb. 20, 1707, *loc. cit.*, f. 26–30. La Vente gave as further reason for his interdiction the fact that the appearance of the chapel was too unseemly, that its condition had mortified him on the occasion of the visit of the Franciscan fathers from Pensacola. La Vente [to Brisacier], July 4, 1708, *loc. cit.*, R 83.

24. *Ibid.* Bienville to min., Feb. 20, 1707, *loc. cit.*, f. 22–25.

of the female inhabitants were charging resulted in the deaths of their babies).[25] Truthfully, Bergier was at a loss as to what to do about La Vente. While he could not uphold the pastor's actions, he nonetheless could not bring himself to upbraid a member of his own order in the presence of so many pro-Jesuits. Instead, he found it more politic to hold his tongue, laboring to institute calm (by his own splendid example) where disorder prevailed. If he did not publicly denounce his *confrère* (as Bienville later claimed),[26] he nevertheless was unable to give his approval of the pastor (even in his 1707 letter to the seminary in Paris).[27]

Bergier had come to an appropriate locale for the practice of asceticism. By February of 1707, supplies were again running miserably low. But the vicar-general had wanted provisions not for himself but for his mission. The commandant had precious little to give him. There was but one course of action to follow: Bergier would remain at Mobile until Easter. In the meantime Bienville would send another ship to Veracruz in an attempt to fill Bergier's request for supplies.

With the *Espérance* destroyed, Bienville had only the brigantine *Aventurier* available for sea duty.[28] Moreover, he had few sailors with which to man the vessel. Again he was forced to call on the Canadians, this time to replace the dead or absent *matelots*.[29] On February 15, Bienville drafted a plea to the Duque de Albur-querque:

> . . . having no hopes of receiving assistance from France, I decided to send a brigantine to Veracruz under command of M. de Châteaugué to ask Your Excellency to send me provisions for at least five or six months; I also need specific ammunitions listed in the letter for which the commissary of this fort, M. de La Salle, is writing Your Excellency. My entire garrison and I are eating corn until the vessel returns with the provisions, which forces me to ask Your Excellency to please order the officials at Veracruz to load and send this vessel as

25. *Ibid.*, f. 24–27. No doubt La Vente refrained from this practice on excessively cold days, but he probably did not fully realize the newborns' vital need for warmth.

26. It is doubtful that Bergier confided in Bienville, as the commandant later intimates. Bienville to min., Feb. 20, 1707, *loc. cit.*, f. 24–25.

27. Tremblay [to Ango Des Maizerets], Jan. 14, 1708, ASQ, Lettres, O 49.

28. Testimonio de Autos hechos . . . , 1707, AGI, *México*, L. 479. La Salle to min., Sept. 12, 1708, AC, C13A, 2, f. 197–98.

29. Bienville to min., Feb. 20, 1707, *loc. cit.*, f. 8–9.

> soon as possible . . . I realize the many difficulties that this shipment may bring, but I also wish to inform Your Excellency that at times of war, these ports are forgotten, and when we receive only one supply ship annually, we are forced to appeal to Your Excellency every year.[30]

On the same day Bienville completed his letter to Alburquerque, La Salle penned a similar note to the viceroy. La Salle's request was more specific, however, mentioning the exact quantities needed by the French colony: six hundred quintals of flour, one hundred quintals of bacon, one hundred quintals of noodles, and four quintals of sugar. La Salle further requested Alburquerque to "give M. de Châsteauguy two copies of the bill for all merchandise that is sent so that one copy can be forwarded to France in order to request payment . . . and the other copy to remain here at Fort Louis so that M. de Châsteauguy can accurately distribute the provisions to the king's stores."[31]

Ten days later, Châteaugué and the Canadians left Massacre Island in the *Aventurier*, arriving in the harbor of Veracruz on the afternoon of the thirteenth of March. That evening, aboard the *Aventurier*, Châteaugué penned his own message to Alburquerque, in hopes of making the viceroy's official see the urgency of the situation:

> . . . I must tell you that our entire garrison is eating only corn; I am hoping that Your Excellency will supply us as soon as he can, without making us wait the forty days that we had to wait the last time; if we have to wait too long, it would be the greatest misfortune that could happen to all our men, many of whom are gravely ill . . . I am imploring Your Excellency with much respect to proceed . . .[32]

The next day at noon Châteaugué dropped anchor at the landing stage and debarked, handing his letter and those of Bienville and

30. Bienbilla al virrey, Feb. 15, 1707, AGI, *México*, L. 479. Bienville also sent his note of February 20 to Pontchartrain on the *Aventurier*. At Veracruz this letter was transferred to one of the French ships in port and transported to Rochefort.

31. La Salle al virrey, Feb. 15, 1707, AGI, *México*, L. 479. *Journal Historique*, p. 101. Carta al virrey, March 14, 1707, AGI, *México*, L. 479.

32. Châteaugué al virrey, March 13, 1707, AGI, *México*, L. 479. The letters from Châteaugué, La Salle and Bienville (translated from French into Spanish) are all contained in Legajo 479 under title of Sup^{or} Gou^{o} Año de 1707, No. 47.

La Salle to the royal officials at Veracruz. The reason for the urgency in his note was that he couldn't be certain that the authorities at Veracruz would fill his order at all. Moreover, he feared the excessive delays that had marked his previous trips, especially the voyage made in the autumn of 1705 which required nearly two and a half months to complete.[33]

Châteaugué was correct in assuming that his order would not ordinarily be handled with sympathy: the French, after all, were still considered intruders on the Gulf Coast; it was chiefly New Spain's fear of the English that gained them what assistance they had previously received.[34] Viceroy Alburquerque was, of course, not in Veracruz but in Mexico City. One of the royal officials, the fiscal officer, Joseph Antonio de Espinosa, received Châteaugué's letters and passed them on to Alburquerque on March 21, along with a note asking the viceroy to "be so kind as to order the royal officers of Veracruz to load, as soon as possible, the provisions needed and turn them over to that commander so that he can bring them to that colony where they are so badly needed." [35]

The next day, March 22, the royal council at Veracruz, anticipating Alburquerque's approval which came a few days later, gave Espinosa permission to begin making arrangements to supply the *Aventurier* and by the 27th of March the loading had begun. By April 11, the storing was completed (exceeding the burden the *Aventurier* could comfortably bear) and Châteaugué departed Veracruz, carrying, besides what was at first requested, additional supplies of rice, lentils and ham. Moreover, Châteaugué extracted a promise from Espinosa to send on another Spanish ship the supplies that were unable to be loaded on the *Santo Rey David*, a vessel Andrés de Arriola was now preparing to sail to Pensacola.[36]

Châteaugué arrived back in Mobile on May 9 with enough provisions to supply the garrison for several months. Upon his arrival he found that a recent vessel from Pensacola had brought additional supplies. He furthermore brought the message (forwarded

33. *Journal Historique*, pp. 93–95. El virrey al rey, June 6, 1706, AGI, *México*, L. 477.

34. The council in Madrid, even at this time, shows its fear of possible French expansion into Mexico. Consejo, May 3, 1709, AGI, *México*, L. 479.

35. Francisco San Juan al virrey, April 16, 1707, AGI, *México*, L. 479. Espinosa al virrey, March 21, 1707, AGI, *México*, L. 479.

36. Alburquerque was later reprimanded and the fiscal (Joseph de Espinosa) fired for the haste and lack of official approval by which the transactions with Châteaugué were carried out. El virrey al rey, Jan. 9, 1708, AGI, *México*, L. 479. Consejo al fiscal, May 3, 1709, AGI, *México*, L. 479.

immediately to Pensacola) that Andrés de Arriola was on his way with relief for the post at Santa María de Galve. His only unsettling news was the report he brought of the death of Payen de Noyan who, according to Frenchmen at Veracruz, died en route to Martinique on the *Aigle* several months before.[37]

Châteaugué's mission to Veracruz had been a complete success. When the additional supplies brought by Arriola to Fort San Carlos were delivered to the French on July 24 by *marinero* Juan Ruiz de Camarena, Mobile was once again prospering (at least as far as foodstuffs were concerned). The Le Moyne brothers, having saved the colony from famine, were once more back in the good graces of the inhabitants. Bergier, given two pirogues filled with provisions, along with two Canadians to man the oars, headed back to his mission among the Tamaroa.[38]

As a result of the calming effect Bergier had on the colony, the chaplain's activity picked up considerably, as did the work of the pastor and his assistant. Moreover, there were numerous baptisms to be performed. Two days before Châteaugué left for Veracruz, Marie-Anne Nadeau, wife of Joussette, *dit* La Loire, gave birth to her second child, Louise, so named by Louise-Marguerite Housseau, wife of Guillaume Boutin. The new surgeon-major, Valentin Barraud, acted as godfather. When the slaves (mostly Chitimacha) were brought to Mobile after Saint-Denis' raid, La Vente was undecided about whether or not to baptize them. He seemed unclear in his authority for such baptisms; but pressed by the new owners of the slaves, and after seeing several of them sick to the point of death, he did not hesitate to approve the performance of such sacraments by Huvé and Le Maire. When two such slaves, one a female, aged 8–9 years, belonging to Marguerite Messier, the other a female, aged 13–14, belonging to Jean Brunet, *dit* Bourbonnois,

37. *Journal Historique*, p. 102. Interrogatoire des habitants, Feb. 25, 1708, AC, C13A, 2, f. 265–66. Francisco San Juan al virrey, April 16, 1707, AGI, *México*, L. 479. La Vente [to Fleury], Aug. 1, 1706, ASQ, Lettres, R 80 (Fleury's attached note).

38. Francisco San Juan y Pedro Carrasco de Aguilar al virrey, Jan. 2, 1708, AGI, *México*, L. 479. Châteaugué, however, returned to Mobile with fewer supplies than La Salle had requested. The final load, including that transported on the *Santo Rey David* by Ruiz de Camarena, totalled 600 quintals of flour, 60 of bacon, 41 of rice and lentils, 16 of ham and 16 of sugar. Summated by Juan Mendo de Urbina, the supplies taken by Châteaugué came to 733 quintals of foodstuffs for which the French colony was billed 5, 328 *pesos*. El virrey al rey, Jan. 9, 1708, AGI, *México*, L. 479. Mendo de Urbina al virrey, Jan. 9, 1708, AGI, *México*, L. 479.

lay near death, La Vente himself performed the baptismal rites.[39]

François Le Maire, whom Bergier had helped place in the role of chaplain, performed his first recorded sacraments on June 11, baptizing four young slaves, all between the ages of three and eight years. One of these was a Negro slave (aged seven) belonging to Bienville whom the commandant named Jean-Baptiste. Young Jean-Baptiste was not the only Negro in the colony. The previous summer, Châteaugué had obtained from Iberville at least six black slaves (though he had hoped for more) that Iberville had seized from the island of Nevis. Bienville and Châteaugué had retained these slaves for themselves. Châteaugué owned a male Negro named François Jacemin whom in January he had moved in with Marie, one of Bienville's Negroes. In October, Marie gave birth to an infant male, named Antoine at a baptismal service performed by La Vente and witnessed by Zacharie Drapeau and Gabrielle Savary.[40]

On June 30, La Vente baptized a slave belonging to Claude Charland, *dit* Francoeur, and four weeks later christened three more slaves, one of whom was a Negro of three years named Joseph, belonging to Bienville. There were nine more slaves baptized that year by La Vente, all savages ranging in age from two to thirteen years, among them those of Christophe Poirier, Charles Dumont, Mandeville and Étienne Burelle. All were dangerously ill when La Vente baptized them and practically all of them died soon after being christened.[41]

In addition, there were numerous celebrations of birth in the colony. On June 19, François Le Maire baptized a child (named Jean-Honoré) of Jeanne L'Ecrüe and master cannoneer Jean-Louis Minuit. After five o'clock on the morning of October 4, Marie Briard gave birth to a daughter of Antoine Rivard, to whom godmother Gabrielle Savary gave her name. Two weeks later, Marie-Élisabeth Des Hayes bore a daughter to her husband, Jean Brunet, *dit* Bourbonnois, who was given the name Élisabeth-

39. ADM, A, Feb. 23, 1707. La Salle to min., July 25, 1707, AC, C13B, 1, No. 7, f. 6v–7v. La Vente [to Brisacier], March 4, 1708, ASQ, Lettres, R 79. ADM, A, May 18, June 9, 1707.

40. La Vente [to SME Dirs.], June 27, 1708, *loc. cit.*, R 82. ADM, A, June 11, 1707. LSMA, DCS, June 4, 1735. Bienville's slave, Georges, was later married to Marie, mother of Antoine. LSMA, DCS, Oct. 1, 1735. ADM, A, Oct. 26, 1707.

41. ADM, A, June 30, July 28, Aug. 13–14, Sept. 22, 25, Oct. 23, 26, Nov. 15, 27, Dec. 1, 1707.

Angélique. And two weeks after that, Marguerite Preau, young wife of Jean Colon, *dit* La Violette (whose Indian wife had died ten months before), gave birth to a male child on whom the next day was bestowed the name Jean by La Rochelle craftsman Jean Bon. On November 27, at eleven o'clock at night, Gabrielle Savary brought forth her third child who the next day was named Jean-Baptiste by godfather Jean-Baptiste Alexandre.[42]

Two days before Christmas, at seven o'clock in the evening, Louise-Marguerite Housseau, wife of anti-Bienvillist Guillaume Boutin, gave birth to an infant male. The next day (Christmas Eve), La Vente had the infant brought to the house serving as the parish church. In the presence of La Salle and his wife Jeanne-Catherine de Berenhardt, La Vente baptized the Boutin infant, named Nicolas by the scrivener.[43]

The baptism of young Nicolas Boutin was the last christening performed that year. On the whole, it had been a productive year for the local clergy, at least as far as baptisms were concerned. La Vente himself had performed twenty-two baptisms, while Bienville's newly-established chaplain, François Le Maire, had performed five. Alexandre Huvé, away for the most part at the villages of the Talimali and the Chato (where Bergier had assigned him), no doubt performed numerous baptisms among the savages that went unrecorded.[44]

In the meantime the discord between Bienville and his arch-adversaries, La Vente and La Salle, though somewhat tempered by Bergier, had by no means been extinguished. Fort Louis was fast rotting to the ground. Bienville wanted to have it repaired (but only as a temporary measure). "It is necessary," he wrote Pontchartrain, "that the king should incur the expense of building this fort anew of brick or of stone, otherwise if it is only reconstructed of wood there will always be expenditures over and over again." In any case, the commandant was determined to keep the fort and the town at its present location (twenty-six miles above the mouth of the Mobile River).[45]

La Vente was just as adamant in calling for the fort's removal,

42. ADM, A, June 19, Oct. 4, 17, Nov. 4, 27, 1707.

43. Interrogatoire des habitants . . . par Dartaguiette, Feb. 25, 1708, AC, C13A, 2, f. 279–87. Bienville to min., Feb. 25, 1708, *loc. cit.*, f. 104–06. ADM, A, Dec. 23, 1707.

44. ADM, A, Feb. 28–Dec. 23, 1707. La Vente [to SME Dirs.], June 27, 1708, ASQ, Lettres, R 82.

45. Bienville to min., Feb. 25, 1708, *loc. cit.*, f. 102–03.

either to Massacre Island or to the base of the river (where present-day Mobile stands).[46] La Salle echoed the pastor's plea, countering with the suggestion that "there should be no hesitation in placing it [the town] at the *Oignoinais*[47]—it is a spot to the east [*sic*], quite spacious, within sight of the bay of Mobile, within reach of the ships—and letting the fort be transferred to Massacre Island with the garrison and the king's magazines where all will be secure and nothing stolen."[48]

Bienville summarily rejected La Salle's suggestion, giving reasons that were more defensive than logical. ". . . the idea of M. d'Iberville," he responded "was that this fort should be close enough to give assistance to the inhabitants who might settle at the bluffs that are above and below this fort. The land on the lower part of this river where it is proposed to build the post is like this land, but the water is brackish there. One is surrounded by swamps. That place is very unhealthy. We have learned that by the many deaths that have occurred at the village of the Chato who are camped where it is proposed to build the post. The opinion of all the inhabitants is that this place where we are now located is incomparably better. There would be only a single advantage of distance which would be but eight leagues. We are here in a better position to receive assistance from the savages."[49]

La Vente, chafed at Bienville's obstinance, launched a bitter but reasoned campaign to change the minds of the authorities, the logic of which he later put to paper in a lengthy report to Briscacier:

> . . . apart from the [aformentioned] argument [the presence of flooding] which seems quite *à propos* when deciding on a site for a permanent establishment there are many others which should not seem any less important if one did not feel himself obliged to maintain an error of judgment which he has committed and which one makes it a point of honor to stand by despite the light by which we are fully illumined from discussion [among the officials]. I consider that for myself the place where we are as a true punishment for the sins of the inhabitants since one had almost to be blind not to be able to locate it in a place more suitable than the one here . . . truly there is no comparison between the two

46. La Vente [to Brisacier], July 4, 1708, ASQ, Lettres, R 83.
47. *Les Oignonets*—"the onion fields."
48. La Salle to min., July 25, 1707, AC, C13B, 1, No. 7, f. 7v–8.
49. Bienville to min., Feb. 25, 1708, *loc. cit.*, f. 102–04.

> places . . . especially since the breeze would always bring the ships easily [to the proposed site] since this breeze ordinarily blows most of the year, while from there to where we are now there are still ten leagues of river so winding that the transports have sometimes been six weeks in making a trip from here to Massacre Island . . . here the land is hilly and full of stagnant water . . . there, it is a spot where a city could be built much taller and larger than Paris . . . here we are athwart the river used by the savages by whom we are at present threatened . . . there, we are out of reach of them because of the location which is fortified naturally by the waters which surround it . . .[50]

La Vente went on to offer numerous other reasons (most of them valid) for transferring the establishment, but Bienville remained unmoved. The commandant did, however, concede the possibility that a large town could later be built on "the lower part of this river, which could serve as a warehousing port." Moreover, he reached somewhat of a compromise with La Salle: with the partial collapse of the chapel, at which time the western curtain and one of the bastions of the fort had also suffered extensive damage, it was quite evident that (in the interest of security) the fort needed immediate repair. Bienville commenced to restore the fort, as he had planned, but agreed to use the propped-up chapel as additional storage space for La Salle. As a further concession to the commissary, he consented to begin construction of a new and larger warehouse on Massacre Island.[51]

This new *magasin* for which La Salle had long been pleading was built close to the water (within a hundred feet of the shoreline). Measuring fifty-five feet in length by twenty-six feet in width, it was fourteen feet high between two sheds, surrounded by a stockade and nicely covered with wooden shingles. The new warehouse, however, impressive as it was, was to remain largely unused for nearly a year. During the summer of 1707, the English-made brigantine, *Aventurier*, languishing in the Massacre Island harbor for the several months after Châteaugué's return from Veracruz, had been continually under attack from worms and wood borers. Despite all measures taken to protect her vulnerable hull, she finally began taking on water and eventually sank. The rigging and equipment of the captured vessel was taken off and

50. La Vente [to Brisacier], July 4, 1708, *loc. cit.*, R 83.
51. *Ibid.* Bienville to min., Feb. 25, 1708, *loc. cit.*, f. 130.

stored in the warehouse, along with what equipment remained from the *Espérance;* but the *Aventurier* was the last of the vessels at Massacre Island capable of making voyages to Havana, Cap-français or Veracruz.[52]

Despite Bienville's concessions to La Salle, relations between commandant and commissary did not vastly improve. In March, La Salle sent precise statements of expenses to the court which he claimed were owed the king by the Le Moynes. For five voyages to Veracruz and Havana "which were made under the pretext of serving the king but which went to sell merchandise in said places and to transport M. d'Iberville's pelts," La Salle listed 71,750 *livres* as the amount to be reimbursed to the crown. For other goods belonging to the king that Iberville had sold, La Salle totaled 14,124 *livres.* For outfitting a brigantine sent to Veracruz, fully loaded with merchandise which La Salle claimed was sold for the sole profit of Bienville and Châteaugué, the scrivener listed 21,537 *livres,* plus another 11,099 *livres* for goods which were delivered from the king's magazine to Bienville who sold it from his own warehouse at more than 600 percent increase during the years 1702–1706. Coupled with various other credits, "all these statements of expenses rise to the sum of 133,682 *livres,* without counting the harm all these voyages have done to the advancement of the colony, which is no further along than on the first day of its settlement."[53]

La Salle complained further that the flour recently obtained from Veracruz was unmilled, of almost unusable quality, and that "the bran which is derived from it has always been left to the profit of a certain Humery [Jacques Leméry], the quartermaster appointed by Bienville."[54] According to La Salle, when warehouse-keeper Christophe Poirier refused to fill an order requested by Bienville, the commandant "treated him with the utmost cruelty, striking him with a stick accompanied by blows in the stomach . . . and me, for not having approved this action, he put in the guardhouse like some poor wretch, during which time he took

52. Dartaguiette to min., Feb. 26, 1708, *loc. cit.*, f. 58. La Salle listed the dimensions as 52 x 20 feet but since Dartaguiette had been sent to Mobile to gather exact information, his figures are presumably more accurate. La Salle to min., July 25, 1707, AC, C13B, 1, No. 7, f. 6–6v. Dartaguiette to min., Feb. 26, 1708, *loc. cit.*, f. 59–60. Bienville to min., Feb. 25, 1708, *loc. cit.*, f. 109–10.

53. La Salle to min., July 25, 1707, AC, C13B, 1, No. 7, f. 4v–5.

54. *Ibid.*, f. 8–8v.

the liberty of going through our desks and pilfering the daily journal . . . of the foodstuffs sent from Veracruz."[55]

Bienville countered that La Salle had refused to reimburse Châteaugué for the last voyage he had made to Havana and that when he attempted to have an order filled for clothes for the chief of the Choctaw that the commissary had ordered Poirier to tear up the request, claiming he had nothing in stock for such demands. Bienville confessed that, to get to the truth of the matter, he and Boisbriant had entered the warehouse, had "examined" the records of which La Salle was speaking. He admitted threatening La Salle with taking away his position as scrivener but to no more, certainly not to the accusation of violence. Bienville further claimed that it was actually the commissary who was in debt to the king (for 2,400 *livres*) but that "La Salle had answered that all of that amount was due him for his lodging and for three rations that he had not taken from the warehouse and for a voyage that he had made to Pensacola."[56]

Bienville further charged that La Salle had taunted him, gloating that since the death of Iberville the commandant no longer had any support. "He must also be complaining," Bienville wrote, "that he has no authority over the garrison and that no inhabitant respects him. It is true, my lord, that no matter what I do I cannot cause him to have any. I have often warned him of his bad conduct without his having been willing to change, so that I do not think that, since he is known by us to be the sort of man he is, he will sustain himself long in his office which another could occupy more worthily than he. At least, if he is to be continued in service, let him be reprimanded in such a way that he will follow in the line of his duty."[57]

The wrangling between Bienville and La Salle continued unabated during the spring and summer of 1707. In August, by a ship from Pensacola, La Salle sent the letter he had written charging the Le Moynes with flagrant and exorbitant theft, but by that time a new crisis was confronting the colony which was spreading fear and alarm to every colonist.[58] In the spring of 1707, Bienville learned from a Choctaw woman who had escaped the English

55. Ibid., f. 9v.

56. Bienville to min., Feb. 20, 1707, *loc. cit.*, f. 19–23. La Salle to min., July 25, 1707, AC, C13B, 1, No. 7, f. 9v.

57. Bienville to min., Feb. 20, 1707, *loc. cit.*, f. 21–22.

58. La Salle to min., July 25, 1707, AC, C13B, 1, No. 7, f. 1–10v. La Salle to min., March 4, 1708, AC, C13A, 2, f. 154–56.

that a number of native villages in the east were joining the English "in order to devour a village of white men." Receiving this news, Bienville invited the Tomeh to attack a village of the Alabama for the purpose of taking prisoners in order to learn the latest English plans for aggression. Shortly afterwards, Tomeh warriors brought Bienville two young Koasati prisoners from whom Bienville discovered after intense interrogation that the English purposed to attack Pensacola that very summer, and after capturing that town, they planned to regroup before launching an assault on Mobile.[59]

In late July, Bienville sent a messenger to Pensacola to warn the Spanish of impending attack. Sebastián de Moscoso, sergeant-major and interim governor (since Guzmán had returned to Veracruz) and former governor Andrés de Arriola tendered their thanks to Bienville's courier, assuring him they would augment their defenses, yet neither of the two officials gave the warning sufficient attention. Two weeks later, on August 11, Arriola left Pensacola for Veracruz, and the next evening at nine o'clock, fourteen headmen, backed by the English, swooped down on an outlying cabin of natives friendly to the Spanish. Capturing several of the Spanish Indians, the invaders proceeded to burn four of the houses in the settlement outside Fort San Carlos before the Spanish infantry managed to drive them off.[60]

The next morning Moscoso sent Captain Gregorio de Quiroga y Losada and a small party to survey the damage and to estimate the strength of the invading forces. By Quiroga's estimate, there had been a sizable number involved in the attack, which caused Moscoso to make immediate plans for emergency defense. Without delay, he ordered the hospital-house of San Juan de Dios and that of San Francisco to be moved inside the fort. The next day, ten Spaniards, including three prisoners, went to the nearby river to wash clothes, but by dusk had failed to return. Two days later, at one o'clock in the morning, some three hundred warriors attacked and set on fire the abandoned houses of the settlement (since the night of the first sortie all the soldiers, women and townsmen had taken refuge inside the fort), then assaulted Fort San Carlos from all sides. A Canadian from Fort Louis, occupied in repairing the ship *San Joseph*, was killed, while a small marine detachment guarding the vessel was driven inside the fort.[61]

59. Bienville to min., Feb. 25, 1708, *loc. cit.*, f. 95–96.

60. *Ibid.*, f. 96–97. El virrey al rey, Feb. 5, 1708, AGI, *México*, L. 633. Junta de 13 de Agosto de 1707, AGI, *México*, L. 633.

61. Moscoso al virrey, Oct. 12, 1707, AGI, *México*, L. 633. Informe de Espinosa, Nov. 10, 1707, AGI, *México*, L. 633.

At dawn of the next day, Moscoso gave orders to burn all the houses in the town in order to prevent the invaders from using them as barriers. Shortly after the fires commenced, the winds changed, endangering the fort, forcing Moscoso to abandon his ruse. No sooner had the burning ceased than the Indians took cover behind the remaining houses and renewed their attack, receiving scarce damage from the cannons of the fort. A single shot from an English-made gun blew off a Spanish sentinel's hand and struck Captain Joseph de Robles in the back. Surrounding the fort, the invaders continued firing, striking numerous soldiers inside the fort, while suffering only minimal damage themselves from the Spaniards' return fire. Later that afternoon, after ransacking the houses in the town and mortally wounding officer Antonio de Padilla, the Indians retired to the woods, leaving the settlement in shambles.[62]

After the natives had retreated, Canadian master carpenter Francois Trudeau, who had been for several weeks working in Pensacola under contract to reconstruct one of the fort's rotted buildings, prepared to return to Mobile, having lost all his clothes and tools and more than two hundred *pesos* in gold coins. After the initial attack, Moscoso had hired Trudeau to supervise the rebuilding of the hospital inside the fort (for 170 *pesos* in wages), but the repeated attacks by the Indians prevented the construction from taking place. Moscoso felt it an opportune time for Trudeau to return to Mobile. Besides losing the hospital's timbers during one of the assaults, the governor's supply of nails was depleted and many of the carriages upon which the cannons were maneuvered had been destroyed. Moscoso gave Trudeau a letter to be delivered to Bienville, by which he informed the French commandant of the invasions and asked that Trudeau be allowed to return to Pensacola with a large supply of nails. He further asked that Trudeau be allowed to construct at Mobile eight carriage wheels for the cannons before returning.[63]

Trudeau left Pensacola in his pirogue on the 18th of August, only hours before the Indians renewed their attack. This time, the invaders set the entire town aflame while brazenly waving an English flag. Moscoso was hard pressed to prevent the fort itself

62. Moscoso al virrey, Oct. 12, 1707, *loc. cit.*, L. 633. Spanish casualties during the attacks of August, September and November totalled eleven dead and fifteen captured. El rey al virrey, Dec. 4, 1709, AGN, *Historia*, 298.

63. *Ibid.* Quoting Spanish manuscripts, I use "peso." French manuscripts use "piastre."

(inside which all the settlement's 374 personnel were gathered) from going up in flames.[64]

The next several months witnessed a cessation of direct assaults by the invaders. Moscoso guessed that the majority of natives had left for Apalache or Carolina to recruit additional forces for a more concerted attack. But he could not be certain exactly how many Indians were still lurking in the nearby forests. The fort was still being attacked at odd moments and the demoralized Spaniards, most of them left with only the clothes they wore on their backs, were afraid to pursue them. Moscoso and his men ventured from the fort only far enough to cut logs from the nearest woods to repair the damaged fort and stockade. Even then they were occasionally ambushed, losing in one encounter one of their most valuable officers "whose body was chopped into numerous pieces," and on another occasion forfeiting a sailor named Pedro Manuel Cabello who was captured and taken off into the forests.[65]

On the tenth of September, Moscoso received a missive from Bienville promising to send Trudeau back to Pensacola with the carriage wheels and requesting that the Canadian be allowed to "pick up the tools and provisions which had been left behind." Bienville further asked for supplies of flour, pitch and tar and other provender, in return for which he promised to send a war party to the Alabama country to gain intelligence concerning the long-range plans of the English and their Indians. Bienville quickly made good this latter promise, dispatching a force of twenty-five Tawasa and fifteen Chato warriors to raid the town of Koasati. Returning to Mobile, the Tawasa and Chato headmen brought four prisoners, who, under intensive questioning, admitted they had seen a hundred Englishmen, some French Huguenots (all on horseback) and some two thousand Indians preparing for a massive assault on Pensacola (with four ships to attack by sea).[66]

64. *Ibid. Journal Historique*, p. 103. Bienville to min., Feb. 25, 1708, *loc. cit.*, f. 98–99. Informe de Juan Mendo de Urbina, Nov. 16, 1707, AGI, *México*, L. 633.

65. Declaración de Pedro Manuel Cabello, Nov. 30, 1707, AGI, *México*, L. 633. Sebastián de Moscoso al virrey, Feb. 10, 1708, AGI, *México*, L. 633. Moscoso blamed Joseph de Guzmán for the poor condition of the fort prior to the August attack, claiming that the absented governor "lived with much confidence and failed to take care of all that was needed for the maintenance and protection of this fortress . . ." Moscoso al virrey, Oct. 12, 1707, AGI, *México*, L. 633.

66. Bienville to min., Feb. 25, 1708, *loc. cit.*, f. 96–99. Moscoso al virrey, Oct. 12, 1707, *loc. cit.*, L. 633. *Journal Historique*, pp. 103–04.

Bienville, believing that Fort Louis was secure enough, turned his attention toward Massacre Island. Should the English be successful in capturing Pensacola, it would be an easy matter to then seize the Massacre Island port, which, if held, would bottle up French shipping indefinitely. Bienville sent Trudeau and a Canadian escort on to Pensacola with the requested supply of nails and carriage wheels, advising Moscoso to "shut himself up in his fort without going out of it." Meanwhile, the commandant would proceed to Massacre Island with eighty of the colony's most able men and some thirty natives from the surrounding villages. From the port, his forces could reach Pensacola in less than a day's time should help be needed.[67]

Bienville had not yet left Fort Louis when Moscoso received the French commandant's message. By that time the Spanish governor had noticed a number of English flags and a troop of Indians with some forty horses milling about through the trees just beyond the fort. Realizing that the siege was about to be renewed, Moscoso immediately dispatched the Canadian who had accompanied Trudeau back to Fort Louis to notify Bienville of the impending attack. Just after noon on that same day (November 27), Moscoso saw an Englishman in a blue coat come out of the trees, moving slowly toward the fort with a white flag in hand. Every ten paces or so, the Englishman stopped and waved the flag before moving closer toward the fort. When the bluecoat reached the fort's entrance, Moscoso sent Captain Gregorio de Quiroga with an armed guard to blindfold him after which Quiroga brought him to Moscoso where the Briton handed Moscoso a written message. When he saw that the message was in English, Moscoso handed the note back, explaining there was no one present who could read it. After a moment's pause, the Spanish governor ordered the Englishman escorted from the fort. A short time later, the Englishman returned with a Huguenot who explained in French (which Moscoso understood) that the English proposed to give the Spanish good living quarters should they agree to surrender without a fight.[68]

Moscoso refused to surrender, however, and the two bluecoats returned to their campsite. At midnight, the English, along with

67. Bienville to min., Feb. 25, 1708, *loc. cit.*, f. 98–99.

68. Moscoso al virrey, Feb. 10, 1708, *loc. cit.*, L. 633. During the preceding two months the English had gathered their Indian forces largely from villages in the Alabama-Apalachicola country. Declaración de Pedro Manuel Cabello, Nov. 30, 1707, AGI, *México*, L. 633.

several hundred warriors, surrounded the fort, launching a violent assault which continued throughout the night. At dawn, the invaders retired to the woods and shortly thereafter the two emissaries returned to the fort waving white flags, this time offering Moscoso his last chance to surrender: if not accepted, the invaders would be forced to set fire to the fort and destroy it completely.[69]

Again, Moscoso refused, proclaiming that he and all the members of the garrison were willing to sacrifice their lives in defense of the *presidio*. When the Englishmen left, Moscoso surveyed his dwindling defense force. The majority of his soldiers were either sick, wounded or dead. As a last resort, he assembled the convicts from the guardhouse, confronting them with a desperate proposition: should they be willing to assist in the defense of the fort, they would be awarded "their freedom as well as money." The convicts were elated at the chance to earn their freedom; when, at dusk, the enemy again charged the fort, the new recruits were decisive in repulsing that night's long assault.[70]

The next evening, the assault was renewed; the attacks went on most of the night. The Spanish lost their guard from the bastion of San Joseph, but succeeded in killing a principal chief of the enemy Indians. It was apparently the loss of this chief that demoralized the Indians, for by early the next morning (November 30), Moscoso could see evidence of a full-scale retreat, an observation that was confirmed when the English freed Pedro Manuel Cabello, the sailor who had been captured on October 4. Just after dawn, Cabello came running from the woods, reporting that the English had given up, having been unable to recruit enough Indians to break the fort's resistance.[71]

At ten o'clock on the morning of December 8, Bienville and his force of 110 French and Indians arrived at Pensacola to offer their assistance. By that time, however, all of the English and most of the enemy warriors had left the vicinity. Moscoso thanked Bienville profusely for his good intentions. After spending a few days at Pensacola, during which time Bienville's Indians searched the

69. *Ibid.* Arriola's reinforcements which were recruited from Puebla, Veracruz and Mexico City had not yet arrived. Instrucción para Don Andrés de Arriola, Dec. 27, 1707, AGI, *México*, L. 633.

70. Informe de Juan Mendo de Urbina, March 7, 1708, AGI, *México*, L. 633. A list of the thirty prisoners who volunteered (and who were later given their freedom plus four *pesos* each) is given in Mendo de Urbina's report of March 27, 1708, AGI, *México*, L. 633.

71. Declaración de Pedro Manuel Cabello, Nov. 30, 1707, *loc. cit.*, L. 633.

countryside for any remaining dangers, the French commandant left with his party for Mobile, leaving with Moscoso three Chato warriors for use in scouting missions. It was the siege of Pensacola that firmly convinced the Spanish of the value of having numerous friendly Indians located near their doorstep, but their loss of the bulk of the Apalache, Chato, Pensacola and Escambe villages was apparently permanent. While Bienville was present in Pensacola, Moscoso had sought his advice on how to attract the natives of Florida back to their former province but Bienville was understandably evasive. In an effort to convince the remaining Chato to transfer to Pensacola, the Spanish governor made them elaborate promises (offering them wool, honey and gold beads) but the natives were simply not interested.[72]

Bienville's conversations with Moscoso left the commandant strangely uneasy about Franco-Spanish co-operation both on the Gulf Coast and throughout the West Indies. Rumors had been adrift for several months now (especially in the port of Veracruz) of a break in relations between the two nations. Moreover, he had learned from Pedro Manuel Cabello that the English and their Indians, upon leaving Pensacola, were planning an attack (possibly a prompt one) on Mobile. Returning with his men to Massacre Island, however, Bienville felt relieved that the immediate crisis was over, and pleased that he had seized the opportunity to demonstrate his good faith and support to the Spanish at no great cost to himself or to the colony. Perhaps he would soon have need to call on Pensacola for special assistance.[73]

Going on to Fort Louis in mid-December, Bienville felt confident of the capability of his forces to resist enemy attack, of his own ability to retain the loyalties of both Spaniard and Indian. He was unaware of events transpiring in Europe that for six months had been moving to divest him of his authority and to jeopardize his future in Louisiana.[74]

72. Moscoso al virrey, Feb. 10, 1708, *loc. cit.*, L. 633.

73. Bienville to min., Feb. 25, 1708, *loc. cit.*, f. 99–100. Declaración de Pedro Manuel Cabello, Nov. 30, 1707, *loc. cit.*, L. 633.

74. Mémoire du Roy, June 30, 1707, AC, B 29, f. 248v–58v.

XVII

Dartaguiette d'Iron

THE ailing Jacques Gravier arrived in Paris in early 1707, intent on pursuing several objectives. One of these (though he still would not admit it) was to obtain expert medical advice concerning the removal of the arrowhead from his elbow. However, the most professional opinion in Paris, he found, was no more encouraging than the least competent in Mobile: the lodged missile could not be removed without the loss of his entire arm. He would have to reconcile himself to this fact: as long as he lived, his elbow would pain him. Frustrated, Gravier turned his attention toward his other purposes—to procure more missionaries for the Illinois fields, to receive permission to establish a Jesuit warehouse at Mobile (to supply the Illinois) as well as a separate place of worship apart from that of the seminary priests, and to serve as Bienville's advocate against the many complaints lodged against him by La Vente and La Salle.[1]

At the time Gravier arrived in Paris, Bienville was surely in need of a skilled apologist. A special commission had by this time been at work for nearly a year seeking to ferret out the guilty parties in Iberville's last campaign, an investigation that already had fully implicated two of the Le Moyne brothers as well as numerous of their close associates. Though the inquest was to drag on for another quarter of a century, by the spring of 1707 Pontchartrain had seen evidence enough. As far as he was concerned, both Iber-

1. Epistola Patris Jacobi Gravier ad Reverendissimum Patrem Michaelem Angelum Tamburini, March 6, 1707, *JR*, *LXVI*, pp. 123–28. Bienville to min., Oct. 10, 1706, AC, C13B, 1, No. 6, f. 8–9. Lettre du Père Lamberville, March 1, 1707, AC, C13A, 1, f. 582. Tremblay [to SQ Dirs.], June 18, 1707, ASQ, Lettres, M 38. Min. to Bégon, Jan. 19, 1707, AM, B2, 196, f. 311–22.

ville and Sérigny were unquestionably guilty of fraud, to the great detriment of the colony at Mobile. If the extent of their guilt was not yet known, the minister was convinced that their conduct had been both dishonorable and damaging.[2]

Iberville's death the preceding summer had both complicated the inquest and necessitated his replacement. In the governing of Louisiana, Pontchartrain had long relied on that Canadian's wisdom, energy and experience. Faced with the commander's loss, the minister was sedulously searching for a successor. Bienville, in a position of command for nearly a decade, may have under other circumstances been a logical choice for the governorship. It is possible that even Iberville's and Sérigny's complicity in the fraudulent expedition would not have removed him from consideration had his own record been *sans reproche*. But the fact that two high officials in Mobile were leveling charges against him similar to those that had been brought against his brothers was too much for Pontchartrain to overlook: where there was so much smoke, was there not certain to be a little fire? Had the Le Moynes too long exercised too much power and influence in the colony for any one family? Surely, it was time for a change. Despite Gravier's good words in behalf of Bienville, he was too late. Pontchartrain had already removed the commandant's name from consideration.[3]

Foiled in his efforts to represent Bienville to the court as an ideal choice for governor, Gravier nevertheless hoped for a salient concession in the question of Jesuit rights in Louisiana. The Mississippi was a vast and fertile field, he claimed, in which the Society of Jesus had been dutifully ministering. But the lines from the Illinois to Quebec were virtually closed. It was only through Mobile that the missions could be supplied and the seminary priests had cut them off at that point. At Gravier's insistence, Jesuit authorities in Paris made a new appeal to Pontchartrain: let the Black Robes have a warehousing depot at Mobile to supply their Illinois missions, and a mission house at Mobile to serve them while tempo-

2. Min. to Bégon, Sept. 22, 1706, AM, B2, 191, f. 325–27. Min. to L'Hostellier, Oct. 10, 1708, AM, B2, 209, f. 178–79. Min. to Clairambault, Nov. 24, 1706, AM, B2, 192, f. 314–15. Comparution de Borie, Dec. 31, 1706, ACM, Prises, B 5921. Min. to Sérigny, Dec. 29, 1706, AM, B2, 192, f. 961–62.

3. Min. to Madame d'Iberville, Sept. 22, 1706, AM, B2, 191, f. 358. Min. to Bégon, May 25, 1707, AM, B 29, f. 241–45. Gravier to min., [1706], AC, C13A, 1, f. 570–77. Gravier to min., Feb. 27, 1707, AC, C13A, 1, f. 578–81. Min. to Brisacier, May 25, 1707, AC, B 29, f. 262–62v.

rarily in the port; such a modest request would answer the needs of the Jesuits while not seriously offending the authority of the seminary.[4]

Pontchartrain listened to this Jesuit proposal thoughtfully, remembering his last conversation with Bishop Saint-Vallier in 1704, shortly before the bishop's ship was captured by the British. It was true that on this occasion Saint-Vallier had hinted that perhaps the Jesuits could be useful in his diocese's southern province. Had the bishop been on the verge of modifying his rigid 1703 stance on the question of a separate sector for the Jesuits? Pontchartrain possibly thought so, but the sensitive bishop was at this time still captive in England. Communications were difficult, and in view of the necessity for prompt decisions, the minister did not wish to stir unruffled waters. A Mobile mission house for the Jesuits would best be disallowed. Even when Gravier suggested that a chapel could be erected on Massacre Island that would have no connection with the parish church of Mobile, Pontchartrain remained unmoved: the Jesuits were to be allowed a depot, but in no wise was a chapel or church to be maintained. If masses were to be said, then they must take place in the regular parish church or in the chapel of Fort Louis with the approval of the appointed parish priest or chaplain. After all, if a depot for connecting their Illinois missions with the outside world was their main objective, as the Jesuits claimed, it was not absolutely essential that they have a separate place of worship. Gravier, rebuffed again, retreated for the moment. But neither his tongue nor his brain was long idle. If he could not remain in a position of influence at Mobile, himself, his hated arch-rival La Vente was not going to remain either, at least not without authorities being apprised of the pastor's fulsome conduct. Before returning to Louisiana, the indignant Jesuit would do what he could to besmirch the *curé's* reputation.[5]

Meanwhile, Pontchartrain was deeply involved in the task of choosing a new governor for the young colony. Among those mentioned as possibilities were Henri-Joseph Beaumont d'Eschilais, *capitaine de vaisseau*, who was to command the next ship for Louisiana; Charles-Gaspard Piot de Langloiserie (Boisbriant's

4. Gravier to min., Feb. 27, 1707, AC, C13A, 1, f. 578–79. Min. to Lamberville, May 25, 1707, AC, B 29, f. 244–45.

5. Min. to La Chaize, June 18, 1704, AM, B2, 175, f. 824v–25. Min. à l'évêque de Québec, June 29, 1707, AC, B 29, f. 30–30v. Gravier to min., Feb. 27, 1707, AC, C13A, 1, f. 578–79. Mémoire du Roy, June 30, 1707, AC, B 29, f. 273v–76v.

brother-in-law), lieutenant of the king at Quebec; and even Iberville's older brother Charles Le Moyne, Baron de Longueuil. But Beaumont d'Eschilais showed no interest in the governorship and the latter two men had both been too closely associated with Iberville and Sérigny. By the first of May, 1707, over the strenuous objections of the Le Moyne faction, the king had decided in favor of Nicolas Daneau de Muy, former town-major of Quebec and recent recipient of the cross of Saint-Louis. Daneau de Muy was no doubt a splendid compromise choice, a man capable of bringing order and harmony into the colony (a nonpartisan who would favor neither Jesuit nor seminary priest). The fifty-six-year-old native of Picardy had been serving in His Majesty's army since 1674, first in Normandy, then, since 1685, in Canada where he had distinguished himself in numerous engagements against the English, the Mohawk and the Iroquois. In Canada he married first into the family of Pierre Boucher, then when his wife Marguerite (by whom he had seven children) died in 1698, he wedded Catherine, sister of Pierre d'Ailleboust d'Argenteuil, by whom he had one son. After serving in Newfoundland, Nicolas returned to the interior where he served for several years as commandant of Fort Chambly before being appointed garrison adjutant at Quebec in 1704. Several years later, Daneau de Muy brought his family to France, in quest of a higher appointment. His timing was excellent; his availability was soon brought to the attention of Pontchartrain who had been searching for a capable, experienced and available Canadian officer not connected with the Le Moynes.[6]

Having chosen Daneau de Muy as governor, the king lost no time in apprising his appointee of the situation in Louisiana regarding the need for Negro slaves, the building of a mill (for which three thousand *livres* had been appropriated), the boundary disputes with the Spaniards, etc. Most importantly, the new governor was to help determine whether or not Commandant Bienville was guilty of the charges of profiteering leveled by La Salle. The king seemed at this time to take it for granted that Bienville was culpable. On June 30, 1707 he wrote Daneau:

6. *DGFC, I*, pp. 71, 152, 156. Min. à Mssrs. Vaudreuil et Raudot, June 30, 1707, AC, B 29, f. 47. AC, F1A, 17, f. 93–95. Min. to Brisacier, May 25, 1707, AC, B 29, f. 261v–62v. Brisacier to min., June 4, 1707, AC, C11A, 27, f. 34–34v. Tremblay [to SQ Dirs.], June 25, 1707, ASQ, Lettres, M 38. AC, F1A, 14, f. 55. Tremblay, however, from reports he received, judged Daneau impetuous and acquisitive. Tremblay [to SQ Dirs.], May 8, 1707, ASQ, Lettres, M 37.

> His Majesty is giving orders to Sieur de Bienville who commands at present in Louisiana, who also knows that country, to bring him [Daneau de Muy] up to date on the affairs of that colony. He is certain that he will do so in good faith and that the said Sieur de Muy will be satisfied with him concerning that matter. When he thinks he is sufficiently informed about what he needs to know, he will deliver to the said Bienville His Majesty's order enclosed herewith by which he [Bienville] is to return to France on the vessel that the king is sending to that country . . .[7]

Pontchartrain received this approved "mémoire du roi" and enclosed it with his personal instructions, both of which he had delivered to the governor-designate, then still in Paris. The minister, in his own directive, did not specifically order Bienville to return to France. He did, however, notify Bienville of the king's intention on this point:

> His Majesty has seen fit to appoint M. de Muy to the governorship of Louisiana. He desires that you render him an account of the state of affairs on his arrival and that you make him acquainted with all the business of that colony in order that he may be able to follow them and render His Majesty an account of them. He [His Majesty] approves, after M. de Muy has gained from you the information he desires, that you embark on the vessel that is bringing him [Daneau], according to His Majesty's order which he is transmitting to you.[8]

In mid-July, Pontchartrain received further complaints from Commissary La Salle, which were apparently even more damaging to Bienville than ones previously received.[9] These letters, however, seeming to make Bienville's recall even more imperative, must have

7. Mémoire du Roy . . . June 30, 1707, AC, B 29, f. 248v. On that same date, the king also wrote Bienville that he was to return to France (only with Daneau's permission, however) and ordered Beaumont d'Eschilais to receive him on board. Mémoire du Roy . . . à M. de Bienville, June 30, 1707, AC, B 29, f. 263v–64. Mémoire du Roy . . . à M. d'Eschilais, July 23, 1707, AC, B 29, f. 277–77v.

8. Min. to Bienville, June 30, 1707, AC, B 29, f. 262–62v.

9. Min. to M. de Muy, July 23, 1707, AC, B 29, f. 277v. These letters, apparently not extant, must have been written after Sept. 8, 1706, since Pontchartrain had on June 30 acknowledged receiving La Salle's letters of Sept. 7, 8, 1706. Min. to La Salle, June 30, 1707, AC, B 29, f. 264. Min. to La Salle, July 23, 1707, AC, B 29, f. 280.

caused Pontchartrain to reflect on the king's initial order. Perhaps the minister read something between the lines. Perhaps something in La Salle's increasing urgency caused the minister to wonder if possibly these new charges were not the ravings of someone a little beside himself. In any case, after communications with the king, the minister sent Daneau de Muy additional instructions, impressing on the governor-select the need for a more thorough investigation:

> If all that is contained in them [La Salle's letters] is true, the said Sieur de Bienville is extremely culpable and deserves punishment. His Majesty desires that you examine carefully, together with Sieur Dartaguiette, commissary of the marine, who is making the voyage with you . . . all the facts contained in these letters and that you have all the possessions of said Sieur de Bienville seized if you provide proofs that he has betrayed his trust in his functions and that he has appropriated to himself the effects of His Majesty. He also wishes, in case you find him guilty in such a way that you are both convinced of it after having conferred with each other about it, that you have him arrested and that you send him as a prisoner to France, according to the order that you will find enclosed herewith; but be careful to adopt this course only after it has appeared clear to both of you that he deserves this treatment, and not otherwise.[10]

The king's original instructions were thus modified: Bienville was not to be sent back to France forthwith, but only if a rigorous inquiry found him blameworthy. The fact that the court was now even more determined to discover the truth of La Salle's charges could make matters worse for the commandant (should he be found guilty); nonetheless it would also provide him a chance to be defended before presumably disinterested parties.

The young man mentioned in Pontchartrain's latest communication to Daneau de Muy who was to jointly conduct the court's inquiry upon his arrival at Mobile was Jean-Baptiste-Martin Dartaguiette d'Iron, a native of the parish of Mendionde (diocèse de Bayonne) in the old province of Basse-Navarre in the south of France. Son of Jean-Baptiste-Martin Dartaguiette, Baron d'Aguerre de Hélette, and Marie de Harriet d'Iron, Dartaguiette, only twenty-four years of age at the time of his selection, had been

10. Min. to M. de Muy, July 23, 1707, AC, B 29, f. 278.

in charge of the impressment service (as commissary of classes) at Bayonne for several years (1704–1707) prior to this appointment. Reared in the Château d'Iron, Dartaguiette was "a man of good family" and, despite his youth (he was two-and-a-half years younger than Bienville), was considered capable and thorough.[11]

In a letter drafted three weeks after the commissary's appointment on June 5, Louis XIV spelled out his instructions to Dartaguiette in detail:

> As soon as he [Dartaguiette] arrives he will have an account rendered by the Sieur de La Salle, the clerk performing the functions of commissary there, of all funds which have passed through his hands. He will determine whether they have been used economically and whether the expenditures have been real. He will examine thoroughly the conduct that the said Sieur de La Salle has observed in the functions of his office. He will draw up with him the accounts of each year and will report vouchers in due form for all the expenses to be transmitted to the general treasurers of the Marine so that they may be able to have their accounts for their fiscal year drawn up.[12]

In addition to auditing the account books, Dartaguiette was to inspect the warehouses and the statements of the *gardes-magasin*, to examine the agreements with the Spanish at Pensacola, and to investigate the general needs of the colony and the various statements made by La Salle and Bienville.[13]

After Pontchartrain received his most recent reports from La Salle, he enlarged Dartaguiette's responsibilities (as he had broadened those of Daneau de Muy), directing the *commissaire* to work in conjunction with the new governor in determining the truth of La Salle's charges. Dartaguiette was given the task of filing the official reports:

> You must send me a *mémoire* in great detail about everything that you will have learned about the conduct of the said Sieur de Bienville, both about the new facts that the said Sieur de

11. Min. to Dartaguiette, June 30, 1707, AC, B 29, f. 284–85. Dartaguiette was born in Mendionde on Nov. 5, 1682. AM, C 7, 9. LSMA, DCS, Aug. 23, 1730. AN, MC, XCVI–273, April 22, 1723. Dépôt d'extrait mortuaire, Oct. 25, 1720, AN, MC, CVIII–347. Mémoires pour Martin Dartaguiette, BN, f° FM, 4429–4431. Min. to Dartaguiette, July 23, 1707, AC, B 29, f. 278v–79v. AN, V1, 141, 162.

12. Mémoire du Roy, June 30, 1707, AC, B 29, f. 266v–67.

13. *Ibid.*, f. 267v–72.

> La Salle advances, and about all the points that concern him which is mentioned in your instructions, together with the proofs that you are able to obtain. I am convinced that nothing will prevent you from rendering me a faithful and exact account of everything you will learn and that I will have reason to be pleased with you in all of this.[14]

His responsibilities thus fixed, Dartaguiette, with his twelve-year-old brother, Bernard Dartaguiette, and an even younger brother, Pierre, left Bayonne for Rochefort from where the *Renommée* was scheduled to depart for Louisiana by late summer. With the appointments of a new governor and a competent commissary to bring order into the accounts, plans for a more skillfully administrated colony seemed set. There remained but one rather delicate question: what action, if any, was to be taken with regard to the parish priest, Roulleaux de La Vente? If La Salle had been successful in hanging a cloud over the conduct of Bienville, the commandant (backed by the sworn testimonies of Boisbriant, Gravier and numerous inhabitants) had been even more successful in damaging the reputation of the parish priest. Should La Vente be summarily recalled; or could so many witnesses be so mistaken (or biased) regarding his customary demeanor? If he were recalled, whom did the seminary have available to replace him? [15]

Aware of the derogatory reports being received by the ministry of marine, and suspecting that Gravier was busy adding aspersion to injury, the seminary directors submitted a report (soon after the Jesuit's arrival in Paris) in vigorous defense of their Mobile pastor. Those at the seminary who knew La Vente intimately could not swallow the charges currently being made, especially since the majority of attacks seemed inspired by the "arch-plotter" Gravier and by a brother of the scandalous Le Moynes. In all truth, the information being circulated about La Vente was of a side of the pastor the directors knew not at all. Until his transfer to Louisiana, La Vente had been noted for his zeal, decorum and eloquence, and little else.[16]

14. Min. to Dartaguiette, July 23, 1707, AC, B 29, f. 278v–79.

15. Min. to Bégon, July 6, 1707, AC, B 29, f. 273. At Rochefort Dartaguiette demanded and eventually received private quarters on the *Renommée*. Dartaguiette to min., Aug. 6, 1707, AC, C13A, 2, f. 49–52. Min. to Brisacier, May 25, 1707, AC, B 29, f. 262–62v. Min. to Demuy, June 30, 1707, AC, B 29, f. 260v–61. Tremblay [to SQ Dirs.], May 8, 1707, ASQ, Lettres, M 37.

16. SME Dirs. [to min.], March, 1707, AC, C11A, 27, f. 41–41v.

Upon receiving the seminary's message, Pontchartrain suggested that its defense of the pastor seemed unsupported by fact, that the directors ought to "recall a man of such ill temper that even his *confrères* suffered from it." The minister tartly added that in addition to replacing La Vente, the seminary would do well to send more missionaries into the field since it was "receiving funds enough for this enterprise." Some weeks later, Pontchartrain sent Daneau de Muy to confront Brisacier in person on the matter, at the conclusion of which meeting Brisacier offered a surprising suggestion: that La Vente be treated in much the same way as Bienville. Upon the new governor's arrival in the colony, he should look carefully into the matter. If, in Daneau de Muy's judgment, the facts merited La Vente's removal, then the pastor should also be sent home on the return voyage of the *Renommée*.[17]

Pontchartrain wasted little time in agreeing to Brisacier's proposition. It was fair enough of the seminary to suggest it, and the minister had confidence enough in his new governor to believe that he would view the facts "with prudence and for the harmony and good service of the colony." With this complication apparently resolved, Pontchartrain proceeded with his final instructions for the officials soon to leave for Mobile.[18]

By the late summer of 1707, the new governor, the commissary and his younger brothers, and a host of other personnel were all at Rochefort, waiting to embark on the *Renommée*, a ship which had made two previous voyages to the colony, captained now by Beaumont d'Eschilais and seconded by the Sieur La Popilière. Besides Daneau de Muy and the Dartaguiette brothers, the shiplist included Daneau's twelve-year-old son, Jacques-Pierre, Jacques Gravier, the shipbuilder Jacques Le Roux, thirty-four soldiers and three officers, and a young habitant-to-be from Mont Louis (archbishopric of Tours-en-Tourain) named Nicolas Bodin. The *Renommée*, substantially overburdened, was to be accompanied by a smaller ship, the *Indien*, commanded by Nicolas-Gédéon de Voutron.[19]

The outfitting of the ships suffered innumerable delays; it was

17. *Ibid.*, f. 41v. Min. to Brisacier, May 25, 1707, AC, B 29, f. 261v–62. Brisacier to min., June 4, 1707, AC, C11A, 27, f. 34–34v.

18. Min. to Brisacier, June 15, 1707, AC, B 29, f. 264–64v. Min. to Demuy, June 30, 1707, *loc. cit.*, f. 258v–62.

19. Min. to Bégon, July 6, 1707, AC, B 29, f. 273. Bienville to min., Feb. 25, 1708, AC, C13A, 2, f. 111–12, 114. Min. to Demuy, July 6, 1707, AC, B 29, f. 274. Min. to Bégon, July 13, 1707, AM, B2, 198, f. 129–30. Min. to Bégon, Nov. 2, 1707, AM, B2, 199, f. 487.

not until October 24 that they finally departed Rochefort. Just before departure, Captain Deschilais had shifted ten of the thirty-four soldiers to a merchant ship from La Rochelle, the *Branche d'Olivier*. On the sixteenth of November a storm separated the merchant ship from the *Renommée* and several weeks later when the *Renommée* and *Indien* arrived at Cap-français, Dartaguiette was uncertain as to whether the missing ship had been wrecked. Accordingly, he convinced the governor of Saint-Domingue, the Comte de Choiseul-Beaupré, to replace at least five of the lost recruits, bringing the total of desperately-needed soldiers to twenty-nine.[20]

By the last week in January, the *Renommée* was approaching Havana where the officers were to disembark for a conference with Spanish authorities and to make arrangements with Jean-Baptiste Ducasse, former governor of Saint-Domingue and currently *générale des armées navales*, for the ship to receive merchandise on her return trip from Mobile. Before reaching port, however, Governor Daneau de Muy took sick and died aboard ship (on January 25) and was apparently buried at sea.[21]

The death of the governor quite naturally threw plans of the ship's authorities into disarray. The stunned officers now looked to young Dartaguiette for direction. After several days in Havana, Dartaguiette grew anxious to set sail for Massacre Island; yet one final detail remained: what arrangements were to be made regarding the disposal of the late governor's papers? Apparently Daneau's instructions were appropriated by Ducasse, who, after examining them, brought them to his quarters for safe-keeping. It is possible that Ducasse made copies of portions of the instructions and sent them on to Bienville (although Bienville more than once denied it), or at least sent the commandant a note warning him of what the instructions contained. In any case, the papers were eventually given over to Dartaguiette before he left Havana, the commissary already having had a fairly precise idea of their contents.[22]

20. Dartaguiette to min., Feb. 26, 1708, AC, C13A, 2, f. 237–38. Both Beaumont d'Echilais and Voutron were subsequently accused of boarding merchandise for their own profit. Min. to Bégon, Nov. 23, 1707, AM, B2, 199, f. 765–71.

21. Min. to Deschilais, Aug. 17, 1707, AC, B 29, f. 287. Dartaguiette to min., Feb. 26, 1708, *loc. cit.*, f. 237–40. AC, F1A, 17, f. 95. No entry appears in the Havana burial registers for Nicolas Daneau de Muy. Archivo de la Catedral de San Cristóbal de la Habana, Registro de las Sepulturas, año de 1708.

22. Antoine Laumet, *dit* Lamothe Cadillac, soon-to-be governor of Louisiana, in fact, made such a charge against Ducasse. Cadillac to min.,

On the second of February the *Renommée* finally weighed anchor and on the eleventh day of that same month reached Massacre Island. Shortly after landing, Deschilais informed Dartaguiette that he planned to leave the port by the first of March, which prompted Dartaguiette to make plans for a quick trip to Fort Louis. Besides making arrangements with La Salle for the reception of the new cargo into the fort's warehouse, the commissary wished to set the stage for his inquiry so as to be able to submit a preliminary report to Pontchartrain by the *Renommée's* return voyage. Contrary winds prevented the commissary from leaving Massacre Island until the seventeenth. By eleven o'clock on the evening of the nineteenth, Dartaguiette had reached Fort Louis, in the company of Bienville and Châteaugué, both of whom had come down to the port to receive him. Bienville was quick to suggest that the commissary lodge with Châteaugué (since Châteaugué occupied a large, comfortable dwelling), an offer that Dartaguiette readily accepted; but the next day Dartaguiette left again for Massacre Island, to maintain as best he could close surveillance on the transference of goods, since the dispensation of merchandise was a cardinal point of his investigations.[23]

The unloading had been proceeding much slower than expected. After several days' observation, Deschilais assured Dartaguiette that the *Renommée* would not be able to leave on schedule, that the commissary, if he hurried, would have time enough to complete his preliminary reports. Dartaguiette, having observed closely the procedures used in transporting the goods from the Massacre Island warehouse to Fort Louis, then prepared to return to the fort. Already he had a suggestion for avoiding the waste about which La Salle had so loudly complained:

> For the thefts that they [La Salle and La Vente] say were made of the effects of the king in the transporting of goods from Massacre Island to Fort Louis, it can hardly be caused except by the negligence of him who loads them at Massacre Island and of the one who receives them at the warehouse at

Oct. 26, 1713, AC, C13A, 3, f. 60–62. The close relationship between Ducasse and the Le Moynes was well known. Iberville to min., Dec. 31, 1698, AM, B4, 19, f. 376–77. Ducasse to min., Jan. 13, 1699, AC, C9A, 4, f. 1–2v. Although Bienville denied having received copies from Ducasse, he did seem to exhibit prior knowledge of some of the specifics contained in the instructions. Bienville to min., Feb. 25, 1708, *loc. cit.*, f. 90–92, 102–03, 105–09, 111–15.

23. Dartaguiette to min., Feb. 26, 1708, AC, C13A, 2, f. 239–41.

> Fort Louis. The first one should send a list of what he loads, and the other should make out a receipt for the goods which should conform to the list sent. When goods cannot be accounted for, a statement should be made of what is lacking in order to make those pay who were responsible for transporting them. It actually should be easy to maintain control here since those who do the transporting are all Canadians or sailors on the wages of the king from whom one has only to retain the value of the lost goods from their wages as the penalty due for their crime.[24]

The next day, Dartaguiette sailed upstream toward the fort, wondering no doubt how such an obvious solution had escaped both Bienville and La Salle. In any case, no goods as yet seemed to have been lost on these early transferences. Back at the fort on the twenty-third of February, Dartaguiette readied himself for what would prove to be four of the most active days of his three years' stay in Louisiana. Early the next morning, he set up quarters in La Salle's office and with M. La Popilière, *capitaine-en-second* of the *Renommée*, as attestant, began preparing to call witnesses for the first day's preliminary inquiry. In the meantime, La Salle's assistant, Christophe Poirier, was occupied in supervising the reception of merchandise at the fort, while Bienville and Gravier were on their way to Massacre Island for a final conference with Captain Deschilais.[25]

Faced with the problem of deciding which of the inhabitants to interrogate, Dartaguiette was somewhat at a loss. Before he left for Massacre Island, however, Bienville had approached Dartaguiette on the matter. The commandant showed him the letter he had recently received from Pontchartrain in which the minister had rather bluntly discussed the charges against him. After Pontchartrain had informed Bienville that the king was sending a new authority to supercede him, the minister had added:

> . . . I shall only tell you that he [Daneau de Muy] has been informed that on the arrival of the vessel *Aigle* you used His Majesty's crews and boats to transport your own goods and those of the officers of the ships, goods which were then sold to the inhabitants at an exorbitant price; that you sent a great

24. Mémoire de Dartaguiette, Feb. 26, 1708, AC, C13A, 2, f. 63–64.

25. Dartaguiette to min., Feb. 26, 1708, *loc. cit.*, f. 239–41. La Salle to min., March 4, 1708, AC, C13B, 1, No. 8, f. 2. Lettre du P. Gravier, Feb. 23, 1708, *JR*, *LXVI*, p. 143.

> deal of merchandise and brandy to Pensacola for your own profit; that you have taken from His Majesty's warehouses everything you have thought fit; that the crews of the small vessels that are at Mobile have almost always been used for the account of Sieur d'Iberville and of your other brothers to transport their goods to Veracruz and to take the peltries coming from the Mississippi *coureurs-de-bois* to His Majesty's vessels for the purpose of transporting them to France; and lastly that you have been carrying on open commerce by which it is claimed you have made vast profits. If you have followed such a course of conduct, His Majesty has great reason to complain of you and will punish you severely.[26]

After showing this letter to Dartaguiette, Bienville informed the commissary that he did not doubt that Dartaguiette had an order to make an investigation of all accusations his enemies had seen fit to make against him; that, if this were the case, Dartaguiette was welcome to subpoena any witnesses he needed, with his [Bienville's] full co-operation. The commandant, in passing, commented that while Divine Providence had seen fit to allow him to continue in office, that he was perfectly willing under the circumstances to share that power with Dartaguiette, and that he would henceforth make no major decisions without Dartaguiette's advice and consent. No doubt Dartaguiette was moved by Bienville's unusual show of courtesy, of deference to the young commissary's position. However, Bienville had recognized from the beginning that Dartaguiette was holding the reins of power, that his future was now almost entirely dependent on the report that the commissary would file. "Time will show the truth of all things," Bienville confidently told Dartaguiette before leaving for Île Massacre.[27]

Bienville's statement that Dartaguiette was welcome to call "any witnesses he needed," was, notwithstanding, an empty gesture. Bienville was only telling Dartaguiette what he already knew. The question was, *which* witnesses would best be called? "I have begun with the *habitants* who appeared to me least interested in the private quarrels," Dartaguiette wrote a few days later, but he could not know at the time (being as yet unfamiliar with the per-

26. Min. to Bienville, June 30, 1707, AC, B 29, f. 262v–63.
27. Dartaguiette to min., Feb. 26, 1708, *loc. cit.*, f. 239–41.

sonalities involved) that four of the seven choices he made were among Bienville's staunchest supporters.[28]

The first witness to appear before the inquest was Joseph Chauvin, *dit* Léry, one of three Chauvin brothers presently in the colony and one for whom on several occasions Bienville had done favors. Léry was quick to disclaim any knowledge of possible wrongdoing in connection with the voyages made to Veracruz and Havana (possibly because he may have, along with his brother Jacques, been one of those Canadians sending items aboard the ships to be sold at those ports). He was also quick to deny knowledge of any other activity that may have connected the Le Moynes to illicit commerce, although he admitted buying a number of articles from Bienville's warehousekeeper, Jacques Allemand. On all occasions, Léry claimed that whenever he obtained anything from the king's storehouse, it was always by a note from Bienville and with the consent of La Salle. When questioned by Dartaguiette as to whether or not he was satisfied with Bienville's administration of the colony, the Canadian replied that he "was so very well pleased he would never want any other authority as long as he lived in these lands." [29]

With this strong testimonial, Dartaguiette ended the interrogation for the day. The next morning, the twenty-fifth of February, the commissary called his second witness. Like Chauvin, *dit* Léry, François Trudeau was a native Canadian and staunch Bienvillist whom the commandant had especially favored by allowing him to work for the Spaniards in Pensacola. By such employment, Trudeau had earned a good deal of hard cash. He returned the favor by purchasing goods from Bienville (in one instance, a Negro slave for one hundred *piastres*), a fact he stated under cross-examination. But also like Léry, he denied knowledge of anything

28. *Ibid.* f. 240–41. Dartaguiette's use of the word *habitants* indicates by what standard he actually made his selection of witnesses; he chose them exclusively from the list of those few (eleven) who were not on the wages of the king. Mémoire de Dartaguiette, Feb. 26, 1708, *loc. cit.*, f. 59–60. AC, F1A, 13, f. 113–19v.

29. Another Chauvin brother, Nicolas, *dit* La Fresnière, was at this time in La Rochelle. La Vente [to Fleury], Aug. 1, 1706, ASQ, Lettres, R 80. Dénombrement du 20 déc., 1724, AC, G1, 464. Léry, a bachelor, was nearing his thirty-fourth birthday. *DGFC, I*, p. 123. Interrogatoire des habitants, Feb. 24, 1708, AC, C13A, 2, f. 255–61. Léry further stated that Bienville often sent him wine, when he needed it, from his own supply. *Ibid.*, f. 258–59.

unlawful on Bienville's part and upheld him in the strongest terms.[30]

One of La Salle's charges that especially interested Dartaguiette (and one on which Trudeau was to shed some light) was the claim that Bienville had on several occasions intercepted certain letters bound for Paris and Versailles, especially those letters intended for delivery by the vessel *Aigle*. Both La Vente and La Salle had made this accusation against Bienville, and the king, through Pontchartrain, had instructed Dartaguiette to determine the truth of the matter. Pontchartrain had, in fact, mentioned this accusal by La Vente in his most recent letter to Bienville. The commandant, upon reading Pontchartrain's words, was enraged. Confronting La Vente with Pontchartrain's letter, in the presence of a group of officers, Bienville demanded an explanation. At first, La Vente denied knowing anything about the accusation, then later mentioned that he thought La Salle may have made that charge "on a mere suspicion." Pressed for details, the pastor admitted that since the time the accusation had been made, that both he and La Salle had learned by reports from Havana that the letters were still on board the *Aigle* when that vessel called at the Spanish port; that, in fact, François Le Maire had personally delivered the letters to Ensign Dauberville when the *Aigle* was leaving Massacre Island. La Vente finally confessed that he had been mistaken about the entire matter and that "we shouldn't think about it any longer," but Bienville was not about to lose his advantage. The accusations had been made in writing; the commandant would make certain that testimony supporting his innocence would also be recorded. In the presence of witnesses, Bienville took an affidavit from François Le Maire, and when, a few days later, the question was put to François Trudeau (who had also been an eye-witness to the exchange of the letters in 1706), the matter seemed settled, as Trudeau testified he had seen La Vente's rowboat arrive at the port with letters known to be those of the pastor. This testimony, coupled with Le Maire's affidavit, was enough to convince Dar-

30. Interrogatoire des habitants, Feb. 25, 1708, AC, C13A, 2, f. 263–66, 69. Moscoso al virrey, Oct. 12, 1707, AGI, *México*, L. 633. The testimony of Jean-Baptiste Saucier, scheduled for Feb. 24, was apparently never taken. Interrogatoire des habitants . . . par M. d'Artaguiette, Feb. 27, 1708, AC, C13A, 2, f. 249–53. Perhaps Saucier was one of those Bienville was accused of "sending away."

taguiette that Bienville was almost certainly innocent of one of the major charges fostered against him.[31]

Still, the question of illicit commerce remained. The testimonies of Léry and Trudeau had failed to produce decisive evidence. After Trudeau's attestations had been read back to him and approved, Dartaguiette called Jean-Baptiste Joussette, *dit* La Loire, another Canadian who staunchly supported Bienville. La Loire's statements echoed the majority of responses made by the two preceding witnesses. On La Salle's charge that Bienville had traded goods the king sent as presents for the savages (in return for the savages' deermeat which was subsequently sold by Bienville for his own profit), La Loire flatly declared that "nothing of the sort had ever been practiced." La Loire admitted he had purchased certain goods from Bienville (a cask of wine, a supply of Rouen linen), but denied that Bienville ever had a warehouse under another name than his own. Nor did he substantiate the charge that Bienville drank and sold wine sent by the king for the purpose of nourishing the sick, another claim made by La Salle.[32]

Later on that afternoon Dartaguiette called his final witness of the day, Guillaume Boutin. Like the three previous witnesses, Boutin was a Canadian, but unlike Léry, Trudeau and La Loire, he was no supporter of Bienville. Hot-tempered, rebellious, Boutin was, in fact, a sworn antagonist of the commandant. More than once the Canadian had come under Bienville's fire for acts of insubordination, and Bienville had responded by threatening him with chains, labeling him "the most seditious man in the colony." Lately, Boutin had petitioned the government to be allowed to remove with his wife and family to Cap-français, but Bienville had spitefully blocked that request. Here, then, was an inhabitant who had reason to testify *against* the commandant, who would not fail to tell what he knew.[33]

The difficulty was, as Dartaguiette was to discover, Boutin

31. Min. to Bienville, June 30, 1707, AC, B 29, f. 263v. La Salle to Bégon, Aug. 10, 1706, AC, C13A, 1, f. 569. La Salle to min., Sept. 7, 1706, AC, C13A, 1, f. 490–92. Min. to Bégon, Jan. 19, 1706, AM, B2, 196, f. 311–21.

32. Interrogatoire des habitants, Feb. 25, 1708, AC, C13A, 2, f. 272–73, 275.

33. *DGFC, I*, p. 82. AC, F1A, 10, f. 284. ADM, A, Dec. 23, 1707. Bienville to min., Feb. 25, 1708, *loc. cit.*, f. 105–06. Min. to M. Demuy, Sept. 27, 1707, AC, B 29, f. 288. Bienville had removed Boutin from the pay of the king as early as 1704. AC, F1A, 11, f. 73, 220–20v.

didn't know very much, at least not much that could be treated as evidence. He charged the commandant with using one of the king's vessels, the *Espérance*, to transport his Canadian supporters' cattle from the Mississippi to Mobile, an uncalled-for show of favor that led to the loss of that ship in a squall. However, he could offer no supporting facts. He testified that he had purchased numerous articles from Bienville's warehousekeeper, but could give no information on a "secret" *magasin* that the commandant may have been operating. He claimed that Bienville had sold wine to La Loire and François Lemay, but he was unable to specify how much had been purchased or for what price. He swore that on the arrival of the *Aigle* Payen de Noyan and his officers had put ashore a substantial amount of vendibles, such as brandy and linen, and that Bienville and Châteaugué had bought the whole lot, but again he was unable to give details concerning the alleged transactions. On the question of whether Bienville had used the king's ships to sell any of these commodities at Veracruz, Boutin maintained that "he had heard that it was so," but could not offer "definite proof."[34]

Boutin's testimony left Dartaguiette somewhat disconcerted. The Canadian had made serious charges, corroborating several of La Salle's accusations, but he was unable to be very specific about any of them. Too, having been so personally hostile to Bienville, Boutin was not exactly among the "least interested" of witnesses. Perhaps his testimony was too biased to be taken seriously. Still, Dartaguiette's suspicions had been aroused.[35]

The next day, Étienne Burelle, a native Parisian who had spent most of his adulthood in Canada, took the oath. Burelle, François Trudeau's father-in-law, was no doubt uneasy about being called to testify. While he disliked Bienville personally, Burelle's two Canadian sons-in-law (the other being Claude Trépanier) were staunch supporters of Bienville. Too, the Mobile merchant was nearing fifty-two years, an age too advanced to be making enemies of such powerful men as the Le Moyne brothers. As a local businessman, he well knew who best could scratch his back.[36] Upon being asked whether he was pleased with Bienville's conduct of the government and whether he knew anything damaging against

34. Interrogatoire des habitants, Feb. 25, 1708, AC, C13A, 2, f. 279–80, 282, 285.

35. *Ibid.*, f. 280–81, 283–84.

36. *DGFC*, I, p. 96. ADM, A, Nov. 27, 1707; A, March 17, 1708. AC, F1A, 13, f. 117v. Bienville to min., Feb. 25, 1708, *loc. cit.*, f. 104.

Bienville's character or conduct, Burelle answered that he knew nothing at all against the commandant, that he was well satisfied with his administration and that he prayed God he would never live under any other. Burelle further testified that he knew nothing about a separate warehouse belonging to Bienville, and that far from selling the king's wine meant for the sick, that the commandant had often given the sick some from his own supply. While he did admit that he had purchased supplies from Bienville and Châteaugué, as well as a good deal of merchandise from Payen de Noyan, Burelle's testimony was perhaps the strongest yet in favor of the commandant, which must have puzzled Dartaguiette somewhat in view of what the commissary had discovered the day before of the cool relationship between Burelle and Bienville. Had the Parisian merchant been intimidated by the power and influence of the commandant? Dartaguiette could well wonder.[37]

When Jacques Chauvin took the witness chair later that same day, Dartaguiette could almost anticipate his responses. This illiterate Canadian, like his younger brother Léry, denied knowing anything detrimental to Bienville's reputation, maintaining from the start that he had always been well-pleased with Bienville's conduct of the government. He did, however, confess that, as a private individual, he had sent for sale (with Bienville's consent) a small number of articles (a few dozen pairs of stockings, fourteen pieces of Brittany linen, two or three pounds of thread, etc.) to Veracruz on one of the king's ships, an admission that caused Dartaguiette to wonder if other of the inhabitants had not done the same thing, and, if so, how much had actually been sent at the king's expense? And while Chauvin disclaimed any knowledge of Bienville's warehouse, he did admit that the late Iberville had goods sold from such a *magasin*.[38]

The final witness called by Dartaguiette was the Rochefort gunsmith René Boyer, thirty-two-year-old husband of Marie-Catherine Christophe, and a man Bienville had twice put in irons. Boyer, bitter at Bienville for having punished him so severely, was perhaps even more resentful at having been removed from the king's pay only two months prior. Under questioning, the gunsmith charged that indeed Bienville had operated a warehouse under a name other than his own, that he himself had purchased several articles, that

37. Interrogatoire des habitants, Feb. 26, 1708, AC, C13A, 2, f. 287–89, 291, 293–94.

38. *Ibid.*, f. 296–97, 299–301.

these goods were sold from a building that was situated near the river, formerly belonging to Iberville, and that since the time that the *Aigle* sailed back to France it had been managed by Madame Le Sueur (Marguerite Messier) for both Bienville and Châteaugué. Furthermore, Boyer claimed, the Le Moyne brothers had regularly sent merchandise on the voyages to Veracruz and Havana for their private gain.[39]

His curiosity piqued, Dartaguiette asked what sort of wares Boyer was referring to. The gunsmith answered: "All kinds of goods—brandy, linen, hats, shirts, shoes, etc." When the commissary then questioned how Boyer knew that these articles belonged to Bienville and Châteaugué, Boyer replied that he had seen them being unloaded and that the two brothers took great pains to have them marked—always with a "B." Spurred by Dartaguiette's questioning, Boyer went on to describe how, two years before, numerous articles had been landed from the *Aigle* on Payen de Noyan's account, how Iberville, during the years 1702–1706, had always kept his warehouse full, and how both Bienville and Iberville had in past years sold huge amounts of gunpowder belonging to the king's powder magazine. According to Boyer, he himself, along with another gunsmith, had been employed privately by the Le Moynes (even while in the pay of the king) to assemble thirty guns which were later sold to the Spanish for ten or twelve *piastres* each, all for the Le Moynes' profit. He further charged that numerous of the king's weapons had been ruined because those responsible for their care were continually occupied in the service of Iberville and Bienville. Prodded for further details, Boyer estimated that more than three hundred rifles had been lost because of this practice, that nevertheless he was instructed to assure those who offered to buy them that the guns were in good condition although in reality they were practically worthless.[40]

Despite Boyer's pointed testimony on the aforementioned counts, the gunsmith refused to commit himself on a major charge set forth by La Salle: that the Canadians were selling at exorbitant prices goods sold them at moderate cost by Bienville from the

39. ADM, A, June 19, 1707. AC, F1A, 13, f. 119v. Bienville to min., Feb. 25, 1708, *loc. cit.*, f. 106–07. Interrogatoire . . . , Feb. 27, 1708, AC, C13A, 2, f. 303–04.

40. *Ibid.*, f. 305–07, 309, 311–12. After Boyer's testimony, Dartaguiette personally inspected the warehouse kept by the widow Le Sueur under the pretext of renting it. Mémoire . . . par Dartaguiette, Feb. 25, 1707, AC, C13A, 2, f. 72.

king's warehouse. In fact, when questioned by Dartaguiette as to whether or not it were true that Bienville had the Canadians sell those same goods back to the king at four hundred per cent above the price at which they had been given them, Boyer gave a flat "no" response. Nevertheless, the whole of Boyer's testimony, coming as it did from an eyewitness, a participant, and a former private employee of the Le Moynes, cast grave doubt on the honesty and good faith of both the commandant and Châteaugué.[41]

Dartaguiette's task, however, was not to press charges against Bienville (his was not the role of public prosecutor), but to acquire information that would enable him to file an accurate report on the validity of La Salle's accusations.[42] He must be concerned about Bienville's innocence as well as his guilt, and the weight of personal testimony, prejudiced as it may have been, seemed in support of the commandant. Of the seven witnesses, only two had made serious charges against Bienville and of these (Boutin and Boyer) only Boyer could offer anything like concrete details. No doubt Dartaguiette's suspicions of Bienville's conduct were aroused (he had quickly been convinced of the guilt of Iberville and Bienville's brother-in-law, Payen de Noyan); they were stirred even further when Bienville, hearing the names of the witnesses who were testifying, challenged their testimony without knowing what they had said. Dartaguiette must have wondered, for example, why Bienville spoke so harshly of Étienne Burelle when in fact Burelle, by his testimony, had strongly supported him. Were some of these witnesses being subtly intimidated? [43]

Dartaguiette's specific instructions from Pontchartrain had been "to examine together with M. de Muy the accusations made against M. de Bienville, and, in case of mutual agreement as to proof of guilt, that the said M. de Muy is to have him arrested and sent to France as a prisoner [aboard the *Renommée*]." [44] The

41. Interrogatoire . . . , Feb. 27, 1708, *loc. cit.*, f. 307–08.

42. Mémoire du Roy, June 30, 1707, AC, B 29, f. 266v–71. Min. to Dartaguiette, July 23, 1707, AC, B 29, f. 278v–79v.

43. Interrogatoire . . . , Feb. 27, 1708, AC, C13A, 2, f. 249–53. Bienville to min., Feb. 25, 1708, *loc. cit.*, f. 104. However, when Dartaguiette summarized his findings in his memoirs of Feb. 25 and 26, he had not yet taken the testimony of René Boyer. Both La Salle and La Vente maintained that the witnesses were afraid to speak out since Bienville remained in command, a charge with which Pontchartrain wholly agreed. La Salle to min., March 4, 1708, AC, C13A, 2, f. 155. Min. to Dartaguiette, July 11, 1709, AC, B 30, f. 185–86.

44. Min. to Dartaguiette, July 23, 1707, *loc. cit.*, f. 279.

investigator's immediate difficulties, then, were two-fold: Captain Deschilais' insistence on embarking as soon as possible after the ship's unloading did not leave Dartaguiette nearly enough time to reach so consequential a judgment as Pontchartrain would have liked; he had not yet even had time enough to examine La Salle's account books. Secondly, the death of Daneau de Muy had immeasurably hampered the entire investigation. Even if Dartaguiette had been fully convinced of Bienville's guilt, his authority to act on his findings was severely limited. Only the late governor had been empowered to order Bienville's arrest; without the governor's consent, the commissary himself was without authority to remove the commandant under any circumstances, a fact Bienville would have no doubt been quick to point out (after demanding to see Dartaguiette's instructions). The commissary, an immensely practical man, thus saw clearly what must transpire: barring accident, disease or murder, Bienville would remain in command of Louisiana, at least until the next ship arrived from France, and, excluding a radical order from Pontchartrain, probably much longer. And Dartaguiette, who planned to remain in the colony only until the next vessel's arrival, had best conform to that reality.[45]

In truth, Dartaguiette had been favorably impressed with Bienville's ability as well as with his attitude. The more he saw of him the more certain he was that the young Canadian was the best man available to exercise authority over the colony. The commandant, contrary to those reports sent by La Vente and La Salle, seemed exceptionally open and without guile. Had he not allowed Dartaguiette to read an unusually personal and disparaging letter from Pontchartrain? He even seemed to possess a degree of humility: upon the arrival of the *Renommée*, Bienville had proposed that Captain Deschilais allow his second-in-command, the Sieur La Popilière, to command in his (Bienville's) place. When Deschilais demurred, Bienville offered to share all his authority with Dartaguiette. In every way possible the commandant seemed unusually co-operative. Apart from this, in lodging with Châteaugué and dining daily with him and Bienville, Dartaguiette was able to hear without interference the Le Moynes' version of the whole affair—their good intentions and high aspirations for the growth of the colony. In short, Dartaguiette was being wooed and won, La

45. Dartaguiette to min., Feb. 26, 1708, *loc. cit.*, f. 238–41. Mémoire de Dartaguiette, Feb. 26, 1708, *loc. cit.*, f. 57–58.

Vente and La Salle having little chance to approach the commissary on any intimate terms.[46]

When the majority of the testimonies had been concluded, Dartaguiette hurriedly drafted several memoirs to accompany the abstracts of the declarations and sent them on to Captain Deschilais. He admitted that the investigation was incomplete but promised to continue gathering evidence (at a more leisurely pace). Nevertheless, the co-commissary had finally succeeded in procuring more exact information on a number of other questions raised by Pontchartrain and had arrived at some tentative conclusions. First of all, La Salle had failed to render exact accounts. To unsnarl this complexity would demand close attention, inasmuch as the scrivener had allowed a singular degree of disorder to creep into his registers. In regard to La Salle's charge that Bienville's kitchen was situated next to the warehouse in the fort, allowing Bienville's servants easy access, Dartaguiette gave a detailed description of the relationship of the buildings, demonstrating that the servants did indeed have convenient entrance; but whether or not they actually took advantage of the opportunity would require further inquiry.[47]

On the charge made by La Salle that Bienville had been receiving the venison brought by the savages and selling it for his own profit, Dartaguiette reported that all the witnesses in the inquest (including both Boutin and Boyer) had testified that the meat was never sold but given away to those who needed it most.[48]

On La Salle's claim that Bienville had "tortured and burned alive an Alabama female prisoner at the gates of Fort Louis," Dartaguiette reported that "the charge is false in all its particulars," that in fact the woman was still alive and living in Mobile.[49]

And on the charge made by La Salle that Bienville had guaranteed certain favored Canadians (among them Antoine Rivard and

46. Dartaguiette to min., Feb. 26, 1708, *loc. cit.*, f. 239–40. La Salle to min., March 4, 1708, AC, C13B, 1, No. 8, f. 2. Pontchartrain's answer to La Salle's report that Dartaguiette was daily dining with the Le Moynes was that "it was very difficult for that to be otherwise in a wilderness like Louisiana." Marginal note on the extract of La Salle's letter of March 4 (AC, C13A, 2, f. 155).

47. Mémoire de Dartaguiette, Feb. 26, 1708, *loc. cit.*, f. 57–69. Dartaguiette to min., Feb. 26, 1708, *loc. cit.*, f. 237–48. Mémoire . . . par Dartaguiette, Feb. 25, 1708, AC, C13A, 2, f. 71–75.

48. Mémoire de Dartaguiette, Feb. 26, 1708, *loc. cit.*, f. 65–67.

49. La Salle to min., Sept. 7, 1706, AC, C13A, 1, f. 474–75. Mémoire de Dartaguiette, Feb. 26, 1708, *loc. cit.*, f. 66–67.

François Dugué) any merchandise they needed without requiring payment, Dartaguiette reported that the promises made by Bienville were only general ones: the commandant would provide *any* potential settler with the means to cultivate the land should he pledge to pay back the king when he was able. In Dartaguiette's opinion, this policy of Bienville's (if slightly irregular) had much to recommend itself, especially if the rich lands at Lake Pontchartrain were to be developed for the benefit of the colony.[50]

In summary, Dartaguiette concluded, from what he could thus far determine, that the bulk of the charges against Bienville were too vague, too unsubstantiated to warrant an outright statement of guilt. While the testimony on several points had indeed been disturbing, the commissary could only promise to continue the investigation and report to Pontchartrain as he uncovered additional facts. Much of the difficulty in the colony, he asserted, stemmed from private quarrels between Bienville and La Salle and there was little way to reconcile contentions of this nature.[51]

If the conducting of an inquest had been damaging to Bienville's authority and prestige among the inhabitants of Mobile, it proved even more injurious to Nicolas de La Salle. Bienville had made numerous charges against the commissary, but the commandant's complaints were general in nature; he alluded to La Salle's pettiness, his sloth and incompetence, etc. But La Salle's charges against Bienville had been much more specific; as a result they could be more easily disproven if false (though the reverse would not prove true). In the course of Dartaguiette's inquiries, La Salle had been caught in two outright fabrications. His charge that Bienville had been instrumental in blocking passage of correspondence between Mobile and France was shown to have been entirely false (at least by all available evidence), and his complaint that Bienville had cruelly burned at the stake a native female prisoner was apparently a malicious lie. Moreover, in his limited association with La Salle, Dartaguiette had already come to have little respect for the *écrivain's* manner of conducting business. His records were in disarray (although, as La Salle justifiably claimed, this was not entirely his fault), his morale was low, and his disposition was fractious. More importantly, his judgment seemed deficient. He overestimated, in Dartaguiette's opinion, the time and difficulty of transporting

50. *Ibid.*, f. 63–65.

51. Interrogatoire des habitants . . . , Feb. 27, 1708, *loc. cit.*, f. 249–53. Mémoire . . . par Dartaguiette, Feb. 25, 1708, *loc. cit.*, f. 76.

goods from Massacre Island to the fort. He demonstrated little initiative or imagination concerning measures needed to safeguard the warehouses at Fort Louis and at the port. "He complains," Dartaguiette wrote Pontchartrain, "that the warehouses are open at all hours of the day. He merely had to order, as I did, that in winter they should be open [only] from two in the afternoon until five, and, in summer, from seven until ten in the morning and from three until six in the afternoon. When that has once been made known those who require anything will conform to it." [52]

Furthermore, on La Salle's suggestion that the king employ a scrivener to serve on the ships going from Mobile to Veracruz and Havana, Dartaguiette responded to Pontchartrain with patient derision: "It seems to me very useless to send a scrivener to Louisiana to serve on the traversiers when these vessels make only one voyage per year to Havana or Veracruz, even less whenever they are employed only to transport the effects from Massacre Island to this fort. One need only appoint one trustworthy man out of those who are already on the wages of the king. It is the same with the guards for these boats; the sailors who are paid all the year by the king can guard them by taking care to have them [the sailors] remain at Massacre Island [only] part of the time . . . whenever there is a vessel there." [53]

With Dartaguiette's preliminary reports completed and delivered to Deschilais, the situation at the fort regarding the colony's high authorities appeared temporarily settled. Both Bienville and La Salle would continue in office, hopefully kept at bay by the young man acting as co-commissary and, in some measure, as co-commandant. Down at Massacre Island, Deschilais was still not prepared to weigh anchor. Much of the merchandise on the *Renommée* had yet to be unloaded. Jacques Gravier, among others, had difficulty in getting his goods transported to the fort. The cost of transference was high (Gravier paid forty-six *livres* for moving his goods) and with only small boats (often overloaded) at hand, the transportation was suffering indefinite delays.[54]

The retardment of the embarkation gave Nicolas de La Salle an opportunity to finish a hasty report giving his own interpretation

52. Mémoire de Dartaguiette, Feb. 26, 1708, *loc. cit.*, f. 65–67. Dartaguiette to min., Feb. 26, 1708, *loc. cit.*, f. 240–41. Mémoire . . . par Dartaguiette, Feb. 25, 1708, *loc. cit.*, f. 75.

53. Mémoire de Dartaguiette, Feb. 26, 1708, *loc. cit.*, f. 66–67.

54. Lettre du P. Jacques Gravier, Feb. 23, 1708, *JR, LXVI*, pp. 124–25. *Journal Historique*, pp. 106–07.

of events transpiring since Dartaguiette's arrival. After complaining that none of the inhabitants had found the courage to speak the full truth against Bienville, because of the fact that the commandant was still in power, La Salle notified Pontchartrain that much of the comestibles aboard the *Renommée* had been lost, and that he was including an official report of the matter. Despite Dartaguiette's precautions, he hinted, it was not so easy as the new commissary thought to prevent the loss of merchandise in this country. He was also sending, he said, the original letter that Iberville had sent him from Nevis two years before which he claimed would further incriminate the Le Moyne family. He furthermore mentioned that two letters had been found among the papers of the late Alexis Guay, warehousekeeper at Massacre Island (whom the Le Moynes had appointed), which would prove sufficiently the illicit commerce that Bienville and Châteaugué had been carrying on in concert with Iberville.[55]

The delay in the ship's departure also gave La Vente a chance to complete a hurried report to Pontchartrain, a letter actually begun some months before. The question of the seminary priest's recall had died for the moment with Daneau de Muy at Havana. Only the governor-designate had been empowered to deal with La Vente; the pastor's fate had not been a part of Dartaguiette's instructions, had not in fact even been mentioned. Thus, the Divine Providence that for the moment had rescued Bienville had also saved La Vente.[56] A week before completing his letter, however, La Vente had changed his mind about remaining at Mobile. Upon seeing that neither the justice of God nor of king was to fall on the objects of his wrath, La Vente had decided to return to France to present his complaints in person. Although utterly discouraged about immediate prospects for a fruitful mission in Louisiana, the passionately bitter priest hoped to at least make the way easier for those who would serve after him, as well as to set the record straight concerning the conduct of Gravier and Bienville. Possibly his revelations could even effect the latter's recall. With these purposes in mind, the pastor made his way to Massacre Island in the company of Albert Davion who had recently returned from the Mississippi.[57]

55. La Salle to min., March 4, 1708, AC, C13B, 1, No. 8, f. 1v, 2v–4.

56. La Vente to min., March 2, 1708, AC, C13A, 2, f. 160–64. AC, F1A, 17, f. 95. Brisacier to min., June 4, 1707, AC, C11A, 27, f. 34–34v. Min. to Brisacier, June 15, 1707, AC, B 29, f. 264v. Mémoire du Roy, June 30, 1707, AC, B 29, f. 260–61. Mémoire du Roy, June 30, 1707, AC, B 29, f. 266v–72.

57. La Vente [to Brisacier], March 4, 1708, ASQ, Lettres, R 79.

It was Marc Bergier who the previous year had suggested to La Vente that a voyage to France might result in the procurement of more material support for his mission as well as give him the opportunity to voice his objections to Jesuit encroachment. La Vente rejected the proposal at first, believing that strongly-worded written pleas might accomplish the same purposes without his having to face the perils of the sea. Moreover, Iberville's replacement as governor, he felt, would surely keep both the Jesuits and the Le Moynes in their proper places. But the death of Daneau de Muy and the return of Gravier had caused the pastor to reconsider. Before leaving the fort, La Vente had brought the matter up in the presence of Bienville and La Salle. Both officials agreed La Vente had the right to make the trip. On first thought, Bienville was elated at the prospect of being rid of the pastor. Once settled in France, the commandant guessed, La Vente would never return. After the pastor had left for the port, however, Bienville had occasion to discuss the matter with Père Gravier. Out of the Jesuit-commandant conversations came a disturbing thought: as irritating as was La Vente's presence in the colony, he could do infinitely more harm in Paris and Versailles. What damage he could accomplish in person to both Jesuit and Le Moyne ambition might be destructive indeed. Would it not be safer to keep the pastor in Mobile, at least until after the selection of a new governor?[58]

Journeying to Massacre Island in late February, Bienville and Gravier found La Vente already aboard ship. A word to Deschilais brought the following result: La Vente was informed by the *Renommée's* captain that without a specific order from the commandant he could not receive him as a passenger. When La Vente turned to Bienville for the order, Bienville refused, smugly replying that "only M. de Muy had the authority to do that." La Vente was enraged at this refusal, realizing the contrivance by which he had been duped: until the last minute he had been led to believe he would be allowed to sail, the disallowance of which, in reality, blocked a crucial communication with Pontchartrain. Tremblay had written him by the *Renommée* that his reputation was suffering immeasurably at court, that to salvage it he must forward to Pontchartrain an extensive, carefully-worded explanation of the entire situation at Mobile. Though ill, La Vente had begun work on this "repugnant task" as soon as he had received Tremblay's

58. Mémoire général des marchandises, [1707], ASQ, Lettres, R 78. La Vente [to Brisacier], March 4, 1708, *loc. cit.*, R 79. Lettre du P. Jacques Gravier, Feb. 23, 1708, *op. cit.*, pp. 138–39.

exhortation. Having obtained Bienville's permission to return to France, however, the pastor had put aside his partially written letter, believing he could present his explanations more effectively in person. Now, at this late hour, there was little time left for drafting a "carefully-worded defense." The *Renommée* was preparing to depart.[59]

La Vente berated Bienville and Gravier for their machinations, then turned on Captain Deschilais for serving as "the commandant's tool" and for "declaring falsely that he could not take me aboard without an order."[60] When Bienville demanded to know the "real reason" La Vente desired to return to France, the pastor fell uncharacteristically silent. Yet there was no need for an answer; they both knew why. His silence, however, allowed Bienville to justify his reasons for refusing the pastor passage:

> . . . M. La Vente is asking me for permission to return to France for some reason or other that he has not sufficiently explained. Because he has no orders from his superiors in France, and as he occupies the position of pastor here, I have been unwilling to permit him to do so, since there is present here only one missionary [Davion] capable of replacing him, who would have been forced to abandon his mission which is more than a hundred leagues from here.[61]

Without Bienville's consent, La Vente was forced to leave the ship. "That is how we are the plaything of men," the pastor moaned to Brisacier, "and how we are in a sort of prison from which we cannot escape." Returning to Fort Louis in a huff, after persuading Deschilais and La Salle (but not Bienville) to sign an affidavit of refusal, La Vente was able to hastily finish his letter to Pontchartrain, though it was anything but a carefully-worded defense. In slapdash, unorganized fashion the pastor attempted to apprise the minister of the commandant's duplicity, then, admitting that his real reason for wishing to return was to vindicate himself in person because of the fear of his letters being intercepted (thus renewing a charge he had only a few days before disavowed), La Vente settled back to brace himself for continued conflicts with the commandant and the newly-returned Jacques Gravier. Doubt-

59. La Vente [to Brisacier], March 4, 1708, *loc. cit.*, R 79. Mémoire de Dartaguiette, Feb. 26, 1708, *loc. cit.*, f. 57–58.

60. La Vente [to Brisacier], March 4, 1708, *loc. cit.*, R 79.

61. Bienville to min., Feb. 25, 1708, *loc. cit.*, f. 111.

less his humor was not improved by the gradual realization that his great haste had been unnecessary. In mid-March the *Renommée* was still resting in port, not to leave until a full three weeks behind the original schedule.[62]

62. La Vente [to Brisacier], March 4, 1708, *loc. cit.*, R 79. La Vente to min., March 2, 1708, *loc. cit.*, f. 160–61. *Journal Historique*, pp. 106–07.

XVIII

Threats from Within and Without

ONE of Dartaguiette's first acts on reaching Mobile was to assemble, in Bienville's presence and with his consent, the Canadians who were still on the payroll of the king.[1] When the Canadians were gathered at the fort (on the twenty-fourth day of February), Bienville read them verbatim the orders he had just received from Pontchartrain:

> He [His Majesty] has strongly disapproved of your having continued to have provisions furnished to the Canadians whom you have received orders to discharge. He has [furthermore] given orders to the Sieur De Muy not to have any more [rations] furnished to them in the future.[2]

Two years before, Bienville had received similar orders from Pontchartrain, but believing support for this group to be absolutely essential for the welfare of the colony, he had neglected to carry out the minister's wishes. In following such a course, the commandant had benefited the settlement (as well as himself, since comrades with credit gave him additional play in his private commerce), and, as a result, had retained the Canadians' singular devotion. But the recent, strongly-worded directive from the minister, as well as the presence of Dartaguiette (who knew, of course, what Daneau de Muy's instructions had been) left Bienville no choice but to order the Canadians removed from the payroll. They were to be stricken from the list as of the first of March.[3]

1. *Journal Historique,* p. 106. Mémoire sur la Louisiane par M. de Mandeville, April 29, 1709, AC, C13A, 2, f. 475. *FLC,* p. 121.
2. Min. to Bienville, June 30, 1707, AC, B 29, f. 263.
3. Bienville to min., Feb. 20, 1707, AC, C13A, 2, f. 9–13. Min. to Bienville, June 30, 1707, *loc. cit.,* f. 263. AC, F1A, 13, f. 117v–18. Min. to La Salle, June 30, 1707, AC, B 29, f. 264. La Salle to min., March 4, 1708, AC, C13B, 1, No. 8, f. 6.

The Canadians were understandably perturbed on receiving notice of their dismissal. How were they to survive without the king's support? Many of them such as Gilbert Dardenne and Vincent Alexandre, *dit* Chenet were married and doing their best to provide for their families. Some, like Jean Colon, *dit* La Violette and Jean-Baptiste Saucier, had several children. The wives of Antoine Rivard and Jean Bourbonnois had recently given birth (each to the second of their children) and François Dupré and Claude Trépanier both had pregnant spouses.[4]

Loudly objecting, those of the Canadians who were unmarried asked for temporary leaves, either to live with the natives or to trap and trade on the Mississippi. If refused, they threatened to desert the colony altogether, some to return to Canada, others to become permanent *coureurs-de-bois*, and still others to defect to Pensacola where their services would surely be in demand. If Pontchartrain's intention was that this dismissal would force the Canadians to become diligent tillers of the soil it seemed apparent that the minister had been grossly mistaken. Far from settling them down, the announcement seemed certain to have the opposite effect.[5]

Indeed this was a crisis for Bienville and Dartaguiette. Both officials realized that only wives would settle the Canadians down permanently; they equally well grasped the fact that without this stalwart group the colony's defense would be immeasurably weakened. The fort would then be protected only by two deficient companies of young soldiers, most of them barely beyond adolescence. There would remain no qualified men for the expeditions and the French would be in grave danger of losing their influence with the natives, which the Canadians with their skill and endurance had helped to maintain.[6]

Bienville and Dartaguiette acted to make the best of a tenuous situation. Between them, using both coercion and appeasement, they strove to convince the Canadians to remain in the colony and to plant, to at least give the soil a chance. The king would aid them as much as possible, they promised. But the king had not yet aided

4. Mémoire sur la Louisiane . . . , April 29, 1709, *loc. cit.*, f. 475. ADM, A, April 2, 1710. ADM, B, Feb. 6, 1726. Dénombrement, Aug. 1, 1706, AC, G1, 464. ADM, A, Oct. 4, 17, Nov. 4, 1707; A, April 8, Oct. 15, Dec. 8, 1708; A, March 12, 1709.

5. Dartaguiette to min., Feb. 26, 1708, AC, C13A, 2, f. 241–44. Mémoire sur la Louisiane . . . , April 29, 1709, *loc. cit.*, f. 475.

6. Dartaguiette to min., May 25, 1708, AC, C13A, 2, f. 319–20. Bienville to min., Feb. 20, 1707, *loc. cit.*, f. 10–13.

them at all, the Canadians retorted. Besides removing them from the rolls of credit, the crown had not even paid them their past wages (in cash) for the years 1705 through 1707. This, of course, Dartaguiette could not deny. It had been past practice for the court to send specie on the supply ships from France which on its arrival was to be distributed to the inhabitants on the payroll (minus deductions for goods supplied from the warehouse). But due to the uncertainty of sea voyages during war time, neither the *Aigle* nor the *Renommée* had carried any specie. The Canadians in particular had been anxiously anticipating payment, needing cash to purchase certain supplies (especially clothes) not available from the *magasin.* By the early spring of 1708 most of the Canadians and their families possessed only garments that had been worn to threads by constant usage over a period of several years. Despite the recent orders of the court, then, one thing seemed clear to the majority of Canadians: if they were to establish themselves with any degree of comfort or well-being, surely they would require some sort of supplement from the crown.[7]

Bienville had little choice but to give some of the Canadians (Jean La Barre and Zacharie Drapeau, for example) permission to live among the natives until the next ship arrived. Furthermore, he distributed to them (with the consent of both Dartaguiette and La Salle) fifty crowns worth of goods at one hundred percent above the price in France, as well as orders on the warehouse for the back salaries due them for the past two years. Moreover, he guaranteed the issuance of certain tools, such as axes, mattocks and handsaws, to those who would attempt to cultivate the land.[8]

Not pleased but at least mollified with this arrangement, the majority of Canadians agreed to remain in the colony; but with Bienville's permission a small number began in the spring of 1708 to move out from Fort Louis (where even the commandant agreed the soil was not suitable for cultivation) to localities where the land showed more promise. Guillaume Boutin moved to the northern bank of the mouth of the *rivière-aux-poules;* Nicolas Bodin, a thirty-one-year-old recently-arrived settler from Mont Louis in France, traveled downstream to the southwesternmost corner of the bay near where the same *rivière-aux-poules* forked to form a

7. Bienville to min., Feb. 25, 1708, *loc. cit.*, f. 91–92. La Vente [to SME Dirs.], June 27, 1708, ASQ, Lettres, R 82. La Salle to min., Sept. 12, 1708, AC, C13A, 2, f. 193–96. Dartaguiette to min., Feb. 26, 1708, *loc. cit.*, f. 241–43.

8. Dartaguiette to min., Aug. 18, 1708, AC, C13A, 2, f. 332–35.

veritable island.[9] Vincent Alexandre, *dit* Chenet, recently married to Marie Preau, moved with his wife to the same vicinity. A few more Canadians moved to the *Oignonets* to join Charles Rochon and Pierre Leboeuf, while Charles Aigron, *dit* Lamothe, André Renaud and François Guillory (among others) transferred to Massacre Island where they began to plant vegetable crops and where they hoped to take advantage of the commercial opportunities certain to arise out of their closer location to Pensacola and to the incoming ships.[10]

But the greatest promise appeared to be at the lands near the Indian villages of the Biloxi and the Colapissa on Bayou Saint-Jean between the Mississippi River and the shores of Lake Pontchartrain. Both Bienville and Dartaguiette (although the latter as yet knew those lands only from hearsay) reported them to be "the finest in the world for raising crops," and Dartaguiette, even at this early date, envisioned the bayou as a site "at which a large settlement could be made to carry on considerable commerce with New Spain and the West Indies." Shortly before the founding of Mobile, Bienville had moved the friendly Biloxi Indians to this location in order to afford the new Fort La Boulaye some measure of native support. After the abandonment of the fort in 1707, Saint-Denis and a few men of his garrison had transferred to a place near the Biloxi village site in order to monitor Indian activities in that district. It was Saint-Denis who first reported to Bienville (and later to Dartaguiette) on the richness of these lands and who was largely responsible for its subsequent development.[11]

9. This island, settled by Bodin (a native of Mont Louis, Tours-en-Tourain), retains the name of Bodin's birthplace in the form of "Mon Louis Island." The original establishment, later called "Miragoane," was one league below the mouth of Fowl River, though Bodin later had another house built at Grosse Pointe. LSMA, DCS, Feb. 1, 1725. ADM, C, Feb. 6, 1746. Carte (ca. 1712), BN, Cartes de la Marine, 13–10–3. Relation de la rivière de la Mobile, AC, C13C, 2, f. 166-66v. *FLC*, pp. 130–31. Carte de la coste de la Louisiane . . . par M. de Sérigny aux années 1719 et 1720, BN, Cartes et plans, 38–1–10 (C11188). The "contrat de cession," signed by Bienville and Dartaguiette on Nov. 12, 1710 and ratified by Cadillac on Sept. 15, 1713, included the entirety of the island from Fowl River to Oyster Pass. Lowrie, *Documents* . . . Vol. III, pp. 19–20. According to Bodin's heirs, the grant consisted of 14, 360 arpents.

10. ADM, A, entry following May 30, 1709. AC, F1A, 13, f. 117v–18. *FLC*, p. 119, 121. *DGFC I*, p. 292.

11. Mémoire pour servir d'instruction au Sieur de Bienville . . . , April 25, 1702, AC, F3, 68, f. 3–3v. Dartaguiette to min., Aug. 18, 1708, AC, C13A, 2, f. 334–35. Bienville to min., Feb. 20, 1707, *loc. cit.*, f. 14. FLC, pp. 121–22.

In the spring of 1708, five aspiring planters (among them Antoine Rivard de La Vigne, François Dugué, Jean-Baptiste Poitié and Nicolas Delon), along with their few Indian slaves, received tools and supplies from the warehouse and journeyed to Lake Pontchartrain to establish themselves at a point where Bayou Tchoupitoulas joined Bayou Saint-Jean. Bienville gave provisional grants of land to each of them (four arpents along Bayou Saint-Jean by thirty-six arpents in depth) on the promise that they would work to cultivate it. The aspiring farmers quickly cleared the land and began to plant wheat, the first seeds for which had been brought from Mobile. Later on that year, Dartaguiette was able to report that "the wheat was coming along very beautifully," although the grain had not yet been harvested.[12]

By a joint effort, then, Bienville and Dartaguiette had averted disaster, had kept the undisciplined Canadians at least temporarily in harness by providing them the means to subsist and perhaps advance themselves by their own vigor and initiative. Although neither the commandant nor the co-commissary were confident they had achieved any permanent solution, they could at least presume that the Canadians would remain in the colony until additional women could be sent, which eventuality they both agreed would be the only hope for making valuable *habitants* out of unbridled woodsmen.[13]

It was fortunate that Pontchartrain's order to dismiss the Canadians came at a time when supplies were relatively plentiful. Although the *Renommée* had not brought sufficient man-power nor additional missionaries nor any specie, she nevertheless delivered a fairly large supply of merchandise. Goods were more abundant now than at any time since the arrival of the *Pélican* in mid-1704. A month prior to the mooring of the *Renommée*, a small French vessel sailing from Havana had anchored at Massacre Island loaded with tobacco, bacon and brandy which was quickly sold to the more able of the colonists. Three weeks later, another French ship (an eighty-ton vessel out of Nantes) reached Port Massacre, bringing more vendibles. The landing of the *Renommée* with a large amount of supplies had not only replenished the settlement but it served to point out one of the colony's most pressing problems—

12. Dartaguiette to min., [extraits, 1708–09], AC, C13A, 2, f. 433–36. La Salle to min., May 12, 1709, AC, C13A, 2, f. 397–98. These "cessions" were not signed until Oct. 28, 1708.

13. Bienville to min., Feb. 25, 1708, *loc. cit.*, f. 92–93. Dartaguiette to min., May 25, 1708, *loc. cit.*, f. 318–21.

the need for suitable vessels to more rapidly transport incoming goods from the port to Fort Louis. Since the loss of the *Espérance* and the *Aventurier*, there had been no medium-sized vessels available to help transfer large amounts of supplies to the town, much less to make vital voyages to Veracruz or Havana. The necessity for using numerous pirogues and canoes to transport the goods from the *Renommée* resulted in heavy fees, as well as losses in time and merchandise. Jacques Gravier was forced to make several trips to oversee the transfer of his belongings to the fort (at an inordinate cost) and La Vente was charged over a hundred *livres* for the transport of his supplies.[14]

The lack of ships was a problem Dartaguiette and Bienville sought immediately to correct. Fortunately, the *Renommée* had brought a shipbuilder from Rochefort, a second-master constructor named Jacques Le Roux who specialized in the building of small craft. Le Roux had come to the colony once before, in 1702, and had immediately begun work on a riverboat, but he had returned to France before the vessel was completed and since that time the hull had rotted on the ways. Back in the colony now, Le Roux was immediately given a contract to construct a flat-bottomed barge of thirty-five to forty tons, capable of transporting goods over the sometimes shallow bars between the fort and Massacre Island. Three thousand *livres* were allotted for this purpose, part of the sum to be paid to the fifteen workers (mostly Canadians) who would assist Le Roux. The contract having been drawn up by Dartaguiette and sent to Pontchartrain, the work of construction began near the small hospital on the creek just north of town. By the first week in June, the barge, constructed mostly of green oak to ward off the insects and wood borers, was ready to be launched. Finished, she measured forty-five feet in length by fourteen feet wide and was capable of carrying some thirty to thirty-five tons burden (slightly less than the contract called for). She drew no more than one foot of water unloaded and three to four feet at her dead load. When the barge successfully completed her maiden voyage to Massacre Island later that summer, Bienville and Dartaguiette were satisfied that the problem which plagued the

14. *Journal Historique*, pp. 104–05. Lettre du P. Gravier, Feb. 23, 1708, *JR, LXVI*, pp. 124–25. La Vente [to Brisacier], March 4, 1708, ASQ, Lettres, R 79. Andrés de Arriola al virrey, Feb. 26, 1708, AGI, *México*, L. 633. Vessels such as the *Espérance*, however, could go only as far as Dog River.

Renommée in 1708 would not be present on the arrival of the next ship from France.[15]

Another problem, although not quite as immediate, was the lack of a mill to aid the colonists in grinding their grain. Ever since the colony's beginnings, the inhabitants had been forced to pound their maize in wooden and stone mortars. Although the *Loire* had brought some mill parts from Rochefort in 1703, the mill had never been completed because of the death of the craftsman responsible for its construction. Bienville had made a bargain with a group of six Canadians to assist in the work for five hundred *livres* and two barrels of flour each, but after the death of the craftsman the project was abandoned. Both Daneau de Muy and Dartaguiette had been instructed to investigate progress on the mill and to determine whether it was actually necessary to have one built. On his arrival at the fort, Dartaguiette quickly concluded that its construction was imperative, a number of the inhabitants having claimed that it was the absence of a mill that was preventing them from beginning cultivation. Dartaguiette, once deciding on its necessity, began immediately to renew construction efforts, but the absence of qualified workers over the next several years would make it a difficult undertaking.[16]

At the same time that Dartaguiette was sharing executive authority with Bienville (at Bienville's request), and overseeing La Salle's work as commissary, he had also been continuing his investigations into the past conduct of the colony's affairs, but not with the diligence that he had promised the minister. He seemed to be getting along well enough with the commandant, and Bienville did not appear outwardly to object to the intrusion into his command. Other than the entry of Dartaguiette into the picture, little change had occurred among the colony's officers and officials during the last several years. Antoine-François Ruette d'Auteuil de Monceaux, young son of the attorney general of Canada and a half-brother of Madame Iberville, had been appointed *aide-major*

15. La Salle to min., Sept. 12, 1708, AC, C13A, 2, f. 203–05. Bienville to min., Oct. 12, 1708, AC, C13A, 2, f. 178. *FLC*, p. 127. Dartaguiette to min., May 25, 1708, *loc. cit.*, f. 322–24. Dartaguiette to min., Aug. 18, 1708, AC, C13A, 2, f. 335–38. Min. to La Salle, May 10, 1710, AC, B 32, f. 49.

16. Bienville to min., Sept. 6, 1704, AC, C13A, 1, f. 463. Bienville to min., July 28, 1706, AC, C13A, 1, f. 526–27. La Salle to min., Sept. 7, 1706, AC, C13A, 1, f. 492. Mémoire du Roy, June 30, 1707, AC, B 29, f. 251v. Mémoire de Dartaguiette, Feb. 26, 1708, AC, C13A, 2, f. 67. Min. to Dartaguiette, May 10, 1710, AC, B 32, f. 45.

by the court on Oct. 21, 1705. He died the next year, however, a month after his arrival at Mobile and Bienville had replaced him with Jacques Barbazant de Pailloux (an appointment that aroused the ire of both La Salle and Pontchartrain: Barbazant, accused of Protestant persuasions, had in years past actually borne arms against the king during an uprising in the upper Cévennes concerning religion and taxes).[17]

Aside from Barbazant, Bienville depended on his old coterie of officers—Boisbriant, Châteaugué, Daraque, Saint-Denis, Mandeville, Antoine Siré and Philippe Blondel (who had been serving as lieutenant in Châteaugué's company in place of Canadian Louis-Joseph Morel de La Durantaye who had been appointed to that position some years before but who had never appeared in the colony). The staff suffered a questionable loss on the twenty-fourth of May with the death of Valentin Barraud, the surgeon major. For years Bienville had requested a qualified surgeon for the colony, a request that was supposedly realized when Barraud arrived on the *Aigle* in 1706. However, Barraud proved anything but the answer to the colony's medical needs. By almost unanimous agreement the surgeon was "ignorant, incompetent and a drunkard who sells [for his own profit] the medicines and everything else intended for the sick." Barraud had married Hippolyte Mercier shortly after his arrival, and François Le Maire had baptized the first product of that union, Jeanne-Marguerite, on January 30. The inhabitants were doubtless not too pained to see the surgeon's passing, especially those of the unmarried Canadians who had remained at the fort; for, a young widow, even one with an infant daughter, was a precious commodity in woman-scarce Louisiana.[18]

The late winter and spring of 1708 witnessed the presence of five religious at Fort Louis—one Jesuit and four seminary priests. Albert Davion had returned to Mobile in February at the insistence of Marc Bergier who some months before had ordered him to make arrangements to receive supplies from the expected ship

17. AC, F1A, 13, f. 113v; 15, f. 60v. AC, D2C, 222. Min. to Bienville, May 10, 1710, AC, B 32, f. 41. *DGFC, I*, p. 159. Bienville to min., Oct. 27, 1711, AC, C13A, 2, f. 585–86. Duclos to min., Oct. 12, 1713, AC, C13A, 3, f. 287–88. Mémoire de Nicolas-Ignace de Beaubois, [1726], AC, C13A, 12, f. 263.

18. Bienville to min., Oct. 27, 1711, *loc. cit.*, f. 584–88. AC, F1A, 13, f. 113–14; 15, f. 60v–61. *DGFC, I*, p. 443. AC, D2C, 222. La Salle to min., March 4, 1708, AC, C13B, 1, No. 8, f. 6v–7. Dartaguiette to min., May 25, 1708, *loc. cit.*, f. 321–22. ADM, A, July 20, 1707; A, Jan. 30, 1708.

from France. Moreover, Bergier was concerned about the increasing hostility of the natives in Davion's district. The presence of Davion in Mobile stimulated La Vente's thinking that he could return to France without the colony's suffering, but Bienville's refusal to allow the pastor passage had squelched that scheme.[19] Unable to go, La Vente comforted himself with the rationalization that he was just as happy to stay:

> I do not lack reasons for wanting to leave this place, but since I do not know the purity or impurity of their [his enemies'] motives, I confide them all to the sovereign will of God in the firm hope which I have that God is too good and too compassionate to abandon me to a place contrary to His good pleasure, seeing that He knows no bond which holds me there. As He is wise, that suffices; and as He is good, that is enough to hearten all persons who seek only Him in the center of the greatest storms. And He is so merciful that in the midst of all these tempests into which He has permitted us to drift He has not failed to allow us to enjoy from time to time calmer moments so pleasant that we are abundantly recompensed for all that we may have suffered before.[20]

La Vente's pleasant moments were indeed only "from time to time." His *confrère* Huvé was almost invariably ill and even when well, the pithless priest's behavior was nothing of which La Vente could be proud. The missioner was away in the village of the Apalache most of the time, laboring ineffectively; he only came to the fort on occasion: when he was sick, and once to baptize a young Chitimacha slave belonging to the seminary. As chaplain, François Le Maire seemed more like a lost scholar cursing the wilderness; his lack of zeal, his morose attitude, did nothing for La Vente's "spirit" nor for the reputation of the seminary missioners in Mobile. Almost grudgingly, Le Maire turned from his books and his dinner table to baptize six Indian slaves belonging to Marie Grissot, Étienne Burelle, Jean-Baptiste Saucier and the seminary priests.[21]

Perhaps La Vente found some measure of cheer in being called

19. *Journal Historique*, pp. 105–06. La Vente [to Brisacier], March 4, 1708, *loc. cit.*, R 79.

20. La Vente [to Brisacier], July 4, 1708, ASQ, Lettres, R 83.

21. Lettre du P. Gravier, Feb. 23, 1708, *JR, LXVI*, pp. 130–31. Mémoire de Le Maire, Jan. 15, 1714, AC, C13C, 2, f. 109–18, 121–34. La Vente [to Brisacier], July 4, 1708, *loc. cit.*, R 83. ADM, A, April 7, 1708.

by Nicolas de La Salle on the afternoon of March 22 to officiate at the baptism of La Salle's newly-born son. La Vente visited La Salle's quarters within hours after being notified of the delivery, but the hour was late. Dame Jeanne-Catherine had given birth at one-thirty and La Vente preferred to postpone christening until the next morning. The baptism was largely a family affair. With La Salle's young son Simon (now a cadet in Vaulezard's company) acting as godfather and Marie Linant serving as godmother, La Vente baptized the infant (who was named Henri after the pastor) at the house now serving as a church.[22]

But such moments were rare indeed. La Vente's customary state of mind could best be summed up by a few sentences he wrote to Brisacier three weeks before the baptism of La Salle's son:

> We are under such great oppression that we can never escape . . . always the target of *procès-verbaux* against us. Ever since we have exercised the functions of chaplain they have deprived us of rations, which the Jesuits always received. They deprive us . . . of servants while they assign them to a surgeon, to a carpenter, to a cannoneer and to numerous others, on the king's orders—and half of them for no good purpose. We can only cry aloud and do nothing for lack of support. They welcome all sorts of the most injust and false proceedings against us. They write all manner of calumnies against our honor to which credence is given without even our knowing in what way our defense will be heard. They want Messieurs the governors to be free to send us away or to keep us at their whim. We are not permitted to shake the dust from our shoes.[23]

As disappointed as La Vente may have been by the demise of Daneau de Muy and by what he considered the inordinate tolerance of Bienville by Dartaguiette, he was infinitely more troubled by the return of his hated adversary, Jacques Gravier. No doubt the pastor would have been elated to know the disillusionment Gravier had suffered in France, but of the Jesuit's blighted hopes he was not yet fully aware. He only knew that the source of a great deal of his difficulty was now back in the colony as testy as ever. It was true that Gravier had been highly disappointed at Versailles, but apparently the Jesuit had not taken Pontchartrain

22. ADM, A, March 22, 1708.
23. La Vente [to Brisacier], March 4, 1708, *loc. cit.*, R 79.

at his word. Believing both king and minister to be pro-Jesuit at heart, Gravier (even at this late date) clung to his faith that the Jesuits would one day make inroads back into the Gulf Coast colony. "I do not know whether the time for which the Reverend Father Goüye leads us to hope is near," he wrote, shortly after arriving, "but I do know that the inhabitants here are greatly dissatisfied with these gentlemen [La Vente, Huvé and Le Maire] . . . A fort is to be built at Massacre Island; the chaplain is to have no connection with that of Mobile or with the *curé;* and this post would suit us well." [24]

Despite Gravier's hopes, he no doubt realized that any such change in policy must await Saint-Vallier's release from captivity in England. His first days back in the colony were occupied with transferring his goods to the fort with the assistance of his young slave and his *frère coadjuteur*, the aged Guillaume-Richard Fortin. Brother Fortin was ill, however, with "quartan fever" and it was all the brother could do to transport himself. When he finally arrived (on the last day of February) Fortin was "like an old man of eighty years . . . unable to take two steps without being out of breath." Gravier suspected that the same disease that had besieged his *confrère* was lurking in his own system, but he was much too preoccupied with affairs at the fort to give the possibility due consideration. Dartaguiette had just begun his investigations and Gravier was elated at La Vente's inability to gain the ear of the new commissary. Yet he was certain that the pastor's failure would not stop him from making further mischief. "The regret that M. La Vente feels," he wrote, "at not being able to substantiate all his calumnies before Monsieur Dartaguiette will induce him to invent others against Monsieur de Bienville, against myself, and against all who may be opposed to him." [25]

La Vente's attempt to turn Dartaguiette against Bienville and the Jesuits was intensified when Gravier revealed the contents of several letters recently delivered from the Illinois country. From Gabriel Marest, Gravier received news that Marc Bergier was attempting to restrict the Jesuits' ministry in that area to the natives, Bergier claiming that the Jesuits had no authority over the

24. La Vente to min., March 2, 1708, AC, C13A, 2, f. 161. Mémoire du Roy, June 30, 1707, AC, B 29, f. 273v–76v. Lettre du P. Gravier, Feb. 23, 1708, *JR, LXVI,* pp. 130–31, 141.

25. Interrogatoire des habitants . . . , Feb. 27, 1708, AC, C13A, 2, f. 249–53. Lettre du P. Gravier, Feb. 23, 1708, *op. cit.,* pp. 124–25, 135, 138–39.

French and Canadians settled among them. Moreover, Bergier was further charging that Gravier actually had no power of vicar-general among those missions because Bishop Saint-Vallier, before he was imprisoned, had removed his authority at the time of the Tamaroa affair.[26]

Gravier was inflamed by Bergier's statements; but his full wrath was directed toward the seminary priests in Mobile and toward La Vente in particular. Had not Bergier spent several months in Mobile the previous year? What devilment had the local pastor put in Bergier's ear while Gravier had been absent in France? Moreover, the Jesuit priest discovered that La Vente had been accusing him of having told Bienville that he would himself seize any letters written by La Vente or Le Maire on first opportunity, a charge La Vente claimed he could prove in writing by Gravier's own hand as well as from certain letters written from Havana.[27]

Gravier had originally planned to leave for his Illinois mission soon after his return to the colony, but Dartaguiette's inquest and La Vente's truculent behavior made him decide to remain at Mobile until matters were more settled.[28] He acceded to a request by Bienville and Châteaugué (no doubt suggested by Gravier himself) to tarry until spring in order to deliver the Easter sacraments to the inhabitants. In explanation of Gravier's violation of Pontchartrain's expressed will, Bienville no doubt tested the minister's patience:

> The Reverend Father Gravier, a Jesuit, has arrived here with instructions from your lordship to lend him men to transfer him to his mission. He urges me to send him promptly, but as all my garrison and three-fourths of the inhabitants did not receive their Easter sacraments last year because of the small amount of confidence they had in the gentleman of the Foreign Missions, I am asking him to remain here until Easter in order that all the people of this colony may have liberty of conscience. I am certain that no one in the colony this year will miss the opportunity this father will give them to perform their Easter duty since no one ever failed to do so while only the Jesuits were here.[29]

26. *Ibid.*, pp. 126–29.
27. La Vente [to Brisacier], March 4, 1708, ASQ, Lettres, R 79.
28. Min. to Lamberville, May 25, 1707, AC, B 29, f. 244.
29. Bienville to min., Feb. 25, 1708, *loc. cit.*, f. 110–11.

The Easter season [April 6–8] arrived without incident. Gravier performed the paschal sacraments, then left for Massacre Island. La Vente, hoping the Jesuit was departing at last for his Peoria mission, was nonetheless puzzled by circumstances surrounding the supposed journey. Gravier, he found out, was shortly expected to return from the port. Moreover, Brother Fortin had remained at Fort Louis along with most of Gravier's supplies and personal belongings. A week later, Gravier was indeed back in Mobile, looking haggard and apparently stricken with a debilitating fever. On the night of April 16, La Vente visited him in his dwelling by the river, and the Jesuit appeared gravely ill. La Vente attempted to converse with him, but Gravier, now in a state of utter delerium, could only babble hysterically, bellowing how the inhabitants of Mobile, in order to make the way clear for the oncoming of the Jesuits, would once and for all gather together and drive the renegade seminary priests from the colony. La Vente listened for awhile, noting "how strange were such words from a missionary who to all appearances would be very soon before the judgment of God," then went home. Having noticed that Brother Fortin, sleeping in the next room, was in no condition to aid his brother Jesuit, La Vente decided to return the next day. The following morning, Fortin, upon being awakened, ushered the pastor into Gravier's room. Together, they discovered that the *curé's* arch rival had passed away during the night, quietly and alone. The man whom La Vente had described as "the instrument by which God punishes me," would threaten him no more.[30]

Gravier's funeral was held that same day, La Vente officiating. Now that his hated adversary was gone, the pastor, no doubt relieved by the removal of "the hand which smote us," formalized his regrets to the seminary:

> We cannot, as Christians, but be very touched by his death since it deprives us of a great source of merit; but God will supply others of his kind, provided we remain faithful.[31]

If the death of Gravier perhaps softened the pastor's attitude toward the Jesuits for a time (there being no more of that order present, the threat of Jesuit encroachment was considerably reduced), it did nothing to lessen his antipathy for the commandant.

30. La Vente [to Brisacier], July 4, 1708, *loc. cit.*, R 83. ASJ, Fonds Brotier, 105. ARSI, Gallia, 110II, f. 269–273v. La Vente [to SME Dirs.], June 27, 1708, *loc. cit.*, R 82.

31. La Vente [to Brisacier], July 4, 1708, *loc. cit.*, R 83.

Shortly after Gravier's funeral, Albert Davion, who had lent somewhat of a temporizing influence to clergy-officer relationships, left Mobile to return to his mission and once again the Louisiana post was beset with wrangling among its officials. "Nothing can equal the disaccord there is here," Dartaguiette wrote Pontchartrain in mid-May, "among Monsieur de Bienville, commandant, and the Sieurs La Vente . . . and La Salle . . ." And not even that able interagent could lessen the rivalry. La Vente taunted Bienville in public with the charge that the commandant had submitted a number of accusations to Pontchartrain in writing against him while at the same time closing an agreement whereby each agreed to refrain from openly accusing the other. When Bienville denied making written accusations, La Vente produced extracts of the charges he had obtained from Brisacier (who had received them from Pontchartrain), to which Bienville replied that such extracts were not taken from any letters *he* had sent the minister. When La Vente asked Bienville to put his denial in writing, the commandant, not about to be trapped into prevaricating against the court, abruptly retreated.[32]

La Salle, too, was busy denouncing Bienville. He rebuked the commandant for allowing a large number of Canadians and *voyageurs* to live with the natives on the Mississippi, charging that the libertinism arising from this practice was irreparably damaging to French-Indian relations. The dangers inherent in Bienville's policy were apparent to all, but as La Salle well knew, in times of low food supplies, the sending of Canadians to the native villages to curb the drain on the storehouse was the only realistic solution. Perhaps more justly, the commissary renewed a charge he had made two years before—that Bienville was dealing too personally with the natives, that when the savages brought meat and skins to Mobile they delivered them directly to Bienville's house and Bienville in return had supplies presented to the natives from his own dwelling rather than from the king's warehouse. Such practices, La Salle claimed, had the effect of creating a personal alliance between Bienville and the savages rather than developing a French-Indian relationship. Thus, the natives were coming to depend more on Bienville himself than on the French as a nation; the com-

32. Dartaguiette to min., May 25, 1708, *loc. cit.*, f. 324–25. Bienville to min., July 28, 1706, AC, C13A, 1, f. 532–38. Bienville to min., Oct. 10, 1706, AC, C13B, 1, No. 6, f. 3–5v. La Vente [to Brisacier], July 4, 1708, *loc. cit.*, R 83.

mandant was seeking, at the expense of the colony, to make himself the indispensable man.[33]

La Salle was especially bitter over Bienville's attempt to establish himself and the Canadians as the only men capable of conducting expeditions or carrying on commerce with the natives. "Nothing will ever be accomplished in this country," he warned Pontchartrain, "as long as the least officer of the family of the late Monsieur d'Iberville is left here. It is necessary to send some good Frenchmen. The belief is exaggerated that it is imperative to have Canadians here or men who have served in Canada. We do not lack interpreters; two of my sons know the Indian languages quite well. Besides this, it is to be presumed that since I have spent twelve years in this country myself I understand the manners of these savages and their languages better than those who came here only at a later time. Added to this, I am the one who has traveled in all the lands of Louisiana and who knows best the extent of it, the situation of the rivers, of the nations, and of the proper locations to place the fort and the inhabitants." [34]

More to the immediate point, as supplies were beginning to diminish, La Salle was concerned as always about the security of the king's storehouse: Jean Delisle, sergeant in Châteaugué's company and personal secretary to Bienville, had stolen twenty-eight pounds of beads before deserting to Pensacola. Bienville, embarrassed at such a flagrant violation of his confidence, dispatched a contingent to Fort San Carlos to retrieve Delisle. Immediately upon the French party's arrival, Sebastián de Moscoso delivered up the *deserteur;* Delisle, on being returned to Mobile, was thrown into irons.

In addition, La Salle charged Bienville with secretly entering the warehouse himself while the detachment was away in Pensacola and marking fifty barrels of the best gunpowder with the letters "D. I." which he later sold from the warehouse managed by the widow Le Sueur. As a consequence, there was very little powder left for the defense of the fort. Bienville's theft was extraordinarily serious, charged La Salle, because of the imminence of Indian attack, and jeopardized the security of the entire settlement.[35]

33. La Salle to min., Sept. 12, 1708, AC, C13A, 2, f. 198–204.

34. *Ibid.*, f. 202–05.

35. La Salle to min. [extraits de 12 sept. et 16 oct., 1708], AC, C13A, 2, f. 213–24. La Salle to min., Sept. 12, 1708, *loc. cit.*, f. 205–09. Delisle, however, was listed with Vaulezard's company in 1706. AC, F1A, 13, f. 117.

The threat of enemy attack mentioned by La Salle was no creation of the commissary's imagination; real enough, it loomed constantly during the summer of 1708. The previous summer and autumn had seen the English-backed Indians almost constantly at the gates of Fort San Carlos in Pensacola. Although the greater part of the invaders had retreated to the interior by early December, there remained in the forests surrounding the fort scattered bands of warriors which periodically attacked Spanish soldiers venturing too far from the fort. Now that the English had the Spaniards boxed in (due to lack of supporting natives in the area), they were proceeding with plans for an assault on Mobile. But such an offensive would not be a certain success, as the Carolinians well knew. The numerous small villages surrounding Fort Louis would preclude a surprise attack, and since Bienville could presumably count on aid within two weeks from the Choctaw and Chickasaw, a long term siege seemed out of the question.[36]

French reliance on large-scale assistance from their two principal allies was not absolutely certain to save them, however. Both Chickasaw and Choctaw had on occasion wavered in their support and the French had no assurance that the number of savages the English could rally would be limited to the number that had attacked Pensacola. Reports reaching Mobile from various sources led French officers to fear that over two thousand natives might possibly be gathered for a direct attack on the fort. Bienville doubted the likelihood of this; nevertheless the reports made him a bit uneasy.[37]

The advance English strategy, as Bienville had learned of it from Indian spies and the several Canadians located in the native villages, became quite apparent by the spring of 1708. If, by eloquent promises and huge numbers of presents, the Carolina agents could persuade the Choctaw and Chickasaw nations to join them (or at least to remain neutral), the French, with mostly adolescent soldiers and small buffer villages, could be blockaded even more effectively than were the Spaniards. Apprised of the strategem, Bienville confided to Pontchartrain:

> The English of Carolina are doing everything possible to win over all our Indian allies. This past spring two Englishmen,

36. Bienville to min., Feb. 25, 1708, *loc. cit.*, f. 96–99. Declaración de Pedro Manuel Cabello, Nov. 30, 1707, AGI, *México*, L. 633. Moscoso al virrey, Oct. 12, 1707, AGI, *México*, L. 633.

37. La Vente [to Brisacier], Oct. 4, 1708, ASQ, Lettres, R. 84.

> envoys of their governor, arrived at the village of the Chickasaw to ask them to deliver presents to all our allies. One of these two came to the grand village of the Choctaw and was not very well received although he gave them a very large present. The proposal that he made to them in his speech stunned them: it was to aid them to destroy all the small nations that were nearest to our fort—the Tomeh, Apalache, Mobile, Tawasa, Chato, Pascagoula and Pensacola . . .[38]

But the Choctaw refused to come to terms with the Englishman (who then immediately returned to Carolina). His comrade, however, left the Chickasaw village and went to the village of the Yazoo where he spoke to a congregation of Tensa, Natchez, Tunica, Arkansas and Koroa. Offering peace to the assembled nations, the Englishman vigorously invoked their co-operation. The French at Mobile, he claimed, were in reality only refugees from France whom the mother country would no longer support. This was the reason for "the dearth of presents the French had to offer." The natives of the lower Mississippi villages made no reply to the harangues of the Englishman, but from several Canadians present at the affair, Bienville and Dartaguiette learned that the Carolinians were planning an assault on Mobile the approaching winter.[39]

When Bienville received the news of English activity in the interior villages that summer he was certain there was no immediate danger of attack. However, he was equally positive that an offensive would eventually come and the French with their dwindling supplies and rotting fort were in no position to resist such an invasion. The state of the fort was of primary consideration. Just the previous year he had "repaired it so it will last two years longer," but now, little more than a year later, it was already beginning to rot again. The bastions could hardly support the cannons and only the past May a windsquall had destroyed the warehouse which had also served as a curtain. Moreover, the size of the fort was barely adequate to shelter the inhabitants (in the event of emergency) whereas Bienville wanted one large enough to include the five or

38. Bienville to min., Oct. 12, 1708, AC, C13A, 2, f. 180–81.

39. Dartaguiette to min., Oct. 1, 1708, AC, C13A, 2, f. 341–42. Bienville to min., Oct. 12, 1708, *loc. cit.*, f. 181–83. The Canadians present at the village of the Yazoo were probably part of Daraque's small party sent to the Illinois country in the spring of 1708 to restrain the activity of certain renegade Canadians who were trying to gain slaves by turning native against native. *FLC*, pp. 122–23.

six hundred neighboring savages as well. The rebuilding and enlarging of the fort to the extent Bienville had in mind would be a huge undertaking for which there was no appropriation. By whom and by what means would the work be accomplished? In the sizzling months of July and August, there were few healthy men willing to labor for pay, much less for nothing.[40]

While mulling over this situation, Bienville was faced with a further dilemma: what was to be done with the Chickasaw chief and a number of his warriors who were sojourning in Mobile? If the English had successfully aroused some of the Choctaw villages against the French, it would not be safe for the Chickasaw to return to their village through Choctaw country. After obtaining the promise of the Chickasaw chief that his nation would not only remain loyal to the French but would drive out any Englishmen remaining in their villages, Bienville, on August 24, sent Châteaugué and twenty-five men to escort the chief and his warriors through the Choctaw country. On passing through the lands of the Choctaw, Châteaugué was to attempt to dissuade the chiefs of that nation from doing business with the English. In support of this maneuver, Bienville sent along two young Frenchmen, one of whom was to remain in the village of the Choctaw, the other to stay with the Chickasaw, to learn the respective languages and above all to keep Bienville informed on the political and commercial activities of each nation.[41]

Meanwhile, Bienville had solved part of his problem of having the fort enlarged. On the fourth of July he sealed a bargain with twenty Apalache natives to do the heavy labor on the fort. For nine *livres* worth of munitions and merchandise the Apalache would cut and dress all the timbers for a large stockade as well as the planks for the bastions. This agreement worked well enough and the Apalache soon proved themselves diligent laborers. Nevertheless, there still remained the skilled work necessary for the completion of the bastions and the dilapidated buildings serving as curtains for the fort. With none of Mobile's craftsmen volunteering their services, where would the manpower come for this task? [42]

40. Bienville to min., Feb. 20, 1707, AC, C13A, 2, f. 9. Mémoire sur la Louisiane . . . par Mandeville, April 27, 1709, *loc. cit.*, f. 473–74. Dartaguiette to min., Feb. 26, 1708, AC, C13A, 2, f. 247–48. AC, F1A, 15, f. 59–63v.

41. Bienville to min., Oct. 12, 1708, *loc. cit.*, f. 183–85. La Salle to min., Sept. 12, 1708, AC, C13A, 2, f. 210–11.

42. *Ibid.*, f. 202–05.

In mid-September, two Mobilian savages who had married among the Alabama got wind that several nations east of the Alabama country were planning a joint attack on the villages surrounding Fort Louis and after that were purposing to burn the fort itself. When the two Mobilians fled the Alabama nation and reported the plan to the French, Bienville and Dartaguiette, though each believed the warning premature, spread the word of impending danger among the inhabitants.[43] La Vente, lodged in the seminary quarters on the outskirts of town, and unsuspecting of the two officials' artifice, described his dismay to Brisacier:

> I must tell you that we have suffered a great alarm, believing the English with more than two thousand savages about to fall upon us. As quickly as possible we have had our most valuable possessions carried to the fort, because as you can see by the map I sent you, we are more exposed to the enemy than anyone else. It was thought necessary for us to hire laborers to transport our valuables, although [the work was carried out] with much difficulty and loss. We have even slept in the fort for one night, abandoning to Divine Providence what we could not take with us. We have had other alarms before but none quite like this one.[44]

The attack, as Bienville and Dartaguiette suspected, did not occur. But the two officials were now able to use the alarm to jolt some of the inhabitants from their lethargy. With the aid of a group of volunteer Canadians who had families to protect, together with the services of several of the French carpenters, the work on the bastions and interior buildings commenced. As much as possible of the original timber was saved, and in ten days' time the task was practically completed. The new fort was one-third larger than the former one (although the increase in size related primarily to the stockade rather than to the fort proper), and was capable of holding the five or six hundred Indians for whom Bienville had made allowance.[45] By the second week in October the commandant was able to describe his accomplishment to the minister, not neglecting to justify the fort's enlargement:

43. *FLC*, p. 123. Dartaguiette to min., Oct. 1, 1708, *loc. cit.*, f. 346–47.
44. La Vente [to Brisacier], Oct. 4, 1708, *loc. cit.*, R 84.
45. La Salle to min., Sept. 12, 1708, *loc. cit.*, f. 202–05. Bienville to min., Oct. 12, 1708, *loc. cit.*, f. 180. Mémoire sur la Louisiane . . . par Mandeville, April 27, 1709, *loc. cit.*, f. 473–74. Dartaguiette to min., Oct. 1, 1708, *loc. cit.*, f. 45–47.

> I have had this fort enlarged and remade like a new fort with four bastions, each provided with seven cannons, which has cost the king very little since I have persuaded the colonists to give several days' work on their part. It is somewhat large for the garrison that is presently here, but I do not doubt, my lord, that your lordship will respect what I have had the honor of reporting to him; that two companies as shabby as these were not enough to protect this colony, especially while guarding a fort at the port of Massacre Island as it is absolutely necessary to do in order to preserve this country well.[46]

With the completion of the fort and the return of Châteaugué from the Chickasaw country with his detachment of twenty-five men, Bienville and Dartaguiette felt much better prepared for the Indian attack they were certain would eventually come. But there were still further considerations for the defense of Fort Louis. Six soldiers had died that summer and Dartaguiette, on the last day of September, was able to count only one hundred and thirty men (which included officers, Canadians, soldiers and craftsmen) capable of bearing arms in times of emergency. Too, there was a crucial lack of armaments, especially gunpowder. To remedy the lack of gunpowder, Bienville looked to Pensacola to supply his needs. In September he had sent envoys to Fort San Carlos bearing his request.[47]

By the end of the summer, however, Pensacola was in no shape to aid anyone. With its sergeant-major, Joseph de Guzmán, still in Mexico, the fort was being commanded by Sebastián de Moscoso, captain of infantry, now serving as provisional governor. Moscoso, since the siege of Pensacola the previous autumn, had quite naturally been primarily concerned with defense. With the aid of Andrés de Arriola, he had been successful in convincing authorities in New Spain to send fresh recruits and the means to reconstruct Fort San Carlos.[48] In late January of 1708, additional

46. Bienville to min., Oct. 12, 1708, *loc. cit.*, f. 180. The seven cannons per bastion was an increase of twelve pieces over the original sixteen installed in 1702.

47. Dartaguiette to min., Oct. 1, 1708, *loc. cit.*, f. 346–47. Bienville to min., Oct. 12, 1708, *loc. cit.*, f. 184. La Salle to min., Sept. 12, 1708, *loc. cit.*, f. 206–09. Min. to Bienville, July 11, 1709, AC, B 30, f. 181–82.

48. Junta, March 13, 1708, AGI, *México*, L. 633. Sebastián de Moscoso al virrey, Feb. 12, 1708, AGI, *México*, L. 633. Captain Pedro de Bilbao arrived in Pensacola on Jan. 29, 1708 with recruits (which included convicts) taken from Puebla and Veracruz. Bilbao al virrey, Feb. 15, 1708, AGI, *México*, L. 633.

men and supplies reached Santa María de Galve and work was immediately begun on the fort. After three weeks, Moscoso was able to submit a detailed progress report to Alburquerque:

> . . . the curtain which goes down to the precipice on the sea, the bastion of Pólvora and of San Joseph have all been completed, but we are still working on the bastion of San Francisco . . . the stakes of the stockade are half a yard higher than the old ones, and in the bastions which are finished and those which form the curtains I have removed the mounded parapets of sand (having realized that these cause the stakes to rot) and have made a platform of logs in the form of a rampart so that on the top the sentinels can watch and the soldiers fight with more safety, comfort and have a better view, all of which will be of greater cost to His Majesty, but it will be better, stronger and will last longer since the stakes are thicker and joined together from top to bottom and will not allow bullets to penetrate . . .[49]

The Spanish, then, were concentrating on defense at the expense of all else. The ship which arrived in January had carried supplies mostly for that purpose and Moscoso was not even allowing houses to be built outside the fort for fear that the enemy would burn them or otherwise use them as barriers as they had done previously. The garrison, composed in large part of hardened criminals, was sleeping in the open air, suffering from critical shortages of food. When Moscoso called on Bienville for aid, the commandant (with an eye toward Pensacola's munitions supply) responded by sending twelve quintals of beef, fifteen hundred pounds of flour and sixty bushels of corn, though the French could ill afford to spare such loans.[50]

In June, however, Yellow fever struck the Spanish settlement and the epidemic which raged throughout the summer was made worse by the fact that so many of the garrison were sleeping out-of-doors, making them easy prey for the infected mosquitoes. Between the eighth of June and the seventh of September, twenty-two men were lost, including four artillerymen, two sailors, eleven infantrymen and five convicts. Among the dead was the veteran paymaster, Pedro García de Vinuesa, who succumbed on the

49. Moscoso al virrey, Feb. 14, 1708, AGI, *México*, L. 633.

50. Francisco San Juan y Pedro Carrasco Aguilar al virrey, Sept. 9, 1708, AGI, *México*, L. 633. Moscoso al virrey, Sept. 7, 1708, AGI, *México*, L. 633. Moscoso al virrey, Feb. 14, 1708, AGI, *México*, L. 633.

twelfth of July.[51] Felipe de Arboloes, in charge of the hospital, was pleading for more mattresses, sheets, pillows and blankets for thirty more beds in addition to the ones already there.[52] In view of the desperate situation at Pensacola it was no wonder that the Spanish were not able to offer the French any aid. In fact, the Spanish, themselves fearing an attack from the Indians, had borrowed muskets from Bienville earlier that summer and claimed they had no powder to lend at present. Although the *Nuestra Señora de la Soledad* at Veracruz was being outfitted to relieve Pensacola, that ship was not to sail until the thirteenth of January.[53]

Bienville, confident that the expected attack on Mobile would not come until mid-winter, was not overly concerned for the moment. He was far more worried about the longer range problems of defense, about when the next supply ship from France, hopefully with an ample supply of gunpowder, would arrive. When in early October a vessel from Saint-Domingue anchored at Massacre Island in search of Indian slaves to take back to Cap-français, Bienville saw an opportunity to send an envoy to Versailles to lobby in person for supplies and perhaps (since Bienville knew Pontchartrain would be seeking a replacement for Daneau de Muy) to slip in a complimentary phrase in his behalf. François Philippe de Mandeville was the first to volunteer. For nearly a year Mandeville had been seeking compensation for supplies he had lent the colony (and the Apalache Indians) during the expedition to aid Pensacola at the time of the 1707 siege, but La Salle had nothing with which to reimburse him. Mandeville, while not Bienville's warmest admirer, was convinced by the commandant that a voyage to France would result in his being recompensed by the crown, that while doing so, he could render valuable service to the colony and perhaps receive a promotion. Mandeville left Fort Louis for Massacre Island on October sixteenth, along with twenty-five soldiers Bienville sent to protect the ship while in port, and in twelve days was on his way to France via Havana. Meanwhile, the colonists dug in for the winter, to await a possible attack.[54]

51. Moscoso al virrey, Sept. 7, 1708, *loc. cit.*, L. 633. Junta, Oct. 5, 1708, AGI, *México*, L. 633. By the first week in October the disease was still raging and Bienville reported the total dead at fifty-five. Bienville to min., Oct. 12, 1708, *loc. cit.*, f. 185.

52. Junta, Oct. 5, 1708, *loc. cit.*, L. 633.

53. Andrés de Arriola al virrey, Oct. 28, 1708, AGI, *México*, L. 633.

54. Mémoire sur la Louisiane . . . par Mandeville, April 27, 1709, AC, C13A, 2, f. 471. Min. to Bienville, July 11, 1709, AC, B 30, f. 181.

The state of the settlement had become increasingly desperate by the fall of 1708. The shortage of food and gunpowder, the bickering among officials, the fear of a surprise attack by marauding Indians all served to demoralize the inhabitants. "There is nothing so sad as the situation of this poor colony," Dartaguiette reported to the minister. "Every day we discover plots to desert that are being formed among the sailors and soldiers." [55] Moreover, many of the Canadians taken off the payrolls in March (even those that were married) showed a reluctance to begin plantations because they had no assurance of having been legally granted lands. Bienville and Dartaguiette, lacking a governor's authority, had no power to confer any sizable concessions, although they did issue several "contrats des cession" in October to Antoine Rivard and those Canadians who went to Lake Pontchartrain. But these were only temporary grants; they were issued with the understanding that they must later be approved by the new governor.[56]

Still, there was some reason for the inhabitants to be hopeful. Bienville was perfectly confident that with the reconstruction and enlargement of Fort Louis, the French could withstand any attack (provided the supply of gunpowder was sufficient). Moreover, the colony showed definite signs of growth. La Salle, who had taken a census at the beginning of August, recorded twenty-eight women in Mobile, twenty-five children and eighty Indian slaves. When the total number of Frenchmen, including Saint-Denis' small detachment and the nearly sixty Canadians and *coureurs-de-bois* on the Mississippi, were included there were approximately 345 Frenchmen in lower Louisiana by October of 1708 which was nearly double the number present in 1704. Moreover, the number of livestock had markedly increased: there were now forty head of cattle and fifty milch cows in the town, four bulls, eight oxen, fourteen hundred pigs and nearly two thousand chickens.[57]

Too, the number of births was gradually increasing the population. In early spring Geneviève Burelle, wife of Claude Trépanier, gave birth to a daughter, Marguerite; and Marie-Marguerite Dufresne bore a son, François, to Dieppe carpenter Jean-Baptiste Alexandre. Later on in the spring, Marie-Thérèse Brochon, wife of

55. Dartaguiette to min., Aug. 18, 1708, AC, C13A, 2, f. 327.

56. Bienville to min., Oct. 27, 1711, AC, C13A, 2, f. 598–99. Dartaguiette to min., Aug. 6, 1712, AC, C13A, 2, f. 705–06. *Cf.* Appendix VII.

57. Bienville to min., Oct. 12, 1708, *loc. cit.*, f. 184. Min. to Bienville, July 11, 1709, AC, B 30, f. 183. Dénombrement du 12 août de 1708 . . . par M. de La Salle, AC, C13A, 2, f. 225–27.

French master-mason Pierre Brossard, gave birth to their second child, a son, named Pierre by Pierre Alain. Jean Roy, a master cannoneer from La Rochelle had married Renée Gilbert of Tours in 1704 and that marriage had produced one of the first sons of those early unions by August of the next year. Roy, a six-year veteran in the colony, had served on board the ships during his early years in the colony, but after becoming a husband and father, he had settled down to till the soil. In the spring of 1708 when a number of Canadians moved to Massacre Island, Jean Roy also brought his family to that port where on the eighteenth of May Dame Renée gave birth to a second son. Six days later, François Le Maire arrived at the port and the next day, in what was probably the first such ceremony to take place on Massacre Island, Le Maire baptized the week-old infant in the presence of pilot Simon Coussot and godmother Marguerite Messier. Philippe Blondel, officer in Châteaugué's company, served as godfather and the child was named Jean-Philippe.[58]

Aside from the baptisms of a few Indian slaves (one a sixteen year-old savage named Jeanne, belonging to the aforementioned Roy; the other a newly-born Tensa owned by Guillaume Boutin), there were three Caucasian baptisms taking place in the autumn. Marie-Madelaine Oüanet, wife of François Dupré, gave birth to a daughter, called Marie-Thérèse; André Pénigault's spouse, Marguerite-Catherine Prévost, bore him a son whom René Boyer gave the name René-André. And Marie Briard bore Antoine Rivard (still away at Bayou Saint-Jean) his third child whom godmother Geneviève Burelle named Marie-Geneviève.[59]

Apart from the births, baptisms and deaths of 1708, that year also witnessed two marriages. Jean Le Caën, master locksmith, who had been one of the first inhabitants to bring his family to the colony, had been living alone for over a year in his house at the corner of the rue Saint-Joseph and the rue de La Salle. La Caën's wife, Madelaine Robert, and his several children were all dead now, his last remaining son, Jean-François, having died the previous year. Prospects for a new wife for the fairly prosperous locksmith seemed faint indeed: the crown was not planning to send any additional shipments of girls until the war in Europe was over. Yet

58. ADM, A, April 8, 18, 1708. Dénombrement, Aug. 1, 1706, AC, G1, 464. AC, F1A, 11, f. 69v–72v; 13; f. 220–20v, 223. ADM, A, Aug. 16, 1705; A, May 18, 1708.

59. ADM, A, June 29, July 9, 1708. AC, F1A, 13, f. 117v. ADM, A, Oct. 15, 27; A, Dec. 8, 1708.

there were present in the colony at least six single women. The aging "nursing sisters," widows Marie Linant and Marie Grissot, could be ruled out as possibilities for marriage; so too could the high-born Mademoiselle Boisrenaud (at least as far as Le Caën was concerned), as well as the demented Gabrielle Bonnet whose husband had deserted her three years before. Among the remaining eligibles, however, was an enterprising widow from Quebec only recently arrived in the colony after the death of her husband a few years before in Canada. Marie-Madelaine Mérienne, *dit* La Solaye, like Le Caën, had no children. After she took up residence in a house next door to Le Caën, which she had purchased from Jacques Chauvin, a romance began to develop. By the nineteenth of May, she and Le Caën were appearing before the local notary to sign their marriage contract (the terms of which specified that in case they had no children, all their property, in the event of the death of one, would accrue to the other). Shortly after signing the contract, Le Caën and Marie-Madelaine married; but the union, which was to last but five years due to Le Caën's death, was childless.[60]

A few months later, another marriage took place, this time between Joseph Chauvin, *dit* Léry and Hippolyte Mercier, recent widow of Valentin Barraud. For Dame Hippolyte this was the third significant ceremony in which she had been involved within a period of nine months. In January she had witnessed the baptism of her daughter, Jeanne-Marguerite, and in May she had attended the burial of her husband. Now, in the autumn of 1708, she married Chauvin, *dit* Léry, thirty-four-year-old brother of Jacques Chauvin and a fairly well-established Canadian merchant who had begun his career as a "Canadian" at Fort Maurepas and who by skillful and energetic trading had made himself independent of the crown's subsidy. The Léry-Mercier union, while the origin of only one of the Louisiana Chauvin lines, was to spawn more than its share of illustrious descendents.[61]

60. ADM, A, Oct. 4, 1704. AC, F1A, 10, f. 283; 11, f. 218–19. Dénombrement, Aug. 1, 1706, AC, G1, 464. Mémoire de M. Hubert, June, 1718, AM, B1, 30, f. 429–29v. ADM, A, March 20, 1710. Cadillac to min., Oct. 26, 1713, AC, C13A, 3, f. 75–76. *DGFC, I*, pp. 341–42, 426. ADM, A, March 23, 1709. Mémoire du Roy, May 13, 1710, AC, B 32, f. 66v. LSMA, DCS, April 27, May 3, July 17, 21, 23, 28, Aug. 6, 1725.

61. Dénombrement, Aug. 1, 1706, AC, G1, 464. ADM, A, Jan. 30, 1708. *DGFC, I*, p. 123. AJM, Greffe de Adhémar, Nov. 6, 1695; May 26, 1696; Sept. 30, 1700. Dartaguiette to min., May 25, 1708, AC, C13A, 2, f. 321–22. Interrogatoire . . . de 24 fév., 1708, AC, C13A, 2, f. 255–61. Dénombrement, Dec. 20, 1724, AC, G1, 464. ADM, A, Oct. 16, 1709. SLCA, Mariages, Book I (1720–30), May 27, 1726.

The aforementioned marriages performed by La Vente were no doubt among those few "bright moments" mentioned previously by the pastor. Aside from marriages and births, La Vente was currently elated over the total number of masses he had been able to perform. From July 1, 1706 until July 1, 1708, he recorded (he claimed to both Tremblay and Brisacier) four hundred and fifty masses, together with Le Maire and Huvé. The number, he was confident, would eventually rise at an even higher rate as the colony continued to grow, although (because of the state of his health) the pastor was beginning to have some reservations about how much longer he himself would be present.[62] Due to a debilitating fever which lingered into the early weeks of October, La Vente had even more doubts about his missionary to the Apalache:

> I had related in my first letter on this occasion that M. Huvé was ill. He had [for a brief while] regained his health, but this was not for long. He fell dangerously ill again more than ten days ago, and since Divine Providence decrees that we may not have a surgeon who knows his business, we are unable to learn what is the nature of his sickness and what is necessary to cure it. One time he believes it is a colic, other times he thinks it is rheumatism and on other occasions he tends to believe it is a disease of the spleen. You see the state in which Divine Providence places those who abandon themselves completely to His service. What God wills, one must perform without any hope of human remedy; but this absence of natural cures is a blessing since it obliges us to do something better, which is to place all our hope in God alone . . .[63]

Unlike La Vente, Bienville preferred to place more reliance on his own ability to solve his ills (both physical and political). Before Dartaguiette's arrival, the commandant had earnestly sought to return to the continent, complaining that only the clear air of France would relieve him of his "sciatic rheumatism . . . hepatic colic and gout." Even after the new commissary's arrival, Bienville remained convinced that a timely voyage to France would benefit his ailing body as well as his languishing reputation.[64]

Yet the death of Daneau de Muy, his subsequent close friendship

62. La Vente [to Brisacier], Oct. 4, 1708, ASQ, Lettres, R 84.

63. *Ibid.*

64. Bienville to min., Feb. 20, 1707, AC, C13A, 2, f. 29. Bienville to min., Feb. 25, 1708, *loc. cit.*, f. 90.

with Dartaguiette and the threats of the English Indians to the fort pushed any immediate thoughts of returning to France from Bienville's mind. For the moment it seemed to his personal advantage to remain in Louisiana and to press his case and his requests to the court by proxy and by good example. Once before, he had personally but in vain petitioned the minister for the governorship of Louisiana. Hurt and humiliated by Pontchartrain's refusal, Bienville was nonetheless quick to perceive the reasons behind his failure to advance. Undaunted, he hoped to quietly work his way back into eventual consideration. In mid-October of 1708, he more humbly invoked the minister's blessing:

> If M. De Muy had lived I should now be justified and in position to declare to you that I have had the honor to serve the king for eighteen years, nine years in the *gardes de la marine*, serving constantly as an officer on the vessels, having been in seven separate combats, the marks of which I bear today; and for nine years I have been in command in this colony with all the troubles and disappointments in the world, having continually been forced to perform all kinds of duties because of a lack of officers. It is because of this that my health has been reduced to its present state. Except for all the slanders that have been made to you about me, I might have expected from your justice to have been made a naval lieutenant or captain of a fireship, an office that I should perform worthily, since I am a seaman.[65]

Toward late autumn, Bienville settled back with the inhabitants to await the winter and the possible onslaught of the English Indians. If he knew anything of defense the commandant felt assured that Fort Louis was invulnerable to capture by a direct assault. Moreover, he was convinced that the Chickasaw and Choctaw would remain loyal to the French and that the enemy savages were unaware of the careful preparations he had made for Mobile's protection. Despite Bienville's assurance, however, the inhabitants would not, over the coming months be able to escape the anxiety of unknown threats.

65. Bienville to min., Oct. 12, 1708, *loc. cit.*, f. 185–86

XIX

The Colony on Its Own

FOR several years now, Pastor La Vente had been gravely concerned over the physical well-being of his fellow missioner Marc Bergier, vicar-general in the Illinois country. Receiving reports of the ascetic's haggard condition, La Vente had written to Bergier several times during the years 1705–06, urging him to devote more attention to his health. When Bergier arrived in Mobile in early 1707 La Vente was shocked at the vicar-general's appearance. The *curé* begged him to cease his fasting, to take sufficient rest—importunities which had not the slightest effect.[1]

While La Vente was somewhat put off by Bergier's less than enthusiastic support of his own methods and policies as pastor, the *curé* deeply respected his zeal and dedication. More than that, La Vente was proud of the universally high repute in which Bergier was held. Sensitive to the lack of regard the inhabitants had for Huvé, Le Maire and Davion, La Vente took great pleasure in being an associate of a man whose good name enhanced his order's reputation. Here, at least, was one seminary missioner even Bienville was forced to admire.[2]

Since Bergier's departure from Mobile in the spring of 1707, La Vente had received little news of the vicar-general. "I have received no direct reports from Mgr. Bergier," La Vente wrote Brisacier in the summer of 1708, "hence I do not know whether he is dead or alive."[3] La Vente's uncertainty was shortly clarified. Canadians returning from the Illinois country on November 9, 1708, brought a letter from Gabriel Marest, missionary at Kaskas-

1. La Vente [to Brisacier], Feb. 5, 1709, ASQ, Lettres, R 86. Bienville to min., Feb. 20, 1707, AC, C13A, 2, f. 24–25. La Vente [to Brisacier], July 4, 1708, ASQ, Lettres, R 83.
2. *Ibid.* Lettre de Marest, April 25, 1709, ASQ, Missions, 48.
3. La Vente [to Brisacier], Aug. 10, 1708, ASQ, Lettres, R 84.

kia, describing the details surrounding Bergier's death one year previous: the ailing priest had been severely weakened by continual fasting when toward summer's end an epidemic swept the village of the Tamaroa, resulting in widespread fatalities. Bergier saw this plague as a godsend, an opportunity to confront the medicine men of the surrounding country who, in seeking to retain their influence among the natives, had steadfastly opposed Bergier's missionary efforts. Bergier walked the village night and day, exhorting the natives to reject their savage gods, promising them that should they place their faith in the Gallic deity, that He would give them the power to dispel their afflictions. A small number of natives were converted and when the epidemic passed they attributed the "miracle" to Bergier's god.[4]

But Bergier himself paid dearly for those few conversions. His "eviscerated" body soon found itself "replete with sores from within and without." With no doctors or surgeons to treat him, Bergier soon realized it was to be his "last sickness, but the one which would free him from all ills." He summoned the closest religious, Jesuit Gabriel Marest, from the nearby Kaskaskia village and from him "received the sacraments and the holy viaticum, made his testament and submitted himself entirely to the sovereign will of God." The only other Frenchman present in the village opened one of his abscesses from which flowed "a great deal of water" after which Père Marest returned to his own village. Bergier lingered on for several weeks, never relinquishing his crucifix, until on the ninth of November, 1707, he died in the company of the Frenchman, without the presence of a fellow religious. Marest returned on November 12 and found that Bergier had been dead for three days. The missioner was then forty years of age.[5]

La Vente was sorely distressed on receiving the message of Bergier's passing. In a letter written several months later the pastor described his regret to Brisacier:

> . . . M. Bergier finished a life which ought to be regarded by most people as exemplary; thus, considering this precious death before God, it seems to me that I see much resemblance to, not to say something more excellent than, the death of the

4. La Vente [to Brisacier], Feb. 5, 1709, ASQ, Lettres, R 86. La Vente [to Brisacier], July 4, 1708, ASQ, Lettres, R 83.

5. ASQ, Polygraphie, IX, 26–27. La Vente [to Brisacier], Feb. 5, 1709, ASQ, Lettres, R 86. Lettre de Marest, April 25, 1709, ASQ, Missions, 48.

> apostle to the Indies, Saint-François Xavier. For there is this difference: that the latter died after ample recompense for his works in this world in the form of a great harvest he made in a large number of conversions among various nations . . . M. Bergier died almost without any consolation for his efforts save an indefatigable patience. He labored mightily with hardly any other recompense but to work for Jesus Christ in pure faith without the gift of languages and with no miracle save that of laboring purely by faith.[6]

The death of Jacques Gravier (though he was an odious rival) had brought somewhat of a moderation of antagonism (however temporary) between the Jesuits and the seminary priests. The death of Bergier, however, had no such effect, at least not between the Mobile missioners and the Illinois Jesuits, due to a misunderstanding between Marest and the pastor of Mobile. Some months before Bergier's demise, La Vente, suspecting that the vicar-general might be gravely ill (if not already dead), wrote to Marest to make an inventory of all of Bergier's and the mission's effects should Bergier pass away. Upon Bergier's death, Marest had these articles transferred to Kaskaskia where he sold most of them at auction before sending Bergier's strictly personal effects to the seminary at Quebec. The sale of the mission's goods totaled only five hundred *écus*, a sum which La Vente claimed did not remotely approach the possessions' true value. The pastor was incensed at Marest's presumptive act, which he saw as a deliberate attempt on the part of the Jesuits to destroy what little chance remained of continuing Bergier's Illinois mission. La Vente had hoped that this excellent site (located on the Mississippi not too distant from the mouth of the Missouri) could be re-established, possibly by Jean-François Buisson (relative of the murdered Saint-Cosme) or Goulven Calvarin (La Vente's former colleague at Île-de-Bourbon). But Marest's sale of the mission's possessions at "give-away" prices would render such prospects extremely unlikely. The seminary, already discouraged at the lack of success in the Mississippi Valley, was rapidly losing its enthusiasm to support *any* Louisiana mission much less one that would require any extraordinary expenditures. La Vente, more embittered than ever, drew into his shell, nursing a still greater enmity for the Jesuits.[7]

6. La Vente [to Brisacier], Feb. 4, 1709, ASQ, Lettres, R 86.

7. La Vente [to Brisacier], Aug. 10, 1708, ASQ, Lettres, R 84. *JR, LXVI*, p. 262. AAQ, Registres d'insinuation, B 244. ASQ, Chapitre, 40. Lettre de

The news of Bergier's death did not strike Bienville so forcefully as it had La Vente, although the commandant was no doubt disappointed that another French mission had been lost. A good seminary priest was, after all, better than no religious at all; he would have welcomed a man such as Bergier in lower Louisiana. Bienville, however, was presently much more concerned with the state of the colony at Mobile than with the future of the seminary priests at the Illinois; for, as the dawn of the year 1709 approached, Mobile was still in a woeful condition. Anticipating a concentrated attack or at the least an extended siege (such as was still taking place at Pensacola) the colonists grew steadily disconsolate; many began expressing a desire to return to France. Yet even this alternative was not for the moment possible. It had been nearly a year since the *Renommée* had left Massacre Island and there was no reason to expect another vessel anytime soon.[8]

Survival, then, was the present preoccupation of the inhabitants; yet the principal foe was not the threat of Indian attack but famine. Pontchartrain was not unaware of Louisiana's food shortage. With the war in Europe still raging, the minister had been unable to supply the colonists with unlimited shipments of foodstuffs. Yet he had not been too eager to support them, even to the extent of his ability; he had no doubt been misled concerning the land's potential (particularly the availability of large game) by early advocates of colonization who feared abandonment by the crown. Intending to compel the inhabitants to make their own way, he had taken the Canadians off the payroll the previous year, hoping this might force them to produce from the land and attain a certain degree of independence. The colony would never reach its full capacity, he felt, until it was able to support itself. Thus the shortage of supplies sent to Mobile was in some measure deliberate.[9]

Discouraged as they were, the inhabitants nevertheless commenced to plant; were they to survive they had no other choice. Some, such as Vincent Alexandre, began to plant tobacco, a crop that seemed to thrive fairly well; yet the lack of ships made the

---

Marest, April 25, 1709, ASQ, Missions, 48. Marest pretended to misread "encan" for "inventaire," according to La Vente. La Vente [to Brisacier], Feb. 5, 1709, ASQ, Lettres, R 86.

8. Dartaguiette to min., Feb. 12, 1710, AC, C13A, 2, f. 531–35. Dartaguiette to min., June 20, 1710, AC, C13A, 2, f. 541–43, 547.

9. Min. to Demuy, June 30, 1707, AC, B 29, f. 268. Min. to Dartaguiette, July 11, 1709, AC, B 30, f. 184–85. Min. to Bégon, Oct. 17, 1708, AC, B 30, f. 49.

marketing of this product especially difficult. Since food was the primary need, however, the majority directed their efforts toward the cultivation of edible crops. Maize, or "Indian corn," was the most successful produce, and had the colonists planted that crop with greater diligence, it no doubt would have attained for them the independence for which Pontchartrain was hoping.[10]

Rivard, Poitié, Dugué and Delon had been at Bayou Saint-Jean since the previous spring, earnestly laboring to develop plantations of wheat. They had failed once; now they were trying again. Their personal aspirations coincided with official ambitions for the colony; if they succeeded, many more inhabitants would follow them; the rich fields below Lac de Pontchartrain (which would later become New Orleans) would then be transformed into a virtual breadbasket, yielding more than enough grain to support the colony, the surpluses to be marketed to Pensacola and Mexico. Just before the end of the year 1708, Dartaguiette pirogued to Bayou Saint-Jean to personally inspect the progress of the wheat that Rivard and his Canadian associates had planted. To all outward appearances the crops were progressing well. The five inhabitants had planted one arpent each, which Dartaguiette described as "coming along very beautifully." The grain, of course, had not yet appeared, but the stalks and leaves seemed unusually healthy. Dartaguiette returned to Mobile highly optimistic, yet the wheat crops at Bayou Saint-Jean were months away from harvest and the inhabitants of Fort Louis needed food immediately. Bienville was afraid that if more food were not located, the colonists would soon be reduced to eating acorns.[11]

The inhabitants somehow struggled through the long, frigid winter of 1708–09, the "most severe they had faced since coming to Louisiana." The clothes of the majority of men and women were threadbare, the colonists not having received any new garments for several years, and the young soldiers, their uniforms literally in rags, were reduced to wearing skins of deer and muskrat killed by the natives. Even the deer were scarce, not nearly as plentiful as earlier reports had claimed, and as a dependable source

10. Min. to Dartaguiette, May 10, 1710, AC, B 32, f. 42. Dartaguiette to min., May 12, 1712, AC, C13A, 2, f. 805. Bienville to min., June 21, 1710, AC, C13A, 2, f. 549–50.

11. Mémoire du Roy, May 13, 1710, AC, B 32, f. 63–64. Dartaguiette to min., Aug. 18, 1708, AC, C13A, 2, f. 334–35. Dartaguiette to min., Dec. 29, 1708, AC, C13A, 2, f. 433. La Salle to min., May 12, 1709, AC, C13A, 2, f. 398. Dartaguiette to min., May 11, 1709, AC, C13A, 2, f. 464–65.

of food, were scarcely worth consideration. By late winter all that was available to the poor hunters were a few drawn, scraggly squirrels hardly worth the ammunition required to bring them in. Cut off from Cuba and Mexico (for lack of traversiers) the colony was enmeshed in a predicament for which there seemed no immediate solution save another ship from France. Jacques Le Roux had recently finished construction of another vessel, a small seaworthy ship of only twelve tons burden, which Bienville and Dartaguiette planned to send to Havana as soon as the choppy winter waters of the gulf subsided. Yet this hope, like the wheat at Bayou Saint-Jean, was but a promise of the future.[12]

In the midst of the colony's misery, life, howsoever impoverished, went on; indeed, new life appeared, bringing brief moments of cheer into the otherwise solemn community. On the fifth of February, 1709, Geneviève Burelle, wife of Claude Trépanier, gave birth to a daughter which Madame Trépanier's sister Jeanne named Geneviève. François Le Maire conducted the baptismal service that same day, the rites being witnessed by merchant Jean-Claude Poithier (who served as godfather) and by old Étienne Burelle (now several times a grandfather), as well as by the infant's uncle, young Louis Burelle.[13]

Three days later, Angélique Drouin, one of the last-wed "*Pélican* girls," bore a son to Jean-Baptiste La Croix, *dit* Grimauld, the carpenter from Havre de Grâce. Grimauld had come to the Gulf Coast in late 1701 with Iberville, but for the past year had been living on Massacre Island. Much in demand as a carpenter, Grimauld had made fairly good wages during the early years and was considered a "good catch" when the group of eligible girls from Paris arrived in 1704. Bienville removed him from the king's payroll later that year, however, and since his marriage to Angélique, Grimauld had lost several children by early deaths. As soon as his wife was up and about, Grimauld boarded a pirogue from Massacre Island and headed for Fort Louis with his new-born son. The weather was almost unbearably cold, the waters thrashing. On February 23, the carpenter and his wife reached Mobile

12. Mémoire de Le Maire, Jan. 15, 1714, AC, C13C, 2, f. 114–60. Min. to La Salle, May 10, 1710, AC, B 32, f. 45. Mémoire de Mandeville, April 29, 1709, AC, C13A, 2, f. 476–77. Dartaguiette to min., Feb. 12, 1710, AC, C13A, 2, f. 532–38.

13. ADM, A, Feb. 5, 1709. *DGFC, I,* p. 96. Liste des filles et des deux familles qui doigent passer à la Louisiane, 3 octobre, 1704, AC, B 25, f. 9–10. AC, F1A, 11, f. 223–23v.

and the next day François Le Maire baptized the sixteen-day-old infant which *habitant* François Dupré named Jean-Baptiste. Godmother Marie Philippe, Dupré and Grimauld, all illiterates, made their marks, before Grimauld and Angélique took their son back to Massacre Island a few days later.[14]

Two weeks afterwards, on March 11, Marie Preau, wife of Vincent Alexandre, *dit* Chenet, gave birth to a daughter, named Anne by Chenet's mother-in-law, Anne Prévost (a durable widow who had recently married the forty-two-year-old gunsmith and tool-maker Jean Bon of La Rochelle).[15]

Four days before Anne Alexandre's birth, Angela Orsseau, wife of François Lemay, *dit* Poudrier, gave birth to a son. Angela had already borne Lemay at least four children but two had died and the newborn infant was dangerously ill. Midwife Marie Grissot, having assisted in the delivery, baptized the infant herself at Lemay's home since at birth it appeared the child was near death. However, two weeks later on the fifteenth of March (his condition markedly improved) young Lemay was brought to François Le Maire for baptism. On this occasion, Marie Le Sueur acted as godmother and Bernard Dartaguiette, younger brother of the commissary, now serving as a cadet in Châteaugué's company, served as godfather, naming the child François-Bernard.[16]

Although the new births brought a ray of light into the lives of some of the families, relations between many family members were irreparably damaged by factors arising from the current poverty. André-Joseph Pénigault, thirty-one-year-old carpenter from La Rochelle, specializing in small boats, had been in Louisiana since 1700, having come with Iberville on the *Renommée*. Indentured for three years to Pierre-Charles Le Sueur, along with Jean Bon, François Dumery and Louis Bidet, Pénigault had traveled widely in Louisiana; he had served on numerous expeditions and explorations, his particular skills with boats having made him a valuable man to have along. When Le Sueur went back to

14. AC, F1A, 10, f. 283; 11, f. 70. ADM, A, Feb. 8, 1709; July 26, Dec. 20, 1710. Liste des filles . . . *loc. cit.*, f. 9.

15. ADM, A, March 12, 1709. AC, F1A, 13, f. 119v. Jean Bon was, along with André Pénigault, one of those craftsmen indentured to Pierre-Charles Le Sueur in 1699. ACM, Rivière et Soullard, 1699–1700, 72 ff. ADM, C, March 7, 1736.

16. ADM, A, March 15, 1709; March 19, 1710. AC, F1A, 13, f. 118. *DGFC, I*, p. 376. AM, B1, 8, f. 285–86. Min. to Bégon, July 6, 1707, AC, B 29, f. 273–73v.

France with Iberville in 1702, Pénigault remained in the colony; Bienville, anxious to keep him, placed him on the king's payroll where he remained for several years. By 1706 he was married to Marguerite-Catherine Prévost, a close relative of midwife Marie Grissot.[17]

All had gone well in this family during the early years. Marie Grissot, along with Marie Linant (widow Duman), had come on the *Pélican* in 1704 as a "nursing sister" and chaperon for the girls from Paris. She had been chosen primarily to fulfill these responsibilities but also to assist as a midwife in case there was need. No salary had been provided for either Grissot or Linant. However, when Catherine Moulois, employed as the colony's midwife, died shortly after arriving, Dame Grissot was elevated to the vacant position at a salary of four hundred *livres* per year, a job she held for the next several years without unusual incident. In the meantime, Pénigault, after being converted to Catholicism by La Vente, had married Catherine Prévost and relations between carpenter and midwife were exceptionally cordial. When in April of 1708 François Le Maire baptized an Indian slave belonging to Grissot, the *sage-femme* asked Pénigault to serve with her as one of the godparents. The slave, in fact, was named André by the converted Calvinist. Moreover, in October of 1708, Marie Grissot helped deliver Pénigault's first son, René-André, and her close associate, Marie Linant, served as godmother.[18]

17. ACM, Rivière et Soullard, 1699–1700, 72ff. *FLC*, pp. 1–2, 114. F1A, 11, f. 70v, 218v; 13, f. 118v, 119–19v. ADM, A, Oct. 27, 1708. Testament de la dame Grissot, 22 déc., 1718, LSMA, DCS, Dec. 22, 1718. Pénigault, son of Jean Pénigault, an illiterate butcher, and Élisabeth Aymery, was born on Dec. 30, 1677 in La Rochelle and baptized on Jan. 5, 1678 by Calvinist minister Jacques Detendebaratz at the Protestant Temple. His godfather was André L'Ortie, a renowned minister and prolific author who two years after Pénigault's baptism was forced to flee to England with his wife and three children. No doubt the fact that his godfather had been an author in part inspired the carpenter, years later, to try his own hand at the craft of writing. BMLR, Registres des familles Protestantes, A, Jan. 5, 1678; B, July 20, 1670. Denizations, Dec. 4, 1681; Sept. 28, 1682, PRO, State Papers of Charles II, Entry Book, 67. Denizations, Aug. 6, 1684, PRO, Patent Rolls. Huguenot Society of London, Quarto Series, Vol. XVIII, 1911. Pénigault's older brother Jacques had abjured the Protestant faith by 1686.

18. Liste des filles . . . 3 octobre 1704, AC, B 25, f. 10v. BN, FF, 22813, f. 133–34, 141–42. Dénombrement . . . 1 août 1706, AC, G1, 464. AC, F1A, 11, f. 218; 12, f. 108; 13, f. 115. ADM, A, April 7, Oct. 27, 1708. André L'Ortie would have no doubt shuddered had he known his name was being passed on to an American savage by his converted namesake through a Roman Catholic baptism.

Over the past two years, Bienville had been earnestly searching for ways to reduce expenditures. With so many men off the king's payroll and a dearth of funds for hiring construction workers, Bienville's attention fell on the capable *charpentier de navire* and the well-salaried *sage-femme* (still on the payroll at four hundred *livres* per year). With such a crying need for ships and small boats in the colony, it was a misappropriation of funds, the commandant felt, that such a craftsman as Pénigault could not be better employed, while a midwife (whom he felt was little better than useless) was drawing a substantial salary. Consequently, Bienville informed Marie Grissot that she was being dropped from the payroll, seeing how there was actually little need for her services.[19]

On receiving this notice, Marie was understandably furious. When she demanded an explanation, Bienville replied that her skills were not exceedingly useful, certainly not worth four hundrd *livres* at a time when the fortunes of the colony were at such a low ebb. In her own defense, Grissot asked whether or not the preservation of the lives of infants were a useful enterprise: had not the commandant himself been highly upset at the prevalence of premature deaths during the settlement's early years? And had not the incidence of such deaths markedly declined since Marie had been serving as midwife? [20]

This, Bienville could not deny, but he argued that to assist in childbirth had been only one of the functions for which the crown had sent her to Louisiana. Among her other responsibilities was to take care of the sick, in particular the soldiers who were presently suffering from an outbreak of scurvy. She was greatly needed for this task, Bienville complained, but she was not performing it. In rebuttal Grissot denied that the court had ever mentioned her attending any hospital. Such an order would not make sense, she claimed. Would the commandant have her run the risk of infecting delicate newborns with the diseases of the sick? Seeing that Bienville was bent on removing her, Grissot approached two of her defenders, La Vente and La Salle. Though outraged themselves, the two officials could only suggest Dartaguiette as the man most likely to effect any change in Bienville's

19. AC, F1A, 13, f. 115. Bienville to min., Oct. 27, 1711, AC, C13A, 2, f. 583–84.

20. La Salle to min., May 12, 1709, AC, C13A, 2, f. 440–43. Dartaguiette to min., Feb. 26, 1708, AC, C13A, 2, f. 242–47. Marie Grissot to min., [1708?], AC, C13A, 2, f. 447–50. Cadillac to min., Oct. 26, 1713, AC, C13A, 3, f. 19–21.

order. Dartaguiette, not wishing to interfere, yet in sympathy with the midwife's complaints, agreed to approach Bienville on the matter, the result of which conference was a compromise: since the charge Bienville made related to Grissot discharging but half her responsibilities, her salary would be cut proportionately. Henceforth, she would receive but two hundred *livres* per year while the remaining two hundred *livres* would go to Pénigault to assist Jacques Le Roux in the construction of the sorely-needed vessels.[21]

Marie Grissot was plainly dissatisfied with this solution. While appreciative of Dartaguiette's efforts in saving at least half of her salary, she wrote immediately to Pontchartrain, denouncing Bienville as a *debauché* and as a man unfit to govern the colony. She claimed, moreover, that Bienville had been persecuting her for several years, that his actions stemmed not so much from her so-called "uselessness" but from the fact that several years earlier she had refused to add her testimony to the charges promoted by Bienville and his officers of La Salle's incompetence.[22]

The charge of political persecution was one to whet the curiosity of Minister Pontchartrain. Ever since the *exposé* of Sérigny and Iberville he had been convinced that Bienville's hands were not entirely clean. He was equally convinced that Bienville was using his power to prevent the truth from coming to light. Being so far from the scene, however, he could only rely on the judgment of Dartaguiette whom he ordered to "investigate the charges the *sage-femme* is making and give me a full report on the matter." To Bienville he wrote in an unusually firm manner:

> I have been informed that you were ill-treating the woman named Marie Grissot, a midwife, and that you tried to keep her from performing the duties for which she was appointed, under the pretext that she is not useful in Louisiana. I must tell you that since this woman has been sent there by order of the king, His Majesty's intention is that she should remain there, that she should serve there and that you should take care not to mistreat her.[23]

Upon receiving the minister's reprimand, Bienville was quick to deny the complaint; he also found it politic to more than once

21. Mémoire du Roy, Dec. 18, 1712, AC, B 34, f. 145–45v. Min. to Dartaguiette, May 10, 1710, AC, B 32, f. 324v.

22. Marie Grissot to min., [1708?], AC, C13A, 2, f. 448–50.

23. Min. to Bienville, May 10, 1710, AC, B 32, f. 39v.

mention the role that the minister's chosen representative had played in his ultimate decision:

> The woman called Marie Grissot . . . was quite improper in making complaints to your Lordship of the alleged ill treatment I gave her, since I have never committed any wrong against her or against anybody. It is quite true, my Lord, that since we observed that this woman who was sent to this country to assist in cases of childbirth and to care for the sick, had refused to perform the latter function although we asked of her (concerning the objection she raised against caring for the men) only that she share the responsibility, the administration of which we were forced to delegate to a soldier since we had no hospital or person put aside for that purpose. M. Dartaguiette and I believed it worthless to have a salary given to a person for no service at all in view of the fact that she has always made the women whom she has delivered pay. It is on the basis of those complaints that M. Dartaguiette and I have cut off half her salary and have given it to a carpenter who is much more useful, in addition to which, my Lord, I have not done any further wrong to her. M. Dartaguiette will be able to give you testimony about it.[24]

Pontchartrain, as did Marie Grissot, found it curious that Bienville could insinuate (as he earlier did) that the midwife was perfectly able to subsist on the inhabitants' private payments, while at the same time pointing out the colonists' scarcity of money. The commandant had made that statement after accusing Grissot of charging the child-bearing women fees in addition to the salary she was receiving from the king. Nevertheless, the minister had little choice but to accept Bienville's decision until he heard further from Dartaguiette; the matter would rest thusly for the next several years: Grissot was to remain as midwife (Pontchartrain was adamant about this point), but at a monthly salary of only 16.67 *livres*. Although she steadfastly refused to tend the sick soldiers, she volunteered her associate Marie Linant to serve in that capacity, an arrangement that was eventually accepted (after which Grissot was restored to her full salary five years later).[25]

24. Bienville to min., Oct. 27, 1711, AC, C13A, 2, f. 583–84.

25. Marie Grissot to min., [1708?], AC, C13A, 2, f. 147–50. Min. to Dartaguiette, May 10, 1710, AC, B 32, f. 324v. Mémoire du Roy, Dec. 18,

In early 1709, however, Marie Grissot was very much distraught, not only with Bienville but with her brother-in-law André Pénigault as well. Pénigault, she suspected, was guilty of promoting the idea of her removal in the first place, and by doing so was traitorous to his own family as well as to the clan of anti-Bienvillists. Yet Pénigault, by tradition and upbringing an anti-Jesuit, had little in common with those Canadians who supported Bienville. Highly literate (at least by Louisiana standards), a Frenchman himself, married to a continental Frenchwoman, he was closely associated with some of Bienville's most severe critics, notably Jean Le Caën, Guillaume Boutin and René Boyer. Boyer, in fact, had served as godfather for his first son which Boyer had named René-André. Yet Pénigault knew well where the power lay and in a time of vile poverty, he, with three mouths to feed (and soon to have a fourth), was not one to refuse the two hundred *livres* Bienville offered him. But he did so at the lasting expense of his sister-in-law's good will; for henceforth the midwife would ever denounce him; even on her deathbed in 1718 she would disavow the carpenter, cutting him completely out of her will, leaving most of her possessions to Pénigault's only surviving child, René-André.[26]

Pénigault's Protestant background did not become an issue during his quarrel with Marie Grissot. Even had the carpenter never made an "abjuration des erreurs de Calvin," or even had Soeur Grissot attempted to use his past against him, the charge would have carried little force. Protestantism was simply not a "problem" in colonial Louisiana and few were really concerned about it.

Yet there were no doubt more than a few men of Protestant background in Mobile during the colony's first decade of existence, just as there had been a significant number in Canada

---

1712, AC, B 34, f. 144–51. Duclos to min., Oct. 9, 1713, AC, C13A, 3, f. 262. Cadillac to min., Oct. 26, 1713, AC, C13A, 3, f. 19–21. Duclos to min., Oct. 12, 1713, AC, C13A, 3, f. 288.

26. ADM, A, Oct. 27, 1708, March 23, 1709. By late 1718, Pénigault's first wife, Marguerite-Catherine, and his second son Jacques, were dead. Testament de la Dame Grissot, 22 déc. 1718. LSMA, DCS, Dec. 22, 1718. ADM, A, March 20, 1710. Unable to work because of poor eyesight and lacking in funds, was Pénigault involved in the tampering of the administration of Marie Grissot's estate before he left Louisiana in 1721? LSMA, DCS, Oct. 31, 1726.

(notably the Barré, Gaudin, Chalifour, Grimard, Baudouin, Bédard and Duteau families) and in the French Antilles.[27] Indeed, it would have been remarkable had there not been, considering the prevalence of Calvinism in La Rochelle and the surrounding towns of Saint-Martin (Île-de-Ré), Bordeaux and Saint-Jean d'Angély from whence the majority of Mobile's sailors, soldiers and craftsmen hailed. Besides Pénigault, there were at least nine or ten residents at Mobile (including soldiers and sailors) who had been baptized into the Reformed Church and numerous others whose families in France were of Calvinist background, such as Bécancour's former pilot, Jacques Bernard, *dit* Matagon, and *matelot* Rodolphe Direxen de Galambourg, goldsmith Louis Doré, *habitant* Jean Bon and Canadian Jean Brunet, *dit* Bourbonnois. François Lemay's mother, for example, was of Protestant parentage, and officer Jacques Barbazant de Pailloux's Calvinism was well known to the authorities. It is certain that if any one of several residents at Mobile had been suddenly transported to Huguenot settlements in Massachusetts, New York or Carolina, he would have found himself not only among familiar faces but among blood relatives as well.[28]

Despite the existence of such *religionnaires*, however, little was made of their presence during Louisiana's first decade. La Vente, in fact, was the only missioner to even make mention of the existence of Calvinists in Louisiana.[29] Had any one Protestant risen to a position of power or influence, his enemies might well have tried to use it against him (as in a case in Quebec involving La Rochelle merchant Gabriel Bernon who became unusually affluent, whereupon the Bishop of Quebec persuaded the governor to order him home). However, none of those Protestants in

27. *DGFC, I*, pp. 221, 376. BMLR, Registres des familles protestantes, A, Sept. 1, 1631; Dec. 11, 1639; June 18, 1647; B, March 20, 1644; C, Nov. 6, 1648; A, Sept. 7, 1668.

28. AC, F1A, 11, f. 70, 283. BMLR, Registres des familles protestantes, A, Oct. 5, 1617; Aug. 14, 1633; April 25, 1636; Aug. 25, 1639. Several of those artisans engaged to Le Sueur in 1699 were of Protestant families. ACM, Rivière et Soullard, 1699–1700, 72ff. In fact, notaries Rivière and Soullard themselves were of Protestant "heritage." BMLR, Registres des familles protestantes, A, April 13, 1613; C, March 1, 1682.

29. La Vente [to Brisacier], June 25, 1704, ASQ, Lettres, 74. Despite the lack of complete statistics, the almost total absence of some of the more common Protestant given names such as Élie, Samuel, Solon, etc. would seem to indicate that the number of Calvinists present at Mobile was not much greater than the estimates given. AC, F1A, Vols. 10–16.

Mobile had risen to a high station; they were not threatened because they were no threat themselves.

The winter of 1709 had been almost unbearably long and severe. Somehow the colonists struggled through it, and, as springtime came to the Mobile River, the inhabitants' frigid attitudes as well as their bodies began to thaw. "We are a little more tranquil than we have been in the past," La Vente wrote Pontchartrain in early May, "because of the presence of M. Dartaguiette, who inspires in us a little more reserve than is ordinary." More important, the colonists were highly optimistic concerning the end of the near famine: the latest reports from Lake Pontchartrain indicated that the wheat plants were healthy as ever; the vegetable crops, planted a few months before, would begin to yield in only a few weeks. Although the bacon in the storehouse was almost gone, there was still perhaps a two-months supply of flour, enough to last until harvest time. Moreover, the colony had just gained a traversier. During the first week in May a small one-deck sloop arrived from Cap-français, which her master quickly offered for sale. None of the colonists were individually in a position to purchase the vessel, but Bienville and Dartaguiette, seeing that she could be used for voyages to Veracruz and Tampico, as well as to Havana, persuaded a number of officers to pool their resources to procure her. This being done, Bienville planned to send her to Havana at the first opportunity in order to bring back some livestock.[30]

Prospects for an improved situation thus seemed suddenly more promising. Missionaries Huvé and Le Maire had been busy baptizing Indian slaves, among them two young Chitimacha belonging to René Boyer and Chauvin, *dit* Léry. And there were a number of pregnant women at the fort: Jeanne-Catherine de Berenhardt, wife of Nicolas de La Salle; Marie Philippe, spouse of Pierre Alain; and Marguerite Preau, wife of Jean Colon. François Trudeau's spouse, Jeanne Burelle, was in the last stages of pregnancy and merchant Pierre Charly owned a savage slave (pregnant by him) who was about to give birth.[31]

30. La Salle to min., May 12, 1709, AC, C13A, 2, f. 395–96. Dartaguiette to min., May 11, 1709, AC, C13A, 2, f. 461–65.

31. ADM, A, March 23, 30, May 30, July 27, Aug. 21, 24, 30, Sept. 19, 1709.

What new tranquility was present in the spring of 1709, however, was abruptly shattered during the first week of May by the sound of gunshots upriver. Could this be the long awaited invasion from the Alabama country? Bienville thought possibly so. If true, it was coming at an unusually unpropitious moment, for the French had even less gunpowder at hand than had been in store the previous winter when an attack appeared more imminent.[32]

Bienville sent scouts out to verify his suspicion, then began moving the women and children inside the fort. The inhabitants, especially the women and their husbands were thoroughly alarmed. The scouts returned sooner than expected. In fact, they had ascended only a few miles upstream when they were met by two fleeing Indians who quickly verified the commandant's fears: numerous bands of savages were assaulting the village of the Mobilians at the fork of the Mobile and Tensaw rivers. The extent of damage was not presently known, but a massacre was greatly feared from reports of the size of the invading forces. Bienville hastily organized a relief party of sixty or seventy French soldiers and Canadian volunteers and, with Boisbriant and Châteaugué, began to prepare for a quick voyage to the battle site some thirteen miles upriver.[33]

Meanwhile, the fighting was heavy and hot at the Mobilian village. The invaders, five to seven hundred in number, had come down the Alabama in pirogues, arriving at a point near the confluence of the Alabama and Tombigbee the night before. Several hundred had remained near the junction, while the greater number moved silently downriver, both groups to simultaneously attack the villages of the Mobilians and the Little Tomeh at dawn. When the assault came, however, the Mobilians were only momentarily surprised. Bienville had warned them the previous winter that sooner or later an attack must come, and though hopelessly outnumbered, the Mobilians were at least fairly well-armed. Nevertheless, the Alabama warriors moved quickly, setting fire to the cabins in the villages. The Mobilians, firing rapidly, retreated hastily but in organized fashion into the woods behind the village. The Alabama, advancing, were unable to succeed in slaying large numbers of Mobilian headmen. However, they did manage to

32. Bienville to min., Aug. 12, 1709, AC, C13A, 2, f. 407–08. *FLC*, pp. 123–25.

33. La Salle to min., (Extract of May 12, 1709), AC, C13A, 2, f. 439–40. Bienbilla a Guzmán, June 17, 1709, AGI, *México*, L. 633.

capture some twenty-six to twenty-eight women and children. Several hours later, the Alabama retreated to their pirogues, carrying with them their Mobilian captives, and headed back upriver.[34]

It was nearly noon when Bienville, Châteaugué and Boisbriant arrived at the village of the Mobilians with their relief force. The cabins were still burning, but the Mobilians had come out of the woods and were working to extinguish the fires. Bienville noticed only a few Mobilian dead, but from a captured Alabaman it was learned that the invaders had lost fourteen men, an estimate that later proved substantially correct by a check of bodies in the woods north of town. Bienville was undecided about his next move. Short of powder and bullets, he was reminded by Boisbriant and Châteaugué that the safeguarding of Fort Louis should be his primary concern, that an extended pursuit could leave him without any resources at all in case the attack were renewed.[35]

Nevertheless, as Bienville well knew, there were other considerations not to be ignored: the Mobilians were incensed and spoiling for revenge; with each passing moment the Alabamans were moving farther upriver with Mobilian wives and children. Should the French refuse to lead an immediate pursuit, they would surely run the risk of permanently alienating their closest ally and principal buffer nation. In the final analysis, then, the commandant saw little alternative: the Alabama must be pursued, vigorously and immediately. After the captured Alabaman was tortured and burned at the stake, the combined French-Mobilian forces boarded their pirogues and headed upriver, joined at the rivers' junction by a contingent of Tomeh and Little Tomeh whose villages had suffered but slightly.[36]

Only several hours behind the fleeing Alabama, the French-Mobilian-Tomeh forces gained rapidly on their enemy. The Alabama pirogues, laden with the extra weight of prisoners, were forced to move much slower. The next morning, however, on the right bank of the river the pursuing party came upon a grisly sight: the Alabama, having realized they were soon to be over-

34. La Salle to min., May 12, 1709, AC, C13A, 2, f. 395–96. Dartaguiette to min., May 11, 1709, AC, C13A, 2, f. 462–65.

35. Bienville to min., Aug. 12, 1709, AC, C13A, 2, f. 407–08. Dartaguiette to min., 1708–09 (Extracts with marginal notes), AC, C13A, 2, f. 428–30. Dartaguiette to min., May 11, 1709, *loc. cit.*, f. 462–64.

36. *FLC*, pp. 124–25. [Bienville] a Guzmán, June 17, 1709, AGI, *México*, L. 633.

taken, had given up the river route and had taken to the woods. On the bank of the river they had hacked their pirogues into pieces then massacred the remaining Mobilian women and children.[37]

When Bienville and his forces came upon the mangled bodies, the commandant, enraged as he was, could only conclude that further pursuit into the swamp-like forests would be utterly futile. Moreover, being now far from home, he began to be apprehensive about the security of the fort which had been left virtually unprotected. The Mobilians, however, griefstricken and inflamed, were more determined than ever to avenge the acts of the Alabamans. After some reflection, Bienville decided to return to the fort, along with Boisbriant and the Canadians. But he left Châteaugué in charge of the French soldiers, Mobilians and Tomeh and ordered him to pursue the Alabamans as long as there was any hope of engaging them.[38]

A week later, Châteaugué returned to Fort Louis in triumph, sporting thirty-four scalps and five prisoners, all of which he had taken a few days after Bienville had left to return to Mobile. After gaining what intelligence he could from the captives, Bienville was ready to dispose of them, spurred by the cries of vengeance from the Mobilians. Remembering Pontchartrain's disapproval of French use of the savage method of execution, however, Bienville sent the Mobilians with their captives back to their village site where the Mobilians roasted them over a slow fire. The commandant could thus report with perfect truth that the prisoners had been burned by the Mobilians in the Mobilians' village, failing to mention his own role in arranging the executions.[39]

Bienville, though satisfied at the performance of his "buffer villages" in defending themselves, was beset with disturbing information coming as a result of Châteaugue's mission; he well realized that the Alabama, had they been able to brush past the Mobilians and the Tomeh with token resistance, could have launched a direct assault on Fort Louis.[40] From what he knew of the strength of the invading force he was confident of the fort's

37. La Salle to min., May 12, 1709, AC, C13A, 2, f. 396–98.

38. *FLC*, pp. 124–25. Guzmán al virrey, Aug. 25, 1709, AGI, *México*, L. 633.

39. Bienville to min., Aug. 12, 1709, *loc. cit.*, f. 407–08. Bienville to min., (extract of Aug. 12, 1709 with the minister's marginal notes), AC, C13A, 2, f. 418–19. In this document, the dates Aug. 12 and Sept. 1, should be reversed.

40. La Salle to min., May 12, 1709, AC, C13A, 2, f. 396–97.

ability to have withstood such an attack; he had nevertheless learned from Châteaugué's captives of further English plans to assault the fort—on the next occasion with much more sizable forces.[41] Two months after the attack by the Alabama, Bienville spelled out the situation to Pontchartrain:

> The English in Carolina are sparing nothing to have our savages assaulted by their own. They continually come against us in large forces which [so far] has not accomplished anything. I have also sent our savages against them in order to avenge themselves. A short time ago our savages brought me some prisoners who reported that the English are preparing to attack again this autumn. In the last few days an Irishman who has fled Carolina has come here and confirms this news; he assures us he has seen the English bringing overland three iron cannons to the Alabama where he also saw two boats ready to be put in the water. They are planning to come via the Alabama River in October, forty Englishmen and twenty-five hundred Indians. I am taking necessary measures to repulse them with the aid of my savages. I venture to repeat to you, my Lord, that it is absolutely necessary to fortify the port of Massacre Island and to increase this garrison with two companies in order to sufficiently protect this colony. I have only seventy soldiers here, one-fourth of whom are only children. It is necessary to have an additional force of twenty-five men to complete the companies and it is necessary to send them [our soldiers] clothes, as they are all destitute.[42]

As uneasy as Bienville may have been about the English threat, he showed no compunction in mentioning an unlikely number of potential assailants, purely for the minister's benefit. Privately, he believed the English could not raise near the number he quoted Pontchartrain. He was far more concerned about the immediate lack of powder in the fort, for without powder he could not expect to ward off even a small number of invaders. Furthermore, since powder was the chief necessity desired by the natives, the

41. Dartaguiette to min., Aug. 6, 1709, AC, C13A, 2, f. 458–59. Min. to Bienville, May 10, 1710, AC, B 32, f. 37.

42. Bienville to min., Aug. 12, 1709, AC, C13A, 2, f. 408–09. The Irishman mentioned in Bienville's letter claimed he was to have been beheaded by the English. [Bienville] a Guzmán, Aug. 17, 1709, AGI, *México*, L. 633.

commandant constantly needed a large supply to retain the loyalty of his allies. Nonetheless, Bienville, along with Dartaguiette and La Salle, hoped that the lack would shortly be remedied. The Spanish at Pensacola, frequently long on munitions and short on food (since they raised none themselves), would be a ready market for the vegetables and Indian corn which by late summer would hopefully be plentiful in Mobile. Too, once the new crop of wheat from Bayou Saint-Jean was harvested (the first planting had failed), one of the two small ships now owned by the colony could be sent to Veracruz where that port would willingly exchange powder for grain.[43] It was, then, with keen regret that the French at Mobile shortly learned that the wheat at Bayou Saint-Jean had once again been a failure. The year before, the ill success had been somewhat understandable: the planting had not taken place at the ideal time of year, the seed had been inferior and it had been a new undertaking for Rivard and his associates. Complete success had been expected for the new crop of 1709, yet the failure of the Bayou Saint-Jean planters in the late spring and early summer of that year brought bitter disillusionment. Although the wheat grew admirably on the stalk, just before harvest time it fell prey to the extreme heat and heavy humidity, the reddish brown fungus causing it to apparently "rust" just before reaching maturity. In any case, the failure now caused Rivard and Poitié to request land farther inland, near the Grand Village of the Natchez. The dream of a breadbasket in lower Louisiana was shattered and the colony was forced to seek success with other crops were they to market food in Pensacola and Veracruz.[44]

It was perhaps some small consolation to Bienville to discover that Pensacola presently had no powder to trade anyway. When, in August, Governor Guzmán sent his ship's boat to Mobile, Bienville was informed that Fort San Carlos was as lacking in munitions as was Mobile. Still plagued by hostile natives in the surrounding woods, the Spanish were afraid to leave their fort for any length of time. Moreover, for two months they had been reduced to "subsisting on biscuits of unmixed barley soaked in

43. Bienville to min., (extracts of Aug. 12 and Sept. 1, 1709), AC, C13A, 2, f. 415–21. Dartaguiette to min., Feb. 12, 1710, AC, C13A, 2, f. 537–38.

44. Dartaguiette to min., June 20, 1710, AC, C13A, 2, f. 546–47. La Salle to min., June 20, 1710, AC, C13A, 2, f. 520–21.

water," and would soon be forced to "live along the seashore on oysters."[45]

Guzmán, in desperate need of provisions, especially corn and flour, wanted to borrow the *Vierge de Grâce*, the small vessel Jacques Le Roux had built, in order to send it to Veracruz to report his *presidio's* misery to Alburquerque. Bienville, assured that a ship from Veracruz would eventually reach Pensacola with a surplus of gunpowder, stripped the storehouse almost bare by lending Guzmán twenty barrels of Indian corn and two barrels of flour. As for the loan of the *Vierge de Grâce*, Bienville was ready to give his consent, believing Guzmán would return the favor by lending him powder when the aid sought from Alburquerque came. Dartaguiette blocked the fulfillment of that request, however, proposing instead to sell Pensacola what supplies it needed (other than foodstuffs) from the colony's warehouse. As far as food was concerned, the co-commissary told Guzmán, the corn and flour Mobile had given Pensacola should last until the next supply ship from Veracruz.[46]

In late August, a bilander sent by Alburquerque arrived at Santa María de Galve, laden (according to reports received by Bienville) with two months emergency foodstuffs and eleven thousand pounds of gunpowder. Bienville believed the problem of gunpowder was solved since the Spaniards apparently now had a large supply. When he requested from Guzmán a loan of one thousand pounds, however, the Pensacola governor (still smarting from Dartaguiette's decision) demurred, claiming he only had enough for himself. Stunned at Guzmán's refusal, Bienville began to see in the governor's attitude "evil designs" on the part of the Spanish, suspecting them now of failing to have delivered his letters the previous January to Captains Du Dresnay de Pennaru and Joseph d'Oroigne, captains of the ships *Triton* and *Apollon* stationed at Veracruz, letters by which the commandant had urgently requested gunpowder. Were such actions manifestations of some change in policy of the Spanish towards the French? Bienville was not certain, but he could offer no other reason for the failure of Du Dresnay and Oroigne to respond to his pleas. He only knew that Alburquerque had not answered his recent appeal

45. Bienville to min., Aug. 12, 1709, AC, C13A, 2, f. 406. The previous November 23, the Spanish had lost seven more men (four killed and three captured) by ambush. Moscoso al virrey, Jan. 4, 1709, AGI, *México*, L. 633.

46. Dartaguiette to min., Aug. 6, 1709, AC, C13A, 2, f. 457–58. Bienville to min., (extract of Sept 1, 1709), AC, C13A, 2, f. 415–18.

for assistance and that Guzmán's apparent ingratitude was "sharper than a serpent's tooth."[47]

Still, there remained the matter of gunpowder. In desperation, Bienville and Dartaguiette sent the *Vierge de Grâce* to Cap-français to request Governor Choiseul-Beaupré for assistance and for fifteen hundred pounds of powder. To emphasize their desperation for this commodity, Bienville and Dartaguiette asked for nothing else save a few small provisions (believing that a new supply ship from France must surely be in the offing). Due to a storm, however, the *Vierge de Grâce* never reached Cap-français; she put in at San Carlos de Matanzas, then called at Havana where in early October she managed to load some merchandise belonging to the director of the Company of the Assiento at Havana, Jean-Baptiste Jonchée, and four barrels of powder left by Dugué de Sainte-Thérèse, now commander of the fireship *Nymphe*. Thus, Mobile finally received her long-needed gunpowder. Though the supplies were not nearly adequate and were preciously expensive (total costs amounted to 2,451 *livres*), Bienville hoped they would suffice until another ship from France arrived.[48]

The return of the *Vierge de Grâce* brought an explanation of the fate of one of Bienville's earlier requests to Oroigne and Du Dresnay which had been made by a voyage of the sloop that the officers had purchased in May. The sloop had been captured in the gulf by the English and the crew put ashore near Havana. Besides the loss to the officers (for the cost of the ship), the king had spent 1,524 *livres* for the pay of the crew and the ship's provisioning. Despite the gain of gunpowder, the colony was again reduced to a single vessel.[49]

In addition to the loss of the colony's sloop that summer, tragedy also struck in the form of a fever. Christophe Poirier, Philippe Minette, Chauvin, *dit* Léry and others all lost young slaves to disease. And the Le Sueur family witnessed the death of their beloved little Vin-d'Espagne. On August 24, Jeanne-Catherine de Berenhardt gave birth to Nicolas de La Salle's

47. *Ibid.*, f. 416–18. Dartaguiette to min., 1708–09, AC, C13A, 2, f. 432–35. Guzmán reported that Bienville had actually asked for two thousand pounds of powder. Guzmán al virrey, Aug. 25, 1709, AGI, *México*, L. 633.

48. Cadillac to min., Oct. 26, 1713, AC, C13A, 3, f. 64–66. Dartaguiette to min., May 11, 1709, AC, C13A, 2, f. 461–62. Dartaguiette to min., Feb. 12, 1710, AC, C13A, 2, f. 537–38.

49. Cadillac to min., Oct. 26, 1713, AC, C13A, 3, f. 65–66.

first and only daughter, which Marie-Françoise de Boisrenaud named Marie. But six days later young Marie died and François Le Maire buried the child in the parish cemetery alongside La Salle's first wife, Madelaine Chartroux. Only a few days before, La Salle had lost a young Natchitoche slave and the day before Marie died, Chauvin, *dit* Léry saw the death of another of his slaves.[50]

In the midst of this summer epidemic, however, came brighter moments. On the same day that La Salle's daughter died, François Le Maire baptized Marie Alain, daughter of Pierre Alain, Canadian *taillandier*, and Marie-Catherine Philippe. Three weeks later, Alexandre Huvé baptized a young son of Jean Colon, *dit* La Violette and Marguerite Preau. It was Huvé himself, serving as godfather, who named Colon's son Isaac. And several weeks later, on October 16, Le Maire baptized Hippolyte Mercier's first child by Joseph Chauvin, *dit* Léry. The infant son (born at seven o'clock the previous evening) was named for his father by his uncle Louis Chauvin, *dit* Beaulieu, the event being witnessed by close friends Claude Trépanier and his wife Geneviève Burelle (who served as godmother).[51]

There were three Chauvin brothers present in Mobile in mid-1709 when young Joseph was born—Jacques, Joseph and Louis. There was shortly to be a fourth. Nicolas Chauvin, *dit* La Fresnière, one of the youngest of the eight sons of Pierre Chauvin and Marthe Autreuil of Montreal, had actually been present in the colony before.[52] Following his older brothers and numerous other relatives who had been active in the fur trade in the Great Lakes and upper Louisiana regions (in the days before Iberville's presence on the Gulf Coast), La Fresnière had served in Mobile as a "Canadian" during the years 1702–1706, along with Joseph Simon, *dit* La Pointe (thirty-seven-year-old native of Quebec and son of Hubert Simon and Marie Viez) and Jean-Baptiste Baudreau

50. ADM, A, entry preceding July 27, 1709. ADM, A, Aug. 24, 25, 1709. The entry of the burial record by Le Maire into the register of baptisms suggests that a separate burial register may not have been kept during these early years. ADM, A, Aug. 30, 1709.

51. ADM, A, Aug. 30, Sept. 19, Oct. 16, 1709.

52. La Vente [to Louis-Charles Fleury], Aug. 1, 1706, ASQ, Lettres, R 80. *DGFC, I*, p. 123. AJM, Greffe de Basset, Sept. 30, 1658; Oct. 31, 1660. AJM, Greffe de Adhémar, May 26, 1696; Sept. 30, 1700. AC, F1A, 10, f. 284v; 11, f. 71v.

de Graveline. By 1706, La Fresnière, then thirty years old and unmarried, was discouraged about his future, especially after Bienville was forced to remove him from the payroll. His two older brothers, Jacques and Joseph, in Louisiana since 1698, had become established as traders in a small way and his younger brother Louis had recently come to Mobile by way of Detroit and Kaskaskia with a load of beaver skins which he hoped to sell in France.[53]

La Fresnière, with ideas for furthering commerce between Louisiana and France, had asked Bienville for permission to return to La Rochelle on the *Aigle*. La Pointe, who had also been interested in such commerce, was already in La Rochelle, having returned on the *Pélican*. La Fresnière had only a small amount of capital and it was not sufficient, even when added to his brothers' resources to purchase a seaworthy vessel to transport furs. But there were two other merchants in the colony with greater funds at their disposal: Graveline, and a thirty-eight-year-old Frenchman, Pierre Babin, *dit* La Source.[54]

La Source, son of Michel Babin and Michelle Derbré, hailed from the village of Laval (diocèse du Mans) in France. Shrewd, experienced in business, unmarried and possessing a modicum of venture cash, La Source was eager to join the Chauvin brothers.[55] His offer was readily accepted. Still there was not sufficient capital to purchase an ocean-going vessel. To supply the remaining funds, Jean-Baptiste Baudreau de Graveline proved the answer. In his thirty-sixth year, Graveline, even at this time, possessed more resources than any other merchant in the colony. A native of Quebec where his father, Urbain Baudreau de Graveline, served for a time (1663–66) as procureur-syndic de Montréal and left a considerable estate, Graveline had been one of those vigorous

53. AC, C13C, 2, f. 15–15v. *DGFC, I*, pp. 123, 549. AC, F1A, 10, f. 284v; 11, f. 71v, 220v. Cadillac to min., Oct. 26, 1713, AC, C13A, 2, f. 92. Hubert to Conseil, Oct. 26, 1717, AC, C13A, 5, f. 51. Recensement de Canada, 1681, AC, G1, 460.

54. AC, F1A, 11, f. 228v. *DGFC, II*, p. 92. AJM, Greffe de Adhémar, May 5, 1699. Unlike Graveline and La Fresnière, La Source was no doubt literate. In his 1708 contract he signs with a clear, forceful hand. AJM, Greffe de Adhémar, April 23, 1708.

55. La Vente [to Louis-Charles Fleury], Aug. 1, 1706, ASQ, Lettres, R 80. *DGFC, II*, p. 92. La Vente [to Brisacier], Oct. 6, 1708, ASQ, Lettres, R 85.

Canadians active in the establishing of Fort Maurepas and Fort Louis. On the king's payroll from 1698 to 1701, he had early been dropped from the lists, having become rather prosperous by crafty buying and selling. By lending his capital to the planned enterprises of La Source and the Chauvin brothers Graveline hoped to increase his holdings substantially.[56]

Graveline, La Fresnière, La Source and François Guyon Des Prés Derbanne, a Canadian merchant who earlier had been active in the search for minerals on the upper Mississippi (as an *engagé* to Le Sueur in 1698–99), left on the *Aigle* with Payen de Noyan in August of 1706. At Havana they were switched to the English-made vessel, the *Coventry*, on which a few months later they arrived at La Rochelle. Before they left, Pastor La Vente (who had shipped four hundred pounds of beaver skins on the *Aigle* to be sold at La Rochelle) entrusted La Fresnière and La Source with several billets to be delivered to Louis-Charles Fleury, merchant and commissary of the Foreign Missions at La Rochelle. When the *Aigle* reached La Rochelle, the beaver skins were no longer on board, having been lost when the *Aigle* was unloaded at Martinique. Moreover, La Source and La Fresnière, after collecting for the billets, failed to send La Vente an exact accounting.[57]

La Source and La Fresnière were apparently not overly concerned with their responsibilities as La Vente's agents. The whole of the matter amounted to only a few hundred *livres*. Along with Graveline, they were busy trying to purchase a small ship and to make arrangements to carry on a profitable beaver traffic between Louisiana and France. Acting as La Vente's agents, however, had given them a chance to meet Fleury who purportedly was interested in any potentially profitable scheme. It was through Fleury that the Louisianians made contact with Antoine Pascaud, former Montreal merchant and brother-in-law of François-Marie Bouat (who had escorted several travelers to Mobile), as well as with

56. AJM, Greffe de Cabazié, Dec. 3, 1686. *DGFC, I,* p. 31. AJM, Greffe de Adhémar, Nov. 21, 1689; Sept. 2, 1696; Jan. 17, 1699. AJM, Greffe de Basset Des Lauriers, Dec. 28, 1689. AJM, Greffe de Maugue, Oct. 31, 1694. AC, F1A, 10, f. 290. AC, C13A, 1, f. 256–57. AC, C13C, 2, f. 15.

57. Clairambault to min., Feb., 1707, AM, B3, 147, f. 115. Min. to Néret and Gayot, Feb. 2, 1707, AM, B2, 196, f. 681. Clairambault to min., Feb. 4, 1707, AM, B3, 147, f. 112. La Vente [to Louis-Charles Fleury], Aug. 1, 1706, *loc. cit.*, R 80. Min. to Clairambault, Dec. 22, 1707, AM, B2, 192, f. 821–23. Clairambault to min., May 9, 1707, AM, B3, 147, f. 335–39.

Martin de Lino, recently arrived from Quebec as a representative of the Compagnie de la Colonie.[58]

From these officials, however, the Louisianians received discouraging news. The assets of the Compagnie de la Colonie had recently been liquidated and the beaver monopoly was being transferred to the French syndicate of Aubert, Néret and Gayot. It was expected that Pontchartrain would prohibit any additional beaver exports to come from Louisiana in order to protect the fur trade in Canada. Indeed the minister had already written (on June 30, 1707) to governor-designate Daneau de Muy to "apply yourself to encouraging another trade than that of the skins of beavers because it is not advisable in view of the Canadian situation." [59] Backed by Fleury and a group of La Rochelle merchants, however, Graveline pressed the court to relent. After due consideration, Pontchartrain, having consulted with Aubert, Néret and Gayot, was set to allow Graveline and the Louisianians to transport their beaver to La Rochelle, the skins to be sold to the French syndicate at six *sols* per pound. But the Louisianians, as well as the La Rochelle merchants, objected to such an arrangement. Since the merchants of Quebec had been receiving three times that amount, the so-called compromise amounted to nothing less than a prohibition. The Louisianians renewed their requests, asking to have price limits raised to twenty *sols*. Pontchartrain, now undecided, chose Michel Bégon to review the entire question and come to a decision himself.[60]

While the beaver issue was being re-examined, Pierre Babin, *dit* La Source petitioned Pontchartrain for permission to sail to Montreal on the next ship for Canada. He was, he claimed, going to Montreal to be married, before returning to Mobile. La Source's request was in accordance with a scheme worked out by Graveline and his Louisiana associates. Whether the beaverskin trade worked out or not, Graveline was convinced there were fortunes to be

58. *DGFC, I*, pp. 69, 457. Mémoire de Pascaud, 1706, AC, C11A, 25, f. 290–91. AJM, Greffe de Raimbault, Oct. 1, 1718. AJQ, Greffe de Duquet, April 2, 1685. King to Vaudreuil and Raudot, June 30, 1707, AC, B 29, f. 55.

59. Min. to Demuy, June 30, 1707, AC, B 29, f. 261.

60. Min. to Néret, Nov. 29, 1707, AC, B 29, f. 290. Min. to Néret and Gayot, April 4, 1708, AM, B2, 207, f. 75. Min. to Bégon, April 11, 1708, AM, B2, 207, f. 93–96. By 1701 the price of beaver had already dropped from previous highs of 3–5 *livres* 10 *sols* to 1 *livre* 10 *sols* per pound. *Cf.* Vaudreuil and Bégon to min., Nov. 12, 1712, AC, C11A, 33, f. 15–46.

made by supplying France with Louisiana's resources. Perhaps there was more to be gained from minerals than from beaver. In Montreal, Graveline had two brothers who might be interested in investing in such enterprises, one of whom, Paul, had been active in discovering minerals near Lake Champlain. The other, Gabriel, had a ready supply of risk capital. La Source, on his journey to Montreal, would convince Graveline's brothers to make the journey with him down the Mississippi to Mobile. In any case, Graveline, with the ship he was about to purchase, was certain he would be able to supply France with any number of skins and minerals.[61]

La Source left La Rochelle in the late summer of 1707, arriving in Montreal on October 27. By late November he had wooed and won Marie-Françoise-Angélique Jallot, twenty-five-year-old spinster daughter of the late master surgeon of Repentigny, Jean Jallot. They were married in the church of Notre-Dame de Montréal on December 1, 1707, and shortly after the first of the year began preparations for the long journey to Mobile.[62]

La Source had married into a distinguished Canadian family. Marie-Françoise's grandfather, Médard Chouart Des Groseilliers, an early explorer and one of the founders of the Hudson's Bay Company, was one of Canada's most respected men, while her grandmother was a half-sister of the renowned Radisson. Her father had died heroically at the hands of the Iroquois in the summer of 1690 and her younger brother Médard was shortly to make a name for himself with Louis Juchereau de Saint-Denis in the wilds of Louisiana and Mexico.[63]

During his stay in Montreal, La Source was able to convince Graveline's older brother, Gabriel, not only to invest substantially in lower Louisiana but to come personally and bring his family with him as well. The La Sources and the Baudreaus would travel first to Detroit, then, after a short stay there, would move on to

61. Mémoire du roy à MM. de Vaudreuil et Raudot, June 30, 1707, AC, B 29, f. 41–42v. Min. to Bégon, July 6, 1707, AC, B 29, f. 273–73v. Min. to Demuy, July 6, 1707, AC, B 29, f. 274–75.

62. ANDM, registres des mariages, 1 déc. 1707. *DGFC, II*, p. 92; IV, p. 578. AJM, Greffe de Raimbault, April 24, 1708. ADM, B, Feb. 2, 1726; A, Sept. 1, 1715. Vaudreuil and Raudot to min., Nov. 15, 1707, AC, C11A, 26, f. 32.

63. *DGFC, I*, pp. 129, 317. *FLC*, pp. 197–202, 220–27. AJM, Greffe de Adhémar, Dec. 10, 1695. Cadillac to Conseil Supérieur, Jan. 2, 1716, AC, C13A, 4, f. 509–21.

the river Mississippi where they would begin investigating possibilities for commerce (in particular, minerals). Gabriel, with his wife, Marie-Catherine Forestier, and two young daughters, began preparations for the journey. On Feb. 14, 1708, at the office of royal notary Antoine Adhémar de Saint-Martin, Gabriel signed on Antoine Simon of Pointe-aux-Trembles to accompany him and his family to Mobile. Simon's services would be obligated to Gabriel for a period of two years, during which time Gabriel would be responsible for all food and supplies.[64]

Five days later, Gabriel signed on five other young men—Étienne Étienne, Laurent Blot, Jean-Baptiste L'Escuyer, Joseph Girardy and Jacques Mainville—several of whom were related to him and all of whom were in their twenties. For a salary of 150 *livres* the *engagés* were, for a one-year period, to "do absolutely all that the said M. Graveline wishes them to do," to "work on the black lead of the Mississippi if he deems it profitable" and "not to leave their services without written consent." With his six *engagés* Gabriel was now ready to depart, having already received permission from Governor Rigaud de Vaudreuil. There were to be further delays, however. Gabriel's younger brother, Paul Baudreau, who had decided to accompany the party, had signed a marriage contract with Marie Tessier that same morning. The next day the marriage ceremony took place in Montreal; it would require a few weeks for the young couple to gain permission from Vaudreuil to leave the country and for them to make personal arrangements.[65]

In the meantime, Babin, *dit* La Source had engaged François-Marie Bouat, brother-in-law of Pascaud (with whom La Source and Graveline had negotiated in La Rochelle) and a veteran *voyageur* who had already made at least two trips to Mobile. For the sum of 1778 *livres* and 15 *sols* Bouat was to provide a large canoe and to escort La Source and his bride. This was on April 23. The day following, Gabriel signed on five more *engagés*—Joseph Carrière, who already had two older brothers at Mobile (both of whom had recently established at Bay Minette), Étienne Campot, Nicolas Cadieu, Jean Alarie and Pierre Bourdon (brother of

64. Bienville to min., Feb. 20, 1710, AC, C13B, 1, No. 9, f. 1v–3. *DGFC, I*, p. 31; II, p. 150. AJM, Greffe de Adhémar, Feb. 14, 1708. *DGFC, I*, p. 549.

65. AJM, Greffe de Adhémar, Feb. 19, 1708. *DGFC, I*, pp. 57, 78, 225, 387; VI, p. 50. Vaudreuil and Raudot to min., Nov. 15, 1707, AC, C11A, 26, f. 48–49. AJM, Greffe de Adhémar, Feb. 19, 1708.

Jacques who had already brought some ore to Mobile from the Wabash and who was presently in Pensacola having it tested).[66]

By the first week in May, the parties were assembling at Lachine (at the southern edge of Montreal) where the acknowledged leader, Gabriel Baudreau de Graveline, was making final preparations. By mid-May the combined group of twenty people (including Gabriel's two young daughters and his wife, now three months pregnant) was leaving Lachine, heading upriver toward Detroit some five hundred miles in the distance.[67]

They had not planned to stay in Detroit (a recently established post even smaller than Mobile) for very long, but the journey was long and tiring. The fort's commandant, Antoine Laumet, *dit* Lamothe Cadillac, hoping to enlarge his post, tried to persuade them to stay. Most of them did stay for a time, long enough for Madame Baudreau to bear another daughter to Gabriel. Marie-Louise was baptized at Detroit on Nov. 24, 1708, and shortly thereafter the main party prepared to push on to Kaskaskia where Gabriel (who had already left Detroit with several of his men in search of more minerals) planned to meet them. Cadillac, disgruntled at the thought of potential settlers leaving his post (Was Detroit to be nothing more than a rest stop for a mass migration to Louisiana?), stepped up efforts to persuade them to stay. When persuasion failed, Cadillac resorted to more devious tactics, ploys he had used before against Canadians attempting to pass through his settlement. Refusing to provide escorts through hostile Indian country, Cadillac had established an understanding with the nearby Miami: they were free to plunder any French parties passing their way without a certain "mark of permission" on their person, provided no life was expended. Afterwards, the natives were to force the "unauthorized" travelers back to the fort.[68]

Without hesitation, the Miami attacked the Baudreau party (since the Canadians had no "mark of permission") and brought them back to Cadillac's fort, the Miami women having seized some of Madame Baudreau's merchandise. Over loud objections, Cadillac claimed that such a precaution was necessary to keep

66. AJM, Greffe de Adhémar, April 23, 24, 1708. *DGFC, I,* p. 78. SLUA, Kaskaskia parish records, I, July 26, 1704; Jan. 19, 1707. Dartaguiette to min., Feb. 26, 1708, AC, C13A, 2, f. 241–45.

67. AJM, Greffe de Adhémar, April 24, 1708.

68. Mémoire du Roy à MM. de Vaudreuil et Raudot, June 6, 1708, AC, B 29, f. 321–29. *DGFC, II,* p. 150. Cadillac to min., Oct. 26, 1713, AC, C13A, 3, f. 21–24.

down desertions but that he had no authority himself to issue any sort of "passports." Smugly, he pointed out the uncertainty of the wilderness and that it would probably be safer for travelers to remain near a fort.[69]

If Cadillac had no authority to give the Canadians permission to travel, however, he had no authority to hold them at Detroit either. After four days, the Baudreau party set out once more, this time eluding the usually vigilant Miami. Some months later, the weary group reached Kaskaskia where the *engagés* began searching the rivers for potential sites for mines.[70]

It had been decided at Detroit that Madame Baudreau would remain at Kaskaskia with her two young girls and new-born child. Gabriel, with his *engagés*, would press on toward Mobile. Having sooner than expected found suitable samples of ore along the Wabash and central Mississippi, however, Gabriel turned back to Kaskaskia from whence in late November the party embarked together. By early January 1710, the group was approaching the mouth of the Arkansas, moving swiftly downstream toward Mobile.[71]

In the meantime, Gabriel's brother, Jean-Baptiste Baudreau de Graveline, had managed to purchase a ship of 35–40 tons, the *Marguerite*, by which he returned to Mobile with Des Prés Derbanne, a small crew and a load of merchandise, turning, soon after his arrival, a relatively good profit. La Fresnière had remained in La Rochelle. Without delay, Graveline sent the *Marguerite* with a small load of cargo back to France, where La Fresnière, acting as agent, sought to arrange for more merchandise to be sent to Louisiana to be sold at Mobile and Pensacola. This time, La Fresnière had difficulty in securing a crew for the *Marguerite*, as well as a sailing permit. At this point, however, merchant Fleury, believing that good profits could be obtained in the venture, interceded for the Louisianians. Helping secure the permit, he invested in outfitting the ship himself. Moreover, he was able to convince the minister that, because only Louisianians would be

69. Bienville to min., Feb. 20, 1710, AC, C13B, 1, No. 9, f. 1v–3. Min. to Bienville, Sept. 2, 1710, AC, B 32, f. 197–98. Cadillac to min., Oct. 26, 1713, AC, C13A, 3, f. 21–23. Dartaguiette to min., Feb. 12, 1710, AC, C13A, 2, f. 534–35.

70. Madame Baudreau that same year witnessed the baptism of Pierre Chabot. SLUA, Kaskaskia parish records, Vol. I, Nov. 16, 1709.

71. Dartaguiette to min., Feb. 26, 1708, AC, C13A, 2, f. 242–46. SLUA, I, Jan. 19, 1707.

used as crew members, such passports would not be a drain on local man power. In the summer of 1709, therefore, the *Marguerite* sailed again for Louisiana, carrying La Fresnière, Joseph Simon, *dit* La Pointe, his wife Marie Foucault and three-month-old daughter Élisabeth, and several Canadian crewmen.[72]

Graveline had every intention of continuing his commerce between Mobile and La Rochelle but when the *Marguerite* returned to Mobile in the fall of 1709, he still had heard no word either from his brother Gabriel or La Source. The colony, moreover, was in dire straits as far as food and powder were concerned. Not knowing whether Gabriel or La Source would ever reach Mobile nor even if they had decided to leave Montreal, Graveline finally gave in to an offer from Bienville and Dartaguiette to purchase the *Marguerite* for the colony's use. In late 1709 Graveline sold the ship to Bienville and Dartaguiette for two thousand *livres*. The two authorities then chartered it to the king for fifteen hundred *livres* and sent it to immediately to Veracruz.[73]

In January 1710, Baudreau and La Source finally arrived at Mobile, but hopes for immediate commercial ventures were temporarily abandoned since by then the vessel had been sold. La Source and his wife, Françoise Jallot, and several of the *engagés* whose terms were ended remained at Mobile, but Gabriel with his family and the remaining *engagés* soon returned to Kaskaskia to extend the search for minerals, while Graveline awaited prospects for purchasing another ship by which to continue his commerce.[74]

72. Min. aux officiers de l'amirauté de La Rochelle, July 6, 1709, AC, B 30, f. 176. Min. to Beauharnois, Oct. 6, 1712, AC, B 34, f. 127. ACM, Amirauté, B 5584. Min. to Massiot, July 6, 1709, AC, B 30, f. 176–77. ADM, C, March 30, 1752. SLCA, Marriages, Book I (1720–30), June 24, 1724. BMLR, Extrait du registre de act de baptême et de mariage de la Paroisse de Saint-Jean, April 16, 1709.

73. Dartaguiette to min., Feb. 12, 1710, AC, C13A, 2, f. 534–35. Cadillac to min., Oct. 26, 1713, AC, C13A, 3, f. 66. Min. to Crozat, Nov. 20, 1712, AC, B 34, f. 134.

74. Bienville to min., Feb. 20, 1710, AC, C13B, 1, No. 9, f. 1v-2v. ADM, A, March 19, 1710.

XX

La Vente and La Salle: Last Days

BY the time Baudreau and La Source had arrived at Mobile in early 1710, Roulleaux de La Vente was nearing the end of his career in Louisiana. Prevented by Bienville and Deschilais from returning to France in 1708, La Vente had for a time resigned himself to remaining at Mobile (seeing as there was little he could do about it). Yet as the months wore on and advancing arteriosclerosis further incapacitated him, the pastor fell deeper into despair.[1] The lack of support from both the crown and the seminary, the seeming decline of moral behavior in the settlement, the widespread disrespect among the officers and inhabitants for his authority all acted to increase his desire to return to France. "I consign everything to the sovereign will of God," he had written Brisacier a year and a half earlier.[2] By the spring of 1710 he could confide to the same official with equally apparent resignation (but not without a subtle touch of venom for his adversaries):

> As I have tried to love the hand which has justly punished me, [so] have I labored to extend my love even to the rods with which it has chastised me. M. de Bienville and the king can actually benefit me more by their actions than by the hatred they have shown for me. One must await the orders of Divine Providence with patience; and although I am told that while I was [lately] at Massacre Island they have again made charges against me, I await tranquilly all that Providence will decide. Do not, my dear Monsieur, be so bothered over the affairs which concern my person. There is really nothing in me which merits such solicitude. Leave me abandoned to Divine Providence and I shall be at the pinnacle of joy on earth.[3]

1. La Vente [to Brisacier], Feb. 5, 1709, ASQ, Lettres, R 86.
2. La Vente [to Brisacier], July 4, 1708, ASQ, Lettres, R 83.
3. La Vente [to SME Dirs.], June 27, 1708, ASQ, Lettres, R 82.

The suspicion in which La Vente now held the king was a new facet of his paranoia; and if he considered the commandant one of those rods to which he was extending his affection he had a peculiar way of showing it. It was not without a good deal of provocation that Bienville had described the pastor as "the blackest-hearted man in the world." [4]

Bienville and La Vente had been at loggerheads almost since La Vente's arrival in 1704. But for a few minor exceptions, the dissension had been petty rather than idealogical: despite their differences, both were trying to advance the king's young colony; both were interested in thwarting the progress of the English; and both were attempting to further the practice of religion among the inhabitants. There was one question, however, which went beyond the bounds of personal contention, an issue which at least bordered on the idealogical. It concerned a subject about which Bienville considered no individual in France or America to have the insight to question his judgment, much less a stodgy pastor who had hardly left the confines of Mobile the entire six years he had been in the colony; it concerned the subject of the American Indians and their relationships with the French.[5]

Bienville had been forced from time to time during periods of near famine to send large numbers of the inhabitants, mostly Canadians, to live with the natives in their villages in order to relieve the drain on the local food supply. It was not a move of which he thought well; it was a matter of simple necessity. As soon as a new ship arrived or large amounts of supplies were received from the Spanish or local crops were harvested, the Canadians were recalled from the villages. Supported by crown policy, Bienville repeatedly warned of the dangers of too intimate a personal association with the natives. If the colony were to grow and develop, the majority of Canadians must be kept close at home —to develop the land, to begin families and to aid in defense. Too great a scattering would mean a lessening of Bienville's (as well as the crown's) authority. Since the natives far outnumbered the French, there was the long-range danger of assimilation.[6]

There were other more immediate dangers. Undisciplined Cana-

4. Bienville to min., July 28, 1706, AC, C13A, 1, f. 538.

5. Bienville to min., June 21, 1710, AC, C13A, 2, f. 554.

6. *FLC*, pp. 104–15. Bienville to min., Feb. 20, 1710, AC, C13B, 1, No. 9, f. 1v–2v. Mémoire du Roy . . . à M. de Lamothe Cadillac, May 13, 1710, AC, B 32, f. 63v. Bienville to min., Oct. 10, 1706, AC, C13B, 1, No. 6, f. 4v–5. Dartaguiette to min., June 20, 1710, AC, C13A, 2, f. 545.

dians could severely injure Bienville's *Pax Gallica*, just as unregimented Carolinians and Spaniards had earlier driven entire villages into the hands of the French. This possibility had recently become all too apparent. Early in the year 1709, an expected ship from France failing to appear, Bienville was once again forced to send some of the inhabitants (even some of the married men) into the interior to subsist. To the village of the Colapissa went carpenter Pénigault; to several villages farther up the Mississippi went numerous Canadians, among whom was Jean La Barre, off the payroll since 1706.[7]

La Barre, a seven-year veteran of the French occupation of Louisiana, was, like other of his Canadian comrades, unruly, lustful and hopeful of gaining slaves in order to trade them at Mobile to those aspiring planters who would use them to try to acquire Negro slaves from Cap-français and Léogane. At the village of Yanagoyochee, La Barre (by trading articles to the chiefs) acquired three native women, one of which he took as his concubine. On his way back to the fort where he planned to sell all three of them, La Barre, dissatisfied by the quality of his concubine's sexual performance, beat and abused the young savage unmercifully; but before they reached the fort she murdered La Barre in his sleep. To eliminate witnesses, the *sauvagesse* also murdered La Barre's other two slaves then made a hasty retreat. A passing Frenchman, however, captured her soon after and brought her on to the fort. For Bienville this was only one of several such incidents reported to him. Angered more by the dead Canadian's actions than by the act of the Yanagoyochee, Bienville nevertheless felt he must hold to the frontier custom of "a life for a life." He summarily had the woman's head broken, then sent Ensign Daraque up the Mississippi to order the Canadians home before more such incidents could disturb the peace.[8]

To his credit, La Vente deplored the action of the commandant in executing the young woman. The whole incident he saw as unnecessary and not uncommon; it was to him but one more manifestation of a too-prevalent French attitude toward the American

7. *FLC*, p. 105. Bienville to min., Feb. 20, 1710, AC, C13B, 1, No. 9, f. 1v–2. AC, F1A, 13, f. 117v. Min. to Bienville, May 12, 1710, AC, B 32, f. 39.

8. La Salle to min., May 12, 1709, AC, C13A, 2, f. 441–45. AC, F1A, 10, f. 284v; 11, f. 71v, 220v. Min. to Bienville, May 12, 1710, AC, B 32, f. 39. Mémoire du Roy . . . à M. de Lamothe Cadillac, May 13, 1710, AC, B 32, f. 63v. Min. to Dartaguiette, May 10, 1710, AC, B 32, f. 325.

savage that did neither French conscience nor French fortune any credit.

For years La Vente had harped on the subject of officers and Canadians living "in shameless dissolution" with native girls purported to be "housekeepers." He had partially succeeded in removing official toleration of this custom although the practice had not nearly been eliminated. Many of these relationships were still producing children long after Pontchartrain had voiced his disapproval. Pierre Charly and Des Prés Derbanne were among those whose offspring by native women were recorded in the parish register as late as 1710 and 1711, but few others bothered to bring such issue to the pastor for baptism.[9] Had they done so, La Vente would have doubtless shown no reluctance to receive them. Although he may have questioned his authority to baptize such children, in practice he did not refrain from doing so whenever the occasion arose.[10] The longer La Vente remained in Louisiana, the more highly he regarded the American savage in comparison to the "civilized" European. In his condemnation of Canadian licentiousness, he saw the natives in a position similar to his own—as being the victims of French abuse and oppression:

> Among these nations, as crude as they are, and full of the baleful traits of sin . . . it seems to me that there still remains something of a fine Natural Law which God hath graven in the heart of a people in a state of innocence . . . [Christianity], while being professed by persons more enlightened than they, is a true subject of confusion among them in that [the French], it turns out, are actually less Christian than the very savages who have no knowledge of Jesus Christ.[11]

La Vente was impressed by the natives' social efforts to aid one other ("an almost pure and workable communal system"), the rarity of adultery, jealousy and malevolence. "Trust is such a rule among them," he wrote, "that they judge it unnecessary to put or keep locks on the doors of their cabins . . . they are savages in name only." [12] The trait he most admired in them was their uni-

9. La Vente [to Brisacier], March 4, 1708, ASQ, Lettres, R 79. Mémoire du Roy . . . à M. de Lamothe Cadillac, May 13, 1710, AC, B 32, f. 63v. ADM, A, Aug. 21, 1709; July 26, 1710. Dartaguiette to min., Sept. 8, 1712, AC, C13A, 2, f. 799. Cadillac to min., Oct. 26, 1713, AC, C13A, 3, f. 13.

10. La Vente [to Brisacier], March 4, 1708, ASQ, Lettres, R 79. ADM, A, Aug. 13–14, 1707; June 29, 1708; Aug. 25, 1709; March 20, 1710.

11. La Vente [to Brisacier], July 4, 1708, ASQ, Lettres, R 83.

12. *Ibid.*

versal respect for the aged, a characteristic he no doubt would have liked to see more of in his arrogant young adversaries.

As long as he confined his activities to "questionable baptisms," protracted rhetoric, even to using the pulpit to voice his personal rancor, La Vente was practically invulnerable. In advocating marriage between European and savage, however, he began treading on more dangerous ground. His reasoning for such an allowance was simple and credible: the absence of French women was a fact that apparently would not soon be remedied; in the absence of wives, the Canadians lacked the restraint to control their natural passions, the result of which would be continued debauchery, hazardous relations and repeated births of illegitimate children. Granted this reality, would it not be wiser to marry French and Indian? If not a perfect solution, would not this at least help to settle down Canadians more surely than they were being settled at present? As for the ultimate results of such marriages, La Vente had no reservations concerning the quality of the offspring. "We do not see," he wrote Brisacier, "that the blood of the *sauvages* will have any ill effect on the blood of the French . . . in certain cases [comparing the natives with several inhabitants of southern French ancestry], the whiteness of the offspring is equal to that of the French themselves."[13]

La Vente, convinced of the rightness of his convictions, was ready to put his beliefs into practice, but not before soliciting by letter the opinion of Gabriel Marest from Kaskaskia. Knowing in advance what Marest's reply would be (assuming that the Illinois Jesuit preached what he practiced), La Vente went ahead: a Canadian merchant-carpenter had approached La Vente with plans to marry one of the Mobile Indians, unaware that one of his own brothers (among many others) had previously had sexual relations with this "public woman." Indeed, according to Bienville, one of the brothers intended to protest the marriage, but La Vente agreed to bless the union. Soon thereafter, the pastor brought the Canadian and the *sauvagesse* together at the makeshift church and blessed the marriage one morning before dawn, without posting the required banns. On discovering what had transpired, Bienville was angered at La Vente's audacity and secrecy. Nevertheless, he was probably pleased with its occurrence, for it gave him an op-

13. La Vente [to Brisacier], March 4, 1708, ASQ, Lettres, R 79. La Vente [to Brisacier], July 4, 1708, ASQ, Lettres, R 83. Bienville to min., Feb. 25, 1708, AC, C13A, 2, f. 116–17.

portunity to strike a double blow against the pastor's diminishing prestige: in performing the ceremony, La Vente had violated the expressed wishes of both the commandant and the court; in performing the act without publishing the banns, he had violated requirements of his own church. In view of this, could either state or church now support his conduct?[14]

La Vente, however, had answers for both complaints: how could Bienville justly condemn the pastor's actions, when his precious Jesuits, Gravier and Marest, had performed so many similar acts in the Illinois country? And what did the commandant think of the letter La Vente had recently received from Marest in which the Jesuit confessed that in view of French libertinage, wilderness clergy had little alternative but to recommend sacramental marriages were they to preserve any guise of moral behavior? As for the pre-dawn ceremony and the failure to publish marriage banns, was not secrecy justified when a pastor was obliged to minister under duress? [15]

Bienville's report to Pontchartrain of the pastor's covert ceremony was not in itself a lethal blow to La Vente. When the minister received it, he did not even immediately comment.[16] He was much more concerned at the moment with La Salle's report of the Jean La Barre incident.[17] Nevertheless, it appeared to him as one more indication that the pastor of Mobile was unable or unwilling to contribute to harmony in the colony. Perhaps La Vente had a point in his accusations that he was compelled to perform his functions under duress (after all, he *was* backed by more than one dissident in the colony); but in the place of being there himself, Pontchartrain must rely on Dartaguiette's judgment. And Dartaguiette, for the present, had not in any way echoed the complaints of the pastor.

The *causa finalis*, as far as La Vente's removal was concerned, was, however, contained in the same letter Bienville had written the minister in complaint of the marriage incident. After calling at-

14. Lettre de Marest, April 25, 1709, ASQ, Missions, No. 48. Bienville to min., Aug. 20, 1709, AC, C13A, 2, f. 413. The Canadian merchant-carpenter could possibly have been Jacques Chauvin but more likely it was one of the brothers Carrière.

15. SLUA, Kaskaskia parish records, March 20, Oct. 4, 1692; July 26, 1704; Feb. 7, 1708; Sept. 9, 1709. Lettre de Marest, April 25, 1709, ASQ, Missions, No. 48.

16. Bienville to min., [résumé of Aug. 12, 1709], AC, C13A, 2, f. 424.

17. Min. to Bienville, May 10, 1710, AC, B 32, f. 39–39v. Min. to Dartaguiette, May 10, 1710, AC, B 32, f. 325.

tention to the difficulties he usually had in getting space on the supply ships for his own personal goods, Bienville penned these fateful lines:

> The Gentlemen of the Foreign Missions obtain easily the quantity of goods they wish from your Lordship on the vessels under the guise of [being] poor missionaries. They misuse it [this privilege] since M. de La Vente, the *curé* of this place and superior of the missions, is keeping open shop and selling at higher prices than anyone else. He sells a quart of brandy for as much as six hundred *livres*, a barrel of wine for two hundred and twenty-five *livres* [and] the rest likewise. In all this country they have only one missionary who lives on maize. Last year M. de La Vente sold [all] his flour, and now that our assistance from France has been so long delayed he takes it from the king's warehouse. Now he is asking ten quintals from me, which I am granting him in order to remove from him every reason for claiming I am letting him die of starvation.[18]

When Pontchartrain came across these words in Bienville's letter, he wrote with disgust and finality in the margin: "Point out to M. Brisacier, attend to it and replace this man."[19] In short order, the minister's secretary followed up this note with a curt directive to Brisacier:

> It is the will of His Majesty that you have M. de La Vente replaced by one whose integrity, fervor and impartiality be known well . . . be assured that you cannot be too careful in the choice you make for this post.[20]

Pontchartrain's orders to Brisacier left no room for conciliation or compromise. La Vente was out and he would stay out. But there was more: Bienville's August letter (carried to Havana by the *Vierge de Grâce*) was long in coming into Pontchartrain's hands. When it finally arrived the minister was already deeply involved in making other important changes in Louisiana's personnel.[21] Despairing of success in the colony and deeply involved in

18. Bienville to min., Aug. 12, 1709, AC, C13A, 2, f. 411–12.

19. Bienville to min., (abstract of letter of Aug. 12, marginal note), AC, C13A, 2, f. 422. *Cf.* Min. to Brisacier, May 5, 1710, AC, B 32, f. 5.

20. Min. to Brisacier, Oct. 15, 1710, AC, B 32, f. 385–85v.

21. Commission de M. de Lamothe Cadillac . . . May 5, 1710, AC, F3, 241, *n.p.* Min. to Bégon, May 5, 1710, AC, B 32, f. 5.

the war in Europe, Pontchartrain had for several years been searching for a way to relieve the crown of supplying Mobile by granting a commercial monopoly to some wealthy merchant or private company.[22] The difficulty was that no such investor could be found. As long as a nonentity such as Bienville, a mere king's lieutenant, was the colony's chief authority, and as long as the colony failed to even support itself, Pontchartrain was not likely to find interested parties. However, should the minister be able to appoint as governor a well-known person who was in addition a successful merchant himself, perhaps he could attract suitable backing.

Since Daneau de Muy's death in early 1708, several individuals had been seeking the appointment as governor of Louisiana, among them Messieurs Picou, Jamain and Antoine-Alexandre de Rémonville. Of these Pontchartrain politely weighed the merits of Picou and Jamain, then dropped them from consideration. As for Rémonville, who had years earlier been active in promoting Louisiana —to him he gave more attention but finally rejected him also. Bienville, of course, was out of the question. None of these possibilities had the prestige or ability Pontchartrain was searching for.[23]

In the early part of 1710, Pontchartrain's eye fell on Antoine Laumet, *dit* Lamothe Cadillac, then serving as commandant of the fort at Detroit. Cadillac's record as military man and administrator presented somewhat of a puzzle to the minister, as it did to numerous others who had known him personally. Emigrating to Canada at the age of twenty-four, Cadillac had succeeded in marrying into the enterprising Guyon family through whose influence he was able to gain a certain respectability which eventually led to his appointment as commandant of Michilimachinac in the Great Lakes region. While serving at this post he was able to acquire a sizable fortune in the fur trade before going on to Detroit where he hoped to develop a thriving colony which would eventually grow into a sovereign polity with himself as governor.[24]

22. Min. to Jonchée, Feb. 2, 1707, AC, B 28, f. 358. Min. to Bégon, Oct. 17, 1708, AC, B 30, f. 49. La Lève to min., Nov. 18, 1708, AM, B3, 169, f. 352.

23. M. de Picous to min., May 20, 1708, AC, C13A, 2, f. 365–66. M. de Jamain to min., Jan. 2, 1709, AC, C13A, 2, f. 451. Liste des sujets . . . , AC, D2C, 51, f. 3. Min. to Bégon, Sept. 28, 1710, AC, B 30, f. 203–04. Min. to M. de Rémonville, Sept. 14, 1710, AC, B 32, f. 208.

24. Cadillac saw his first service in Canada under his future brother-in-law, privateer François Guyon. *DGFC, I,* pp. 169, 294, 296. AJM, Greffe de Lepailleur, Jan. 19, 1702.

The colony at Detroit, however, did not mature as rapidly as Cadillac had envisioned. He was consistently at odds with Jesuits, *habitants*, traders, Indians and the authorities in Canada. Even while Baudreau and La Source were having difficulties passing through his sector, a government investigator, François Clairambault d'Aigremont, was busy filing a report which presented Cadillac as a tyrannical, self-seeking administrator who had grossly exaggerated his accomplishments. Moreover, his handling of delicate Indian affairs was such as to endanger French control and influence in the entire Great Lakes region. Pontchartrain, though he had earlier been impressed with the witty opportunist, was soon convinced of the necessity of removing him from Detroit (a post he now believed to be a liability anyway) before he could do further damage.[25]

Nonetheless, perhaps the restive Gascon could still be put to good use. Despite his shortcomings, Cadillac possessed certain traits that interested Pontchartrain. Imaginative, persuasive, persistent—who else could better promote private investment in Louisiana? Disregarding his pervasive reputation as a tyrant, his self-indulgent attitude, was he not a man who got things done? With far fewer Frenchmen at Detroit than Mobile, did he not already have over three hundred acres under cultivation, in comparison with Bienville's meager achievement? If he could do nothing more than cajole Mobile's inhabitants into planting, he would have accomplished far more than the Le Moyne brothers had done in a decade.[26] Moreover, his anti-Jesuit record might be considered an asset: the seminary's enthusiasm for its Louisiana mission had been waning in recent years. With a governor in office more sympathetic to their order's presence, would not the Rue de Bac be willing to step up its support? [27] No doubt Pontchartrain considered the appointment of Cadillac a possible *coup de maître*. With one stroke he would solve the problems of both Louisiana and Detroit.

25. Duclos to min., Oct. 9, 1713, AC, C13A, 3, f. 224–25. Dartaguiette to min., Feb. 12, 1710, AC, C13A, 2, f. 534–35. Clairambault d'Aigremont to min., Nov. 14, 1708, AC, C11A, 29, f. 26–57. Min. to Daigremont, July 6, 1709, AC, B 30, f. 170–73. Min. à M. de Lamothe Cadillac, July 6, 1709, AC, B 30, f. 163–64.

26. Mémoire de M. de Lamothe Cadillac, [1699], AC, C11E, 14, f. 40–44. AC, D2C, 51, f. 3. Clairambault d'Aigremont to min., Nov. 14, 1708, AC, C11A, 29, f. 29–71. Min. to Dartaguiette, July 11, 1709, AC, B 30, f. 184–85.

27. Silvy [to Tamburini], Nov. 14, 1707, ARSI, Gallia, 110, 2. Tremblay [to Glandelet], June 5, 1712, ASQ, Lettres, O 53.

Accordingly, on May 5, 1710, the Gascon was duly commissioned governor.[28] Eight days later, the king, through Pontchartrain, forwarded his new appointee the following instructions:

> . . .His Majesty is issuing an order to Sieur de Bienville who is presently commanding in Louisiana [and] who is familiar with that country to acquaint you with all the affairs of the colony. He is convinced that he will do so in good faith . . . His Majesty recommends to you to devote yourself to the furthering of the Catholic religion, to seeing that the worship of God be conducted there with edification, to maintaining the country in a good condition, and to requiring that the inhabitants live in unity and on pleasant terms . . .[29]

Cadillac was further instructed to investigate commercial possibilities (particularly those relating to cowhides and tin mines), to maintain peace among the natives (in fact, to effect a truce with the Alabama whom Pontchartrain believed were now begging for terms) and to attempt to come to some conclusions about the complaints made against Bienville. As for La Vente's conduct, Cadillac was to investigate the pastor's behavior and to render an account of it. Although Pontchartrain wanted this report for the record, it would not in the least affect his order to recall the missionary.[30]

The instructions to Cadillac completed, Pontchartrain, that same day, drafted a curt note to Bienville, informing him of the court's decision to supersede him:

> The king has judged it proper to institute M. de Lamothe Cadillac in charge of the government of Louisiana. His Majesty wishes that you render him an account of the condition of everything on his arrival and that you acquaint him with the business affairs of this colony so that he may attend to it and report to His Majesty. He desires that you stay on good terms with this governor and give this your greatest attention in order to deserve the favors that His Majesty might grant

28. Commission de M. de Lamothe Cadillac . . . May 5, 1710, AC, F3, 241, *n.p.*

29. Mémoire du Roy pour servir d'instruction à M. de Lamothe Cadillac, May 13, 1710, AC, B 32, f. 58v, 66v.

30. *Ibid.*, f. 60–60v, 63v–65, 65v–66v.

you when you have vindicated yourself against all the charges that have been leveled against you.[31]

Although Pontchartrain had made his decisions in May of 1710, they would not be known in the colony until several years later. In the meantime, Cadillac, after having requested permission from Pontchartrain to return to France, was preparing to leave his settlement at Detroit (unaware also of Pontchartrain's decision that he was to be replaced at that settlement by former Parisian clerk François Dauphin de La Forest). Bienville, still hoping for the governorship, had his hands full with local problems. Short of food and supplies and expecting another attack from the English in the autumn, he was preparing to send Châteaugué and Barbazant de Pailloux on an urgent voyage to Veracruz.[32] As far as La Vente was concerned, the Mobile pastor was still plodding along, knowing he was under fire at Versailles but not suspecting the full pitch of events.[33] On March 20, he conducted a mass baptism of Indian slaves—seven boys and three girls, all of them between the ages of two and eleven, belonging to Dartaguiette, Pénigault, Christophe Poirier, *Soeurs* Grissot and Linant and soldiers Jean Marest Dupuy and Michel Danti, *dit* L'Auvergne.[34] Five weeks later, at nine-thirty in the evening of April 28, Gabrielle Savary gave birth to Jean-Baptiste Saucier's fourth child. The next morning, the infant male was taken to the house serving as a church and with La Vente officiating, carpenter Jacques Le Compte named the child Jacques (Geneviève Burelle serving as godmother). It was the Mobile pastor's last recorded sacrament.[35]

For nearly nine months now, La Vente had been under an harrassment that was becoming increasingly difficult to bear. Bienville, believing he had fatally wounded the pastor's prestige at court, was no longer afraid of any damage La Vente might do him in France. Consequently, he now had no qualms about threatening to deport the pastor. For a long while, mostly out of spite, La Vente

31. Min. to Bienville, May 13, 1710, AC, B 32, f. 57v–58.

32. Cadillac to min., July 21, 1709, AC, C11A, 30, f. 410–11. Mémoire du Roy . . . à M. de La Forest, May 5, 1710, AC, C13A, 2, f. 555. Bienville to min., June 21, 1710, AC, C13A, 2, f. 555. Bienville to min., June 21, 1710, AC, C13A, 2, f. 551–52.

33. La Vente [to SME Dirs.], June 27, 1708, ASQ, Lettres, R 82.

34. ADM, A, March 20, 1710.

35. ADM, A, April 28, 1710.

had been determined to remain at Mobile, seeing how much Bienville desired his departure. Yet even his virulent hatred was insufficient to sustain him indefinitely in this regard. Eventually, at La Vente's request, Albert Davion came down from his mission at the Tunica to relieve the pastor, while La Vente prepared to return to France.[36]

The difficulty was, however, that in the spring of 1710 there was no ship by which La Vente could be transported home. Both pastor and commandant were waiting in vain for the supply vessel Pontchartrain had promised them. So also were a leading Chickasaw chief and ten of his warriors (as well as several of the Tunica who had come with Davion) whom Bienville had invited to Fort Louis several months previous to receive presents when the ship should finally arrive. In a last-ditch effort to dissuade the Chickasaw from joining the English, Bienville had extended the invitation, hoping that the promised vessel would arrive on time.[37] Finally in mid-June of 1710, a bilander from Martinique anchored at Massacre Island and La Vente prepared to board ship for the West Indies.

On June 21, the day the bilander left Massacre Island, Bienville rose early to finish drafting a letter to Pontchartrain. Informing the minister of La Vente's departure, Bienville could not resist making one last joust at the pastor and, not incidentally, at the seminary in Paris. Although La Vente was leaving with Bienville's consent, with even his encouragement, the commandant charged: "He is abandoning his curacy to one of his priests who was filling a [vital] mission at the Tunica with the result that the gentlemen of the Foreign Missions do not have a single missionary in all this country."[38]

At this point, however, Bienville was far more concerned with his own career than he was with La Vente's fate. Four months earlier, he had informed Pontchartrain that he had learned "with a great deal of regret, that you are still seeking for someone to command in my place," that he had trusted in "your justice, that you will take into consideration my twelve years of service in which I have sacrificed the best years of my life in such an ungrateful

36. Bienville to min., June 21, 1710, AC, C13A, 2, f. 553. La Vente [to SME Dirs.], June 27, 1708, *loc. cit.*, R 82. Davion [to La Vente], Oct. 20, 1711, ASQ, Missions, No. 46.

37. Mémoire sur l'état présent de la colonie de la Louisiane suivant ce que j'ai appris par M. de La Vente, [Sept., 1710], AC, C13A, 2, f. 565.

38. Bienville to min., June 21, 1710, AC, C13A, 2, f. 553.

country as this, separated from formal pleasures and friends in order to achieve some measure of success which has not yet materialized . . ." [39] Believing that the minister was still searching for a governor (but unaware he had found one), Bienville, in a show of importunity, made one last plea for consideration:

> Allow me, my lord, to bring to your attention that I have been serving the king for twenty years with all possible devotion without any selfishness. In the twelve years I have been in [a position of] command I have gone into debt to the amount of fifteen thousand *livres*, having always done honor to my office which pays me a salary of but twelve hundred *livres* which is not nearly enough in a place where everything is extremely expensive . . . I have no doubt at all that your Lordship is now fully informed that far from having carried on commerce I have never received any provisions since I have been in this land except what I received by the frigate *Aigle* at which time I received a few articles of furniture for my personal use. This gives me confidence, as regards my services, that you will make no provision for the nomination of a third governor and that you will do me the honor of granting me a cross of the knight of the Order of Saint-Louis. I venture to predict to you that when I am relieved of the burden of civil administration no one will better govern the colony or [more skillfully]manage the savages . . .[40]

With Bienville's appeal signed and sealed, La Vente's ship left for Martinique, from whence, joined by the *Indien*, she proceeded to France. By July 28, after an unusually quick voyage, the pastor arrived in La Rochelle where he heard talk that Bienville was soon to be replaced as the highest authority in Louisiana, words that rewarded him well for his thirty-eight days at sea. He also heard, with a good deal of consternation (yet surely with a modicum of relief) that he himself would not be returning to the colony. Worse still, as he would begin to realize over the next several months, the seminary (due in large part to the lack of his mission's success) was not seriously interested in replacing him.[41]

Before leaving La Rochelle for Paris, La Vente had a short conference with M. Rémonville who was preparing to command the

39. Bienville to min., Feb. 20, 1710, AC, C13B, 1, No. 9, f. 3v.

40. Bienville to min., June 21, 1710, AC, C13A, 2, f. 553–54.

41. Mémoire sur l'état présent . . . [Sept., 1710], AC, C13A, 2, f. 563–64.

Renommée on her long overdue voyage to Mobile. Rémonville found the former pastor "interesting . . ." and the information he secured from him ". . . useful."[42] The polite judgments were descriptive of the nature of La Vente's future service. Sensing the end of his career in Louisiana, the pastor journeyed to the seminary in Paris where he would spend the rest of the seven years left to him in a somewhat vague advisory capacity. Deprived of his mission and far from the conflicts of Mobile, his vision would become clearer and his spirit more temperate as his health slowly declined.[43]

La Vente's absence left only three missioners in lower Louisiana, all of them at Mobile Bay. Davion, now acting as pastor (and quite discontented in the position), did not even perform any baptisms for several years. Huvé, ill most of the time, thinking only of returning to France, kept busy during the summer of 1710 baptizing dying slave-children. On July 5, during a visit upriver to the Apalache village of Talimali, Huvé baptized the three-week-old daughter of a native couple, Carlitos and Teresa. Several weeks later, on a trip to Massacre Island, he christened two Indian slaves, one belonging to Des Prés Derbanne and the other owned by Dartaguiette. In early August, on his way back to Fort Louis, Huvé stopped by the small settlement near the mouth of the river where he baptized slaves belonging to Claude Parent and Charles Rochon. By the end of the month he was back at the fort where on August 30 he baptized eighteen slaves owned by such newcomers as Thomas Desercy and Dartaguiette's young brother, Bernard. Most of these slaves died. Summer's end had witnessed the ravages of a widespread epidemic, and winter brought yet another. Dartaguiette, who possessed a group of fourteen young slaves, watched helplessly as ten of them succumbed to dysentery. "It is heartrending," he reported, "to see them die like this for lack of a remedy." The dysentery proved even more calamitous than the summer epidemic.[44]

42. *Ibid.*, f. 563–66.

43. Min. to Brisacier, Oct. 15, 1710, AC, B 32, f. 214. Mémoire sur la conduite des français en la Louisiane, 1714, AC, C13A, 3, f. 389–95. La Vente died at the seminary in Paris on July 9, 1717 of complications arising from "acute apoplexy." Lettre de M. de Brisacier, Oct. 31, 1716, ASQ, Missions, No. 45. Montigny [to Guignes], Sept. 25, 1717, AN, MM, 531, f. 246.

44. Bienville to min., June 21, 1710, AC, C13A, 2, f. 553–54. ADM, A, June 29, July 5, 26, 29, Aug. 10, 30, Sept. 10, 1710. Davion [to La Vente], Oct. 20, 1711, ASQ, Missions, No. 46. Dartaguiette to min., Jan. 10, 1711, AC, C13A, 2, f. 639.

Like Huvé, François Le Maire was highly discouraged, wanting desperately to return to France. Still serving as chaplain of Fort Louis, Le Maire performed only one baptism at the fort that summer. On July 20, he baptized Philippe Alexandre, son of Jean-Baptiste Alexandre and Marie-Marguerite Dufresne. Later that autumn, he would journey to Massacre Island to baptize children belonging to pilot Simon Coussot and artisan Jean La Croix, *dit* Grimauld, yet for now he was but miserably frittering away time at Mobile, helplessly watching the epidemic reach its peak before gradually beginning to recede.[45]

Of the three missioners, Davion was perhaps the most distraught. Shortly after La Vente arrived at the seminary in Paris, the former pastor had written a letter, dated October 12, addressed jointly to the three missionaries of Mobile. On hearing from La Vente that he had been joyously received in Paris and that the seminary was possessed with renewed optimism (exaggerated, of course, by La Vente), Huvé was persuaded to postpone his plans to leave Mobile and remain for at least another year. As for Davion, La Vente's report only made him begin thinking of journeying to France rather than to Quebec whence he had recently received a letter from Abbé Charles de Glandelet (who in Saint-Vallier's absence was now administering affairs of the diocese) asking him to return there.[46] Indeed, Davion, who admitted "coming for the savages and not for the French," preferred to return to Canada, but a voyage up the Mississippi was an even more gruelling trip than a voyage to Europe. To La Vente he confessed:

> I am completely resolved to leave here as soon as possible, unable as I am to resign myself to stay in a colony where there is so much licentiousness, which we have not been able to correct, and which is going from bad to worse every day . . . I look at you, Monsieur, as being very fortunate to have been able to return to France and I beg you by the bowels of compassion of our Lord Jesus Christ to work at procuring me some good fortune, seeing how useless I am in this colony . . .[47]

45. ADM, A, July 20, Nov. 19, Dec. 20, 1710. Le Maire à son oncle, Oct. 10, 1711, AM, 2 JJ 56, 20.

46. Min. to Brisacier, Oct. 15, 1710, AC, B 32, f. 385–85v. Davion [to La Vente], Oct. 20, 1711, ASQ, Missions, No. 46. ASQ, Chapitre, 30–32; Polygraphie, II, 28. The venerable Bishop Laval had died on May 6, 1708, Glandelet pronouncing his funeral oration. *DGFC, I,* p. 172. ANDQ, Sépultures, May 9, 1708.

47. Davion [to La Vente], Oct. 20, 1711, ASQ, Missions, No. 46.

With La Vente back in Paris, Bienville was rid of his most hated and energetic personal adversary. However, his most dangerous enemy, the man who had done him the most damage at court, was still present: *Commissaire* Nicolas de La Salle. The commissary had watched La Vente's departure for France with grave uneasiness. Although he hoped that the pastor would be able to successfully plead the case of the anti-Bienvillists in Paris (and possibly at Versailles), he nonetheless felt forlorn without the intrepid, outspoken La Vente to second him in local confrontations. Yet La Salle was not to shrink from launching new charges against the commandant. Sometime before La Vente left Massacre Island, La Salle wrote Pontchartrain, describing one of Bienville's recent maneuvers: Jacques Leméry, former warehouse guard whom Bienville had appointed some years ago (against La Salle's advice), was seeking to learn the art of forging La Salle's signature. Leméry, after a rift with Bienville in 1706, had been dismissed by the commandant. For the past several years he had been regarded by almost everyone as a drunken pariah. However, according to La Salle, Bienville was at present encouraging the ex-warehousekeeper to "hang around" the *magasin* under pretense of "helping out" since La Salle was short of assistance, but in reality to learn how to make La Salle's signature, or, in the event he was unable to accomplish that, to make certain deletions from the account books.[48]

Before complaining to Pontchartrain, La Salle had rejected Leméry's offer of aid, then lodged a protest to Dartaguiette. On the same ship which carried La Vente, La Salle submitted an accounting to the crown for 8,140 *livres* and 10 *sols*, principally for provisions (including 108 quintals and 99 pounds of fresh pork, 34 quintals of fresh beef and 116 barrels of Indian corn) which had been furnished for the subsistence of the garrison by some of the Mobile merchants between April 1, 1709 and May 23, 1710 during the period of near famine.[49] Bienville signed the statement with La Salle, but he could not know that in the letter La Salle drafted to accompany the account, the commissary was also blatantly accusing the commandant:

> It is also clear that in this provisioning, M. de Bienville . . . is included as having borrowed fifteen quintals of fresh beef,

48. La Salle to min., May 12, 1709, AC, C13A, 2, f. 445–46. Min. to Dartaguiette, May 10, 1710, AC, B 32, f. 46–47. Mémoire du roy . . . à M. de Lamothe Cadillac, May 13, 1710, AC, B 32, f. 63–63v.

49. Rélevé des vivres . . . [June, 1710], AC, C13A, 2, f. 529–30.

> fifty-nine quintals of fresh pork and fifty quintals of Indian corn . . . in order to avoid paying off his original debt, which he has owed the king's storehouse since the beginning of this establishment.[50]

La Salle further complained that in recently dispatching Ensign Daraque and two Canadians to the Illinois country Bienville's stated purposes for the expedition (to take the savages presents and to order the Canadians back to the fort) was not his true aim. In reality, La Salle claimed, Daraque's mission was to trade in furs and slaves (for which Bienville would reap the larger profits) to be sold at Martinique and Cap-français, the commerce to be at the colony's expense. "It would be helpful," he went on, "if your Lordship should issue an order forbidding us to allow these men their salaries for the several months they are absent . . . Otherwise Messrs. the naval officers and those serving inland would be able to claim the same privilege when they travel to Paris or to the provinces to tend to their private affairs; it is quite necessary that the commissioner who is in charge of this matter give strict orders in writing for the officials to confine themselves to guarding the land and the ports which they command." [51]

Pontchartrain's reaction to La Salle's new charges was fairly predictable: he took the commissary's accusations seriously, but he felt incapable of deciding on the accuracy of them "from such a distance." Apparently he believed (or was trying desperately to believe) the worst. However, since Bienville was soon to be replaced as the chief authority in Louisiana, he was not quite as consumed with the question of Bienville's guilt or innocence as he had been previously. Yet if Bienville were to continue to occupy some position of command in the colony commensurate with his abilities, Pontchartrain still wanted the facts. On this point, the minister was no less determined than before; yet, possibly hoping to catch Bienville off guard, he refrained from mentioning La Salle's complaints in subsequent letters to the commandant.[52] He was careful, however, to reaffirm his feelings on the matter to Dartaguiette on whom he was still placing his trust to come to a resolution:

50. La Salle to min., June 20, 1710, AC, C13A, 2, f. 524.
51. *Ibid.*, f. 525–26.
52. Min. to Bienville, May 10, 1710, AC, B 32, f. 36v–41. Min. to Bienville, Sept. 2, 1710, AC, B 32, f. 197–98v. Min to Bienville, Sept. 9, 1710, AC, B 32, f. 206.

> I have received the initial reports that you have sent concerning the complaints of Sieur de La Salle against Sieur de Bienville. It is probable that no proof can be gained against the latter as long as he remains as the highest authority in the country; so it is necessary to wait until there is a new governor to shed further light on the charges that have been made. I am certain that you have found many contradictions in all the facts that have been brought out on both sides. It is for you to verify them on the spot since it is not possible for me to do this . . .[53]

As far as Dartaguiette's role in the continued investigation of Bienville was concerned, the co-commissary had long since lost interest in pursuing the matter. His first reports, made in February of 1708 almost immediately upon his arrival, were, he thought, fairly detailed and specific, despite the haste with which he was compelled to submit them.[54] Although they failed to give Pontchartrain the full coverage he wanted, the reports promised of more precise information to come. Three months afterwards, Dartaguiette had indeed sent further word: M. de Bienville had not distributed one-fourth of the presents that had been sent for the savages; he had given only enough to supply the chiefs and those warriors that accompanied the chiefs to the fort.[55] The remark must have further piqued the minister's suspicion: by failing to fully distribute the supplies sent for the savages, was Bienville keeping the merchandise for himself to trade for his own profit? The assumption was natural enough, perhaps; but Bienville had by this time abandoned such obvious tactics, especially with the minister's representative so close at hand. According to Dartaguiette, the commandant was using the goods intended as gifts to trade evenly with the natives for maize whenever the colony's flour was lacking. What he did not trade to the Indians, he sold to the more affluent of the inhabitants, the proceeds accruing to the king. At the same time he was withholding the savages' presents, Bienville had managed "to maintain their good faith and loyalty." From this latter reference to Bienville's success, Pontchartrain must have suspected even at this early date that Dartaguiette was being

53. Min. to Dartaguiette, June 11, 1709, AC, B 30, f. 185–86.

54. Interrogatoire des habitants . . . par M. d'Artaguiette, Feb. 24, 25, 26, 27, 1708, AC, C13A, 2, f. 249–312. Mémoire d'Artaguiette, Feb. 26, 1708, AC, C13A, 2, f. 57–69.

55. Dartaguiette to min., May 25, 1708, AC, C13A, 2, f. 318.

won over by the commandant; yet in the same letter, Dartaguiette promised the minister:

> I neglect nothing in order to inform myself of the truth of everything; and I hope that upon the arrival of the first vessel, there will remain nothing to be desired from me to make you a sincere report of all your Lordship will desire to to know . . .[56]

In letters written later that year, Dartaguiette submitted only some additional evidence he had found against Iberville.[57] While further promising to continue his investigations, he again found occasion to praise the commandant: "M. de Bienville works without ceasing in order to place this fort in a state of preparedness."[58]

By the year 1710, both Pontchartrain and La Salle had given up on Dartaguiette's being able to produce any conclusive evidence against Bienville. Dartaguiette, in fact, had already requested to be allowed to leave Mobile. Pontchartrain, having just appointed Cadillac, contented himself with the hope that further inquiry would show more success in the hands of the new governor. In giving permission to Dartaguiette to return to France he had hopes of learning more from the co-commissary in person, but that would remain to be seen.[59] For the moment it was perhaps natural that Dartaguiette, as a realist, would be lenient in his judgment of Bienville. Without food, the inhabitants demoralized, what leader present was more likely to hold the colony together? With a dearth of gunpowder, menaced by alien Indians, with the colony's native allies continually threatening to join the English, who could better hold the shaky Chickasaw and Choctaw alliances, without which the colony would be practically defenseless? If Bienville were a sloven civil administrator, if he were an erratic military leader, if he were contentious, overweening, opportunistic, even a petty thief, did it matter so much under such conditions as these? He could also be decisive, inventive, even inspirational. He was, with all his faults, a leader and the man in whom at least a majority

56. *Ibid.*, f. 318–19, 324–25.
57. Dartaguiette to min., Aug. 18, 1708, AC, C13A, 2, f. 38–40.
58. Dartaguiette to min., Oct. 1, 1708, AC, C13A, 2, f. 342.
59. Min. to Dartaguiette, May 10, 1710, AC, B 32, f. 42–45. Mémoire du Roy . . . à M. de Lamothe Cadillac, May 13, 1710, AC, B 32, f. 59–59v, 61–61v. Cadillac would later complain that Dartaguiette had not seriously pursued the case against Bienville. Cadillac to min., Oct. 26, 1713, AC, C13A, 3, f. 59.

of the able-bodied inhabitants still had the most confidence. More important, he commanded the undying respect of the two most influential groups in lower Louisiana—the Canadians and the Indians.

Throughout his tenure, La Salle had clung tenaciously to a rigid standard: Bienville was using the company storehouse, the king's men and supplies for his own use. The mere fact that the commandant's aims frequently coincided with the crown's (*i.e.*, what was good for Bienville was good for the king) was not acceptable. Dishonesty was dishonesty, however great or small. Small liberties taken now would be greater liberties in the future, and where would it all end? In the mind of the bookkeeper, there was no allowance for improvisation.

If La Salle had little conception (and still less tolerance) of the tactics of frontier politics, he nonetheless had the king's interests at heart: his vigilance in such matters no doubt helped restrain Bienville from taking further advantage of the king's supplies. Yet La Salle was never a forceful personality. Unlike the commandant, his ways were not winning; he had made few personal friends while in the colony. Vindictive, given to wild exaggeration, he had tried to make Bienville the whipping boy for the colony's financial ills; but Bienville, with greater force of personality, had been far more successful in making *him* the scapegoat. Unable to reach Dartaguiette, La Salle had, since 1708, been living in a state of extreme depression, which was reflected in his work. Indeed Dartaguiette, upon his arrival, had criticized him severely for failing to keep accurate records, a charge however that was not altogether deserved. After this, La Salle had become progressively dispirited, believing that nothing he could do would remedy the situation.[60]

If La Salle had kept the interests of the king at heart, the king (through Pontchartrain) had never done a great deal for La Salle. In the early years, Pontchartrain (on the recommendation of Iberville) had raised his salary from six hundred *livres* per year to eight hundred, but the minister had never seen fit to grant the commissary the piece of land La Salle had wanted to develop farther down the bay; nor had he granted the commissions La Salle had re-

60. La Salle's own son, Simon, served as godfather at the baptism of the commissary's children, Henri and Marie. ADM, A, March 22, 1708; Aug. 24, 1709. La Salle himself was recorded only once as having served in the capacity of godfather. ADM, A, 1704–1711. Mémoire de Dartaguiette, Feb. 25, 1708, AC, C13A, 2, f. 75–76. Dartaguiette to min., Feb. 26, 1708, AC, C13A, 2, f. 57–58. Min. to Dartaguiette, May 23, 1710, AC, B 32, f. 111–11v.

quested for his sons, Nicolas and Simon. At times, even, Pontchartrain rebuked him without just cause.[61]

At the same time Pontchartrain was appointing Cadillac as governor and ordering La Vente replaced, his attention was also directed toward the position La Salle occupied. Over the past several years he had been receiving unfavorable reports about the commissary from Dartaguiette, reports which were strikingly similar to those given by Bienville and Boisbriant.[62] Perhaps he also received additional intelligence from officer Mandeville, currently in France, who admired neither La Salle nor Bienville. In any case, Pontchartrain was forced to depend on his emissary Dartaguiette for advice in such matters, and Dartaguiette was opposed to La Salle. With some hesitancy, the minister wrote to Intendant Michel Bégon, notifying him of the further criticisms of La Salle he had received from Dartaguiette and questioning the commissary's fitness to serve.[63] After finding a suitable replacement in the person of a certain Sieur Jamin, Pontchartrain came to a decision: for Louisiana's better harmony, a clean sweep was in order; along with La Vente and Bienville, La Salle should also go.[64] In notifying Dartaguiette of his verdict, however, he left the final question of La Salle's future up to his Mobile agent:

> In view of everything you have written me concerning the question of Sieur de La Salle I have deemed it advisable to have him returned to France and to send someone else in his place. Sieur Jamin, who has been ordered to embark as a scrivener on a corvette that is accompanying the *Renommée* to Louisiana, is quite capable of filling the position of Sieur de La Salle. I am sending you an order to establish him in this position, so that if you still have the same opinion of Sieur de La Salle you may be able to make use of him; but I bring it to your attention that it appears to me that the personal conflict which exists between Sieur de Bienville and Sieur de La

61. La Salle to min., Sept. 7, 1706, AC, C13A, 1, f. 477–80, 488–91. AC, F1A, 10, f. 282; 13, f. 113. Min. to La Salle, Nov. 4, 1705, AC, B 27, f. 7–8.

62. Bienville to min., Feb. 25, 1708, AC, C13A, 2, f. 93–94. Mémoire de Dartaguiette, Feb. 25, 1708, AC, C13A, 2, f. 75–76. Boisbriant to min., Feb. 28, 1708, AC, C13A, 2, f. 159.

63. Mémoire . . . par M. de Mandeville, April 27, 1709, AC, C13A, 2, f. 471–80. Min. to Bégon, April 29, 1710, AC, B 32, f. 4. Min. to Bégon, May 5, 1710, AC, B 32, f. 5–5v.

64. *Ibid.*, f. 5v. Min. to Bégon, May 23, 1710, AC, B 32, f. 104–05.

> Salle has played a large part in everything that you have written against the latter. If this is the only reason to have him return or if it is possible that Sieur de Bienville might in the future be placed elsewhere [in the colony], you should give a great deal of consideration to this change. Otherwise, I leave the matter up to you.[65]

But La Salle was not to receive word of Pontchartrain's order. In the late autumn of 1710, he was still performing, however perfunctorily, the functions of commissary at Fort Louis, unaware that orders for his replacement had been placed on board the *Renommée*, still in port at La Rochelle. In early December, La Salle's wife, Jeanne-Catherine de Berenhardt, became gravely ill, possibly from an unusually severe case of influenza. In a few days she was dead, the second of the commissary's wives to die at Fort Louis. It was only one of many tragedies suffered by La Salle in Louisiana. A year or so after his first wife, Madelaine Chartroux, had died in late 1702, his five-year-old son, François, had passed away. Following the death of another son (by his second wife) born in 1705, his only daughter, Marie, had died (only fifteen months before Jeanne-Catherine). Yet, for the La Salle children, the worst was not over: La Salle, himself, who had been ill most of the month of December with influenza, died on the last day of the month while the *Renommée*, with orders for him to return to France, was en route to Louisiana.[66]

Immediately following notification of La Salle's death, Christophe Poirier went to the commissary's home near the fort and placed the king's seals on his front door. On the first of January, 1711, the commissary's body, after a short service conducted by the venerable Albert Davion, was laid to rest in the cemetery on the outskirts of town, next to his departed wives and children. The day after the funeral, Dartaguiette removed the seals and made an inventory of the dead man's effects. The worth of La Salle's belongings proved to be very little, but as the law provided, the officials began preparing them for the auction which was to be

65. Min. to Dartaguiette, May 23, 1710, AC, B 32, f. 111–11v.

66. La Salle to min., June 20, 1710, AC, C13A, 2, f. 519–27. Dartaguiette to min., Jan. 10, 1711, AC, C13A, 2, f. 637–38. Min. to Beauharnois, Nov. 19, 1710, AM, B2, 223, f. 435–36. AC, F1A, 11, f. 223. *Journal Historique*, p. 107. ADM, A, Aug. 30, 1709. AC, C13A, 2, f. 639. Min. to Beauharnois, Dec. 1, 1710, AC, B 32, f. 226–27.

held two weeks later, the possessions to be sold "to the last and highest bidder." [67]

La Salle left five survivors, all male. The two oldest, Nicolas, aged seventeen, and Simon, aged sixteen, were now serving in Vaulezard's company. Of the three remaining, ranging in age from two to five years, all were now orphans to be reared by the few friends of their dead parents.[68] Dartaguiette, touched by the appearance of the foundlings, made a special plea to the minister:

> Aside from his [La Salle's] affairs, I beg you, Sir, to have pity on the five children this man leaves behind, who will without your assistance soon be reduced to begging. There are three very appealing ones who are well worthy of your charity.[69]

Surely Bienville, like Dartaguiette, was moved at the sight of these poor waifs losing both mother and father in such a short period of time. But equally as certain, he must have been relieved by the absence of the man who more than any other had thus far prevented him from gaining the governorship of Louisiana.

With the removal of Bienville's last formidable adversary, the commandant felt a new sense of freedom. To be sure, he still had enemies present (Davion, Huvé, Le Maire, Boyer, Boutin, etc.), but none of these men had real force, nor did they pose any serious threat. Even Christophe Poirier, who would now succeed La Salle as acting commissary, would present no special problem. As the new year began, Bienville could look forward to closer co-operation from his officials than at any time since the spring of 1702. Perhaps, he hoped, the next ship from France would bring news of a promotion, an increase in salary, a cross of Saint-Louis—perhaps even the governorship itself.[70]

67. Dartaguiette to min., Jan. 10, 1711, AC, C13A, 2, f. 637–39.

68. AMT, État civil, GG, 87, 92, Aug. 30, 1693; Dec. 22, 1694. ADM, A, March 22, 1708. La Salle to min., July 25, 1707, AC, C13B, 1, No. 7, f. 10v. La Salle to min., Sept. 7, 1706, AC, C13A, 1, f. 478–79, 488–91.

69. Dartaguiette to min., Jan. 10, 1711, AC, C13A, 2, f. 638–39.

70. La Salle to min., July 25, 1707, AC, C13B, 1, No. 7, f. 10v–11. Bienville to min., Feb. 25, 1708, AC, C13A, 2, f. 113–14. AC, F1A, 13, f. 114. Bienville to min., Oct. 27, 1711, AC, C13A, 2, f. 593.

XXI

The Spanish Grow Cold

THE removal of Bienville's arch political enemies saw a certain congeniality return to the colony's local administration. Yet such accord brought little relief to the inhabitants themselves. Canadians Denis Durbois and Pierre de Launay were just as discontented as they had been the previous year; soldiers Nicolas L'Anglois and Henri Berteau were no less ragged than they had been since 1707. If there were renewed harmony in the upper echelons of command, there nonetheless remained a good deal of grumbling and muttering among the multitudes.[1] In view of the state of affairs, Dartaguiette could graphically complain to the minister:

> There is no more bacon here; we are reduced to slaughtering the bulls that are in this colony since it is not possible to live only on Indian corn. The majority of soldiers are wearing animal skins and this gives the natives a wretched impression of us. There is nothing in the warehouse for these savages. They are just as impatient as we at having to wait [so long] for the ships. Should a large squadron anchor at Havana, it might be necessary to allow our neighboring chiefs to view it. This would give them a more favorable impression of us without incurring much expense.[2]

In the absence of sufficient food and clothing, morality showed a rapid decline. Theft increased markedly and the practice of religion diminished to a new low. Libertinism prevailed to such an extent that Dartaguiette found it necessary to devote a separate

1. Bienville to min., June 21, 1710, AC, C13A, 2, f. 549–54. Bienville to min., June 20, 1711, AC, C13B, 1, No. 11, f. 1–3v. AC, F1A, 13, f. 116, 119v.
2. Dartaguiette to min., June 20, 1710, AC, C13A, 2, f. 543.

memoir to proposing ideas for its prevention. "Of all the remedies," the commissary observed, "the most certain is to send women; otherwise it will be exceedingly difficult to stop the concubinage of the *coureurs-de-bois* and the soldiers." [3] As Dartaguiette recognized, the problem of libertinism was not merely a question of sexual immorality, but one directly related to the survival of the colony. Unmarried men, given to pursuit of the native women, were not likely to settle down and work the land, the only solution to the colony achieving self-sufficiency in its food supply.

Yet Dartaguiette could not agree with Pontchartrain that the production of large supplies of Indian corn would best enable the colonists to subsist, at least not in a satisfactory way. The majority of inhabitants, especially the continental Frenchmen (more especially the French women) despised the taste of maize. "I have urged the colonists to plant wheat," Dartaguiette advised, but he early conceded that the much-desired crop could not be harvested at either Fort Louis or farther down the bay. After the failure of Rivard and the Bayou Saint-Jean planters on the lower Mississippi, those farmers requested permission to try their luck farther inland, near the site of the Grand Village of the Natchez—"the finest lands on this continent." Permission was granted and the failed planters tried again. In 1710, at the lands of the Natchez, they made an unusually desperate effort, experimenting in planting every month of the year. Once more, however, the attempt ended in failure. As at Mobile and Bayou Saint-Jean, the wheat grew well on the stalk, but at harvest time, "the plant was all wet, the grains so tiny and so small that there was nothing but a hull without flour." Dismayed, Rivard and his comrades returned to Mobile. As far as Dartaguiette was concerned, the question of raising wheat on the Gulf Coast was decided: the crop was necessary to the survival of the colony, but it would have to be grown and harvested much farther north (at least as far away as the Wabash), then floated down the Mississippi on flatboats to the Gulf Coast settlements.[4]

The situation in the colony appeared bleaker than ever by late 1710. The lack of support from the crown had forced the colonists to "make do for themselves" were they to survive; but, demoral-

3. Mémoire de M. d'Artaguiette, Sept. 8, 1712, AC, C13A, 2, f. 799.

4. Mémoire d'Artaguiette, May 12, 1712, AC, C13A, 2, f. 804. Dartaguiette to min., June 20, 1710, AC, C13A, 2, f. 546–47. Cadillac to min., Oct. 26, 1713, AC, C13A, 3, f. 11. La Salle to min., June 20, 1710, AC, C13A, 2, f. 520.

ized as they were, the majority of inhabitants were unwilling to work any more than necessary to insure themselves the barest subsistence. Even the officials at Martinique and Saint-Domingue seemed not terribly interested in their fate, and authorities in Canada were too far away to lend assistance even had they been willing (which they were not). There remained only one immediate source to which the French could turn in their hour of most desperate need—the Spanish at Pensacola, Veracruz and Havana.[5]

In earlier years relations between Mobile and Pensacola had been cordial and mutually beneficial. Each post had been willing to help the other with supplies of food and ammunition in times of famine or siege, confident the favor would be returned upon the arrival of a new ship from France or Veracruz. In the earliest years, Mobile had carried the greater burden of assistance. During the English invasion of Apalache, Bienville had sent generous supplies of arms and ammunition. When Pensacola suffered a series of disastrous fires, the commandant had loaned food, supplies and even craftsmen (among them, François Trudeau and Guillaume Boutin) to aid the Spanish in rebuilding their *presidio*. And when Sebastián de Moscoso notified Mobile in 1707 that Pensacola was under siege, Bienville had hastened to the rescue himself with a large force of Canadians, soldiers and Indians.[6] Bienville and Francisco Martínez had once sent a joint French-Spanish expedition to the Baye de Saint-Bernard upon receiving reports that an English force had fortified that area of the gulf.[7]

On the local level, the custom of mutual assistance was the result of what each outpost hoped was only "temporary necessity." On higher planes of authority (in France and Mexico), this close co-operation of garrisons was tolerated, even encouraged, because of both countries' fear of English aggression. The Carolinians had for the moment driven the two Latin posts into each other's arms. Toward the end of the first decade of Mobile's existence, however, the pendulum was beginning to swing in the other direction. Mobile was poverty-stricken. Pensacola, while not prosperous, was

5. Bienville to min., June 21, 1710, AC, C13A, 2, f. 549–52.

6. Sebastián de Moscoso al virrey, Oct. 12, 1707, AGI, *México*, L. 633. Informe de Juan Mendo de Urbina, March 7, 1708, AGI, *México*, L. 633. Moscoso al virrey, Feb. 10, 1708, AGI, *México*, L. 633.

7. Declaración de Felipe de Mendoza, Oct. 4, 1703, AGN, *Provincias Internas*, 28. Martínez a Joseph de Guzmán, Feb. 1, 1702, AGI, *México*, L. 618.

faring much better than before. The 1707 siege had convinced Spanish authorities that unless considerably more aid were given that *presidio*, New Spain was in grave danger of losing "the finest natural port on the gulf." Men, ships and *piastres* (even a few families) began flowing into Santa María de Galve.[8] Bienville was confident that past sacrifices in favor of Pensacola would now be returned with gratitude. Yet as the months wore on, he detected a cool detachment on the part of the Spanish. They did not now seem as anxious to maintain close contact.

Despite the outward co-operation of past years, there had nonetheless always been a certain suspicion between the French and Spanish, going back to the days when Andrés de Arriola had threatened the French at Fort Maurepas.[9] That latent distrust was not lessened by France's repeated efforts to convince Spain that Pensacola would best be placed in French hands.[10] Nor had it been moderated by the results of the joint expedition to the Baye de Saint-Bernard in 1703: the year after the founding of Mobile, Francisco Martínez, having received reports of a European settlement near the site of Cavelier de La Salle's old post, sent Felipe de Mendoza and two Spaniards to Mobile with the suggestion that Bienville provide an equal number of men to reconnoiter the location. Bienville, not wishing to relinquish any of his men from Fort Louis, sent the Spaniards on to Fort La Boulaye with instructions for Commandant Saint-Denis to provide three men from that garrison. At the Mississippi fort, one of the Spaniards took ill and had to stay behind, but the remainder of the expeditioners proceeded up the Mississippi to a large tributary which they followed to the west, eventually making their way back to the coast. When Mendoza's Spanish comrade attempted to break away from the main party to make his own reconnaissance, the French pursued and killed him. Mendoza, believing his own life in danger, then stole away himself, several months later reaching the Spanish Mission of San Juan Bautista. One of the three Frenchmen was killed by the Indians, the rest eventually returning to Mobile. Mendoza was taken on to Mexico City where he gave a deposition of

8. Declaración de Pedro Manuel Cabello, Nov. 30, 1707, AGI, *México*, L. 633. Instrucción para Don Andrés de Arriola, Dec. 27, 1707, AGI, *México*, L. 633.

9. Jakob Franck al virrey, June 4, 1700, AGI, *México*, L. 618. Andrés de Arriola to Surgères, March 23, 1700, AC, C13A, 1, f. 243–46.

10. Consulta del Junta de Guerra, June 6, 1701, AGI, *México*, L. 633. El rey al virrey, Nov. 24, 1703, AGN, *Historia*, 298.

all that had happened, reporting no trace of a European settlement at the Baye de Saint-Bernard.[11]

The testimony of Mendoza convinced the Spanish that there was no immediate English threat to the Gulf Coast from the west, but the murder of the Spaniard by the French did nothing to alleviate Spanish distrust of Mobile. It was even suspected (by those unaware of Martínez's precise role) that Bienville had concocted the whole scheme himself in order to determine (with Spanish assistance) if there were any remnants of La Salle's lost colony. Moreover, the fact that Mendoza had been able to travel overland from Florida to Mexico caused Alburquerque to wonder whether or not the French, having established the possibility of a land route to New Spain (it was assumed that at least some of the Frenchmen had returned safely to Mobile), would attempt to introduce unlawful trade into the Texas country and possibly gain access to Mexico's rich mining regions.[12]

During the years 1703–1707, when the Carolina threat against the Gulf Coast settlements was at its peak, such wariness was temporarily put aside. When, however, the siege of Pensacola was successfully thwarted in late 1707 and Fort San Carlos was placed on fairly firm footing, the old suspicions returned. Sebastián de Moscoso, sergeant-major and hero of Pensacola's successful defense, returned to Mexico covered with commendations but complaining that his efforts had physically and emotionally sapped him of his strength. He was replaced by his predecessor, the veteran sergeant-major who had succeeded Francisco Martínez as acting governor in 1704—Joseph de Guzmán.[13]

Unlike Martínez and Moscoso, Guzmán was not so sympathetic toward the French. It was Guzmán who had been in command at Pensacola when the British had ravaged Apalache, who had stood by helplessly while the refugee Indians from that province deserted his district for the Mobile Bay area, thereby frustrating his plans to retake Apalache and stripping him of the sort of buffer

11. Bienville to min., Sept. 6, 1704, AC, C13A, 1, f. 457. Declaración de Felipe de Mendoza, Oct. 4, 1703, AGN, *Provincias Internas*, 28. Informe de Dn. Gregorio de Salinas y Varona, Oct. 12, 1703, AGN, *Provincias Internas*, 28. Carta de Joseph Antonio de Espinosa, Nov. 23, 1703, AGI, *México*, L. 618.

12. *Ibid.* Consulta del Consejo de las Indias, May 7, 1709, AGI, *México*, L. 479. Cadillac to min., Sept. 18, 1714, AC, C13A, 3, f. 526–27.

13. Carta del Duque de Alburquerque, Feb. 5, 1709, AGI, *México*, L. 633. El rey al virrey, Dec. 4, 1709, AGN, *Historia*, 298.

villages that so well protected Fort Louis. Although authorities in Mexico considered Guzmán "fully experienced, brave and of great esteem," Moscoso had laid on him the charge of "not being foresighted and not adequately preparing the *presidio* for defense." Without adequate support and deprived of neighboring savages, Guzmán felt the charge unmerited and laid part of the blame on the French. Back in Pensacola in 1709, Guzmán resolved to further strengthen Pensacola's defenses, reclaim his lost Indians and perhaps eventually regain Apalache for Spain.[14]

Upon Guzmán's return to Pensacola, the question of boundaries re-surfaced. Authorities in New Spain, who had always regarded the French as intruders, were insistent that if the French remained on the Gulf Coast at least their easternmost boundary should be the east side of the Mobile river and bay. In pursuit of this claim Guzmán had once, several years before, attempted to salvage a wrecked French vessel because it lay on a sandbank just east of the Mobile River channel. Bienville had used a small show of force to prevent Spanish salvage operations. Nevertheless, Guzmán continued to maintain that the Mobile River was the proper line of demarkation. Bienville, not wanting any Spanish outpost facing him from across the bay, claimed the territory as far as the Perdido River. When the commandant went to the relief of Pensacola in 1707, he had brought the question up to Sebastián de Moscoso who promised to solicit Viceroy Alburquerque's opinion on the matter. The viceroy's answer to Moscoso's query was that the Spanish governor should not dispute the French claim at the present time.[15] After Dartaguiette received word of the viceroy's response and communicated it to Pontchartrain, the minister sent Bienville his instructions on the point:

> Sieur Dartaguiette has informed me that the governor of Pensacola has notified you that he has received instructions from the viceroy of Mexico not to engage in any controversy about our boundaries which extend as far as the Perdido River. It is necessary that you have markers bearing the king's arms set up so that they may serve to distinguish our [right-

14. Junta de 3 de Junio, 1710, AGI, *México*, L. 633. Carta del Duque de Alburquerque, 14 de Abril, 1708, AGI, *México*, L. 633.

15. Mémoire de M. d'Artaguiette, Feb. 25, 1708, AC, C13A, 2, f. 316. Mémoire du Roy . . . à M. de Muy, June 30, 1707, AC, B 29, f. 248v–49v. *FLC*, pp. 117–19.

ful] boundaries in order to eliminate any future cause for dispute.[16]

But the instructions coming from Alburquerque had been received and communicated to Fort Louis by Sebastián de Moscoso who was now no longer in command. Bienville had no precise idea of the feelings of Guzmán on this subject or whether in fact there had been a recent change of heart on the part of the viceroy. In any case, he did not immediately pursue setting up the boundary markers.

Aside from this issue, Bienville had good reason to suspect that Spanish policy had not changed regarding Pensacola's effort to gain back their lost Indians. Even Moscoso admitted he would attempt to accomplish this (by means of bribery, if necessary) and even went so far as to ask the commandant the best means of reaching the natives. Guzmán, Bienville assumed, would certainly continue the attempt; but on this question he also had the will of the minister at hand:

> Regarding the complaints that the governor of Pensacola has made to you, that you have been attracting to the region around the Mobile fort the savages that were formerly neighbors of his, His Majesty has approved of the answer that you have given him [Moscoso]. He wishes that you always answer him with courtesy but that you retain these savages . . .[17]

Pontchartrain added, however, that the Spanish must be allowed to court the natives as they wish and that Bienville, although he was to make every effort to retain his allies by diplomatic entreaties, must not use force to keep them. But Bienville had little concern on that point. He knew his Talimali and Chato; he had confidence that the same factors which brought them to Mobile in the first place would keep them in the vicinity, regardless of Guzmán's overtures.[18]

Despite these bones of contention, peaceful co-operation between Mobile and Pensacola continued with no sign of interrup-

16. Min. to Bienville, May 10, 1710, AC, B 32, f. 40–40v. Although Bienville claimed that he had earlier posted boundary markers on the Perdido, this was probably carried out for the first time in November of 1711. Bienville to min., Oct. 27, 1711, AC, C13A, 3, f. 583.

17. Min. to Bienville, July 11, 1709, AC, B 30, f. 183.

18. *Ibid.* Mémoire du Roy . . . à M. de Lamothe Cadillac, May 13, 1710, AC, B 32, f. 62.

tion until the summer of 1709 when Dartaguiette refused to lend the recently-built *Vierge de Grâce* to Guzmán for a trip to Veracruz. Although Bienville had dipped deeply into the colony's storehouse to provide Guzmán with much-needed Indian corn and flour, the Pensacola governor was highly irritated by Dartaguiette's refusal and when a few weeks later Guzmán received an ample shipment of gunpowder from Veracruz he refused to lend Fort Louis any at all, claiming he had only received a small amount. After that, relations between Pensacola and Mobile began to deteriorate and suspicions increased. Bienville began to believe there was a move afoot to sabotage French efforts on the Gulf of Mexico.[19]

To clear the air and in anticipation of settling some overdue accounts with the Pensacola garrison, Bienville and Dartaguiette invited the Pensacola governor to Fort Louis in late 1709. Hopefully Dartaguiette and La Salle could settle up the accounts with Guzmán's new paymaster and Bienville and Guzmán could come to some friendly terms concerning long-range policies. Perhaps, too, Guzmán would see his way clear to lending Mobile a supply of powder from the liberal amount Bienville was certain was stored in his *almacén.*[20]

In early January of 1710, Guzmán sent word to Fort Louis that he and his paymaster and several officers and men would arrive in Mobile the following week. According to Guzmán he had been requested by Alburquerque himself to "go and observe this settlement." Bienville, anxious to fulfill Pontchartrain's instructions to "live on good terms with the Spanish," was ready for the governor's arrival. When Guzmán and his men reached Fort Louis on the eighteenth of January, the governor was welcomed by the firing of cannon and the discharge of muskets from the garrison. Visibly impressed by the ceremonious greeting, Guzmán, after a short tour of the town, was escorted to quarters inside the fort where he bedded down for the night.[21]

The next day Guzmán entered into serious discussions with

19. Dartaguiette to min., Aug. 6, 1709, AC, C13A, 2, f. 457–58. Bienville to min., (extract of Sept. 1, 1709), AC, C13A, 2, f. 415–18. Dartaguiette to min., 1708–09, AC, C13A, 2, f. 432–35. Joseph de Guzmán al virrey, August 25, 1709, AGI, *México,* L. 633.

20. La Salle to min., June 20, 1710, AC, C13A, 2, f. 522–26. Bienville to min., (extract of Sept. 1, 1709), AC, C13A, 2, f. 415–16.

21. Dartaguiette to min., Feb. 12, 1710, AC, C13A, 2, f. 535. Min. to Bienville, May 10, 1710, AC, B 32, f. 36v. *FLC*, p. 104.

Bienville, La Salle and Dartaguiette. The accounts were nearly balanced, La Salle reported. Until the previous year the Spanish had owed Mobile a total of 692 *piastres* the majority of which had been repaid the past autumn. When the subject of the local Indians was brought up, Bienville replied that the Chato, Pensacola, Talimali and Tawasa were free to go wherever they chose. As long as force was not used, the Spanish could entice them by any method they pleased. Guzmán could not quarrel with this attitude, but on another matter he had a special favor to ask: the Spanish had two buildings in need of construction at Santa María de Galve but lacked the skilled craftsmen necessary to erect them. Could Bienville let him have two French carpenters to direct the operations? He would pay them well in hard cash. Bienville readily agreed, suggesting Jean Le Caën and François Trudeau, both of whom had previously labored at Pensacola.[22]

At the same time Bienville gave his assent for Trudeau and Le Caën to return to Pensacola, he mentioned his need for gunpowder. Guzmán took the hint and promised the commandant twenty-five quintals. As for the question of boundaries, Guzmán made no mention of it, and Bienville, not wanting to put a damper on the meeting, did not even bring up the subject. From past experience he knew Guzmán's feelings on the matter only too well: in the Pensacola governor's opinion the area of his jurisdiction extended from Pensacola to Veracruz (including Mobile Bay), a claim he indeed stated to Dartaguiette (but not to Bienville) after that same conference was concluded. Furthermore, Guzmán promised to send Dartaguiette a copy of Alburquerque's directive on the matter, which to the co-commissary sounded somewhat ominous, for it differed considerably from the instructions Sebastián de Moscoso claimed he received from the viceroy two years before.[23]

For the moment, however, the question of boundaries went unmentioned. Guzmán had been invited to Mobile to be appeased, for the French desperately needed his good will in their hour of

22. La Salle to min., June 20, 1710, AC, C13A, 2, f. 523–26. Bienville to min., Feb. 25, 1708, AC, C13A, 2, f. 99–100. Min. to Bienville, Sept. 2, 1710, AC, B 32, f. 198–98v. Bienville to min., Oct. 27, 1711, AC, C13A, 2, f. 577, 582–83. *FLC,* pp. 104–05. El rey al virrey, Dec. 4, 1709, AGN, *Historia,* 298.

23. *Ibid.* Bienville to min., (extract of Sept. 1, 1709), AC, C13A, 2, f. 415–16. Bienville to min., Oct. 27, 1711, AC, C13A, 2, f. 567–68, 582–83. Dartaguiette to min., Feb. 12, 1710, AC, C13A, 2, f. 535–36. Bienville to min., June 21, 1710, AC, C13A, 2, f. 550.

crisis, just as Guzmán had been dependent on the French several years before. Later on that same day, the nineteenth of January, Guzmán received a visit from an old acquaintance, one who had spent a number of weeks in Pensacola in years past helping reconstruct buildings that had been damaged in the fires. Guillaume Boutin, Canadian carpenter, had just received word that his wife, Louise-Marguerite, had given birth to a daughter. Would the governor consent to serve as godfather in the baptismal service that was shortly to take place?[24]

Because they were friends, Guzmán was happy to assent. Moreover, Guzmán had not forgotten that Boutin and Bienville had long been at odds and that the commandant had once sent soldiers to remove the carpenter from Pensacola. On that occasion Bienville had placed the Pensacola governor in a discomfiting position. Quite fond of Boutin, Guzmán had been forced to turn him over to Bienville's soldiers (on Bienville's strict orders) when he had wanted to keep him at Pensacola. By now agreeing to serve as the Boutin infant's *parrain*, Guzmán could in part atone for his inability to come to Boutin's rescue as well as repay the commandant for having embarrassed him. The baptismal service, scheduled to take place in the fort, was to be one of the most ceremonious that had yet taken place at Mobile. With Chaplain François Le Maire performing the rites, Boutin's infant daughter was baptized Marie-Marguerite by Dame Marguerite Messier (widow Le Sueur). When the ceremony ended, Guzmán, with elaborate strokes, signed the register, then marched out of the chapel with his attendants, while Bienville remained quietly in the background, obviously miffed. The soldiers of the garrison, having been put under arms, fired three volleys from their muskets as Guzmán emerged from the chapel, one of his attendants tossing several hundreds of *piastres* to the bystanders and soldiers of the garrison.[25]

Several days after the baptismal ceremony, Guzmán and his aides departed for Pensacola. The fanfare which accompanied his

24. *Ibid.* Bienville to min., Oct. 27, 1711, *loc. cit.*, f. 568. Bienville to min., Feb. 25, 1708, AC, C13A, 2, f. 105–06. *FLC*, pp. 104–05.

25. Min. to M. Demuy, Sept. 27, 1707, AC, B 29, f. 288. Bienville to min., Feb. 25, 1708, *loc. cit.*, f. 105–06. *FLC*, pp. 104–05. Pénigault dates this incident in 1706. The Mobile register of baptisms suggests that Guzmán's visit and the baptism of Boutin's daughter took place in 1709 but this is due to the fact that Le Maire made the entry in an empty space on a page bearing 1709 baptisms. ADM, A, entry (year not given) following Jan. 6, 1709. Dartaguiette to min., Feb. 12, 1710, AC, C13A, 2. f. 535–36.

arrival—the cannon and musket fire, the beating of the drums—was no less evident on his leaving. Before his departure, Guzmán made one last request: during his stay at Fort Louis, he had reviewed the guardhouse where he spotted several French prisoners whose faces he knew. After deserting to Pensacola the Frenchmen had been seized by Guzmán and sent back to Mobile (in accordance with an agreement he had made with Bienville). When the prisoners saw Guzmán they begged him to speak to Bienville about their release. When Guzmán asked Bienville to pardon them, the commandant, not wishing to offend the governor at this point, reluctantly honored his request.[26]

After Guzmán's departure Bienville breathed a little more freely. Relations with the Spanish seemed more amiable than they had been in many months and despite the report from Dartaguiette on Guzmán's boundary claim, Bienville felt the Spanish would continue to be co-operative, a belief that was substantiated a few weeks later when the long-needed gunpowder was delivered.[27]

Unknown to Bienville at that time, however, changes were indeed taking place in governmental circles in Madrid and Mexico City—in policy as well as in personnel. Less than four months after Guzmán's departure from Mobile, a new viceroy was nominated to succeed the Duque de Alburquerque. The Francophile *virrey* had recently been reprimanded for his failure to more strenuously enforce measures designed to curtail illicit trade. In 1708, Spanish Admiral Andrés de Pez had brought numerous and specific accusations that Alburquerque and his subordinates were profiting immensely from a huge contraband trade with the French at Veracruz to the ruin of merchants in Mexico and the commerce of the regular *escuadra*. Moreover, the viceroy had been strongly criticized by the Council of the Indies for having allowed Châteaugué in 1707 to receive on credit alone goods valued at 5,328 *pesos*. On the sixteenth of May, 1710, Fernando de Alencastre, Duque de Linares, was nominated to replace the viceroy and by mid-November Alburquerque had handed over the reins of government.[28]

26. *FLC*, pp. 104–05.

27. Bienville to min., Oct. 27, 1711, AC, C13A, 2, f. 568. Bienville had refused to buy the powder outright, the price of which was "too dear." The agreement was for the French to make repayment by an equal amount of powder as soon as the next ship from France arrived. Bienville to min., July 21, 1710, AC, C13A, 2, f. 550.

28. Carta del Almirante General Dn. Andrés de Pez [1708], AGI, *México*, L. 377. Cartas del virrey de la Nueva España [*s.d.*], AGI, *In-*

Changes in personnel were also underway as far as Pensacola was concerned. Guzmán had been serving only as acting governor since he replaced Sebastián de Moscoso. But authorities in Madrid were determined to strengthen that *presidio;* in support of such a policy it was deemed necessary to send a commissioned governor. On May 16, 1709, Captain Gregorio de Salinas y Varona, former governor of Coaguila and presently serving as governor of Honduras, was appointed to supercede Guzmán though he was not to arrive until several years later. Salinas y Varona, an experienced soldier and administrator, had served in Europe for over a decade before coming to New Spain in 1687. As an explorer he was quite familiar with Mobile, Pensacola and the various inlets of the Gulf Coast, having sounded those bays long before Bienville or Iberville saw them. Moreover, as governor of Coaguila, he had been unusually successful in the conversion and management of the local Indians. In choosing him, authorities in Madrid were serving notice that they had no intention of allowing Pensacola to wither away. Rather, they intended to develop it and hoped that Salinas' experience with the Indians would be a valuable asset in the proposed re-conquest of Apalache.[29]

Meanwhile, Bienville and Dartaguiette, for the most part unaware of changes taking place in Spanish policy and personnel, were still helplessly mired in poverty, desperately awaiting the arrival of a supply ship. In December of 1710, the two leaders jointly decided on a contingency plan: should a merchant ship arrive from Martinique or Cap-français they would purchase the entire shipload on credit, then attempt to sell or trade the merchandise at Veracruz for supplies for the colony; that is, provided the ship's captain were willing to hire his vessel out for the voyage. In view of the fact that the colony, in its present situation, was obviously unable to purchase any ship's cargo outright, it was hoped that the longed-for merchant or his agent might be sympathetic to such an arrangement.[30]

---

diferente general, L. 5. Consulta del consejo de las Indias, May 7, 1709, AGI, *México,* L. 479. El virrey al rey, Jan. 9, 1708, AGI, *México,* L. 479.

29. Relación de Servicios del Capitán Dn. Gregorio de Salinas y Varona, June 20, 1701, AGI, *México,* L. 1424. Informe de Dn. Gregorio de Salinas y Varona, Oct. 12, 1703, AGN, *Provincias Internas,* 28. Salinas y Varona al virrey [Nov. 1712], *AGI, México,* L. 632.

30. Dartaguiette to min., Jan. 10, 1711, AC, C13A, 2, f. 636–38. *Journal Historique,* p. 107. Dartaguiette to min., Feb. 23, 1711, AC, C13A, 2, f. 365–66.

In late January of 1711, the *Profond*, a merchant bilander from Fort Saint-Pierre on the island of Martinique, moored at Massacre Island, captained by one Jean Béranger. The ship, belonging to Martinique merchant Jean Gachet, carried a hefty and precious cargo. Apart from smaller items which were sold to some of the Massacre Island inhabitants, the lading included choice Rouen cloth, broad Brittany linen, fine Bayeux thread, 550 pounds of steel, over three and a half tons of flat and square Biscay iron and one cardboard crate of black Pontardement lace.[31]

No sooner had Captain Béranger anchored the *Profond* than Bienville approached him with the colony's proposal. Since Béranger, as agent for Gachet, was promised by the commandant a profitable sale for the merchandise, the scheme was viewed by him with some enthusiasm. There was just one drawback: suppose the king refused to stand good for the value of the cargo in the event the Spanish seized it or it were lost at sea. Despite the unlikelihood of this, there would have to be an additional personal guarantee. In the face of this demand, Bienville stood almost helpless; he himself was already too deeply in obligation. Dartaguiette, however, showed no reluctance to offer a personal warranty. It was unthinkable that the king would refuse to honor the obligations of his colony, especially as it involved only necessaries. If that possibility occurred, however, Dartaguiette himself would stand accountable.[32]

On the first of February, Bienville drafted a note to the viceroy outlining the colony's proposal, including with his letter a list of the merchandise to be sent and a list of supplies needed. The value of the shipment totaled 10,748 *livres* in French currency, consigned to the viceroy and the royal officials of Veracruz.[33]

On the twenty-fourth of February Béranger weighed anchor and sailed toward Mexico. By March 4, the *Profond* was mooring in the harbor of Veracruz, and shortly thereafter Béranger was negotiating with the royal officials of that port. The officials at Veracruz were somewhat perplexed at the proposal Bienville was

31. Réponse de M. Duclos au mémoire des officiers Royaux de la Veracrux . . . du 13 août 1714, AC, C13A, 3, f. 610–12. Mémorandum des marchandises envoyé à la Veracrux du 23 fév. 1711, AC, C13A, 2, f. 717.

32. Dartaguiette to min., Feb. 23, 1711, AC, C13A, 2, f. 365–67. Bienville to min., June 20, 1711, AC, C13B, 1, No. 11, f. 1v–3v.

33. Dartaguiette to min., April 27, 1712, AC, C13A, 2, f. 701–03. Réponse du duc de Linarès, March 27, 1711, AC, C13B, 1, No. 10, f. 1–1v. Sns. Bienvilla y Dartagette al rey, [n.d.], AGI, *Indiferente general,* L. 6.

making them. While Felipe V had not recently disapproved of allowing small amounts of necessary supplies to be sold to Mobile, the fiscal of the Consejo de las Indias now regarded any act of trade as damaging to His Majesty's claims on the Gulf Coast. Morever, the substantial amount of goods now resting on the *Profond* was considered by the Veracruz officials to represent much more than the meager commerce which had previously been allowed.[34]

After some discussion the port officials submitted the matter to Viceroy Linares together with the recommendation that the numerous royal decrees on the question of contraband trade left them no choice but to confiscate the *Profond's* merchandise. Toward the latter part of March, Linares received the appropriate documents along with the port officials' opinions. To guide him in his judgment he had before him the recent decree of King Felipe ordering strict observance of the present regulations against contraband commerce in America.[35] With this in hand and given the situation, Linares felt he had no alternative but to abide by the recommendations of the officials at Veracruz. He therefore ordered the merchandise on the *Profond* confiscated, then directed only a minimum of foodstuffs to be sent back to Mobile. On March 27, he wrote to Bienville justifying his actions:

> I was greatly vexed not to have been able to contribute to your needs because of specific orders of the King, my master, which I found to absolutely prohibit any commerce in foreign merchandise, so much so that by resolution of the Council and so not to evade the King's intentions it was necessary to confiscate the aforesaid merchandise as per the decree hereby enclosed; but as I moreover cannot be lacking in respect for all that concerns His Very Christian Majesty's service nor in the special affection which I have for the French nation, I have ordered the governor of Veracruz to send you immediately and by the same ship at least the flour and foodstuffs for which you are asking. I assure you that I will take

34. Mémorandum des marchandises . . . 23 fév. 1711, AC, C13A, 2, f. 717. Dartaguiette to min., April 27, 1711, AC, C13A, 2, f. 701–02. Consulta del Consejo de las Indias, May 7, 1709, AGI, *México*, L. 479. Cartas del virrey de la Nueva España, [n.d.], AGI, *Indiferente general*, L. 5.

35. S.M. manda se obserben inviolablemente las Leyes y ordenanzas que prohiben los ilizitos comerzios en las Yndias . . . , March 10, 1710, AGI, *México*, L. 377. El rey al virrey, May 30, 1714, AGN, *Historia*, 298.

> pains to supply you in all the occasions in which necessity may place you; and while waiting, if you consider it appropriate to apply to the court in Madrid as well as that in Paris for the restitution of this [confiscated] merchandise and to obtain an order to that effect, I shall be quite delighted to execute it. I have also given orders to the governor [of Veracruz] to send you a small gift, for yourself, and to demonstrate the esteem I hold for your fine qualities and for all that concerns France.[36]

Over Béranger's strenuous objections, the *Profond* was unloaded (a task the officials at Veracruz seemed delighted to stretch out over a period of nearly six weeks) and sent back to Mobile with only one hundred barrels of flour. When Béranger anchored at Massacre Island in June, Bienville was enraged at the sight of the meager cargo on board. "Messieurs the royal officers," he complained to Pontchartrain, "to whom I had turned for help confiscated our goods on the specious protest that we were desirous of establishing [illicit] commercial relations, as if these goods would have been sent to them if they were not directly allied with my master who is desirous only in trading fairly with them. In any case, they [the Veracruz officials] were asked only for provisions and not money. They maintain they have never [before] refused us. That may be true, but they have always acted with so much bad grace that one has to be reduced to the direst necessity before applying to them." [37]

Bienville was highly chafed over the turn of events; even so, his feelings were more subdued than Dartaguiette's. The commissary, who was now held accountable for the value of the merchandise, was in his own words "ruined, if Your Excellency is unable to have the goods released through the court of Spain." With high emotion he poured out his passions to the minister:

> This action astounds me, the purity of my intentions not having allowed me to foresee this result . . . I had appealed to the royal officers themselves, as well as to His Excellency, Monseigneur the Duque de Linarès. I know not what may be the orders from the king, their master . . . I hold responsible only the evil interpreters of his intentions in Veracruz—hard,

36. Réponse du duc de Linarès, March 27, 1711, AC, C13B, 1, No. 10, f. 1–1v.

37. Bienville to min., June 20, 1711, AC, C13B, 1, No. 11, f. 1v–3.

greedy men, solidly partisan, who demanded bribes to permit this exchange . . .[38]

Aside from lodging complaints to higher authorities in France and Spain there was little that Dartaguiette and Bienville could do for the moment. On the same vessel by which Béranger was returning to Martinique, Dartaguiette posted a heated complaint to the French Ambassador in Madrid. But the situation at Mobile remained practically the same except for the temporary surplus of flour. "We have arrived at the point where we can no longer bear our own poverty," Bienville groaned. "It is so great that I cannot describe it." And fearing that the long overdue supply ship had been lost, the commandant made plans to try to charter a vessel to France "to report what we cannot set down on paper." Meanwhile, the colony must wait and hope and wonder what were the causes of the promised ship's delay.[39]

Pontchartrain had begun preparations for a supply ship to Louisiana in April of 1709 as he had promised Dartaguiette nearly two years before.[40] To equip the vessel he had secured the services of Antoine-Alexandre de Rémonville, seigneur de Rochebonne, a merchant long interested in the commercial possibilities of Louisiana. After the discrediting of the Le Moyne family and the death of Daneau de Muy, Rémonville's interest in the colony had been renewed. In recent years he had been active in privateering, but he now hoped to be named by the minister as governor of Louisiana. With high expectations, Pontchartrain had written to Bienville in the summer of 1709 that the *Renommée* would shortly be under way.[41]

Rémonville and Pontchartrain, however, early ran into difficulties. Rémonville was unable to bear the full expense of the voyage, and Pontchartrain, because of the war, was unable to lend much support. For assistance the two men looked to the merchants of La Rochelle. The La Rochelle merchants, however, failed to view the venture with a great deal of enthusiasm. The primary objective

38. Dartaguiette to min., June 20, 1711, AC, C13A, 2, f. 641–42.

39. *Ibid.*, f. 642–43. Bienville to min., June 20, 1711, *loc. cit.*, No. 11. The French were eventually reimbursed for the confiscated merchandise in 1716 by an order of Felipe V. Minutes de Conseil, May 11, 1716, AM, B1, 10, f. 150.

40. Min. to Bégon, April 24, 1709, AC, B 30, f. 113.

41. Rémonville to Villermont, Feb. 18, 1704, BN, FF, 22814, f. 52–54. BN, FF, NA, 9295, f. 13–19. Min. to Bienville, July 11, 1709, AC, B 30, f. 181.

of the voyage, as far as Pontchartrain was concerned, was to assist an impoverished colony and since most of the supplies aboard ship were destined for that purpose it did not leave a great deal of opportunity for private profit. By late 1709, the ship was still not provisioned and Pontchartrain found local exporters unwilling to accept the ministry's promise of payment in ordinances.[42]

It was not until May of 1710 that the *Renommée* appeared ready to sail. By that time, however, Rémonville's funds had nearly been exhausted and he was obliged to discharge his crew because he was unable to supply them with food. His capital depleted, Rémonville was now out of the question as a successor to Daneau de Muy and Michel Bégon matter-of-factly suggested that he turn over his crewmen to another ship. It was at this point that Pontchartrain had appointed Cadillac as governor of Louisiana.[43]

In the face of such misfortunes Pontchartrain no doubt expected Rémonville to abandon the enterprise. But Rémonville had gone too far. Heavily in debt, the aging privateer felt he had already invested too much time, energy and capital in the venture; he could not quit now. Just as all seemed lost (for the expedition and for Rémonville), a Tonnay-Charente merchant named Simon Guérinet came to the rescue, agreeing to furnish the hardtack necessary for the voyage and to aid in providing additional funds. In the meantime Rémonville went even deeper into debt to provide for the salaries of workers to refit the ship and for the subsistence of the sailors.[44]

Nevertheless, the eventual embarkation now seemed assured. Rémonville was to captain the *Renommée* himself. Due to his inexperience in oceanic voyages, however, the privateer was provided by the court with a highly capable navigator, Maximien Tivas de Gourville, and a council aboard ship to whom he was ordered to pay strict attention. The next few months were destined to be spent boarding the necessary personnel as well as certain officers and inhabitants scheduled to return to Louisiana. Besides the veteran François Philippe de Mandeville, the ship was to transport

42. Bégon to min., June 18, 1707, APR, 1 E 400, f. 256v–57. Lusançay to min., Oct. 15, 1709, AM, B3, 171, f. 394–96. Min. to Rémonville, Feb. 19, 1710, AM, B2, 220, f. 623.

43. Bégon to min., May 10, 1710, APR, 1 E 402, f. 159–60. Min. to La Mothe Cadillac, May 13, 1710, AC, B 32, f. 55–56v.

44. Min. to Bégon, April 16, 1710, AM, B2, 221, f. 211. Min. to Rémonville, May 7, 1710, AM, B2, 221, f. 577. ACM, Amirauté, Prises, B 5924, l. la Mignonne. Min. to Beauharnois, June 18, 1710, AM, B2, 221, f. 1234–35.

Jean-Baptiste Valigny, a long-time captain-of-arms in a marine company at Rochefort, and François Juchereau de Vaulezard, a Canadian whose company had been stationed at Mobile for nearly six years. In addition, several families seeking to establish themselves in Louisiana were given passage; but the number of artisans requested by Bienville and Dartaguiette had to be limited because of Rémonville's inability to assure them sufficient food during the voyage.[45]

The outfitting of the *Renommée* suffered further delays. By the end of the summer the vessel had still not sailed. Yet Pontchartrain was confident that the hour was near. On Sept. 25, he informed Beauharnois de La Chaussaye (who had succeeded the recently deceased Michel Bégon as intendant at Rochefort):

> The Sieur de Rémonville writes me that the Sieur Guérinet will probably finish up this week with supplying the provisions destined for the crew of the frigate *Renommée;* thus I expect that she will be able to leave during the first days of next month. I am quite pleased that you have had embarked on her the provisions, munitions, clothes and apparel consigned to Louisiana. Do not fail to send along the twenty-five soldiers from the new levee and an equal number to the cape [Cap-français].[46]

Two weeks later, the minister wrote to Beauharnois again, this time setting October 15 as the deadline for embarkation.[47] The month of October came and went, however, with the *Renommée* still in port. Vaulezard was refusing to board ship and Valigny could not be found. Moreover, Rémonville was taken ill and there was not enough room for all of the twenty-five soldiers requested. On November 12, Pontchartrain wrote Beauharnois a third time, ordering him to see that operations were hastened.[48]

It was not until several weeks later that the *Renommée* finally weighed anchor at La Rochelle and set sail for the West Indies,

45. Min. to Beauharnois, June 4, 1710, AM, B2, 221, f. 1023. Min. to Beauharnois, June 21, 1710, AC, B 32, f. 124–24v. Min. to Rémonville, July 13, 1710, AC, B 32, f. 136. Min. to Dartaguiette, Sept. 2, 1710, AC, B 32, f. 200. Min. to Rémonville, Aug. 10, 1710, AC, B 32, f. 193–94.

46. Min. to Beauharnois, Sept. 25, 1710, AC, B 32, f. 209–10.

47. Min. to Beauharnois, Oct. 8, 1710, AC, B 32, f. 212.

48. Min. to Beauharnois, Oct. 24, 1710, AC, B 32, f. 238. Min. to Beauharnois, Oct. 27, 1710, AC, B 32, f. 217. Min. to Massiot, Nov. 26, 1711, AM, B2, 223, f. 491.

accompanied by a merchant vessel, the *Agathe*. By this time Rémonville had recovered his health and Valigny had finally boarded ship, but the full number of soldiers requested by Bienville was not aboard nor was Vaulezard, who after futile attempts to find a replacement for himself, ultimately refused absolutely to embark.[49]

The voyage was to be a protracted and controversial passage. After stopping by several Spanish mainland ports, including La Coruña, the *Renommée* sailed for Martinique where she anchored at Fort Royal in April, after capturing several prizes along the way, one of which, the *Catherine*, Rémonville planned to bring to Louisiana in hopes of selling it to the colonists. Once in the West Indies, however, the *Renommée* suffered further delays, a heated conflict erupting between Rémonville and the officers and private passengers. Navigator Tivas de Gourville was brutal in blaming Rémonville for the unnecessary tardiness (which he attributed to poor administration), chiding the captain for personal cowardice and incapacity in seamanship. In the summer of 1711 the *Renommée* was yet floundering in the French Antilles and Mobile was still waiting desperately for her arrival.[50]

49. Min. to Beauharnois, Nov. 12, 1710, AC, B 32, f. 220. Min. to Beauharnois, Oct. 24, 1710, AC, B 32, f. 238.

50. Min. to Rémonville, Feb. 4, 1711, AM, B2, 226, f. 439. Min. to Tivas de Gourville, March 18, 1711, AM, B2, 226, f. 988–89. Vaucresson to min., April 26, 1711, AC, C8A, 18, f. 1–2. Phélypeaux to min., May 9, 1711, AC, C8A, 18, f. 4–9. Tivas de Gourville to min., Dec. 7, 1711, AC, C13C, 2, f. 67–70.

XXII

Moving Downstream

SINCE the return of Graveline, La Fresnière and Des Prés Derbanne from La Rochelle in 1709, the infant settlement on Massacre Island, begun soon after the dismissal of the Canadians the year before, had shown a surprising rate of growth.[1] By any reasonable standards, however, there was little to recommend the location as a site for a permanent settlement. What little game existed was small, such as squirrel, duck and muskrat. The land would barely support even simple vegetable gardens much less staple crops. There was little possibility of trade with the Indians, for the natives rarely even visited the island. The risk of storms also added to its undesirability: while a full-blown hurricane had not struck the port in the eight years the French had occupied it, the inhabitants were well aware of the threat, their only protection being the large sand dunes near the seashore. When Dartaguiette arrived in 1708, there were only a few buildings on the island, including the large, recently rebuilt warehouse used to store goods unloaded from the ships. Even the name "Massacre," stemming from the 1699 discovery of a large burial mound at the western end of the island, suggested an unsavory, even lurid, locale.[2]

Aside from its disadvantages, however, Massacre Island *was* the colony's chief anchorage point and next to Pensacola was perhaps the outstanding natural harbor on the Gulf Coast.[3] Dartaguiette would describe its potential to Pontchartrain on his return to France the following year:

1. *FLC*, p. 133. Dartaguiette to min., Jan. 10, 1711, AC, C13A, 2, f. 633–35.
2. Dartaguiette to min., Feb. 26, 1708, AC, C13A, 2, f. 57–58. *FLC*, pp. 11, 56, 60. Cadillac to min., Oct. 26, 1713, AC, C13A, 3, f. 1–7. Bienville to min., Oct. 27, 1711, AC, C13A, 2, f. 599–600.
3. Mémoire d'Artaguiette . . . du 12 May 1712, AC, C13A, 2, f. 805. *FLC*, p. 56.

> The port at Île Massacre is secure, the anchorage is excellent, quite easy to protect. There are always twenty feet of water in the channel which, to be certain, is narrow; but once we have [capable] pilots, there will be no risk in entering it. The anchorage on the outside, when the winds are not favorable for entering, is very good. In the port there are five and one-half to six fathoms of water, very little swell, and the bottom is all sand and mud. It is capable of containing more than fifteen vessels of forty to fifty cannons and many other smaller ones.[4]

It was the commercial advantages of the island that ultimately caught the eye of Graveline. As long as he was confined to the forests around Fort Louis there was little chance to advance himself, but after moving to the mouth of the bay, his new location near the port opened varied trading possibilities for him. Spanish Pensacola, which from Massacre Island was only a day's voyage, offered a ready market for produce. Even if his plans for developing commerce in furs and ore should come to naught, there was a definite possibility of raising substantial numbers of cattle on the island, with the excellent grasslands to the northwest of the harbor. On each of his two trips from La Rochelle, Graveline had stopped by Havana to purchase cattle, the first time procuring a bull, by which he was able to begin a herd. Though he had recently sold the *Marguerite* to Bienville and Dartaguiette, he would no doubt soon find opportunity to replace the vessel. By that time his herd would have increased to the extent that he could supply beef not only to Pensacola and Apalache (should that province be regained by the Spanish) but to the French as well.[5]

By the late summer of 1710, there were some sixteen settlers (many with families) gathered around a small lagoon just back from the seashore. Graveline himself, though he owned two buildings near the lagoon, was not among these; upon his return from La Rochelle he had built a house less than two miles to the northwest of the warehouse near the edge of a large, logy inlet (today called Graveline Bay) where the grasslands were abundant. This house, "the finest private home in the colony," was a building of

4. Mémoire d'Artaguiette . . . du 12 May 1712, AC, C13A, 2, f. 805–06.

5. Min. aux officiers de l'amirauté de La Rochelle, July 6, 1709, AC, B 30, f. 176. Min. to Clairambault, May 18, 1707, AM, B2, 197, f. 879. ACM, Amirauté, B 5584, July 6, 1709. Min. to Demuy, July 6, 1707, AC, B 29, f. 291. Cadillac to min., Oct. 26, 1713, AC, C13A, 3, f. 66.

two stories, costing Graveline over two thousand *livres*. Yet even by Canadian standards it was not an unusually elaborate structure.[6]

To share his new home, Graveline had brought with him his wife Suzanne whom he had married while in La Rochelle. Like a considerable portion of the population at La Rochelle and a significant number of the residents of Mobile, Suzanne hailed from a Protestant background. But unlike the majority of the Mobile *religionnaires*, she took her Protestantism seriously. No sooner had she arrived at Massacre Island than she began to instruct her servants in the beliefs of her denomination. If Suzanne were anxious about eventual repercussions stemming from the practice of her faith, she had little to fear for the moment. In the colonial Louisiana of 1710 few other than the seminary priests were concerned with religion at all. As Davion, with doddering hand, was to write the next year, "Religion is entirely ignored here, if [indeed] it has not already been lost . . ." Already pregnant with her first son, Suzanne, with Graveline's fine house and herd of cattle, had visions of a peaceful and prosperous life on the island.[7]

Besides Graveline, Canadian André Renaud was also established at a location not too far distant from the warehouse. With his wife and young son, François, Renaud had managed to accumulate a small herd of cattle himself and was further occupied in raising poultry and vegetables.[8]

The majority of the Île Massacre inhabitants were huddled near

6. Mémoire sur les déclarations de La Vente, [Sept., 1710], AC, C13A, 2, f. 565. Carte du baye de la Mobile, [*s.d.*], BN, 138, 10, 3. Relation de la rivière de la Mobile, AC, C13C, 2, f. 166–67. Min. to Beauharnois, Oct. 6, 1712, AC, B 34, f. 127v. Min. to Crozat, Oct. 24, 1712, AC, B 34, f. 131.

7. Min. to Clairambault, May 18, 1707, AM, B2, 197, f. 879. Min. to Demuy, July 6, 1707, AC, B 29, f. 291. ADM, B, March 1, 1734; A, May 4, 1736; Jan. 13, 1742. Cadillac to min., Oct. 26, 1713, AC, C13A, 3, f. 22. Davion [to La Vente], Oct. 20, 1711, ASQ, Missions, No. 46. Suzanne died on Massacre Island in late October, 1713 [Cadillac to min., *loc. cit.*, marginal note to f. 14] three years after giving birth to Graveline's only son, Jean-Baptiste. If Suzanne's religion caused her no serious difficulty, however, the same would not hold true for her son. For many years into his manhood young Jean-Baptiste was unable to act in private sales, being civilly nonexisting. To enable him to inherit, the senior Graveline was finally successful in having his son legitimated. The son, however, was broken on the wheel some ten years before his father died, due to his association with an insurrection. LSMA, DCS, Sept. 20, Oct. 7, 1747; Oct. 6, 1753.

8. AC, F1A, 11, f. 220v; 13, f. 118. Role de la garnison du fort de Biloxy, May 26, 1700, AC, C13A, 1, f. 257–58. Dénombrement du 1 de août 1706, AC, G1, 464. ADM, A, March 19, 1710.

the seashore in a long, unvaried line of houses facing the lagoon: Jean Roy and his wife Renée Gilbert and children; Jean La Croix, *dit* Grimauld and wife Angélique Drouin; Pilot Simon Coussot and wife Marie-Marthe Flein and young daughter Hippolyte. A number of the more recently-arrived, Jacques Allemand and his wife, and daughter Marguerite, and Guillaume Boutin and his family (who had, however, not yet permanently transferred from the mouth of Fowl River) were anti-Bienvillists, seeking refuge from what they felt was personal and governmental tyranny.[9] Some of these settlers had moved to the island before the return of Graveline. Others, such as La Pointe, La Fresnière and Basque tanner Jean Arnaud, had returned with him on the *Marguerite.* And, for the moment, Graveline's brother, Gabriel Baudreau, and close friends, La Source and Angélique Jallot, were situated near the warehouse, Baudreau soon to be returning to the Illinois country. There was no priest assigned to the settlement as yet; however, François Le Maire and Alexandre Huvé both made occasional visits to baptize slaves and newborns.[10]

The most important official stationed on Massacre Island was the keeper of the warehouse, François Guyon Des Prés Derbanne. Derbanne, after years of travel on the Mississippi and in the Great Lakes region with such Canadian *voyageurs* as Mathurin Moquin, Jacques Le Moine and the brothers Chauvin, had finally been persuaded to settle at Mobile. After ascending the Missouri river several hundred leagues in 1706 (so he claimed), Derbanne, of an old and influential Canadian family (his grandfather had been the renowned explorer Nicolas Marsolet de Saint-Aignan who had served with Champlain; his first cousin, Marie-Thérèse Guyon, was married to governor-designate Cadillac), had sailed to La Rochelle with Graveline and on his return was made *garde-magasin* at a salary of six hundred *livres* per year.[11]

After his return to Massacre Island, Derbanne, "a good and honest man," took into his household a Chitimacha slave called

9. *FLC,* p. 133. ADM, A, May 18, 1708; Feb. 24, 1709; March 19, July 26, Nov. 19, Dec. 20, 1710.

10. *FLC,* p. 133. ADM, A, March 19, July 26, Dec. 20, 1710. On Dec. 20, 1710, Jean Arnaud had been ceded a plot of ground on Massacre Island measuring 447 feet by 1,087 feet. Lowrie, *Documents* . . . p. 15.

11. *DGFC, I,* pp. 294–95. AJQ, Greffe de Duquet, Nov. 15, 1672; Greffe de Rageot, Oct. 23, 1671. AJM, Greffe de Basset, April 16, 1696; Adhémar, May 27, 1701. Relation de Derbanne, AM, 3 JJ 276, 3. AC, D2C, 51, f. 6–8. Duclos to min., Oct. 25, 1713, AC, C13A, 3, f. 287–88.

Jeanne de la Grande Terre with whom he lived. By early 1710, Jeanne had given birth to a male child which Derbanne began calling Jean-Baptiste. Six months later, during a visit to the island by Alexandre Huvé, Derbanne decided to have his bastard son baptized. Huvé, who was in the process of christening slaves belonging to Dartaguiette and *habitant* Alexandre Bloquien, assented. On July 26, with Nicolas Bodin and Louise-Marguerite Housseau acting as godparents, Huvé baptized the six-month-old Jean-Baptiste. Although Derbanne was not at this time wedded to his Indian slave, he decided later to marry her; they subsequently lived a long life together, producing numerous children.[12]

Despite its disadvantages, Massacre Island seemed to be developing into a fairly prosperous settlement by mid-1710. The authorities at Mobile, while in disagreement over numerous other questions, were in unanimous accord regarding the necessity for fortifying the island to protect the port. Bienville and La Salle had both requested funds for this purpose. Almost immediately after Dartaguiette's arrival in 1708, the co-commissary warned Pontchartrain that ". . . it is absolutely necessary to have a fort built at L'Isle Massacre in order to defend the entrance to the port and to guard the warehouse of the king."[13] Pontchartrain, with firm confidence in Dartaguiette's judgment but suspicious of any of Bienville's recommendations requiring royal funds, had first commissioned Daneau de Muy, then Cadillac, to look into the matter; but since Cadillac had not yet arrived in the colony, the fort remained unbuilt and the island remained defenseless as there were not even any batteries constructed to protect the harbor.[14]

Six weeks after Huvé baptized Derbanne's young son, disaster struck the island. On September 9, a brigantine appeared three-quarters of a league offshore bearing a French flag. The inhabitants gathered together in the middle of the settlement, watching the ship tossing in the outer waters. When the vessel fired two cannon

12. Dartaguiette to min., Jan. 10, 1711, AC, C13A, 2, f. 636–37. Archives of the Church of the Immaculate Conception (Natchitoches, La.), Vol. I, Burials, Oct. 24, 1735; Dec. 20, 1740. Marriages, April 8, 1736; April 19, 1746. ADM, A, July 26, 1710.

13. Mémoire du Roy pour servir d'instruction à M. Lamothe Cadillac, May 13, 1710, AC, B 32, f. 62–62v. La Salle to min., Sept. 8, 1706, AC, C13A, 1, f. 545–46. Dartaguiette to min., Feb. 26, 1708, AC, C13A, 2, f. 58–60.

14. Mémoire du Roy pour servir d'instruction à M. Demuy, June 30, 1707, AC, B 29, f. 255–55v. Mém. du Roy . . . à M. de Lamothe Cadillac, May 13, 1710, AC, B 32, f. 62–62v.

shots, the settlers decided the ship must surely be in distress, perhaps lodged on one of the sand bars near Pelican Island. In the distance now they could see two ship's boats being lowered into the water. Half an hour later when the boats reached the beach, two Frenchmen stepped ashore, where they persuaded warehousekeeper Derbanne and Ensign Philippe Blondel, the only two officials on the island at the time, to return with them to their ship. As soon as Blondel and Derbanne stepped aboard the brigantine, they realized they had been hoodwinked: the brigantine was in reality an English corsair from Jamaica, captained by a Protestant buccaneer who had once landed at Massacre Island on a ship from Martinique. Blondel and Derbanne were kept as hostages aboard the vessel while some thirty to forty pirates descended on Massacre Island in rowboats.[15]

With their two leaders held captive, the Massacre Island inhabitants, surprised and disorganized, were powerless to resist. The port was taken without the firing of a single shot.

The next day, September 10, a few additional pirates came ashore, bringing Derbanne and Blondel with them, Derbanne because he knew the whereabouts of the key to the warehouse. Once inside the magazine, the pirates found it filled with merchandise. The cargoes of three recent ships from Martinique were stored away; there were eight or nine thousand deerskins and more than fifteen thousand racoon skins and other small peltries. The plunderers further discovered cables, rigging and sails of the few ships present in the harbor, as well as seventy-one barrels of flour which Châteaugué had recently brought back from Veracruz and which he had temporarily stored in the warehouse, part of which was to provision the small boats used to transport goods to Fort Louis.[16]

The inhabitants were herded into several houses, as the pirates spent that entire day and the next transferring the contents of the warehouse by rowboats to the brigantine. At the end of the third day, the looters prepared to leave the island, having succeeded in loading most everything of value. Before they left, however, the

15. ADM, A, July 26, 1710. AC, F1A, 13, f. 113v. Bienville to min., Oct. 12, 1710, AC, C13A, 2, f. 190. Min. to Bienville, May 10, 1710, AC, B 32, f. 40v. Dartaguiette to min., Jan. 10, 1711, AC, C13A, 2, f. 633–34. *Journal Historique*, p. 107.

16. Dartaguiette to min., Jan. 10, 1711, AC, C13A, 2, f. 634–35. Duclos to min., Oct. 25, 1713, AC, C13A, 3, f. 287–88. Bienville to min., June 21, 1710, AC, C13A, 2, f. 551–52.

pirates tortured the inhabitants they believed to be holding back cash, then set fire to all the buildings (including the warehouse) except those in which the inhabitants were held captive. These and the houses of Graveline, Guillory and Renaud (being some distance from the main settlement) were spared. The pirates then boarded their boats, leaving the community in flames. As they were leaving, a Canadian *voyageur*, having landed his small boat near the house of Renaud, approached the burning settlement. Seeing the fires, but unaware of what had transpired (or of the superior number of the enemy), the *voyageur* found one lingering looter near the warehouse and shot him dead in his tracks. The embarking pirates, hearing the gunfire, stopped for a moment, then, suspecting the arrival of a substantial relief force, continued quickly on their way.[17]

The suddenness by which the Massacre Island inhabitants were taken captive had prevented them from sending a plea for help to Fort Louis. As darkness descended on the island now, Blondel sent two men in a canoe to call for assistance. In the meantime the hapless colonists were hoping the pirate ship would shortly be weighing anchor, at least by the next day.

The following morning, however, the brigantine was still present, though she had rounded Pelican Island and was now resting near the eastern end of the island near the point where Canadian François Guillory had built his small dwelling. Two days before, while the looters were busy ransacking the warehouse, several of the inhabitants had noticed the pirates' interest in Graveline's grazing cattle. In particular the privateers' leader had seemed interested in seizing his bull. One of the inhabitants had overheard words to the effect that the marauders might come back the next day and take the bull then slay the remaining cattle.[18] Yet now the pirates seemed much more cautious. They could not be sure that the French had not received reinforcements during the night and, if they had, how many. The failure of one of their number to return to ship, coupled with the sound of gunfire, indicated that the missing comrade had probably been killed and they were certain they had seized all the guns in the inhabitants' possession. Should they wish to come back for the bull, there was nothing to do but

17. Dartaguiette to min., Jan. 10, 1711, AC, C13A, 2, f. 634–36. *Journal Historique*, p. 107. Mémoire d'Artaguiette, May 12, 1712, AC, C13A, 2, f. 803–04. Tivas de Gourville to min., June, 1712, AC, C13A, 2, f. 739.

18. AC, F1A, 13, f. 118v. Cadillac to min., Oct. 26, 1713, AC, C13A, 3, f. 2–5, 7.

test the colonists' capacity to resist. Later that morning a small group of pirates was sent ashore near Pointe à Guillory to see what fire they would draw. Meanwhile, Graveline, Blondel, Renaud and Guillory gathered at the island's edge with four guns that had escaped seizure, which, added to the rifle of the *voyageur*, made a total of five weapons. As the pirates' small party came ashore, the inhabitants opened fire, causing the pirates to turn back toward their boat. Three of the men then quickly crawled behind some underbrush to a point some fifty feet away and opened fire again as the two others moved to an opposite location, the gunfire from several different directions creating the illusion of more than mere token opposition. Satisfied that a substantial relief force was now present on Massacre Island (if not sufficient to repel them at least capable of doing them considerable damage), the Jamaican pirates shortly weighed anchor and left for the open sea.[19]

Graveline's cattle had been saved, but almost everything else of value on the island had been seized or destroyed. Dartaguiette later estimated that the total loss of property ran to eighty thousand *piastres*.[20]

The destruction of the Massacre Island settlement had hit the colony particularly hard, coming at a time when the fortunes of Louisiana were at such a low ebb. Not only were the island settlers in a woeful condition but the colony as a whole was enormously affected by the loss of the warehouse, the ships' rigging and by the fact that the island's inhabitants, previously almost self-sufficient, would now cause a further drain on the resources at Fort Louis. Bienville and Dartaguiette complained bitterly to Pontchartrain while Derbanne and his neighbors began to rebuild their settlement. For the moment the damage was done, but the incident set Bienville and Dartaguiette to planning extensive moves, to take effect with or without the consent of the minister.[21]

At Fort Louis, meanwhile, conditions were faring little better than at Massacre Island. It had now been three years since the colonists had seen a supply ship from France. Bienville wondered if one would ever arrive and Dartaguiette was worried about rumors that the *Renommée* had been captured by the English.[22]

19. *Ibid.*, f. 3–7. Dartaguiette to min., Jan. 10, 1711, AC, C13A, 2, f. 634–37.
20. *Ibid.*, f. 634–35.
21. *Ibid.*, f. 633–40. Bienville to min., June 20, 1711, AC, C13B, 1, No. 11, f. 1–3. Dartaguiette to min., June 20, 1711, AC, C13A, 2, f. 644–45.
22. *Ibid.*, f. 645.

"The distress is great," the commissary fretted. "Everyone [here] is dissatisfied . . . it is pitiful to watch them [the soldiers], as they are all naked and for the most part are reduced to living on crushed and boiled Indian corn with only an occasional piece of meat. Two suits of clothes and four sets of accessories are due them . . ." [23]

If the soldiers were in penury so were the majority of inhabitants. Dartaguiette added: "The colonists are languishing; they are few in number. They are unable to undertake anything of consequence. Besides all this, their wives are ruining them by their desire for luxury." [24] The extreme want, aside from its immediate effect on the colonists, was to have other, more far-reaching consequences. Bienville was ready to throw up his hands in despair:

> We can no longer bear up against the affliction of the presents which the English give to our savages nor their inducements to abandon our side, and if we have had the natives' loyalty up until now I protest to you that it has not been possible without many accomodations and deprivations. For two years now we have given them nothing and we have kept them hoping from one month to the next. I have no more ammunition. I dare not tell you what I have left. I have asked for some from Martinique, but they will do as they have done before; that is, they will pay no attention to our entreaties.[25]

The Carolinians were not uninformed on the deteriorating condition of Mobile. To take advantage of the situation, the English had begun in the year 1710 to instruct their Indians to refrain from doing any harm to captured French soldiers, a tactic that La Salle had interpreted as a sincere desire for peace on the part of the natives, but which Bienville was quick to see through.[26] In an impoverished colony, the English reasoned, there would be a heightened tendency for poor soldiers to desert. The chief deterrent now preventing large-scale desertions to the English or to Pensacola was the fear of being captured by the enemy and put to the stake. The English ban on persecution and torture of straying Frenchmen proved moderately successful once news of the policy became widely known and believed. "The soldiers are deserting

23. Dartaguiette to min., May 12, 1712, AC, C13A, 2, f. 803.

24. *Ibid.*

25. Bienville to min., June 20, 1711, AC, C13B, 1, No. 11, f. 1–2.

26. Mémoire d'Artaguiette, May 12, 1712, AC, C13A, 2, f. 803. Bienville to min., Oct. 27, 1711, AC, C13A, 2, f. 576–77.

to the Indian enemies," Dartaguiette lamented, "and from there they are going to Carolina. The fear that they hitherto have had of being burned at the stake has up until now restrained them but since the English have forbidden their Indians to do them harm we are unable to hold them here." [27]

The colonists were indeed demoralized; but perhaps their dejection was due more to rank uncertainty of the future than to their dire poverty. To plant, to create an establishment, required long hours of toil and sacrifice. This they were admonished to do by the crown but they had no official assurances that their establishments, once made, would be permanent. Moreover, there was much talk of a private company assuming control of the colony and even rumors (given further credence by the failure of supply ships to appear) that the colony would be abandoned altogether.[28] Even if none of these fears proved true the inhabitants were almost certain that the town would eventually be moved to a different location and the fruits of their labors wasted. Granted, they had finally begun to plant Indian corn in the spring of 1710 and 1711, but this was a matter of pure necessity. The majority abhored the taste of maize, harvesting only that which was necessary to sustain them.

For several years now the inhabitants had been listening to the subject of transferring the town being debated among the colony's officials. La Salle and La Vente had long been in favor of moving to another site.[29] Even in the very first years the colonists had privately expressed their dissatisfaction with "living in a mud hole." [30] As long as Iberville had been alive, there was little question of leaving the site. The commander had approved the location himself, and apparently he meant to maintain it, despite all objections. Bienville and Gravier had strenuously supported Iberville's decision and no amount of criticism would sway them. As evidence of Bienville's determination to keep Fort Louis at its river location, he had gone to some expense in 1707 to repair it and in 1708 to rebuild it almost completely, resorting even to falsely alarming the inhabitants of an Indian attack in order to get the work done.

27. Mémoire d'Artaguiette, May 12, 1712, AC, C13A, 2, f. 803.

28. La Salle to min., Sept. 7, 1706, AC, C13A, 1, f. 477–79. Bienville to min., June 20, 1711, AC, C13B, 1, No. 11, f. 1v–3. Dartaguiette to min., Aug. 6, 1712, AC, C13A, 2, f. 705–06.

29. La Vente [to Brisacier], July 4, 1708, ASQ, Lettres, R 83. La Salle to min., Sept. 7, 1706, AC, C13A, 1, f. 477.

30. Extrait d'une lettre du neveu de M. Lefèvre, 15 mars 1702, BN, FF, 9097, f. 123v–24. Lettre, 10 sept. 1704, BN, FF, 9097, f. 141–45.

After the death of Iberville, La Salle and La Vente began their criticisms anew.[31] Just two months after Iberville's death La Salle complained to Pontchartrain: "Already some *habitants* have left the unfavorable location of Fort Louis and established themselves along the bay. They have had more success there in four months than we have had in the five years we have been at this fort. This is the worst possible land that could have been chosen . . . we can count on nobody and have no amenities in the middle of the woods where M. d'Iberville has put us . . ." [32]

By early spring of the following year, La Vente was noting such high water that "more than thirty inhabitants were obliged to abandon their homes and we ourselves were constrained to leave our church on which planks there were about two feet of water and people were obliged to get about almost everywhere in the town by pirogues." [33] In that same dispatch to Brisacier, La Vente testily observed:

> . . . God permitted this establishment for the punishment of some and the humiliation of others . . . but although those who at present hold the reins of government have sufficient influence so that their personal authority prevails on the public I can say with assurance that this location will change even if it takes thirty years or even if someone of good sense never comes . . .[34]

When Dartaguiette arrived in 1708, the young commissary was quick to note that the topography was much more suitable at the mouth of the river than it was where Fort Louis was situated; he promptly suggested the advisability of having the fort moved. Yet, despite almost unanimous opposition (Bienville was supported only by Châteaugué, Boisbriant and a few officers), the commandant, as late as March of 1711, was still adamant about keeping the settlement in the same location. As the rainy season approached, the increasingly impatient inhabitants could well question the basis of their leader's reasoning.[35]

As to what the commandant's reasons were, La Vente had con-

31. La Salle to min., Sept. 8, 1706, AC, C13A, 1, f. 546–47. La Vente [to Brisacier], July 4, 1708, ASQ, Lettres, R 83.

32. La Salle to min., Sept. 7, 1706, AC, C13A, 1, f. 476–77.

33. La Vente [to Brisacier], July 4, 1708, ASQ, Lettres, R 83.

34. *Ibid.*

35. Dartaguiette to min., Feb. 12, 1710, AC, C13A, 2, f. 531–32. Dartaguiette to min., [extracts of Aug. 18 and Oct. 1, 1708], AC, C13A, 2, f. 353–54.

jectured that Bienville was merely too proud and too stubborn to admit his initial mistake. After all, Bienville (along with Sérigny and Levasseur) had been the first French present on the site and Iberville, in ordering the establishment to be built at that location, had relied principally on Bienville's judgment. In offering his own explanation, La Salle had been less charitable: it was his outspoken opinion that Bienville desired to keep the fort and the town as far from Massacre Island as possible so as to afford his agents opportunity to abscond with the king's goods in the long and cumbersome procedures involved in transferring merchandise from the ships to the warehouses and finally to Fort Louis. Were the colony moved to Massacre Island or even to the mouth of the river, Bienville and his brothers would have much less leeway to work their circuitous schemes.[36]

Just how much truth there was to La Salle's accusation had eluded Dartaguiette; yet he viewed the commandant's early practices with grave misgivings. How else could one explain the many discrepancies between goods boarded in La Rochelle, Cap-français and Havana and merchandise eventually received at Fort Louis? Iberville's and Sérigny's guilt had been well (if not yet fully) established by this time. Was it reasonable to assume they would have sent illicit freight to Mobile unless they had been confident of Bienville's co-operation in handling such merchandise? [37]

Nevertheless, by late 1710, La Salle's accusations even if true would not fully explain the commandant's reluctance to move downstream. By this time, Bienville was aware that Dartaguiette had set up a system of accounts that had virtually eliminated the possibilities of fraud. Realizing he was being carefully watched, Bienville had put aside (for the moment at least) any plans of using the warehouses for his own private purposes. Too, the basic idea for locating a fort upstream still seemed to him a sound one. There were bluffs all along the river well above the confluence of the Alabama-Tombigbee arms, plateaus adequate enough for small settlements, and it was surely not reasonable to expect settlers to develop lands contested among the natives without the protection

36. La Vente [to Brasacier], July 4, 1708, ASQ, Lettres, R 83. La Salle to min., July 25, 1707, AC, C13B, 1, No. 7, f. 1, 7v–8. La Salle to min., Sept. 8, 1706, AC, C13A, 1, f. 545–47.

37. Min. to Châteaugué, June 30, 1707, AC, B 29, f. 289v–90. Min. to Pajot, Nov. 23, 1707, AM, B2, 199, f. 778. Min. to L'Hostellier, Feb. 29, 1708, AM, B2, 206, f. 697–98. Min. to Bégon, May 25, 1707, AC, B 29, f. 241–42.

of a nearby fort. Moreover, close relations with the interior nations was still an all-important facet of French colonial strategy. Would not moving in an opposite direction from their village sites show a decided weakness? Or, worse still, would it not indicate a lack of desire for maintaining commercial relations? Assuredly the question of transference was not so incomplex as La Salle and La Vente would have made it appear; yet the fact remained: the inhabitants could not live in a quagmire; they must move somewhere, but move they must.[38]

The turning point came during April of 1711: the spring rains fell incessantly, continuing even into May, swelling the little creek that ran behind and to the northwest of the fort; the overflowing waters, unable to escape, glutted the low places behind the bluff on which the fort stood. By the end of the first week in May they had risen even higher than had the waters of 1707 and 1710.[39] Nearly two-thirds of the houses were completely flooded. "The waters have risen so greatly this spring," Dartaguiette wrote, "and with so much force that most of the houses in this village were submerged to the ridgepole in five or six days; this lasted almost a month."[40]

The inhabitants, particularly Jean Le Caën, François Hayot and Charles Dumont, whose houses were located in the lowest areas of town, were dismayed. Out of desperation they demanded a hearing with the officials, while at the same time privately pouring out their complaints to Dartaguiette. Though his own opinion on the matter had not changed, the commissary had thus far refrained from interfering. After three years in Louisiana, the mutual respect that had grown between him and Bienville was still unimpaired. The commandant was in awe of the younger man's sophistication, education and solid judgment whereas Dartaguiette greatly admired Bienville's resourcefulness and mastery of native diplomacy.[41] At this point, however, Dartaguiette felt compelled to confront Bienville with some plain talk. Laying before him the complaints of the inhabitants, the commissary pointed out the hopelessness of

38. *FLC*, p. 128. La Vente [to Brisacier], July 4, 1708, ASQ, Lettres, R 83.

39. Bienville to min., June 20, 1711, AC, C13B, 1, No. 11, f. 1–3. *FLC*, p. 128. *Journal Historique*, p. 107.

40. Dartaguiette to min., June 20, 1711, AC, C13A, 2, f. 643–44.

41. Plan de la ville et du Fort Louis, sur la Mobile, AN, Section Outremer, DFC, 120B. Dartaguiette to min., Aug. 18, 1708, AC, C13A, 2, f. 330–31.

remaining where they were. After only three years the fort was again rapidly decaying. Of necessity it must soon be rebuilt (at considerable expense), so that at no greater cost it could just as well be constructed at another location. Furthermore, the recent attack on the Massacre Island settlement should be evidence enough that the distance between the principal establishment and the port ought to be considerably shortened, for the port was equally as important as the fort. Finally, the dissatisfaction among the inhabitants was reaching a crescendo. As long as the settlement remained at its present location, the colonists would refuse to labor. The sooner it was moved, the sooner the inhabitants would begin to work and plant in earnest.[42]

Faced with Dartaguiette's opposition, Bienville had little choice but to relent. He had, he confessed, been slowly coming over to the commissary's opinion himself, having recently been informed by the natives that the lands were capable of filling even higher with water. In fact, he had not failed to inform Pontchartrain the previous year of the late winter flood that had destroyed the Indian corn the *habitants* had grudgingly planted. Nevertheless, he pointed out to Dartaguiette, he himself had no authority to move the settlement. Indeed he did not; but no doubt only because he had never requested it. Yet, according to Dartaguiette, at the request of Commissary La Salle, Pontchartrain had ordered the late Daneau de Muy to investigate the possibilities of such a move. Since neither the minister nor the appointed governor was present, it was permissible, even mandatory, that in times of crisis, those in authority use their own discretion. Was this in fact such a crisis? Dartaguiette assured the commandant it was; the minister would surely approve such a decision concerning which there was unanimous agreement.[43]

Convinced of Dartaguiette's good judgment, Bienville agreed to proceed with plans for abandoning the settlement. There was no question of moving the principal establishment to Massacre Island, but Dartaguiette and Bienville agreed that plans were to be made

42. *Ibid.*, f. 353. Dartaguiette to min., June 20, 1711, AC, C13A, 2, f. 643–44. Bienville to min., June 20, 1711, AC, C13B, 1, No. 11, f. 1v–2v. La Vente [to Brisacier], July 4, 1708, ASQ, Lettres, R 83. Extrait d'une lettre du neveu de M. Lefèvre, March 15, 1702, BN, FF, 9097, f. 123–23v. Lettre, Sept. 6, 1704, BN, FF, 9097, f. 140.

43. *FLC*, pp. 128–29. Bienville to min., June 21, 1710, AC, C13A, 2, f. 551. Mémoire du Roy pour servir d'instruction à M. de Muy, June 30, 1707, AC, B 29, f. 255–55v.

as soon as possible to fortify that port, the construction to begin as soon as the next ship from France arrived. As for the proper location for the new town, there was no question either; there was only one suitable spot: at the mouth of the Mobile River at the place called the *Oignonets*.[44]

By mid-May of 1711, Bienville and Dartaguiette had journeyed to the mouth of the river to investigate more closely the new site for the town.[45] With them went Châteaugué, Boisbriant, and Jacques Barbazant de Pailloux, a French officer with some knowledge of engineering and a man whom Bienville greatly admired for his "strict manner of discipline." [46] The proposed site was some eight leagues (25.9 miles) downriver from Fort Louis near the vicinity where in 1700 Charles Levasseur had planted his cross. The land there was sandy, the soil not much different in fertility than the land at the present site. Moreover, the water was more brackish. Yet overall it was a site much more desirable for a large town. Though the small bluff back from the marsh along the riverbank was only half as high as the bluff on which Fort Louis stood, the plateau behind it was broad and expansive, extending several miles into the woods. What was of greater importance, the new site did not seem likely to suffer from poor drainage and in fact those who were familiar with the area over a long period of time (the Mobilians and the Little Tomeh) had never known it to overflow.[47]

The vicinity was not unoccupied. A few hundred yards to the north a village of Chato Indians had been encamped since the summer of 1704. Three quarters of a league to the south of the plateau where the town was to be transfered, a group of Canadians had formed a small settlement where a few of them had been living since 1706. Among these *Québecois* dwelling in the area was a backwoodsman who had sailed on the *Renommée* with Iberville in 1701 and who for five years had remained on the king's payroll as

44. Davion [to La Vente], Oct. 20, 1711, ASQ, Missions, No. 46.

45. *FLC*, pp. 128–29.

46. *Ibid.* ADM, A, Jan. 30, 1715. La Chaise [to Dirs. of the Company of the Indies], Sept. 6, 1723, AC, C13A, 7, f. 22–23. Bienville to min., Oct. 27, 1711, AC, C13A, 2, f. 569.

47. *Ala. River Navigation Charts*, Sept., 1972, pp. 1–2. The soil at both Old and New Mobile was of a "fine sandy loam" (Eulonia at Old Mobile and a mixture of Eulonia and Dunbar at New Mobile). Yields of most crops average slightly lower for the Eulonia, and Dunbar is the best-drained of the two. Williams, *Soil Survey* . . . pp. 26–29. La Vente [to Brisacier], July 4, 1708, ASQ, Lettres, R 83.

a Canadian—Pierre-René Leboeuf. Pierre had been present at the founding of Old Mobile, had served continuously from that time until 1706. When Bienville was forced to dismiss him from the payroll that year Leboeuf moved down to the base of the river, built a modest home and later took up residence with his young Tensa slave named Marguerite.[48] In early June of 1711, Leboeuf would succeed in having his concubine baptized (by Alexandre Huvé). The following year he would marry her, and the next year she would bear him a son, Claude.[49]

Leboeuf had been joined at the river's mouth by Gilbert Dardenne and his wife Marguerite Burelle who brought with them their three children, among whom were two daughters (one, a five-year-old; the other, named Jeanne, born the year before). Close by the Dardennes was Claude Parent, thirty-four-year-old master edge-tool maker from Quebec, son of Pierre Parent and Jeanne Badeau. The preceding August, both Le Maire and Huvé had witnessed the baptism of one of Parent's slaves at Claude's house.[50]

Another early settler at the base of the river was Charles Rochon, native of Quebec and descendant of a Canadian family originally from Saint-Côme-le-vert in Mans. Rochon's family connections in Canada had been numerous and influential: the Guyons, the Buissons de Saint-Cosme and the Gaulins (his first cousin, Antoine, was presently a priest of the Séminaire de Québec).[51] Leaving his family at an early age, Rochon had for years traveled on the Mississippi, exploring with Henri de Tonti and dealing in furs. During the colony's very early years, he, along with Jean Brunet, *dit* Bourbonnois and numerous other Canadians, had drifted into Mobile where Bienville enticed him to remain and placed him for a short time on the king's payroll. When Pontchartrain's orders to discharge the Canadians came, Rochon was released. His first thought was to return to the life of the trapper; but he was then in his thirty-fifth year, a widower with at least one child. Since he had accumulated a fair amount of capital he decided to remain at Mobile. Shortly after 1708 he went downriver

48. ADM, A, Dec. 24, 1708; Oct. 10, 1714. *FLC*, pp. 125–26. *DGFC, I*, p. 357. AC, F1A, 10, f. 285; 11, 220v; 13, f. 117v–18v.

49. ADM, A, June 3, 1711; Feb. 11, 1713.

50. Dénombrement du 1 août 1706, AC, G1, 464. *DGFC, I*, p. 158. LSMA, DCS, May 14, 1723. ADM, A, April 2, Aug. 4, 1710. AC, F1A, 11, f. 220.

51. *DGFC, I*, pp. 54, 294, 525. ANDQ, Registres des baptêmes, July 5, 1673. Dénombrement de mars 1725, AC, G1, 464. ADM, C, March 22, 1733.

to join Claude Parent and Pierre-René Leboeuf and built a house, a fair-sized structure measuring twenty by twenty-seven feet. The house was a duplex (estimated value: eight hundred *livres*) which Rochon built in conjunction with a certain Marchand, a trader and probably a kinsman.[52]

After long conversations with Rochon and his neighbors, Bienville and Dartaguiette decided with finality to move the entire town to the river's mouth, the removal to begin immediately. Further plans were then made to re-situate some of the area's buffer villages. The Little Tomeh were to be left at their original site at Nannahubba Bluff, but the Chato were to be moved farther down the bay and up Dog River a quarter of a league above the old warehouse situated at the mouth of that stream. This removal would take effect immediately as would another one: one of the smaller villages of the Talimali (a refugee tribe from the province of Apalache), then located upstream from the present town site just below the Little Tomeh, would move to the south side of the mouth of the rivière Saint-Martin (presently Chickasabogue or Chickasaw Creek) just above the new town site. From this location, the Talimali, judged to be the most skilled and the most diligent of the nearby allies, would be in better position to aid in constructing the new fort.[53] Moreover, the Mobile Indians would be asked to move downstream from their ancient location at the fork of the Mobile and Tensaw rivers to occupy the area just north of the site the French were abandoning.[54]

Bienville and Dartaguiette had left Barbazant de Pailloux in charge at the new site. While the two leaders were preparing the settlers to leave, Pailloux, with his aides, was laying out the new

52. Mémoire [Montigny to Tremblay], 1700, ASQ, Missions, 107. AC, F1A, 13, f. 118. Davion [to LaVente], Oct. 20, 1711, ASQ, Missions, No. 46. ADM, A, Aug. 4, 1710; Jan. 5, 1716.

53. *FLC*, pp. 125–26, 128–29. Bienville to min., June 20, 1711, AC, C13B, 1, No. 11, f. 1v–3. Floride Occidentale, AM, 4040 C, 32. [Baye de la Mobile], BN, Cartes et Plans, D 4387. Relation de la rivière de la Mobile, [before 1720], AC, C13C, 2, f. 166v–67. The new site of the Apalache was precisely where the International Paper Co. stands today. The Tawasa were moved to the present Bayou Sara which runs into the stream known in colonial times as the rivière à Boutin (actually a western branch of the Mobile River).

54. The Mobilians, however, would later refuse this site, preferring instead to occupy the location some seven miles above the fort near what is now Seymour's Bluff. Carte de la Louisiane, par Danville, 1732, BN, Cartes et Plans, Collection Danville.

town according to the specifications he had been given, the new fort to be just back from the edge of the marsh on the first rise of ground. The town was to be more regularly shaped than the old town. Except for larger lots given to Bienville and the seminary priests, the new assignments were all practically the same size—approximately 80 by 160 feet, or about the size of some of the smaller lots at the old site such as those occupied by Zacharie Drapreau and René Boyer.[55]

Back at Old Mobile the settlers were delighted with the news that the removal was to proceed immediately. In actuality, there was no reason for delay. What few crops had been planted had already been ruined by the floods and at this late date it was not considered feasible to begin replanting.[56]

The complexities of moving an entire town raised considerable problems. The inhabitants were fortunate in that some of the land on the new site had already been cleared. They were fortunate, too, in that the distance to be traveled was relatively slight (twenty-six miles) and all of it downriver. Yet transportation presented a formidable obstacle. The colony's flatboat, though sizable, could bear only a limited load and would be used mostly for transferring the "official" supplies and those belonging to Bienville, Dartaguiette and the officers. The inhabitants must provide their own transportation and labor.[57]

Although there was an Indian path (to which the modern Saint Stephens Road roughly conforms) leading from Old Mobile to the new site, it was a path little used even by the savages themselves. In this part of the wilderness, transportation by water was by far the most efficient mode of travel and in this particular enterprise an absolute necessity. Most of the inhabitants, despite the difficulties, would find it more feasible to disassemble their houses, float them down to the new site, then reassemble them there than to fell and hew new timbers.[58]

The colonists began to dismantle their dwellings as soon as Bienville informed them they were moving. Those who owned

55. *FLC*, pp. 128–29. Plan de la Ville et Fort Louis de la Louisiane établies par les françois en 1711, BN, Cartes et Plans, 138,10,2 (D 6210).

56. Dartaguiette to min., June 20, 1711, AC, C13A, 2, f. 643–44.

57. Davion [to La Vente], Oct. 20, 1711, ASQ, Missions, No. 46. *Ala. River Navigation Charts*, Sept., 1972, pp. 1–7.

58. Journal de Bertet de la Clüe, 1720, Museum of the City of Mobile, Manuscripts and Documents. Bienville to min., Oct. 27, 1711, AC, C13A, 2, f. 579.

pirogues and small boats proceeded immediately to load their lumber and head downstream. After depositing a shipment at the new site the movers returned upstream for another load until after numerous exhausting trips they had completed transference of their notched timbers and, in some cases, foundation bricks. Then began the process of reassembling the structures. When those families who owned boats were finished, they loaned, or in some cases, rented them to other inhabitants who, after disassembling their houses proceeded to transport the parts downstream. During the last week in May and the first weeks in June the river was almost continously crowded with canoes and small boats, those headed downstream loaded almost to the point of sinking, the others empty on their way back upstream.[59]

The work of removal was cumbersome and tedious, but it was being carried out remarkably fast. By the twentieth of June nearly half the inhabitants had succeeded in transferring their dismantled dwellings and Bienville could report to Pontchartrain that "the work was proceeding well" and that "the inhabitants were all building" at the new location. Bienville at this point went down to Massacre Island to see a ship off for Martinique, leaving Dartaguiette in charge of the operations at New Mobile. As for the missionaries, two of them were also preparing to depart the old site. For the next year their efforts would be largely divided: Huvé would serve the settlement at Massacre Island, Le Maire would remain at the old fort with the garrison and Davion would come down to the new location to serve as pastor. Davion, in fact, had just made arrangements for his lodging so as "not to be forced to sleep out under the stars." The man named Marchand, who with Charles Rochon had built the duplex near the new site some years before, intended to return to France as soon as the next ship arrived. Anticipating his departure, Davion arranged to buy Marchand's half of the duplex for 240 *livres* (on Tremblay's credit), and shortly thereafter moved in next to Rochon.[60]

During the hectic spring and summer of 1711, Davion, though plainly dispirited, was struggling mightily to maintain some sem-

59. *Ibid. FLC*, pp. 128–29. Dartaguiette to min., June 20, 1711, AC, C13A, 2, f. 643–44. *Journal Historique*, p. 107. The abandoned site was to remain unoccupied until granted by Governor Carondolet to Louise Rochon in 1792. Mobile County Probate Court, Conveyances (Caro's Translated Records), Vol. II, Oct. 5, 1792.

60. Bienville to min., June 20, 1711, AC, C13B, 1, No. 11, f. 1–3. Davion [to La Vente], Oct. 20, 1711, ASQ, Missions, No. 46.

blance of religion in the colony. Missionary activity was slight during those months, Huvé and Le Maire apparently preoccupied with their personal affairs. Yet their efforts were not nonexistent. In May, Le Maire baptized a young Chitimacha belonging to Corporal Jacques Châtillon, and in July, he baptized a Chitimacha belonging to Bienville, while Huvé christened Leboeuf's concubine wife-to-be in June. Davion, while he performed no baptisms, himself, was holding masses and preaching whenever he could, efforts that did not go unrecognized by Dartaguiette. "M. Davion," the commissary reported, "has by his mildness, his pleasant conversation and his apostolic discourse, brought many strayed sheep back to their duty. Truly this man is so strongly imbued himself with what he preaches to others that the lowest criminals cannot but believe in the eternal truth he espouses . . ." [61]

If the work of the town's removal was going well, there remained difficulties that seemed almost insurmountable. While the move was taking place, there were some twenty to thirty Chickasaw at Old Mobile, impatiently awaiting the supply ship's arrival in order to receive their presents. The Chickasaw were not favorably impressed with the recent turn of events: Bienville had promised to build a fort on the Tombigbee, in their direction; instead, the French were moving the other way. Perhaps the Carolinian traders had been correct: were the French but a dying nation? Merely the remnants of a civilization the English had already virtually destroyed? If the foregoing were not enough, one of the Chickasaw villages had recently been persuaded by the English to launch a surprise attack on the Choctaw, once more breaking the peace.[62] Dismayed, Bienville confided to the minister:

> Regardless of the measures I have taken to maintain relations with our savage allies, I have not been able to furnish them the assistance that would protect them against the entreaties that the allies of the English make to them . . . the Chickasaw, with whom I have always maintained a close understanding have let themselves be seduced by the considerable presents of the English and have excused themselves for this action by the justification that since the French have not been able to

61. ADM, A, May 23, June 3, July 17, 1711. Dartaguiette to min., Jan. 10, 1711, AC, C13A, 2, f. 639.

62. *Journal Historique*, p. 107. Bienville to min., Feb. 20, 1707, AC, C13A, 2, f. 7.

answer their needs they have had by necessity to turn to the enemy . . .[63]

Bienville was hoping that the arrival of the *Renommée* would bring sufficient presents for the Chickasaw to enable the French to weather this crisis. If the natives now at Mobile could return to their villages with a considerable amount of goods, it might be enough to win the Chickasaw back before it was too late. Even so, additional gifts would be required to appease the now-aroused Choctaw. Assuredly, hopes for the reception of sufficient amounts of presents seemed far-fetched; by the middle of July the ship had still not arrived, and if rumors of the *Renommée's* capture by the English proved true, it might be years before the colony saw another vessel.[64]

By late July, Bienville and Dartaguiette felt they could wait for the *Renommée* no longer. On the twenty-ninth, the two officials sent Barbazant de Pailloux to Veracruz to attempt to obtain additional foodstuffs from the Spanish, hoping that Pailloux would have better success than had Béranger and Châteaugué on previous voyages. Meanwhile, they could do little but trust in Linares' compassion, while at the same time continuing the work of removing to the new site. The majority of colonists were by this time lodged at the *Oignonets*, but some twenty-five inhabitants still remained at the fort, along with Le Maire and the major part of the garrison.[65]

During the time the *Oignonets* was being settled, Bienville found that by means of gunshots and smoke signals between the two native villages and the various settlers along the bay, concise messages could be sent from Massacre Island to New Mobile in less than an hour's time. In case of an attack against the port, Bienville would be able to dispatch a relief force on the same day the emergency occurred. One morning in early September, a signal went out from Massacre Island to Vincent Alexandre's place, the first establishment on the mainland. Alexandre promptly relayed the shots to Nicolas Bodin who in turn signalled Guillaume Boutin

63. Bienville to min., Oct. 27, 1711, AC, C13A, 2, f. 570–72.

64. Bienville further complained that while he had been able to supply his savage allies with only 10,000 *livres* worth of presents in ten years, the English had given them over 300,000 *livres* worth. *Ibid.*, f. 575.

65. Mémorandum des marchandise . . . par M. d'Artaguiette, Feb. 23, 1711, AC, C13A, 2, f. 717. Bienville to min., Oct. 27, 1711, AC, C13A, 2, f. 568–69.

who signalled the small Yamasee village farther up the bay. The Chato received the message from the Yamasee and in turn relayed it on to Rochon and Parent who signalled New Mobile, where the message set off a wild celebration, long overdue. After three and a half years, the colony was once again to be supplied: the *Renommée* was finally in port.[66]

Amid the cheers, Bienville set out for the harbor, accompanied by the barge and a number of officers and inhabitants in pirogues and small boats. Arriving at the island Bienville was met by Captain Rémonville and several officers he had not seen in years—Mandeville, who had left the colony in 1708 and Louis Bécart de Granville, a Canadian officer of long acquaintance who had been active in the founding of Mobile in 1702. Moreover, there were several new faces to greet him: an engineer, Guillaume-Philbert Chevillot, who would aid in the construction of the new Fort Louis and the fortifications at Massacre Island, and Jean-Baptiste Valigny, a seasoned veteran with a wooden leg. But there were three men missing from the new arrivals, which highly disappointed Bienville: Vaulezard, Louis-Joseph Morel de La Durantaye and Bienville's nephew, Jacques Le Moyne de Sainte-Hélène. Vaulezard, in fact, had been due in the colony for nearly seven years, and Sainte-Hélène, who was supposed to be accompanying the *Renommée* in a small ship coming from Martinique had been separated from the larger ship in a storm and was feared lost.[67]

There were other disappointments as Bienville was to soon discover. The supplies aboard the *Renommée* were not near the quantity he expected. Most of the flour was missing; much of the merchandise had been damaged due to poor packing; there were not enough nails or canvas; and none of the four thousand pounds of bullets Bienville had requested from Rochefort was aboard. Moreover, a large number of uniforms for the soldiers were corroded with rust, after having been packed in the kegs of nails. Perhaps the biggest disappointment was the absence of cash with

66. Mémoire de M. Dartaguiette, May 12, 1712, AC, C13A, 2, f. 806. Carte de la Louisiane . . . par Danville, 1732, BN, Cartes et Plans, Collection Danville. *Journal Historique*, p. 108. *FLC*, pp. 128–33. The *Renommée*, after two weeks in Havana, had required 27 days to reach Massacre Island (normally a week's voyage). Tivas de Gourville to min., Dec. 7, 1711, AC, C13C, 2, f. 67.

67. *Journal Historique*, pp. 108–09. Bienville to min., Oct. 27, 1711, *loc. cit.*, f. 584–92. *DGFC, I*, pp. 42, 380. Cadillac to min., Oct. 26, 1713, AC, C13A, 3, f. 77.

which Bienville had expected to reimburse those inhabitants to whom the king was in debt.[68]

Nevertheless, the return of the *Renommée* was a welcome sight—the most exhilarating event to transpire in the colony since that same ship's 1708 mooring. Despite the missing items and men, she brought more supplies than the colony had seen since Dartaguiette's arrival, as well as a captured English-made vessel, the *Catherine.* Of equal importance perhaps, the *Renommée's* appearance was ample proof to the colonists that the court was not abandoning the colony; it gave them the uplift in morale they needed to speedily complete the work on the new town.[69]

As soon as the merchandise was transferred to the Massacre Island warehouse, Bienville issued the Chickasaw their presents and sent Châteaugué and a handful of men to escort them back to their homes through the Choctaw country. Perhaps, Bienville hoped, there was still a chance to save that alliance from complete destruction. Soon after Châteaugué left, the nearby Apalache, having recently completed the harvesting of a portion of their crops, went back to work on the new fort (which, however, would not be ready for occupancy until well into the year 1712).[70]

Rémonville, with whom Bienville and most of the inhabitants were keenly impressed, went out of his way to help put the colony back on its feet. Besides volunteering the services of Bécart de Granville to command Vaulezard's company, Rémonville replaced some of the missing merchandise from his own supply, which would enable the work on Fort Louis and the fortifications at Massacre Island to be completed. Furthermore, in answer to some of the colonists' requests, the privateer promised two hundred *piastres* to Davion to finance the building of a church on Massacre Island. He delivered one hundred and fifty *piastres* on the spot, then agreed to sign a promissory note for the remaining fifty.[71]

Soon after the arrival of the *Renommée*, Barbazant de Pailloux

68. Bienville to min., Oct. 27, 1711, *loc. cit.*, f. 571–72, 600–01. Tivas de Gourville to min., Dec. 7, 1711, AC, C13C, 2, f. 68–68v. Mémoire de M. d'Artaguiette, May 12, 1712, AC, C13A, 2, f. 803.

69. Bienville to min., Oct. 27, 1711, *loc. cit.*, f. 567–68, 570–71.

70. *Ibid.*, f. 570–71. *Journal Historique*, p. 108.

71. *FLC*, pp. 132–35. Davion [to La Vente], Oct. 20, 1711, ASQ, Missions, No. 46. Bienville to min., Oct. 27, 1711, *loc. cit.*, f. 602. Tivas de Gourville, however, painted a highly unflattering picture of Rémonville's character and ability. Tivas de Gourville to min., Dec. 7, 1711, AC, C13C, 2, f. 67v–70.

returned from Veracruz, bringing additional supplies (mostly foodstuffs), which, added to those brought by the *Renommée* and those donated by Rémonville, put the colony for the time being on fairly sound footing. Bienville was forced to send on to Pensacola (as repayment for past debts) much of the gunpowder that Rémonville had brought, but Sainte-Hélène finally arrived in his ship with an extra supply.[72] In the autumn of 1711, Mobile was on the soundest basis it had been since 1704; Bienville reported the progress with reserved optimism:

> The assistance that M. de Rémonville has brought us, altogether quite moderate, provides us courage and gives us hope against the fear we have had of being forced to abandon this colony, which by my care and by my efforts is beginning to take some shape . . . the entire colony appears to me quite well pleased with the change that we have made and each one is working in emulation of the others on his own establishment. There now remains at Fort Louis only five or six houses which are being prepared for immediate transfer to the new site. Only the garrison will remain at the old site until the fort is completed . . .[73]

Her mission accomplished, the *Renommée* now prepared to return to France after an over-extended stay in port. Though only fourteen years old, the "vaisseau de 4ème rang" was in a baleful state of repair. Already she had made four voyages to Louisiana, the second having brought Iberville and those who were instrumental in the founding of Mobile. The return voyage home was to be her last.[74]

During the third week in October, Bienville went down to Massacre Island to see Captain Rémonville off. With him went the man who had done so much for the commandant as well as for the colony—Jean-Baptiste-Martin Dartaguiette d'Iron. Dartaguiette was leaving with Rémonville for France, his principal assignment largely unaccomplished (at least as far as Pontchartrain was concerned). Yet the commissary had played a vital role in the colony's administration; he had won the respect and admiration of almost everyone, had put more order in the colony's business affairs than the late La Salle was ever able to institute, and he had kept up the

72. Bienville to min., *loc. cit.*, f. 567–68.

73. *Ibid.*, f. 567–68, 578–79.

74. *Journal Historique*, pp. 108–09. AM, G, 13. Tivas de Gourville to min., Dec. 7, 1711, AC, C13C, 2, f. 67–67v.

colony's morale when its fortunes had been at lowest ebb. Bienville, of course, was considerably in Dartaguiette's debt. A man of different persuasion or temperament could have severely damaged the commandant's career.[75]

Before Dartaguiette boarded ship he and Bienville had one last conference. Together they had agreed on moving the colony downstream and on beginning the fortifications on Massacre Island. Now they would jointly propose two additional changes. In mid-1707 the minister, in his instructions to Daneau de Muy, had expressed displeasure over the name "Mobile" that was being applied to the establishment. The appellation suggested a lack of stability and Pontchartrain asked the governor-designate to consider "a more suitable one." [76] When Dartaguiette mentioned this to Bienville, the two of them discussed the matter, then suggested that the new establishment should be called "Immobile," a perfectly logical if seemingly frivolous proposal. Furthermore, they agreed that since the name "Île Massacre" sounded a bit ominous it should best be changed to Île Dauphine and the name of the port to Port Dauphine, both after the new dauphine of France, news of whose recent ascendency had reached Saint-Domingue only shortly before the *Renommée* left Cap-français for Mobile. Dartaguiette could not have brought up the subject of nomenclature (his own instructions from the court contained no such directives) without mentioning the fact that he had all along had in his possession the late Daneau de Muy's orders, instructions Bienville must have wondered about on numerous occasions. At this point, however, Dartaguiette felt at liberty to reveal their contents. Indeed just before leaving, Dartaguiette handed over the originals of these orders, then on the nineteenth day of October he boarded ship and the next day was on his way to France via Havana.[77]

75. Bienville to min., Oct. 27, 1711, *loc. cit.*, f. 592–94, 599–602. *FLC*, pp. *xxxi*, 120–42.

76. Min. to M. de Muy, June 30, 1707, AC, B 29, f. 261v.

77. Bienville to min., Oct. 27, 1711, *loc. cit.*, f. 569, 599–600. Davion [to La Vente], Oct. 20, 1711, ASQ, Missions, No. 46. The year following, the king notified Cadillac of his disapproval of the proposed name "Immobile," preferring to retain the old name "Fort St. Louis." He did approve of the switch to "Île Dauphine," in honor of his beloved granddaughter-in-law, Marie-Adélaïde de Savoye, Duchesse de Bourgogne, who had become dauphine in April, 1711. Mémoire du Roy. . . . 18 déc. 1712, AC, B 34, f. 144v. While officials in France and Louisiana thereafter began to use "Île Dauphine," the name "Massacre" continued to be used by the inhabitants well into the nineteenth century. Relation de Le Maire, 1718,

Watching the *Renommée* sail away on that October morning, Bienville saw the departure of one of the last of those men who had been unusually prominent in the life and development of Old Mobile. Indeed, with the exception of the discredited La Vente and Sérigny, Dartaguiette was one of the few who were still alive. Iberville, Le Sueur, Dongé and Limoges lay dead in distant graves, while La Salle, Levasseur, Tonti and Gravier lay buried in the nearly abandoned town upstream. Now, in late 1711, only Bienville, Boisbriant and Châteaugué remained. Bienville, in his thirty-second year, felt for the moment secure in his position. The two letters he had received from the minister made no mention of his being replaced as the chief authority, and though he had recently heard rumors to the contrary, he could still hope that the governorship might yet be given him, especially if Dartaguiette's support be accorded due weight.[78]

Looking around at the settlement on Massacre Island, Bienville felt optimistic about the results of the energy and zeal of the inhabitants who had almost completely rebuilt their settlement. Industrious entrepreneurs such as Graveline, La Source, La Pointe and La Fresnière would soon make something profitable of that place and with the completion of fortifications, the port would be practically impregnable.[79]

Returning to the mouth of the river, Bienville could take heart too at the work of the settlers on their houses and lots. The lands behind the as-yet-unfinished fort were now practically all cleared. Although there was no church at the moment (and there would not be for some time), Bienville was certain that the seminary in Paris would gain renewed interest in its mission field as the war in Europe came to a close and the town began to prosper. Despite the harrowing early years, the crippling poverty, the disorganiza-

---

AC, C13C, 2, f. 153–59. View of a cottage on the Island Massacre near the Mobille, Oct. 1764, British Museum, Map Room, CXXII, 94–2. Dartaguiette to min., March 1, 1712, AC, C13A, 2, f. 697–98.

78. *Journal Historique*, pp. 108–09. In his letter of Oct. 27, 1711, Bienville acknowledged receipt of Pontchartrain's letters of May 10, 1710 and Sept. 2, 1710 but not of the letter of May 13, 1710 in which the minister notified him of the appointment of Cadillac. Bienville's letter, in fact, seems to indicate he had not at this point been officially informed of Cadillac's promotion. Was Bienville pretending the loss of the minister's May 13 letter or did Pontchartrain actually refrain from sending it, having had second thoughts about the appointment? AC, C13A, 2, f. 567–602. AC, B 32, f. 36v–41, 57v–58, 197–98v.

79. Dartaguiette to min., June 20, 1711, AC, C13A, 2, f. 644–45.

tion, the Indian attacks, the epidemics, the lack of support from the crown, Bienville felt a new day dawning. There were some remarkably hearty and enterprising inhabitants present in his colony—men like Saucier, Rivard, La Loire, Trudeau, Trépanier, Rochon, Derbanne, Saint-Denis and the brothers Chauvin—men who had lifted themselves up by their own initiative, who, whatever might lie ahead, would carry the colony forward in this execrable and defiant land.[80]

80. *Ibid.* Bienville to min., June 20, 1711, AC, C13B, 1, No. 11, f. 1–3. Tivas de Gourville, ensign serving on the *Renommée*, envisioned the colony's principal establishment and governor's residence at Bayou Saint-Jean. Tivas de Gourville to min., June, 1712, AC, C13A, 2, f. 739.

Illustrations

Louvre, 65 DN 699

Louis XIV at the time of the founding of Mobile

By Hyacinthe Rigaud, 1701

Musée des Beaux Arts à Rochefort

The port of Rochefort

MV, 3667

Jérôme Phélypeaux de Pontchartrain
1647–1747

MM, 33117

French naval personnel of the late seventeenth century

Ancienne Préfecture Maritime à Rochefort

Michel Bégon de La Picardière
1638–1710

Artist Unknown

Comte Le Moyne de Martigny

Pierre Le Moyne d'Iberville
1661–1706

Artist Unknown (Cf. Appendix VIII)

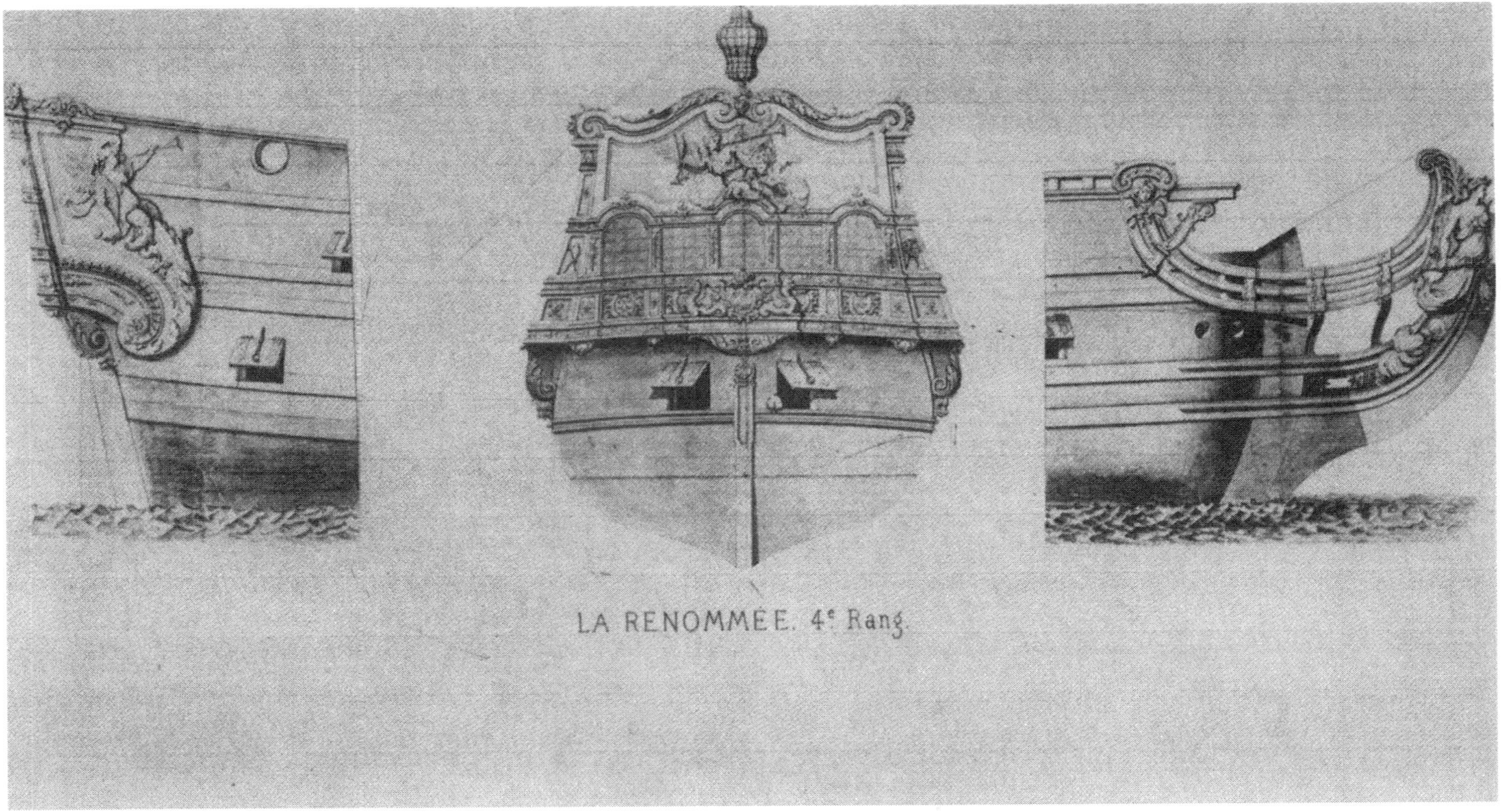

MM, 72743

Three views of the Renommée

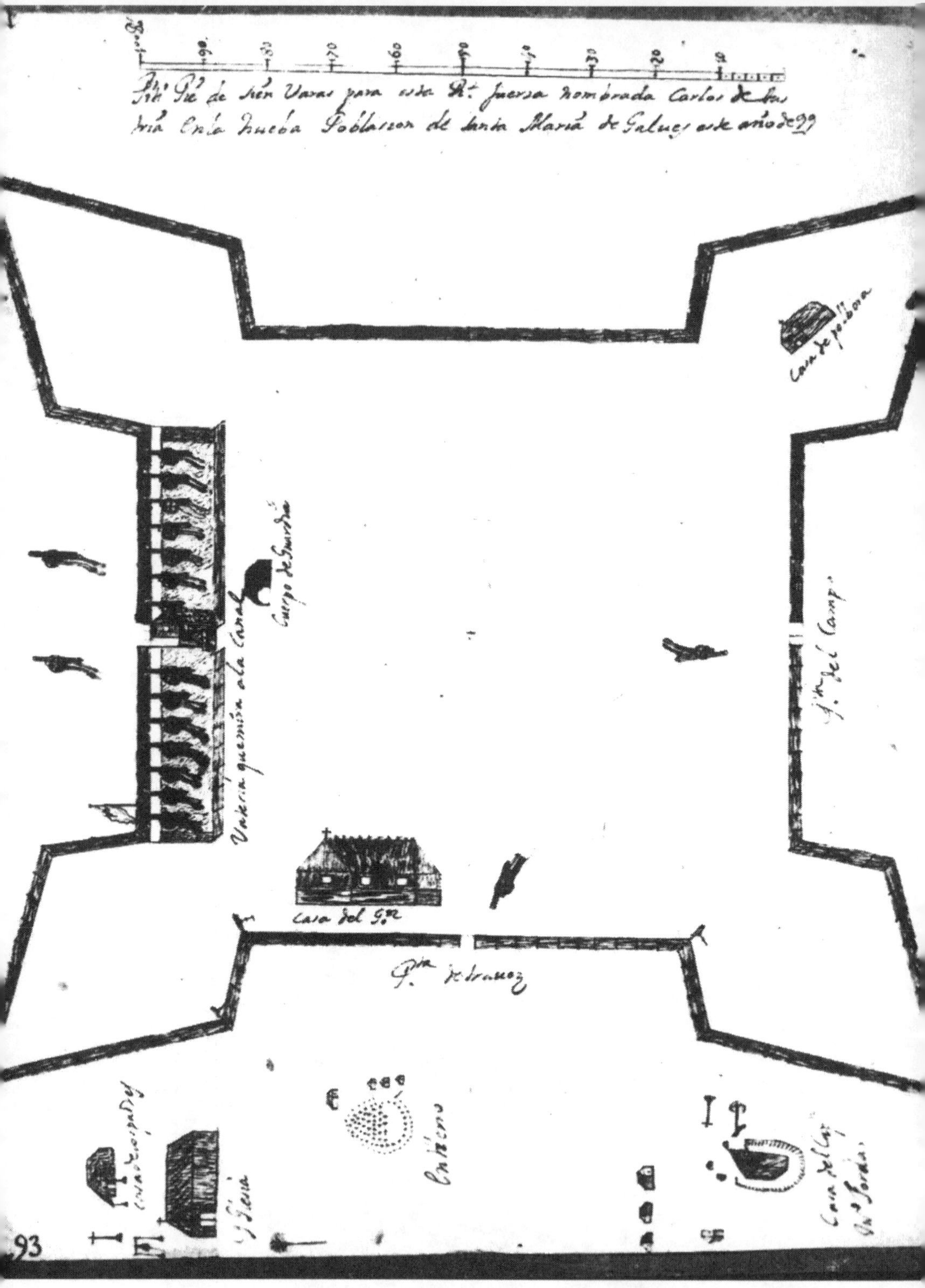

AGI, México, *L. 618*

Fort San Carlos de Austria (Pensacola)
1699

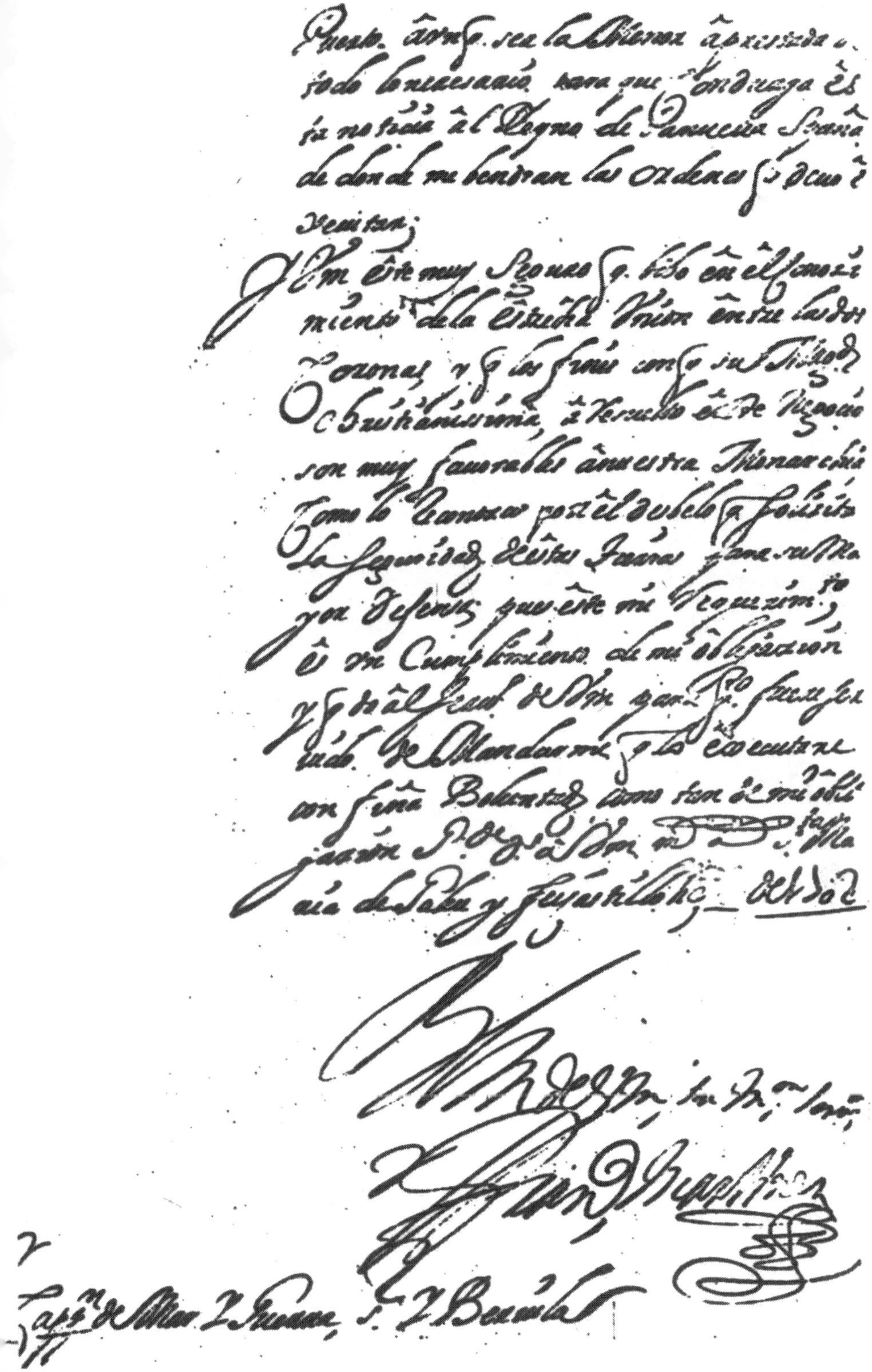

AC, C13A, 1, f. 362

Signature page of Martínez's note to Iberville on the eve of the founding of Mobile.

Comte Le Moyne de Martigny

Joseph Le Moyne de Sérigny
1668–1734

Artist Unknown

Photo by John Freeman Martin, 1974

Site of Fort Louis (1702–1712). View from what was the center of the parade ground, looking toward the middle of town

Photo by John Freeman Martin, 1974

Edge of the bluff where Fort Louis stood. The river has eroded approximately half of the original fort site.

Photo by John Freeman Martin, 1974

The terrain behind the bluff where the fort stood. This area was near the center of town and is typical of conditions during the rainy season.

Photo by John Freeman Martin

From Fort Louis, looking upriver

Photo by John Freeman Martin, 1974

On the site of Fort Louis, looking directly across river

Photo by John Freeman Martin, 1974

From site of Fort Louis, looking downriver

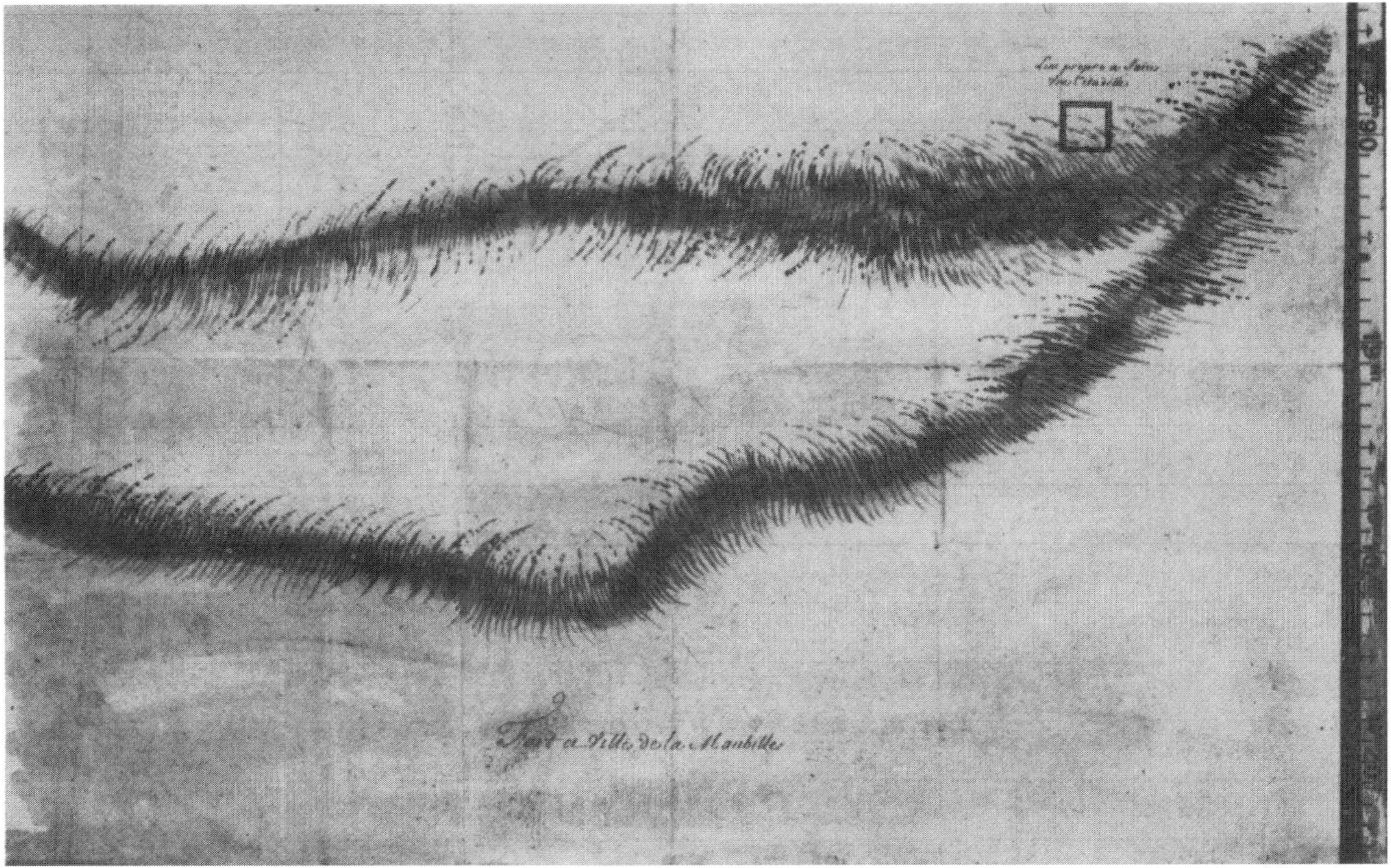

AN, DFC, 119A

Sketch of the bluff on which Fort Louis would be built (January, 1702). Probably by Charles Levasseur

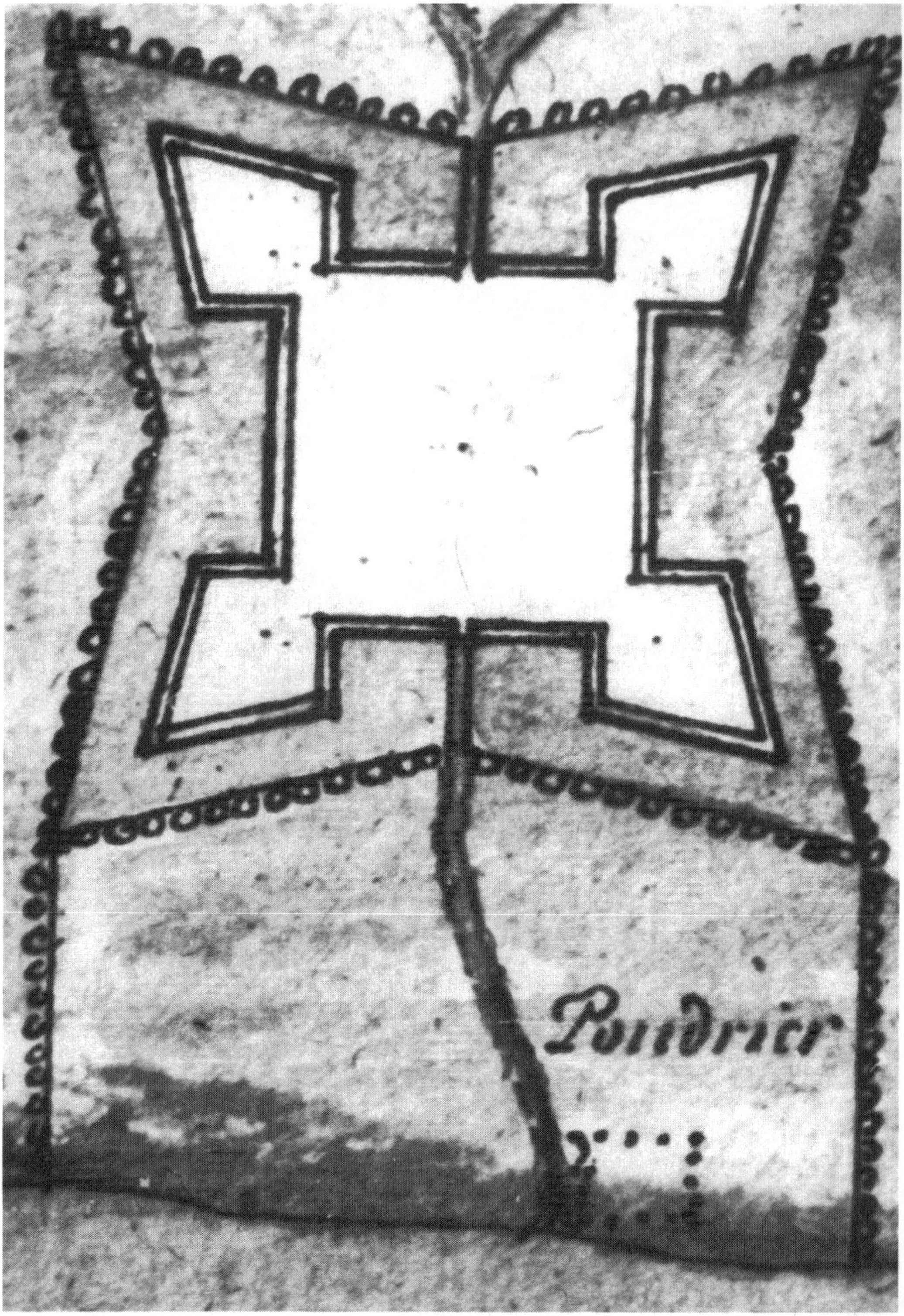

AN, DFC, 119A

Levasseur's plan for the fort in 1702. The construction was carried out approximately according to plan except that the principal entrance was located to the right or northwestern side of the fort.

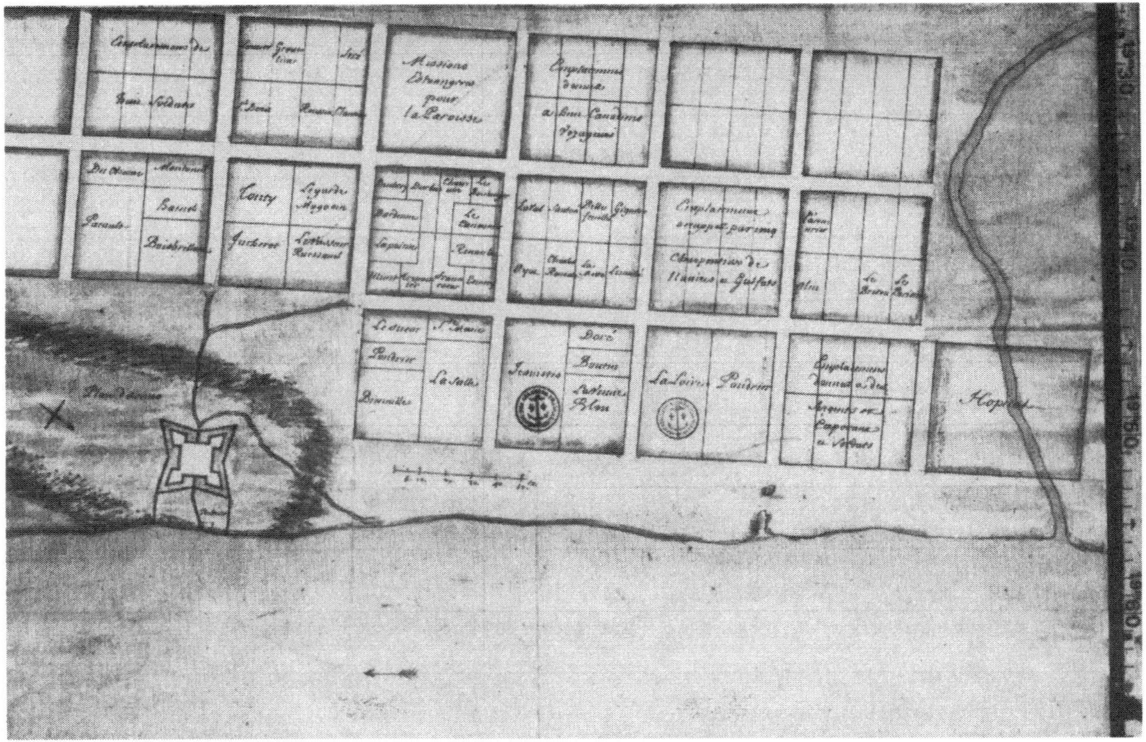

AN, DFC, 119A

Plan for the fort and town of Mobile in early 1702

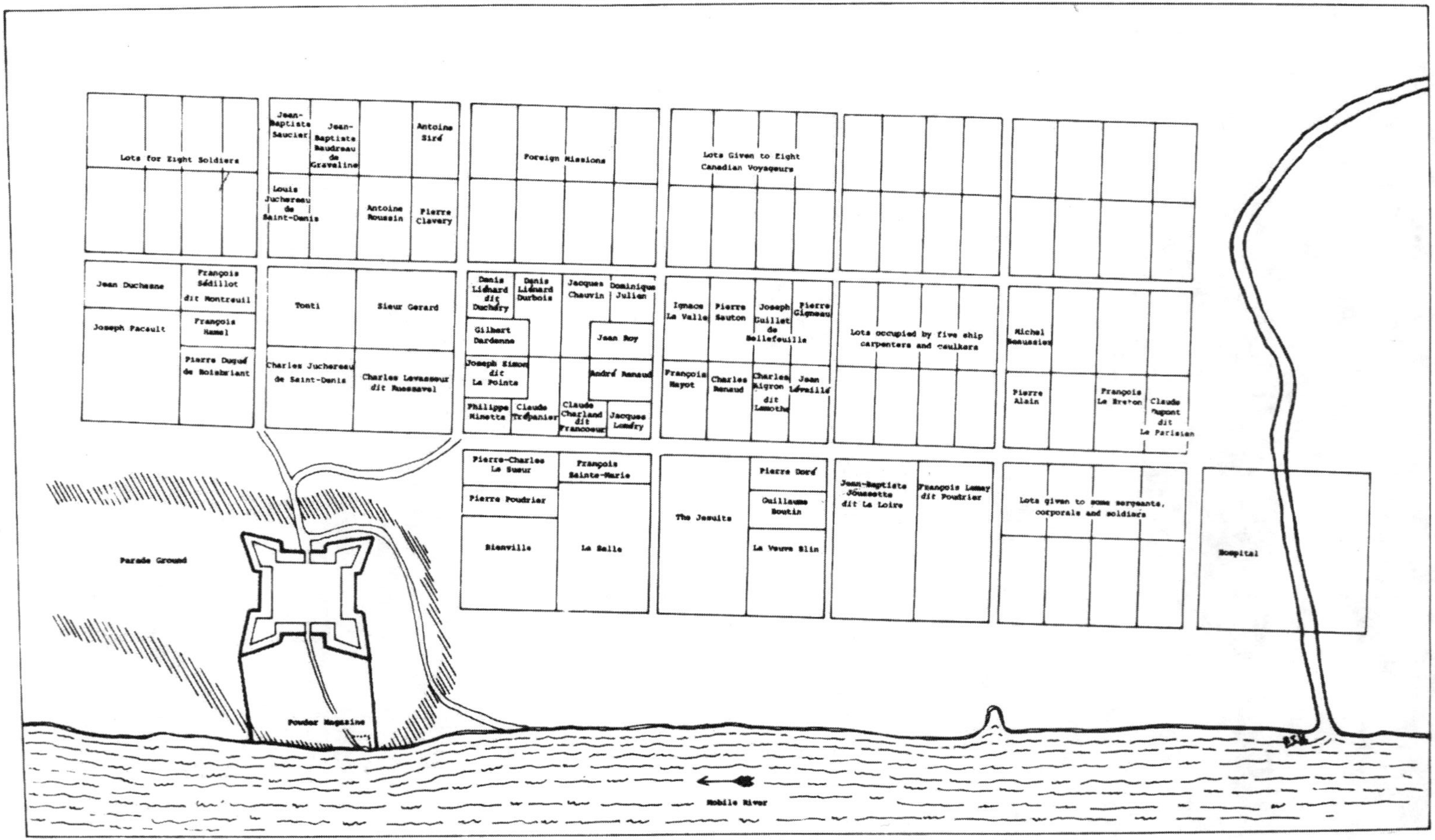

MPL, Maps and Plans

Amplified plan for Mobile during mid-winter of 1702

By Jay Higginbotham

Museum of the City of Mobile

Henri de Tonti
1649?–1704

Artist Unknown

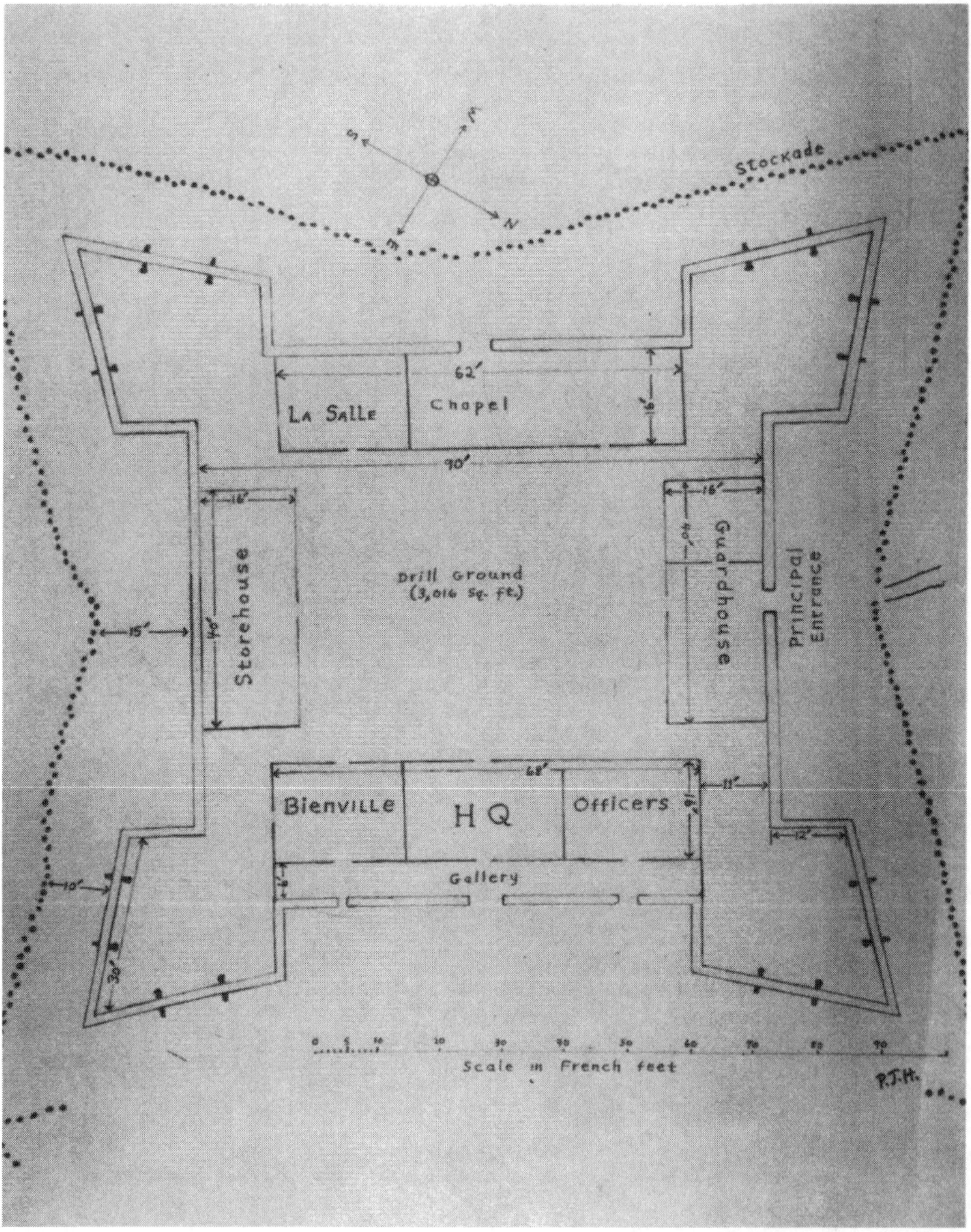

MPL, Maps and Plans

Fort Louis de la Louisiane (1702–1707)

By Jay Higginbotham

ASQ, Missions, 46

Letter of Albert Davion to La Vente, October 20, 1711

Gibbes Art Gallery, Charleston

Sir Nathaniel Johnson
Governor of Carolina
1703–1708

Artist Unknown

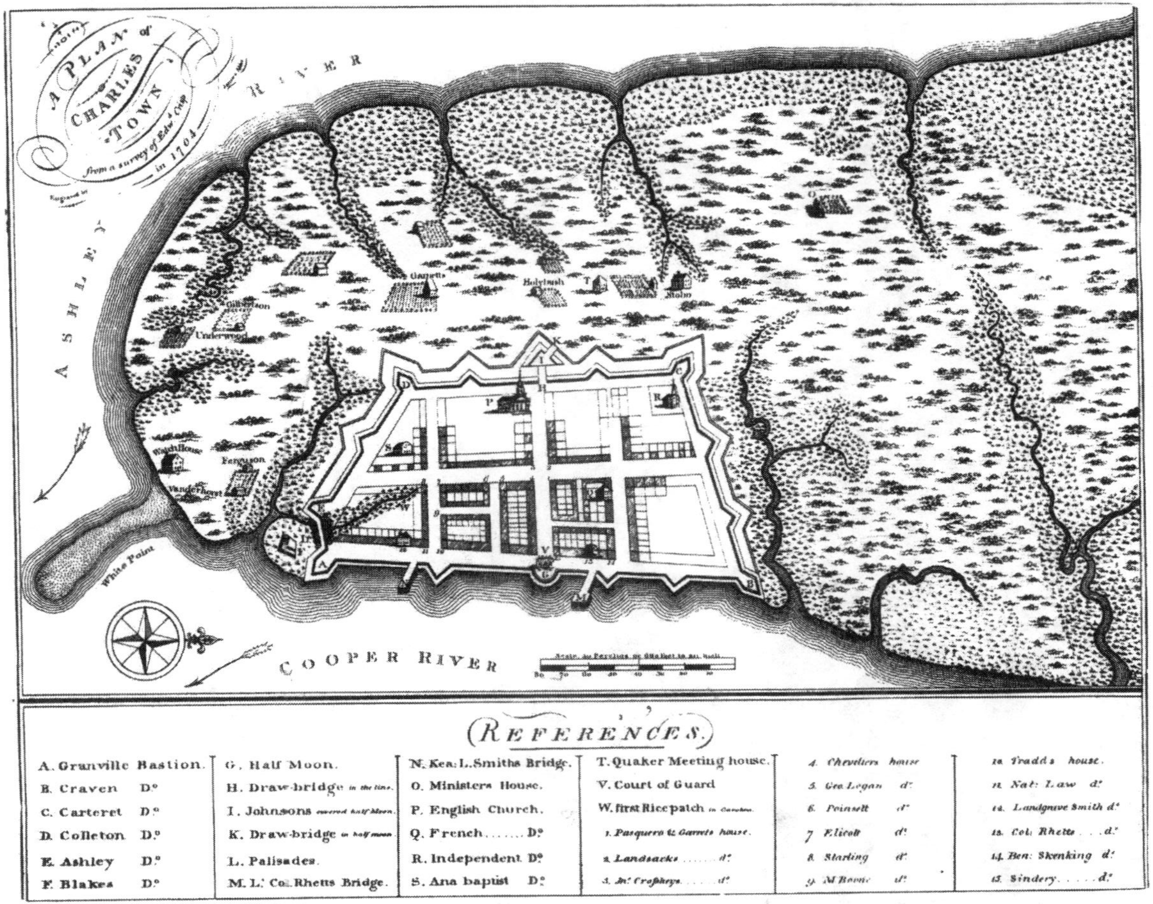

Ramsey, History. . . *II*, 3

Charles-Town in 1704

From a survey by Edward Crisp

Comte Le Moyne de Martigny

Jean-Baptiste Le Moyne de Bienville

Artist Unknown

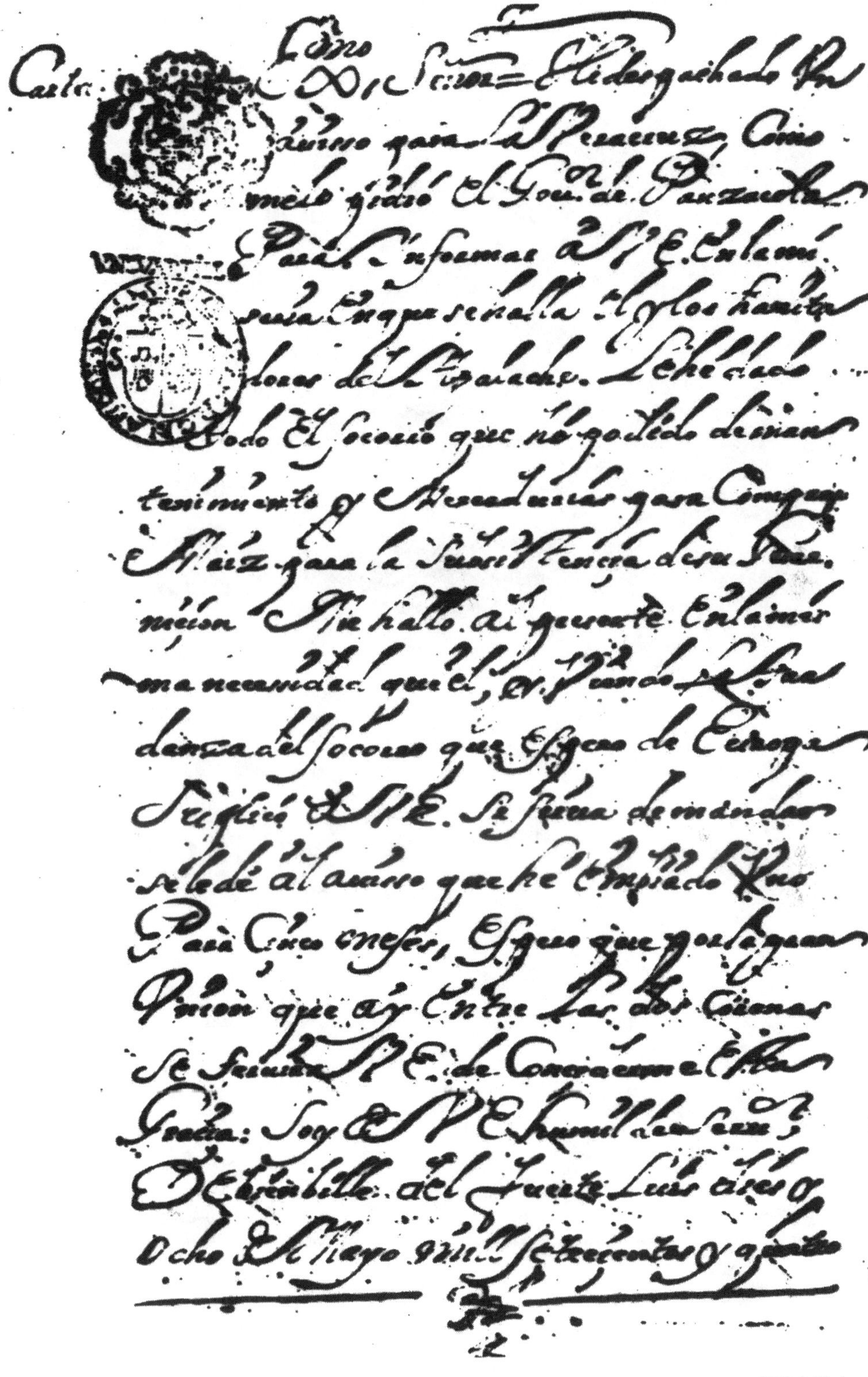

AGI, México, *L. 618*

Spanish copy of Bienville's letter to Alburquerque, May 18, 1704

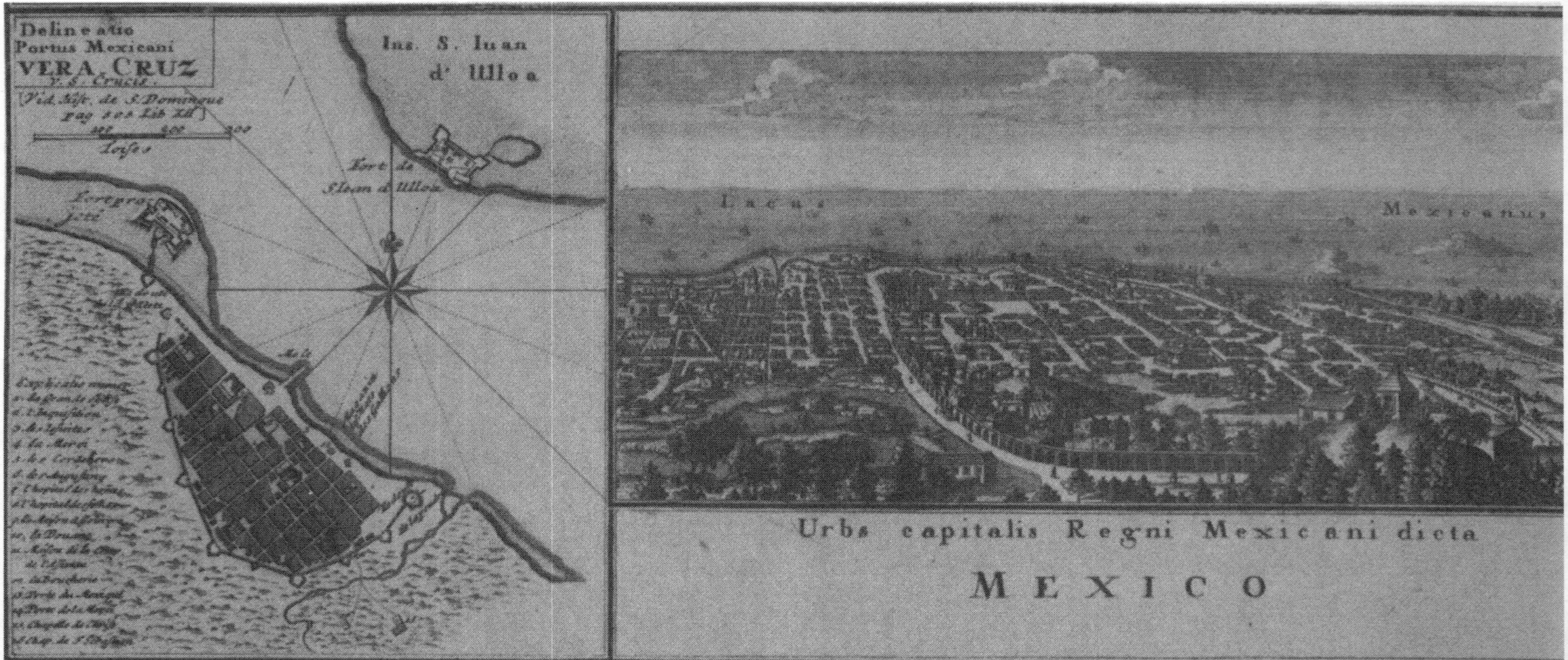

From Homann, Grosser Atlas . . .

The port of Veracruz in the eighteenth century

Ministere des Affaires Culturelles du Quebéc
Oeuvres d'Art, QQQ-12

Jean-Baptiste de La Croix de Chevrières de Saint Vallier
1653–1727

Attributed to Jacques Leblond, *dit* La Tour, ca. 1699

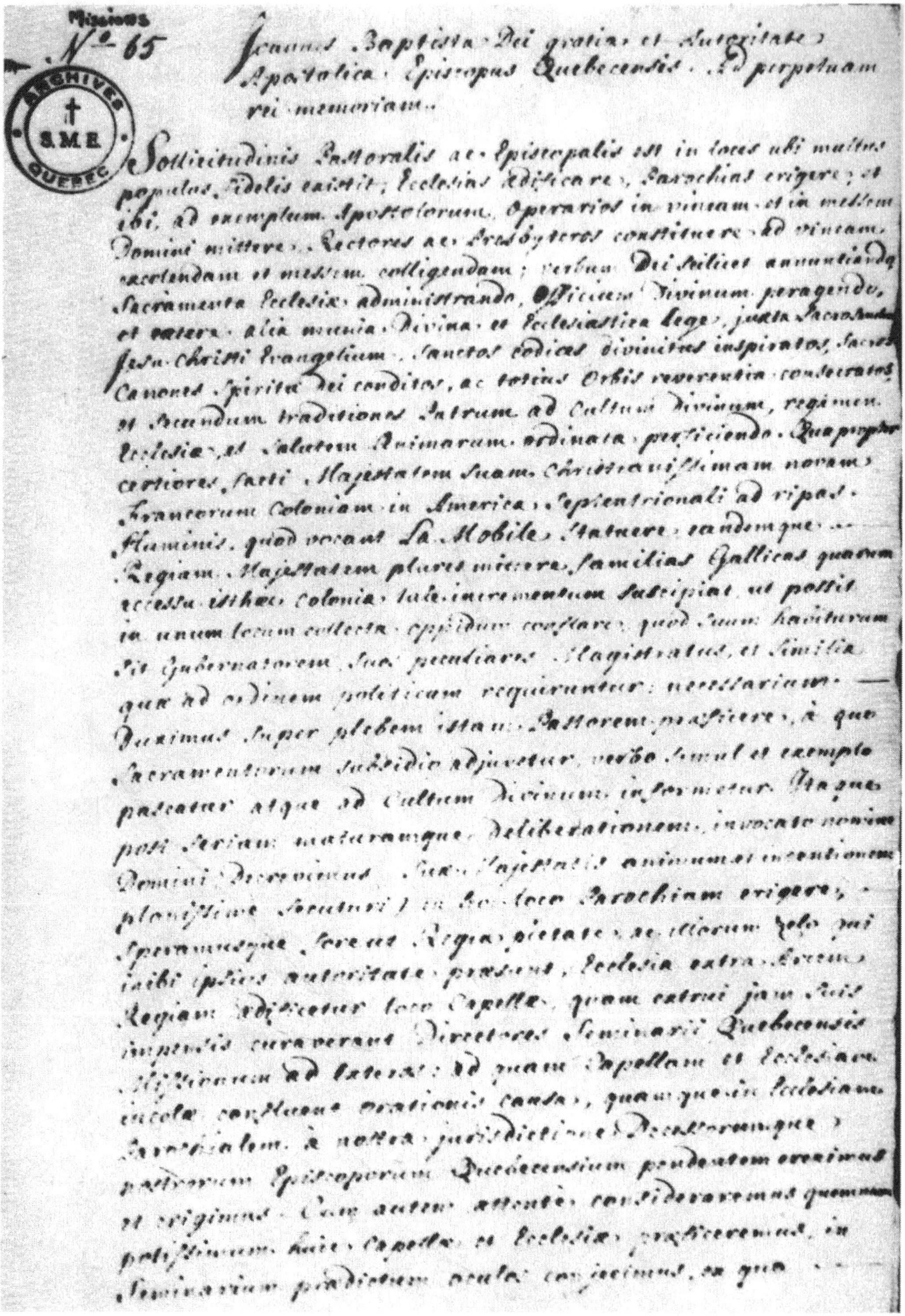
Missions

N° 65

Joannes Baptista Dei gratia et Authoritate Apostolica Episcopus Quebecensis. Ad perpetuam rei memoriam.

Sollicitudinis Pastoralis ac Episcopalis est in locis ubi multus populus fidelis existit, Ecclesias aedificare, Parochias erigere; et ibi, ad exemplum Apostolorum, Operarios in vineam et in messem Domini mittere, Rectores ac Presbyteros constituere ad vineam excolendam et messem colligendam; verbum Dei scilicet annuntiando, Sacramenta Ecclesiae administrando, Officium Divinum peragendo, et caetera alia munia Divina et Ecclesiastica lege, juxta Sacrosanctum Jesu Christi Evangelium, Sanctos codices divinitus inspiratos, Sacros Canones Spiritu Dei conditos, ac totius Orbis reverentia consecratos, et Sanctorum traditiones Patrum ad cultum divinum, regimen Ecclesiae, et salutem Animarum ordinata perficiendo. Quapropter certiores facti Majestatem suam Christianissimam novam Francorum Coloniam in America Septentrionali ad ripas fluminis quod vocant La Mobile statuere, eandemque Regiam Majestatem plures mittere familias Gallicas quarum accessu istha Colonia tale incrementum suscipiat ut possit in unum locum collecta oppidum constare, quod suum habiturum sit Gubernatorem, suos peculiares Magistratus, et similia quae ad ordinem politicum requiruntur: necessarium duximus super plebem istam Pastorem praeficere, a quo Sacramentorum subsidio adjuvetur, verbo simul et exemplo pascatur atque ad cultum divinum informetur. Itaque post seriam maturamque deliberationem, invocato nomine Domini, decrevimus Suae Majestatis animum et intentionem plenissime secuturi, in hoc loco Parochiam erigere, sperantesque fore ut Regia pietate, ac illorum zelo qui ibi ipsius authoritate praesunt, Ecclesia extra Arcem Regiam aedificetur loco Capellae, quam extrui jam fecit impensis curaverunt Directores Seminarii Quebecensis Missionum ad exteras; ad quam Capellam et Ecclesiam incolae confluent orationis causa, quamque in Ecclesiam Parochialem a nostra jurisdictione Successorumque nostrorum Episcoporum Quebecensium pendentem creavimus et erigimus. Cum autem attente consideraremus quemnam possessionem huic Capellae et Ecclesiae praeficeremus, in Seminarium praedictum oculos conjecimus, ex quo

ASQ, Missions, 65

Page one of the Erection of the Parish of Mobile and the Nomination of La Vente as Pastor by Bishop Saint-Vallier

Vereeniging Ned. Hist. Scheepvaart Museum

A Dutch ship of the type of the *Pélican*

Library of Congress, Map Division, 3297

The port of Havana in 1702

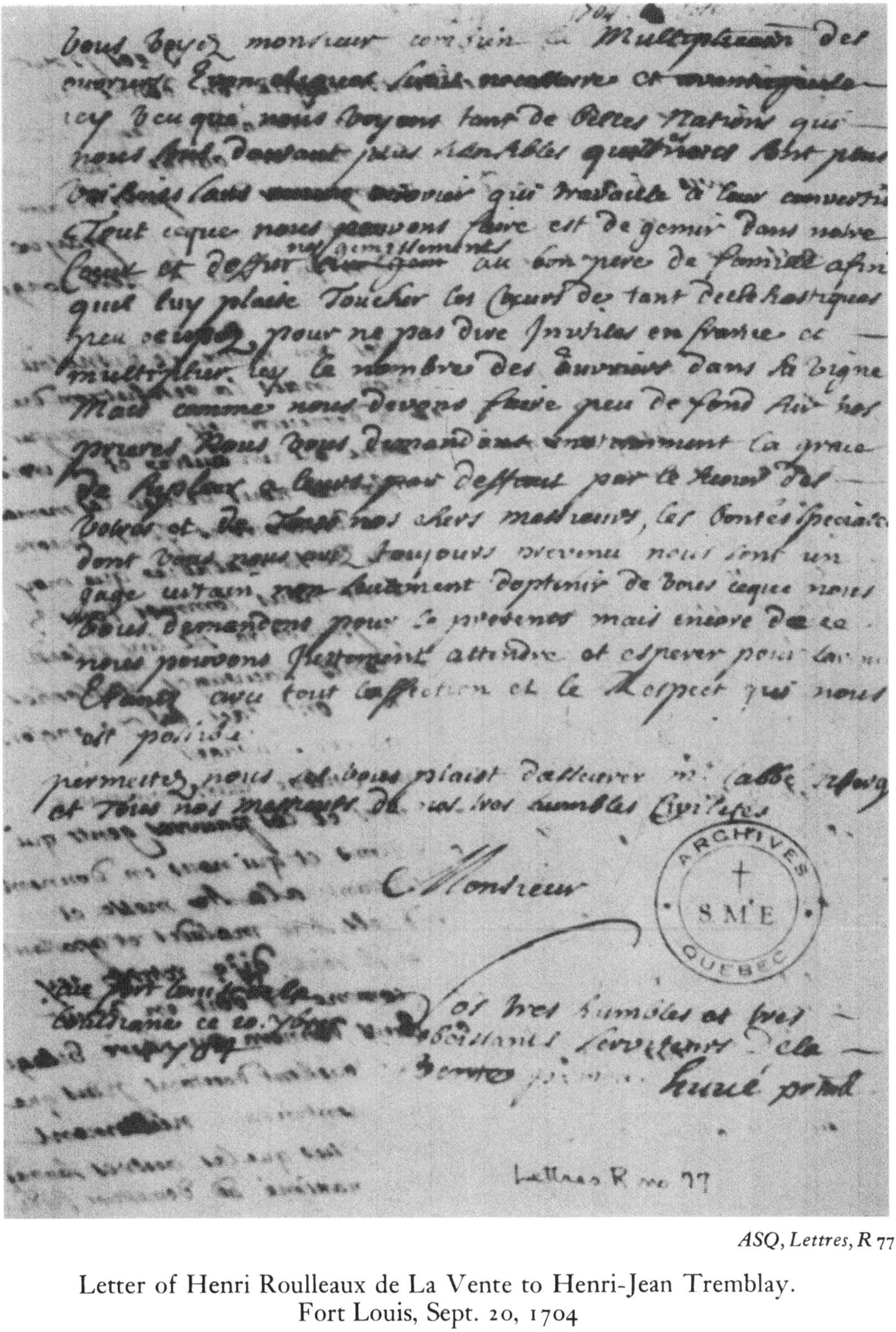

ASQ, Lettres, R 77

Letter of Henri Roulleaux de La Vente to Henri-Jean Tremblay.
Fort Louis, Sept. 20, 1704

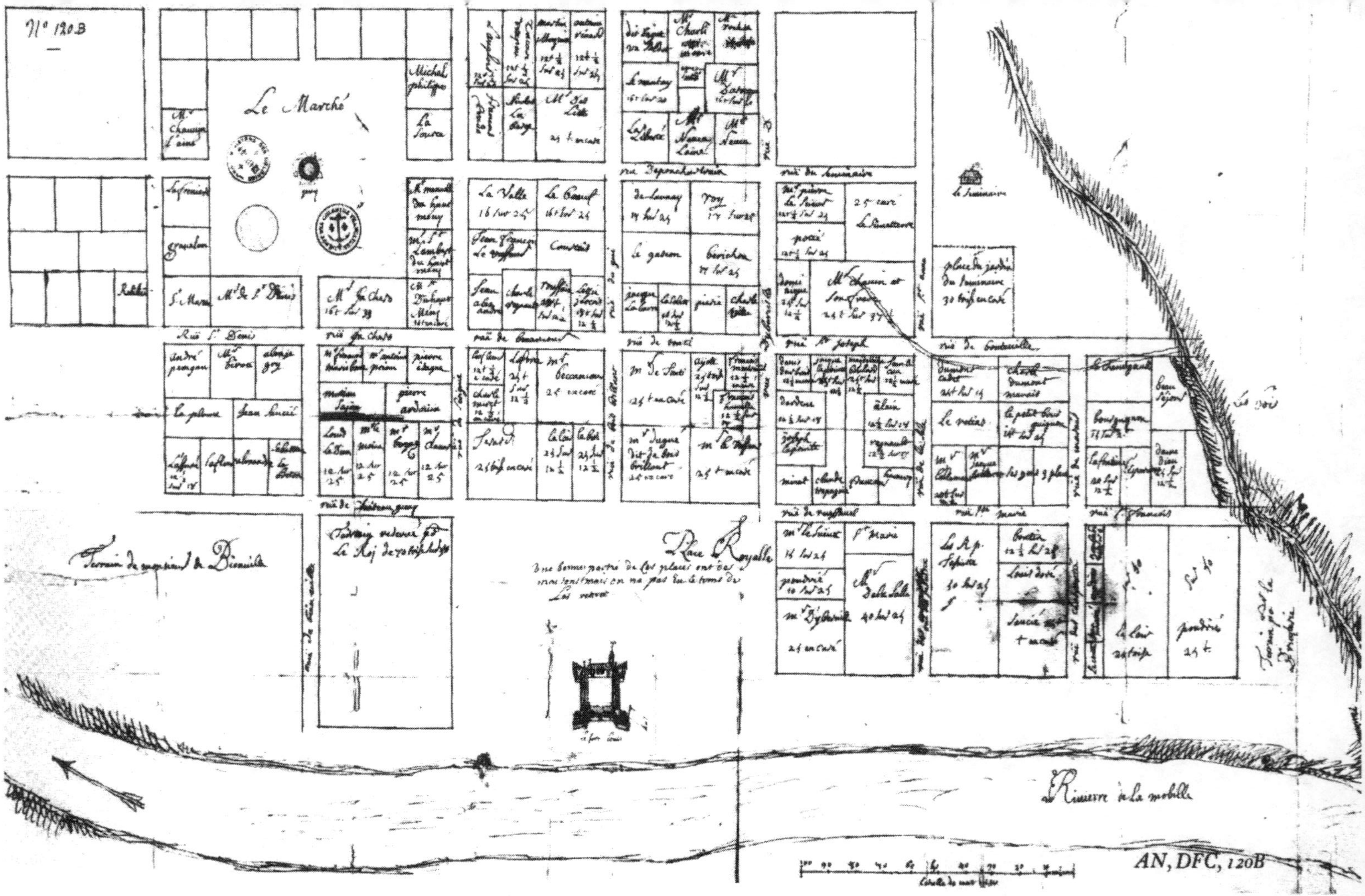

Old Mobile in 1704–05

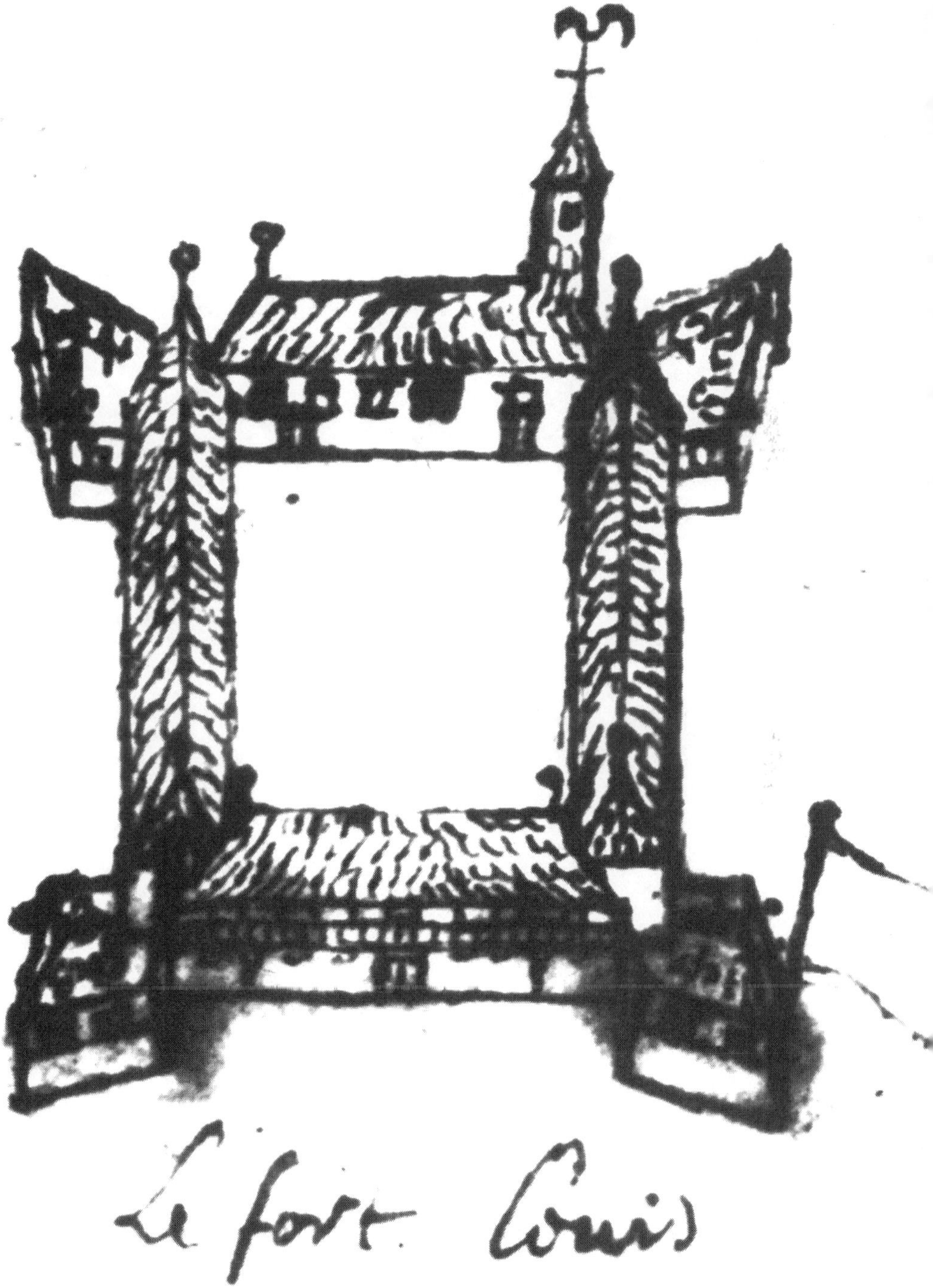

AN, DFC, 120B

Sketch of Fort Louis in 1705 (enlarged)

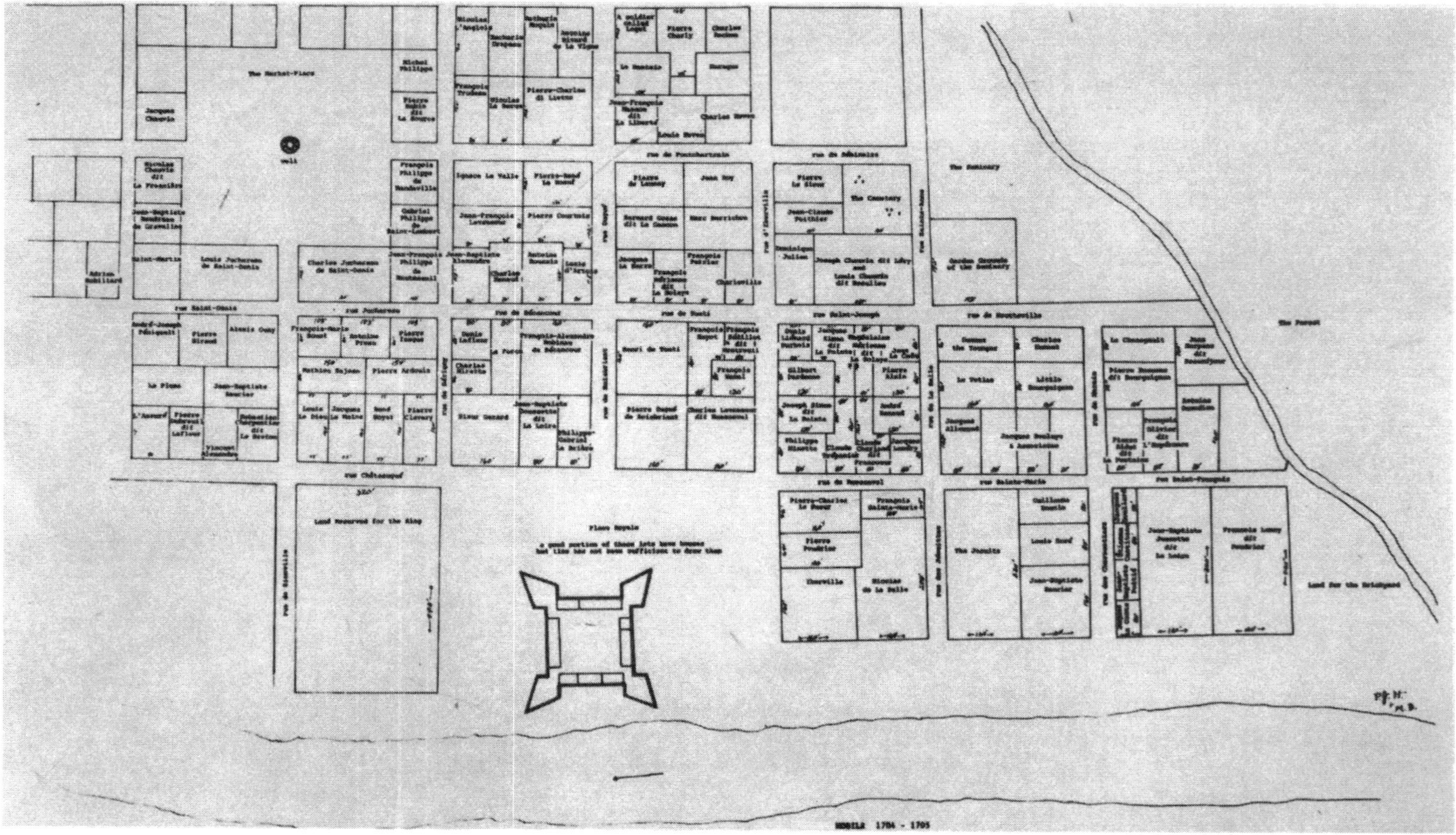

Mobile Public Library, Maps & Plans

Amplified map of Old Mobile of 1704–05

By Jay Higginbotham

Museum of the City of Mobile

Presumably Antoine Le Moyne de Châteaugué
1683–1747

Attributed to Jean-Baptiste Jouvenet

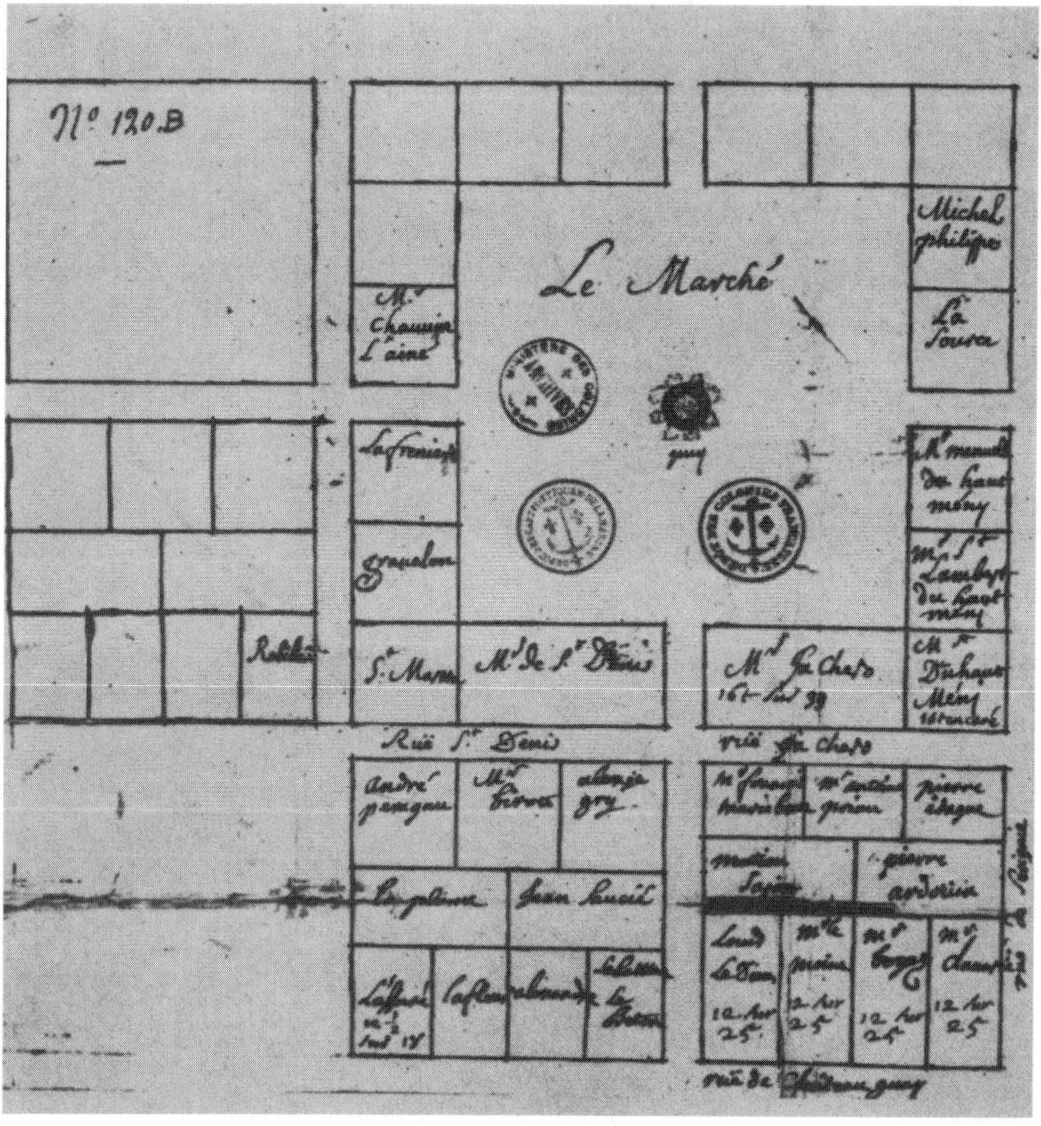

AN, DFC, 120B

Southeastern section of town

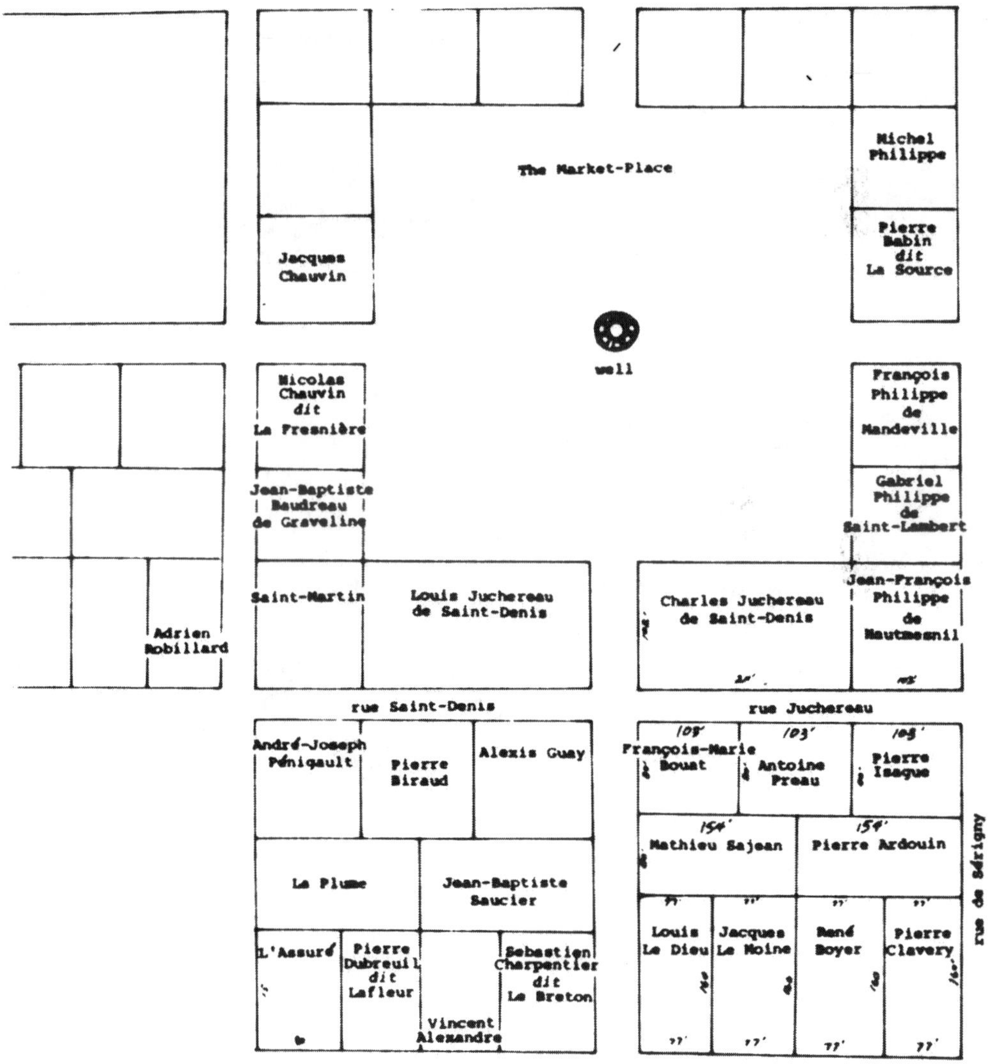

Mobile Public Library, Maps & Plans

Southeastern section of town

By Jay Higginbotham

AN, DFC, 120B

Central section of town

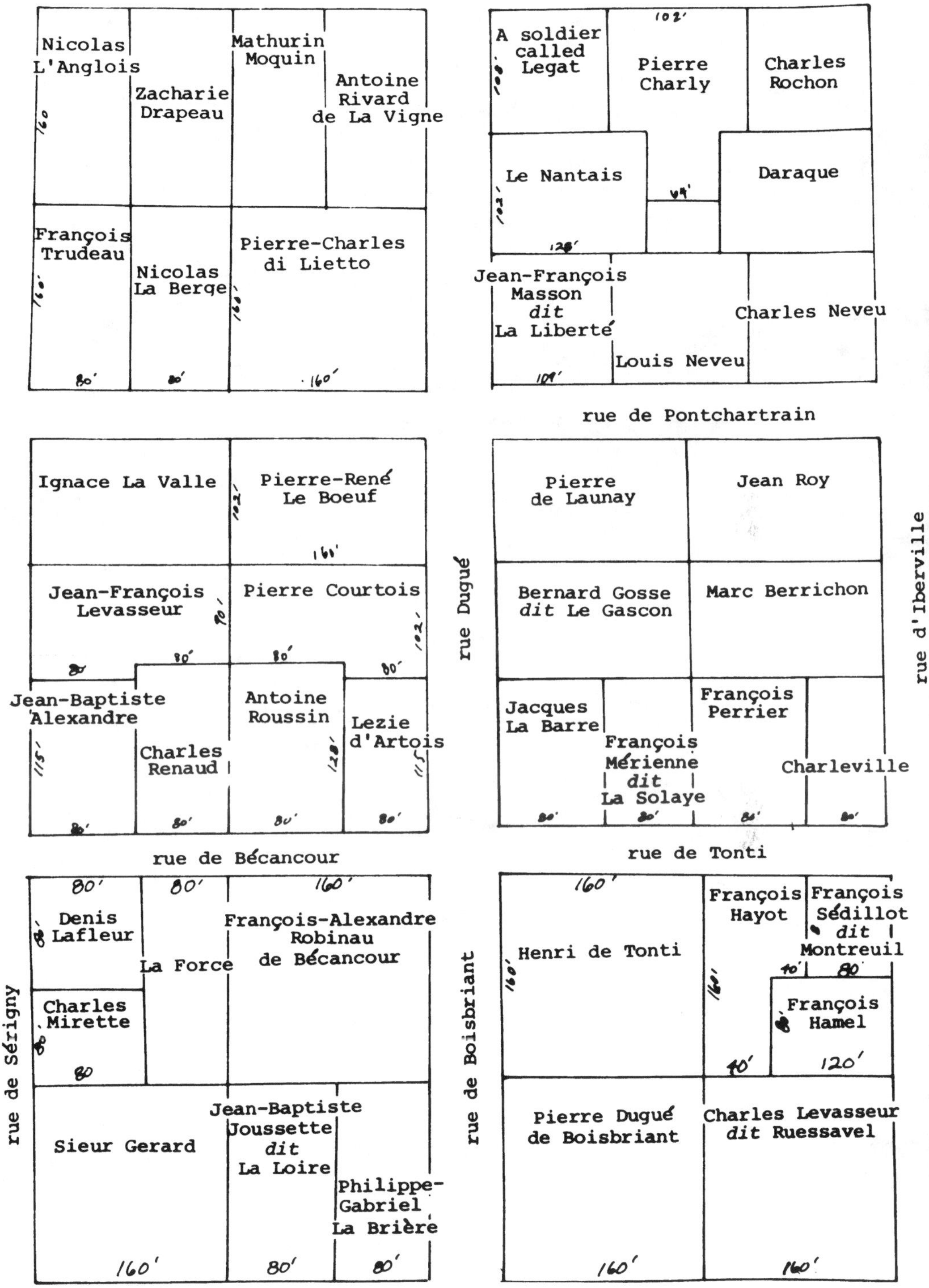

Mobile Public Library, Maps & Plans

Central section of town

By Jay Higginbotham

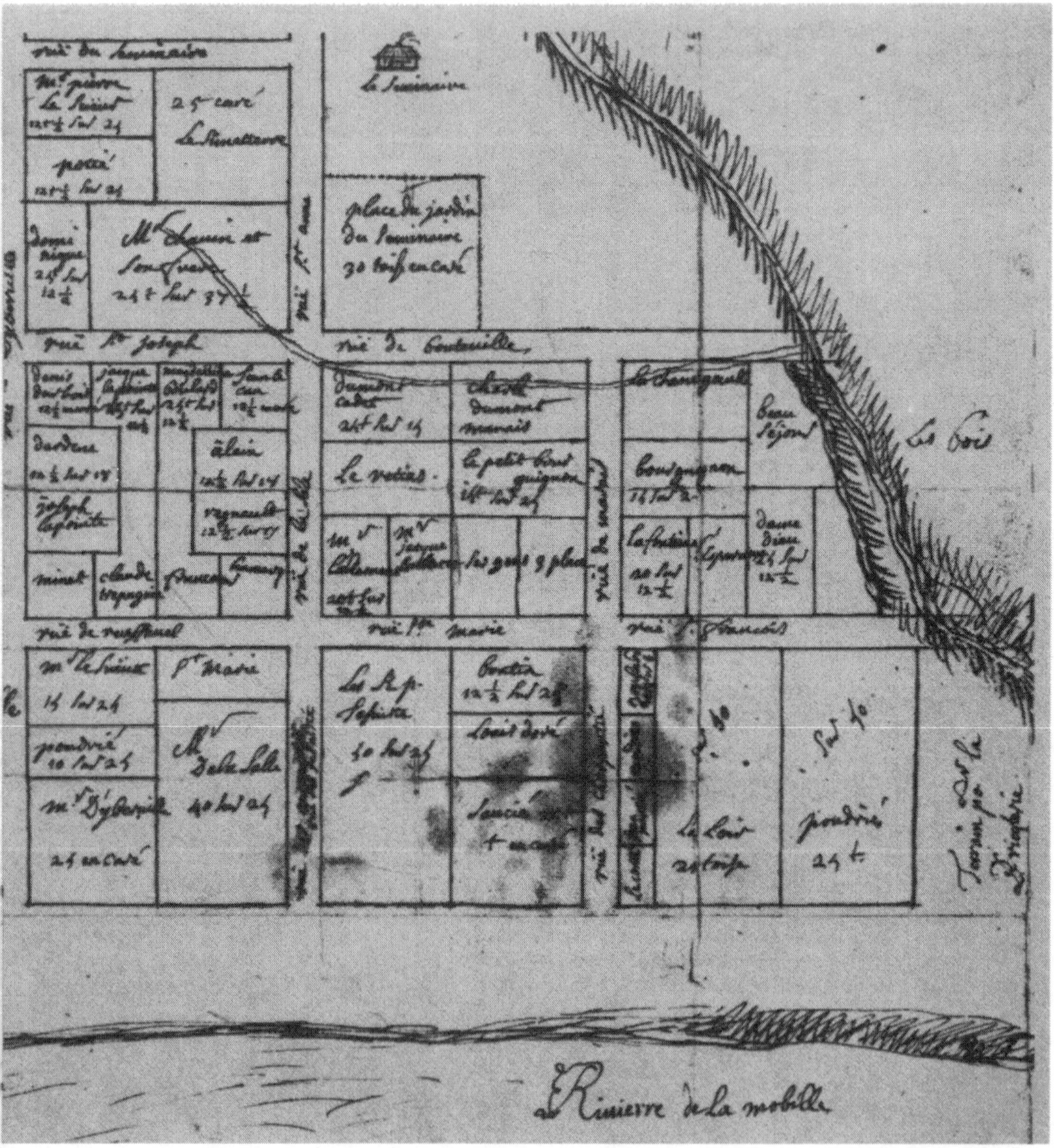

AN, DFC, 120B

Northwestern section of town

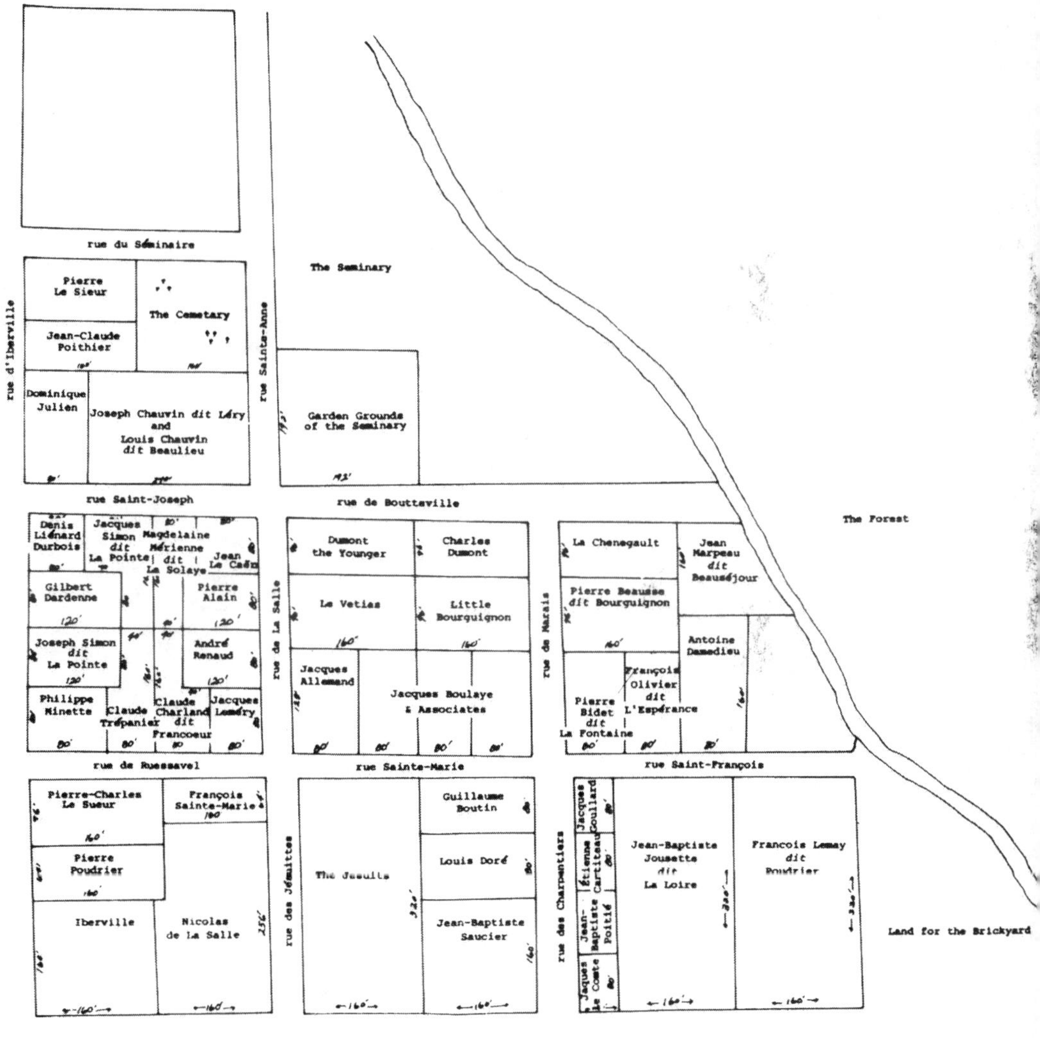

Mobile Public Library, Maps & Plan.

Northwestern section of town

By Jay Higginbothan

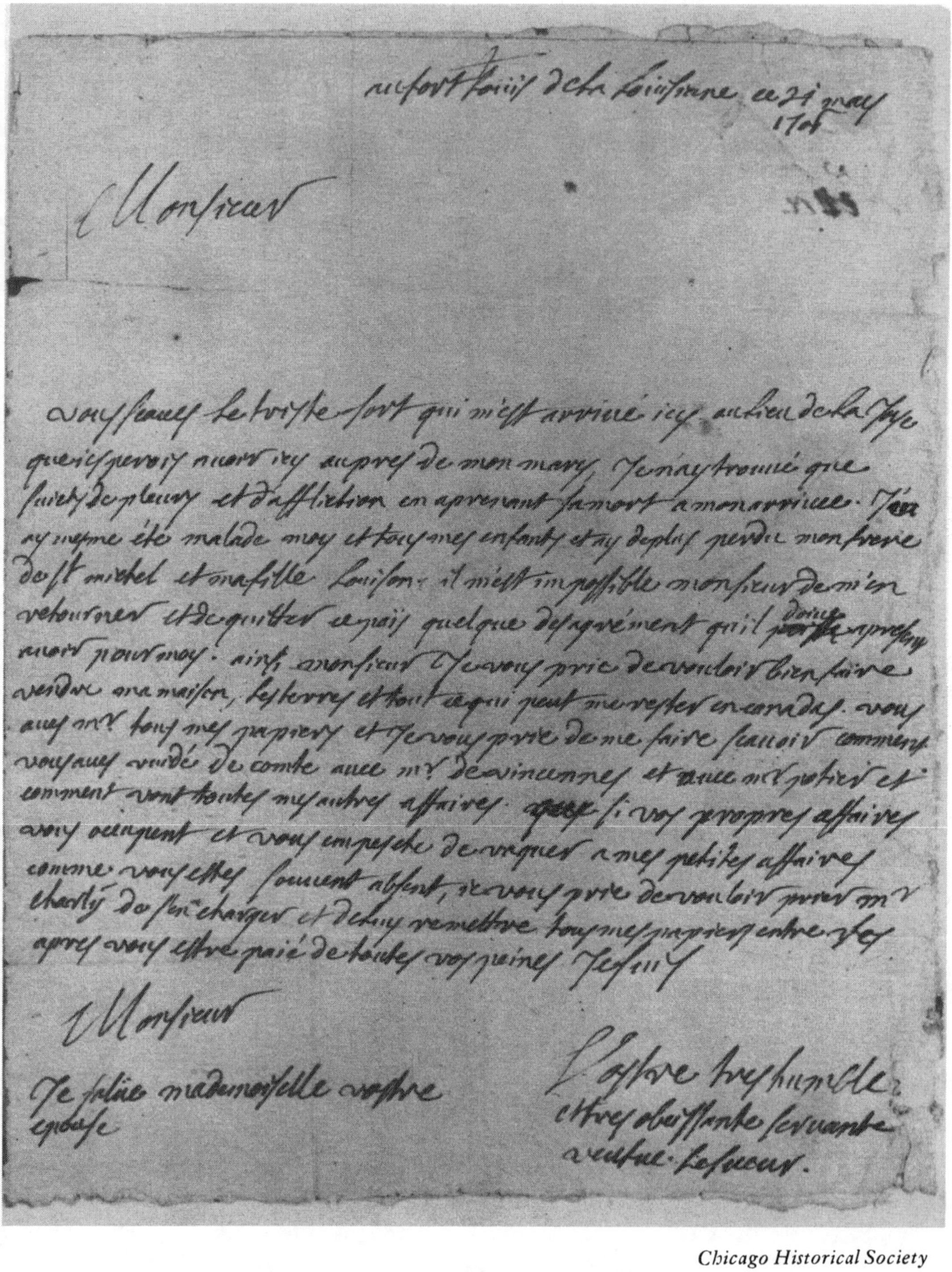
au fort Louis de la Louisiane ce 21 may 1706

Monsieur

vous scaués le triste sort qui m'est arrivé icy au lieu de la joye que je pensois avoir icy auprès de mon mary, je n'ay trouvé que sujets de pleurs et d'affliction en aprenant sa mort à mon arrivée. J'ay mesme été malade moy et tous mes enfants et y ay de plus perdu mon frere de st michel et ma fille Louison. il m'est impossible monsieur de m'en retourner et de quitter ce pais quelque desagrément qu'il doive apres sa mort pour moy. ainsi monsieur je vous prie de vouloir bien faire vendre ma maison, les terres et tout ce qui peut me rester en canada. vous avés mr tous mes papiers et je vous prie de me faire scavoir comment vous avés vuidé de comte avec mr de vincennes et avec mr potier et comment vont toutes mes autres affaires. si vos propres affaires vous occupent et vous empesche de vacquer à mes petites affaires comme vous estes souvent absent, je vous prie de vouloir prier mr charly de s'en charger et de luy remettre tous mes papiers entre ses mains apres vous estre paié de toutes vos peines. Je suis

Monsieur

Je salüe mademoiselle vostre epouse

Vostre tres humble et tres obeissante servante veuve Lesueur.

Chicago Historical Society

Letter of Marguerite Messier (widow Le Sueur) to Maurice Blondeau in Montreal. Written at Fort Louis on May 21, 1706.

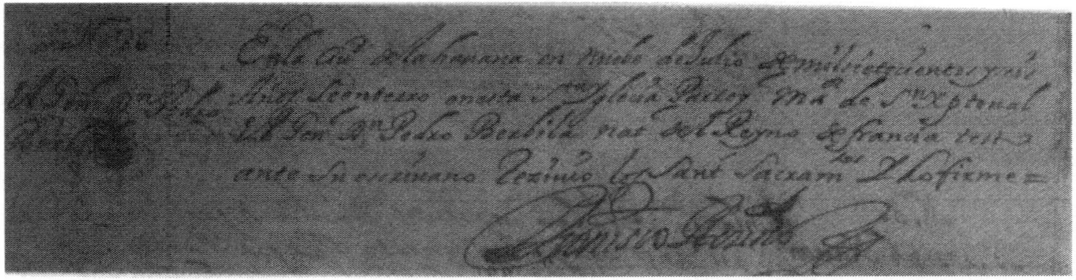

Iberville's burial record at Havana

Catedral de San Cristóbal de la Habana
Registro de las Sepulturas, IV, f. 78, No. 26

MM, 83320

Capture of the *Coventry* by Duguay-Trouin in 1704 Artist Unknown

MM, 7178

Bow of the vessel *Aigle*

MM, 415

Stern of the *Aigle*

MM, 416

Quarter gallery of the *Aigle*

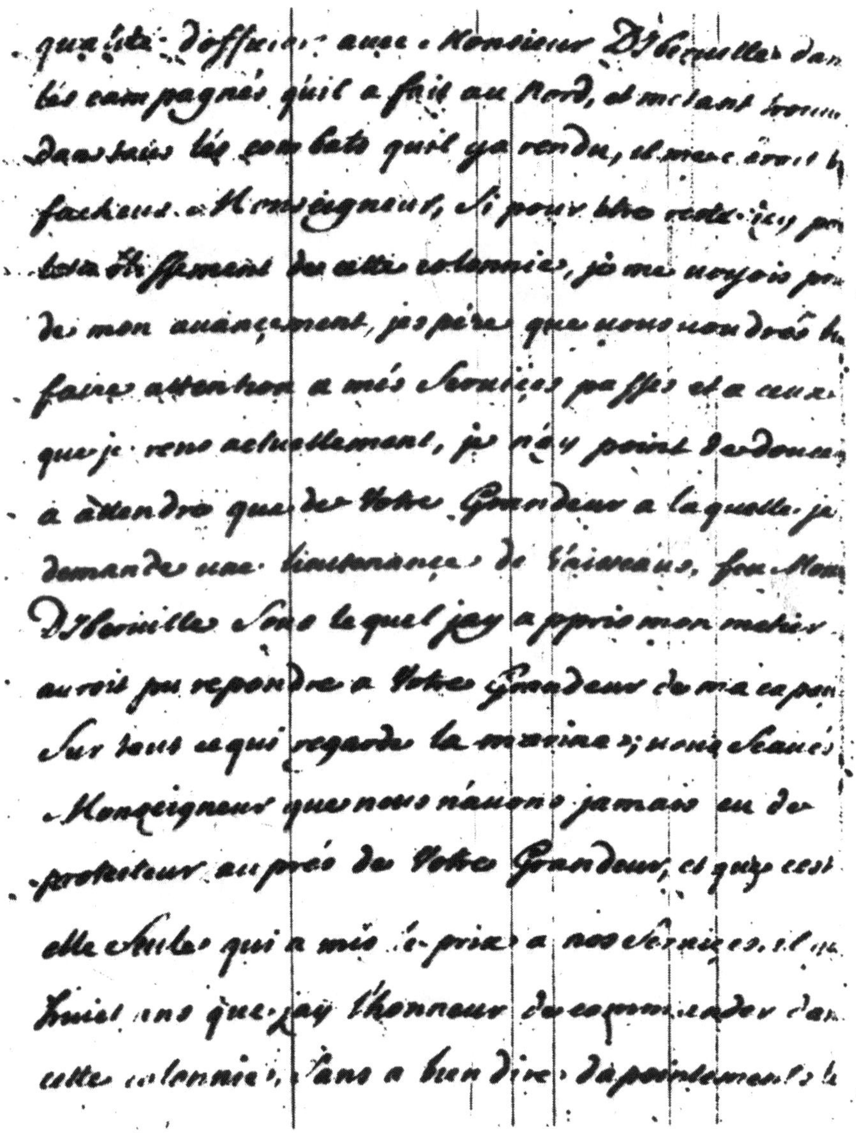

qualité d'officier avec Monsieur D'Iberville dans
les campagnes qu'il a fait au Nord, et m'estant trouvé
dans tous les combats qu'il y a rendu, il m'est arrivé [illegible]
facheux. Monseigneur, si pour vostre seule j'ay [illegible]
tout l'establissement de cette colonnie, je me voyois [illegible]
de mon avancement, j'espère que vous voudrés bien
faire attention a mes services passés et a ceux
que je rens actuellement, je n'ay point d'autre [illegible]
a attendre que de Votre Grandeur a laquelle je
demande une lieutenance de vaisseaux, feu Monsieur
D'Iberville sous lequel j'ay appris mon metier
auroit pu repondre a Votre Grandeur de ma capacité
sur tout ce qui regarde la marine; vous scavés
Monseigneur que nous n'avons jamais eu de
protecteur auprès de Votre Grandeur, et que c'est
elle seule qui a mis le prix a nos services. Il y a
huict ans que j'ay l'honneur de commander dans
cette colonnie, sans a bien dire d'apointements [illegible]

AC, C13A, 2, f. 30

Page of letter from Bienville to Pontchartrain, Feb. 20, 1707

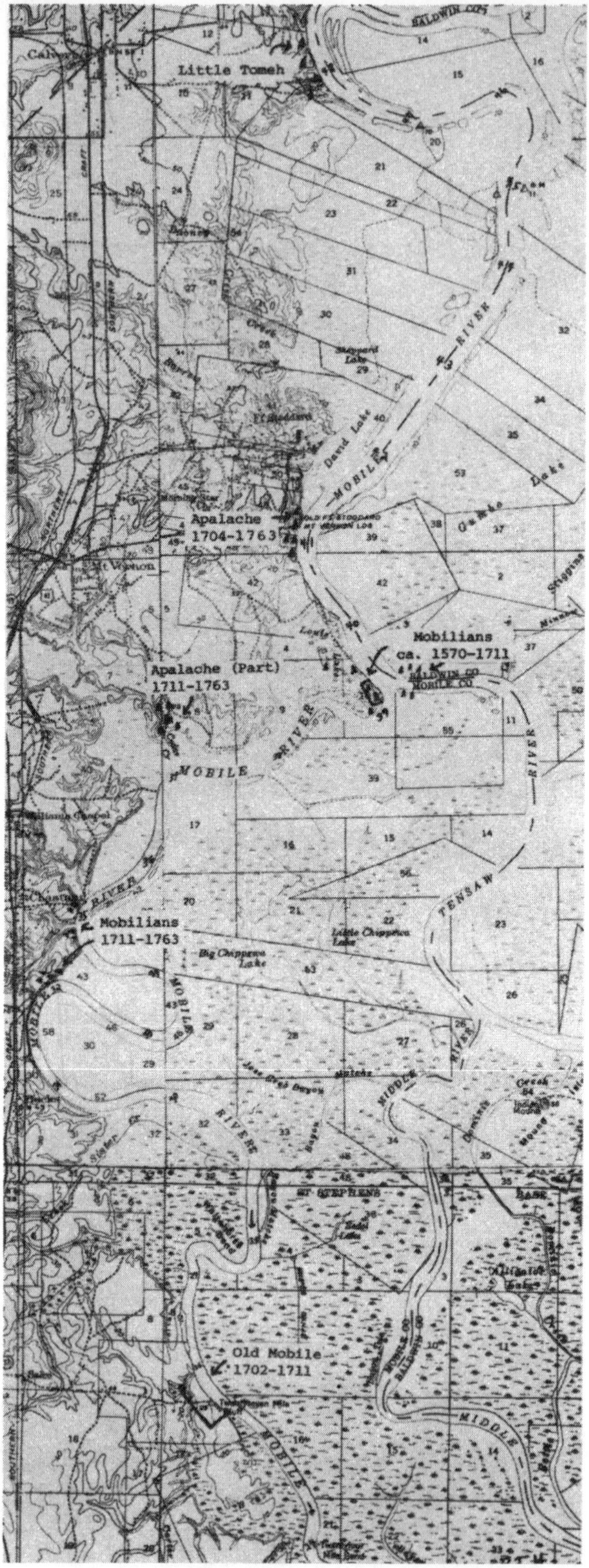

MPL, Maps and Plans

Mobile River Village sites

By Jay Higginbotham

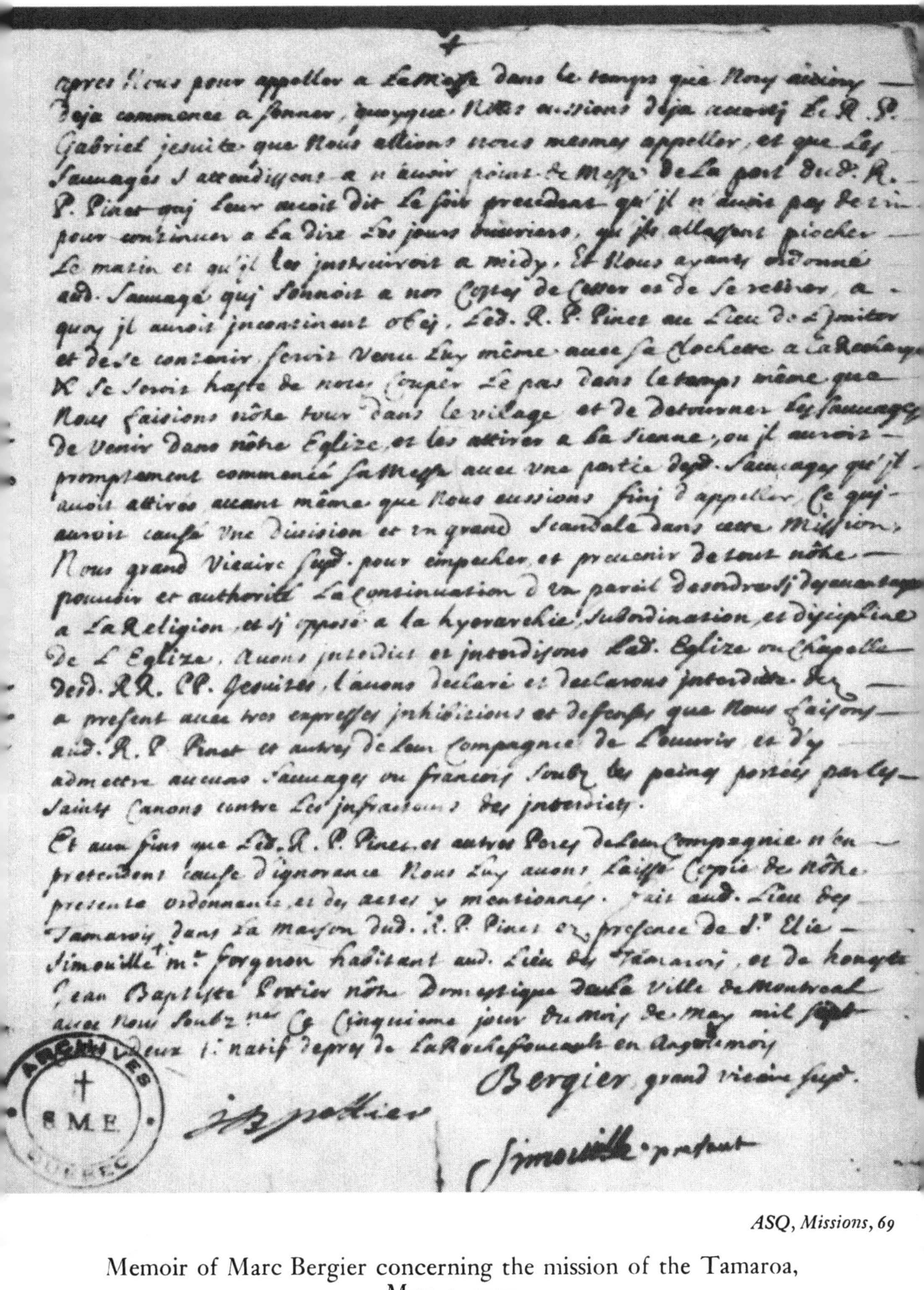

apres Nous pour appeller a la Messe dans le temps que Nous avions
deja commencé a sonner, quoyque Nous eussions deja averty le R. P.
Gabriel jesuite que Nous allions nous mesmes appeller, et que les
Sauvages s attendissent a n avoir point de Messe de la part dud. R.
P. Pinet qui leur avoit dit le soir precedent qu'il n'avoit pas de vin
pour continuer a la dire les jours ouvriers, qu ils allassent piocher
le matin et qu'il les instruiroit a midy, Et Nous ayant ordonné
aud. Sauvage qui sonnoit a nos Coptes de cesser et de se retirer, a
quoy il auroit incontinent obey, led. R. P. Pinet au lieu de l imiter
et de se contenir, seroit venu luy même avec sa clochette a la Rencontre
& se seroit hasté de nous couper le pas dans le temps même que
Nous faisions nôtre tour dans le village et de detourner les Sauvages
de venir dans nôtre Eglize et les attirer a la sienne, ou il auroit
promptement commencé sa Messe avec une partie desd. Sauvages qu'il
avoit attirés avant même que Nous eussions finy d'appeller, Ce qui
auroit causé une division et un grand scandale dans cette Mission,
Nous grand Vicaire susd. pour empecher et prevenir de tout nôtre
pouvoir et authorité la continuation d'un pareil desordre si desavantageux
a la Religion, et si opposé a la hyerarchie, subordination, et discipline
de l Eglize, Avons interdict et interdisons lad. Eglize ou Chapelle
desd. RR. PP. Jesuites, l'avons declaré et declarons interdite dès
a present avec tres expresses inhibitions et defenses que Nous faisons
aud. R. P. Pinet et autres de leur Compagnie de l'ouvrir, et d'y
admettre aucuns Sauvages ou françois soubz les peines portées par les
Saints Canons contre les infracteurs des interdicts.
Et aux fins que led. R. P. Pinet et autres Peres de leur Compagnie n'en
pretendent cause d'ignorance Nous luy avons laissé Copie de nôtre
presente ordonnance, et des actes y mentionnés. Fait aud. Lieu des
Tamarois, dans la maison dud. R. P. Pinet en presence de Sr Elie
Simouille† mtre forgeron habitant aud. Lieu des Tamarois, et de honête
Jean Baptiste Potier nôtre domestique de la ville de Montreal
avec Nous soubz nez Ce Cinquieme jour du mois de May mil sept
cens deux †. natif de pres de La Rochefoucault en Angoumois

Bergier, grand vicaire susd.

J B potier

Simouille present

ASQ, Missions, 69

Memoir of Marc Bergier concerning the mission of the Tamaroa,
May 5, 1702

BN, 62 B 29007

La Rochelle in the eighteenth century

Artist Unknown

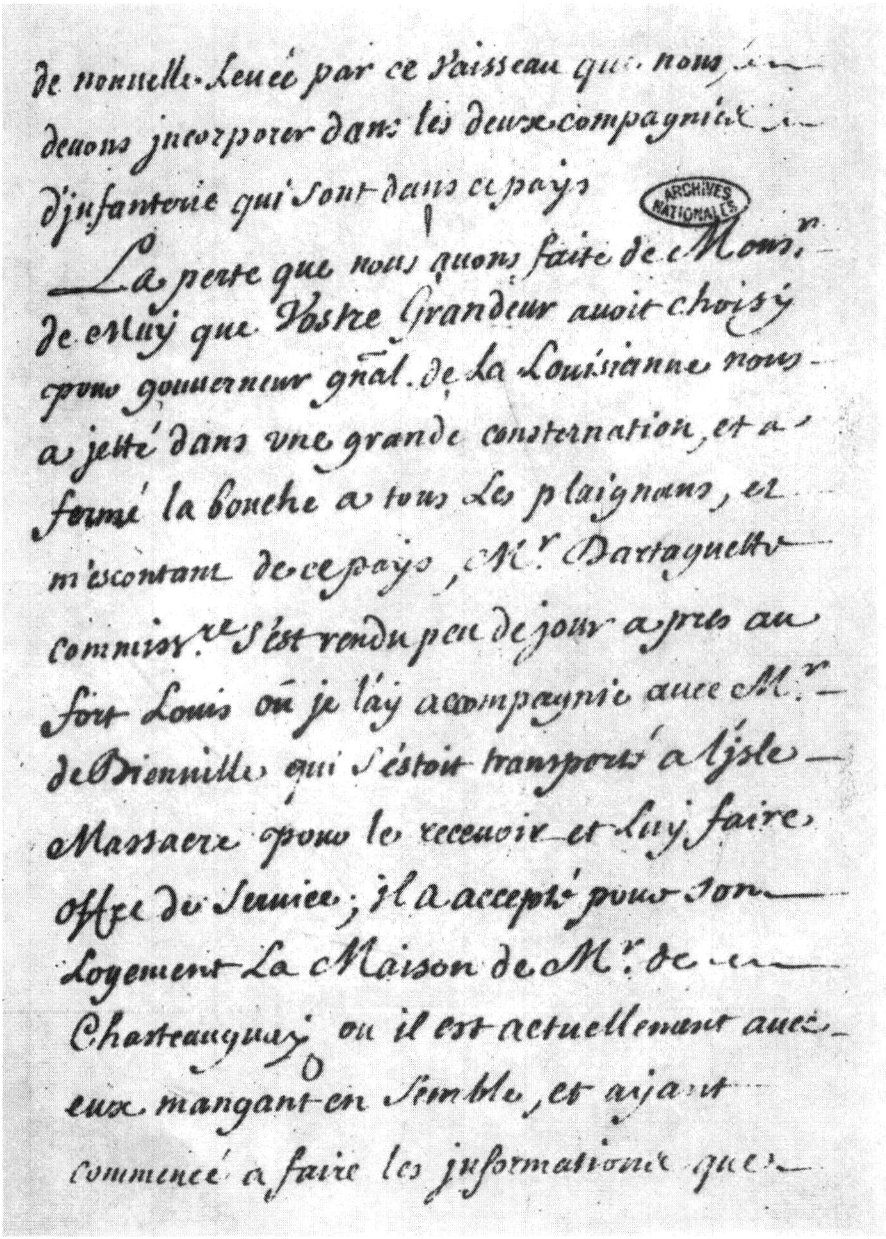

de nouuelle Leuée par ce Vaisseau que nous
deuons jncorporer dans les deux compagnies
d'jnfanterie qui sont dans ce pays
La perte que nous auons faite de Monsr.
de celuy que Vostre Grandeur auoit choisy
pour gouuerneur gnal. de la Louisianne nous
a jetté dans une grande consternation, et a
fermé la bouche a tous les plaignans, et
mescontans de ce pays, Mr. Dartaguette
commisre. s'est rendu peu de jour apres au
fort Louis où je l'ay accompagnie auec Mr.
de Bienuille qui s'estoit transporté a l'jsle
Massacre pour le receuoir et luy faire
offre de Seruice; il a accepté pour son
Logement La Maison de Mr. de
Chasteauguay ou il est actuellement auec
eux mangant en semble, et ayant
commencé a faire les jnformations que

AC, C13B, 1, No. 8

Page of letter from La Salle to Pontchartrain, March 4, 1708

Musée des Beaux-arts de Niort

Jean-Baptiste-Martin Dartaguiette d'Iron
1682–1746
by Alexis Grimou (1678–1740) in 1720

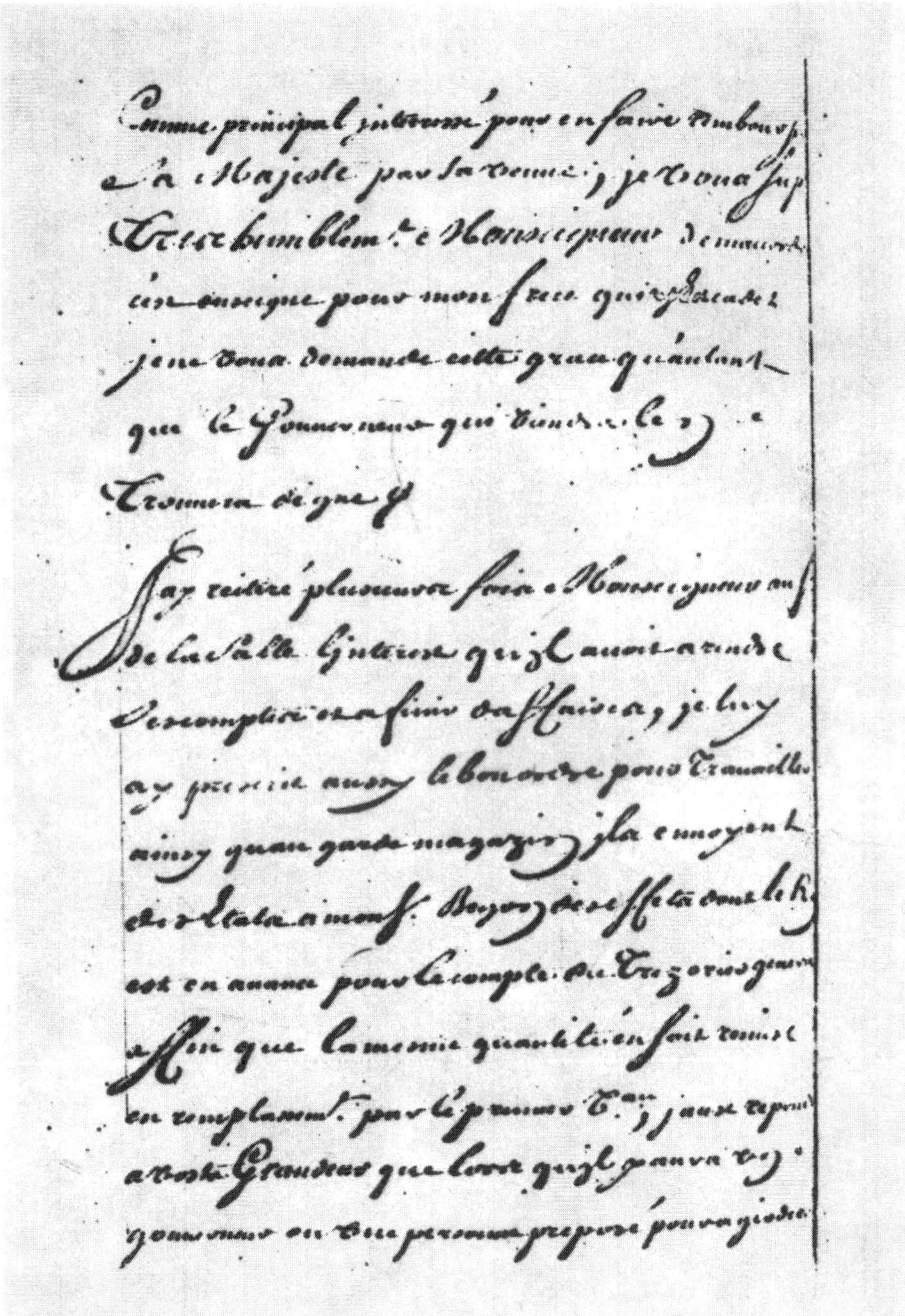

AC, C13A, 2, f. 346

Page of a letter from Dartaguiette to Ponchartrain, Oct. 1, 1708

U.S. Department of Agriculture
0197 175 108-R

Arial view (1975) of the site of Old Mobile

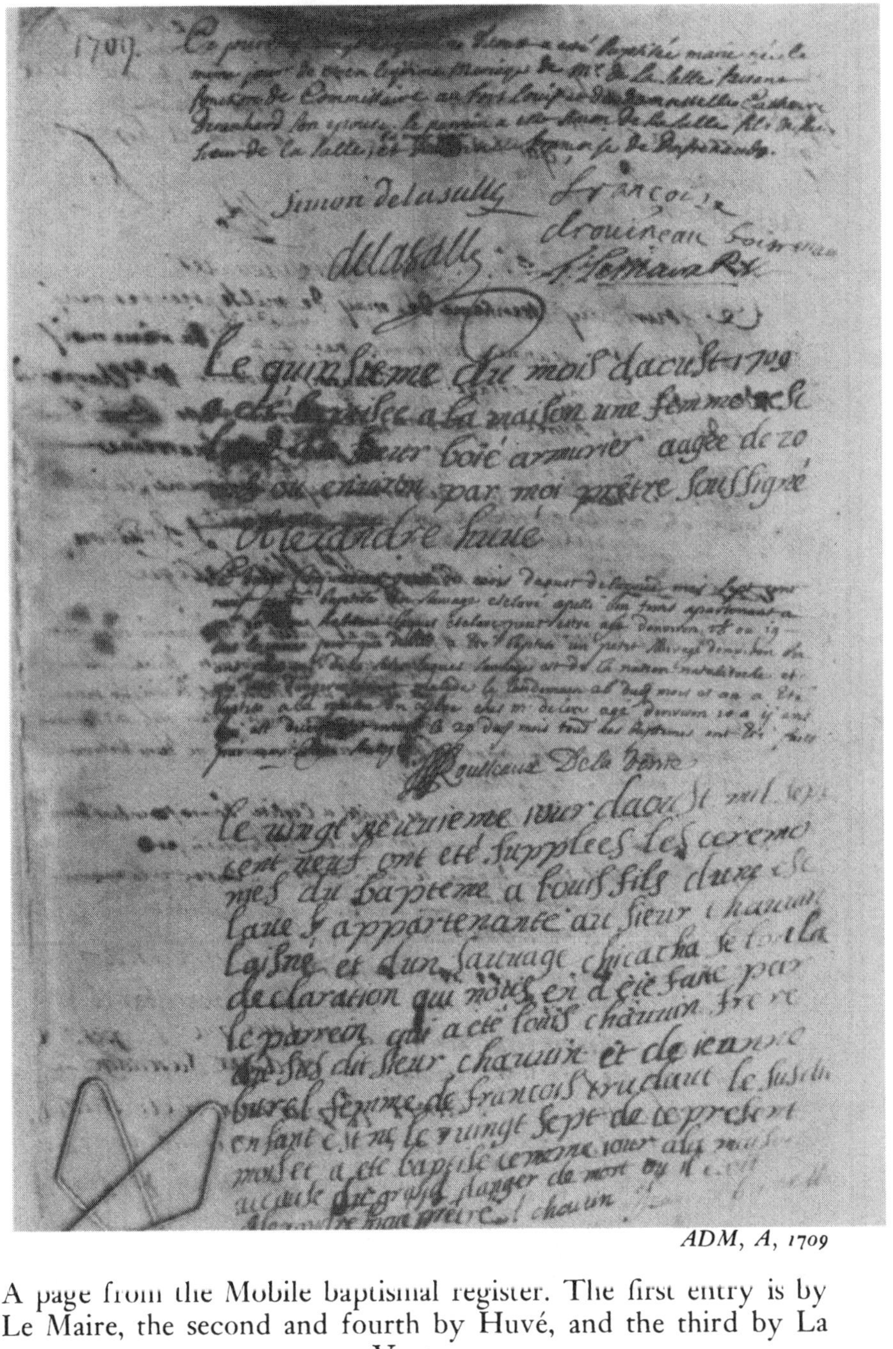

ADM, A, 1709

A page from the Mobile baptismal register. The first entry is by Le Maire, the second and fourth by Huvé, and the third by La Vente.

Castillo de Chapultepec

Juan Fernández de la Cueva y Henriquez, Duque de Alburquerque
Viceroy of New Spain
1702–1710

By Nicolás Rodriquez Xuarez

LSMA, DCS, July 23, 1725

Abstract of the marriage contract between Jean Le Caën and Marie-Madelaine Mérienne at Fort Louis, May 19, 1708.

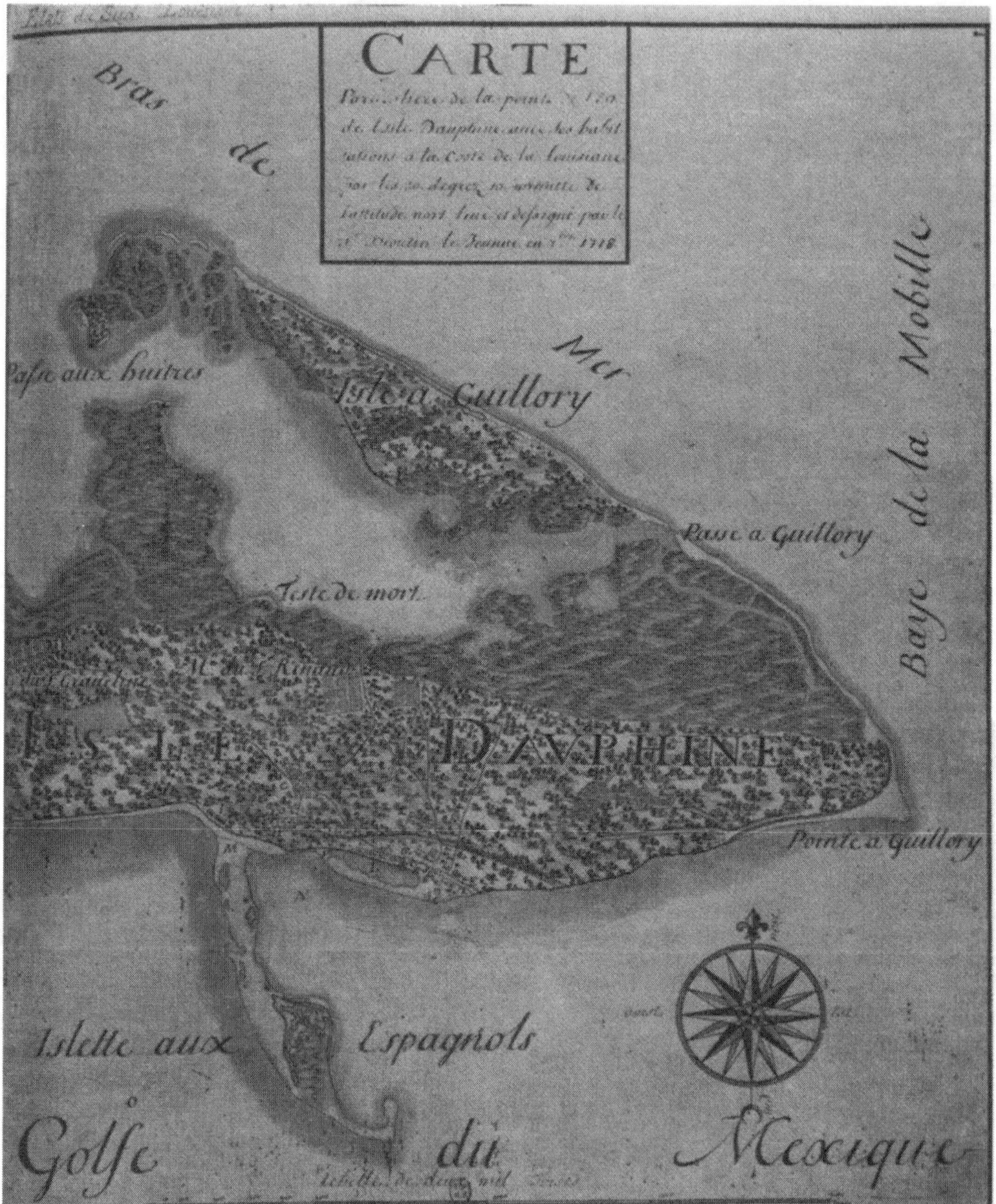

BN, Cartes et plans, C72487

The port and settlement at Massacre Island (Îsle Dauphine)

BN, 64 B 33902

Marie-Adélaïde de Savoye, Dauphine of France, after whom Dauphine Island was named.

Artist Unknown

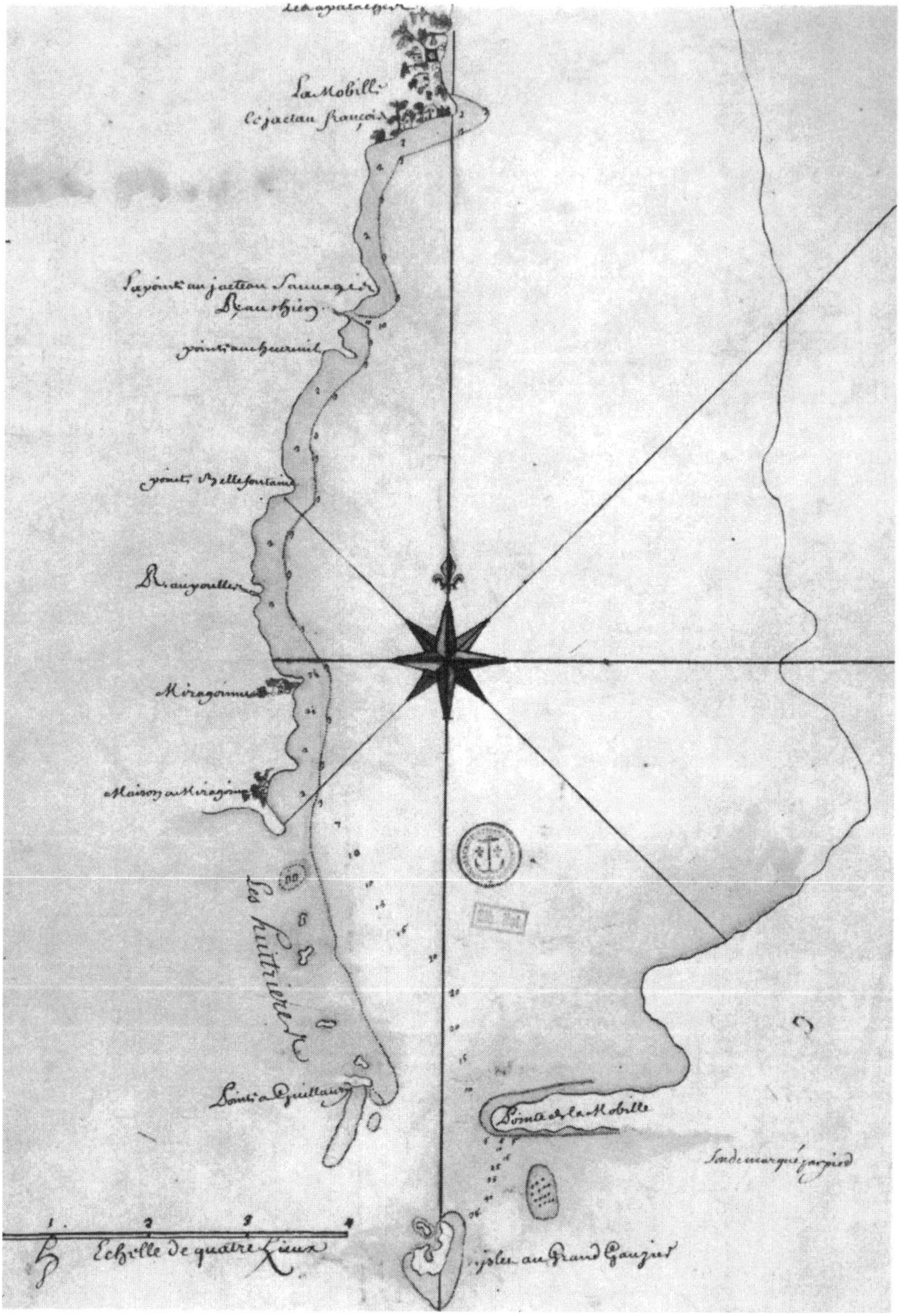

BN, Cartes et plans, D4387

Mobile Bay shortly after transferal to the *Oignonets*

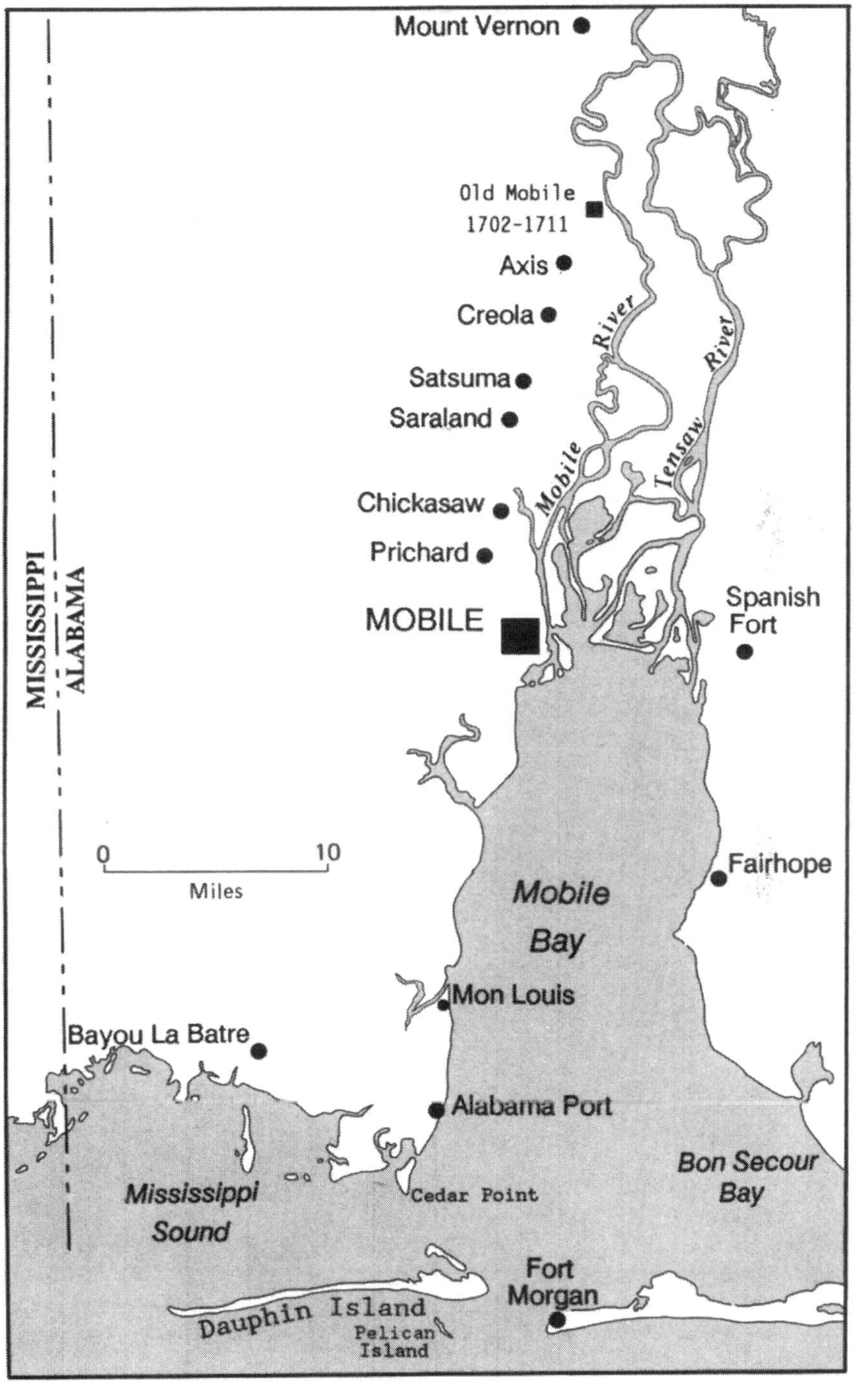

Mount Vernon
Old Mobile
1702-1711
Axis
Creola
Satsuma
Saraland
Chickasaw
Prichard
MOBILE
Mobile River
Tensaw River
Spanish Fort
MISSISSIPPI
ALABAMA
0
10
Miles
Fairhope
Mobile Bay
Mon Louis
Bayou La Batre
Alabama Port
Bon Secour Bay
Mississippi Sound
Cedar Point
Fort Morgan
Dauphin Island
Pelican Island

Appendixes

I. Érection de la cure de la Mobile, son union au Séminaire de Québec et nomination de M. Henri Roulleaux de la Vente, premier curé, 20 juillet, 1703.[1]

Joannes Baptista Dei gratia et autoritate Apostolica Episcopus Quebecensis Ad perpetuam rei memoriam.

Sollicitudinis Pastoralis ac Episcopalis est en locis ubi multus populus fidelis existit, Ecclesias aedificare, Parochias erigere, et ibi, ad exemplum apostolorum, operarios in vineam et in messem Domini mittere, Rectores ac Presbyteros constituere ad vineam et excolendam et messem colligendam; verbum Dei scilicet annuntiando, sacramenta Ecclesia administrando, officium Divinum peragendo, et caetera alia munera Divina et Ecclesiatica lege, juxta sacrosanctum Jesu Christi Evangelium, sanctos codices divinitus inspiratos, sacros canones spirita Dei conditos, ac totius Orbis reverentia consecratos, et secundum traditiones Patrum ad cultum divinum, regimen Ecclesiae, et salutem Animarum ordinata perficiendo. Quapropter certiores facti Majestatem suam Christianissimam novam Francorum coloniam in America septentrionali ad ripas fluminis, quod vocant La Mobile statuere, eandemque Regiam majestatem plures mittere familias Gallicas, quarum accessu isthaec colonia tale inerementum suscipiat, ut possit in unum locum collecta oppidum conflare, quod suum habiturum sit gubernatorem, suos peculiares Magistratus, et similia quae ad cultum ordinem politicum requiruntur; necessarium duximus super plebem istam

1. Archives de Saint-Sulpice, R. 25, Vol. I, No. 21.

Pastorem praeficere, a quo sacramentorum subsidio adjuvetur, verbo simul et exemplo paseatur, atque ad cultum divinum informetur. Itaque post seriam maturamque deliberationem, invocato nomine Domini, Decrevimus (Suae Majestatis animum et intentionem plenissime secuturi) in hoc loco Parochiam erigere, speramus que fore ut Regia pietate, ac illorum zelo qui inibi ipsius autoritate praesunt, Ecclesia extra Arcem Regiam aedificetur loco capellae, quam extrui jam suis impensis curaverant Directores Seminarii Quebecensis Missionum ad exteros ad quam Capellam et Ecclesiam incolae confluent orationis causa, quamque in Ecclesiam Parochialem a nostra jurisdictione Decessorumque nostrorum Episcoporum Quebecensium pendentem ereximus et erigimus. Cum autem attente consideraremus quemnam potissimum huie capellae et Ecclesiae praeficeremus, in Seminarium praedictum oculos conjecimus, ex quo quadraginta abhinc annis tot ac tam eximii prodierunt Operarii in nostra Dioecesi indefesso labori incumbentes, et a quo jam jam ab initio novae hujus coloniae missi sunt Operarii Evangelia ad barbaros terra indigenas fide Catholiqua imbuendos. Itaque Superioribus utriusque Seminarii Parisiensis et Quebecensis, aut eorum alteri his praesentibus Literis jus et facultatem perpetuam concessimus et concedimus nominandi et praesentandi nobis nostrisque successoribus Presbyterum capacem et idoneum qui nostra aliorumque deinceps Episcoporum Quebecensium autoritate, Ecclesiae hujusmodi Parochiali praeficiatur ut Pastor, illamque administret. In cujus concessionis virtute nominatam nobis et praesentatum Magistrum Henricum Roulleaux de la Vente Dioecesis Bajocensis Sacerdotem jam diu in obeundis tam intra Galliam quam apud Indos Missionibus cum laude versatum, primum Ecclesiae Parochialis in loco dicto La Mobile (extra Regiam Arcem) Pastorem instituimus qui omnibus Parochi muniis apud Christianam hanc plebem fungi possit et valeat, Sperantes Christianissimum Regem Ludovicum Magnum semper Pium semperque Beneficus in hujus coloniae primordio pro sua pietate et beneficentia plane Regali suppeditaturum non solum ea qua ad honestam Parochi sustentationem necessaria fuerint, verum etiam sacra tum vasa tum orramenta aliaque omnia quae ad cultum Deo digne exibendum conducere videbuntur. Mandamus porro et injungimus quibuscumque sacerdotibus et Clericis tam sacularibus quam regularibus cujuslibet ordinis et societatis extiterint ut dictum Magistrum Rolleaux de la Vente institatum a nobis primum Ecclesiae Parochialis loci dicti La Mobile Pastorem et Parochum legitimum agnoscant et colant; a quo scilicet omnes hujus loci Incolae Sacramenta suscipiant et sancta documenta quibus pro data ipsi sapientia instruantur ad salutem. Ei autem tanquam Pastori legitimo potestatem damus percipiendi decimas et oblationes, fruendique omnibus juribus curialibus qua ubique gentium ad Parochos spectant: plurimum in Domino confidentes fore, ut quam hactenus apud novam istam Coloniam navare semper studeat, eique verbo et exemplo prodesse satagat. Datum Parisiis, ubi Diaecesis nostra negotiis detinemur, Anno salutis millesimo septingentesimo tertio, die vigesima Julii. Ita subscriptum: Joannes Episcopus Quebecensis et sigillo munitum. De Mandato Illustrissimi ac Reverendissimi DD Episcopi Quebecensis, ita subscriptum Despies.

II. Induction of Roulleaux de La Vente as Pastor of the Parish of Mobile, September 28, 1704.[1]

Jay sousigné prestre et miss. apost. ateste a tous quil appartiendra que lannee du salut mil sept cents quatre le vint huit[e] du mois de 7bre en vertu des lettres de provision et de collation accordee et Scollee de Le vingt[e] de Juillet de lannee derniere, par lesquelles Monseigneur Illustrissime et Reverendissime Eveque De Quebec Erige une Eglise paroissiale dans le lieu dit le fort louis de la louisiane et dont Il donne la Cure et le Soin a m. henri Roulleaux De la Vente miss. apost. Du Diocese de Bayeux, Jay mis led pretre en possession actuelle et corporelle de lad Eglise paroissiale et de tous les droits qui lui apartiennent, apres avoir observé les Ceremonies acoutumees et requises, Scavoir par lentree de Leglise, laspersion de leau benite, le baiser du grand autel, le touché du missel, la visite du tres Sainct Sacrement de lautel et le Son des cloches a laquelle possession Jateste que personne ne sest opposé donné en leglise du fort louis le jour du mois et de lan sud en presence de Jean baptiste de bieville lieutenant du Roy et commandant aud fort, pierre Du Que de boisbriant major, Nicolas de la Sale Ecrivain et faisant faisant fonction de Commissaire de la marine.

davion   Bienville   Boisbriant   delasalle

1. ADM, Miscellaneous French Papers, 1704.

III. Slaveowners, 1702–1711 *

Slaveowner	Indian (Male)	Indian (Female)	Black (Male)	Black (Female)	Total
Charles Aigron, *dit* Lamothe	0	1	0	0	1
Vincent Alexandre, *dit* Chenet	1	0	0	0	1
Jean Arnaud	2	1	0	0	3
Pierre Babin, *dit* La Source	1	1	0	0	2
Jacques Barbazant de Pailloux	2	1	1	0	4
Valentin Barraud	1	0	0	0	1
Jean-Baptiste Baudreau de Graveline	2	1	1	0	4
Philippe Blondel	0	1	0	0	1
Nicolas Bodin	2	1	0	0	3
Françoise de Boisrenaud de Roisneau	0	6	0	0	6
Guillaume Boutin	1	0	0	0	1
René Boyer	0	2	0	0	2
Jean Brunet, *dit* Bourbonnois	0	1	0	0	1
Étienne Burelle	1	1	0	0	2
Charles Bussart, *dit* Saint-Jean	0	1	0	0	1
André Carrière	1	1	0	0	2
Claude Charland, *dit* Francoeur	0	1	0	0	1
Pierre Charly	0	2	0	0	2
Jacques Châtillon, *dit* Châtillon	0	1	0	0	1
Jacques Chauvin, *dit* Mondon	1	2	0	0	3
Joseph Chauvin, *dit* Léry	2	3	0	0	5
Louis Chauvin, *dit* Beaulieu	0	1	0	0	1

* Includes native *domestiques*

Slaveowner	Indian (Male)	Indian (Female)	Black (Male)	Black (Female)	Total
Nicolas Chauvin, *dit* La Fresnière	1	1	0	0	2
Jean Colon, *dit* La Violette	1	0	0	0	1
Michel Danti, *dit* L'Auvergne	2	1	0	0	3
Bernard Dartaguiette d'Iron	1	0	0	0	1
Jean-Baptiste-Martin Dartaguiette d'Iron	12	7	0	0	19
Pierre Dartaguiette d'Iron	1	0	0	0	1
Pierre Dugué de Boisbriant	3	1	1	0	5
Charles-François Dumont	0	2	0	0	2
Jacques Gravier	2	0	0	0	2
Marie Grissot (See *Soeurs*)					
François Guyon Des Prés Derbanne	0	1	0	0	1
François Hayot	1	1	0	0	2
Jean-Baptiste Joussette, *dit* La Loire	2	1	1	0	4
Louis Juchereau de Saint-Denis	3	1	0	0	4
Jean La Barre	0	3	0	0	3
Nicolas L'Anglois	0	1	0	0	1
Nicolas de La Salle	1	1	0	0	2
Pierre René Leboeuf	2	1	0	0	3
Jean Le Caën	1	1	0	0	2
François-Xavier Lemay, *dit* Poudrier	1	2	0	0	3
Antoine Le Moyne de Châteaugué	2	1	1	0	4
Jean-Baptiste Le Moyne de Bienville	14	3	3	1	21

Slaveowner	Indian (Male)	Indian (Female)	Black (Male)	Black (Female)	Total
Marie Le Sueur	1	2	0	0	3
Charles Levasseur, *dit* Ruessavel	2	1	0	0	3
Marie Linant (See *Soeurs*)					
Jean Marest Dupuy	1	0	0	0	1
Marguerite Messier (*Veuve* Le Sueur)	1	1	0	1	3
Philippe Minette	1	1	0	0	2
Missionnaires (La Vente, Huvé, Davion, Le Maire)	7	0	0	0	7
Claude Parent	1	1	0	0	2
André-Joseph Pénigault	0	1	0	0	1
François Philippe de Hautmesnil de Mandeville	0	1	0	0	1
Christophe Poirier	2	1	0	0	3
Antoine Rivard de La Vigne	4	0	0	0	4
Charles Rochon	1	1	0	0	2
Jean-Baptiste Roy	0	1	0	0	1
Jean-Baptiste Saucier	3	2	0	0	5
Joseph Simon, *dit* La Pointe	2	1	0	0	3
Antoine Siré	0	1	0	0	1
Soeurs (Marie Linant & Marie Grissot)	3	1	0	0	4
Henri de Tonti	2	1	0	0	3
Claude Trépanier	2	1	0	0	3
François Trudeau	3	4	0	0	7
Vitrac de La Tour	0	0	0	1	1
Grand Totals	103	80	8	3	194

IV. Population Figures, 1702–1711 [1]

	Officers and Officials	Religious	Craftsmen	Canadians and *Voyageurs*	Soldiers and Sailors	Women	Children (12 and Under)	Slaves and *Domestiques*	Totals
1702	18	5	19	73	47	4	8	5	179
1703	11	4	21	67	43	8	8	7	169
1704	14	4	18	59	79	33	11	13	231
1705	13	3	16	61	72	29	27	11	232
1706	16	4	16	68	81	30	35	26	276
1707	13	3	14	62	76	28	39	64	299
1708	17	5	13	64	97	28	28	87	339
1709	14	3	10	53	94	28	36	93	331
1710	13	4	8	65	91	31	43	98	353
1711	19	3	9	59	106	30	46	76	348

1. The above figures, based on the records cited in the bibliography, are yearly totals. They include all individuals of French descent who were actually at the site of Old Mobile (even for a few days) during a given year, as well as Indian and Black servants and slaves who were more or less permanent residents. They do not include persons at Massacre Island or any of the surrounding settlements. The account registers in AC, FIA add considerable detail, but taken by themselves give only an incomplete picture, even for the years 1702–1706. During the years cited, over 700 individuals of French descent were at one time or another present at the town site and the names of 623 are presently known.

V. Baptisms, 1702–1711[1]

	French	Indian	Black	Mulatto	Total
1702	0	2	0	0	2
1703	1	3	0	0	4
1704	4	7	0	0	11
1705	17	6	0	0	23
1706	11	9	1	0	21
1707	7	17	3	0	27
1708	10	13	0	2	25
1709	11	21	0	0	32
1710	7	42	0	1	50
1711	4	13	1	0	18
Totals	72	133	5	3	213

1. Based largely on ADM registers. Includes settlements at Massacre Island, the *Oignonets* and along the river and bay.

VI. Baptisms by individual religious, 1704–1711[1] (Includes French, Indian and Black)

Albert Davion	3
Alexandre Huvé	56
François Le Maire	53
Henri Roulleaux de La Vente	46
Total	158

1. Based almost exclusively on ADM registers. Actual figures, if known, would be considerably higher.

VII. 1710 Cession to Nicolas Bodin [1]

We, king's lieutenant and commandant of Fort Louis de la Louisiane, and Dartaguiette, king's counsellor and *commissaire ordinaire de la marine*, sent by the direction of the court into this colony, have agreed, for the support of His Majesty's interest in the advancement of this colony, to issue *contrats des cessions* to several inhabitants, namely to M. Nicolas Baudin the area of Grosse Pointe, to commence at and continue along the course of the rivière des poules until it reaches the Passe-aux-huîtres which separates Isle Massacre from the mainland, in order to raise cattle thereon. In regard to the above-mentioned land, we have issued, in the name of His Majestry, the entire cession and transfer, including all circumstances and dependencies, in order that he, his children, heirs or assigns, may enjoy and use it henceforth and forever, without fear of being vexed or disturbed in the peaceful possession thereof, never claiming nonetheless to prohibit any rights and claims which His Majesty might have for the good of His service.

Fort Louis de la Louisiane
November 12, 1710 Dartaguiette Bienville

I, governor of the province of Louisiana approve and ratify the above-mentioned grant.

Fort St. Louis [sic]
September 15, 1713 Lamothe Cadillac

VIII. Notes on the Portraits

Of the six portraits included in the illustrations of persons present at Old Mobile, only one (that of Dartaguiette) presently has sufficient documentation to establish it as having been painted from life. This portrait (13 x 18, oil on canvas), was painted and signed by Jacques Grimou (1678–1740) in Paris in 1720. Entitled "Portrait du Marquis D'Artaguiette," it hangs in the Musée des Beaux-

1. LSMA, DCS, July 16, 1761.

Arts de Niort and is listed in the Bénézit index, Vol. IV, p. 434.

The portraits of Iberville, Sérigny and Bienville were in the possession of French archivist Pierre Margry during the last part of the 19th Century. After Margry's death in 1894, the portraits were acquired by Charles Chadenat of Paris, and sometime after 1904 were re-acquired by the Parisian family Le Moyne de Martigny, the original owners. While they are handsome portraits, it seems unlikely that any of the three were painted from life (with the possible exception of the one of Bienville).

The portrait of Châteaugué presents a puzzle. Entitled "Chateaugay" and signed "J Jouvenet", the work's signature appears to be genuine. However, Châteaugué left La Rochelle in 1704 and apparently did not return to France until the John Law era. Jouvenet lost the use of his right hand in 1713 and died on April 5, 1717 at which time Châteaugué, at thirty-three years of age, was still in Louisiana. If the signature of Jouvenet were falsely added at some later date, this could still be a genuine life portrait of Châteaugué (by an unknown artist); or it may possibly be a portrait by Jouvenet of another Châteaugué entirely unrelated to the Le Moynes. But it is almost certainly not Antoine Le Moyne de Châteaugué by Jean-Baptiste Jouvenet.

The portrait of Henri de Tonti (attributed to Nicholas Maes) is to my mind purely fanciful. The painting, obviously an attempt at realism, shows the iron hook on the wrong hand. In addition, there are other discrepancies too complex for discussion here, such as the painting's suspect background, the inclusion of the never-earned decoration, etc. As to the supposed Maes connection, Tonti left France with La Salle at the approximate age of 27 and never returned to Europe, and there is no evidence to show that Nicholas Maes ever left Holland. Nonetheless, the Tonti portrait, by standards of workmanship, is probably the finest of the six paintings.

The observations made here are casual; they do not result from any detailed research of the origins of the paintings. Such an investigation would be interesting but has never to my knowledge been undertaken.

Bibliography

I. Archival Sources

A. CANADA

Montreal

Archives Judiciaires de Montréal (presently housed at the Archives nationales du Québec à Montréal)
Guides:
Auger, Roland-J., "Le riche dépôt généalogique aux archives judiciaires de Montréal," *Mémoires de la Société Généalogique Canadienne-Française*, VII, pp. 13–18.
État Sommaire des Archives Nationales du Québec à Montréal (Montreal, 1972).
Notaires: Antoine Adhémar, Vols. I–LXI.
Bénigne Basset Des Lauriers, Vols. IV–XXXV.
Jacques Bourdon, Vol. I.
Hilaire Bourgine, Vol. I.
Pierre Cabazié, Vols. I–II.
Michel Lepailleur de Laferté, Vols. I–VII.
Claude Maugue, Vols. I–XII.
Pierre Raimbault, Vols. I–IX.
Jean de St.-Père, Vol. I.
Index des sépultures catholiques, 1643–1721
Registres des audiences, Vols. III–IX.
Registres d'état civil:
Boucherville-Chambly, Vols. I–III.
Contrecoeur, Vol. I.
Laprairie, Vols. I–IV.
Notre-Dame de Montréal, Vols. I–VII.

Sainte-Agnes, Vols. I–II.
St.-Antoine de Longueuil, Vol. I.
Sainte-Famille, Vol. I.

Archives Paroissiales de Notre-Dame de Montréal
Guide:
Maurault, Oliver, *Premier Registre de l'Église Notre-Dame de Montréal* (Montreal, 1961).
Registres des baptêmes, mariages et sépultures
Notre-Dame de Montréal (1642–1708).
Lachine (1676–1691).
Pointe-aux-Trembles (1674–1696).

Quebec

Archives de l'Archevêché de Québec
Guides:
Rapport de l'Archiviste de la Province de Québec, 1939–40, pp. 157–353; *1940–41*, pp. 333–473; *1941–42*, pp. 179–298.
Caron, Ivanhoë, "Les Archives de l'Archevêché de Québec," *Rapport de la Société canadienne d'histoire de l'Église catholique* (*1934–35*), pp. 65–73.
Évêques de Québec, Carton I.
Gouvernement, Carton III (arrêts, proclamations, ordonnances).
Notre-Dame de Québec (parish), Carton I.
Registres d'insinuation, Registres A (1659–1705), B (1675–1782).

Archives du Québec
Guides:
État général des archives publiques et privées du Québec (Quebec, 1968).
Roy, P.-G., *Inventaire des concessions en fief et seigneurie, fois et hommages, aveux et dénombrements conservés aux Archives de la Province de Québec*, 6 Vols. (Beauceville, 1927–39).
Collection de pièces judiciaires et notariales, Vols. XIII–LXXI.
Dossiers du Conseil supérieur, Vols. I–IV.
Insinuations du Conseil supérieur, Vols. I–IV.
Ordonnances des intendants, Vols. III–XVII.
Procès-verbaux des grands voyers, Vols. II–V.

Archives du Séminaire de Québec
Guides:
Baillargeon, Noël, "The Seminary of Quebec: Resources for the History of the French in the Mississippi Valley." In McDermott, J. F., ed., *The French in the Mississippi Valley* (Urbana, 1965).
Maheux, Arthur, "Les archives du séminaire de Québec," *Le*

Canada Français, XXVII, pp. 503–08.
Chapitre: I, Nos. 16–79.
Documents Faribault: I, Nos. 9–43, 57, 112.
Évêques: I, Nos. 158–71.
Lettres: Séries M, Nos. 28–49; N, 110–32; O, 26–58; P, 6–57; R, 26–86; S, 79–131.
Missions: I, II, Nos. 41–77.
Paroisse de Québec: I, Nos. 7–43.
Paroisses diverses: I, Nos. 3–14.
Polygraphie: III–IV, VI–XIII, XXIII–XXVI.
Séminaire: I–III, XXXV, LXIX.
Verreau: XIII.
Manuscrit 429: Recensements de la Nouvelle-France (1666, 1667, 1681).

Archives Judiciaires de Québec (presently housed at the Archives du Québec)
Guides:
Roy, Antoine and Pierre-Georges Roy, eds., *Inventaire des greffes des Notaires du régime Français*, Vols. I–XXI (Quebec, 1943–64).
Roy, P.-G., *Inventaire d'une collection de pièces judiciaires, notariales, etc., conservées aux Archives Judiciaires de Québec*, 2 Vols. (Beauceville, 1917).
Notaires: Claude Auber, Vol. I.
Guillaume Audouart, Vol. I.
Romain Becquet, Vols. I–IV.
Louis Chambalon, Vols. I–II.
Pierre Duquet de la Chesnaye, Vol. I.
François Genaple, Vols. I–II.
Gilles Rageot, Vol. I.

Archives Judiciaires de Trois-Rivières
Notaire: Jean Cusson, Vol. I.

Archives Paroissiales de Notre-Dame de Québec
Registres des baptêmes, mariages et sépultures
Notre-Dame de Québec (1621–1692).
Boucherville (1668–1681).
Château-Richer (1661–1703).
Neuville (1679–1693).
Sainte-Anne de Beaupré (1669–1684).
Saint-Joseph de Lévis (1679–1681).
Trois-Rivières (1635–1689).

B. CUBA

Havana

Archivo de la Catedral de San Cristóbal de la Habana
Registros de las sepulturas (1702–1708).

C. ENGLAND

London

British Museum
Broadsides (1698–1709)
Topographical Collection of George III, CXXII

Public Record Office
Guides:
Andrews, Charles M., *Guide to the Materials for American History, to 1783, in the Public Record Office of Great Britain*, Vol. I, *The State Papers;* Vol. II, *Departmental and Miscellaneous Papers* (Washington, 1912–14).
Guide to the contents of the Public Record Office, Vol. I, II. (London, 1963).
Pugh, R. B., *The Records of the Colonial and Dominion Offices.* Handbook III (London, 1964).
Admiralty.
A1: Admiralty and Secretariat. Correspondence (Incoming), 1701–1715.
A2: Admiralty and Secretariat. Correspondence (Outgoing), 1698–1712.
A6: Admiralty and Secretariat. Registers, returns and certificates, 1702–1714.
B: Admiralty Dimensions books, 1703–04.
Colonial Office
CO5: America and West Indies.
Vols. 286–90. Lords Proprietors' orders and instructions, 1693–1710.
Vol. 292. Lords Proprietors' minute book, 1708–1727.
Vols. 306–07. Miscellaneous Carolina (North) and Florida papers, 1702–1706.
Vol. 382. Miscellaneous Carolina (South) papers, 1699–1724.
Vols. 1258–1265. Carolina and Maryland Proprietary papers, 1699–1720.

Vols. 1288–1293. Board of Trade, Proprieties, Entry books, 1699–1727.
Vols. 1309–1312. Virginia Papers, Board of Trade, 1696–1702.
Vol. 1409. Virginia, Journals of Council, Assembly and Council in Assembly, 1693–1702.
CO 323: Plantations General, Board of Trade.
Vol. 3. Original Correspondence, 1699–1703.
Vol. 7. Original Correspondence, 1710–1719.
CO 391: Board of Trade Journal.
Vols. 9–24. Minutes, 1696–1718.
Colonial Office Library: Maps
North American Colonies (General, Carolina, Florida, West Indies)
Maps and Plans, General
Patent Rolls.
Shaftesbury Papers.
S.P.O. 48: South Carolina Papers.
Papers of Charles II (1680–1715).
WO 1: Correspondence (Incoming).
Vol. 49. West Florida and West Indies (1764)

D. FRANCE

Archives Departementales
Guides:
Berranger, Henri de, *Guide des Archives de la Loire-Atlantique*, Vol. I (Séries A à H), Vol. II (Séries J à Z). (Nantes, 1962–64).
Delafosse, Marcel, *Guide des Archives de la Charente-Maritime* (La Rochelle, 1958).
État général par fonds des Archives départementales: Ancien régime et période revolutionnaire (Paris, 1900).

Archives de l'arrondissement maritime et du port de Rochefort.
Série E: Féodalité, familles, état civil, notaires, communautés d'habitants (1640–1715).
E Supplément: Archives communales déposées aux archives maritime (1680–1707).
1E 50 1, 60 (Dépêches de la Cour à Michel Bégon, *l'ainé*); 338–44, 398–402 (Lettres de Beauharnois et Bégon, *l'ainé*).

Archives de la Charente-Maritime, La Rochelle
Série B: Cours et Juridictions
B 5584, 5590–5595—Correspondance générale (1701–1711).

B 5692–98, 5701–15—Procès-verbaux, interrogatoires, déclarations (1703–1709).
B 5919–5928—Prises (1705–06).
Série E: Notaires
Registres 1699–1710 (Minutes de Maîtres Rivière et Soullard)

Archives de la Gironde, Bordeaux.
Série E: Féodalité, familles, état civil, notaires, corporations, communautés d'habitants (1640–1690).

Archives de la Loire-Atlantique, Nantes
Série B: Cours et juridictions
B 4477–4481—Contrats de propriétés des vaisseaux, receptions de capitaines, pilotes, déclarations (1693–1715).
B 4535–4543—Édits, déclarations, commissions et installations d'officiers, passeports, etc. (1703–1714).
B 4571–4577—Rapports des capitaines au long cours (1698–1716).
B 4675–4684—Passeports pour les colonies et l'étranger (1700–1717).
B 5004—Journaux de bord (1706–1753).

Archives du Var, Draguignan
Série E: État civil
Registre 7—L'acte de mariage de Nicolas de La Salle et Madelaine Chartroux (1692).

Archives Communales et Paroissiaux
Guides:
Baudot, Marcel, "Les archives des villes," *Gazette, 3e trim.*, 1970, No. 70, pp. 145–58.
———, "Les archives municipales dans la France l'Ancien Régime," *Archivum*, XIII, pp. 23–59.
Colnat, Jean, "Les archives des petite communes," *Gazette, 3e trim.*, 1970, No. 70, pp. 161–80.

[Sources in municipal and parish archives and libraries are too numerous to be cited here in detail. These were researched chiefly for personnel and genealogical data. In the Archives Communales, Séries EE (Affaires Militaires, Marine, etc.) and GG (Registres paroissiaux) were especially useful while in the parish archives the registers of baptisms, marriages and burials were, of course, the primary objects of search. The archives of the following townships and parishes have yielded data: Bayonne, Beauchêne, Bordeaux, Carcassonne, Chantilly, Clermont (Parish of St.-Nicolas), Heudin (Parish of Notre-Dame), La Rochelle, Laval, Marseille, Maux, Moulin, Niort, Paris (Parishes of

St.-Germain, St.-Nicholas-des-Champs, St.-Severin, St.-Germain-le-vieux), Rochefort, St.-Denis, St.-Jean d'Angély, Sainte-Marguerite de Saules, Toulon, Tours, Vannes and Vernon.]

Chantilly

Archives de la Province (Société de Jesus) de Paris
Fonds Brotier, 105

Paris

Archives des Colonies (AN)
Guides:
Maurel, Blanche and Étienne Taillemite, eds., *Moreau de Saint-Méry: Description topographique, physique, civile politique et histoire de La Partie Française de l'isle Saint-Domingue*, 3 Vols. (Paris, 1958).
Surrey, Nancy M. Miller, *Calendar of Manuscripts in Paris Archives and Libraries Relating to the History of the Mississippi Valley*, Vol. I (Washington, 1926).
Taillemite, Étienne, "Les archives des colonies françaises aux Archives nationales," *Gazette des Archives* (Paris), XLVI (1964), pp. 93–116.
———, *Inventaire analytique de la correspondance générale avec les colonies, depart, Série B, I, registres l à 37, 1654–1715* (Paris, 1959).
Série B: Ordres du Roi et Dépêches de la Marine. Registers 20 to 34 (1698–1712).
Série C: Correspondance générale.
C8A—Martinique. Registres 16, 18.
C9A—Saint-Domingue. Registres 4–9.
C11A—Nouvelle-France. Registres 16–36.
C11E—Canada, divers. Registre 14.
C13A—Louisiane. Registres 1–5, 9–11, 13–15, 28–29.
C13B—Louisiane. Registre 1.
C13C—Louisiane. Registres 2–3.
Série D: Troupes et milice des colonies.
D2C: Registre 1 (Officiers militaires et civile), 1711–1777.
Registre 18 (État-major), 1672–1744.
Registre 21 (Colonies), 1693–1800.
Registre 28 (Régiments et bataillons), 1669–1803.
Registre 51 (Compagnies Louisiane), 1710–1757.
Registre 57 (Officiers militaires et civile), 1695–1736.
Registre 59 (Canada et Louisiane), 1692–1776.

Registre 221 (Colonies), 1715–1727 *bis*.
Registre 222 (Alphabet Laffilard), 1608–1740.
D2D: Officiers militaires et civile (liste générale), 1685–1789.
Série E: Dossiers personnels.
Série F: Fonds des colonies.
F1A—Registres 8–23.
F2A—Registres 8, 12–13.
F3—Registres 4, 24–25, 68, 241.
F5A—Registre 3.

Archives de la Marine (AN).
Guides:
Bourgin, Georges, *Inventaire des Archives de la Marine—sous série 4JJ* (Paris, 1963).
Neuville, Didier, *État sommaire des Archives de la Marine anterieurs à la Révolution* (Paris, 1898).
————, *et al.*, *Inventaire des Archives de la Marine, Série B: service général*, 8 Vols. (Paris, 1885–1963).
Taillemite, Étienne, *Les archives anciennes de la Marine* (Paris, 1962).
Série B: Correspondance
B1—Registres 1–3, 8–10, 30 (Délibérations du conseil de Marine).
B2—Registres 121–235 (Ordres et dépêches).
B3—Registres 102–230 (Lettres reçues).
B4—Registres 19–25, 29–36 (Compagnes).
Série C: Personnel
C1—Registres 105–7, 151, 153–5, 157, 160–63.
C7—Registres 9, 180.
Série G: Documents divers
Registres 13, 13 *bis*, 14, 18
Série JJ: Service Hydrographique
2 JJ—Registres 55–57 (Collection des papiers Delisle).
3 JJ—Registres 271–279, 387 (Collection des papiers Delisle).
4 JJ—Registre 14 (Journaux de bord).
Dépôt des Cartes de la Marine: Atlas 4040 B, 4040 C, 4044 B, 4044 C.

Archives du Ministère des Affaires Étrangères
Guides:
Archives des Affaires étrangères, *Inventaire sommaire des archives du département des Affaires étrangères*, 6 Vols. (Paris, 1883–1903).
————, *État numerique des fonds de la correspondance politi que de l'origine à 1871* (Paris, 1936).
————, *Inventaire des mémoires et documents: Fonds France et fonds divers des pays d'Europe jusqu'en 1896* (Paris, 1964).
Mémoires et Documents

Amérique:
Registre 1 (1712–1715).
Registre 6 (1693–1732).
Registre 24 (1712–1759).
Angleterre:
Registre 17 (1701–1713).

Archives Nationales
Guides:
État sommaire par séries des documents conservés aux Archives nationales (Paris, 1891).
État des inventaires des Archives nationales, départementales, communales et hospitalières au Ier janvier 1937 (Paris, 1938); *Supplement, 1937–54* by R. H. Bautier (Paris, 1955).
Inventaire sommaire et tableau méthodique des fonds conservés aux Archives nationales, I partie, Régime Antérieur à 1789 (Paris, 1871).
Meurgey de Tupigny, Jacques, *Guide des Recherches Généalogique aux Archives Nationales* (Paris, 1956).

Section Ancienne

Série G: Contrôle général des finances
G7: Cartons 340–42 (Intendants de La Rochelle); 533–535 (Phélypeaux de Pontchartrain).
Série K: Monuments historiques
Cartons 1232, 1374 (Lettres des prêtres des missions étrangères).
Série MM: Carton 531 (Mélanges)
Série V: Grande Chancellerie et Conseils
V1—Carton 141
V7—Carton 214 (Commissions extraordinaires).
Série Y: Châtelet de Paris (Notaires Le Cat et Le Semelier).

Fonds Particuliers

Minutier Central: Notaires parisiens, Études XX, LII, XCVI, CVIII

Section Outre-Mer

Série G: État Civil, recensements et divers documents
G1—Registres 460–61 (Recensements de Canada)
Registre 412 (État Civil); Registre 464 (Dénombrement des familles . . . à la Louisiane, 1706); Registre 465 (Concessions); Registres 466–67 (Recensements).

Dépôt des fortifications des colonies
Cartes et plans: Colonies
Pièces 3, 24–7 (Louisiane).
Pièce 119A (Plan de la Ville et du Fort de la Maubile).
Pièce 120B (Plan de la Ville et du Fort Louis, sur la Mobile).

Archives du Séminaire des Missions Étrangères
Guide:
Mahieu, Bernard, "Les Archives de l'église catholique en France," *Archivum*, IV, pp. 89–104.
Amérique: Vol. 344 (Lettres de Albert Davion).
Vol. 345 (Histoire [MS] de la mission Tamaroa).
Vols. 865, 957–58 (Île de Bourbon).

Archives du Séminaire de Saint-Sulpice
Guide:
Dechêne, Louise, "Inventaire des documents relatifs à l'histoire du Canada conservés dans les archives de la compagnie de Saint-Sulpice à Paris," *Rapport des Archives du Québec*, 1969 (Tome 47), pp. 149–288.

Section Canada

Série I: Les Dossiers
Dossiers VIII–IX, CII
Série II: Manuscrits
Mss. 1236, 1273, 1280

Archives du Service Historique de L'Armée
Cartes et plans: 7 C 213

Archives de la Ville de Paris
Guide:
Vaux de Foletier, François de, "Archives of the Seine and the City of Paris," *Indian Archives*, II, pp. 112–14.
Registres paroissiaux (1651–1698).
Reconstitution des actes de l'état civil (1660–1702).

Bibliothèque de l'Arsenal
Manuscrits Bastille, No. 12472

Bibliothèque Nationale
Guides:
Leland, Waldo G., *Guide to Materials for American History in the Libraries and Archives of Paris, Vol. I, Libraries* (Washington, 1932).
Roy, J.-E., *Rapport sur les archives de France relatives à l'histoire du Canada* (Public Archives of Canada publication No. 6, 1911), pp. 655–848.

Table général alphabetique (Fonds français et F.f., Nouvelles acquisitions), 6 Vols. (Paris, 1931–48).

Cartes et Plans

Portefeuilles 138–138 *bis* (Plans de rades et de fortifications).
Ge DD 2387 et suiv. (Cartes de colonies).
Collection Danville.

Cabinet de Manuscrits

Fonds Clairambault: Registres 495, 1016
Fonds français:
Registre 6453 (Lettre de Gravier; notes sur les Jésuites).
Registre 8989 (Journal de Bénard de La Harpe).
Registre 9097 (Mémoires historique concernant l'Amérique).
Registre 12105 (Mémoire de François Le Maire).
Registre 14613 (Relation de Pénigault).
Registre 21690 (Relation de Levasseur-Ruessavel).
Registres 22800, 22803–22806, 22807–22815 (Lettres addressées à Villermont).
Fonds français, nouvelles acquisitions:
Registres 783–85, 2550, 2610, 5398, 7485, 9294–96, 9310, 9499, 21395, 21399.

Département des imprimés

f° FM: 4429, 4431 (Mémoires pour Dartaguiette d'Iron)

Bibliothèque Historique de la Ville de Paris
Série B: Plans manuscrits

Musée de la Marine
Division des cartes et plans: Colonies (La Louisiane)
Documents iconographiques

E. ITALY

Rome

Archivum Romanum Societatis Iesu
Francia: 9, 17, 23–24, 25I e II, 34, 35I e II, 45.
Gallia: 10, 15I, 110I, II e III.

Archivio della Sacrae Congregazione pro Gentium
Evangelizatione Seu de Propaganda Fide
Acta: 54–57, 72–73, 90–92.
Scritture originali riferite nelle congregazioni generali: 491–92, 546.

F. MEXICO

México, D. F.

Archivo General de la Nación
Guides:
Bolton, Herbert Eugene, *Guide to Materials for the History of the United States in the Principal Archives of Mexico* (Washington, 1913).
Carrera Stampa, Manuel, *Archivalia Mexicana* (Mexico, 1952).
Rubio Mañé, Jorge Ignacio, *El Archivo General de la Nación, México, D.F.* (Mexico, 1940).
I. Sección de Historia
Tomos 27–37, 166, 298–9, 321, 394 (1690–1721).
II. Sección de Minería
Tomos 28–29, 181 (1700–1716).
III. Provincias Internas
Tomo 28 (1700–1703).

G. SPAIN

Sevilla

Archivo General de Indias
Guides:
Índice de documentos de Nueva España existentes en el Archivo de Indias de Sevilla (Mexico, 1928–1931).
Peña y Cámara, José María de la, *Archivo General de Indias de Sevilla: Guía del Visitante* (Sevilla, 1958).
Sección I: Patronato
La Florida—Legajo 19.
Tierra Firme—Legajo 26.
Sección IV: Justicia
México—Legajos 97, 1013.

Sección V: Gobierno
Audiencia de Santo Domingo—Legajos 226, 228, 377, 409, 833, 836, 839–43, 837, 851–54, 856–58, 864.
Audiencia de México—Legajos 97, 477, 479, 615–18, 632–33, 1424.
Indiferente general—Legajos 5–6.

H. UNITED STATES

Chicago

Chicago Historical Society
Otto L. Schmidt Collection
1. Memoir of Le Page du Pratz.
2. Letter of Marguerite Messier (*Veuve* Le Sueur), 1706.
3. Journal of Bénard de La Harpe

Newberry Library
Ayer Collection: Manuscripts
No. 262—Du Ru Journal
No. 293—France, Colonies (1702–1750), Vol. 4.

Mobile

Archives of the Diocese of Mobile
[Baptisms]: Reg. A—1704–1778 (including marriages 1724–26 between pages 50–61 [W.P.A. Pagination]).
Libro de Matrimonios: Reg. B—1726–1812.
Registres Mortuaire: Reg. C—1726–1830.
Miscellaneous French Papers, 1704–1764.

Mobile County Probate Court
Conveyances: Translated Records (Caro's Originals).
Vol. I—1715–1812.
Vol. II—1763–1798.

Mobile Public Library
Iberville Historical Society Papers
No. 1043—Relation of Louis de Vendel Chaudron

Museum of the City of Mobile
Manuscripts & Documents: Journal of Bertet de La Clüe, 1720.

Artifacts: Relics from the site of Fort Louis de la Louisiane, 1702–1711.

Natchitoches

Archives of the Church of the Immaculate Conception
Register of Baptisms, Marriages, Burials
Vol. I: Poste St.-Jean-Baptiste (1734–1764).

Natchitoches Parish Records
Conveyances: Vols. I–XVI.

New Orleans

Louisiana State Museum Archives
Délibérations du Conseil Supérieur de la Louisiane
Boxes I–IV, VI, VIII–XVII, XIX.
Spanish Judicial Records (1781)

New Orleans Notorial Archives
Notaries: Andrés Almonaster, Vols. I–XVI.
Jean-Baptiste Garic, Vol. I.
Charles J. Maison, Vol. I.
Miscellaneous Records: Vols. I, II.
Successions: Vols. I, II.

St. Louis Cathedral Archives.
Baptisms: Registers 1731–1733.
Marriages: Registers 1720–1733.
Burials: Registers 1731–1733.

St. Louis

St. Louis University Archives
L'Immaculée Conception de la S.V. (Mission des Illinois).
Registres des baptêmes: Vol. I (1692–1721).

Washington, D.C.

Library of Congress
Geography and Map Division: Group RMR.
Spanish Papers, Vol. VI.

II. Published Sources.

Atlases, Dictionaries & Documents

Bellin, Jacques-Nicolas, *Hydrographie Françoise* (Versailles, 1756–1802).

———, *Le Petit Atlas Maritime*, Vol. II (Paris, 1764).

Boislisle, A. M. de, ed., *Correspondance des Contrôleurs-Généraux des finances avec les intendants des provinces, 1683–1715*, 3 Vols. (Paris, 1874–97). Vol. II.

Chéruel, A., *Dictionnaire historique des institutions, moeurs et coutumes de la France*, 2 Vols. (Paris, 1855).

Colección de documentos inéditos relativos al descubrimiento, conquista y colonizatión de las posesiones españoles en América y Oceania [sic], *sacados, en su mayor parte, del Real Archivo de Indias*, 42 Vols. (Madrid, 1864–84). Vol. XXVIII.

Colección de documentos inéditos relativos al descubrimiento, conquista y organizatión de las antiguas posesiones españoles de Ultramar, 25 Vols. (Madrid, 1885–1932). Vol. XVIII.

Conrad, Glenn R., ed., *The First Families of Louisiana*, 2 Vols. (Baton Rouge, 1970).

Depping, G. B., ed., *Correspondance administrative sous le règne de Louis XIV* (Paris, 1850–55).

De Ville, Winston, *The New Orleans French, 1720–1733: A collection of marriage records relating to the first colonists of the Louisiana Province* (Baltimore, 1973).

Dictionnaire biographique du Canada, 2 Vols. (Québec, 1966, 1969).

Édits, ordonnances royaux, déclarations et arrêts du Conseil d'état du roi concernant le Canada, Vol. I (Québec, 1854).

Fernández de Navarette, Martín, *Colección de los Viajes y descubrimientos que hicieron por mar los españoles desde fines del siglo XV, con varios documentos inéditos concernientes à la historia de la marina castellana y de los establecimientos españoles en Indias*, 5 Vols. (Madrid, 1825–37). Vol. III.

Fernández de Oviedo y Valdés, Gonzalo, *Historia general y natural de las Indias, Islas y Tierra Firme del Mar Océano*, Vol. II (Madrid, 1852).

Ferrière, Claude de, *Dictionnaire de Droit et de Pratique*, Vol. II (Paris, 1771).

Homann, Johann Baptist I, *Grosser Atlas über die gantze welt . . .* (Nuremberg, 1737–53).

Huguenot Society of London, *Quarto Series*, Vol. XVIII (London, 1911).

Jugements et délibérations du Conseil souverain de la Nouvelle-France, 1663–1716, 6 Vols. (Québec, 1885–91). Vol. III.

Lowrie, Walter, ed., *Documents, Legislative and Executive, of the Congress of the United States in relation to the Public Lands*, 8 Vols. (Washington, 1834).

Margry, Pierre, ed., *Découvertes et établissements des Français dans l'ouest et dans le sud de l'Amérique septentrionale (1614–1754): Mémoires et documents originaux*, Vol. III (Paris, 1878).

Marion, Marcel, *Dictionnaire des Institutions de la France aux XVIIe et XVIIIe siècles* (Paris, 1923).

Moll, Herman, [*Atlas*], (London, *ca.* 1717).

Ordonnance de la Marine du mois d'Aoust, 1681 (Paris, 1747).

Ottens, Reiner and Joshua, *Atlas sive geographia compendiosa*, Vols. I & II (Amsterdam, *ca.* 1775).

[Peypus, Frederick], *Praeclara Ferdinãndi Cortesii de Noua maris Oceani Hyspanica Narratio* (Nuremberg, 1524).

Provost, Honorius, *Le Séminaire de Québec: Documents et biographies* (Québec, 1964).

Rapport de L'Archiviste de la Province de Québec pour 1925–1926 (Québec, 1926).

Salley, Alexander S., *Journal of the Commons House of Assembly, 1692–1735*, 21 Vols. (Columbia, 1907–46).

Seller, John, *The English Pilot: West India Navigation . . . The Fourth Book* (London, 1689).

Serrano y Sanz, Manuel, ed., *Documentos históricos de la Florida y la Luisiana*, siglos XVI al XVIII (Madrid, 1913).

Tanguay, Cyprien, *Dictionnaire généalogique des familles canadiennes depuis la fondation de la colonie jusqu'à nos jours*, 7 Vols. (Montréal, 1871–90).

Thwaites, Reuben G., ed., *The Jesuit Relations and Allied Documents: Travels and Explorations of the Jesuit Missionaries in New France, 1610–1791*, 73 Vols. (Cleveland, 1900). Principally Vols. LXIV–LXIX.

U. S. Army Corps of Engineers, *Alabama River Navigation Charts* (Mobile, 1972).

———, *Black Warrior-Tombigbee Rivers Navigation Charts* (Mobile, 1972).

[West India Atlas], (London, 1741–1807). In Library of the National Maritime Museum, London.

Early Relations & Memoirs

Adair, James, *History of the American Indians* (London, 1775).

Alonso de Benavides, [Fray], *Memorial Que Fray Juan de Santander de la Orden de san Francisco, Comissario General de Indias, pre-*

senta a la Magestad Catolica del Rey don Felipe Quarto nuestro Señor (Madrid, 1630).

Barcia Carballido y Zúñiga, Andrés G., *Ensayo cronológico para la historia general de la Florida, 1512–1722* [Por Gabriel de Cárdenas Z. Cano, pseud.] In *Conquista del Nuevo Mundo,* Vols. VIII & IX (Madrid, 1829).

Boimare, A.-L., ed., *Journal Historique de l'Etablissement des Français à la Louisiane* (Paris, 1831).

Bossu, Jean-Bernard, *Nouveaux Voyages aux Indes occidentales; Contenant une Relation des differens Peuples qui habitent les environs du grand Fleuve Saint-Louis, appellé vulgairement le Mississipi; leur Religion; leur gouvernement; leurs moeurs, leurs guerres et leur commerce,* 2 Vols. (Paris, 1768).

Esteynefer, Juan de, *Abogados para toda clase de enfermedades del florilegio medicinal* (Mexico City, 1712).

Garcilaso de la Vega, el Inca, *La Florida Del YNCA: Historia del Adelantado Hernando de Soto, Gouernador y capitan general del Reyno de la Florida, y de otros heroicos caualleros Españoles è Indios; escrita por el Ynca Garcilasso de la Vega, capitan de su Magestad, natural de la gran Ciudad del Cozco, cabeça de los Reynos y provincias del Peru* (Lisbon, 1605).

Labat, [Jean-Baptiste], *Nouveau Voyage aux Isles de l'Amérique,* 8 Vols. (Paris, 1743).

Laval, [Antoine], *Voyage de la Louisiane fait par ordre du Roy en l'année mil sept cent vingt: Dans lequel sont traitées diverses matières de physique, astronomie, géographie et marine* (Paris, 1728).

McWilliams, Richebourg G., trans. and ed., *Fleur de Lys and Calumet; Being the Pénicaut Narrative of French Adventure in Louisiana* (Baton Rouge, 1953).

Relaçam verdadeira dos trabalhos q̃ ho governador dõ Fernãdo de souto e certos fidalgos portugueses passarom no descobrimẽto de provincia da Frolida. Agora novamẽte feita per hu fidalgo Delvas (Evora, 1557).

Relación que dio Alvar nuñez cabeça de vaca de lo acaescido en las Indias en la armada donde yua por gouernador Pamphilo de narbaez desde el año de veynte y siete hasta el año de treynta y seys que boluio a Seuilla con tres de su compañia (Zamora, 1542).

Studies & Accounts

Bézard, Yvonne, *Fonctionnaires maritimes et coloniaux sous Louis XIV: les Bégon* (Paris, 1932).

Blois, Theodore de, *Histoire de Rochefort* (Paris, 1733).

Clowes, William L., *The Royal Navy, a History from the Earliest Times to the Present,* 5 Vols. (London, 1897–1903).

Coste, P., *Les Filles de Charité* (Paris, 1933).
Cumming, William P., *The Southeast in Early Maps* (Chapel Hill, 1958).
Dawson, S. E., *The Saint Lawrence Basin and its Borderlands* (London, 1905).
Debien, Gabriel, *Le peuplement des Antilles françaises au XVIIe siècle: Les engagés partis de La Rochelle, 1683–1715* (Le Caire, 1942).
Delanglez, Jean, *The French Jesuits in Lower Louisiana, 1700–1763* (Washington, 1935).
———, *El Rio del Espíritu Santo: An Essay on the Cartography of the Gulf Coast and the Adjacent Territory during the Sixteenth and Seventeenth Centuries* (New York, 1935).
Delmas, Louis, *L'église réformée de La Rochelle* (Toulouse, 1870).
Deschamps, Hubert, *Méthods et doctrines coloniales de la France* (Paris, 1953).
Douville, Raymond et Jacques Casanova, *La Vie Quotidienne en Nouvelle France* (Paris, 1964).
Fleury, Michel, and Louis Henry, *Nouveau manuel de dépouillement et d'exploitation de l'état civil ancien* (Paris, 1965).
Giraud, Marcel, *Histoire de la Louisiane Française, Tome Premier: La règne de Louis XIV, 1698–1715* (Paris, 1953).
Glasson, M., *Histoire du Droit et des Institution de la France*, Vol. VIII (Paris, 1903).
Guérin, L., *Histoire maritime de la France*, 6 Vols. (Paris, 1851–59).
Hemelin, Jean, *Économie et Société en Nouvelle-France* (Québec, 1960).
Harris, Donald A., *An Archaeological Survey of Fort Louis de La Mobile, Final Report* (Mobile, 1972).
Janin, Joseph, *La Religion aux colonies françaises sous l'ancien regime* (Paris, 1942).
La Roche, René, *Yellow Fever, considered in its historical, pathological, etiological and therapeutical relations*, 2 Vols. (Philadelphia, 1855).
Lévy-Valensi, J., *La médecine et les médecins français au XVIIe siècle* (Paris, 1933).
McDermott, John Francis, ed., *The French in the Mississippi Valley* (Urbana, 1965).
Mémain, R., *La marine de guerre sous Louis XIV: Rochefort, arsenal modèle de Colbert* (Paris, 1937).
Milfort, Le Clerc de, *Mémoire ou coup-d'oeil rapide Sur mes différens voyages et mon séjour dans la nation Crëck* (Paris, 1802).
O'Neill, Charles Edwards, *Church and State in French Colonial Louisiana: Policy and Politics to 1732* (New Haven & London, 1966).
Ramsey, David, *History of South Carolina* (Charleston, 1809).
Trudel, Marcel, *Le Terrier du Saint-Laurent en 1663* (Ottawa, 1973).

Valin, René-J., *Nouveau commentaire sur l'ordonnance de la marine*, 2 Vols. (La Rochelle, 1766).

Williams, B. H., *et al., Soil Survey of Mobile County, Alabama* (Washington, 1936).

Articles

Bonnault, Claude de, "Les Protestants au Canada avant 1760," *Bulletin des Recherches Historique*, LXIII, pp. 5–33.

Bugher, J. C., "The pathology of yellow fever." In Strode, G. K. (ed.), *Yellow Fever* (New York, 1951), pp. 137–63.

Chambolle, François, "Observations sur la Fièvre Jaune recueilles à la Guadeloupe pendant l'Épidémie de 1825, avec des Réflexions," *Annales de la Médicine Physiologique*, X, pp. 391–92.

Chatard, M., "Notice Succincte du Typhus, & C., qui se manifesta à Baltimore au moi de Juillet, 1819," *Observateur des Sciences Médicales de Marseille*, V, p. 333.

Crane, Verner W., "Projects for Colonization in the South, 1684–1732," *Mississippi Valley Historical Review*, XII, pp. 23–25.

Delafosse, Marcel, "La Rochelle et les Îles au XVIIe Siècle." *Revue d'histoire des colonies*, XXXVI, pp. 238–81.

Elton, N. W., Romero, A., and A. Trejos, "Clinical pathology of Yellow fever," *American Journal of Clinical Pathology*, XXV, pp. 135–46.

Falardeau, Jean-Charles, "Paroisses de France et de Nouvelle-France au XVIIe siècle," *Cahiers de l'École des sciences sociales, politiques et économiques de Laval*, II, pp. 20–38.

Giraud, Marcel, "Marins et ouvriers des ports devant la crise de la fin du règne de Louis XIV," In *Eventail de l'histoire vivante: hommage à Lucien Febvre*, 3 Vols. (Paris, 1953).

Godbout, Archange, "Les Robinau de Bécancour," *Mémoires* (Société généalogique canadienne-française), IV, pp. 158–62.

Lanctot, Gustave, "Les Débuts du Christianisme en Louisiane," *Annual Report of the Canadian Historical Association* (1924), pp. 54–65.

Leclerc, Paul-André, "Le Mariage sous le regime français," *Revue d'Histoire de l'Amérique Française*, XIII, pp. 230–46, 374–401, 525–43; XIV, pp. 34–60, 226–45.

McCusker, John J., "Les equivalents métriques des poids et mesures du commerce colonial aux XVIIe et XVIIIe siècles," *Revue Française d'histoire d'outre-mer*, LXI, pp. 349–65.

Massicotte, Édouard-Zotique, "Les colons de Montréal de 1642 à 1667," *Mémoires de la Société royale du Canada, VII*, pp. 3–65.

Pietraszek, Bernadine, "Anglo-France Trade Conflicts in North America, 1702–1713, *Mid-America*, XXXV, new series, Vol. 24, no. 3, pp. 144–74.

Rand, Earl, "The Structural Phonology of Alabaman, a Muskogean Language," *International Journal of American Linguistics,* XXXIV, pp. 94–103.

Roy, P.-G., "La famille Dugué de Boisbriand," *Bulletin des Recherches historiques,* XXIV, pp. 161–73.

Trickey, E. Bruce and Nicholas H. Holmes, Jr., "A Chronological Framework for the Mobile Bay Region, revised, 1970," *Journal of Alabama Archaeology,* XVII, pp. 115–28.

Wedel, Mildred M., "The Bénard de La Harpe Historiography on French Colonial Louisiana," *Louisiana Studies,* XIII, pp. 5–67.

Wilson, Samuel, Jr., "Colonial Fortifications and Military Architecture in the Mississippi Valley," in McDermott, J. F., ed., *The French in the Mississippi Valley,* pp. 103–22 (Urbana, 1965).

Index